LIBRARY
PLANO SENIOR HIGH School 11th & 12th
PLANO, TEXAS 75075

AF412477

# Readings in
# SPECIAL
# EDUCATION

### Revised Edition

WITHDRAWN

## Special Learning Corporation
42 Boston Post Rd. Guilford, Connecticut 06437

# SPECIAL LEARNING CORPORATION

Publisher's Message:

The Special Education Series is the first comprehensive series designed for special education courses of study. It is also the first series to offer such a wide variety of high quality books. In addition, the series will be expanded and up-dated each year. No other publications in the area of special education can equal this. We stress high quality content, a superb advisory and consulting group, and special features that help in understanding the course of study. In addition we believe we must also publish in very small enrollment areas in order to establish the credibility and strength of our series. We realize the enrollments in courses of study such as Autism, Visually Handicapped Education, or Diagnosis and Placement are not large. Nevertheless, we believe there is a need for course books in these areas and books that are kept up-to-date on an annual basis! Special Learning Corporation's goal is to publish the highest quality materials for the college and university courses of study. With your comments and support we will continue to do this.

John P. Quirk

©1980 by Special Learning Corporation
Guilford, Connecticut 06437

All rights reserved. No part of this book may be reproduced, stored, or communicated by any means--without permission from Special Learning Corporation.

First Edition

1  2  3  4  5

ISBN No.  0-89568-120-X

# SPECIAL EDUCATION SERIES

* ●Abnormal Psychology: The Problems of
    Disordered Emotional and Behavioral
    Development
  ●Administration of Special Education
  ●Autism
* ●Behavior Modification
    Biological Bases of Learning Disabilities
    Brain Impairments
  ●Career and Vocational Education for the
    Handicapped
  ●Child Abuse
* ●Child Psychology
  ●Classroom Teacher and the Special Child
* ●Counseling Parents of Exceptional Children
    Creative Arts
  ●Curriculum Development for the Gifted
    Curriculum and Materials
* ●Deaf Education
    Developmental Disabilities
* ●Developmental Psychology: The Problems of
    Disordered Mental Development
* ●Diagnosis and Placement
  ●Down's Syndrome
  ●Dyslexia
* ●Early Childhood Education
  ●Educable Mentally Handicapped
* ●Emotional and Behavioral Disorders
    Exceptional Parents
  ●Foundations of Gifted Education
* ●Gifted Education
* ●Human Growth and Development of the
    Exceptional Individual

  ●Hyperactivity
* ●Individualized Education Programs
  ●Instructional Media and Special Education
  ●Language and Writing Disorders
  ●Law and the Exceptional Child: Due Process
* ●Learning Disabilities
  ●Learning Theory
* ●Mainstreaming
* ●Mental Retardation
  ●Motor Disorders
    Multiple Handicapped Education
    Occupational Therapy
  ●Perception and Memory Disorders
* ●Physically Handicapped Education
* ●Pre-School Education for the Handicapped
* ●Psychology of Exceptional Children
  ●Reading Disorders
    Reading Skill Development
    Research and Development
* ●Severely and Profoundly Handicapped
    Social Learning
* ●Special Education
  ●Special Olympics
* ●Speech and Hearing
    Testing and Diagnosis
  ●Three Models of Learning Disabilities
  ●Trainable Mentally Handicapped
  ●Visually Handicapped Education
  ●Vocational Training for the Mentally Retarded

●  Published Titles    *Major Course Areas

# TOPIC MATRIX

| MAJOR TOPICS | RELATED ARTICLES | RELATED SPECIAL LEARNING CORPORATION READERS |
|---|---|---|
| **I. ISSUES** | | |
| **A. History** | 1. Special Education: Past, Present and Future<br>2. Mainstreaming: Merging Regular and Special Education | Readings in Administration of Special Education<br>Readings in Individualized Educational Programs<br>Readings in Law and Special Education: Due Process |
| **B. Legislation** | 4. The Barriers Ahead<br>6. Public Law 94-142 and Section 504: What they say About Rights and Protections<br>7. Teachers Ask About Handicapped Children and the New Laws | |
| **C. Appropriations** | 5. Federal Legislation for Exceptional Children: Implications and a View of the Future | |
| **D. Labelling** | 34. A Community Alert for Children with Learning Problems | |
| **II. METHODOLOGY** | | |
| **A. Mainstreaming** | 3. Impressions of Special Education in America<br>8. First Things First<br>17. Put on a Handicap<br>20. Mainstreaming the Mildly Handicapped Secondary Student: Another View | Readings in Mainstreaming<br>Readings in Behavior Modification<br>Readings in Instructional Media |
| **B. Special Education Programs** | 9. Evaluating Special Education Programs<br>10. The Montessori Approach to Special Education<br>11. Our Special Children are People Too: A Parent's View<br>12. Successful Programs for Young Handicapped Children<br>14. The Sexual Needs of the Handicapped<br>15. Therapy and Leisure Education<br>16. Critical Issues in Career Education for Handicapped Students | |
| **C. Therapy Techniques** | 13. The Road to Self-Expression<br>30. The Medicine Pots: A Motivation Operation<br>31. Behavioral Blockbusters<br>32. Georgia's Rutland Center | |
| **III. MENTALLY HANDICAPPED** | | |
| **A. Definition** | 18. What is Mental Retardation?<br>19. Teaching the Invisible Retarded<br>21. Definitions of Severely Handicapped: A Survey of State Departments of Education | Readings in Mental Retardation<br>Readings in the Educable Mentally Handicapped<br>Readings in Trainable Mentally Handicapped<br>Readings in Down's Syndrome<br>Vocational Training for the Mentally Retarded<br>Developmental Psychology: The Problems of Disordered Mental Development<br>Mentally Handicapped: A Reference Book<br>Readings in Special Olympics |
| **B. Curriculum** | 22. Toward a Curriculum for the Profoundly Retarded and Multiply Handicapped Child<br>23. The Education and Community Support of Severely Handicapped People | |
| **IV. EMOTIONAL DISORDERS** | | Readings in Emotional and Behavioral Disorders<br>Readings in Hyperactivity<br>Readings in Autism<br>Abnormal Psychology: The Problems of Disordered Emotional and Behavioral Development |
| **A. Adolescent Behavior Problems** | 24. Understanding and Evaluating Adolescent Behavior Problems<br>25. Educating Adolescents with Emotional and Delinquency Problems | |

# TOPIC MATRIX

| MAJOR TOPICS | RELATED ARTICLES | RELATED SPECIAL LEARNING CORPORATION READERS |
|---|---|---|
| **B. Autism** | 26. New Light on Autism and Other Puzzling Disorders of Childhood | Readings in Autism<br>Readings in Hyperactivity<br>Readings in Abnormal Psychology: The Problems of Disordered Emotional and Behavioral Development |
| **C. Hyperactivity** | 27. Hyperactivity: Diagnosis<br>28. Hyperactivity: Treatment<br>29. Hyperactivity: The Scandalous Silence | |
| **V. LEARNING DISABILITIES** | | |
| **A. Identification** | 33. Why?<br>35. The ABC's of Learning Disabilities<br>36. When a Child has a Learning Problem<br>37. Bright Child, School Failure | Readings in Learning Disabilities<br>Readings in Motor Disorders<br>Readings in Reading Disorders<br>Readings in Language and Writing Disorders<br>Readings in Three Models of Learning Disabilities<br>Readings in Perception and Memory<br>Learning Disabilities: A Reference Book |
| **B. Remediation** | 38. School Before School can be the Answer<br>39. A Working Model for Developing Instructional Materials for the Learning Disabled | |
| **VI. PHYSICALLY AND SENSORIALLY HANDICAPPED** | | |
| **A. Deaf** | 40. Sound Minds in a Soundless World<br>41. Cued-Speech Keeps Deaf Pupils Ahead<br>42. My Deaf Child Leads a Full Life | Readings in Deaf Education<br>Readings in Physically Handicapped Education<br>Readings in Visually Handicapped Education<br>Readings in Speech and Hearing |
| **B. Blind** | 43. Mainstreaming: It Can Work for Blind Children<br>44. Importance of Precision Teaching in the Education of Visually Impaired Students Being Mainstreamed into the Public Schools-Part II | |
| **C. Orthopedically Impaired** | 47. Developing IEP's for Physically Handicapped Students: A Transdisciplinary Viewpoint<br>48. Mainstreaming a Child with Spina Bifida | |
| **D. Speech Impaired** | 45. Help for 10 Million Americans Who Suffer Speech Problems<br>46. St-st-st-st-st-st-stuttering | |
| **E. Health Impaired** | 49. Involuntary Deviance: Schooling and Epileptic Children<br>50. What are Health Impairments? | |
| **VII. GIFTED EDUCATION** | | |
| **A. Identification** | 52. The Gifted Child<br>53. The Brightest Kids<br>55. How to Tell if Your Child is Gifted<br>57. Growing Up Gifted and Getting Along | Readings in Gifted and Talented Education<br>Readings in Foundations of Gifted Education<br>Readings in Curriculum Development for the Gifted |
| **B. History** | 54. The Gifted Child in the United States and Abroad | |
| **C. Curriculum** | 51. The Many Paths for Gifts and Talents<br>56. Enhancing Self-Concept in Gifted Black Students | |

# CONTENTS

# Focus  102

# 3. Mentally Handicapped



# 4. Emotional and Behavioral Disorders

## 5.  Learning Disabilities

**Overview**





## 6.  Physically and Sensorially Handicapped

# 7. Gifted and Talented

# GLOSSARY OF TERMS

**accelerated programs** Programs for gifted students where the child may work or be placed in a higher grade than he/she would normally be placed according to chronological age.

**accountability** Idea where schools are held accountable for producing set results.

**advocacy** A program in which individuals or organizations act on behalf of the interests of other persons who are in some way developmentally disabled.

**aggression** Physical or verbal behavior with the intent to injure or destroy.

**agnosia** Loss of or an impairment of the ability to recognize objects or events when presented through various senses.

**allegation** Charge or complaint which is proven true or false at a trial or hearing.

**amniocentesis** An examination of the genetic composition of the amniotic fluid in which the fetus is suspended.

**anoxia** Inadequate supply of oxygen to the brain. This can cause mental retardation if prolonged.

**anomia** Inability to appropriately name objects, persons and/or activities.

**aphasia** Inability to understand and/or use language efficiently.

**articulation** The movements of speech organs employed in producing a particular speech sound or consonant.

**articulation-speech problem** Inability to articulate words clearly without noted problems.

**assessment** A battery of tests (formal and informal) to evaluate a person's performance.

**ataxia** Impairment of muscular coordination characterized by a lack of balance.

**attention span** The ability to attend to a stimulus.

**auditory acuity** The sensation level of hearing. It denotes how well a person is able to hear an auditory stimulus in terms of decibel level.

**auditory discrimination** Ability to discriminate between closely related sounds or spoken words.

**auditory memory** The ability to produce or retain auditory units and/ or remember what one needed to learn through hearing and remember what he/she has heard.

**Barrier-free design** The thought that all buildings must be designed so that they are accessible to the handicapped.

**BIF model** (Black Identity Facilitation Model) The curriculum model designed to help gifted Black students have a positive Black identity.

**blindness** The complete loss of sight.

**brain damage** A general term referring to any injury to the brain.

**Bureau of Education for the Handicapped** Governmental agency which assists States, colleges and universities, and other institutions and agencies in meeting the educational needs of the handicapped.

**behavior modification** A current technique of behavior control applied to learning situations. It is a technique which involves altering undesirable behavior to a more appropriate state.

**central nervous system** In humans, the brain and spinal cord to which sensory impulses are transmitted.

**cerebral palsy** A qualitative motor disorder caused by damage to the brain before or after birth.

**child development** Pattern of sequential stages of interrelated physical, psychological, and social development in the process of maturation from infancy and total dependence to adulthood and relative independence.

**childhood schizophrenia** A childhood disorder characterized by onset after age 5, consisting of unusual body movements, extreme emotional abnormalities and peceptual disorders.

**chromosome** Structures in the cell nucleus which carry the genes.

**closure** Used in reference to creative thinking. It is the ability to delay completing a task long enough to make the mental leap that makes it possible to produce original ideas.

**cognition** The process or act of knowing. Thinking skills and processes are often considered cognitive skills.

**conceptualization** The highest level of learning a man achieves. After having developed sensation, perception, memory and symbolization, the individual can use these facilities to form concepts.

**cranium** The skull.

**cued speech** A manual supplement to sign language. It consists of 8 hand shapes which are used in 4 positions to make all the sounds of the English language look different either on the lip or hand.

**deafness** Sensory handicap which is the partial or total loss of hearing.

**decibel** A relative measure of the intensity of sounds, zero decibel represents normal hearing.

**decoding** The ability to understand what is expressed verbally or visually.

**depression** A disorder characterized by deep gloom and a slowing down of physical and mental processes.

**developmental disabilities** A group of handicapping conditions which often require special services. It is a disability which originates before age 18, continues indefinitely, and constitutes a substantial handicap.

**deviant behavior** Behavior which is different from the "norm".

**diagnostic teaching** The day-by-day teaching or evaluation session in which the teacher or therapist on an informal basis determines, through observation and follow-up, a child's specific learning strengths and weaknesses.

**directionality** The ability of perceiving directional characteristics such as right, left, up or down.

**directional problem** The inability to distinguish up from down, right from left, or forward from backward.

**discrimination** The ability to perceive differences among stimuli presented visually (shapes) or auditorily (sounds).

**distractibility** Attention given to insignificant stimuli rather than to what is relavant at the time.

**Down's Syndrome** A condition caused by an extra number 21 chromosome in each cell of the body characterized by specific physical characteristics; occurs in all degrees of retardation severity. Once known as mongolism.

**dysarthria** A severe speech impairment in which the defect in articulation is usually caused by central or peripheral nerve damage.

**dysgraphia** A disorder of written language in which the child is unable to transfer visual to motor patterns. (Specific writing disability)

**dyslexia** Impairment in the ability to read.

**echolalia** The meaningless repetition of speech sounds and words and is a normal developmental process in a young child's learning of language.

**edema** Swelling caused by excessive amount of fluid in the body tissues.

**emotional disorder** A learning handicap caused by problems with feeling not derived from cognitive and volitional states of consciousness or reason.

**encode** The expression of meaning in symbols or codes.

**enrichment courses** Technique for teaching gifted children. The student remains in his/her own grade level but is able to pursue specialized

interests through independent study or Saturday morning or afternoon classes at a more intensified and advanced level.

**environmental disabilities** A problem of learning caused by exposure to surroundings which are detrimental and/or inappropriate.

**epilepsy** A disease of the nervous system sometimes characterized by seisures.

**exceptionality** That which causes a child to deviate from the "norm" in mental, physical, social, or emotional behavior.

**Feingold Diet** Diet devised by Dr. Ben Feingold which helps to control hyperactivity in children.

**figure-ground perception** The ability to attend to one part of a stimulus in relation to the rest of the field.

**fine motor** Relates to the use of the hands to perform manipulative and writing tasks.

**finger spelling** Technique for communicating with the deaf which involves literally spelling the word with the fingers.

**formal diagnosis** consists of evaluation by a team of professionals who utilize various psychological instruments to determine a child's learning strengths and weaknesses and overall adjustment.

**gene** Those parts of the chromosome which transmit hereditary characteristics.

**gross motor skills** Skills which relate to the use of the large muscles of the body in performing acts of motion such as turning, jumping, and running. They also relate to the ability to coordinate large muscle movements.

**gustatory** Relating to the sense of taste.

**handicapped** Those who deviate from the average in mental, physical or social characteristics to such a degree that they require modifications in school programs or methods in order to develop to their maximum potential.

**health impaired** Impairment which limits strength, vitality or alertness due to chronic or acute health problems.

**hydrocephalus** Head enlargement due to abnormal increase in the amount of fluid on the brain and exerting pressure on the brain possibly causing mental retardation. Can be prevented surgically.

**hyperactivity** Disorganized, disruptive and unpredictable behavior; overreaction to simuli. Person's behavior is characterized by lack of purpose or need.

**hyperkinesis** See hyperactivity

**I.E.P.** Individualized Educational Program; a formal written program developed by school personnel, a child's parents, and when appropriate the child himself/herself, in order to delineate assessment, placement, goal setting, special services, and evaluation procedures.

**impairment** Refers to the actual physical disorder.

**informal diagnosis** See diagnostic teaching.

**in-service training** Professional oriented programs given to personnel while they are teaching or involved in public or private practice.

**involuntary deviance** When a child deviates from the norm unwillingly because of a physical or mental handicap.

**I.Q.** Intelligence Quotient; the number used to identify the relative intelligence of a person. It is determined by dividing the mental age by the chronological age and mutiplying by 100.

**kinesthetic** Pertaining to the muscular sense.

**language** The utilization of symbols for the purpose of communication. Can be of three types: spoken, written, or read.

**language experience approach** An approach to reading in which the material to be read is directly related to the child's language experiences.

**laterality** Refers to a person's differentiation of the two sides of his body.

**learning disability** Disorder of one or more of the basic psychological processes used in understanding or in using language.

**least restrictive environment** L.R.E.; The "most normal education program" that a child can receive, including instructional services outside the classroom.

**linguistics** A scientific and systematic study of the components of our speech and language system.

**mainstreaming** The placement of a handicapped student into education programs with normal functioning children.

**malnutrition** Being undernourished, can cause learning disabilities and/or emotional disorders.

**maturation** The process of becoming fully developed in character and mental capacity.

**megavitamins** Huge doses of various vitamins used in drug treatment with varied rates of success.

**mentally handicapped** Persons who are limited in their ability to learn and are generally socially immature.

**Mentorships** Gifted education technique which pairs a gifted child with a highly skilled adult from the community who is working in the area which is of interest to the child.

**mild mental retardation** See Educable Mentally Handicapped.

**minimal brain dysfunction** A mild neurological impairment that causes learning difficulties in the child with near-average intelligence.

**modality** One of the sensory processes through which learning occurs.

**moderate mental retardation** see Trainable Mentally Handicapped

**multisensory** Describes learning experiences in which several sensory modalities are used to reinforce one another.

**negative reinforcement** Behavior which results in the removal or termination of events that are unpleasant in consequence.

**neurological** Refers to the central nervous system.

**non-verbal** The inability to talk. The cause may be physical, psychological or intellectual.

**olfactory** Relating to the sense of smell.

**orthopedically impaired** Severe skeletal disorder which affects the child's educational performance.

**overlearn** To learn something so well that one's responses become "automatic".

**overloading** Occurs when the brain is required to make more discriminations or associations at any one given time than it is capable of doing.

**peers** Group to which one belongs determined by either age, grade, or social standing.

**perception** The process of organizing or interpreting stimuli received through the senses.

**perceptual disabilities** Disability where one fails to understand stimuli.

**peripetologists** ·Specialists who teach orientation and mobility to blind children.

**perservation** The inability of a person to restructure his thinking quickly. The child with perservation persists with a response that is no longer appropriate.

**PL 94-142** Education of All Handicapped Children Act of 1975.

**positive reinforcement** Strengthened behavior through receipt of pleasurable consequences or the removal of unpleasant consequences.

**Profound Mentally Handicapped** Historically defined when intelligence testing scores fall more than 5 standard deviations below the norm on a standard I.Q. test. As with the severely retarded the profound retarded will exhibit severe adaptive behavior problems and may also be physically or sensorially disabled.

**psychological evaluation** Evaluation which includes diagnostic instruments that measure a child's native intelligence for learning, perceptual tests, and apperception tests of emotional maturity.

**psychomotor** The motor effects of psychological processes.

**psychosis** Severe mental disorder characterized by personality disintegration and loss of contact with reality.

**psychosomatic disorder** Physical symptoms, often including actual tissue damage, that may result from the continued mobilization of the body during sustained stress.

**regression** A maladaptive response to stress in which earlier modes of behavior are resumed.

**rehabilitation** Restoration of a skill or restoration of efficiency to a level compatible with partial or complete vocational and social independence.

**resource room** A special feature of many schools. It is a special room where exceptional children can go for most or part of a day or week and receive special individualized or small group instruction. As in the case of gifted students the room can be used for accelerated study in subjects that are not normally taught in the regular classroom.

**sensation** The lowest level of learning experience and refers to the activation of sensory-neural structures.

**sensorimotor** Pertaining to the actions that depend upon the combined activity of sensory organs and muscles.

**sequentialization** The ability to order and structure events in a pre-designated sequence.

**Severe Mentally Handicapped** Historically defined when intelligence testing scores fall 5 standard deviations below the norm on a standard I.Q. test. The severely retarded person has an obvious incapacity to exercise the expected controls of reason and of personal management necessary for normal living in any given culture.

**sign language** Communication with deaf individuals using a kind of short hand using the hands and facial expressions.

**social perception** The recognition and perception of social interrelationships and structures.

**somatic** Pertaining to the body.

**spasticity** Increasing tone of the muscles, making it difficult for the person to control the extremities.

**spatial orientation** A child's or person's ability to locate himself in a space world. It deals with correlates such as right, left, in, on, under, on top, etc.

**speech impaired** Inability to articulate sounds of our language for some physical or psychological disorder.

**spina bifida** Congenital gap in the wall of the spinal canal. It causes the loss of feeling from the waist down.

**stimuli** An external event which causes physiological change in the sense organs.

**stuttering** A speech impediment in which the flow of words is interrupted by hesitations, rapid repetition of speech elements, and or spasms of breathing.

**tactile** Relating to the sense of touch.

**therapy** Remedial treatment of a disorder.

**Trainable Mentally Handicapped** Defined historically as the degree of mental retardation when intelligence testing scores fall 3 to 4 standard deviations below the norm. According to law the child must also be evaluated according to behaviors. The TMH child will respond to training in various self-help skills and can learn simple communication skills.

**visual discrimination problem** Inability to distinguish shapes when both are of the same relative size.

**visual handicap** Inability to understand what is seen by the eye.

**visual perception** The ability to identify, organize and interpret what is received by the eye.

**vocational training education** That part of the curriculum concerned with the competencies involved in successful employment and vocational choice.

**writing disorder** Disorder where a person is unable to express oneself through written language.

photo: Office of Human Development Services, DHEW

# PREFACE

Special education is changing rapidly. Educators and parents are now finding themselves involved in obtaining the best education possible for the handicapped. Recent law mandates that the handicapped be given a free and appropriate education in the least restrictive environment. For many exceptional children this means being mainstreamed into regular classes along side their peers for all or part of the day. For educators this law means retraining to obtain the skills necessary to successfully educate the exceptional child. This law spells out hard work for all, teachers, parents and administrators. It is through these groups that the handicapped can be educated to the fullest extent possible.

*READINGS IN SPECIAL EDUCATION* gives an overview into this vast field. Designed for in-coming special education students and regular teachers returning for retraining classes, the book will discuss such topics as the history of special education, the law, current methodology, and will look at each exceptionality, the mentally handicapped, emotional disorders, learning disabilities, physically and sensorially handicapped, and gifted and talented.

photo: Office of Human Development Services, DHEW

# PERSPECTIVES

Special education has changed drastically over the past half century. Looking back to the 1920's one would find literally no appropriations for special children in the regular schools. The handicapped were kept at home or placed in institutions.

Later, as World War II was over and many veterans were returning home disabled, rehabilitation programs began. This led way to the development of special education programs in the 1950's and 1960's. These programs were, however, according to Reynolds and Rosen in "Special Education: Past, Present and Future," "based on categorical handicaps and conducted apart from the regular education classes..."

Special education today has shifted gears, so to speak, and is working to provide a place for the handicapped in both the school and the community. Several forces led to these changes. In the article entitled "Mainstreaming: Merging Regular and Special Education," Hasazi, Rice and York discuss such factors as educators, parent-advocacy groups, courts and federal litigation. Together these forces helped to bring about the law as it stands today (PL94-142) and the present status for equal education of the handicapped.

The first section of this book will examine the history and the law affecting special education. The articles in this section give interpretations of the law from various viewpoints. An Englishman, Trevor J. Tebbs, gives his impressions of how mainstreaming is implemented in the United States. Then a view from the government is presented in the form of an article by Dr. Martin LaVor, senior legislative associate for the House Education and Labor Committee of the U.S. Congress. Along with a Focus page which reviews all the various laws affecting exceptional children passed from 1950 to present, the section concludes with two articles using a question answer format which attempt to spell out the law in clear, concise terms.

# Special Education: Past, Present, and Future


MAYNARD C. REYNOLDS
SYLVIA W. ROSEN


MARY is in the first grade this year, in the same classroom as her neighborhood age mates. Like them, she is learning to read and write. However, while her classmates are poring over print, Mary is learning to read braille. She was born blind. Nevertheless, Mary will be able to keep up with her age group all through school because special education teachers will help her to acquire the special skills she needs to compensate for her lack of vision. Furthermore, they will supply her with essential equipment, such as braille textbooks, braille writer, tape recorder, and typewriter, and help her classroom teachers to learn some techniques for managing her day-by-day educational program. Mary will receive training in mobility from a special teacher which will enable her to live and function as an independent, competent person. Mary's training in independence actually began when she was an infant; special workers from the state office for the blind visited her home and helped her parents to adjust to her lack of vision and to enrich her experiences. Because of all the help they have received, Mary's parents have learned to treat her like a child who is normal in every respect but vision.

If Mary had been born 100 years ago, her blindness would have set her apart from other people. The local community would have sympathized with her parents, but it had no facilities or services to offer them. At school age, if there had been room, Mary would have been enrolled in a state residential school for the blind, a difficult separation,

---


Maynard C. Reynolds is professor and chairman of the Department of Psychoeducational Studies and director of the Leadership Training Institute/Special Education at the University of Minnesota. Sylvia W. Rosen is publications editor for the Leadership Training Institute/Special Education.

sometimes, where she would have learned to interact with other blind children. The school staff, who were learning by doing, might have taught her to read and write braille (a recently developed skill at that time); play a musical instrument, perhaps; take care of her bodily needs; and perform simple repetitive tasks, like basket weaving. At best, Mary would have been equipped to function only in a sheltered environment outside the mainstream of life.

If Mary had been born 200 years ago, her blindness might have been regarded as divine retribution. Like all handicapped children of that day, she would have been considered uneducable and untrainable, and she would have been completely dependent on her family or charity. From birth on, her life would have been one of helplessness and hopelessness, a burden to herself, her family, and the community in which she lived.

The Marys and other handicapped children of the United States have come a long way since the establishment of the nation: from silent neglect and lack of opportunities to acceptance in local schools and community support for a variety of social services. The change reflects not only the development of knowledge, techniques, and materials to accommodate in classrooms children with different kinds of physical, neurologic, and emotional handicaps but, and perhaps more basic, the expansion of our definitions of equality and freedom. As with all cultural concepts, our definitions reflect societal beliefs at a given time. On the basis of current judicial utterances and legislative enactments, we can say that we have progressed from conceptualizing freedom and equality in terms of the majority to conceptualizations in terms of the individual. Differences from the norm are no longer regarded as valid reasons for depriving persons of opportunities to develop optimally and maximally.

Massive changes are underway in our schools at present to bring educational practices in line with our expanded definitions of the two concepts. The changes are occurring on many fronts and especially in relation to student rights and the provision of educational services. As defined by the courts in recent adjudications, the purpose of education is no longer the benefits that may accrue to society but, rather, the benefits that may accrue to each child. Schools may no longer exclude or demit children without due process procedures, they bear the responsibility of providing educational services for all children, regardless of handicap or status, and they must provide individualized educational programs for all handicapped children.

The children most affected by the changes are those with severe to moderate handicapping conditions and behavioral and learning problems. Where such children were previously institutionalized, the institutions are returning many of them to the communities; where such children were isolated in special classrooms, the rooms are now emptying out to the regular classroom; and where such children were excluded from schools because programs were not available, programs must now be provided for them. In large part, these changes impinge upon the interface of special and regular education and can be subsumed under the term "mainstreaming." To understand the significance of the movement represented by the term, it is essential to look at the rise of special education and the ways in which educational services have been delivered to handicapped children (or children who were labeled "handicapped" because they were hard to teach) until recently.

### A Little History

As a professional field, special education is relatively new, although the handicapped children it serves have been with us always. The seeds of the profession were planted in the early nineteenth century by a handful of European and American pioneers who proved that children with handicaps were capable of learning and could be taught. Because the children were usually the victims of massive neglect and rejection, they were collected in residential schools where they could be provided with nurturant environments as well as education and training. By mid-century, state-funded institutions for "the blind," "the deaf," and the "mentally retarded" were proliferating across the country. Following the Civil War, the nation was caught up on a wave of strong optimism stemming from the idea of cultural progress. The belief was widespread that the judgment and intelligence of handicapped children, especially of those who appeared to be mentally subnormal, could be increased by improving their simple sensory discrimination processes.

The optimism gave way to pessimism about handicaps near the end of the century, however, with the publication of Galton's work on eugenics. Although Mendel's laws of heredity had not yet been rediscovered, handicaps came to be viewed as genetic defects inherited from progenitors and capable of being passed on to descendants. It was at this time that the phrase "mental defectives" came into the common parlance. After the turn of the century, Lombroso's widely publicized

theories of criminality and its relation to mental subnormality led to the adoption of compulsory sterilization policies in a number of states. In *Buck* v. *Bell*, Supreme Court Justice Oliver Wendell Holmes, Jr. supported the policy as follows:

> It is better for all the world, if instead of waiting to execute degenerate offspring for crime or to let them starve for their imbecility, society can prevent those who are manifestly unfit from continuing their kind.[1]

During the first half of the twentieth century, programs for handicapped children were established in local schools at the behest of parents. This community movement developed slowly. At first, many children were not acceptable under the standards formulated for admission and most were admitted for minimal periods only. Some school systems organized what were called "special" classes or "opportunity" rooms for the handicapped pupils, and the terms quickly took on derogatory overtones. The first teachers in these programs came from residential schools and brought their categorical skills and techniques with them. As the community programs increased in number and population, a few colleges and universities around the country began training teachers for the education of the handicapped in programs that were separated out of the regular curriculum as "special education." Still following the pattern initiated in the residential schools, training was organized strictly around the handicap categories.

Innovative though the community program movement may have been, at its best it was merely tolerated in the public schools. Children and teachers were isolated in remote classrooms or separate buildings. Because the materials needed for the children's education were expensive, budgetary discussions centered on whether it was fair to spend public funds on a minority of children rather than to improve the programs for the majority. In those days, of course, the public schools were not prepared or expected to serve all children at all grade levels. Given that the purpose of schooling was conceptualized as preparing pupils to become contributory members of society, children were expected to stay in school only long enough to acquire the skills they would need as adults. Furthermore, although school attendance was mandatory for children, the schools were not mandated to provide educational services for all children, and uncounted numbers of children were left unserved.

# 1. PERSPECTIVES

World War II was a watershed for special education. Toward the end of the 1940s a number of states organized broad, public school programs to provide educational services, although still in isolated, categorical special education classes, for children with many different kinds of handicaps and learning problems. Institutions of higher education responded with numerous teacher-training programs in special education. This movement was given impetus during the 1950s when many states launched special "excess cost" funding programs for local schools that provided special education services; even greater impetus was provided during the 1960s when the federal government began its generous support of research and training programs in the areas of exceptionality and began to make direct grants to states and school districts for special education.

In 1948, no one knew exactly how many handicapped children there were in the nation although, generally, an estimate of 10 to 12 percent of the total child population was used. In that year, the special education classes enrolled a population of 442,000; by 1963, the number increased to 1,666,000,[2] and by the 1971-72 school year, 2,857,551 handicapped children were on the public school rolls (estimate, USOE Bureau of Education for the Handicapped). Thus, in the twenty-five years following World War II, the number of children identified as handicapped and served in special school programs increased sixfold. The sudden expansion of programs at the local school level for handicapped children resulted not from technological discoveries or conceptual changes but, rather, from a concatenation of circumstances at a particular time in our history.

The United States came out of World War II with an enlarged definition of democracy that included the concept of "freedom from fear and want" (Atlantic Charter, the statement signed by President F. D. Roosevelt and Prime Minister W. Churchill, August 14, 1941; endorsed by the United Nations Declaration of January 1, 1942). At the same time, the maimed veterans of the war refused to accept the prospect of merely living out their lives in forgotten custody. In response to their clamor, the federal government authorized a massive rehabilitation program that called upon such university and college disciplines as psychology, physical medicine, prosthetics, and vocational guidance to enhance the ability of the young veterans to return to society independently and competently. Some of the expertise developed under this program was extended to children with handicaps.

For example, mobility techniques devised for blinded war veterans were found to be applicable to blind adolescents; and the clinical psychology programs developed to treat veterans with emotional problems led to increased interest in treating the emotional and behavioral problems of children in school. A major effect of the veterans' rehabilitation program, and a not surprising one, in retrospect, was increased community acceptance for persons with different kinds of handicaps.

Medical research teams began to delve into the causes of birth defects and found that while some handicaps are genetic in origin, many result from intrauterine and birth accidents. For example, rubella during the first trimester of pregnancy was discovered to be, perhaps, the greatest single cause of mental retardation, blindness, or multiple handicaps; and retrolental fibroplasia, resulting from the overexposure of premature infants to large amounts of oxygen, was found to be the cause of much blindness in children. The public response to these findings was one of great sympathy.

Parents who had long despaired over the lack of services available in the public sector for handicapped—especially severely handicapped—children began to form categorically based organizations which soon became national in scope, such as the National Association for Retarded Citizens. These organizations became a powerful goading force in maintaining and improving special education services for children in schools and institutions.

The burgeoning special education programs of the 1950s and 1960s were still preponderantly based on categorical handicaps and conducted apart from the regular education classes; nevertheless, for the first time, many children with many different kinds of exceptionalities were schooled in the same buildings at the same time. Thus, it became possible for special educators to look across all categories and to note the similarities and differences among the learning problems of handicapped children. Furthermore, by the beginning of the 1970s, it became evident to a number of educators—special and regular—that a sizable percentage of the children who were being placed in special education classes were not so much handicapped as hard to teach. Special educators in particular began to reexamine their goals and purposes. Given the time, this reexamination might have led to a gradual change in the delivery of services to handicapped children. In the early 1970s, however, time ran out.



Because of the experience gained during the proliferation of special education classes in the twenty-five years following World War II, the field of special education has shifted its emphasis. Currently, it is negotiating a more integrated place for handicapped children in both public schools and communities under the aegis of mainstreaming. The movement is supported by a number of factors: the activities of militant parents' groups; the decrease in population growth; the cost of maintaining two parallel education systems; the political climate, which has led to increased concern for children who are identified as handicapped and "disadvantaged"; a general disillusionment with the prospects of "curing" human ailments through the ministrations of specialists in clinical environments; technical developments in measurements and observation systems; and value changes that emphasize "payoff" for the individual rather than institutions or society.

*Parent Organizations.* Parents of handicapped children began to organize about thirty years ago to obtain educational facilities for their offspring and to act as watchdogs of the institutions serving them. At first, the organizations concentrated on political action; since 1970, however, they have turned to the courts. This fact may be more important than any other in accounting for the changes in special education that are occurring now and are likely to occur in the near future.

The first major case brought by a parent organization was a landmark. It resulted in the extension of the *Brown v. Board of Education* integration mandate to handicapped children. In the case of the Pennsylvania Association for Retarded Children,[4] a consent decree established the principle that every child, no matter how seriously handicapped he may be, has *the right to education.* In other words, public schools are obligated to provide appropriate education for literally all children, either in existing facilities or by arrangement with other agencies. The appropriate function of public education was described as the equipping of handicapped children with "life skills," a principle that goes far beyond the goal of imparting academic skills. In addition, the court clearly indicated that the enhancement of individual development rather than potential returns to society is the critical object of education.

The PARC case also established the right of parents to participate in major decisions affecting their handicapped children. The state secretary of education in

Pennsylvania was directed to train "hearing officers" to conduct proceedings for parents and school representatives on such matters as school placement whenever there were serious disagreements about the proper course for a child. The court expressed a clear preference for the placement of handicapped children in regular classrooms with displacements to special classes and schools requiring extraordinary justification. Further, the court ordered that the education provided to all children be based on programs that are *appropriate* to the needs and capacities of each child.

Another set of influential cases, developed mainly in the context of institutional placements, has established the individual's *right to treatment,* which was defined as including education. The Wyatt-Stickney case[5] has prompted special interest because it helped to establish the principle that lack of funds is not an acceptable rationale for failing to provide treatment; public agencies are required either to raise sufficient funds or to reallocate existing resources to fulfill their treatment responsibilities to patients.

For parents' groups the PARC case has had an unexpected aftermath: the stamp of judicial approval on mainstreaming. Traditionally, the memberships of these organizations, mostly white, middle-class, and relatively affluent parents of severely handicapped youngsters, have been interested primarily in increasing the provision of special education services for their children. It happened, however, that their efforts had great impact on urban, poor, minority group children in ghetto schools; the influx of special education funds from state and federal sources made possible the establishment of "educable mentally retarded" and "emotionally disturbed" programs—the two categories that probably carry more stigma than any other—to which the ghetto children were frequently shunted because they were found to be hard to teach. Unlike the categorical parents' groups, however, the minority group parents resented and resisted the special class placements; they fought against the testing, classification, and labeling systems employed in the schools and for the return of their children to the mainstream.

The President's Committee on Mental Retardation[6] determined that children from impoverished and minority group homes are fifteen times more likely to be diagnosed as retarded than are children from higher income families, and that three-fourths of the nation's mentally retarded are found in the isolated and impoverished urban and rural slums. Because of the court actions of minority group parents, the administrators of school systems in our largest cities are under a virtual mandate to reverse the expansion of special education programs and to eliminate the testing, categorizing, and labeling practices which are associated with placement in such programs.

In associations of professionals, such as The Council for Exceptional Children, minority group members have also voiced their concern for the excessive allocations of minority group children to programs that remove them from the mainstream of education, and they are working within their associations for changes in the policies and operations of the schools. In fact, there is a rising and very broad demand among special educators for the elimination of any activities that degrade and stigmatize children. The minority groups and professionals who challenge the special placements and simple categorization of children have taken a position that is, in fact, discordant with the strictly handicapping categories or concepts on which parents' groups are organized.

While associations of parents of handicapped children are seeking to expand the services of special education for their children, minority group members are tending to take strongly negative attitudes toward almost every activity conducted in the name of special education which involves negative labeling of children. This opposition is particularly a problem in our largest cities where the future of special education as a separate service has been placed in doubt.

*Mainstreaming.* Mainstreaming in the schools is one manifestation of a much larger social phenomenon. Broadly speaking, the phenomenon can be characterized as de-institutionalization, that is, the maintenance in the community with supportive services of qualified persons who, otherwise, would be committed to hospitals, prisons, or other institutions for exceptions to the social norms. In a sense, the movement can be seen as a reversal of the two-box theory of treatment in which a person is either normal and law-abiding and needs no treatment, or he is sick, poor, disturbed, asocial, or old and institutionalized for treatment or care. Some of the support services that make this kind of mainstreaming possible are community psychiatric programs, day care centers, AA (Alcoholics Anonymous), half-way houses, probation and parole officers, Meals on Wheels (for aged home-bound persons), foster homes, and social welfare agencies.

In the schools, the two-box theory was characteristic of the separation of pupils into those placed in regular education classrooms and those placed in special education settings; every child was classified as either normal or handicapped and placed accordingly. Mainstreaming does not require such classifications. Just as it has been possible to deliver supportive services and treatments to enable persons with unusual needs to be maintained in the larger community, so in the schools it has become possible to deliver special education services to most children with learning problems while they are maintained in the regular classroom. With mainstreaming, it is possible to treat the learning problems of most children without regard for whether they are medically or legally handicapped.

Because the kind of handicap a child bears is less important educationally than the kind of learning problem presented by the child, mainstreaming permits the treatment of the problem without isolating, labeling, or stigmatizing any child. Thus, special education services can be delivered to pupils who are suffering temporary learning problems, and a large proportion of so-called normal children undergo such experiences, as well as do pupils whose problems are long-lived.

Mainstreaming is a set or general predisposition to arrange for the education of children with handicaps or learning problems within the environment provided for all other children—the regular school and normal home and community environment—whenever feasible. It needs to be said immediately that most of the action required for mainstreaming is not the reallocation of children to regular schools—tossing them back to regular schools and classrooms without adequate provisions can be a cruelty to both children and teachers—but the changing of the mainstream so that it is able to accommodate the individual educational needs of children with many kinds of learning differences, including those who, otherwise, would be labeled "handicapped" and segregated in isolated settings.

When mainstreaming is implemented properly, each placement is made on an individual basis. That is, all children with handicaps or learning problems are not dumped indiscriminately in regular classrooms and there permitted to struggle as best they can. Mainstreaming is based on a philosophy of individual programming. Each child is placed in the educational setting, whether regular classroom for part or all of the day, special class, or special school, which is best suited to meet his needs for optimal development at a particular point in time. At the same time, the goal of each placement is to return the child to a more normal setting as soon as possible. Every placement, therefore, is a two-way street in that the child can be moved out of it as easily as she or he is moved into it. Regular reviews of children's progress are essential, consequently.

Obviously, mainstreaming makes new demands on both regular classroom and special education teachers. In the past, a regular education teacher was expected to know enough about handicapping conditions to be able to identify children with such problems for referral out of the classroom into special education settings. At the same time, special education teachers were trained to work directly with children with certain specific handicaps (as in the days of residential schools) in separate special settings.

Under mainstreaming, different roles are demanded of both kinds of teachers. The trend for training special education teachers for indirect resource teacher roles rather than narrow specialists is well established in many preparation centers.[7] Concurrently, programs are under way to provide regular education teachers with training in the identification of learning problems. At the local school level, regular and special education teachers in mainstreamed programs are no longer isolated in separate classrooms. They work together in teams to share knowledge, skills, observations, and experiences to enhance the programs for children with special problems, whether the children are permanently or temporarily handicapped. Thus, it has become essential for special teachers to learn the skills of consultation and for both teachers to learn techniques of observation as well as communication.

Many special educators now conceptualize their field as covering a broad continuum or cascade of administrative and instructional arrangements, varying from regular class placements to resource room plans, itinerant teaching arrangements, part-time special classes, full-time special classes, local day schools, residential schools, treatment centers, and hospitals. In the past, handicapped children tended to be rejected automatically to special stations, with the most seriously handicapped rejected all the way down to end-of-the-line residential centers. Under mainstreaming, these special stations are not eliminated, but a more careful evaluation process, involving parents, is followed before children are placed in them. At its best, mainstreaming permits the thrilling discovery that public schools can indeed accommodate handicapped pupils at some level of

service and can become part of the broad community mainstream support structures for the children who are different.

It should be noted that the mainstreaming of handicapped children is not a concept originated by the courts. Mainstreaming systems were already established in some school districts before the Pennsylvania PARC decision. In fact, the involvement of the courts in the mandating of mainstreaming may hinder the development of the concept in some areas because it demands too many changes too fast. Furthermore, although the courts can hand down mandates, they cannot provide resources to implement their mandates. For many school districts, the combination of court or legislative orders and inadequate appropriations have resulted in the production of fine programs in the files and token implementation in practice.

*Parent Involvement.* Out of the social change which has been fermenting in this country for the past decade or two has come the message that the people served by institutions should participate in the decisions that affect them. College students have asserted their right to influence organizational and academic policies; welfare recipients, how the agencies serving them are operated; and parents, the establishment of local school policies. This movement has led to the decentralization of school operations, that is, the formation of neighborhood councils in which are vested some of the authority for the operations of local schools that were formerly held in central school offices. Examples of such decentralized school operations can be seen in many of the nation's largest cities (e.g., New York, Philadelphia, Chicago, and Detroit).[8]

In the placement of children who have special needs, the concept of shared authority is being expressed in due process procedures; that is, in informal and formal meetings and in formalized avenues of hearings and appeals through which parents participate in determining the way their children are educated. Because of the extraordinary opportunities special educators have had to work with parents individually and in groups, they seem to be in the position to help lead the way to develop school-wide systems to provide for the participation of all persons affected by school decisions. If one believes that the authority for basic policy formulation ought to rest with the people affected by the policies—not everyone sees this principle as positive—then special educators have a special responsibility in helping school systems to restructure policies and operations to include parental inputs.

*Individuality.* Despite the long-standing, compulsory school-attendance laws in virtually all states, a sizable group of children in the past have been either not admitted to or expelled from attendance. In most communities, no one really knew how many children were out of school at a given time. For example, in Pennsylvania, after the consent decree in the PARC case began to be implemented, 15,000 children were found who were not being served by the public schools; of this number the majority (52 percent) were only mildly or moderately mentally retarded.[9]

We are seeing radical changes in the implementation of the school attendance laws in most states because, in part, of the activities of students themselves in seeking their rights to education. Individual students have been aided by lawyers, civil libertarians, and professionals to use the courts to secure these rights. Many legislatures have removed categorical bases for the demission of children from schools, such as the repeal of laws permitting the exclusion of the trainable mentally retarded. Consequently, schools have been forced to deliberate each proposed demission on the basis of individual merits and following due process procedures. Educators are being mandated, not only to enroll all children who are presented to the schools and to place them in appropriate programs, but actively to seek out all children for enrollment, including those with special needs. Implicit in this movement is the concept that the rights of the individual supersede institutional and even societal concerns and values.

The emergence of individual priority is reflected in the conceptualization of programs in terms of individual rather than social reward and in the de-emphasis of the statistical norm. For example, in measuring and monitoring, there is a growing tendency for schools to rely on domain- and criterion-referenced rather than norm-referenced testing.[10] New management systems, such as IGE (Individually Guided Education), stress individual development; curricula stress individual adaptations, as in IPI (Individual Prescribed Instruction); and a number of systems for the individualizing of instruction through computerized assistance are being developed. The applied behavior analysts now working in the schools, following the principles developed by Skinner, Bijou, Lindsley, Haring, and others, give preeminence to data on and instruction for the individual.

Special educators, more than regular educators, have long been concerned with the individualization of education programs for their clientele and they are currently in a position to help implement the principle in mainstreaming programs. Indeed, individualization is a key element in the mainstreaming of handicapped pupils.

### THE FUTURE

If education is still conceptualized as a pupil on one end of a log and a teacher on the other end, then the judiciary is now the fulcrum between the two. It is difficult to believe that the condition is a permanent one, however. In extending the protection of the Fourteenth Amendment first to minority group children (*Brown* v. *Board of Education*)[11] and then to handicapped children (*PARC* v. *Pennsylvania*)[12] the courts paved the way for additional litigation in which remedies could be sought against failures to implement the mandates and subsidiary principles could be clarified. But the courts do not concern themselves with the day-to-day operations of institutions. In the PARC case, for example, the court mandated the establishment of due process procedures through which parents and students can participate with school personnel in the planning of individual educational programs and in the resolution of any disagreements that might arise.

In some states, it seems, these consultation procedures are not yet in wide use.[13] On the surface, it appears that a lack of familiarity with the procedures and the persistence of old patterns of behavior account for the disuse. Parents are not accustomed to participating in making educational decisions and they may need some education in their rights to do so. With time, however, we can expect that the consultation and due process procedures will become the customary avenue for parents and older students to share with educators the responsibilities for determining not only individual programs but school policies as well.

Although in the large cities many minority group parents have fought the placement of their children in special education classes with their derogatory labels, they are not antagonistic to intensive educational services in more normal settings. If in the past special education fell into disrepute, it was because of the anomalous position of handicapped children in the school systems and the excessive separation of special from regular education. All parents are eager for their children to receive whatever services they need, providing the services do not carry discriminatory overtones. In the future, it appears that special and remediation services will become resources for every teacher and child in the schools.

New roles for all teachers can be predicted. Special education teachers more often will work cooperatively with regular teachers. The training of regular education teachers will include components on handicapping conditions as well as on techniques for the individualization of educational programs. Teachers will be encouraged to work together in teams in order to share experiences, expertise, and decision-making. More important, perhaps, teachers will be encouraged to individualize their teaching styles and modes of operation. Teacher-training programs, it is hoped, will exemplify the principles that teachers will use in the classrooms.

In the future, schools will place less emphasis on the kind of handicap a child has and more on the child's learning problems. Since many children have need of special services for a temporary period at some time in their school careers, they will be able to receive special help on the basis of their problems. One far-reaching consequence of this change is that special education funding will need to shift away from systems that produce dollar flow only as individual children are placed in labeled categories. So far, it seems, special education funding has had strong political appeal because it is directed to individual children who are handicapped: the mentally retarded, the blind, the deaf, and so on. Undoubtedly it will be a difficult job to shift the payoff to a different unit, such as personnel employed in programs or major cost elements themselves (such as diagnosis, transportation, resource rooms), but some states have now shown that it is possible to move categorical funding to new, less troublesome units.

Traditionally, in the United States, schools have been operated as local enterprises and federal supports for the schools have been limited in nature. The rationale for the customary mode of operation has been that with local controls and financing the schools would be more responsive to local needs. Unfortunately, however, not all states or local districts have the same resources for the support of education and, thus, differences occur. If equality of educational opportunity is to become a national standard, then it is almost inevitable that the federal government will intervene to upgrade schools, teacher training, and educational programs in those areas of the country where educational opportunities do not meet the national standard.

School districts are also unequal in access to educational expertise. Should the federal government intervene in the financing of schools to equalize educational opportunities, it is also quite likely that it will show some concern for the equalization of technical assistance to school administrators. In agriculture, medicine, and other segments of the economy, for example, the federal government has established support systems to assure the equal dissemination of information and technical assistance to all practitioners. During the late 1960s, the USOE Bureau of Education Personnel Development established a series of leadership training institutes in special education which proved that support systems in education are both feasible and profitable. Through support systems, the professional and technical resources of the nation can be mobilized in any quantity or specialty needed to facilitate change of any kind in a particular area. Support systems not only assure that federal funds are expended on the purposes for which they have been granted, but that the purposes are achieved.[14]

Federal funds in the future will be made available also to support preschool activities for all children. Just as in the past the age of compulsory school attendance was extended upward to eighteen years in most states, so we believe the age will be extended downward to perhaps three years. Handicaps and learning problems do not appear full-blown when children enter first grade, and the earlier the handicapping conditions are identified, the sooner compensatory measures can be introduced and the more effective they are. The results of the Head Start and Follow Through programs indicate the effectiveness of such programs in, for example, raising the potential of children from disadvantaged homes for success in school and increasing the language facility of children who are deaf.[15] For many children, early educational intervention obviates the necessity for later and more expensive special services.

Like all social institutions, schools serve the society in which they exist. The future of our schools, therefore, is inexorably related to the future of the nation and to the directions it takes politically, economically, socially, ecologically, and industrially. The priorities we set determine the purposes for which public monies will be raised and appropriated. We define and redefine the concepts on which the nation was established. Right now we can look back to the founding of the nation and take satisfaction in the growth of equality and individuality, in the increased

# 1. PERSPECTIVES

recognition given to individual differences and needs, and in the determination of education as a constitutional right. It will take considerable vigilance to maintain these gains. Rights, like muscles, atrophy when they are not exercised.


### Notes

1. 274 U.S. 200, 207 (1927).

2. R. P. Mackie, "Spotlighting Advances in Special Education," *Exceptional Children* 32 (1965): 77-81.

3. 347 U.S. 483 (1954).

4. *PARC* v. *Pennsylvania,* 334 F. Supp. 1257 (E.D. Pa., 1971).

5. *Wyatt* v. *Aderholt,* 334 F. Supp. 1341 (M.D. Alabama, 1971).

6. President's Committee on Mental Retardation, *MR Priority Report: The Retarded Victims of Poverty* (Washington, D.C.: Government Printing Office, 0-310-156, 1954).

7. E. N. Deno, ed., *Instructional Alternatives for Exceptional Children* (Reston, Va.: Council for Exceptional Children, 1973).

8. M. C. Reynolds, ed., *Special Education and School System Decentralization* (Minneapolis: Leadership Training Institute/Special Education, University of Minnesota, 1975).

9. Thomas K. Gilhool, "Changing Public Policies: Roots and Forces," *Minnesota Education* 2 (Winter 1976).

10. W. Hiveley and M. C. Reynolds, eds., *Domain-Referenced Testing in Special Education* (Reston, Va.: Council for Exceptional Children, 1975).

11. 347 U.S. 483 (1954).

12. 334 F. Supp. 1257 (E.D. Pa. 1971).

13. Gilhool, "Public Policies."

14. For a discussion of educational support systems see the contributions to M. C. Reynolds, ed., *National Technical Assistance Systems in Special Education: Report of the Conference in Washington, D.C., May 1974* (Minneapolis: Leadership Training Institute/Special Education, University of Minnesota, 1976).

15. H. H. Spicker, N. J. Anastasiow, and W. Hodges, eds., *Early Childhood Development and Education of Children with Special Needs* (Minneapolis: Leadership Training Institute/Special Eduction, University of Minnesota, forthcoming).

# Mainstreaming: Merging Regular and Special Education

## Forces Influencing Change in Special Education

**O**ver the past two decades, theory and practice in special education have undergone major changes. These changes have been the result of four powerful forces: educators themselves, parents and advocacy groups, the courts, and government policy and legislation. These various forces have acted together to produce rapid and profound changes in special education delivery systems.

### Educators

Special educators themselves were among the first to question the way the special education delivery system was organized. In 1968 Lloyd Dunn, a leading authority in special education, questioned the efficacy of placing mildly handicapped children in special classes. The work of Dunn and others in the 1960s stimulated many forces within the profession that were gathering momentum.

Elementary and secondary teacher preparation programs began to include training for teaching children with learning problems. Research was being translated into practice in the development of more effective teaching strategies. The concepts of individualized instruction and heterogeneous grouping moved out of educational textbooks into regular classrooms. Improvements in assessment techniques assisted educators in more accurately describing and providing for the individual differences demonstrated by each child. Specialists such as speech and language therapists and guidance counselors assisted classroom teachers in developing and implementing instructional programs. Our schools began to open their doors and welcome paraprofessionals, parent volunteers, and high school-aged tutors. All of these

**Susan E. Hasazi,**

**Paul D. Rice,**

**and Robert York**

Mainstreaming: Merging Regular and Special Education, Susan E. Hasazi, Paul D. Rice, and Robert York, *Phi Delta Kappa Educational Foundation*, 1979, ©1979 Phi Delta Kappa Educational Foundation.

# 1. PERSPECTIVES

developments in regular education encouraged learning environments designed to meet the needs of each individual child. Teachers began to accept, and expect, wide ranges of skill levels within each classroom. Children learning to work together in spite of their differences was recognized as a worthy goal.

Our technology has advanced so that we now have the skills and knowledge necessary to educate most children within the public schools. The barriers to providing such a broad spectrum of education are largely attitudinal. Through increased knowledge about and experience with handicapped children, nonhandicapped children will hopefully learn one of the most important lessons our educational system can teach—the value and acceptance of individual differences.

## Parents and Advocacy Groups

A leading parent advocate once said that her young handicapped child would be the light of her life if she didn't have to think about her child's future. Parents, faced with exclusion and uncertainty regarding the educational opportunities available to their children, have made a powerful impact on the educational system. Initially, these groups were formed to provide support for and encourage communication among parents of handicapped children. As a result of increased communication, concerned parents began to focus their attention and efforts on changing social policies. They no longer accepted their children's exclusion from educational opportunities because there were no programs available or was not enough money to fund appropriate services. Advocacy groups such as the National Association for Retarded Children launched public information campaigns that influenced state legislatures and eventually the courts.

Professional associations such as the Council for Exceptional Children provided a forum for special educators to broadcast their fundamental belief, "as that of recognizing every child as a unique composite of potential abilities and learning needs for whom an individual educational program must be designed." Further, the Council stated "that the purpose of special education was to enlarge the variety of educational programs for all children whatever their needs" (*Policy Statements of the Council for Exceptional Children*).

Parent-initiated court action and federal and state legislation have required that parents and educators work together to develop appropriate educational plans for each child. It is only through such joint efforts that the promise of mainstreaming will become a reality.

## The Courts

Parent advocacy groups have been successful in bringing their case to the courts. In 1971 the Pennsylvania Association for Retarded Children (PARC) filed suit on behalf of 13 retarded children who were not receiving educational services. Thomas Gilhool, the attorney representing PARC, argued that "every child, every exceptional child, every retarded child, is capable of benefiting from an education. There is no such thing as an uneducable and untrainable child." The court, through a consent agreement, found in favor of PARC, thus establishing the principles of right to education, due process, and least restrictive environment. These three principles were to become highly significant in the ensuing development of special education and mainstreaming.

In the *PARC* decision relating to the principle of least restrictive environment, the court ordered that:

> . . . access to schooling was to be accorded to all of those children within the context of a presumption that placement in a regular class is pre-

ferred to placement in a special class and placement in a special class is preferable to placement in any other program whether homebound, itinerant, or institutional.

In other words, the child must be educated within the closest approximation to the typical classroom as the child's particular conditions dictate. Placement options that allow for interaction with nonhandicapped children are required.

Another principle affirmed in the *PARC* decision was that of due process. This principle assures that parents must be involved in any decisions related to placement of their child. It requires that prior to assessment, program change, or service implementation, parents be informed and agree to the program for their child in writing. Further, it requires specification of a formal system for dealing with any disagreement in a child's program that should arise.

Later in 1971 the Federal Court in the District of Columbia ruled in *Mills* v. *Board of Education* that the right to an education is available to all handicapped children, not just the retarded. Further, in responding to the defendants (the board of education) who claimed that such action would be impossible given limited financial resources, the court said:

> The District of Columbia's interest in educating the excluded children clearly must outweigh its interest in preserving financial resources. If sufficient funds are not available to finance all of the services in programs that are needed and desirable in the system, then the available funds must be extended equitably in such a manner that no one child is entirely excluded from a publicly supported education consistent with his needs and ability to benefit therefrom. The inadequacies of the District of Columbia public school system, whether occasioned by insufficient funding or administrative inefficiencies certainly cannot be permitted to bear more heavily on the exceptional or handicapped than on the normal child.

*PARC* and *Mills* were landmark cases, but current special education policies and procedures have been influenced by a number of other cases since 1970 as well. *Wyatt* v. *Stickney* established the principle of right to treatment. The court ruled that citizens residing in state schools and hospitals had the right to individually designed treatment programs including an education designed to meet their specific needs. Further, the court ruled that programs must be reviewed often and revised if necessary. *Diana* v. *State Board of Education* and *Larry P.* v. *Riles* questioned the procedures used to determine eligibility for assignment in special education classrooms. The defendants in both cases claimed that current practices were culturally biased and resulted in a disproportionate number of certain minority groups in special education classrooms. These two cases have resulted in injunctions against group testing, development of tests to measure more accurately achievement levels of minority group children, and parent consent prior to placement in special education programs.

## Federal Policy and Legislation

The changes that have taken place in special education in the 1960s and 1970s could not have happened without the active involvement of the federal government. While federal support for education of the handicapped goes back more than a century (Gallaudet College for the deaf was established in 1864), it was not until the late 1950s and early 1960s that significant federal support for special education was begun. The funding of the Cooperative Research Act in 1957, which was primarily aimed at special education research, is typically cited as the critical point in the history of government support for special education. In the 10 years following, a series of laws was passed extending research

# 1. PERSPECTIVES

funding, providing support for teacher training, creating a network of university-affiliated research and training centers, and culminating in the creation by law of the Bureau of Education of the Handicapped in 1967. Throughout this exciting period in the history of special education, the influence of two prominent political leaders cannot be underestimated. John F. Kennedy, both as senator and President, consistently supported special education and brought its importance to the awareness of the American people. Likewise, Hubert H. Humphrey, throughout his political career, was a strong and faithful supporter of important legislation for the handicapped. The leadership of two men, both of whom had handicapped children in their own families, helped to set a climate conducive to federal level support that has continued to this date.

From 1974 to 1978 the impact of legislation upon special education has been profound. Public Law 93-380, the Education Amendments of 1974, guaranteed due process procedures in placement, nondiscriminatory testing, and confidentiality of school records. Further, it established the principle of least restrictive environment, which requires that to the greatest extent possible, handicapped children be educated with nonhandicapped peers. In November, 1975, Public Law 94-142, the Education for All Handicapped Children Act, was passed, expanding upon Public Law 93-380. This important law serves as a statement of national policy. Once and for all it insures that every handicapped child, regardless of handicapping condition, has the right to a publicly supported, appropriate education. To help attain this goal, Congress has provided the states with additional federal dollars to build a full continuum of services for all children.

As a result of federal legislation, the children in our public schools represent a broader range of humanity than ever before. Edwin Martin, director of the Bureau of Education for the Handicapped, quotes a "wise teacher" as saying "when people conceived the world to be flat, they feared sailing off the edge, but when they conceived it as round, exploration and discovery became possible" (Martin, 1973). Educators must now become explorers in researching, planning, and implementing programs for the handicapped.

# IMPRESSIONS OF SPECIAL EDUCATION IN AMERICA

## TREVOR J. TEBBS

*Trevor J. Tebbs is a special education teacher certified in education and the handicapped child. He has served as co-ordinator of the Ways and Means project in the United Kingdom and is consultant to continuing Ways and Means projects. Until recently, he served as deputy head master of a special school in the United Kingdom. He has just completed an extensive tour of the United States examining the mainstreaming programs there. This article, his view of the mainstreaming programs, was written expressly for our publication.*

To have a special need, whatever the nature of that need, however caused or perpetuated, whether it be physical, mental, environmental or cultural, is a handicap. It is a handicap in that the individual with that special need is less able, perhaps even, never able to fully play his or her part in the multifarious aspects which make up life, both in terms of the quality of life in the individual and in society in general. In times past, in the United States, Great Britain[1] and doubtless many other countries, to be handicapped was something one had to suffer, accept and live with. Little, if any, quarter was afforded to anyone who was in some way considered "different" from the accepted "norm". Those mildly disabled or "slow" probably muddled through life, but it was practically unheard of that anyone properly handicapped could or should have any potential or contribution to make as a member of society. Equally, mass public opinion was that society should not contribute to the alleviation or servicing of the handicapped, and so those with special needs were largely ignored, put away, used or mocked. Not so today, particularly in America.

Equality of opportunity is legally endorsed and "enforced" by withdrawable federal funds. It is evident that many inequalities, especially with regard to education and the right of the handicapped to education, have been forced into the open. Pressure and legislation brought about by parents, professionals and the handicapped themselves have focused the attention of the educators and public upon the needs of the child who is in some way disabled. It is evident to the visitor that the handicapped, their parents and the various other agencies involved in the well-being of the handicapped, are a force to be reckoned with in American society. The handicapped are in the limelight and their cause is widely publicised. Things are happening for them. They are becoming a political platform and an emotive issue. People appear to be bending over backwards to facilitate their needs, provide all manner of opportunities and clear their way, quite literally, with wide doors, ramps, special facilities, jobs, etc. It is their day. The educational needs of the exceptional child are manifestly special and it would appear that those special educational needs have been recognised and are being serviced

as never before. Special education has consequently become an obvious and integral part of schooling, pre-school through to higher education and teacher training. Those delivering the service have also taken on a new importance. The training and expertise of special education are becoming an essential ingredient in American Education.

## IMPLEMENTATION OF PL 94-142

It would be impossible to present one's impression of American Special Education without direct and detailed reference to PL 94-142. Already in previous paragraphs, indirect reference has been made with regard to equality of opportunity, the right of the handicapped to full educational facilities, and consequent growth in special education. Education and the cause of the handicapped are evidently issues bonded together, there is no separating them. The cement is PL 94-142, it's related rules and regulations and foregoing resolutions, e.g. Chapter 766 enacted in Massachusetts.

It is not difficult to see that PL 94-142 has had a most profound and far reaching effect upon both teacher and student at whatever level and in whatever corner of the U.S.A. To call the law controversial would perhaps be an understatement, but it will do to describe it's prime effect. It certainly has caused and will continue to cause controversy, but more importantly, it has caused many educators to look closely at provision made for the education of children with special needs. Many questions have been asked, many opinions have been expressed, many voices have been raised in protest, and even more have spoken in favour of equal educational opportunity.

The autonomy of each of the states is at first a little hard for a visitor to appreciate, but when it is realised that each state has had the power to make it's own laws and regulations with regard to educational services, the diversity of provision made in the various states and even local education authorities throughout America is understandable. All manner of rearrangements, alterations, ammendments, policy changes, reallocation of funds and children, have been required by law to take place. The state

# 1. PERSPECTIVES

of Pennsylvania, for example, cares for children with special needs, in particular, the TMH* and EMH* child, in special education centres. These centres have trained staff, the facilities are geared to the special needs of the children, the buildings are each on a separate campus and each serves a large area of the state. The state education department has spent considerable time and effort in the past convincing the public of the importance and qualities inherent to these centres. In the considered opinion of the providers of education, the separate centre was best and most appropriate for the children with special needs. PL 94-142 cast a different light upon the matter and considerable confusion is the result. Undercurrents of feeling from all directions make the administrator's job difficult. Anxieties in both special and regular classroom teachers surface. Job security and "mainstreaming" become constant topics of conversation. Newly PL 94-142 aware and stigma conscious parents breathe threatingly down superintendent's neck.

On the other hand, in Washington State, one particular school district,[2] doubtless known by many, has been working to the letter and spirit of PL 94-142 for many years, before there even was mention of the possibility of education for the handicapped in the majority of the states. The staff of that district now present in-service training to teachers and administrators throughout the states, in hope that their experience, of over twenty years, might ease the minds and help solve the problems presented by the regulations of PL 94-142.

Between the two examples mentioned lay variations of provision, including virtually no provision at all, especially for the more severely handicapped child. PL 94-142 has changed that, or rather, has started a process of change. For what the law demands is really quite considerable, and to have immediately complied with the letter of the law would have been humanly impossible. It is my impression that despite the law being signed by President Ford in 1975, 1979 is only just beginning to see a move in the direction of meaningful compliance. In the days of steam trains, I used to watch the engines move off from the station, wheels spinning on the rails and despite a full head of steam, making slow progress at first. The situation in the U.S. appears to be very similar-the order to move forward has been given, but the wheels are only just beginning to bite into the rails and momentum is gathering. The move forward and impetus in different states, down through to individual schools, is varied depending much upon the enthusiasm, the commitment and the attitude of those involved.

It is in fact doubtless that both PL 94-142 and the practical outworkings of it will provide a tremendous example to many countries in the Western World who are considering the place and opportunities afforded their handicapped citizens. The phrase "that handicapped students be educated with non-handicapped students", "mainstreaming", is not the whole story, only a part. Read on from that phrase and discover, "... be educated with non-handicapped students to the extent appropriate." PL 94-142 legislates for much more than purely mainstreaming or integration. In fact, as I visited various areas, met with teachers and administrators, it was evident that the term "mainstreaming" is a misused term and fast losing ground in the eyes of those responsible for the planning and organisation necessary to be in compliance with the law. "Mainstreaming" can and does give the wrong impression as to what in reality PL 94-142 is about, "... to the extent appropriate..." is really a very important phrase in my mind. It alerts one's attention to the greater part of the law. The phrase infers that the education of the handicapped student with the non-handicapped students may not be wholly appropriate in some instances. It infers an alternative provision. In fact the law speaks of the necessity of alternative provision. Each agency is required to have various alternative placements available, including special schools, home instruction and instruction in hospitals and institutions.

The law speaks of the provision of the "least restrictive environment", the L.R.E. L.R.E. was something I heard frequently referred to and it's use indicates an increasing awareness and understanding of the law. It clearly shows that the enormous differences and needs of individual children are not expected to be coped with by one person, in one place, at one time. To provide "the least restricted environment" for children with special needs has given the authorities an element of flexibility. It has given opportunity for the provision of the wide variety of educational facilities forming a continuum, each designed, manned, organised and serviced with due regard to the spirit and letter of the law, and with due regard to the needs unique to each child. I must be frank, compared with what there is to be seen and observed, I have only scratched the surface. However, from the observations made in the states and schools visited, many of the facilities are being housed under the same roof; and so "mainstreaming" is taking place to the extent that the school principal is responsible for the education of the handicapped and the non-handicapped in one building.

The provision of this sort of environment is less "restrictive" in that, in theory at least, every opportunity is provided for them to work with non-handicapped fellows. The handicapped are allowed access to the mainstream, they need not be restricted forever by their handicap and are afforded equal opportunity to succeed if by any means they "make the grade" or are thought able to "make the grade."

---

*Trainable Mentally Handicapped. Educable Mentally Handicapped

During my visit in the United States, I was able to observe the two types of integration, these being what I suppose are the first steps towards full compliance of PL 94-142. The first type of integration, is what the Warnock Report* calls "locational" integration, that is children, regardless of handicap, are grouped in one common location. It may be the case however, that despite locational integration, in reality the handicapped may be segregated as totally as if they were housed on a separate campus. This may be due, in part, to the time-tabling, the use of play areas at different times than non-handicapepd students or the arrival and departure to and from school at different times.

The second type of integration is, again in Warnock terminology "social and (semi)-functional integration." Social, in that handicapped and non-handicapped do meet with each other and are given the opportunity to socialise, talk with, play with, etc. and share in their contribution to every day activities, especially the non-academic aspects of the school life.[4] Semi-functional, where, as well as social integration taking place, disabled students considered able to "make the grade" in certain aspects of the curriculum are put into mainstream classes and educated on equal terms with their non-handicapped colleagues.

It is my impression that only the most capable EMR or EMH and LD children are presently included in mainstream classroom situations on a regular semi-functional basis. I have met teachers of the hearing impaired who have expressed great pleasure and satisfaction at having members of their classes moved either into regular classes, on a full-time or part-time basis, or into EMR classes. Also, I have met with the situation where TMH students have been placed for varying lengths of time with EMR groups. This same concept applies to the gifted. In Silver City, New Mexico, I met a teacher responsible for a special part-time course for gifted children. There the children worked in regular classes but were given special tutoring each day. It is evident that there is flexibility which facilitates vertical movement within a school situation, in other words the "cascade" system in action. This to my mind, is the essence of PL91-142, provision and opportunity to enjoy that flexibility, regardless of national origin, sex, economic status, race, religion, and phyiscal or mental handicap.

## PARENTAL INVOLVEMENT

A lasting impression will be the real power of the attorney. The accountability of educators, whether at the "chalk face" or at administration office is somewhat awesome to one whose country is still basically passive with regard to teachers and the education of children.[5] One wonders how long it will before the British parent has as much legal say in certain educational matters as does the American parent. It is my impression that although their complete involvement is regarded as a legally endorsed and essential ingredient in their children's education, especially the education of their handicapped children, a minority take full advantage of their rights. Those who do, it can be supposed, are sufficient to make administrators and teachers err on the side of caution in terms of provision, placement and programming.

This brings me to the all important document, the I.E.P. I mention it now in respect of the parents' involvement especially with respect to the production of the programme, for it is here that advantage of their rights would appear not to be taken in full. Doubtless the degree of involvement is bound to vary



depending upon the area in which the child and his parents is situated. It may also reflect the degree to which the parents are actively concerned with the child and his development.

Disinterested and apathetic parents are surely a universal problem. It could also, however, reflect a degree of intimidation by officialdom over the child's parents. Although my experience of conferences included a meeting where only teacher, psychologist and parent came together to discuss the educational well-being of the child, the I.E.P. and the placement, technically several other professionals have the right to attend. Teachers have indicated that the array of professionals eligible to attend an I.E.P. or evaluation meeting, may well prove to be just too formidable for the more humble and less able parents. Despite this, it is my opinion that the parents' contribution is recognised as being vital to the development of the child and is openly and unquestionably sought by special educators. In the U.K., workshops have been set up in special schools where the parents of mentally handicapped children can actively take part in their children's education, following activities, programmes and methods devised in conjunction with teachers and other parents, in a home environment after school hours and during vacation periods.[6] The parents' contribution, however, is not sought after in the same way or to the same extent as in the U.S. Of course, the British parent, once aware that their child is in need of special educational services, technically at least, have the choice as to where and in which special school their child is educated. In practice they are limited to one suitable school in one area, often there only being one special school serving an area which includes several large towns and villages. Their interest in the child whilst it is at school is highly valued by the teachers, but "consent" is not required in the same way as it is in the U.S. with regard to the child's programme. I quote from the Illinois Regulations governing special education--they would appear to be typical of similar regulations produced in the other states:

> "Consent" --The parent(s) 1, has been informed of all necessary information, 2. understands and agrees in writing to carrying out the activity for which consent is sought and 3. understands that the granting of consent is voluntary on his or her part and may be revoked at any time."

As I have said, the parents' input is very important, but one wonders if the power that the parent has to revoke consent and demand a new programme or replacement of a child into alternative provision might not be something of an inhibiting factor in the work and attitudes of a teacher.

The need for accuracy in the screening and identification process, the extensive diagnosis, assessment and programming procedures is of grave importance to the education of the handicapped. This must be fundamental to the whole process of delivery of special education and it is good to see that it is undertaken by a multi-disciplinary team. That such a team should work together to establish the child's present level of educational performance, annual goals and short term instructional objectives, specific special education and related services, etc. is an important concept. It is bound to produce a clearer picture of the exceptional child and, therefore, provision made for him or her is going to be more precise and appropriate. This in turn is going to benefit the child, teacher, school, parent and society alike. Diagnosis and assessment certainly would appear to be one of the strengths of American special education. Teachers seem to be more aware of the structure of a child's development than many teachers int the U.K. and one wonders if it might be so because of the pressure put upon American teachers to work in a more accurately structured and programmed style, by the existence of grades and the I.E.P.

## SPECIAL EDUCATION RESOURCES

A great deal of thought is evidently being given to the important aspect of related services in special education. The federal government, State Education Departments and local authorities would appear to be making every effort to provide the adequate back-up of all varieties demanded by law. This back-up might include financial assistance, trained personnel, resources, or funding of research projects related to the needs of the exceptional child. All this has the tendency to leave the visitor a little wide-eyed!

The amount of money budgeted to date and the expenditure detailed for future development in special education is simply colossal. The American experience must cause other countries to look hyper-critically at their own plans for integration of the handicapped into the mainstream of education and on into society. Although many may disagree, financial commitment might in the end be indicative of the depth of concern, a measure of the social and ideological commitment to the cause of equal opportunity for the handicapped and less priviledged in any one society. Finance must be heavily available to even consider enacting such a law as PL 94-142, for without proper resources, personnel with specialist skill and knowledge, and other facilities, the concept of integration would seem likely to remain but an attractive idea.

There are two particular resource developments which I found interesting and which warrant close examination. The first is the Meeting Street School Project, co-ordinated by Martha Robinson in East Providence, Rhode Island and the second Dr. Hal Chew's Resource Centre at Gibsonia, Pennsylvania.

First, the Meeting Street School Project. As an educator who is amongst other things, concerned with strategies which can be used to increase positive attitudes towards exceptional children, I found the concept central to this project wholly good and exciting. Many readers may already know of the project and perhaps they will concur with my enthusiastic recognition of its importance to special and regular education equally. The Meeting Street School Project is about giving non-handicapped children an insight into the world of the handicapped, in order that the school environments newly opened to the disabled child is "least restrictive" in terms of attitude as well as opportunity. The project was to "assist elementary school children in developing positive attitudes and greater understanding of children with special needs." The project was founded on the precept that "when ordinary children understand the causes, visible effects and consequences of disabilities, they will try to treat disabled children as they would anyone else." The ways and means used to further this project are well documented in literature available from the school.[7] Workshops are run on a regular basis for adults taking the theme into other states, school districts, etc. and for children in schools within travelling distance of the Meeting Street School. The project seems to be a novel, yet thoroughly logical approach to drawing recipients of regular and special education together now, and of course bodes well for future attitudes in children and adults.

The Resource centre at Gibsonia, directed by Hal Chew, was extremely impressive and it represented a particularly positive area of development in the wide spectrum of provision under the auspices of special education. Teaching children with a "disability" of whatever nature whether gifted or severely handicapped intellectually, is a most demanding occupation. One cannot always rely on the child's own initiative, drive, curiosity, response, or development to feed or stimulate you, the teacher. This is quite unlike teaching the "regular" child where there is often a two way flow of ideas and mutual stimulus. Consequently the special educator is often very quickly drained of ideas and energy. A resource book, or better still, a resource centre is of great assistance, at such times. It can re-fire thought, provide new ideas, restimulate and reactivate a tired, but dedicated mind. The wealth that the commercial interest and investment in educational products is extremely keen and now that special education is such an integral part of education as a whole,

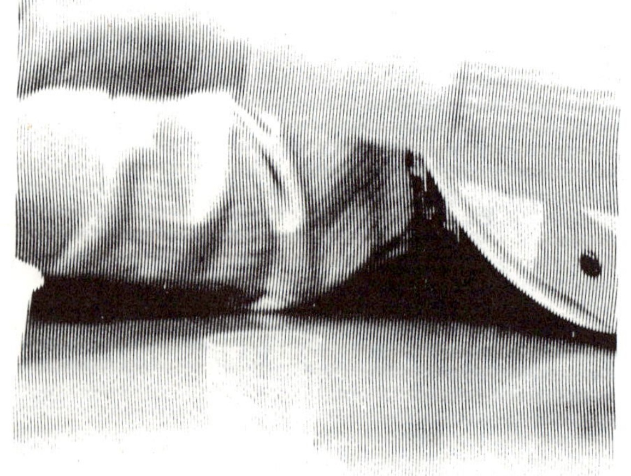

commercial suppliers have not been slow to produce and market a great number of materials, aids and systems designed for use by teachers of exceptional children. Many of the articles available for purchase are products resulting from careful educational and market research, perhaps based on ideas developed by teachers in classroom situations. The sum total of these products presents an attractive and stimulating array of resources at the disposal of the teacher, but their very abundance causes problems. Questions arise, such as, "What can I use?" "Where can I find it?" "What is best?" The development of resource centres is crucial, as they provide important back-up for teachers and principals complying with PL 94-142 as the law itself states that "appropriate materials and equipment" may be seen, studied, touched borrowed or rejected; seminars, workshops, and courses can be arranged; problems and promising practices can be discussed and shared. As with the Meeting Street School project, the concept central to this particular aspect of special education in America, seems wholly good and worthwhile. An interesting point was made by Dr. Hal Chew. His comment underlines the important fact that special education has much to give to education as a whole, in terms of methods, techniques, attitudes and many other facets. "At first the centre was open to teachers in special education only. It was soon discovered by teachers in regular education that so much material provided for children with disability in learning was relevant to their children, having no particular handicap. It is now used equally by teachers of non-handicapped and handicapped children." Evidence of the need and growing importance placed upon the resource centre is found in the willingness of the Federal Government to fund the facility. The number of resource centres being established across the U.S. is indicative of the value they are proving to be at a time when many teachers are constantly in the position of having to seek new ways and means to tackle new and old problems in the classroom.

In order to have specially trained and skilled people in schools, special training facilities are necessary to provide that training, appropriate courses and personnel are required in colleges and universities. America seems to be in a similar state in regards to lecturing staff in institutions of higher education as is the U.K. Generally speaking, for decades, colleges and universities have employed staff who are subject-oriented in respect of teacher training. After years of giving instruction in the techniques of teaching "regular" non-handicapped students, the onset of provision for and interest in the education of the handicapped has caused major problems for many in higher education. Special education courses demand qualified presenters in that field, but there is a definite shortage of adequately experienced men and women capable of providing insight into the needs of exceptional children.

It cannot be an easy thing to change horses in midstream, suddenly being required to put emphasis on areas basically unexplored and unknown. Project RETOOL, a national effort to develop models for updating practicing teacher educators, is of particular interest in this respect. This project, along with matters relating to Dean's Grants in various regions of America, was presented at the C.E.C. Conference at Dallas. The need for inservice updating of professionals involved in teacher education, is pressing and there is a move to assess those needs and develop effective delivery systems to remediate, ameliorate and alleviate needs as they are found. Devlopment in this particular area of special education seems most profitable and something from which others may learn.

Most, if not all, the universities in the U.S. have their department of special education where highly trained and qualified people conduct research, lecture and generally equip the young teachers to face the problems liable to be encountered in special and regular classrooms, resource rooms and units. Once more though, the impression of a gulf presents itself and according to one professor presenting at the C.E.C. Conference these departments are subject to negative attitudes by colleagues in other departments. The same man, a director of special education, felt that considering the profound effect of PL 94-142 upon the education scene in the States, his department is incredibly small, five staff members, in the light of the task it is required to undertake. One wonders if higher education authorities are less forward in their provision of instruction than might be expected. Not that the picture is depressingly black as it is obvious that state universities and other colleges and organizations are designing programmes, courses, workshops and summer schools entirely devoted to the preparation of teachers who may be meeting new and challenging problems day by day in the classroom.

To make up the anticipated short fall in training, PL 94-142 requires "a comprehensive system of personnel development," in essence "in-service training." Surely, in-service training is of the most fundamental importance as far as enactment of the law goes. It is one of the prime means by which new skills can be learnt; skills, ideas, thoughts, problems can be pooled and shared and eventually it must be a most valuable means by which the gulf previously mentioned can in part, at least, be bridged. The growth of the "comprehensive system of personnel development," as undertaken on a local level, would look to be dependant upon the enthusiasm of individuals, teachers groups and assocations.

## 1. PERSPECTIVES

At one in-service training session I attended, four serving teachers in special education presented material gathered from a workshop held on a previous occasion. The material was relevant to prevocational training and career training of children in elementary schools. The relevance and use of I.E.P. was also reiterated. Those attending the meeting were a mixed group of special and regular education teachers and by coincidence the group included those from a local school in which I had spent the day. From comments and conversation throughout the day one could gather the real drive and enthusiasm was tilted in favour of the special education teachers. It was just one example of something which has shown itself in both the U.S. and the U.K., that is the dedicated nature of those involved with the education of the child with special needs. They seem to possess qualities which set them aside in many ways. The depth of commitment, the ability to relate and communicate with exceptional children, in short, real dedication, is fundamental to the provision of special education and it perhaps is at this level where problems will arise, however much one legislates, funds or trains. It seems to me that wherever there is a handicap, there are going to be people who can and are willing to relate and understand the problems concomitant with the difficulty. Conversely there are those who can't, won't, or are not able for a thousand reasons. Teachers are people too!

## CONCLUSION

It will be interesting to see how other countries tackle the problems at present being faced by American educators. There are substantial differences between various societies and cultures, but there are also many similarities, especially with regard to the handicapped. The problems connected with provision and attitudes are therefore, similar. It seems reasonable to assume that much can be learnt from the experience of colleagues in the U.S. Strategies and procedures adopted to expedite PL 94-142 could conceivably form the basis of accepted practices in other countries especially in Europe. Along with Sweden's policies, a country quite advancd in attitude towards the exceptional child and the handicapped citizen, the American special education scene is bound to be subject to close scrutiny by governmental and university research groups.

To sum up my impressions of American Sepcial Education, I feel it necessary to go back a little in the history of the country. My impression is that American educators have made a brave and bold stand with regard to handicapped citizens, their rights and opportunity. The country's educationalists have faced the problem of mandatory integration with courage and determination. To the mind of a visitor there is a definite flavour of the "pioneer spirit." It does not ring too false, the Mississippi has been crossed and there is no going back. No-one is really certain of what lies ahead. New ground is being broken, new advances made, some people along the way are hostile, some people find the going easy, some find it hard, some make smooth headway, others lag behind. The analogy could be extended ad nauseum, and so suffice it to say, that special education seems to be both wagon and horses driving towards a promised land. In the eyes of an observer, the wagons seem well equipped and the horses fresh and well shod. When combined with the driving force found in all those determined to reach the goal, one can only feel confident of the success of the venture and visualise many following on behind.

## REFERENCES


1.  Report of the Snowdon Working Party, *Integrating the Disabled,* N.F.P.C.D., England.

2.  Tacoma Schools, Washington: See *Readings in Mainstreaming,* Special Learning Corporation, Barbara Milbauer, The Mainstreaming Puzzle : Beyond Emotional Problems-Through Opportunities for Learning, C.E.C. Dallas, 1979.

3.  Warnock Report, *Special Educaitonal Needs-Report of the Committee of Enquiry into the Education of Handicapped Children and Young People, H.M.S.O., London,*

3.  *Warnock Report, Special Educational Needs-Report of the Committee of Enquiry into the Education of Handicapped Children and Young People*, H.M.S.O., London, 1978.

4.  James T. Crawford, *A Touch of Hands,* University of Pittsburgh, U.C.I.R. Hillman Library, Pittsburgh, PA 15260

5.  See *Readings in Mainstreaming,* Special Learning Corporation, "The Changing Mandate for Special Education," Larry Molloy.

6.  *Working with Parents-Developing a Workshop course for Parents of Young Mentally Handicapped Children,"* cc. Cunningham & D.M. Jeffree, N.S.M.H.C. (NMW Region) 1 Brazennose Street, Manchaester M25FJ, U.K.

7.  Susan R. Bookbinder, *Mainstreaming-What Every Child Needs to Know About Disabilities,* Exceptional Parent Press, Boston, 1978.

8.  Somerset Education Authority, *Ways and Means: A Resource Book of Aids and Methods Materials, and Systems for Use with the Language Retarded Child,* Globe Education, Basingstoke, U.K.

# The barriers ahead

## Despite landmark laws and decisions, some will continue to be deprived of education rights unless we act

By Stanley Herr

*This article is based on a recent address given by the author before the Massachusetts Association for Children with Learning Disabilities. Herr is an instructor and visiting scholar at Harvard Law School. He is also a research fellow for the Research Institute on Legal Assistance of the Legal Services Corporation, studying the delivery of legal services to residents of mental-retardation facilities. He participated as a counsel in Mills v. Board of Education, Wyatt v. Stickney, NYSARC v. Carey, and other significant cases affecting rights of disabled people. As a former Joseph P. Kennedy, Jr., Fellow and a Rosemary F. Dybwad Award recipient, he completed national and international studies on the civil and human rights of the mentally disabled.*

Eighty-five years ago the highest court of Massachusetts allowed the schoolhouse door to be closed to the mentally disabled. The Cambridge School Committee (board) excluded a boy named Watson on the ground that he was "too weak-minded to derive profit from instruction."

Perhaps more to the committee's distress, Watson was reported to be "troublesome to other children, making unusual noises, pinching others, etc. He is also found unable to take ordinary, decent physical care of himself."

To the justices of the Massachusetts Supreme Judicial Court of 1893, the School Committee's determination was final. No tribunal could call this total exclusion into question, and a jury could not inquire into the actual facts of Watson's presence in school. *(Watson v. City of Cambridge, 32 NE 864)*

In that day, Massachusetts was not unique in extinguishing the educational rights of the handicapped. Consider the all too brief education of Merrit Beattie, age 13. The Wisconsin Supreme Court tells us he was "slow and hesitating in speech," had uncontrollable facial contortions, and drooled. It was also claimed, on the part of the School Board, that "his physical condition and ailment produce a depressing and nauseating effect upon the teachers and school children . . ."

With that School Board claim, the schools washed their hands of Merrit Beattie, and the court refused to review that discretion. Except Justice Eschweiler, dissenting. The justice bravely reminded his colleagues of 1919 that the Constitution intended to "secure to every child a substantial and fundamental right to attend the common schools." *(State ex rel Beattie v. Board of Education, 172 NW 153 (Wis 1919)*

We happily live in a time when Eschweiler's proposition has gained acceptance, and when the Watsons and the Beatties of this generation cannot be discarded by some unreviewable administrative fiat.

Six years ago the school-excluded children of the District of Columbia--learning disabled, emotionally disturbed, mentally retarded, disciplinary problems, whatever their cause of exclusion or condition--won a great victory in the U.S. District Court. Their victory announced that exceptional children were Constitutionally entitled to a specialized education program suited to their individual needs.

As a matter of due process of law, they, their parents, and their advocates were further entitled to identification, hearing, and other procedures and provisions to explore fully the contours of those needs.

Moreover, in the funding of required special education services, the court explicitly rejected any rationing system that would leave these children's schooling to some later day. Wrote the court, in *Mills v. Board of Education,* "If sufficient funds are not available to finance all of the services and programs that are needed and desirable in the system, then the available funds must be expended equitably in such a manner that no child is entirely excluded from a publicly supported education."

And in Pennsylvania, to similar if narrower effect, a three-judge Federal court permanently enjoined state and local officials from denying or postponing a free public program of education and training to any of the state's mentally retarded children.

Upon the model of these two cases–*Mills v. Board of Education of the District of Columbia* and *Pennsylvania Association for Retarded Citizens v. Pennsylvania*–litigation in well over 30 states erupted. Public Law 94-142, the Education for All Handicapped Children Act, essentially codifies those judicial results and goes on to promise subsidies for states conforming to its mandate of all-inclusive education, individualized educational planning, and procedural safeguards.

As Sen. Edward Kennedy of Massachusetts recognized back in 1973, PL 94-142 provided a "clear, straightforward legislative remedy," a remedy which in his words would "implement the (then) recent decision of U.S. District Court Judge Joseph Waddy, who declared that the handicapped child and emotionally disturbed have the same Constitutional right to equal educational services as any other child within the District of Columbia."

As Sen. Kennedy acknowledged, Massachusetts in 1973 was ahead of other states, even though 10,000 children received essentially no services at all in the school system. With the passage of its Chapter 766, pioneering legislation establishing mainstreaming principles, Massachusetts lengthened that lead.

It is now six years after the landmark court decisions, four years after the coming into effect of Chapter 766, three years after 94-142 reinforced those judicial standards with Federal regulations and Federal dollars, and one year after Section 504 added a Federal stick to a Federal carrot. The laws have increased geometrically, the advocacy resources have not. Where do we stand, and where might we be going?

## The barriers ahead

Every child's and every adolescent's right to education should be dear to us. From long and painful,

experience, however, we can well predict those who will be most frequently missed by our special educational services. The poor, the racial minorities, and the institutionalized will fare most poorly in the competition for those services.

Permit me to quote at length from the findings of a U.S. District Court judge reciting the expert testimony on educational provisions for the 350 teenagers confined to a so-called state training school. Here is that shocking testimony concerning the school, referred to as OTS:

> **OTS students are not evaluated to determine their educational needs. The majority of incoming students arrive without any school records, and, for approximately 50% of the students, prior school records are never received. As a result, OTS has no way to identify students with learning disabilities or other educational problems which need special attention and has no means of developing an education program to meet the individual needs of each student. An extremely high percentage of OTS students are retarded or have other problems which require special education services. However, OTS has virtually no special education programs for those students. At present, there is only one special education teacher who teaches approximately 20 students. There are no special education services or classes for the trainable mentally retarded, students with specific learning disabilities, emotionally handicapped youths, or hearing and visually-impaired students. OTS students who have these problems receive no services designed to meet their needs. (Morgan v. Sprout. 432 F. Supp. 1130, 1151)**

And that is not Dickens describing a 19th Century Bleak House, but a conservative Federal jurist writing in 1977 of a publicly supported American institution, purporting in the words of a statute to be "concerned with the care, protection, and rehabilitation of the child in question." If this is rehabilitation, then what is punishment?

Bear this further in mind: The state has isolated these young men from all other sources of education, and then provides only one special education teacher for 350 students, of whom 90% are in need of some special education for learning disabilities or mental retardation.

Can you possibly doubt that countless thousands of children and young people in our mental hospitals, reformatories, mental retardation facilities, institutions--by whatever name they are called–are desperately in need of the professional services of special educators, lawyers, school administrators, or concerned citizen advocates?

When was the last time you considered the potential discriminatory impact of programs that erroneously label children in need of special education? In August, 1975, the U.S. Department of Health, Education, and Welfare issued a memo on "Identification of discrimination in the assignment of children to special education programs." Chief state school officers and local superintendents were advised that violation of Title VI or IX of the Civil Rights Acts **might** be indicated by the "disproportionate over or under-inclusion of children of any race . . . national origin, or sex in any special program category."

The memo also required assistance for students who have been placed erroneously when they are returned to regular classes. It cited a number of other special problems to be corrected, such as a lack of "uniform nondiscriminatory criteria for referral for placement" and failure to meet other procedural and substantive requirements. School districts have, of course, a continuing responsibility to abide by this memo to remain in compliance with Title VI and Title IX.

Let me go back to the problem of poverty and unequal access to special education services. A case recently before the U.S. Supreme Court involved the denial of full tuition payments in violation of the rights of poor handicapped children to the equal protection of the laws. A three-judge District Court panel in *Kruse v. Campbell* was faced with Virginia's system of partial reimbursement of educational costs through tuition grants. Parents of exceptional children could get 75% of private school tuition paid when a free and appropriate special education could not be provided in a public school or institution. The way this system operates, children could be totally excluded from the benefits of an appropriate education when their parents were without resources to supplement the grant.

The District Court found that this discrimination produced an absolute deprivation of educational opportunity for poor handicapped children, whereas other children--handicapped and non-handicapped-- were accommodated in the public schools, or, if affluent and handicapped, in private schools if their families were able to afford to take advantage of the tuition program. Some poor handicapped children were effectively excluded from any program.

In a four-line memo, the U.S. Supreme Court vacated this judgment and remanded the case to the District Court with the cryptic instruction to decide the claim on the basis of Section 504 of the Rehabilitation Act. Presumably this reflects the long-standing jurisprudential rule that cases be resolved on statutory grounds whenever a Federal Constitutional determination might prove unnecessary.

A similar finding appears in what may prove the most significant litigation to date focusing exclusively on education for the learning-disabled. U.S. District Court Judge Newcomer has indeed proved a welcome newcomer to the growing ranks of jurists focusing increased attention on the educational needs of learning-disabled children.

In the case of *Frederick L. v. Thomas,* the court held that the school district of Philadelphia had failed to meet its obligations under state law to provide learning-disabled students with a minimally appropriate education. Accordingly, the court ordered, and the Third Circuit Court of Appeals affirmed, procedures mandating identification of all learning-disabled students in the district. [419 F.Supp. 960 (1976); 557 F.2d 373 (3rd Cir. 1977)]

The facts were these: Eight thousand children in the Philadelphia school district were thought to suffer from specific learning disabilities. The district could only identify 1,300 of them. That violated a clear statutory and regulatory duty to identify all learning-disabled students.

As a matter of law, the District Court found that children with learning disabilities are entitled to proper education and training, and that the district had breached that duty by failing to identify those children and provide them with appropriate education in accordance with an approved plan, and by not enforcing the special education laws.

The court noted that "mainstreaming" is a preferred technique under the state regulations, but leaving it to chance that unidentified learning-disabled children find their way into appropriate programs was not mainstreaming.

As a first step in crafting a remedy to all this mess, Judge Newcomer appointed a master (an expert receiving her compensation through the court) to oversee and monitor the implementation of court-ordered relief.

The first stage of that relief required the defendant school district to submit a plan "reasonably calculated to identify all of its learning-disabled pupils." Later stages envisaged interim and final plans for appropriate placement of the identified students.

The court's orders as to identification have already been upheld by the Third Circuit. The appeals court reasoned: "Identification is a means to the end of assuring that those children who are entitled to special educational services receive them."

The court emphasized the deficiencies in relying on a teacher-referral method for identifying learning-disabled students: Namely, a lack of ordinary teacher training in identifying the cause of students' problems, a tendency to make psychological referrals only for disruptive students, and not making referrals where the classroom teacher does not believe there is a suitable program in which to place the child.

Community Legal Services provided counsel for the plaintiff children and their class, a reflection of the disproportionally large number of poor persons in Philadelphia's school district without appropriate services. Public interest lawyers had also represented the Delaware Valley Association for Children with Learning Disabilities, a plaintiff intervenor in this case.

To sum up, while the past decade has seen enormous gains in legal rights and the resources to attain them, these gains have--for the most part--not filtered down to those most in need of them. Focused strategies of judicial, legislative, and political organizing action must be developed and targeted for the poorest, most stigmatized, and most isolated of those you would wish to serve.

Consumers must press for the creation of effective legal advocacy systems in every state to carry out such strategies. In a handful of states--Minnesota and Vermont most conspicuously--those systems are operational. Those systems link disabled consumers, lawyers, lay advocates, and other rights-oriented citizens in common cause.

The surrogate-advocate program required under Public Law 142, the Boston special education enforcement suit with its compensatory education services and its attorney's fees, and the new Developmental Disabilities Law Center under Public Law 94-103 should be stimulants to further action.

If we together--parents, teachers, disabled persons and their organizations, lawyers, and concerned administrators--will not hear the voices of frustrated children and young people asking us to share the benefits of our literacy, then who will? For we are all moral actors bound by Albert Camus's timeless injunction:

> *"Perhaps we cannot prevent this world from being a world in which children are tortured. But we can reduce the number of tortured children. And if you don't help us, who else in the world can help us do this?"*

# Federal Legislation for Exceptional Children: Implications and a View of the Future

*Martin L. LaVor is currently senior legislative associate for the House Education and Labor Committee of the U.S. Congress. Some of his responsibilities in this position include overseeing all aspects of legislation from introduction to final passage in areas concerned with education of the handicapped, vocational rehabilitation, child abuse, Head Start programs, runaway youth, aging, and others.*

*Dr. LaVor's professional preparation includes a B.S. degree in industrial arts from Trenton State Teachers College in 1958, an M.A. degree in special education from Seton Hall University in 1962, an M.A. equivalent in rehabilitation counseling from Seton Hall University, and an Ed.D. degree in special education from the University of Alabama in 1969. His early professional positions were with the Southeast Office of Economic Opportunity in Atlanta, Georgia, the Alabama Technical Assistance Corporation in Montgomery, and the Guild Training and Placement Service for the retarded and physically handicapped in Newark, New Jersey. A selected bibliography of works by Martin L. LaVor is found on pages 269-70.*

On November 29, 1975, the Education for All Handicapped Children Act became Public Law 94-142. This law represents the most complete legislative action ever taken by the federal government in the field of education of the handicapped.[1] Although as many as thirty bills affecting the handicapped have become law in a single year, none has had the scope of this one.

## HISTORICAL PERSPECTIVE

The large number of laws in this area indicates a very substantial federal role; however, this movement has only emerged in the last twenty years. Federal laws for the handicapped during the nineteenth century were primarily designed to meet the problems of specific disability groups such as the deaf and the blind. It wasn't until the 1920s that programs designed to provide services for all handicapped persons were enacted. This was achieved primarily through vocational rehabilitation legislation which was the result of the need to assist the great number of people disabled during World War I, or injured while working in the rapidly growing industries. With the exception of periodic extensions to

[1] The words "disabled" and "handicapped" do not have the same meanings. It happens that in most federal legislation the term "handicapped" has been used in place of or interchangeably with the term "disabled." This chapter will use the term "handicapped" even though "disabled" may be the proper term.

# 1. PERSPECTIVES

the Vocational Rehabilitation Act, legislation for the handicapped over the next forty years was primarily, though not exclusively, focused on services and special exemptions for the blind.

In 1958, the federal government through the National Defense Education Act, began providing funds for general education. Prior to that legislation, there was virtually no federal money going to finance general education. As part of that law, captioned films for the deaf were authorized.

In 1965, the Elementary and Secondary Education Act became law. As part of that act, a program was established to assist children in state operated or supported schools serving the handicapped.

In 1966, ESEA was amended to establish the Bureau of Education of the Handicapped in the U.S. Office of Education. In addition, funds were provided for states to expand, either directly or through local educational agencies, programs or projects to meet educational and related needs of handicapped children.

ESEA was amended again in 1967, and Regional Resource Centers to provide testing to determine special educational needs of handicapped children were established.

In 1968, the Handicapped Children's Early Education Assistance Act designed to establish experimental preschool programs for the handicapped became law.

The 1969 amendments to ESEA included the Gifted and Talented Education Assistance Act and the Children with Specific Learning Disabilities Act.

1972 marked the first time in federal history that a law for the handicapped ever received a negative vote in the Congress, and the first time a bill for the handicapped was ever vetoed by the president. The Vocational Rehabilitation Act of 1972 was vetoed, as was its successor in 1973. The revised amendments to the Vocational Rehabilitation Act finally became law (PL 93-112) later in 1973. The Congress that year took significant action in revising the original law by requiring that first priority for rehabilitation services be given to individuals with "the most severe handicaps."

In the Education Amendments of 1974, the Congress significantly increased the authorization level of the basic state aid program for meeting special needs of handicapped children. More importantly, the 1974 law included for the first time language directing states to move toward the goal of guaranteeing the rights of exceptional children and their parents and provided a detailed timetable for achieving this goal.

Fourteen months later, PL 94-142 became law. The purpose of PL 94-142 was to assure

1. that all handicapped children have a free appropriate public education which emphasizes special education and related services designed to meet their unique needs;
2. that the rights of handicapped children and their parents or guardians are protected; and
3. that states and localities provide for the education of all handicapped children.

In order to qualify for assistance under the law, each state must demonstrate that the following conditions are met:

1. It has in effect a policy that assures all handicapped children have the right to a free appropriate public education.

2. It sets forth in detail the policies and procedures which it will undertake or has undertaken in order to assure that:

   (a) there is established (i) a goal of providing full educational opportunity to all handicapped children; (ii) a detailed timetable for accomplishing such a goal; and (iii) a description of the kind and number of facilities, personnel, and services necessary throughout the State to meet such a goal;

(b) a free appropriate public education will be available for all handicapped children between the ages of three and eighteen within the State not later than September 1, 1978, and for all handicapped children between the ages of three and twenty-one within the State not later than September 1, 1980, except that, with respect to handicapped children aged three to five and aged eighteen to twenty-one, inclusive . . .

(c) all children residing in the State who are handicapped, regardless of the severity of their handicap, and who are in need of special education and related services are identified, located, and evaluated, and that a practical method is developed and implemented to determine which children are currently receiving needed special education and related services and which children are not currently receiving needed special education and related services;

(d) it has established . . . procedures to assure that, to the maximum extent appropriate, handicapped children, including children in public or private institutions or other care facilities, are educated with children who are not handicapped, and that special classes, separate schooling, or other removal of handicapped children from the regular educational environment occurs only when the nature of severity of the handicap is such that education in regular classes with the use of supplementary aids and services cannot be achieved satisfactorily;

(e) . . . procedures are established for consultation with individuals involved in or concerned with the education of handicapped children, including handicapped individuals and parents or guardians of handicapped children, and . . . there are public hearings, adequate notice of such hearings, and an opportunity for comment available to the general public prior to adoption of the policies, programs, and procedures required.

These words represent the culmination of years of consideration, extensive hearings, thorough research, debates, trade-offs and compromises by the United States Congress. They reflect an awareness of and concern for handicapped children and their goal of achieving full rights as citizens. The law represents a significant commitment by the federal government to assist them in gaining full educational opportunities; it has been hailed as the most far-reaching legislation for the handicapped ever enacted by the Congress and, in the minds of handicapped individuals, their parents, and persons who work with them throughout the nation, it is.

While PL 94-142 represents a significant national commitment, it should not be perceived as the only one. An earlier amendment (contained in PL 93-112) to the 50-year-old Vocational Rehabilitation Act many would argue is equally potent in its implications. Section 504 of the Rehabilitation Act of 1973 (PL 93-112) parallels and complements PL 94-142. Section 504 has been characterized as a bill of rights for the handicapped. It requires that:

No otherwise qualified handicapped individual in the United States . . . shall, solely by reason of his handicap, be excluded from the participation in, be denied the benefits of, or be subjected to discrimination under any program or activity receiving Federal financial assistance.

Any student of American statutory law well knows that the gap between a law and its enforcement, between mandate and fulfillment, between

# 1. PERSPECTIVES

promise and practice can be considerable. And where the guarantee of constitutional rights is involved, closing that gap may be aggravating and prolonged.

PL 94-142 set in motion a mandate which *should* guarantee that all handicapped children in America will receive a complete education. As a result of Sec. 504 of the Vocational Rehabilitation Act, the handicapped of America *should* have access to education and jobs, and *should not* be denied anything that any other citizen is entitled to or already receives. Although legislative language can be cumbersome and difficult to understand at time, words in these two laws are not. The laws are sufficiently direct and specific to satisfy anyone interested in the well being of the handicapped. In fact, there are many who, upon reading the laws, will relax in the confidence that everything necessary has been accomplished; that it is just a matter of time until all of the requirements in the law are implemented. This attitude is self-deluding and will hamper the attainment of the goals of meeting the needs of handicapped persons.

It must be noted that for all of the features of these laws which brought satisfaction and hope to so many, PL 94-142 was not received with open arms by everyone. When he signed the law, President Ford said·

> Unfortunately, this bill promises more than the Federal government can deliver and its good intentions could be thwarted by the many unwise provisions it contains. Everyone can agree with the objective stated in the title of this bill—educating all handicapped children in our Nation. The key question is whether the bill will really accomplish that objective.
>
> Even the strongest supporters of this measure know as well as I that they are falsely raising the expectations of the groups affected by claiming authorization levels which are excessive and unrealistic.
>
> Despite my strong support for full educational opportunities for our handicapped children, the funding levels proposed in this bill will simply not be possible if Federal expenditures are to be brought under control and a balanced budget achieved over the next few years.[2]

Criticism was not limited to the White House. The education agencies responsible for carrying out the new law claimed that it imposed heavy administrative burdens on state and local school districts and did not provide adequate new funds for implementation. For a multitude of reasons, such features as the individualized education program, the due process procedures, the state-local program dollar split, and the relatively low (compared to state) federal funding all found disfavor somewhere. There were claims that the law was so extensive that it could not be enforced. The majority of persons interested in and knowledgeable about the new law, however, viewed it as far-sighted, progressive, and very positive. Only time will tell which side is right and whether PL 94-142 can achieve its purposes.

Similarly, it is not yet clear when or whether Section 504 of the Vocational Rehabilitation Act, which became law on September 30, 1973, will be implemented and its intended impact felt. At the time this chapter was published (Feb. 1977), final regulations interpreting this Section had still not been promulgated by the Department of Health, Education and Welfare; thus, over three and one-half years after the provision was signed into law, it was still not being enforced.

A major cause of confusion and difficulty in the development of the regulations was the lack of legislative history and specific Congressional intent. As a result the Office of Civil Rights in HEW, which drafted the regulations, had no guidance for interpreting the broadly stated Congressional desire to eliminate discrimination against the handicapped.

---

[2] From the veto message signed November 29, 1975.

Publication of very detailed "proposed Sec 504 regulations" in May, 1976, became the subject of a national controversy. Opponents claimed they were too wide-ranging and detailed, would cost hundreds of millions of dollars to implement, and were unenforceable at any cost. Supporters argued the proposed regulations were too limited and contained inadequate penalties.

The issue involved in parts of PL 94-142 and Sec. 504 is the capacity or willingness of the federal government to enforce its laws. With these laws, new *civil rights* mandates have been enacted while some already on the books remain unenforced. Unlike grants-in-aid, civil rights not only provide a right or benefit to an individual, but they impose a correlative duty on someone else, and enforcing that duty is not easy. If voluntary action could achieve this goal, a law would not have been necessary; therefore, some legal requirement for those who have not complied voluntarily is needed. Such a workable mechanism does not exist at this time.

It is clear that the mere passage of a law does not guarantee that its objectives will be met. It is too early to label these laws "success" or "failure"; they were highlighted here because they represent a new concern and awareness by the Congress about the needs of the handicapped.

## ISSUES AND UNRESOLVED QUESTIONS

Through the years, as more and more focus is placed on the needs of the handicapped and as the funds appropriated by the Congress to carry out programs rise, numerous questions and issues are being raised.

### ACCOUNTABILITY

It is generally contended that special education is the forerunner of activities and procedures which will eventually be adopted in regular education programs. Small class sizes, supplementary services, special equipment, and individualized education are examples of approaches that started in and are part of special education and have been adopted in varying degrees by regular education. When education is scrutinized, special education is often singled out to justify itself more than any other educational area. Also, when budgets are cut back, special education programs are often the first to be reduced. In spite of the fact that general education cannot prove its cost efficiency and effectiveness, special education is usually asked to do so. Whether this demand is fair or not, one of the most critical issues facing programs for the handicapped over the next few years is accountability. How can taxpayers be assured they are getting the most for their dollars? How can they be assured that greater fiscal investment results in improving the future of handicapped individuals? As more money is made available by federal, state, and local governments, greater fiscal accountability will be required, and it is reasonable to suggest that the demands on special education will increase in direct proportion to the demands it makes on those funding sources.

Questions concerning the best ways of financing, the most effective ways to spend public funds, the degree to which such funds produce desired results, the relationship between the child, learning, and costs involved, and most important, the kinds of benefits that are accrued by society will have to be addressed. One of the vehicles which may provide some answers to accountability questions is a provision in PL 94-142 which calls for an individualized education program. As defined in law:

> The term "individualized education program" means a written statement for each handicapped child developed in any meeting by a representative of the local educational agency or an intermediate

educational unit who shall be qualified to provide, or supervise the provision of, specially designed instruction to meet the unique needs of handicapped children, the teacher, the parents or guardian of such child, and, whenever appropriate, such child, which statement shall include (A) a statement of the present levels of educational performance of such child; (B) a statement of annual goals, including short-term instructional objectives; (C) a statement of the specific educational services to be provided to such child, and the extent to which such child will be able to participate in regular educational programs; (D) the projected date for initiation and anticipated duration of such services, and appropriate objective criteria and evaluation procedures and schedules for determining, on at least an annual basis, whether instructional objectives are being achieved.

This requirement in the eyes of many is one of the most important features of the new law in that it will give local education agencies an opportunity to develop plans designed to meet the unique needs of each handicapped child and determine the specific services needed. It is anticipated that through successful implementation of the plans and evaluation of outcomes, it will be possible to find out what children are learning so that a clearer view and judgment as to what the end product in special education is, and whether or not goals are being achieved, can be ascertained.

It is claimed that special education is unique because each child has unique problems. If this statement is true, then special education based on these plans should be able to provide unique results. Unfortunately, as special education works with each individual and his or her problems, the costs for providing extra services may increase at a time when the public is clamorous for greater results with fewer resources. It is possible that costs may decrease as a result of individualized planning.

Accountability in education goes far beyond the education of handicapped children; nevertheless, special education will probably become the laboratory in which the answers will first be sought.

## CLASS SIZE

One of the first and most obvious questions about special education relates to class size: Why are classes so small? Or How does one determine the optimum class size? There is no doubt that it is difficult to work with most handicapped children who require special services, but one must also ask, Isn't it just as difficult to handle large classes in regular education? Optimum class size appears to be a relative term. It is generally acknowledged that special education class size should be small because of the unique and often complex needs of the students; but does this mean that it is easier to teach "normal" kindergarten or regular elementary school class students with 25-35 students in each class? Almost any teacher with 35 children in a class would probably say, "If I could only get my class size down to 25, I would really be able to do a first-rate job." A teacher with 25 wants to get down to 20 "in order to reach every individual"; a special education teacher with 15 may want to get down to 10. The question of what constitutes an appropriate class size and the related cost implications will have to be addressed.

Since the largest disability group being educated today is the mentally retarded, focus here will be placed on the class size of educable and trainable children. Table 1 (*page 254*), compiled from the *Digest of State and Federal Laws: Education of Handicapped Children*, illustrates the minimums and maximums, laws, rules, or guidelines, which each state generally follows in serving these populations.

Table 1 clearly shows that the maximums for each group vary significantly from state to state. The question is, Does an educable mentally retarded individual in one state which has a maximum class size of 12 receive a better, the same, or a worse education than an indi-

Table 1: Class size of educable and trainable children.

| State | Special classes | | | |
| | Educable mentally handicapped Class size | | Trainable mentally handicapped Class size | |
| | Minimum | Maximum | Minimum | Maximum |
|---|---|---|---|---|
| ALABAMA | 10 | 15 | 10 | 15 |
| ALASKA | — | 15 | — | 15 |
| ARIZONA | — | 15 | — | 10 |
| ARKANSAS | 5 | 15 | 5[1] | 8 |
| Home economics | 5 | 10 | — | — |
| CALIFORNIA | | | | |
| (depending on age spread) | — | 15-18 | — | 12 |
| COLORADO | | | | |
| Elementary—mental age 4 and under | — | 15 | — | — |
| mental age 4 and over | — | 12 | — | — |
| Jr. & Sr. HS— | | | | |
| mental age 4 and under | — | 18 | — | — |
| mental age 4 and over | — | 15 | — | — |
| CONNECTICUT | 9 | 9 | 9 | 9 |
| DELAWARE | 8[2] | 22[2] | 6[2] | 10[2,3] |
| DISTRICT OF COLUMBIA | — | — | — | — |
| FLORIDA | | | | |
| Primary age | 6 | 12 | 5 | 10 |
| Intermediate age | 8 | 15 | 6 | 10 |
| Jr. high school age | 10 | 18 | 8 | 12 |
| Sr. high school age | 12 | 18 | 10 | 15 |
| GEORGIA | | | | |
| Elementary age 6-9 | 12 | 14 | — | — |
| Elementary age 9-13 | 14 | 16 | — | — |
| Secondary Jr. high over age 13 | 16 | 20 | — | — |
| Secondary Sr. high over age 13 | 20 | 20 | — | — |
| HAWAII (based on delivery option) | 12 | 15 | 5 | 8 |
| IDAHO | — | 12[4] | — | 12[4] |
| Resource room | — | 12[5] | — | 12[5] |
| ILLINOIS | — | — | 5 | 10 |
| Age 6-9 | 8 | 15[6] | — | — |
| Age 10 and above | 10 | 15[6] | — | — |
| INDIANA | 10-18-w/para | | 10 | 13[7] |
| Primary | — prof. 18-21 | | — | — |
| Intermediate | —14-16-w/para | | — | — |
| | prof. 23-25 | | — | — |
| Jr. high | 16-18-w/para | | — | — |

Table 1   continued

| State | Special classes | | | |
| | Educable mentally handicapped Class size | | Trainable mentally handicapped Class size | |
| | Minimum | Maximum | Minimum | Maximum |
|---|---|---|---|---|
| Sr. high | — prof. 26-28 | | | |
| | 16-18-w/para | | | |
| | — prof. 26-28 | | | |
| IOWA | — | — | — | 10[8] |
| KANSAS | — | — | 5 | 9 |
| Age spread 3 yrs. or greater | — | 15 | — | — |
| Age spread 2 years | — | 16 | — | — |
| Age spread 1 year | — | 17 | — | — |
| KENTUCKY | 15 | 20 | 6 | 12[9] |
| LOUISIANA | 10 | 15 | 8 | 12 |
| Slow learners | 12 | 18 | — | — |
| MAINE | — | 15[10] | — | — |
| Integrated program | — | 20[11] | — | — |
| Primary C.A. 5-9 | — | — | 3 | 6[12] |
| Intermediate C.A. 10-14 | — | — | 3 | 8[13] |
| MARYLAND | | | | |
| Primary age | — | 10 | — | 7 |
| Intermediate age | — | 15 | — | 10 |
| Jr. & Sr. high | — | 20 | — | 12 |
| Resource teacher | — | 30 | — | — |
| MASSACHUSETTS | | | | |
| Age range less than 1 year | — | 20 | — | — |
| Age range 1 year | — | 19 | — | — |
| Age range 2 years | — | 18 | — | — |
| Age range 3 years | — | 17 | — | — |
| Age range 4 years | — | 16 | — | — |
| Age range 5 years | — | 15 | — | — |
| Age range 6 years | | 14 | — | — |
| MICHIGAN | — | 15 | — | 15 |
| MINNESOTA | 12 | 15 | 5 | 7 |
| MISSISSIPPI | 5 | — | 5 | — |
| MISSOURI | 10 | 20 | 10 | 20 |
| MONTANA | 4 | 15[14] | 4 | 12 |
| NEBRASKA | | | | |
| Elementary or secondary—general | — | 30 | — | — |
| Elementary level with grouping | — | 15 | — | — |
| Elementary level without grouping | — | 12 | — | — |

| State | Special classes | | | |
|---|---|---|---|---|
| | Educable mentally handicapped Class size | | Trainable mentally handicapped Class size | |
| | Mini-mum | Maxi-mum | Mini-mum | Maxi-mum |
| Teacher aide | — | — | — | 10[15] |
| Age range 6 years or greater | — | — | 5 | 6 |
| Age range less than 6 years | — | — | 5 | 10 |
| NEVADA | | | | |
| Preschool | — | 8 | — | 6 |
| Primary | — | 10 | — | 8 |
| Elementary | — | 12 | — | 8 |
| Intermediate | — | 14 | — | 10 |
| Senior high | — | 14 | — | — |
| Elementary 2 or more levels comb. | — | 8 | — | 8 |
| Secondary | — | 10 | — | 10 |
| NEW HAMPSHIRE | — | 15[16] | — | 10 |
| Departmentalized programs | — | 30[17] | — | — |
| NORTH CAROLINA | | | — | 12[18] |
| Primary grades | 12[19] | 12[19] | — | — |
| Elementary grades | 16[19] | 16[19] | — | — |
| Resource teacher daily caseload | — | 24-30 | — | — |
| NEW JERSEY | — | 15 | — | 10 |
| NEW MEXICO | 5 | 15 | 5 | 10 |
| Part-time instructor | — | 5 | — | — |
| Primary grades | 12[20] | 12[20] | — | — |
| Elementary grades | 16[20] | 16[20] | — | — |
| Resource teacher | — | 24-30 | — | — |
| NEW YORK | | | | |
| Elementary | — | 15 | — | — |
| Secondary | — | 18 | — | — |
| Over 12 | — | — | — | 12 |
| Under 12 | — | — | — | 10 |
| NORTH DAKOTA | 5 | 15 | 6 | 12 |
| OHIO[21] | | | 5 | 12 |
| SLOW LEARNERS | | | | |
| Elementary age range 24 mos. or less | 12 | 20 | — | — |
| Elementary age range 24-48 mos. | 12 | 16 | — | — |
| Secondary age range 24 mos. or less | 12 | 22 | — | — |
| Secondary age range 25-48 mos. | 12 | 20 | — | — |
| Secondary unit work study program | 12 | 30 | — | — |
| OKLAHOMA | 8 | 22[22] 23[23] | 5 | 10 |

| State | Special classes | | | |
|---|---|---|---|---|
| | Educable mentally handicapped Class size | | Trainable mentally handicapped Class size | |
| | Mini-mum | Maxi-mum | Mini-mum | Maxi-mum |
| OREGON | | | | |
| Elementary | — | 15 | — | — |
| Secondary | — | 18[24] | — | — |
| PENNSYLVANIA | — | — | 7[25] | 18[25] |
| Primary | 10 | 18 | — | — |
| Work experience ½ day-Secondary | 15 | 18 | — | — |
| Homeroom w/integrated placement-Secondary | 15 | 20 | — | — |
| Resource teacher-Secondary | 15 | 30[26] | — | — |
| Secondary | 15 | 18 | — | — |
| RHODE ISLAND | | | | |
| SPECIAL CLASS[27] | | | | |
| Preschool program | — | 10 | — | 10[28] |
| Primary group | — | 10 | — | — |
| Intermediate group | — | 14 | — | — |
| Jr. high | — | 16 | — | — |
| Sr. high | — | 16 | — | — |
| Elementary age level | — | — | — | 12[28] |
| Elementary age level | — | — | — | 8[29] |
| Secondary C.A. range less than 5 yrs. | — | — | — | 12 |
| Secondary C.A. range greater than 5 yrs. | — | — | — | 8 |
| SOUTH CAROLINA | 10 | — | 8[30] | — |
| SOUTH DAKOTA (Recommended) | — | 10 | — | 6 |
| TENNESSEE | — | — | 8 | 16 |
| Primary | 12 | 14 | — | — |
| Intermediate | 12 | 16 | — | — |
| Jr. high | 12 | 16 | — | — |
| Sr. high | 12 | 16 | — | — |
| Sr. high cooperative schools prog. | 14 | 16 | — | — |
| TEXAS | | | | |
| ½ unit/½ day | 4 | — | 4 | — |
| Unit | 8 | — | 8 | — |
| 2 units | 14 | — | 14 | — |
| No. children for ea. unit above 2 | 14 | — | 14 | — |
| UTAH | 8 | 15 | 8 | 12[31] |
| VERMONT | 12 | 15[32] | — | 10 |
| VIRGINIA | — | 16 | — | 12[33] |

TABLE 1 *continued*

| State | Special classes | | | |
|---|---|---|---|---|
| | Educable mentally handicapped Class size | | Trainable mentally handicapped Class size | |
| | Minimum | Maximum | Minimum | Maximum |
| **WASHINGTON** | | | | |
| Preschool-Kindergarten | 6 | 10 | — | — |
| Primary | 8 | 12 | — | — |
| Intermediate | 8 | 12 | — | — |
| Secondary | 10 | 16 | — | — |
| **WEST VIRGINIA** | | | | |
| Elementary | 10 | 15 | 10 | 15 |
| Secondary | 10 | 15 | 10 | 15 |
| **WISCONSIN** | | | | |
| General school age | 10[34] | 20 | — | — |
| Pre-primary age 4-8 years | 8 | 12 | — | — |
| Primary age 7-9 or 7-10 where no pre-primary exists | 10[34] | 12 | — | — |
| Intermediate 9-12 years | 10[34] | 15 | — | — |
| Ungraded wide range 8-15 years | 10[34] | 15 | — | — |
| Jr. high 13-15 years | 10[34] | 14-16 | — | — |
| Sr. high 16-18 | 10[34] | 20[35], 15[36] | — | — |
| Full-time | — | — | 5 | 10[37] |
| Extended day | — | — | 5 | 9 |
| With teacher monitor | — | — | 12 | 15 |
| Homebound | — | — | — | 4 |
| **WYOMING** | 13 | — | 8 | — |
| With instructional assistant | — | — | 10 | — |

[1] Class size may be adjusted downward when multiply handicapped pupils are enrolled, usually on a 2:1 basis. Each multiply handicapped child is counted as 2 pupils.

[2] Implied by unit funding regulations.

[3] Class may be larger if a teacher aide is employed.

[4] Fifteen when teacher has interim certification and full-time aide; 18 when teacher has full certification and full-time aide.

[5] Not available.

[6] Age range of 4 years or less.

[7] Maximum age range—8 years. These figures represent optimum class size. Exceptions may be made when teacher's aide is employed.

[8] Fifteen with matron, if age range does not exceed 8 years.

[9] Smaller classes may be approved.

[10] Twenty with teacher aide.

[11] No more than 15 in a single class at any one time.

[12] Twelve with teacher aide.

[13] Twelve with teacher aide.

[14] Suggested maximum is 12.

[15] Each qualified teacher will be responsible for supervising no more than 5 teacher aides.

[16] Age range not to exceed 4 years.

[17] No more than 15 pupils are assigned to one teacher at any given time except for music, gym, etc.

[18] Sixteen when demand is great. Teacher aide must be employed if class is larger than 7 children. In classes of 13-16 children, two teacher aides must be employed to help the teacher.

[19] Approximate class size.

[20] Approximate class size.

[21] Class size may be adjusted downward for individual units at any age level where pupils with multi-handicaps are enrolled.

[22] If equivalent of one half-time aide is used.

[23] If one full-time aide is used.

[24] In any one scheduled class period.

[25] An aide may be employed if class size is greater than 8 pupils and fewer than 15. An aide must be employed when class size is greater than 15 pupils.

[26] Not less than 15 children to be in room at any one time.

[27] Each class shall have one full-time teacher and a teacher's aide.

[28] With aide.

[29] No aide.

[30] Average daily attendance minimum.

[31] Aides may be employed as deemed necessary.

[32] A class size of 12 is recommended for early elementary level I educable programs and for programs having one or more children with multiple handicapping conditions.

[33] With aide.

[34] Minimum number of students may be allowed to drop as low as 8 for no more than two consecutive years.

[35] With substantial integration in other nonacademic classes.

[36] With limited integration.

[37] Smaller class may be approved on a proportionate pro rata.

Adapted from Trudeau, E. (Ed.). *Digest of state and federal laws: Education of handicapped children.* Reston, Va.: Council for Exceptional Children, 1973. Reprinted with permission.

vidual with the same disability in another state which allows a maximum of 22 in a class?

The economics of education and the costs of teachers' salaries may force the educational establishment to look at the class size structure particularly with the educable mentally retarded (EMR) to determine what is the best way to work with them. Since no efficacy studies can be found which justify and validate specific class sizes for EMR or trainable mentally retarded (TMR) children; the question of cost may necessitate such consideration. The differences between 10 and 20 students in a class is one teacher's salary and of course, the class sizes of 12, 15, and 18 represent a third, more or less, of a teacher's salary. If a professional teacher with one aide (or paraprofessional) can handle 25 students with results comparable to those achieved in a class half the size with one teacher, what cost savings might occur without diminishing the impact of educational programs for students?

The concept of *segregated* or *special* schools of the handicapped rather than integrated classes in regular schools also warrants consideration in terms of benefits versus economic implications. Another concept, *mainstreaming* (i.e., placing handicapped children in regular classes and providing supplementary services for them), which was once thought to be the obvious way to cut special education costs, is proving to be not necessarily cheaper but in some cases more expensive than special education classes. The question of costs transcends the classroom to include those children in institutions. Is there any way to serve handicapped children who require institutionalization in a cost-efficient manner, and at the same time provide all of the educational services such children require?

A study entitled *Resource Configuration and Costs* (Rossmiller, Hale, & Frohreich, 1970) illustrated the incredible variation of costs in providing special education for handicapped children within each disability group, and among selected cities throughout the country. Table 2 focuses on only two groups considered in that study: the educable mentally retarded (EMR) and the trainable mentally retarded (TMR).

TABLE 2:   Resource configuration and costs.

| School district | EMR Exceptional program cost per pupil | TMR Exceptional program cost per pupil | Regular program cost per pupil |
|---|---|---|---|
| A | $ 1,289 | $ 871 | $ 482 |
| B | 708 | 636 | 509 |
| C | 1,634 | 1,840 | 1,114 |
| D | 875 | 562 | 477 |
| E | 1,012 | 2,321 | 889 |
| F | 1,414 | 2,629 | 600 |
| G | 1,689 | 875 | 795 |
| H | 826 | 1,032 | 484 |
| I | 987 | 1,701 | 468 |
| J | 1,412 | 911 | 860 |
| K | 933 | 1,550 | 653 |
| L | 1,523 | 1,411 | 783 |
| M | 1,543 | 1,553 | 690 |
| N | 1,034 | 2,078 | 734 |
| P | 1,645 | 912 | 828 |
| Q | 910 | 1,755 | 480 |
| R | 1,342 | 1,791 | 656 |
| T | 911 | 1,010 | 615 |
| U | 1,844 | 1,739 | 1,193 |
| V | 2,358 | 2,657 | 734 |
| W | 1,863 | 2,038 | 647 |
| X | 1,197 | 1,821 | 654 |

Adapted from Rossmiller, R. et al. *Educational programs for exceptional children: Resource configurations and costs.* Madison: University of Wisconsin, 1970, pp. 65, 70.

The obvious question is, For a population which is presumed to be identical as far as disability classification, why should the EMR cost per student vary from $708 in one school district to $2,358 in another, and why should the TMR cost per student vary from $636 to $2,657? On the basis of cost alone, can we assume that a child in the EMR class with an expenditure of $2,358 per student receives a better education than the child in the class with the lower expenditure? Special education must begin to address such issues.

## APPROPRIATENESS

Throughout PL 94-142, the requirement of "free appropriate public education" is found. But what is "appropriate" to the education of a child? What does this language mean in terms of what should specifically be provided? What is the yardstick for measuring appropriateness? Children are also required to be served in the "least restrictive environment." What does this really mean in terms of specific services and their settings?

A more important question with the most overwhelming implications is, *What is "appropriate" in terms of dollars?* It must be emphasized that this chapter deals primarily with education and its related costs; it is recognized that health and related expenditures may be far more extensive and that this area should undergo similar questioning and review.

Any parent wants the best money can provide for his or her child. At the same time budget developers have to make hard decisions as to where money should or should not be allocated and as to where cut-offs will be. High costs are receiving considerable attention these days. In Massachusetts, for example, two children are receiving services which cost the public $62,000 per year for each child. It must be noted that as of February, 1976, only 27 children out of 119,000, in special education programs in Massachusetts were in programs which cost in excess of $16,000.

The following are examples of some representative per-pupil estimates on high-cost programs compiled in February, 1976 by the Bureau of Education of the Handicapped of the U.S. Office of Education. It is emphasized that not all of these expenses are solely educational, nor are the programs necessarily funded by the Bureau. They are merely examples of costs. *(See Table 3, page 262.)*

It is possible to dismiss these figures as extreme efforts for a limited number of children and as unrepresentative of actual costs of special education. While this may be true to some extent, such figures of the magnitude represented here are those that attract attention and become the basis for questioning all other traditional or excess costs. As emphasized earlier, special education will be in the forefront of education's financial justification.

If society must provide handicapped children with an appropriate education and assume the full costs, then special education is obliged to justify that the appropriate education is being provided for each child in the *most* efficient manner. If the average per pupil cost in a community is $1,500 per student per year, is $1,500 per year for each handicapped child an appropriate expenditure? Is $3,000, $6,000, $12,000, $24,000, or even $62,000 appropriate to spend on an annual basis to meet a child's needs? Since appropriateness has to be considered in the light of desired or expected outcomes, how much more and what kind of services are needed to meet the objectives? Are expectations (desired outcomes) reasonable and achieveable? Is there any limit as to what educational and/or social services should be provided? What should be the extent of society's responsibility? Should all children be supported, regardless of family income, and provided with any services which are

TABLE 3: Representative per-pupil estimates on high-cost programs for the handicapped.

| Program (Residential) | Per pupil cost | Handicapping condition |
|---|---|---|
| Bell Faire<br>Shaker Heights, Ohio | $ 16,323 | Severely emotionally disturbed |
| Ben Haven<br>New Haven, Conn. | 25,000 | Autistic |
| DeVereux Foundations<br>Washington, Conn.<br>Debon, Pa.<br>Kennesaw, Ga. | 12,000–18,000 | Learning disabled<br>Severely emotionally disturbed |
| Hillcrest Children's Center<br>Washington, D.C. | 18,943 | Severely emotionally disturbed |
| Grove School<br>Madison, Conn. | 16,800 | Learning disabled<br>Severely emotionally disturbed |
| National Children's Rehabilitation<br>Leesburg, Virginia | 16,200 | Severely emotionally disturbed |
| Christ Child Institute for Children<br>Rockville, Md. | 26,299 | Severely emotionally disturbed |
| Perkins School for the Blind<br>Deaf-Blind Department<br>Watertown, Mass. | 24,487 | Deaf–Blind |
| New York Institute for the Education of the Blind<br>Bronx, New York | 19,000 | Deaf–Blind |
| Oak Hill School for the Blind<br>Connecticut | 18,576 | Mentally retarded<br>Deaf–Blind |
| Belchertown State School<br>Massachusetts | 21,076 | Mentally retarded;<br>Deaf–Blind |

required? Finally, the ultimate question is, If a dollar limitation is placed on appropriate expenditures, who will or who should make the judgment as to what is appropriate?

As the issue of what is appropriate in terms of dollars is being considered, the other side of the coin must also be viewed; that is, what will happen when judgments are made on the basis of dollars and parents raise the question that what is proposed to be provided is *not* appropriate or sufficient? Does this portend that future lawsuits against public agencies filed by parents questioning appropriateness will be based on *education malpractice?*

The most significant question that must be answered, however, does not concern what is appropriate in terms of dollars, but whether school systems will be able or willing to provide the broad range of facilities and programs necessary to accommodate the special problems and individual needs of children.

## A View from the Real World

In spite of the new federal and state laws and increased expenditures, some parents are still experiencing difficulty in finding, let alone getting children into, special programs. At the same time, school districts in trying to meet federal and state mandates are experiencing comparable problems, questions, and frustrations. Dr. Gloria Engnoth, Coordinator of Special Education for the Baltimore County (Maryland) schools, in response to my inquiry, provided the following frank and perceptive appraisal of the expenses and problems her school system is facing in attempting to serve *all* handicapped children. Rather than attempt to rewrite or condense her response (with her kind permission), it is inserted with a minimum of change. It should be understood that the concerns noted by Dr. Engnoth are not unique to Baltimore County; similar examples can be found in every state and in almost any school district.

The following is a summary of the philosophical and practical concerns that face a local education agency when trying to implement legislative and judicial directives which state that every handicapped child should be provided with the most appropriate educational program to meet his individual needs. In complying with such a mandate, a local education agency must consider the use of residential facilities as a source of programming for pupils who are severely, profoundly and uniquely handicapped (excerpted from Maryland State Bylaw directive).

As I shared with you, the Board of Education of Baltimore County had appropriated in its 1975–76 special education budget $500,000 to cover the cost of covering such services. This estimate was based on applications during the previous year for this level of service. The figure was derived from the Maryland State Department of Education which directed local education agencies to give priorities to pupils in the following order: (a) to serve all school-age pupils and to finance their educational program in residential settings if this was recommended by the Admission, Review, and Dismissal Committee . . . (b) to continue funding for any handicapped child who had been placed and funded under this service level during the previous year; (c) where possible, to extend residential service appropriate to preschool age levels. I might add that the department in its correspondence indicated that there would be little or no funding support for the infant/preschool group that this service would need to be provided by finances available through the local county government; i.e., board of education. As of this date, in order to comply with these requests the Board of Education of Baltimore County has expended approximately $735,000 for approximately 156 identified pupils. As you can see, our budgeted amount fell very short of the actual expenditure. This led to my staff and I examining very closely the residential programs for handicapped pupils. Attached you will find a breakdown of costs for 25 pupils whose educational program is being paid for in private schools by the State of Maryland Department of Education and the Baltimore County Board of Education. The board felt that we needed to break apart tuition costs in order to identify specific areas where monies were being spent.

A general explanation of the chart is column 1—child; column 2 is total tuition requested by the nonpublic facility; column 3 is instructional costs; column 4 is therapy costs; column 5 is room and board and any requiring extras; column 6 is the name of the nonpublic facility, [changed to letter designation for inclusion in this text]. Perusal of the data raises the following concerns: The Federal Handicap Educational Act, Maryland State Law, and the Special Education Bylaw mandate the payment of educational costs; Question 1—should a board of education direct money intended for instruction to the provision of therapies such as psychiatric treatment? Question 2—when one looks at the total cost to the facility and the costs that parents assume . . . should the use of education monies supplant financial obligations of families toward the rearing of the child? . . . Let me clarify this a little further . . . if a child were living at home, parents would have to pay food costs, transportation, recreation, etc. If one looks at what parents pay in the private facility, it appears that their financial contribution is addressed to laundry, purchase of clothing, spending money.

I think a case consideration needs to be outlined in terms of the dispersal of money across agencies so that educational costs should address instruction and should be paid for through monies allocated to education. Therapy, if it is medical in nature, should be paid for by monies allocated through health and mental health agencies, and room and board at least be partially paid by families requesting service for children in nonpublic schools.

A second aspect deals with a local board of education's obligations to certain categorical types of handicapping conditions. I will describe three special cases, give background data, and then raise the issue that we faced in this particular educational agency.

*Case #1* is fourteen years old, is currently being provided with an educational program at School F, and is being supported by funding from the Board of Education of Baltimore County.

*Descriptive Diagnosis:*   This child's handicap can be described as a severe motor expressive aphasia combined with mental retardation. The pupil's educational service summary is as follows:

| | | |
|---|---|---|
| 1966-67 | School G* | $ 700.00 |
| 1968-69 | School H* | 800.00 |
| 1/1/70-6/70 | School F* | -3,331.14 |
| 1971-72 | School F | 8,100.00 |
| 1972-73 | School F | 8,100.00 |
| 1973-74 | School F | 8,100.00 |
| 1974-75 | School F | 8,100.00 |
| 1975-76 | School F | 9,540.00 |

This case is unique in that the Board of Education of Baltimore County has available classes for children with severe communicative/language disabilities and classes for pupils with communicative/language disorders and mental retardation. However, the child's mother refuses to have the child in the home. When this child returns home, it causes such an upheaval the mother must be hospitalized for psychiatric care. The issue in this case addresses itself to . . . should there again be a shared financial cost across

* Schools F, G, H, I, J, and N are additional schools which do not appear in table.

| Child | Tuition | Instruction | Therapy | Room and board | School |
|---|---|---|---|---|---|
| 1. | $15,000 | $11,460 | $540 | $3,000 | —A— |
| 2. | 11,675 | 4,800 | Inc. | 6,875 | —B— |
| 3. | 11,675 | 4,800 | Inc. | 6,875 | —B— |
| 4. | 11,675 | 4,800 | Inc. | 6,875 | —B— |
| 5. | 11,675 | 4,800 | Inc. | 6,875 | —B–- |
| 6. | 11,675 | 4,800 | Inc. | 6,875 | —B— |
| 7. | 14,400 | 4,800 | 1,200 | 8,400 | —B— |
| 8. | 14,400 | 4,200 | 1,800 | 8,400 | —B— |
| 9. | 11,675 | 4,800 | Inc. | 6,875 | —B— |
| 10. | 11,675 | 4,800 | Inc. | 6,875 | —B— |
| 11. | 14,400 | 4,200 | 1,800 | 8,400 | —B— |
| 12. | 11,675 | 4,800 | Inc. | 6,875 | —B— |
| 13. | 11,675 | 4,800 | Inc. | 6,875 | —B— |
| 14. | 12,480 | 5,800 | 1,620 | 3,539<br>1,521 for recreation, extras | —C— |
| 15. | 14,760 | 6,300 | 1,620 | 3,539 plus<br>extras | —C— |
| 16. | 8,000 | 3,280 | —— | 4,400 +<br>$320—phys. ed. | —D— |
| 17. | 8,000 | 3,280 | —— | 4,400 +<br>$320—phys. ed. | —D— |
| 18. | 8,000 | 3,280 | —— | " | —D— |
| 19. | 8,000 | 3,280 | —— | " | —D— |
| 20. | 8,000 | 3,280 | —— | " | —D— |
| 21. | 18,000 | 7,020 | 8,640 | 2,340 | —E— |
| 22. | 14,100 | 6,345 | 5,640 | 2,115 | —E— |
| 23. | 15,600 | 7,020 | 6,240 | 2,340 | —E— |
| 24. | 13,200 | 5,940 | 5,280 | 1,980 | —E— |
| 25. | 14,400 | 6,480 | 5,760 | 2,160 | —E— |

agencies of the cost of keeping this child in a residential setting? It is a very difficult question to resolve. As you see from the summary cost of School F, if we were to continue this young man through the age of 21, the cost to the educational agency would be $66,500 for these remaining years. This figure is only approximate. It has been our observation that in many cases the tuition cost of nonpublic facilities has arisen several thousand dollars from one fiscal year to the next. The second issue is should a child be continued in a residential program due to the physical and mental health of his family?

*Case #2* raises some difficult questions regarding educational programming in nonpublic facilities. This child is twelve years old and is blind and retarded with an estimated IQ of 25. There is a recurrent history of epilepsy and limited speech and communicative abilities. His performance level is limited progress in self-help skills and group skills. He requires strong staff supervision and direction, has a history of adversive behavior, although some improvement has been noted. Investigations have been made for services within the local school district. The Mental Retardation Administration has indicated that they cannot serve this young man because rentro lental fibro plasia has left him too blind to profit from programs for the mentally retarded. The State School for the Blind has rejected their educational planning for him because he is too retarded. The Vocational Rehabilitation service has indicated that this young man is too handicapped, and therefore could not receive their services. Social Services has indicated that he is still of school age and therefore does not fall within their jurisdiction. Therefore, plans for this young man fall to the educational agency. Therefore, he had his educational program delivered at a residential facility in Chicago which provides services for multihandicapped blind. The cost of provisions of service for this young man has been:

| 1971-72 | School I* | $8,500 |
| 1972-73 | School I | 8,900 |
| 1973-74 | School I | 9,195 |
| 1974-75 | School I | 10,500 |
| 1975-76 | School I | 11,000 |

for a total of $48,095 to date.

We have recently received communication from the family; though the young man will be 21 years of age in November, they are requesting continuation of funding through June of the coming fiscal year. To my knowledge no agency plans to assume responsibility of this young man at the time the educational agency ceases its service. At issue are two aspects: (1) With a young man of age where the educational program is about to cease and little hope of increase in ability to make use of the instructional program, should a local educational agency continue to fund through a year in which the 21st birth date occurs? (2) If there should not again be a coalition of agencies providing service and assuming burdens for services other than educational services, then what services will be available for this child? In this young man's case there are 40 sessions of individual therapy at a cost of $400 and a recreational program of $625. Question: What is a local educational agency's responsibility for continued training of a multihandicapped person till and through the age of 21 who shows minimal progress? Should there be a time when there is realization that the investment of funds for instruction, i.e., $6,835, is not continued and that person continue to have appropriate care? Is every individual entitled to instruction 0–20 years regardless of documentation of progress?

*Case #3* involves siblings. The first, Child X, is fifteen years old and has a diagnosis of cerebral dysfunction manifested by mental retardation with performance in the low trainable range. He was seen at School J* and the following behavioral descriptions resulted: (a) biting fingers/wrist at a rate of 6.6 responses per minute; (b) spitting at a rate of 2.1 responses per minute; (c) biting or pinching others at a rate of 0.3 responses per minute; (d) unintelligible sounds at a rate of 1.4 rpm. Total adversive behavioral responses—9.50 rpm.

*Educational History:*   School J Appraisal: Enrollment behavioral modification program—2 months. 1970-71 School K (day center)—released because too difficult to handle. 2/72 enrolled School L (residential center) length of stay 3 hours—too difficult to handle. 8/72 enrolled School M.

This young man has not cost the board of education anything to date, but his father is exploring the possibility of residential placement. This child and his sibling were also plaintiffs in the Maryland Association for Retarded Citizens class action suit against the State of Maryland.

Child Y is fourteen years old and also has a diagnosis of cerebral dysfunction manifested by mental retardation with performance in the low-trainable range.

*Behavioral Description:*   Adversive behavior occurred at the following rates: (a) cries and chews hands at a rate of 2.50 rpm; (b) puts objects in mouth, that is, uses his tongue as a server, at a rate of 3.5 rpm; (c) grabs others; (d) screams at a rate of 3.50 rpm; (e) acceptable behavior could only be elicited if the young man was reinforced at a rate of 0.25 tokens per minute.

This young man parallels his brother except that he appears to have a bit more potential. He is enrolled in a private facility: 1975–76—School N*—$6,000. The Baltimore County Board of Education assumed responsibility as of this year.

This Office of Special Education has had lengthy and frequent contact with the father of the two boys. He is separated from his wife and has custody of the two boys; however, he indicates that he has no way of providing home care for either child and that residential placement will be essential from now on. Since this young man is 15 years of age we can look forward to paying education and care costs for him for the next six years. Both boys show minimal progress. The private nonpublic school and the public institution have indicated that the prognosis for their educational development is poor. Rather they indicate that the youngsters need tender, loving care. Again, I feel that the Baltimore County Board of Education has an obligation to see that some aspect of educational program is continued with both boys, but should a full cost of care fall to an educational agency alone? Also, what should the parent's responsibility be in the provision of some financial contribution toward their care?

Marty, please be aware that I am not in any way trying to minimize the role that education should play in seeing that severely, profoundly and uniquely handicapped children be provided with an educational program. I am in full agreement with legislation and judicial decisions to insure every individual the opportunity for education. The issues and questions I have raised address themselves primarily to whether it is the sole responsibility of a board of education because a child is of school age to provide all services in order for the individual to live and to supplant parental responsibility during the developing years of their child. As further explanation of that statement, let me say that quite often parents call to say "Well, my kid's been kicked out of the last residential school where you sent him—now, what are you going to do for him? Remember he is of school age and it is your responsibility to see that he gets the appropriate education in the most conducive environment—law and court guarantees this as my right."

## Work and Placement

It is recognized that every individual should have the opportunity to live the fullest possible life with all of the benefits and pleasures that life has to offer. It is recognized, too, that education is one of the vehicles through which fulfillment comes. After education is completed, however, finding and securing employment is yet another difficulty the handicapped must face.

The questions raised in this chapter go beyond the matter of spending levels and go to the basis of special education itself. Because PL 94-142 requires that handicapped children be educated, a re-evaluation of what they will be educated for must be made. The nation is currently faced with high unemployment, a move toward more and more automation, and an increasing elimination of unskilled jobs. When viewed in the light of the anticipated identification and school enrollment of thousands of new severely handicapped children within the next few years, it is obvious that thought must be given to the future placement of these children and their role in society after the schools have completed their work. Special education will have to re-evaluate its programs to determine whether it is properly meeting the needs in today's changing world.

What should handicapped individuals who cannot work in competitive employment do? In five or ten years if there are as few jobs available as there are today, what will become of these individuals? One possibility is sheltered or limited and restricted work structures which provide settings in which individuals perform work skills at their own rates and within their own abilities. Payment is generally below the minimum wage. The question that must be asked now is whether workshops as they presently exist can adequately accommodate or begin to meet the needs of these severely handicapped individuals who will be brought into special education programs within the next few years.

If one assumes that there will not be any more jobs available in ten years than there are today and many of the lower level jobs which exist today will be eliminated, what will become of the severely handicapped individuals who will not be able to compete with able-bodied persons? Should these individuals be placed in sheltered, restricted, controlled work situations which pay less than the minimum wage? Should these settings be required to pay employees at least the minimum wage because of the reality that an individual earning at that level is below the poverty standard and certainly cannot support himself from those wages alone? Should federal, state and/or local governments supplement salaries of handicapped persons working in sheltered employment? Should financial support be given to the agency or organization providing employment to cover costs and salaries or should they be closed altogether and the money which would have gone to them be given directly to each severely handicapped person who might be "employed," thereby eliminating all overhead and operating costs?

## CONCLUSION

In 1954 as the Supreme Court considered the *Brown* v. *Board of Education* case, the problem was unequal access to unequal resources for achieving identical ends. In the early 1960s, we had equal access to equal resources to achieve identical ends. Through compensatory education programs, the move was to equal access to differing resources to achieve identical ends. In the last part of the 1970s, through individualized education, we are entering an era of equal access to differing resources to achieve differing ends.

The old joke, "I have some good news and some bad news," dramatically applies to special education today. The good news is that the dream of having the capacity to serve all handicapped children may finally be realized. The bad news is that there will be greater public scrutiny of how well schools are educating children, how well they are utilizing scarce public resources, and how well handicapped individuals are prepared to lead a meaningful life. To some, these questions may be overwhelming. But it is hoped that those who work with the handicapped will see them as a positive and exciting challenge.

# FOCUS...



### 1954      BROWN V. BOARD OF EDUCATION

Civil Rights court case whose landmark decision stated that education must be available to all on equal terms.

### 1971      PENNSYLVANIA ASSOCIATION FOR RETARDED CITIZENS (PARC) V. COMMONWEALTH OF PENNSYLVANIA

The parties of this case, 14 mentally handicapped children of school age and state secretaries of education, state board of education, public welfare, and 13 school districts, agreed that no child would be denied admission to a public school program without first being notified and given the opportunity of a due process hearing.

### WYATT-STICKNEY V. ADERHOLT (M.D. ALABAMA)

The result of this established the precedent that the lack of funds is not an acceptable rationale for failing to provide treatment to the handicapped. If the agency lacks funds, it must find ways to raise the funds or reallocate existing funds to provide adequate treatment.

### 1972

### MILLS V. BOARD OF EDUCATION, DISTRICT OF COLUMBIA

The outcome of this case guaranteed that the Board of Education of the District of Columbia shall provide to each school age child a free and appropriate public education, regardless of the degree of the child's impairment.

### 1979      SOUTHEASTERN COMMUNITY COLLEGE V. DAVIS

The Supreme Court in this case ruled that Mrs. Davis, a deaf nursing student, not be allowed to participate in the college's associate nursing program. Mrs. Davis contended that under Section 504 of the Rehabilitation Act the college was obligated to admit her to the program. The judges ruling stated that Section 504 gives no requirement upon an educational institution to lower or to affect substantial modifications of standards to accomodate a handicapped person.

---

### 1964      CIVIL RIGHTS ACT

Established the precedent that everyone is entitled to a free-appropriate education regardless of race, color, or nationality. This has been used in later cases to apply to handicapped persons as well.

### 1965      PUBLIC LAW (89-313) PROGRAM

This law ammends the Elementary and Secondary Education Act of 1965 and provides for federal funds to be granted for the special education of handicapped children in state schools and to those handicapped children who have transferred to special education in public schools.

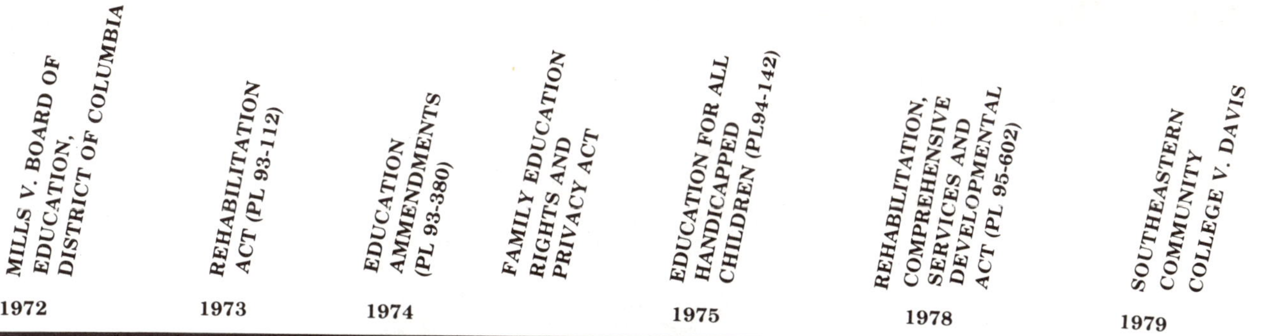


**1968**        **ARCHITECTURAL BARRIERS ACT (PL 90-480)**

Any building constructed or leased by federal funding must be made accessible to and usable by the handicapped. This law was not enforced until the Architecture and Transportation Barriers Compliance Board was established in 1973.

**1970**        **EDUCATION OF THE HANDICAPPED (PL 91-230)**

All handicapped children must have available to them a free-appropriate public education which emphasizes special education and related services designed to meet the handicapped's needs.

**1973**        **REHABILITATION ACT (PL 93-112)**

**SECTION 504:** This law states that no person can be excluded, by reason of handicap, from participating in or be denied the benefits of any program or act receiving federal assistance, if it is found he/she is otherwise qualified.

**SECTION 502:** Develops the Architecture and Transportation Barriers Compliance Board to enforce architectural accessibility as outlined in the Architectural Barriers Act of 1968.

**1974**        **EDUCATION AMMENDMENTS (PL 93-380)**

This act further ammends the Education of the Handicapped Act of 1970. The provisions of this ammendment call for correcting the fact that many handicapped children were not receiving education and required the States to take steps to protect the rights of handicapped children and their parents in placement changes. It also assured that as much education as possible is done in the "regular" classroom. Testing and evaluation materials can not be racially or culturally discriminating. The ammendment also provides for further funds to be available to give full education opportunity to the handicapped.

**1974**        **FAMILY EDUCATION RIGHTS AND PRIVACY ACT**

This act guarantees parents the right to see all official school records involving their children. It also limits the access of these records from outsiders without parental permission. The implications of this act on the handicapped is that it prevents the labelling of handicapped children on school records without the parents knowledge.

**1975**        **EDUCATION FOR ALL HANDICAPPED CHILDREN (PL 94-142)**

Establishes that State and Local Education Agencies must find and locate all school age children not presently receiving public education and provide those children with such an education. All handicapped children should be "mainstreamed" in the least restrictive environment and be given special services where mainstreaming is not applicable. Agencies must provide a written IEP and parents *must be consulted* and *understand* all phases of diagnosis and planning of the child's educational programs.

**1978**        **REHABILITATION, COMPREHENSIVE SERVICES AND DEVELOPMENTAL DISABILITIES ACT (PL 95-602)**

This act extends the vocational rehabilitation program established in the 1973 Rehabilitation Act for four more years and creates a new program for comprehensive, independent living services for the disabled and a new National Institute of Handicapped Research. Also established is the National Council on the Handicapped and expands the enforcement power of the Architecture and Transportation Barriers Compliance Board.

# Public Law 94–142 and Section 504:
# What They Say about Rights and Protections


JOSEPH BALLARD
JEFFREY ZETTEL

JOSEPH BALLARD *is Assistant Director for Policy Implementation, and* JEFFREY ZETTEL *is a Specialist for Policy Implementation, Governmental Relations Unit, The Council for Exceptional Children.*


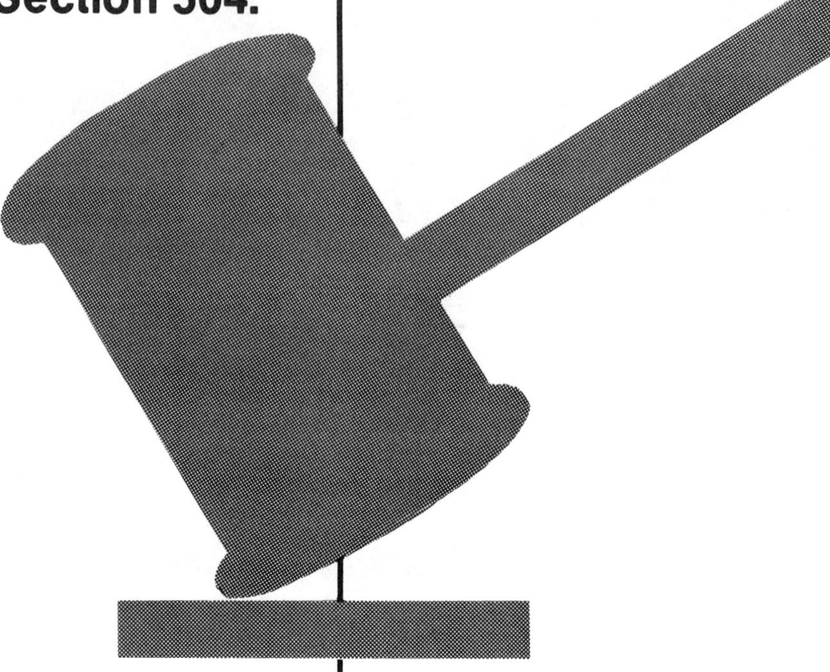

This is the second article in *Exceptional Children* during the current volume year that deals with Public Law (P. L.) 94–142, the Education for All Handicapped Children Act. The primary objective of this series is to provide the reader with a background as well as a substantial understanding of this monumental and most complex piece of federal legislation as it relates to the education of all handicapped children. The October issue of *Exceptional Children* contained the feature article "The End of the Quiet Revolution: The Education for All Handicapped Children Act of 1975."

The purpose of that article was to provide a historical perspective of state and federal litigation and legislation that both directly and indirectly influenced the conception of P. L. 94–142. What follows in this and subsequent articles will be an in-depth analysis of the specific language and principal intent of the law. For the sake of clarity, as well as brevity, the vehicle for the majority of the ensuing discussions will be in the form of a question and answer format. Finally, it should be noted that frequent reference will be made to Section 504 of the Vocational Rehabilitation Act of 1973 with the expectation that the parallels and similarities between the two laws in regard to their potential impact on the education of handicapped children will be apparent.

## Basic Thrust, Objectives, and Target Populations

### What is P. L. 94–142?

P. L. 94–142, the Education for All Handicapped Children Act, is legislation passed by the United States Congress and signed into law by President Gerald R. Ford on November 29, 1975. The "94" indicates that this law was passed by the 94th Congress. The "142" indicates that this law was the 142nd law passed by that session of the Congress to be signed into law by the President.

### What are the purposes of P. L. 94–142?

P. L. 94–142 can be said to have four major purposes:

- Guarantee the availability of special education programing to handicapped children and youth who require it.
- Assure fairness and appropriateness in decision making with regard to providing special education to handicapped children and youth.
- Establish clear management and auditing requirements and procedures regarding special education at all levels of government.


**44**    Reprinted from *Exceptional Children* by Joseph Ballard and Jeffrey Zettel by permission of The Council for Exceptional Children. ©1977 by the Council for Exceptional Children, 1920 Association Drive, Reston, Virginia 22091.

- Financially assist the efforts of state and local government through the use of federal funds (refer to Section 3 of the Act).

**What is Section 504?**

Section 504 is a basic civil rights provision with respect to terminating discrimination against America's handicapped citizens. Section 504 was enacted through the legislative vehicle P. L. 93-112, the Vocational Rehabilitation Act Amendments of 1973. Though Section 504 is brief in actual language, its implications are far reaching. The statute reads:

> No otherwise qualified handicapped individual in the United States shall, solely by reason of his handicap, be excluded from the participation in, be denied the benefits of, or be subjected to discrimination under any program or activity receiving Federal financial assistance.

**To whom do P. L. 94-142 and Section 504 apply?**

P. L. 94-142 applies to all handicapped children who require special education and related services, ages 3 to 21 inclusive. Section 504 applies to all handicapped Americans regardless of age. Section 504 therefore applies to all handicapped children ages 3 to 21 with respect to their public education both from the standpoint of the guarantee of an appropriate special education and from the standpoint of sheer regular program accessibility. Close coordination has thus been maintained between the provisions of P. L. 94-142 and those of the Section 504 regulations (refer to Section 611 of P. L. 94-142 and background statement of the Section 504 regulation).

**What is the relationship of P. L. 94-142 to the older federal Education of the Handicapped Act (EHA)?**

P. L. 94-142 is a complete revision of only Part B of the Education of the Handicapped Act. Part B was formerly that portion of EHA addressing the basic state grant program. The other components of the Act (Parts A-E) remain substantially unchanged and continue in operation. Parenthetically, all programs under the aegis of the EHA, including the P. L. 94-142 revision of Part B, are administered through the Bureau of Education for the Handicapped under the US Office of Education.

**Was there a forerunner to P. L. 94-142?**

Many of the major provisions of P. L. 94-142, such as the guarantee of due process proce-dures and the assurance of education in the least restrictive environment, were required in an earlier federal law—P. L. 93-380, the Education Amendments of 1974 (enacted August 21, 1974). P. L. 94-142 was enacted approximately one year and three months later, on November 29, 1975.

**How are handicapped children defined for purposes of this Act?**

Handicapped children are defined by the Act as children who are:

> mentally retarded, hard of hearing, deaf, orthopedically impaired, other health impaired, speech impaired, visually handicapped, seriously emotionally disturbed, or children with specific learning disabilities who by reason thereof require special education and related services.

This definition establishes a two pronged criteria for determining child eligibility under the Act. The first is whether the child actually has one or more of the disabilities listed in the above definition. The second is whether the child requires special education and related services. Not all children who have a disability require special education; many are able and should attend school without any program modification (refer to Section 4 of the Act).

**If a child has one or more of the disabilities listed in the preceding definition and also requires special education and related services, how does P. L. 94-142 define special education?**

Special education is defined in P. L. 94-142 as:

> specially designed instruction, at no cost to parents or guardians, to meet the unique needs of a handicapped child, including classroom instruction, instruction in physical education, home instruction, and instruction in hospitals and institutions.

The key phrase in the above definition of special education is "specially designed instruction . . . to meet the unique needs of a handicapped child." Reemphasized, special education, according to statutory definition, is defined as being "special" and involving only instruction that is designed and directed to meet the unique needs of a handicapped child. For many children therefore, special education will not be the totality of their education. Furthermore, this definition clearly implies that special education proceeds from the basic goals and expected outcomes of general education. Thus, intervention with a child does not occur because he or she is mentally retarded but because he or she has a

# 1. PERSPECTIVES

unique educational need that requires specially designed instruction (refer to Section 4(a)(16) of the Act).

**How are related services defined in P. L. 94-142?**

Equally important to understand is the concept of related services that are defined in the Act as:

> transportation, and such developmental, corrective, and other supportive services (including speech pathology and audiology, psychological services, physical and occupational therapy, recreation, and medical and counseling services, except that such medical services shall be for diagnostic and evaluation purposes only) as may be required to assist a handicapped child to benefit from special education, and includes the early identification and assessment of handicapping conditions in children.

The key phrase here is "as required to assist the handicapped child to benefit from special education." This leads to a clear progression: a child is handicapped because he or she requires special education and related services; special education is the specially designed instruction to meet the child's unique needs; and related services are those additional services necessary in order for the child to benefit from special educational instruction (refer to Section 4(a)(17) of the Act).

## Rights and Protections

### A Free Appropriate Education

**What is the fundamental requirement of P. L. 94-142, from which all other requirements of this Act stem?**

P. L. 94-142 requires that every state and its localities, if they are to continue to receive funds under this Act, must make available a free appropriate public education for all handicapped children aged 3 to 18 by the beginning of the school year (September 1) in 1978 and further orders the availability of such education to all children aged 3 to 21 by September 1, 1980 (refer to Section 3(c) of the Act).

**What about preschool and young adults under P. L. 94-142?**

For children in the 3 to 5 and 18 to 21 age ranges, however, this mandate does not apply if such a requirement is inconsistent with state law or practice or any court decree. Refer to regulations for further expatiation of this provision (refer to Section 612 (2)(B) of the Act).

**What does Section 504 say regarding the right to an education?**

Section 504 makes essentially the same requirement. However, the 504 regulation says "shall provide." P. L. 94-142 says "a free appropriate public education *will be available.*"

The 504 regulation does not refer to specific age groups per se. Instead, it refers to "public elementary and secondary education," and, therefore, the traditional school age population. With respect to that school age population, the 504 regulation accedes to the September 1, 1978, date of P. L. 94-142 as the final and absolute deadline for the provision of a free appropriate public education. However, the Section 504 regulation also precedes that requirement with the phrase "*at the earliest practicable time* but in no event later than September 1, 1978." (Refer to #84.33(d) of the 504 regulation.)

**What is required with respect to preschool and young adult programs under Section 504?**

The 504 regulation appears simply to say that preschool and adult education programs will not discriminate on the basis of handicap, and further that such program accessibility is to take effect immediately. On the other hand, P. L. 94-142, as previously noted, explicitly states that there shall be available a free appropriate public education for children ages 3 through 5 and youth ages 18 through 21 unless such requirement is inconsistent with state law or practice or the order of any court. Again, P. L. 94-142 does not require such availability until September 1, 1978 (refer to #84.38 of the 504 regulation).

**Since Section 504 and P. L. 94-142 are making, in essence, the same fundamental requirement of a free, appropriate public education, are federal monies authorized under Section 504 as they are under P. L. 94-142?**

No. Section 504 is a civil rights statute, like Title VI of the Civil Rights Act of 1965 (race) and Title IX of the Education Amendments of 1972 (sex).

**Must there be compliance with the fundamental requirement of P. L. 94-142 (as reiterated in Section 504 regulations) if P. L. 94-142 is not "fully funded"?**

It is most important to note that compliance with this baseline guarantee of the availability of a free, appropriate public education is in no way dependent upon whether this Act receives appropriations at the top authorized ceilings, or in other words, is "fully funded." If a state accepts money under this Act, regardless of the amount of actual appropriations, it must comply with the aforementioned stipulation.

### What does "free" education, as required in both P. L. 94–142 and Section 504, mean?

"Free" means the provision of education and related services at no cost to the handicapped person or to his or her parents or guardian, except for those largely incidental fees that are imposed on nonhandicapped persons or their parents or guardian (refer to #84.33(c)(1) of the 504 regulation).

### What if a public placement is made in a public or private residential program?

If both the school and parents jointly agree that the most appropriate educational placement for the child is in a public or private residential facility, then such a program placement, including nonmedical care as well as room and board, shall be provided at no cost to the person or his or her parents or guardian (refer to #84.33(c)(3) of the 504 regulation).

### Does "free" mean that no private funds can be used?

No. Private funds are not prohibited. To reiterate: there must be no cost to the handicapped person or to his or her parents or guardian.

### What does "appropriate" education mean?

"Appropriate" is not defined as such, but rather receives its definition for each child through the mechanism of the written individualized education program (IEP) as required by P. L. 94–142. Therefore, what is agreed to by all parties becomes in fact the "appropriate" educational program for the particular child.

#### Individualized Education Programs

### What are the basic concepts of the IEP?

The term *individualized education program* itself conveys important concepts that need to be specified. First, *individualized* means that the IEP must be addressed to the educational needs of a single child rather than a class or group of children. Second, *education* means that the IEP is limited to those elements of the child's education that are more specifically special education and related services as defined by the Act. Third, *program* means

that the IEP is a statement of what will actually be provided to the child, as distinct from a plan that provides guidelines from which a program must subsequently be developed.

### What are the basic components of an IEP?

The Act contains a specific definition describing the components of an IEP as:

> a written statement for each handicapped child developed in any meeting by a representative of the local education agency or an intermediate educational unit who shall be qualified to provide, or supervise the provision of, specially designed instruction to meet the unique needs of handicapped children, the teacher, the parents or guardian of such child, and whenever appropriate, such child, which statement shall include (A) a statement of the present levels of educational performance of such child, (B) a statement of annual goals, including short-term instructional objectives, (C) a statement of the specific educational anticipated duration of such services, and appropriate objective criteria and evaluation procedures and schedules for determining, on at least an annual basis, whether instructional objectives are being achieved.

(Refer to Section 4(a)(19) of the Act.)

### May others be involved in the development of an IEP?

Good practice suggests that others frequently be involved. However, the law only requires four persons be involved (i.e., the parents or guardians, the teacher or teachers of the child, a representative of the local educational agency or intermediate unit who is qualified to provide or supervise the provision of special education, and whenever appropriate, the child). If a related service person will be providing services, then it seems to make sense that they be as involved as the teacher. Also, good practice indicates that parents often want to bring an additional person familiar with the child to the meeting.

### Who must be provided an IEP?

Each state and local educational agency shall insure that an IEP is provided for each handicapped child who is receiving or will receive special education, regardless of what institution or agency provides or will provide special education to the child: (a) The state educational agency shall insure that each local educational agency establishes and implements an IEP for each handicapped child; (b) The state educational agency shall require each public agency which provides special educa-

# 1. PERSPECTIVES

tion or related services to a handicapped child to establish policies and procedures for developing, implementing, reviewing, maintaining, and evaluating an IEP for that child.

## What must local and intermediate education agencies do regarding IEP's?

- Each local educational agency shall develop or revise, whichever is appropriate, an IEP for every handicapped child at the beginning of the school year and review and if appropriate revise its provisions periodically but not less than annually.
- Each local educational agency is responsible for initiating and conducting meetings for developing, reviewing, and revising a child's IEP.
- For a handicapped child who is receiving special education, a meeting must be held early enough so that the IEP is developed (or revised, as appropriate) by the beginning of the next school year.
- For a handicapped child who is not receiving special education, a meeting must be held within 30 days of a determination that the child is handicapped, or that the child will receive special education.

(Refer to Section 614(a)(5) of the Act.)

## Do the IEP requirements apply to children in private schools and facilities?

Yes. The state educational agency shall insure that an IEP is developed, maintained, and evaluated for each child placed in a private school by the state educational agency or a local educational agency. The agency that places or refers a child shall insure that provision is made for a representative from the private school (which may be the child's teacher) to participate in each meeting. If the private school representative cannot attend a meeting, the agency shall use other methods to insure participation by the private school, including individual or conference telephone calls (refer to Section 613(a)(4)(B) of the Act).

## Is the IEP an instructional plan?

No. The IEP is a management tool that is designed to assure that, when a child requires special education, the special education designed for that child is appropriate to his or her special learning needs and that the special education designed is actually delivered and monitored. An instructional plan reflects good educational practice by outlining the specifics necessary to effectively intervene in instruction. Documenting instructional plans is not mandated as part of the IEP requirements.

## What procedures should education agencies follow to involve parents in the development of their child's IEP?

- Each local educational agency shall take steps to insure that one or both of the parents of the handicapped child are present at each meeting or are afforded the opportunity to participate, including scheduling the meeting at a mutually agreed on time and place.
- If neither parent can attend, the local educational agency shall use other methods to insure parent participation, including individual or conference telephone calls.
- A meeting may be conducted without a parent in attendance if the local educational agency is unable to convince the parents that they should attend. In this case the local educational agency must have a record of its attempts to arrange a mutually agreed on time and place such as: (a) Detailed records of telephone calls made or attempted and the results of those calls, (b) copies of correspondence sent to the parents and any responses received, and (c) detailed records of visits made to the parent's home or place of employment and the results of those visits.
- The local educational agency shall take whatever action is necessary to insure that the parent understands the proceedings at a meeting, including arranging for an interpreter for parents who are deaf or whose native language is other than English.

## When must handicapped children be guaranteed the IEP?

- For handicapped children counted under the fiscal funding formula of P. L. 94–142, not later than the beginning of school year 1977–1978.
- For all handicapped children in each state, regardless of the delivering agency, not later than the beginning of school year 1978–1979.

## What does Section 504 say with respect to the IEP?

As just discussed, P. L. 94–142 requires the development and maintenance of individualized written education programs for all children. The 504 regulation cites the IEP as "one means" of meeting the standard of a free appropriate public education (refer to #84.33(b)(2) of the 504 regulation).

**Least Restrictive Educational Environment**

**P. L. 94-142 requires that handicapped children receive a free appropriate public education in the least restrictive educational environment. What does this mean?**

It is critical to note what this provision *is not*:

- It is not a provision for mainstreaming. In fact, the word is never used.
- It does not mandate that all handicapped children will be educated in the regular classroom.
- It does not abolish any particular educational environment, for instance, educational programing in a residential setting.

It is equally critical to note what this provision *does* mandate:

- Education with nonhandicapped children will be the governing objective "to the maximum extent appropriate."
- The IEP will be the management tool toward achievement of the maximum least restrictive environment and therefore shall be applied within the framework of meeting the "unique needs" of each child.
- The IEP document(s) must clearly "show cause" if and when one moves from least restrictive to more restrictive. The statute states that the following component must be included in the written statement accompanying the IEP "and the extent to which such child will be able to participate in regular educational programs."

(Refer to Section 612(5)(B) of the Act.)

**Correspondingly, what does the Section 504 regulation say with respect to least restrictive educational environment?**

The language of the 504 regulation is, in most important respects, nearly identical to the least restrictive statute in P. L. 94-142. There remains one notable distinction, however. The 504 regulation would seem to consider the "nearest placement to home" as an additional determinant of instructional placement in the least restrictive environment (refer to #84.34(a) of the 504 regulation).

**Procedural Safeguards**

**Under P. L. 94-142, what happens if there is a failure to agree with respect to what constitutes an appropriate education for a particular child?**

States must guarantee procedural safeguard mechanisms for children and their parents or guardians. Those provisions of previously existing law (P. L. 93-380, the Education Amendments of 1974) toward the guarantee of due process rights are further refined in P. L. 94-142, and their scope is substantially enlarged.

Basically, the state education agency must guarantee the maintenance of full due process procedures for all handicapped children within the state and their parents or guardian with respect to all matters of identification, evaluation, and educational placement whether it be the initiation or change of such placement, or the refusal to initiate or change. Interested individuals are strongly urged to read Section 615 of the Act ("Procedural Safeguards") in its entirety.

It should be observed that the P. L. 94-142 refinements take effect in the first year under the new formula, that is, fiscal 1978 (school year 1977-1978). In the meantime, those basic features of due process as authorized in the prior Act (P. L. 93-380) must be maintained by the states.

It should be further noted that, when the parents or guardian of a child are not known, are unavailable, or when the child is a legal ward of the state, the state education agency, local education agency, or intermediate education agency (as appropriate) must assign an individual to act as a *surrogate* for the child in all due process proceedings. Moreover, such assigned individual may not be an employee of the state educational agency, local educational agency, or intermediate educational unit *involved in* the education or care of the particular child (refer to Section 615 of the Act).

**Does the Section 504 regulation also require the maintenance of a procedural safeguards mechanism?**

Yes. However, though most of the major principles of due process embodied in P. L. 94-142 are clearly present in the 504 regulation, *all* of the stipulations of P. L. 94-142 are treated only as "one means" of due process compliance under Section 504 (refer to #84.36 of the 504 regulation).

**What does P. L. 94-142 say with respect to assessment of children?**

P. L. 94-142 carries a provision that seeks to guarantee against assessment with respect to the question of a handicapping condition when such assessment procedures are racially or culturally discriminatory. The statute does not provide a comprehensive procedure of remedy with respect to potential discrimination but does make two clear and important stipulations in the direction of remedy:

- "Such materials and procedures shall be provided in the child's native language or mode of communication."
- "No single procedure shall be the sole criterion for determining an appropriate educational program for a child."

The provision, in effect, orders that assessment procedures be multi-factored, multi-sourced, and carried out by qualified personnel. The regulations governing this provision should therefore be carefully reviewed (refer to Section 612 (5)(C) of the Act).

### What does the Section 504 regulation say with respect to the assessment of children?

The objectives of Section 504 and P. L. 94–142 are identical on this matter, and the regulatory language for both statutes are also identical (refer to #84.35 of the 504 regulation).

### What does P. L. 94–142 say with respect to the confidentiality of data and information?

P. L. 94–142 contains a provision that addresses the question of abuses and potential abuses in school system record keeping with respect to handicapped children and their parents. P. L. 94–142, as did the prior P. L. 93–380, simply orders a remedy and does not go beyond. The governing statutes for this provision are contained in the larger "Family Educational Rights and Privacy Act" (often referred to as the "Buckley Amendments" after the author, US Senator James Buckley of New York). That measure sets forth both the access rights and privacy rights with respect to personal school records for all of the nation's children and youth, and their parents.

Thus, readers should study the Act itself (contained in P. L. 93–380), the accompanying regulations for the "Buckley Amendments," and the modest addendums to those provisions contained in the regulations for P. L. 94–142 (refer to Section 617 (c) and Section 612 (2) (D) of the Act).

### What then, in summary, are the rights and protections of P. L. 94–142 (which, for the most part, are also affirmed in Section 504) that must be guaranteed?

P. L. 94–142 makes a number of critical stipulations that must be adhered to by *both* the state and its local and intermediate educational agencies:

- Assurance of the availability of a free, appropriate public education for all handicapped children, such guarantee of availability no later than certain specified dates.
- Assurance of the maintenance of an individualized education program for all handicapped children.
- A guarantee of complete due procedural safeguards.
- The assurance of regular parent or guardian consultation.
- Assurance of special education being provided to all handicapped children in the "least restrictive" environment.
- Assurance of nondiscriminatory testing and evaluation.
- A guarantee of policies and procedures to protect the confidentiality of data and information.
- Assurance of an effective policy guaranteeing the right of all handicapped children to a free, appropriate public education *at no cost* to parents or guardian.
- Assurance of a surrogate to act for any child when parents or guardians are either unknown or unavailable or when such child is a legal ward of the state.

It is most important to observe that an official, written document containing all of these assurances is now required (in the form of an application) of *every* school district receiving its federal entitlement under P. L. 94–142. Correspondingly, such a public document also exists at the state level in the form of the annual state plan, which must be submitted to the US Commissioner.

# TEACHERS ASK ABOUT HANDICAPPED CHILDREN AND THE NEW LAWS

## *Barbara Aiello*

In a recent report by the National Education Association (*Consensus, Conflict and Challenge*, 1978) a panel of special and regular educators termed Public Law 94-142 "a bill of rights for more than 8 million handicapped children." Yet the report authors admit that the new law, which is almost as significant a piece of legislation as were the desegregation rulings, is greatly misunderstood and misperceived by many professionals.

In a *Learning* magazine poll, a majority of the 577 respondents reported that teachers desperately need more practical information regarding both the spirit and the letter of Public Law 94-142.

The following questions were compiled as the result of those most often asked by a national sample of over 2000 educators. These teachers voiced their concerns about mainstreaming and current legislation and their questions are answered from the perspective of the classroom teacher who may work with children with handicapping conditions of all kinds.

**Q. I've heard about Public Law 94-142. Some of my colleagues are adamant that the law means that all handicapped children must be placed in regular classrooms. Is this true?**

**A.** No. The law is clear when it states that "to the maximum extent appropriate, handicapped children . . . are educated with children who are not handicapped (Section 121a.550)." The key here is the phrase "to the maximum extent appropriate." In practical terms more mildly handicapped children can be educated in regular class settings than can most severely involved children — such as those who are profoundly retarded, for example. However, the law states that placement decisions are made on an individual basis and that the individual educational needs of each handicapped child must be considered before she/he is placed in either a special or a regular class. Moreover, it is essential to regularly assess the child's progress, and when appropriate, move the child towards settings which are less restrictive. All decisions are time-limited.

**Q. How does "mainstreaming" fit into all of this?**

**A.** The term "mainstreaming," which came about a few years prior to the enactment of Public Law 94-142, was used in referring to the placement of mildly handicapped children, such as some learning disabled, emotionally disturbed, and educable mentally retarded children, into regular classrooms on a full- or parttime basis. Before Public Law 94-142 was enacted, approximately 12 of the 50 states had drafted legislation to include mildly handicapped children in regular classrooms. This inclusion was often referred to as "mainstreaming."

Confusion arose when the term "least restrictive alternative" was used in the text of Public Law 94-142, to describe a broader concept. While "mainstreaming" was assumed usually to refer to mildly handicapped children, "least restrictive alternative" is applicable to all types of handicapped children. Let me give you two examples:

Eddy is 17 years old and a resident of a state institution for persons who are mentally retarded. It has been decided that Eddy is competent enough to live outside the institution, in a supervised group home. The "least restrictive alternative" for Eddy is a residential placement in the community. Eddy will not be mainstreamed into a high school algebra class, as some critics of the law would have regular class teachers believe.

Katherine is 5 years old and trainably mentally retarded. Her preschool trainable class has been moved from the basement of a local church into a public elementary school. The least restrictive environment for Katherine and other students in her special class might be a shared snack time or recess with the other kindergarten students in the "normal" class.

Children like Eddy and Katherine will probably not be mainstreamed into regular classes on a fulltime basis because their individual educational needs would not be met in that setting. However, to fulfill the letter and the spirit of the law, the educational environment that is "least restrictive" (i.e., a group home, snack time with normal peers, etc.) must be actively sought for all handicapped children.

**Q. I can understand that a child in a wheelchair, or a deaf or a blind child should be mainstreamed. But what about retarded and emotionally disturbed children? Does this law apply to them?**

**A.** The law requires that educators look beyond the label that a handicapped child carries, to the individual needs of the child. Thus, placement decisions must be made on an individual basis.

If a regular class teacher receives a retarded, a disturbed, a deaf, or cerebral palsied child into the class, that decision should have been made because the individual needs of a particular child can best be met in the regular class setting with nonhandicapped peers.

**Q. How and why did this law come about? Isn't it just another case of "the pendulum swing back?"**

**A.** P.L. 94-142 is the result of the work of many groups of persons who were concerned about the quality of education and the educational opportunities for handicapped children.

By the late 1960s parent groups began to gain national prominence in their quest for equal educational opportunity for their handicapped children. The Pennsylvania Association for Retarded Children (PARC) was the first advocacy group to support a parent in his suit against a state board of education to obtain local school district services for his handicapped child (*PARC* v. *Commonwealth of Pennsylvania, 1972*).

When the Pennsylvania State Board of Education consented to the case, state policy had to be rewritten to include handicapped children in educational programs. Other states followed suit and in 1975 President Gerald Ford signed the "Education for All Handicapped Children Act," known as Public Law 94-142. With the U.S. Office of Civil Rights monitoring states to ensure the civil right of a free, appropriate, public education to all handicapped children, it can be assumed that the law is here to stay and is much more than the backswing of the proverbial pendulum.

**Q.** **I voted for the bond issue that made it possible for a special school for physically handicapped children to be built in our area. Does the "least restrictive alternative" or "mainstreaming" concept mean that schools like this one may be phased out?**

**A.** The law does not mandate that special schools close their doors or that special classes be dissolved. Instead, the law requires that an individual placement decision be made for each handicapped child. Special education facilities, such as schools for severely or multihandicappedd children can be made available to those children for whom such fulltime placement is considered appropriate for some part of their educational program.

**Q.** **There is talk in our district about forming resource rooms to supplement special services. What will happen to the special education classes?**

**A.** Resource rooms can supplement special services in a variety of ways. First, a resource room can permit handicapped children to work with special teachers in a smaller, more structured setting, during part of their school day, and to work in regular classes with their nonhandicapped peers for another segment. In addition, resource rooms often offer flexible scheduling to permit the specialist who operates the room to become a resource to the classroom teachers in the school.

**Q.** **In our district, special education teachers are writing IEPs for handicapped children. What exactly is the IEP?**

**A.** An "IEP" means "Individualized Education Program," and it is a written plan for providing instructional services on an individual basis, to individual handicapped children. An IEP is written during a meeting at which educators, parents, and whenever appropriate, the child, decide on the specially designed instructional needs of the handicapped child. (If the parents or guardians choose not to attend, the professional persons proceed with planning.)

An IEP must contain a statement of the child's present levels of educational performance, a listing of annual goals, including short term instructional objectives, or stepping stones, that will help the child meet the goals.

In addition, the IEP must contain a statement of the specific educational and related services to be provided to the child, and the extent to which the child will be able to participate in regular educational programs. The IEP must contain appropriate, objective evaluation criteria and a schedule for determining on at least an annual basis, whether the instructional objectives are being achieved.

**Q.** **Regular class teachers may be involved in IEP writing. Why regular class people — they're not special educators?**

**A.** Because the law stipulates that teachers must be included in the planning process for handicapped children, it is likely that many regular class teachers will have the opportunity to help develop an IEP. The education of handicapped children is now the dual responsibility of both the special and the regular education communities and if you, as a regular class teacher are referring a child for special services, or receiving a handicapped child into your classroom, you may be asked to help formulate goals and objectives for the new arrival, or to share the strengths and weaknesses of a child who may be in need of special services.

**Q.** **How is anyone, even special education personnel, going to get the job done? Doesn't the IEP process require a lot of extra work?**

**A.** Writing high quality IEPs is not an especially easy task at first, and for this reason it is safe to say that, at the outset, many school districts will be faced with extra work. Yet educators must remember that planning meetings of any kind traditionally have implied extra work for teachers and administrators. Now we are required to devote some of our school planning time to meeting the unique needs of handicapped children.

**Q.** **What happens if a parent doesn't agree with what the committee decides?**

**A.** The committee process represents an avenue for increased cooperation between special and regular educators, and between educators and parents. Parents are invited to participate on the committee as equal members, sharing their thoughts and concerns about the needs and the placement of their handicapped child.

When school people work hard at cooperatively drafting a clear IEP, parents seldom refuse to sign it. In addition, when educators make clear to parents that the IEP is *not* binding and that inappropriate placements can be changed, parents and teachers often are more willing to give the proposed plans a try.

Although it is true that parents must agree to the educational decisions for children by signing the IEP, when the committees function as cooperative forums for shared concerns, the signing process becomes a formality, not a fight.

If however, agreement cannot be reached, both the parents and the school personnel have the right to a due process hearing.

**Q.** I'm concerned about this due process hearing. I've heard that parents can take the whole school system to court. Is that true?

**A.** Due process procedures were instituted as part of the laws to protect the rights of handicapped children and their parents. When either party (parent or school official) disagrees regarding the identification, evaluation, or educational placement, the next step is an impartial due process hearing. During this time, the child remains in her/his original classroom setting until the matter is resolved, unless the complaint involves an application for admission to public school in which case the child must be placed *in* the public school until the matter is resolved. If either party is still dissatisfied after a due process hearing, the case may be appealed to the state educational agency for an impartial review of the hearing. Then if no agreement is reached, any party may bring civil action. Certainly, by means of the processes described, a parent could take a school system to court.

**Q.** Is it true that because of the news laws, it will be almost impossible to get a child into a special class?

**A.** The law states that "special classes, separate schooling or other removal of handicapped children from the regular educational environment occurs only when the nature or severity of the handicap is such that education in regular classes with the use of supplementary aids and services, cannot be achieved satisfactorily (Section 121a.550)." Handicapped children will continue to be placed in special classes but that placement is made only after possible placement in the regular school or regular class is judged inappropriate. Categorical decisions, such as "every educable mentally retarded child belongs in a fulltime, self contained special class," are no longer permitted. A child's placement in a regular or a special class is based upon her/his individual strengths, weaknesses, and needs.

**Q.** Let's say I get a handicapped child in my classroom. I don't feel as though I'm trained to handle those children. What do I do then?

**A.** The requirements of the law are meant to bridge the gap between the regular and the special education communities. Should you receive a handicapped child in your classroom, you should expect consistent help and support from the special services personnel assigned to your school. Clearly, the wholesale "dumping" of handicapped children into regular classes is not the intent of the law. Rather, the placement committee process, IEP development, etc., are means to facilitate the gradual, planned inclusion of handicapped children into regular classes.

Specialists must be ready to prepare regular class teachers for the handicapped child and regular class teachers must request from specialists the help they will need.

**Q.** What can I do about the other children? They can be so cruel at times. And what about teasing, etc.?

**A.** Not only must regular class teachers be prepared for a handicapped child, but the children themselves must be prepared for the handicapped classmates. School systems around the country are including the study of handicapping conditions into social studies and human relations curricula.

Teachers report that when students are prepared for a handicapped classmate, teasing or cruel behavior rarely surfaces. Instead children are especially understanding, helpful, and friendly.

**Q.** Sometime ago, an official at HEW signed another law for the handicapped — he signed it after a sit-in, as I recall. How do these two laws relate to each other?

**A.** In April of 1977 Secretary of HEW Joseph Califano signed the 504 Regulation on the 1973 Rehabilitation Act (Public Law 93-112). The protest to which you refer involved a 23 day sit-in by handicapped individuals at the HEW offices. The sit-in was an attempt to direct public attention to the administrative postponement of signing what is termed the civil rights act for the handicapped.

This law relates directly to Public Law 94-142 in that it also guarantees all handicapped children a free, appropriate, public education, the right to due process, the development of an IEP for each handicapped child, and the placement of handicapped in the least restrictive alternative.

In addition, the 504 Regulation requires that all buildings erected or renovated with federal funds be made accessible to the handicapped. This directive includes public school buildings from elementary schools to colleges and universities. Programs, services, and activities in existing facilities must be made accessible to students as well. The 504 Regulations are comparable to the earlier Civil Rights Act of 1964 and recipients of HEW funds will be monitored by the U.S. Office for Civil Rights to assure compliance. Non-compliance may result in a loss of federal funds or court action if noncompliant recipients fail to take remedial action.

**Q.** Many of us see these laws as a boost for handicapped children and adults. But these days school systems are pinching every penny. Where will the money come from?

**A.** Federal funds are made available to states and to local school districts so that they can carry out the requirements of the law. The amount of general funds allocated to states is determined by the following formula:

| NAE X ____% X | NHC | = | $$$$ |
|---|---|---|---|
| National Average Expenditure per pupil | Number of Handicapped Children | | Amount of federal funds allocated to state for the year |

The NAE is multiplied by a specific percentage. This percentage escalates gradually over a 5 year period which began with 5% in fiscal year (FY) 1977 and will reach a maximum of 40% by FY 1982 if Congress appropriates the necessary funds. Full funding — up to 40% by FY 1982 — seems unlikely in view of the "austerity" policies so evident in 1979.

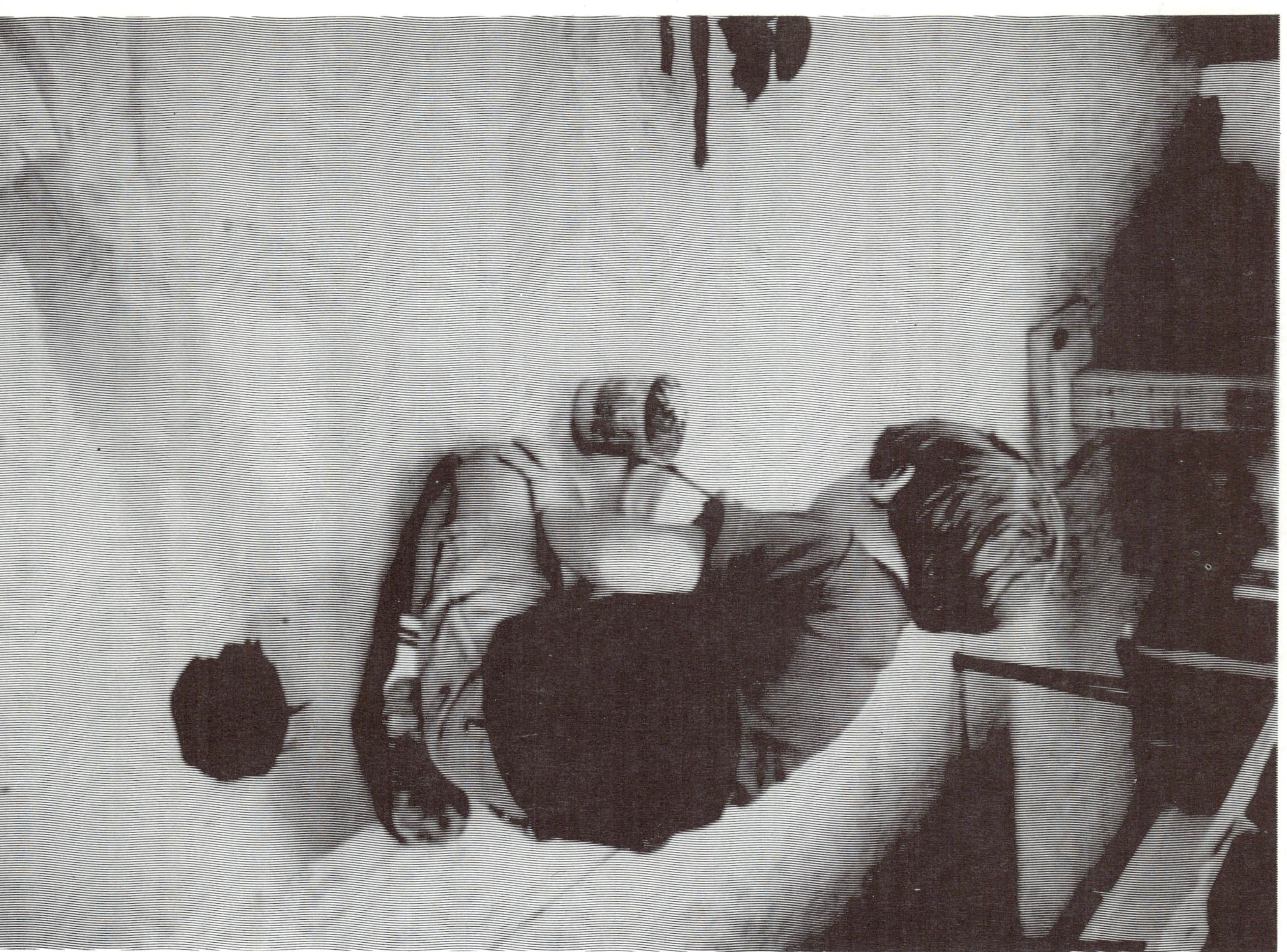

photo: Office of Human Development Services, DHEW

# METHODOLOGY

The impact of PL94-142 has caused educators to look closely at special education and mainstreaming programs. It is through this intense evaluation that new programs and theories for educating exceptional children are derived.

Education of the handicapped is more than the teaching of reading and math to handicapped children. It encompasses all the areas which one is exposed to in life. These areas might include career education or sex education. Also, educators must look at ways they can initiate the non-handicapped to the life of the handicapped. They must develop methods to alleviate the uneasiness in the mainstreamed classroom. Special educators must also assist regular classroom teachers in preparing their classes and curriculum to facilitate the handicapped. Such things as safety and a barrier free classroom are areas which the regular teacher may have never been exposed, yet are extremely important.

It is with these ideas that this section is compiled. Articles are chosen to give an overview into the total educational picture for the handicapped. The section opens with an article which suggests several positive steps a teacher can follow to make mainstreaming easier. The following article then examines one method which can be used to evaluate special education programs.

The section then takes a look at the specific methods used to teach in the areas of education which are not related to basic skills. These articles will examine career education, sex education, leisure education and preschool education programs for the handicapped.

The section closes with two ideas which can be used to help the non-handicapped child become familiar with the handicapped who might be coming into the regular classroom for all or part of the day. All of the ideas presented in this chapter will help educators provide a full educational experience for the handicapped child.

# first things first

Don't think of mainstreaming as being one year away. It's here and now---and there are things you can start doing right away.

**By William Johnson**

Dr. Johnson is a professor of special education at Fairfield (Conn.) University.

Many classroom teachers, aware that recently passed federal legislation concerning special education is scheduled for full implementation in the very near future, have expressed to me their concerns, doubts and questions about mainstreaming. While some classroom teachers have little idea of just what their new responsibilities will be and want to know more, others have already formulated opinions based on hastily and--in far too many cases--thoughtlessly implemented mainstreaming programs.

For these reasons, I would like both to describe the mainstreaming procedures implied by the new federal law and suggest steps to insure their successful implementation. Let's first take a very brief look at the most recent history of mainstreaming, the concepts involved in mainstreaming, and how mainstreaming will affect you in the classroom.

**Litigation and Legislation.** In 1968, a noted special educator, Lloyd Dunn, published an article in the *Journal of Exceptional Children* which had a profound effect on the entire field of special education. In his article, Dunn pointed out that many of the accepted, traditional practices in special education might not be as sacred as people thought. Dunn questioned the need to segregate handicapped children in special classes and the need to apply labels to children in order to provide special services.

The impact of Dunn's article and those that have followed were felt far beyond the confines of special education. Parents of handicapped children, together with advocacy groups, picked up many of the arguments of Dunn (and others) and used them in



Reprinted with permission of the publishers Allen Raymond, Inc., Darien, Conn. 06820. From the May, 1977 issue of *Early Years.*

litigation to force states to provide equal education to handicapped children. This litigation, which gained momentum in the late sixties, is being followed by legislation—by state governments and by the federal government in The Education for All Handicapped Children Act of 1975.

As a result of Dunn's article, the litigation and the legislation of the past few years, we are now at a point where most educators are committed to the notion of mainstreaming, which, as inferred in PL 94-142, means educating handicapped children in ''the least restrictive environment.'' For many *mildly* handicapped children—including many of the learning disabled, the mentally retarded, the socially and emotionally maladjusted, the partially sighted and the partially deaf—this implies being at least partly educated within the regular class setting.

**Four Categories.** According to PL 94-142, handicapped children cannot be removed from or replaced in a regular class program unless recommended by a committee on the handicapped composed of various members of the professional staff and parents. Whatever the terminology employed by the committee, from the point of view of the elementary teacher, children are removed from their class because of problems that fall within four categories of classroom function.

Furthermore, handicapped children are returned to the regular program because of demonstrated improvement in one or more of these categories to the point where they are able to perform again within the limits accepted in the regular class program. The four categories are: behavioral management, instructional methods, instructional materials and curriculum.

But who goes where? To answer this question specifically, let's consider the reasons within each of these categories for removing special children from and returning them to the mainstream.

*Behavior Management.* The question of behavioral management comes up most often in reference to the highly aggressive child or the child who tends to create a great deal of disruption within the classroom. When such behavior gets to the point where it prevents other children from learning, then steps to change the situation must be taken.

First, the teacher must ask herself just what her limits are. Exactly which behaviors are acceptable and which are not? Once the teacher has answered this question, she can request the assistance of the special education teacher in bringing the child's behavior within the acceptable limits. Very often, the special ed teacher has a few techniques up her sleeve which will solve the problem without removing the child from the regular classroom, a step of last resort.

*Instructional Methods.* Sometimes a child is either so slow in a certain area, or so different generally, that the methods used by the teacher with the rest of the class do not seem applicable to a special child. Many teachers, for example, have three or four reading groups within a classroom. Within the lowest group, there may be considerable range of performance; even so, one child may fall so far below the others that participation is no longer feasible. At this point, the teacher must consider alternative methods. The special ed teacher can assist her in finding and implementing methods particularly suited to the child's learning pattern. (Instruction in reading may then be undertaken within a special setting or within the regular classroom, as the situation requires.)

*Instructional Materials.* Materials are the means for achieving educational goals. Some handicapped children require special materials to achieve these ends. Since such specialized materials may involve additional expense and special supervision, it's quite conceivable that a child might be removed from the mainstream because of a lack of necessary funds. However, thanks to PL 94-142, this is not a situation which classroom teachers will encounter frequently.

One of the purposes of the new federal law is to provide the additional money necessary for these materials, so that local educational budgets will not be overly pressed to meet the needs of the special child. Even if the materials are not available, the resource specialist can often find ways to adapt existing materials to the requirements of the child with special learning needs. The materials may be used in the resource room or in a regular classroom, and may be supervised by a special or a regular teacher.

*Curriculum.* Adjustment of curriculum, or educational goals, has the most far-reaching effect on children's educational programs. If, for instance, it is established that a child should undertake a functional reading curriculum involving modification of mainstream reading goals, then the child might well need to be educated outside the regular school program. The regular teacher would not usually be expected to accommodate such an adjustment in her class.

**Positive Steps.** Let's turn now to some of the positive steps that classroom teachers can take before mainstreaming is implemented in the schools. Some of these steps can be taken right away, some will have to wait until your school system has made its own first initiatives to implement mainstreaming, but they can all be taken before the first handicapped child is placed in a regular classroom.

These suggestions are also made to avoid the misguided efforts of school districts to return handicapped children to the mainstream prematurely, without due consideration for the consequences of such actions and without adequate support or preparation of the regular teacher and her class.

To begin with, teachers should request that their

school issue a policy statement regarding mainstreaming. It doesn't have to be a professionally written statement, but it should be fairly complete, including the extent to which mainstreaming is going to go, the types of children that will be placed in regular classrooms and under what conditions, some of the aims and goals, and some of the procedures that will be employed in mainstreaming handicapped children.

Needless to say, a policy statement isn't going to anticipate all of the problems that may arise, but it's a step in the right direction—and a step that should involve the concerted efforts of both the regular and special ed instructional and administrative staff.

Another step you can take personally is to think carefully about the range of variations you feel you can work with in the classroom. In considering behavior, ask yourself what problems have given you trouble in the past, how they were solved and what effect they had on your classroom practices. Once you find out the answers to these questions, you'll be well on your way to discovering what kind of behavior problems will reduce your teaching effectiveness. In considering instructional problems, ask: Which methods work effectively for you? Which ones don't? Are there any learning problems you really feel you can't cope with?

It's a good idea, by the way, to list these questions as a series of your strengths and weaknesses. This list may come in handy later on, when it's time to match up a handicapped child with just the "right" teacher.

**Formal Communications.** Whatever else happens when mainstreaming becomes a reality, you can count on one thing: You *will* be working closely with the special ed teachers in your school. This means that you should establish formal lines of communication between you and the specialists.

These lines, or procedures, should include such things as scheduled consultations, established reporting procedures and agreement on terminology used to describe problems and recommendations. By stressing the formal aspect of communications procedures, I don't mean that you should rule out informality—merely that you'll have to establish certain ground rules which will insure regular and meaningful consultations.

Just when you'll be able to sit down and talk to the special ed teachers depends, of course, on the particular situation in your school system. If the special ed teachers are on hand now, then you can open up a dialogue right away. However, if they're still to be hired, then obviously you'll just have to sit tight until they arrive.

This also applies to the handicapped children you may be teaching. There's nothing you can do until you find out who they are; but once you do find out, you can make a point of trying to establish a relationship with each child in his special ed setting. Working with a handicapped child in a learning center or resource room before he's placed in your classroom can accomplish a number of things:

First, it will enable you to become better acquainted with the child, to understand his problems a little more fully before he joins your class. Second, it will enable the child to become better acquainted with you—a tremendously important consideration when you take into account what a difficult transition he's going to have going from one setting to another. Third, you'll undoubtedly be able to pick up a few valuable pointers about the methods and procedures which are used with a child in a special ed setting.

**Sensitization.** Finally, one positive step you can take before a handicapped child is placed in your classroom is to acquaint your regular students—and their parents—with the characteristics and needs of the handicapped. It's important that your handicapped children develop a positive image of themselves, and it's unlikely this is going to happen if they become the object of ridicule.

How do you get children (and their parents) to appreciate the needs of the handicapped? Well, there are a number of excellent films and books available which deal with the problem; and there's also the possibility of inviting older handicapped people to talk about their own problems and solutions.

As you can see, there are all sorts of positive steps you can take to insure the initial implementation of a mainstreaming program. Some of these steps are easy, while others involve considerable time and effort. But they're all tremendously important—both in terms of how you do your job and how your job is going to affect the handicapped children placed in your care.

Handicapped children have the right to participate in the fruits of our society and to be productive, along with their social and economic peers, in the mainstream of American life. They have to start somewhere, and it so happens that they're going to start with you. You may think that you're going to have problems, but really, it's the opportunity of a lifetime. Both theirs and yours.

# EVALUATING SPECIAL EDUCATION PROGRAMS

*Clifford E. Howe and Marigail E. Fitzgerald*

Dr. Howe is Professor of Special Education, University of Iowa. Mrs. Fitzgerald is Director of Educational Services, University Hospitals and Clinics, University of Iowa.

Material for this article has been summarized from work prepared for the Iowa Department of Public Instruction (Howe & Fitzgerald, 1976). It is not intended as the final word in program evaluation, nor as a cookbook set of procedures. It does outline a model which has been field tested, with the most useful aspects retained.

Iowa has recently reorganized into 15 intermediate units called Area Education Agencies (AEA) to provide special education, media, and other services to areas with school populations ranging from a low of approximately 15,000 to one with almost 130,000 pupils. It seems certain that recent legislation will require more accountability and evaluation procedures for individual children than has historically been the case. Iowa's legislation essentially mandates special education for all handicapped students, and requires annual reevaluation of the appropriateness of the program and student placement (State of Iowa, 1974). It is further indicated that school districts, in conjunction with the Area Education Agency, must develop procedures designed to evaluate and improve special education programs and services.

At the federal level, the Education for All Handicapped Children Act (P.L. 94-142, 1975) mandates that each state obtaining funds under this act must provide for evaluation procedures to ensure the effectiveness of programs designed to meet the educational needs of handicapped children (including evaluation of individualized education programs). Evaluation must be carried out at least annually.

Several models have been proposed in the past decade which focus on evaluation in education. One of the most extensive was that developed by Phi Delta Kappa's Research Advisory Committee under the authorship of Stufflebeam and others (1971). Recognizing that evaluation of educational programs was long overdue, they developed a model which combined knowledge of the process as well as product evaluation. Their model views the roles of evaluation as being made up of context, input, process, and product (CIPP). The outcome of evaluation is seen principally as providing useful information for making decisions about program alternatives.

## 2. METHODOLOGY

Stufflebeam deals with the reasons educational evaluation has either been done poorly or not at all in the past. Included are symptoms such as avoidance (the process is viewed as painful), anxiety (evaluation is viewed as a judgment, often of personal competency), immobilization or lethargy and lack of interest, skepticism regarding whether evaluation can really be done or whether the results are of any use, and a lack of significant differences as the result of much educational research (leading to frustration on the part of the practitioner). Stufflebeam suggests ways in which these difficulties could be overcome and proposes models which will be useful to practitioners (1971).

Popham (1972) proposes a more restricted view of evaluation, and ties it to instructional objectives and criterion-referenced measurement. This handbook provides practical application in the process of constructing and measuring objectives. Emphasis is placed on learner performance data. Evaluation is viewed as a process of determining the desired ends or goals of the educational system, and judging the worth of educational means through both formative (process) and summative (product) assessment. Although his model is not limited to measures of individual student change data, this is the major emphasis.

A third model for educational evaluation is the technique long used by various accrediting associations (NCA, etc.). Stufflebeam (1971) categorizes this as evaluation based on professional judgment. Evaluative criteria are provided, but the major work is done by the schools themselves through a self-study procedure which usually takes about a year. After it is completed, a visiting team of experts and peers comes to the school to observe for a few days, studies the data provided by the school, and renders judgments and recommendations regarding the quality of the program. The major strength of this technique is usually seen in the self-study aspect, where a school and community critically evaluate themselves, thus investing enough of themselves in the evaluation effort to be willing to make and implement decisions for improvement.

An extension of the models above, and one which seems to be very relevant to special education programs, is that of Goal Attainment Scaling (GAS), proposed by Kiresuk and Sherman (1968). These techniques were originally developed from grants by the National Institute of Mental Health, and focused on ways of determining the effectiveness of different treatment approaches for patients in community mental health centers in the Minneapolis area.

In summary, it would appear that successful program evaluation is concerned with two major issues. The first is that of determining the technical approach which appears to have the highest likelihood of yielding useful data to use in making decisions regarding future directions for the program. For the individually-tailored program in special education, it would seem that the use of Goal Attainment Scaling provides promising possibilities.

The second issue which seems critical is that of developing a readiness in the organization to undertake program evaluation. Time should be spent with those involved to reduce defensiveness, develop trust, and reach a consensus regarding both the purpose of evaluation and the process to be used. If educational evaluation can be seen, as Stufflebeam (1971) states, "as the process of delineating, obtaining, and providing useful information for judging decision alternatives," then the effort can be viewed in light of its real purpose.

Figure 1 shows that program evaluation must occur throughout the organization and may take different forms at different levels. While evaluation of individual children is specific to each pupil at Level III, it becomes much more general at Level 1. Middle management in Level II uses techniques from both Levels I and III and helps tie the entire process together.

### SETTING THE STAGE

For change to occur in an organization, some significant member needs to be the instigator and begin the dialogue with key staff members. Most AEAs in Iowa do not now have an organized program evaluation system, and the director of special education would seem to be the logical person to initiate such an effort. The director must first be convinced of the importance of evaluation efforts. Once

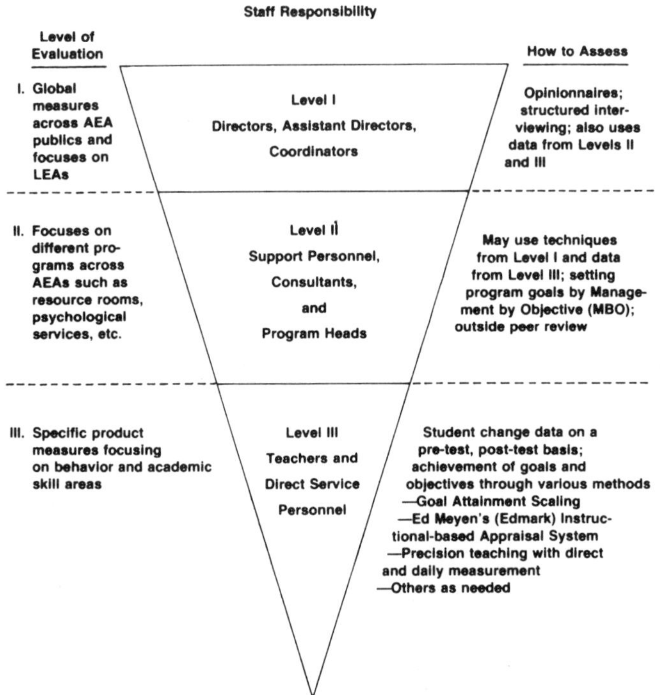

**Figure 1**
### PROPOSED MODEL FOR EVALUATION OF SPECIAL EDUCATION AEAs



this commitment is made by the director, time is needed for informal discussion with the leadership staff.

Our experience suggests that an initial session of not less than two hours is necessary, and that several followup sessions of similar length may be required. During these preliminary discussions, the desired outcome is to overcome resistance to the idea of evaluation and to begin to formulate a plan of positive action. The following topics usually come up in these initial sessions, and need to be resolved:

Q: Are we really going to have to do this sometime in the future in order to get funds, or is this just another passing fad?

A: All signs seem to point in the direction of increasing accountability for appropriateness of programs and to accumulate some evidence showing that the approach used is beneficial. Legislation and Rules in Iowa now require systematic evaluation and will probably become more stringent as the AEAs mature. P.L. 94-142 will become operational in the next year or two, and includes strong statements regarding evaluation plans in order to qualify for these federal funds for the handicapped. It would appear that token evaluation systems won't suffice for the future.

Q: We already have too much to do, and if this becomes another requirement, who is going to do it and where are we going to get the time? How about hiring someone who is a specialist in evaluation?

A: One way to manage an evaluation system is to use "third party" or outside evaluators. This supposedly has the advantage of not adding to the work load of the present staff, and of guaranteeing an objective approach. Many federal projects, such as Title III grants, use this technique. However, there are disadvantages and one of the major ones is that the existing staffs in an AEA may not invest themselves in the operation and instead see it as a one-time effort conducted by outside paid professionals. Another way to view program evaluation is to think of it as a long-term management technique where the evaluation data become a part of the decision-making process on an ongoing basis. Outside specialists can be used for specific tasks occasionally, but the evaluation effort is really a part of the long-term management of the AEA and all leadership staff should contribute to it.

Q: Aren't we really talking about evaluation of staff, and judgments being made about the personal competence of individuals?

A: It would be dishonest to say that program and staff evaluation are completely separate from each other. Both are important, and need to be done. However, the emphasis on program evaluation is broader than an individual teacher, psychologist, or speech clinician. The purpose is to gain information that is program-wide, such as determining the impact of the total program of speech services in an AEA, for example, rather than focusing on the competency of one speech clinician. Obviously, the success of the total program is dependent on the competency of each person, but program evaluation aggregates the results for the total program, and the individual remains anonymous. Evaluation of an individual serves another purpose and should not be confused with program evaluation.

Q: Many evaluation studies gather dust in the files and much research ends up with conclusions of "no significant differences." How do we know we won't be embarking on a similar enterprise?

A: You don't, really, but that is a strong argument for planning it ourselves as a management tool on a long-term basis, of asking evaluation questions that make sense for our AEA, and of using the results for planning for the next year or several years. We have to make these decisions anyway, and evaluation results should be viewed as just another piece of information which will help us when we must set priorities and make hard decisions.

Q: Okay, I'm convinced. How do I begin with my staff of ten consultants, for whom I am responsible?

A: You need to remember that they will have the same, or perhaps even more, misgivings or questions about evaluation that we've struggled with in the past few hours and sessions. Start slowly, allow at least two hours in a beginning session with all of them, and let them voice all their concerns as well as ideas as to what form the evaluation should take. Expect them to feel avoidance, anxiety, and skepticism, and deal honestly with these feelings. Try to develop credibility of the evaluation process and outline the risks involved. One sure way to encounter difficulty, or perhaps even failure, is to present the evaluation scheme in terms of a dictate from the top. An honest approach might be to say that we will be committed to a continuing evaluation effort, but that the form and methods used are matters to be decided by the group.

The following sections are intended to give ideas and examples of how evaluation might be used by an AEA throughout the various levels of the organization. Evaluation moves from specific child change data as a major component in Level III, to much more general attitudinal data for the total program at Level I.

## LEVEL I   EVALUATION PROCEDURES

Level I evaluation is concerned with general views held by consumers throughout the AEA regarding programs and services for the handicapped. The procedure could be likened to a "Gallup Poll" approach, and samples attitudes from a variety of publics. Stratified random sampling procedures are used so that numbers of respondents are manageable in terms of costs, yet yield a reliable and valid picture of the present status of the organization.

Figure 2 shows an example of an opinionnaire which was field-tested in AEA 16 in the spring of 1976 (Johnson, 1976). Questions included were selected as being of high priority by the leadership staff, including the director and assistant director of special education, supervisors, and consultants.

The staff decided there were eight different subgroups that should be canvassed, including:

Local education agency superintendents
Local education agency building administrators
Special education support staff
Special education instructional staff
Regular education instructional staff
Parent groups for the handicapped
Outside agencies (mental health centers, private schools, etc.)
Secretarial staff in the area education agency

Different subgroups could be chosen by another AEA if, in their judgment, the opinions of such groups were important to the success of the AEA. A minimum sample of 40 was selected from each subgroup with populations which were larger than 40. For those groups whose entire population in the AEA approximated 40 or fewer, all were included in the sample. Where sampling was done, a table of random numbers was used.

A total of 217 opinionnaires was mailed, with 168 returned, for an overall response rate of 77%. This level of response is quite high, considering the diversity of populations sampled and the fact that no additional follow-up mailings were made. The rate of return varied among groups from 100% for superintendents, 85% for building administrators and special education instructional staff, to a low of about 50% for regular teachers and parent groups.

Opinionnaires were returned to a neutral agency outside of the AEA to protect anonymity and encourage more honest responses. Data from the opinionnaire were then

# 2. METHODOLOGY

tabulated, using a standard computer program which yielded results for each question in the form of means and standard deviations for each of the eight groups. In addition, percentages of each group responding from 5 (agree strongly) to the other extreme of 1 (disagree strongly) were provided on the computer printout for each item.

From this summary, the 18 questions asked were rank-ordered from high to low in terms of degree of agreement. Inspection of the data also pointed up specific subgroups whose responses varied significantly from the overall group.

This information gave the leadership group in AEA 16 a good indication of the general reaction to various aspects of special education services. It is common practice to stop at this point in the procedure and to use these data as input for planning and decision making. However, it is our feeling that another step should be taken to validate results, probe in more depth the indicated problem areas, and solicit suggested changes for improvement. For this followup, we used the technique of structured interviews.

The leadership staff used the opinionnaire data to derive the questions to be asked during the structured interviews, focusing on those areas where there was disagreement among groups or where responses were most negative by the majority of the groups. The advantage of this particular approach is the ability to narrow the range of questions asked and avoid the "shotgun" effect of including many broad questions or of guessing as to what the critical issues are.

### Summarizing Structured Interview Data

The interview team should meet with the special education director after interviewing has been completed, to share the major themes which emerged. This should be done while the team is intact and before leaving the AEA. Nothing is more devastating to the process than to have the AEA director wait for several weeks before getting any feedback on results.

After the verbal exit interview with the AEA director and whatever additional staff he or she wishes to include, a short written report is usually prepared within the next week, summarizing strengths and weaknesses observed and indicating possible recommendations. As a final step, and if the special education director so wishes, the chairman of the interview team meets with the director and his or her leadership staff to further discuss the results of the opinionnaire and structured interviewing, and to help plan intervention strategies for future change. At this point, all original data have been returned to the AEA for its use.

Evaluation procedures for Level I are AEA-wide, sample opinions of the various publics served by special education, and combine opinionnaire data with followup structured interviewing. Trust and anonymity are important ingredients for the data to be accurate and useful, and for the process to proceed without undue defensiveness. All original data and results are given to the AEA for its use in assessing the current situation and in planning for the future. If done correctly, the entire process takes a minimum of time and yields useful data.

## LEVEL II   EVALUATION PROCEDURES

Level II comprises middle management AEA personnel, including supervisors, consultants, and program heads. They are responsible for an area of support services or type of instructional program. Level II personnel also provide a link between instructional programs in the schools and the overall management of special education programs at the director level.

Program evaluation for Level II can utilize the opinionnaire and structured interview techniques outlined earlier under Level I. Questions asked and opinions sought are more narrowly-focused, and related to a specific program such as psychological services, audiology, resource rooms, etc. Because the focus is more delineated, it is possible to go into more depth, as well as to make comparisons of various approaches to delivery of services. Interviewers can be selected from peers in other AEAs throughout the state.

### Management by Objective (MBO)

Much has been written about MBO, and the general procedures are common knowledge. We encountered some resistance to the technique and made modifications which retained the major concepts but reduced the amount of detail which is usually associated with the technique. Using an MBO approach can add a major component to program evaluation. It makes planned work efforts explicit, establishes timelines, and pinpoints responsibility. Program development can be planned in a more orderly fashion, reducing the likelihood of decision making occurring as a defensive posture. A staff person's time can be better utilized and focused on those objectives which have higher priority. The technique also provides a concrete basis for staff supervision and for coordination among staff at the middle management level.

Another variant, which we believe has considerable potential, combines elements of MBO and Goal Attainment Scaling. Goal Attainment Scaling techniques are outlined in detail in the next section, but a sample of one Goal Scale is included in Figure 3 (p. 8) to show how major work priorities can be scaled (Howe, 1976).

Note that only major activities are scaled and that the form is not filled with a great amount of detail. All management and supervisory positions involve some maintenance activities which are routine and must be done. However, they should not be the most important activities of a manager, and need not be included in a Goal Scale. Some type of monitoring of a clinical nature will usually suffice to ensure that routine chores are completed on time.

Middle management is a critical part of any organization, and program evaluation is particularly important at

**Figure 2**

**OPINIONNAIRE**

**PERCEPTIONS OF SPECIAL EDUCATION SERVICES IN AREA EDUCATION AGENCY 16**

This form is an attempt to get feedback from various groups on selected aspects of special education services provided by AEA 16. The purpose is to learn from you those things which you feel the AEA is doing well, and those which should be improved or discontinued. The results will be used to evaluate our present position and to plan for the future.

Below is a series of statements with which you may agree, disagree, or have not had any basis for answering. Please blacken the appropriate box for each statement and return in the enclosed envelope. It takes only 5 or 10 minutes and will be a great help to us.

| | Agree strongly | Agree somewhat | Neutral | Disagree somewhat | Disagree strongly | No basis on which to answer |
|---|---|---|---|---|---|---|
| 1. More services are being provided for handicapped children as compared to last year | ☐ | ☐ | ☐ | ☐ | ☐ | ☐ |
| 2. Better services are being provided for handicapped children as compared to last year | ☐ | ☐ | ☐ | ☐ | ☐ | ☐ |
| 3. Staff of the AEA are available when I need them: | | | | | | |
|    psychologists | ☐ | ☐ | ☐ | ☐ | ☐ | ☐ |
|    consultants | ☐ | ☐ | ☐ | ☐ | ☐ | ☐ |
|    speech clinicians | ☐ | ☐ | ☐ | ☐ | ☐ | ☐ |
|    social workers | ☐ | ☐ | ☐ | ☐ | ☐ | ☐ |
|    special education administrators | ☐ | ☐ | ☐ | ☐ | ☐ | ☐ |
|    hearing services | ☐ | ☐ | ☐ | ☐ | ☐ | ☐ |
| 4. The AEA Division of Special Education should reduce the number of programs it administers directly and turn these over to local school districts | ☐ | ☐ | ☐ | ☐ | ☐ | ☐ |
| 5. Too much money is currently being spent for special education, often at the expense of regular education | ☐ | ☐ | ☐ | ☐ | ☐ | ☐ |
| 6. Decisions made regarding special education at the AEA central office include about the right amount of consultation with those involved at the local level | ☐ | ☐ | ☐ | ☐ | ☐ | ☐ |
| 7. Sufficient supplies and materials are provided for each handicapped child | ☐ | ☐ | ☐ | ☐ | ☐ | ☐ |
| 8. The quality of consultation provided by the special education AEA staff is high | ☐ | ☐ | ☐ | ☐ | ☐ | ☐ |
| 9. There is a sufficient quantity of consultation and support staff available from the AEA to adequately support instructional programs for the handicapped | ☐ | ☐ | ☐ | ☐ | ☐ | ☐ |
| 10. The time it takes for a handicapped child to be processed, from original referral to placement, is a good investment of effort | ☐ | ☐ | ☐ | ☐ | ☐ | ☐ |
| 11. Staffing children with various professionals meeting as a group is a good idea | ☐ | ☐ | ☐ | ☐ | ☐ | ☐ |
| 12. The system of referral for a child is working well | ☐ | ☐ | ☐ | ☐ | ☐ | ☐ |
| 13. A major reason for AEA providing some services is the lack of program offerings by local school districts | ☐ | ☐ | ☐ | ☐ | ☐ | ☐ |

ADD ANY STATEMENTS THAT YOU THINK SHOULD HAVE BEEN INCLUDED:

| | | | | | | |
|---|---|---|---|---|---|---|
| 14. | ☐ | ☐ | ☐ | ☐ | ☐ | ☐ |
| 15. | ☐ | ☐ | ☐ | ☐ | ☐ | ☐ |
| 16. | ☐ | ☐ | ☐ | ☐ | ☐ | ☐ |

OTHER COMMENTS YOU MAY WISH TO MAKE:

**Figure 3**

# GOAL ATTAINMENT SCALE

| August 1976 | June 1977 | | Student Name |
|---|---|---|---|
| **Start Date** | **Score Date** | | |
| | Howe | | School |
| | **Teacher** | | |
| **Score** | **Percentile** | | Town |
| | ***Entry Level** | × Exit Level | |

| SCALE HEADINGS: | SCALE 1: MONITORING AEA 16 | SCALE 2: NEW PROGRAM DEVELOPMENT | SCALE 3: TRAINING STATE CONSULTANTS | SCALE 4: STATE PLAN |
|---|---|---|---|---|
| **LEVELS:** | (weight 1 = ) | (weight 2 = ) | (weight 3 = ) | (weight 4 = ) |
| **Most unfavorable outcome thought likely** | AEA 16 will abandon current plan and will not invest further in program evaluation efforts. | No new AEAs will participate in program evaluation efforts beyond token involvement. | DPI staff fails to become involved and does not attend any inservice training sessions. | AEAs request more staff and money with no evidence as to effectiveness of current operation. |
| **Less than expected success** | No further refinement of current evaluation plan. | One or two new AEAs will develop segments of an evaluation system. | Minimum of two DPI staff will participate in one or more inservice training sessions. | Majority of requests for staff and funds based on subjective opinion and emotion. |
| **Expected level of success** | AEA 16 will continue evaluation effort and operationalize pilot plans for collecting child change data with monitoring by me. | Minimum of three new AEAs will develop a program evaluation system with me in 1976-77. | Frank Vance, John Lanhan and two consultants will participate with me in inservice training of AEA staff for evaluation. | Evidence of some "outcome data" in state plan and of use of such data in future planning decisions. |
| **More than expected success** | Complete AEA-wide evaluation system will be operational with monitoring by me. | Four or five AEAs will participate in developing an evaluation system. | Several DPI staff will assume leadership in developing and monitoring AEA evaluation systems. | Annual plan and fiscal requests tied to evaluation evidence of current operation. |
| **Most favorable outcome thought likely** | Complete AEA-wide evaluation system will be operational and function without my help or monitoring. | More than five AEAs will develop a system. | State Division of Special Education will require an evaluation system of AEAs and will monitor progress. | Additional positions authorized to AEAs by State Superintendent based on outcome data showing success of program. |

Level II positions in AEAs. The master plan has been developed by the state and the AEA director and his or her staff. It is the job of the supervisors, consultants, and program heads to see that the plan is translated into action and to measure the results.

We see middle management as the key to successful program evaluation. It is the supervisor and the consultant who must deal with the problems of efficient application of technical skills to the teaching process, systematic ordering of the process so that teaching can take place with measurable results, and maintenance of teamwork among the principal participants in the process.

## LEVEL III  EVALUATION PROCEDURES

Evaluation at Level III focuses specifically on child change data. The two most frequent approaches to documenting change in students are the use of pre- and post-test batteries and the recording of progress on specific behavioral objectives. Other useful systems are available commercially, such as the *Instructional Based Appraisal System* (Meyen, 1976) and various remedial curricular programs. Specific behavior recording, precision teaching, and classroom observation approaches may also provide excellent evaluative data on changes in students.

We view evaluation of student progress as primarily a teacher function, since it is most important to the child. The choice of evaluation approach used at Level III depends in part upon the intended use of the results of the evaluation. To meet the intent of recent state and federal legislation for the handicapped, evaluation should provide an annual review of student progress, assist in determining where to go with each child, and should directly relate to the planning and improvement of the instructional program.

An extension of the models cited above, and one which seems to provide promising possibilities to special education programs, is Goal Attainment Scaling as proposed by Kiresuk and Sherman (1968). Goal Attainment Scaling can be viewed as a logical evaluation approach for individualized programs using instructional objectives, prescriptive teaching, and behavior charting methods. It asks the teacher to predict the results for a specified future time and then provides a simple way of scoring the actual outcomes. The method concentrates on the major priorities thought important for each child, and can handle different priorities for different children.

We have piloted Goal Attainment Scaling in a number of communities and with many different types of special education programs. Teachers and support staff have been largely enthusiastic in learning the technique, and have found it a satisfying approach to individualizing program efforts and in evaluating their outcomes. Mastery of the technique comes from actually sitting down and writing scales for individual children. The first ones will be laborious and time-consuming. A complete Goal Attainment Scale can be written in about one-half hour after having done the first five or ten.

### Goal Attainment Scaling Procedures

*Scale Development.* A number of priority areas should be selected for the student. These priorities will not necessarily include all the important work to be done with each child, but should be representative of the major goal areas to be concentrated upon in the special education program during the time covered by the Goal Attainment Scale. Typically, these major problem areas will have been identified in the child's staffing. Goals can then be determined by the teacher and support staff charged with responsibility for planning the child's program.

Once the priority areas for scaling have been identified, each should be given a title. The title may be abstract, theoretical, or vague. It is designed to focus the attention of someone inspecting the scale on the major goal areas being evaluated. The title may also be thought of as the place where the teacher constructing the scale has an opportunity to indicate the general problem area to which the specific variables described in the body of the scale correspond.

When priority areas have been selected and titles identified for the scale, a numerical weight (numbers 1, 2, 3, 4, or 5) can be added to each scale below the title. The weighting system indicates the relative importance of the scale. The scales can also be used without weighting if all goals are judged to be equally important. The higher the number used, the more significant the scale is relative to other scales. The title box can also be used to indicate any special sources of information for the scale, such as normative test data like the KeyMath or Durrell Reading Tests. Figure 4 shows a complete Goal Attainment Scale example where the specific priority areas are not equally important. The scales have been weighted 5, 4, 3, and 4 respectively (Leone, 1975).

The key level for predictive purposes is the expected level, or middle box, on each five-point scale. The expected level presents the best, most realistic prediction possible of the outcome which will have been attained by the student at the score date. The statements ought to be realistic, so that the expected level of each scale reflects what outcome realistically could be attained by the score date, not necessarily what should be attained. The estimate of the expected outcome ought to be independent of the student's current level of functioning. It may be that the expected level outcome would reflect no change or even regression; in spite of the undesirableness of this situation, it belongs in the middle box if this outcome is thought most likely.

The expected level is usually developed first and should be the most likely outcome. The other outcome levels should be constructed after the expected level and should be thought less likely to occur. It is not required that all levels be written in on the scale, but at least one box on each side of the middle box must be specified. Thus, at least three of the five boxes or levels must be completed for each scale.

The "more than expected success" and "most favorable outcome thought likely" levels offer teaching objectives and guide program efforts and planning in the future. Although humanitarian instincts would lead us to hope we could accomplish these higher outcomes, the accurate use of the Goal Attainment Scaling technique would not allow these levels to be reached very frequently. Similarly, the "less than expected success" and the "most unfavorable outcome thought likely" should not occur as frequently as the middle box outcome. Nevertheless, these less favorable outcomes are important to balance the picture of possible outcomes, to pinpoint children and priority areas needing closer evaluation, and to help judge when special needs go beyond the program's capacity to meet them.

We recommend that more than one person be involved in writing the child's Goal Attainment Scale. In Iowa, the child's teacher, the Area Education Agency special education consultant, and the program's supervisor may share this responsibility and periodically meet and confer on the child's progress and the program's usefulness. The team may use this format to clarify and differentiate responsibilities in accomplishing the predicted outcomes.

## Figure 4

# GOAL ATTAINMENT SCALE

| 9-1-75 | 6-1-75 |
|---|---|
| **Start Date** | **Score Date** |

|  P. Leone  |
|---|
| **Teacher** |

| | | |
|---|---|---|
| **Score** | **Percentile** | |
| | ***Entry Level** | **× Exit Level** |

**Student Name**

**School**

**Town**

| SCALE HEADINGS: | COURSE CREDITS | TASK BEHAVIOR | USE OF LEISURE TIME | REGULAR CLASS INTEGRATION |
|---|---|---|---|---|
| **LEVELS:** | (weight 1 = 5 ) | (weight 2 = 4 ) | (weight 3 = 3 ) | (weight 4 = 4 ) |
| **Most unfavorable outcome thought likely** | Will fail all 7th grade classes and/or be excluded from continuing attendance in regular classes. | Almost no work accomplished in spite of continual teacher intervention. | Continual pattern of starting and soon thereafter quitting. | More than 20 hours per week of special class contact. |
| **Less than expected success** | Will fail two regular 7th grade classes. | Completes a quarter to a half of assignments with continual prodding and ultimatums. | Completes most of requirements with frequent adult supervision (3 or more per week). | 12-20 hours of special class contact. |
| **Expected level of success** | Will fail one regular 7th grade class, but will pass on to 8th grade. | Completes half of expected assignments in resource room with frequent prodding. | Joins sports team, league, or club and completes season with periodic adult supervision (once per week). | Maintains appropriate behavior to the extent that he will have only 11 special class contact hours each week during last quarter. |
| **More than expected success** | Will successfully pass all 7th grade classes with D or C average. | Completes most assignments with 1 or 2 reminders. | Continues in 2 or more after-school groups with periodic supervision. | 1-10 hours of special class contact. |
| **Most favorable outcome thought likely** | Will successfully pass all 7th grade classes with a B average. | Completes most assignments with no reminders. | Completes requirements of one team, club, league, or group with no special supervision. | Maintained completely as regular 7th grade student with no direct special class service. |

Having a team of professionals involved in the Goal Attainment Scaling process provides a check and balance mechanism to avoid setting expected level statements unrealistically high or low. If the outcome statements must be agreed to by the program supervisor and the special education consultant, the likelihood of setting expected levels too low to "look good" or too high is minimized. With the use of pre/post normative test data as an additional element in the total evaluation process, the concern and/or likelihood of such an event occurring is reduced.

Learning to write Goal Scales is a developmental process. You learn primarily by experience, and gradually improve in being able to specify level outcomes within priority areas. Although an individual program is written for each student, there is some overlap of scales among students. After having written a number of scales, you will find that you can often draw from the bank of earlier scales for some items.

*Scoring and Interpretation.* The student's level of functioning at the time the scale is developed can be noted on the Goal Scale form by placing an asterisk in each box for entry level. At the followup score date, the scales are marked with an "X" for outcome. Two possible kinds of effectiveness measures can be collected from the Goal Attainment Scaling system: Whether or not the "expected" levels of outcome are reached, and whether or not change occurred. The degree of change can also be documented on the basis of the post-test data or records gathered at the predetermined date. To score the Goal Attainment Scale, scores of $-2$ (most unfavorable), $-1$ (less than expected), 0 (expected level,) $+1$ (more than expected), and $+2$ (most favorable) are given for each final outcome. A formula or calculation table is then used to convert these scores to standard scores with a mean of 50 and a standard deviation of 10.

In order to add composite Goal Attainment Scores of various children or to compare one child longitudinally, some cautions of a statistical nature should be kept in mind. The various goal scales should be done realistically, so that the expected mean value for the group is near zero (standard score = 50) and with a standard deviation approximating one (converted standard score = 10). Stated another way, about two-thirds of the composite scores of the total group should fall within the "expected level of success" on the Goal Attainment Scale; about 10% to 15% should obtain scores of "less than expected success"; 10% to 15% should receive "more than expected success"; and very few (2% to 5%) should achieve scores at the extremes of "most favorable" or "most unfavorable" outcome thought likely. If there is considerable variance from this as a group, the effect is that some composite goal scores will have heavier weights than others and make the comparisons less valid. The cautions just noted should not discourage use of the technique, but should be kept in mind.

*Applications for Use.* As indicated earlier, results from individual evaluation scales are potentially useful in a variety of applications. First, scored scales provide information on individual child changes upon which decisions regarding the student's continuation or change in placement can be initiated and resolved. Secondly, the scored scale in and of itself is a data base on the child's placement that can be inserted into the student's cumulative folder for documentation of placement and subsequent instruction. Thirdly, the scale provides the teacher, the Area Education Agency special education consultant, and the program's supervisor a systematic means to review the achievements of the students served in the program.

The potential for comparing program models as well as types of instructional designs (behavior modifications, use of paraprofessionals and/or associates in instruction, teaching methods, etc.) over the years is an aspect yet to be explored as the implementation of the process proceeds to its conclusion. Indeed, the use of Goal Attainment Scaling as described in this proposed model appears to be most promising.

## REFERENCES


Howe, C. E. *Goal scaling used to evaluate major work priorities.* Unpublished manuscript, College of Education, Division of Special Education, University of Iowa, Iowa City, IA, 1976.

Howe, C. E., & Fitzgerald, M. E. *A model for evaluating special education programs in Iowa Area Education Agencies.* Des Moines, IA: Iowa State Department of Public Instruction, Division of Special Education, 1976.

Johnson, W. *An example of an opinionnaire field tested in AEA 16 in the spring of 1976.* Unpublished manuscript, Director of Special Education, Area Education Agency 16, Mount Pleasant, IA, 1976.

Kiresuk, T., & Sherman, R. Goal attainment scaling: A general method for evaluating comprehensive mental health programs. *Community Mental Health Journal,* 1968, 4(6), 443-453.

Leone, P. *Sample of complete goal attainment scale example where specific priority areas are not equally important.* Unpublished manuscript, Child Psychiatry Service, University of Iowa Hospitals and Clinics, Iowa City, IA, 1975.

Meyen, E. *Instructional based appraisal system.* Bellevue, WA: Edmark Associates, 1976.

Popham, W. J. *An evaluation guidebook: A set of practical guidelines for the educational evaluator.* Los Angeles: The Instructional Objectives Exchange, 1972.

State of Iowa. *Rules of special education.* Des Moines: Department of Public Instruction, 1974.

Stufflebeam, D. L., et al. *Educational evaluation and decision making.* Itasca, IL: Peacock Publishers, 1971.


## ADDITIONAL REFERENCES


Garwick, G. *Guidelines for goal attainment scaling.* (A product of the Program Evaluation Resource Center, T. J. Kiresuk, Director.) Grant No. 1 R12 MH1561902. Washington, D.C.: National Institute of Mental Health, Department of Health, Education, and Welfare, February 1975.

Kiresuk, T. J., & Garwick, G. *Program evaluation project report 1969-73: Basic goal attainment scaling procedures* (2nd ed.). Grant No. 5 R01 1678904 and Grant No. 1 R12 MH2561902. Washington, D.C.: National Institute of Mental Health, Department of Health, Education, and Welfare, 1975.

Neufeldt, A. H. Considerations in the implementation of program evaluations. In Davidson, Clark, & Hamerlynch (Eds.), *Evaluation of behavioral programs.* Champaign, IL: Research Press, 1973, pp. 65-82.

Senf, G., & Anderson, D. *A program evaluation manual for project initiators.* Final Report Project No. H 12-7145B, Grant No. OEG-0-714425. Washington, D.C.: Bureau of Education for the Handicapped, June 1974.

# The Montessori Approach to Special Education

## Lena L. Gitter

Much of the thought of Maria Montessori, Italy's first woman doctor, as reflected in the materials she devised, anticipated the philosophy behind today's development of programmed learning. Summing up work done in programmed instruction for the retarded, Luke S. Watson, Jr. writes: "Characteristics of programmed methods (of learning) include the following: (1) the student receives individual attention and extensive prompting; (2) the subject matter is presented in small well-organized sequential steps; (3) the student gets immediate knowledge of results; (4) the student progresses at the rate he prefers; however, he is not permitted to progress beyond the point of comprehension; (5) programs are designed specifically for a particular group, such as the educable mentally retarded of a given mental age level."

The teacher demonstrates each activity so the child learns the correct way of approaching a given task. There is an efficient way of scrubbing a table or folding a cloth, and the child who has learned this will be able to perform effectively and with genuine pleasure all the necessary tasks which make a livable classroom atmosphere. In addition, he will be able to demonstrate these skills at home and receive much-needed praise given without condescension, for he will be performing these tasks properly and usefully.

Another series of exercises in practical living that provide great emotional satisfaction for children who have been starved for success are those which involve the actual housekeeping of the classroom: washing, polishing, dusting and similar activities. At the same time, these duties are valuable in encouraging a sense of responsibility, of pride in work well done, of pleasure in the orderly environment. They help develop increasing eye-hand coordination on all levels from the simple to the more sophisticated. The child comes to perceive the differences between a clean chair and a dirty one and to take pride in his work, which wrought the change so clearly visible to everyone.

**Dressing Frames**

An exercise of practical value is done with dressing frames. These are simply constructed wood frames with material attached to them. The fabric gives, in simplified and enlarged form, a section of clothing that must be fastened with buttons, snaps, zippers or laces. Many special children cannot fasten their clothes and are old enough to be embarrassed by their inability to do this relatively simple task. These dressing frames, which are not emotionally charged with concepts of the proper age for tying

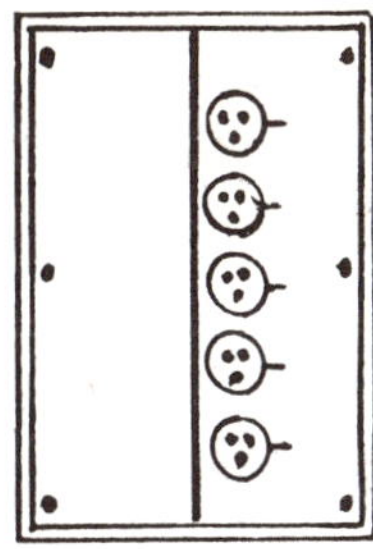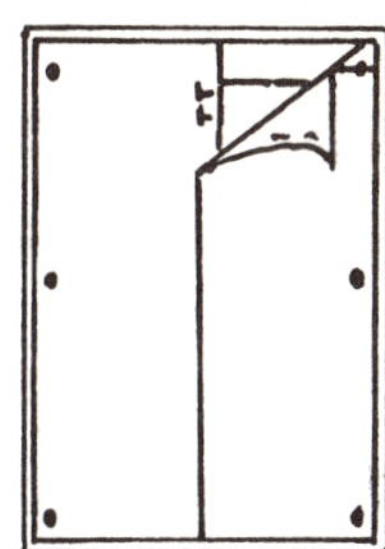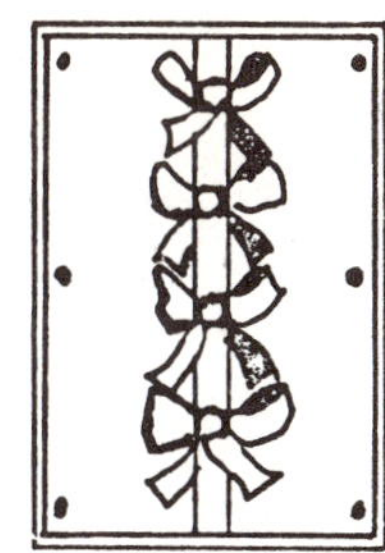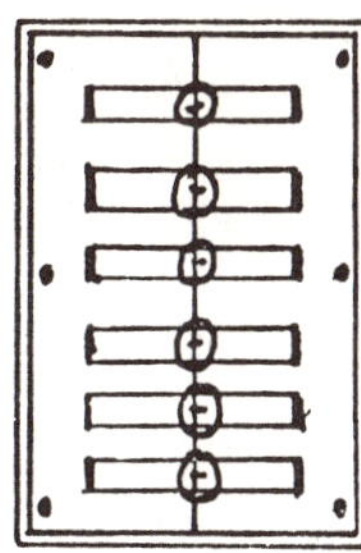

shoes or buttoning buttons, allow the child to work quietly by himself until he perfects a skill without the fear of errors being exposed by others. The self-correcting nature of the frames shows the child where he has gone wrong and enables him to correct his error either alone or with the teacher's assistance. Repeated success with the frames will give him courage to tackle the problem of dressing himself and  fastening smaller buttons or shorter laces.

At the same time the child learns to see himself as successful in performing the exercises of practical life. He is mastering specific skills which have a distinct value of their own. They are preparing him for later work in writing and ultimately for realistic job possibilities

When the child pours grains, such as rice or oats, from one cup to another, he is developing eye-hand coordination as well as learning the skill of controlling the flow of grain when the cup is almost full. At first he will spill the grain. But with practice his perception will be sharpened and his muscular control improved so he will spill less and less and finally, none at all.


**Grace and Courtesy**

Manners are the external signs that reveal we are able to conduct ouselves in accordance with the social norms of a given society or a given group in society. They are not, however, purely external, for they also determine to a considerable extent how we feel about people we meet in social circumstances. They provide valuable clues for our reaction to other people. Manners bind together members of the same social group. Manners are a way of recognizing the individuality of each person we meet.

Normal children learn accepted ways of social behavior in the family group, from precept and observation. A child who makes a social mistake, either with his peers or with adults, quickly learns to observe the signs of disapproval on the faces of others, and to modify his actions accordingly. Children from substandard homes find that lack of knowledge of acceptable manners bars them from society at large.

The same is true of the special child, whether he is mentally retarded, emotionally disturbed, or brain-damaged. He must be taught ways of behavior that are learned naturally by other children. And this part of his education is no less important than that which involves direct academic training, for the special child depends even more than the normal one on the impression he makes on others, who may harbor fears and anxieties about this child and who may be uncertain of their own social attitude towards him. A simple exchange of expected courtesies often may reassure others that this child is indeed capable of the social behavior demanded by the group.

In addition, there are more immediate reasons for observing proper social relations. The classroom is in itself a group situation where the teacher must keep a certain number of children functioning in harmony with each other. And, of course, the relationship between each child and the teacher can unfold in an atmosphere of mutual understanding and respect when the child comes to perceive that the teacher treats him with courtesy and dignity, with care for his individuality.

**Opening Exercises**

Each morning should begin with the teacher greeting each child personally with a hand shake and a few pleasant words. "Good morning, Michael, how are you? My, what a nice green sweater you are wearing!" This brief exchange does many things. It gives the teacher time to observe the child: does he seem tired, unusually disturbed, upset in some way? The child hears his name and has another opportunity to associate his name with himself. He feels good when he hears an appreciative comment about *his* clothes or *his* hair. The pleasant tone of the greeting creates a good atmosphere for the rest of the day, even if the teacher should not have much time to spend with the child. It gives him a chance to tell the teacher anything that is on his mind. Perhaps a grandmother has come to visit, or his mother is ill, or he has received a new toy. Such happenings may affect his behavior for the day and the teacher can be of assistance if she understands the reason for his unusual excitement.

The child, of course, is learning day by day, through this example, how to behave with others when he is meeting them, how to shake hands, how to make the appropriate polite remark. Through the teacher's carefully chosen words he is adding to his vocabulary and also to his understanding of the correct context in which to use particular words.

Finally, in this brief moment when the child is looked at directly and can return this look, when eyes meet and acknowledge the existence of another person, the child is experiencing a vital human exchange. In the life of a special child, such moments may be tragically few. The teacher should not neglect the chance of increasing them.

### The Fundamental Lesson

However, this vast array of exciting material is in itself no guarantee of learning. What is needed in addition are certain techniques, which are used in teaching at every level in the Montessori class, beginning with the sensorial exercises and going on to the academic work. The retarded, brain-damaged or emotionally disturbed child presents a problem that must be met before any learning can take place. This child is easily upset by the presence of extraneous objects, as he is by the sound of many words. because he

---

**"To avoid misunderstanding and confusion, it is essential to isolate the quality the child is to experience in much the same way as teaching machines break down materials to be learned into precise and unambiguous steps."**

---

lacks the power to discriminate between what is and what is not important. Therefore, a way must be found to isolate the material we wish him to learn, to create an empty space around the child except for what is being taught at the time.

Thus the fundamental lesson is the start of all Montessori learning and forms the necessary preparation for what will follow. It is the means by which the teacher demonstrates the child's right to learn and guarantees the freedom in which learning will become possible.

The table on which the child is to work should be clear of all materials, flowers, plants, etc., for what forms a pleasant background for the normal child only disturbs the special child. The teacher's movements as she prepares the table and the child's chair should be quiet and simple. The chair is placed gently by the table. Then the teacher walks to where the material to be used in the lesson is kept and shows this to the child and how to carry it to his work place.

The teacher should make certain that the child's interest is engaged in this work. If not, she waits for a better moment and proceeds from the very beginning.

When the material is placed properly on the otherwise empty table, the lesson starts. The child may work with his material for as long as he wishes after the teacher has demonstrated the correct way of using it. This demonstration will be marked by very little talk. Rather, the teacher will show by appropriate gestures, moving as economically as possible, what is to be done. Then she will refrain from offering additional comments or assistance until the child requests help.

With the special student a great deal of initial demonstration may be necessary. The teacher should be careful not to repeat unnecessarily. She must wait patiently until the child reveals a need for further instruction. The teacher must also be certain to demonstrate the primary purpose of the material, ignoring all the interesting variations possible. Another time will serve for additional points of interest. In this, too, she will be guided by the expressed interest of the child.

When the lesson is completed, the material is returned to its proper place on the shelf by the child.

### Sandpaper Letters

The purpose of Dr. Montessori's use of sandpaper letters was a direct preparation for reading and writing. These letters are also useful in sensory activities.

The letters, in large clear script, are cut out of sandpaper and mounted on cardboard, the vowels on pink and the consonants on blue. These letters are taught to the child until he has mastered the sound of each letter and learned to associate it with the correct shape.

When this happens the teacher takes the child's hand and shows him how to follow with his two forefingers the contour of the letter, just as he would do if he were writing it. At the same time she has him pronounce distinctly the sound of the letter.

By the time the alphabet has been taught with sandpaper letters, the child has learned to associate the sound of each letter with the muscular movements necessary to reproduce it.

Variations can be introduced as the pupil is ready for them. He can be blindfolded, so he learns to recognize the shape of the letters solely by touch. Such modifications and additions, however, will come only after the child has thoroughly mastered the basic exercises and has gained the confidence of achievement.

Thus we find the teaching of motor coordination is part of the direct preparation for reading and writing, as well as for other classroom work. At the same time it has its own value in the development of a positive self-concept. We all know of the poor motor coordination commonly found in retarded and disturbed children. The pupil who trips over his feet also trips over his words and the same metaphor is appropriate to both difficulties.

Once this has happened, he is ready for the next step in his direct preparation for reading and writing. All too often, actual writing must wait until the child has gained sufficient muscular control to handle a pencil. With the special child—as, indeed, with some normal children—small muscle control is delayed until beyond the age when the child is actually emotionally and mentally ready for working with words.

### Walking on the Line

For the special child, exercises that lead to improved muscular coordination are even more important than they are for the normal child. Experiences leading to development of such coordination should be a regular part of the special class. Walking on the line is an exercise of great value that is simplicity itself and can be done in the classroom without any special equipment.

A line is drawn on the floor with chalk or marked out with masking tape if a permanent painted line is not allowed. It should be about one inch wide and in as large an oval as the room will allow. If the room is sufficiently large, a second, smaller oval can be placed inside the first so that slower children or children with impaired muscular control may proceed at their own, unforced pace.

Then the children arrange themselves on the line at equal distance from each other. Through example the teacher shows the children how to walk, placing the whole of their

# 2. METHODOLOGY

feet on the line. Then gradually she encourages them to take smaller and smaller steps until they are walking heel-to-toe along the line in a slow and regular rhythm.

Once the children have mastered this basic exercise, various modifications can be introduced that provide additional challenge and interest. They also refine muscular skills

---

**"Each modification represents a challenge; each challenge once mastered, a victory; each victory marks a step in the child's education."**

---

already learned. The children continue to walk heel-to-toe, not forgetting the initial lessons of posture and rhythm. Walking on the line can be done without music but quiet tunes without a marked rhythm can be played if desired.

The kind of supplementary material to be used is limited only by the teacher's imagination and the children's capacity to respond. They can use flashlights to throw a beam on the line in front of them. Or they may carry small flags which they hold up high as an aid to walking with heads up and eyes away from their feet. They can carry objects on their heads without using hands. If some are available, the children can wear hats which serve not only as objects to be balanced but also as objects which *define*, if well-chosen, as: firemen's hats, nurse's hats, and so on.

Weights can be used, or bells that should not ring, or small glasses filled with colored water that should not spill. Each modification represents a challenge; each challenge once mastered, a victory; each victory marks a step in the child's education.

### The Silence Game

In the Silence Game, the teacher interrupts classroom activity by ringing a bell to gain the children's attention. Or she may draw their attention to a fish bowl or quiet external object on which they can focus their interest. Gradually, the room falls silent. She may also establish silence by writing the word on the board, by speaking the word ever more quietly, by setting an example through her own silence: silent, still more silent, until all the children are quiet.

This is only the beginning. The children then seat themselves at their tables, moving the chairs silently; then they compose themselves for relaxation, each child holding a comfortable position without moving around. Awareness of muscles and control of any troublesome muscles is necessary for quiet performance of these activities.

Slowly, each child relaxes and is silent. Then he becomes aware, perhaps for the first time, of the persistence of background noises: a watch ticking, another child breathing, a bird song. Each background sound is clearly isolated, an especially important sensory experience for a child in our culture, where silence is almost impossible to obtain. Radios, television, or piped-in music are a constant accompaniment to every activity.

Silence also has an emotional or spiritual importance in the life of everyone, especially for the special child, who often lives in the midst of a buzz of confusion or meaningless noise. Silence is not merely the absence of sound but it is in itself a positive sensory experience, a condition of inner tranquility. When it goes along with practice in muscular self-control, it becomes doubly valuable as therapy for the special child.

In addition, the practice of silence is valuable preparation for adult life which may require moving and working quietly and prolonged concentration or listening. The child who has learned to compose himself silently may then go with his family to a movie or to a dinner where he will be required to be quiet and controlled.

When the room is completely silent and each child motionless, the teacher rises noiselessly and walks to one end of the room. Then, speaking as softly as possible, she calls each child by name. The child whose name is called rises, places his chair at the table and walks to where the teacher is standing, all in silence. Here he receives a smile meant just for him.

It is clear that children will enjoy the silence that is necessary for hearing their names called and will respond with pleasure to the sound of their names. But for the special child, who frequently has problems of identification, this acknowledgment of his name and his presence, this opportunity to perceive the relationship between his name and himself, signaled by the teacher's pleasure when he appears in response to his name, has unusual importance.

Establishing silence before his name is called can serve a similar function to the empty table in the fundamental lesson: by removing distractions that are often painful in their intensity, the teacher frees the child to concentrate on the one element in the activity that is of prime importance. Muscular control and awareness of the emotional satisfactions of silence are established through the experience itself without the need for more than minimal verbalization.

# Our Special Children Are People Too:

# A Parent's View

ROSE MARIE STOEBNER

"I continue to stress self worth and a sense of belonging as key ingredients in my classroom as all academic growth hinges on how the children perceive themselves. I have learned a great deal from my oldest son about which I wrote this article, as he has helped me understand the fears and frustrations of failing. I am growing in patience and finding strengths to praise even very slow students. I also can more easily see through the facade of the trouble makers to look for the frustrations that cause such unacceptable behavior."

Rose Marie Stoebner was born and raised on a South Dakota farm and attended a one room rural school. After high school, she went to Sioux Falls College and received a B.A. in education in 1959. She was married after college and began her career teaching fourth grade in Sheboygan, Wisconsin. Ms. Stoebner taught for 2 years then spent the next 5 years as a housewife and mother to her three children. She began teaching again in 1966 in Ipswich, South Dakota. She taught there for 10 years and was instrumental in helping the school establish a nongraded, individualized approach which included team teaching and open classrooms. Through summer school sessions at Colorado State University, Ms. Stoebner received a Masters in Guidance and Counseling in 1971. Last year she set up a junior high remedial reading program in her school. She helped her students build self esteem and a sense of belonging and many were able to make large strides in reading. Ms. Stoebner is currently teaching fourth grade in Hill City, South Dakota.

I am agonizing over the fears, frustrations, and failures faced by my 14 year old son Dean, who is a "slow learner." I want to share his story in hope that something more will be done to help this segment of our school population.

Early in life Dean learned fear. Due to allergies and low resistance, he had infectious diseases of the respiratory system, and had to fight for every breath of air for months. He had his first attack of asthma at 11 months, but through weekly desensitization shots from age 3 through 6, he has overcome that. The high temperatures during his many bouts with pneumonia may even have caused some brain damage. Whether or not it did, his fear of every new situation is grounded way back in the basic fear for survival. He cried whenever he was left with a babysitter and withdrew when he was expected to play with others his age. He had trouble playing with his sister and brother who are 1 and 3 years younger, respectively. He lagged behind in social skills from potty training through kindergarten games, and now the junior high school functions.

With this background let's look at what happens to him in school. He is classified as "dull normal" by several types of tests he has taken. His IQ falls in the low 80's and he always finds himself at the "bottom of the barrell" in class. Much of his emotional energy is spent fearing what others might think of him.

It took him all of first grade to learn the alphabet and a few phonetic sounds. By the end of third grade he was just beginning to unlock the reading process. We thought about holding him back, but in our one track school system that would have put him in the same room with his sister who excels. The other alternative was to



Reprinted from *Teaching Exceptional Children* by Rose Marie Stoebner by permission of The Council for Exceptional Children. ©1979 by The Council for Exceptional Children, 1920 Association Drive, Reston, Virginia 22091.

send him to the Catholic parochial school in town, but Dean's lack of ability to cope with new situations and make adjustments prevented our "keeping him back" then.

So he continued to struggle in a semi-individualized classroom and made some progress. By the end of sixth grade he was reading at the fourth grade level and doing fifth grade math with some glimmer of success. But he was to enter junior high where letter grades are given and he seemed doomed to F's. Faced with the crushing affect that would have on him, we decided he must at least have more time to get ready, so we had him repeat sixth grade. Luckily, he had a new teacher which made it a new experience.

There was some wisdom in our decision as he made some academic growth and is coping with seventh grade even though he gets mostly D's and F's. He has had the benefits of remedial reading, summer school sessions, and caring parents, but this is what he lives with. Every day he goes to school knowing he will fail. Naturally, he's not too crazy about it, but he doesn't let his feelings show in class. He doesn't want to reveal his ignorance, so never asks questions even though he doesn't understand. Then, he comes home with homework, often not sure just what the assignment is. Well, his sister can bail him out because she has all the same courses, except shop. That is another disappointment. Dean signed up for shop hoping to achieve some sense of accomplishment for doing things with his hands. Well, the first semester was all "book learning" and much of it beyond his grasp, like the elements of mass production and basic concepts of economics, not to mention memorizing the 20 or more parts of a micrometer. This did not build his self esteem and the result was another F.

Back to how he acts at home. I try to help him with his assignments. I really push him to do what he can do, like copy the sentences correctly from the English book. Then I help him diagram them—his given assignment. He gets so frustrated he often cries or throws things. He screams and swears. He used to ask why he couldn't go to "special ed" because the regular classroom was so hard. He can't even begin to understand what he reads in social studies. The questions at the end of the chapter included a comparison of the Eastern philosophies. How can he be expected to do that when he doesn't know if Philadelphia is a city or a state? And the science text vocabulary is way beyond him to say nothing of the concepts.

I could give endless examples, but the point is, Dean is expected to cover the same territory and handle the same concepts as his gifted sister, and, although he works harder and worries more, his reward is D's and F's while hers is straight A's.

Needless to say, his self worth is not too high. He compensates by tearing down his brother at every possible opportunity. He bugs him mercilessly about everything from feeding the dog to singing too loud at church. Most attempts at play end in hassles over petty rules. Dean tries desperately to look better or feel superior in at least some little way.

We try to be understanding. We encourage him to hold his own and settle differences himself if we think he can handle it. We praise him for small successes—remembering to brush his teeth, taking out the garbage, sharing his bubble gum, etc. But we are finding it extremely difficult to do enough building to allow him to cope with his life at school.

Our school is no worse than any other school. In fact, in many ways it's better because the teachers know all their students personally. But, when all kids are expected to do the same thing, those that don't perform as well naturally get the D's and F's. And, kids like Dean, who can't possibly perform up to average, become the "scapegoats of the classroom." What does this do to them? If they are finally convinced that they are failures, they strike out against society. They cheat, steal and/or try drugs and often fill up our correctional institutions. What else can we do for them?

I haven't any easy answers but I do have some ideas of what I would hope for my child. I want him to be able to read and understand a newspaper. He should be able to write a letter. I want him to handle money correctly, including a checking account. I want him to know where he lives in relation to other states in this country and other major countries around the world. And I want him to get along with others, respecting their rights and his own. I especially want him to know he has value and ability, even if he doesn't match up to school standards. I want him to be able to hold a job and make a living.

I think these are reasonable expectations for Dean, but he has 5 more years before he gets out of high school, and it seems most of the courses he will be required to take will be college prep oriented and not practical, everyday skills. He is not college material, but can't public education help prepare him for life too? I have read that about 15% of our school population are "slow learners." Don't they deserve more than we are presently offering them? How about a curriculum aimed at their needs? School should help them feel good about themselves and prepare them to go out in the world on their own. If public education is for everyone, can we continue to ignore the needs of this group?

# Successful Programs for Young Handicapped Children

## Garry McDaniels

Probably every reader of this special issue of *Educational Horizons* on "Educating the Very Young" has at one time taken a course in child or human development and has studied texts on individual differences. Some also may have studied abnormal development or developmental disabilities. Scholars and researchers who are now asking us to reexamine some of our treasured assumptions about normal and unusual child development do us a favor by forcing us to review research findings critically and to continue our interest in and study of infants and young children.

Recent studies on development of the human brain (Shneour, 1974) and on the abilities of newborns give us some new perspectives about infants and correct some of our earlier misconceptions. Studies such as Haring, Hayden, and Beck (1976) describe the development of the fetal central nervous system from conception and the establishment of the total number of neurons as early as the second trimester of pregnancy. While the rate of growth is greatest before birth, the major increase in the size of the human brain comes soon after birth, and the brain nearly triples in size during the first year of life. Even though we now recognize the importance of good prenatal care and delivery of the newborn, as well as of the early months and years of life (White, 1975), there are a number of newborn infants—up to 31 percent—who present symptoms of neurological or growth abnormalities that may signal potential developmental problems (Denhoff, Hainsworth, & Hainsworth, 1972).

These infants at risk for handicapping conditions cannot wait until age six, or even age three, before receiving intervention that will help them. If, as we are learning, children as young as one year or less can make fine discriminations, then that is the age at which programs should begin. However, there are stumbling blocks.

### But where are the data?

In the mid-sixties and early seventies, increased funding and support for programs serving the very young and the handicapped resulted in increased demands for accountability and evaluation. Calls for proof that such programs were working came both from the academic community and from funding agencies. Among academicians, there was some scepticism that programs for young children, especially for the disadvantaged or handicapped, were actually producing the results claimed. On the public policy side, the main questions revolved around quality and economics. The cost of early childhood programs was reaching hundreds of millions of dollars and people in government were asking, "What works? What are the best methods? How much should it cost?"

> " . . . children
> with preschool experience
> do better than
> children who needed
> such services
> but did not receive them
> by age five or six."

Unfortunately, the first major studies raised more questions and controversy than they answered. The Westinghouse, Ohio, study (Bissell, 1970) of the effectiveness of Head Start pointed up the "wash-out" effect of gains made during summer Head Start programs, yet went on to say that full-year programs that served the disadvantaged and handicapped could be effective in helping such children maintain higher levels of achievement. Similarly, the Coleman study (1966) raised general concerns about the im-


Successful Programs for Young Handicapped Children, Garry L. McDaniels, *Exceptional Horizons*, Vol. 56, No. 1, Fall, 1977. Reprinted by permission of the publisher and author. ©1977 Phi Lambda Theta, Inc.

pact of special materials, equipment, and programming for school-aged children.

Though these and other highly visible studies did not reduce the level of funding for programs for young children, they did create a climate of caution and concern. This, coupled with Vietnam-era priorities away from education and toward military spending, created a ceiling on early childhood program expenditures that was (and still is) far below what is needed.

### The data are building

Recently, priorities have shifted away from military spending and more toward education and other people-oriented programs. At the same time, the data regarding the success and importance of programs serving young children are building (McDaniels, 1972; Wiekart, 1970). Especially as they impact on increased and continued educational services to young children who are handicapped, the data are particularly important. By extracting ideas from the research literature on the most effective program components, and by supplementing such ideas with observations of successful programs serving young handicapped children, educators and legislators alike should be able to identify successful directions for preschool programs.

Just within the past two years or so, research studies examining the long-term effects of early intervention programs have begun to show that over several years, children with preschool experiences do better than children who needed such services but did not receive them by age five or six. Hayden, Morris, and Bailey (1977) report on the results of a follow-up study of graduates of the Model Preschool Center for Handicapped Children at the University of Washington. Preliminary findings indicate that children who received early intervention are placed in special education programs less often than control children who did not receive early training. The Model Preschool "graduates" maintained the cognitive development gains they made in preschool, and even those graduates placed in special education scored as high on intelligence tests as a great number of the children in regular education. Children placed in regular classes did not repeat grades, but kept up with their normal classmates.

Lazar (1977) reported the results of a twelve-program coordinated effort that indicates that gains made by handicapped children in preschool programs are long lasting, that fewer children who had preschool experiences were placed in special classes or returned to special classes, and that fewer experimental children had to repeat grades.

Hayden and Pious (1977) make the case that now more than ever we need to state and reiterate the case for early programming and we must keep abreast of the current research that indicates the longitudinal effects of early education. If we continue to keep the subject of early intervention vital, then all of us who deal with handicapped children will be more open to the newest research findings as they appear.

### Characteristics of success

Evaluation data that have recently been published or that will be published in the next two or three years discuss the success of handicapped early childhood programs. Summaries of data can be found in Bronfenbrenner (1974) and Lazar (1977). In addition, there are numerous studies that look at the impact of programs for handicapped children, including a recent study by the Battelle Institute (Stock, Wnek, Newborg, Schenck, Gabel, Spurgeon, & Ray, 1976), focusing on the importance of the Handicapped Children's Early Education Programs funded by the Bureau of Education for the Handicapped.

As individual studies are examined, a pattern seems to emerge regarding what characterizes successful programs—programs that are coherent and that include an explicit rationale in their statement of goals of their utilization of time, materials, and training.

***Articulated goals.*** It is a truism to say that people who know where they are going (1) are most likely to get to where they want to be and (2) are most likely to get there efficiently. This appears to apply to educational programs. The more clearly defined the goals of a program and the more specific the expectations, the more likely will be the success. The program administrators, the parents, the teachers, the support staff must all share the same goals for a program to succeed.

> " . . . educational intervention
> as soon as possible
> is not only feasible
> but efficacious."

The educational community has devoted excessive energy to battles between those who feel the process of education is somehow damaged by emphasizing the outcome of interventions and those who support such emphasis. As a result of resistance to clear statements of goals by several segments of the educational and psychological communities, programs often described as behavioral, behavioristic, or programs using behavior modification techniques have been attacked on emotional grounds. The methods of be-

# 2. METHODOLOGY

havioral psychologists and educators require an explicitly concrete statement of goals. As a result, their programs (for example, Bricker & Iacino, 1977; Vincent & Broome, 1977) are increasingly cited in evaluations of effective interventions. Fortunately, the management power of clear goal statements has not gone unnoticed by programs that are more cognitively and affectively oriented. Data from such programs where the goals are clearly articulated (for example, Weikart, Deloria, Lawser, & Wiegerink, 1970; Weikart & Lambie, 1970) produce similar successes.

***Time dimension.*** The importance of time is becoming increasingly apparent in successful programming for children. Time is important in two ways: the time at which the intervention takes place, and the amount of time devoted to accomplishing clearly delineated goals.

The earlier the identification of a handicapping condition, the more successful the intervention. There are two interrelated bodies of literature from which statements evolve of the need to intervene as early as possible with handicapped children. One is based on logical/theoretical grounds, the other on empirical evidence. On the logical/theoretical side a number of well-articulated rationales have emerged (Bricker, Bricker, Iancino, & Dennison, 1976: Bricker & Iacino, 1977; Haring & Bricker, 1976; Caldwell, 1970; Hayden & McGinness, 1977; White, 1975). In general these positions have two major tenents. First, that complex human behavior develops through a continual interaction of internal maturational factors and external environmental inputs (Hunt, 1961; Lewis & Rosenblum, 1974, Piaget, 1970; Piaget & Inhelder, 1969). Secondly, with handicapped children whose specific delays in development are well documented by skill area (for example, Rubin, Rosenblatt, & Balow, 1973), there is a clear need to arrange environmental inputs to attempt to circumvent anticipated problems. Furthermore, since 6.8 percent of the handicapped population can be identified at or near birth (Beck, 1976), and since the bases for many complex cognitive and social skills appear to develop during the first three years of life (White, 1975), the feasibility and need are emphasized to intervene as close to birth as possible.

Empirically, a number of studies demonstrate the effectiveness of early intervention with handicapped children. One landmark study, continually cited in the literature in support of the efficacy of early intervention, was conducted by Skeels and Dye (1939). In this study it was found that institutionalized handicapped infants receiving "mother-child" infant stimulation by institutionalized retarded adults showed significant gains over a contrast group raised within the parameters of minimal adult contact in the institution nursery. In a follow-up study on this same population, reported twenty-seven years later (Skeels, 1966), not only were the initial gains maintained, but all children in the experimental group were self-supporting and not residing in institutions. Another frequently cited early research effort was conducted by Kirk (1958). This study was specifically designed to gain longitudinal information regarding the efficacy of preschool education for mildly and moderately handicapped children. The study essentially demonstrated that children in the experimental preschool group demonstrated significant gains over children in a traditional nursery program and children who remained at home. In addition, gains were maintained upon entry into school. Similar findings were cited by Spicker, Hodges, and McCandless (1966) and Heber, Garber, Harrington, Hoffman, and Falender (1975) with mildly handicapped children.

Much work has been conducted with premature infants, possibly because of the ease of identification and well-documented delays (Ross & Leavitt, 1976). Scarr-Salapatek and Williams (1972) examined a combined hospital and home intervention program. Prior to intervention, control subjects demonstrated significantly higher developmental scores on psysiological and behavioral measures than experimental infants. At the end of the hospital intervention phase, experimental infants showed significantly higher scores than did infants in a control group. By the end of the home intervention phase, experimental infants (X=C.A. 12 mo.) not only maintained these significant gains, but were functioning at age-appropriate levels.

In a study by Williams and Scarr (1971), various methods of home intervention (including no imposed intervention) were compared with premature children in three age groups: a) one-two years, b) two-three years, c) three-four years. From the results of this study it was concluded that only children who received a combined approach of materials and home training showed significant gains. Children whose families were either given materials only or had no form of intervention did not improve significantly.

From both the theoretical and empirical information presented, it can be tentatively concluded that educational intervention as early as possible is not only feasible but efficacious. It is incumbent upon us as educators and program designers to give serious consideration to developing services for handicapped children at the earliest possible age.

---

" . . . the gap between
high and low achievers
can be reduced
if children simply
spend more time in school."

---

Equally important, and until recently, un-noticed, is the importance of spending reasonable amounts of time on the goals being sought. A recent study has shown that the gap between high and low achievers can be reduced if children simply spend more time in school (Hays & Grether, 1969). Similar findings are appearing from other studies (Wiley & Harnischberger, 1974). In the case of handicapped children, the argument is parallel. There simply is not enough time to do everything well. Programs should organize time against their goals; that is a characteristic of success.

***Training.*** The success of any program rests in the hands of the caregivers: the parents, teachers, and other adults who deal directly with the child. In the past, a prevailing myth has been that the broadly or generally educated person probably makes the best teacher. The education of teachers has been characterized as eclectic. A little bit of this and that has been included in curricula to the point where very few training institutions stand for an approach. However, a few exceptions are notable. Bank Street College in New York City has a coherent developmental and psychological position. If you are a "Bank Streeter" your training is expected to represent the reputation established by the College. Similarly, teachers trained at the Experimental Education Unit at the University of Washington graduate with complete training in a particular system of programming for handicapped children.

Looking across these and other successful programs, a common characteristic is that careful attention is given to training. The training is designed to implement a very highly specific program or "treatment." Unfortunately, this highly specific training is found in too few of the college training programs.

***Coherent programs.*** Clearly, specific goals, careful utilization of time, and specific training are characteristics of coherent programs. The author finds these attributes common in the growing success literature that says programs do make a difference if carefully implemented. (Dalta, Weikart, & McDaniels, 1973). These encouraging findings represent the recent literature on programming for young children. However, if the characteristics that contribute to successful programs are the three described above, we must carefully examine both our practices and our training programs. The behaviorally oriented programs are currently in the lead in implementing programs with these characteristics. However, this does not say that behaviorism is the only approach. Rather, this suggests that we need a little less rhetoric and more common sense in some of our other competing intellectual traditions. This will take the hard work and resolve of all of us in the helping professions.

Deaf children live in a world of silence but they can "listen" to their parents with their eyes. Recent discoveries about early childhood, stressing the importance of the gestures and facial expressions which accompany speech, are being increasingly used by parents and teachers to help handicapped children to acquire communications skills. The deaf child is trained to follow the adult's line of vision before lip-reading his or her comments.

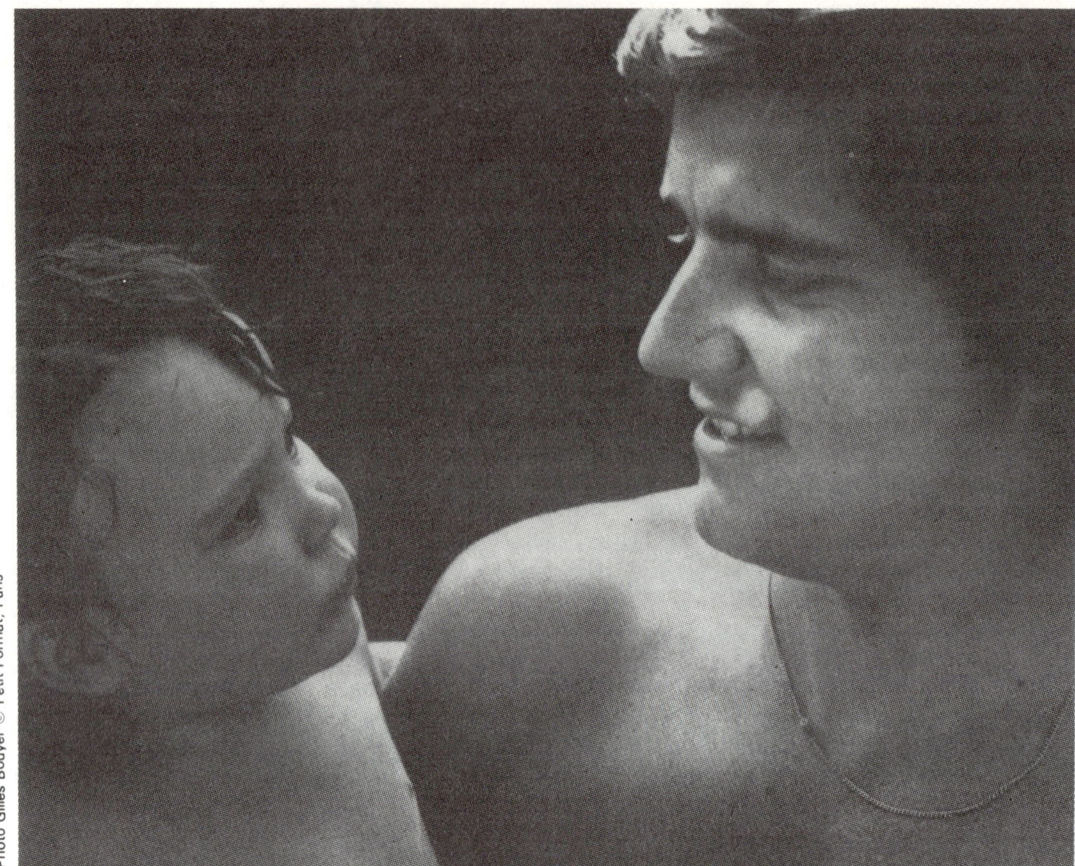


# The road to self-expression

## Awakening the latent language skills of handicapped children

**Anne McKenna**

LET us eavesdrop for a few moments while a normal child talks to his mother after he has just come out of school. He rushes through the door and runs to tell her what he has done since he last saw her, in school and on the way home with his playmates. His conversation carries the outside world into the home, and as his mother listens sympathetically the various strands of his life—school, home and friends—come together for him and interweave to make a new pattern and a new world that he himself has fashioned.

Such fortunate children who have been brought up in happy homes and who possess all their senses unimpaired have taught us so much about the meaning of the world for a child. In giving us these insights, they have given us the opportunity to acquire a new perspective on the rights of handicapped children on their long voyage to adulthood.

We now know that children learn many of the highly complex processes of communication in a very short time early in life, long before they reach school age. During a recent study of a pre-school programme in a socially disadvantaged area of the United



The Road to Self Expression, Anne McKenna, *UNESCO Courier*, January, 1979. Reproduced from the Unesco Courier, January, 1979.

Kingdom, parents were asked whether the programme had helped their relationship with their children. About half of them said that this relationship had improved and most often they attributed this to the child's increased verbal facility.

The children had learned new words which had made it easier for their parents to communicate with them; the pre-school experience had apparently provided topics for conversation. It may seem surprising that parents and children living under the same roof should need to be provided with conversational themes, but the fact is that there are many situations in which language is superfluous.

Eating and sleeping can be supervised by the parent with a great deal of efficiency and even affection, but with very few words. To wrap up a child carefully against the cold you do not need to talk about his red jumper or blue jumper or to differentiate a woollen from a synthetic coat ; and you can tuck him into bed at night without talking about the sun, the moon and the stars.

The language used on occasions like these may often be a one-sided set of terse instructions from parent to child, with an almost total lack of dialogue. To engage in dialogue with the child about the names of things, to perceive, compare and classify their qualities, to create imaginary and hypothetical situations, to relate events in time and space, to discuss the happenings of a familiar story, and to talk about how one feels—all of these activities and many others which form the basis of a good pre-school programme, might also become topics of conversation to try out with mother as well as with teacher. In giving the child conversational pieces to take home, just as we would let him take home his drawings, we are also giving the parent, perhaps for the first time, an opportunity to try out alternative topics of conversation.

But with the child who is handicapped in language development by deafness, developmental delays or low-level linguistic stimulation in the home, we must go back to the beginnings of language. Early deprivation through any form of handicap, either social or physical, can have far-reaching effects and can result in irreversible damage. On the positive side, early enrichment programmes can be highly effective if they are appropriate to the child's age and level of development.

What are the essential elements of a language programme for children who have not yet acquired language? To answer this question we need to know what the normal child has to learn before he can begin to speak. Before language is possible, we must "learn to mean" as one linguist has put it—to make sense of the world and of the people in it—and what other people are trying to do *for* us and *to* us. This is the journey that we embark on from the first breath of life, and children have travelled

far along this road before speech begins, indeed before speech can begin.

One of the first things we know to be essential is the setting up between infant and adult of a common ground, with the adult looking at the same thing as the infant and then commenting on it. This immersion in the same subject, which the American psychologist Jerome Bruner has called "joint attention", is a precious commodity for the language enrichment programme. It is in such conditions that we see the precursor of language and it is to be noted that the adult joins in the child's attention rather than expecting the child to join in his.

A mother does not say: "Pay attention, this is a hat", but when the child involuntarily attends and looks with interest at his daddy's head, so does mother, accompanying this with words like "Oh! look at daddy's lovely hat". Meaning for the child is the total content of the event, the words, the pointing finger, the smile on mother's face and the question in her eyes. The younger the child, the more handicapped the child, the more important is this context where everything that is happening around him is a clue to be snatched up if he is to make sense of the world.

And if the speaker's face expresses impatience at having to repeat the message for, say, a deaf child, this is what the situation "means" to the child. You may be mouthing "Take off your coat", but the frustration or irritation in your eyes is the chief message the child is receiving. So too much of the tone of your voice when speaking to a blind child, like the pressure of your touch, can underline or cancel out a spoken message.

No sooner has the child acquired the ability to speak a three- or four-word sentence to get attention, to procure his wants, to comment on a surprising change, in short to steer him through all the practical interchanges necessary for living, no sooner has he acquired this basic minimum than he shows a joy in experimenting with it. Language becomes something to be played with, an object to be investigated. And in the normal course of events the child is the initiator, pushing the adult into dialogue.

A recent study has revealed just how active and initiating children can be. When the spontaneous speech of four-year-old children in their own homes was recorded, in circumstances in which neither the mother nor the child knew when they were being recorded, it was found that the child initiated speech to the mother twice as often as she initiated speech to him.

This finding has caused all of us to think again about whether we teach language to a child or whether we set up a situation which allows the child to teach himself, and if we do, to ask what sort of situation this should be.

Once the to and fro of real dialogue has

been established, it provides the frame for the child to try out new speech interaction patterns. Here is a sample from an actual dialogue in which a three-year-old child is showing active forward planning, which is revealed when the adult does not say the "lines" he has mentally written for her.

— (Child) Shall I read this?
— (Mother) Yes please.
  (Child) O.K. (pretending to read) There are no monkeys.
— (Mother) Aren't there?
— (Child) No. Say why aren't there.
— (Mother) Why aren't there?
— (Child) Because there is only Jane and Peter.

The question "Aren't there" asks only for a "Yes" or "No" answer whereas a question containing the word *why* asks for a detailed reply, which in this instance the child had already prepared and intended to deliver. This is just one of many examples from our tape recordings of a child, not merely initiating speech but also structuring the form of the dialogue, a dialogue in which the child is the leader and the adult the follower.

What are the implications of this for children who are going through the critical early years in situations which are less than ideal? What kind of language enrichment programme should we have for the deaf, the socially and culturally disadvantaged, the mentally handicapped child? We have to recognize the great value and productivity of those desultory and, to the adult mind, apparently aimless exchanges which go on between an apprentice speaker, a child, and a skilled practitioner, an adult. Furthermore, we should recognize that such exchanges will not take place until the child is sufficiently emotionally secure to disengage from the practical world of real life, to play and experiment with language in his own way and at his own pace.

Are there situations in which the burden of providing for the family is so overwhelming that the providers become sources of anxiety for the child, to be avoided rather than sought out for little chats? In those cultures where the child becomes an economic unit of his family before he has mastered the language learning process, he will no doubt precociously acquire the scaffolding of language, but will there be time and interest—his own and that of his parents—to draw out the richness of language that he possesses? The child needs a listener—a listener with plenty of time: one who appreciates that language itself is a great adventure for the human spirit and not just a tool to make children more conforming, more hard-working—or even less talkative.

In this, the International Year of the Child, we should be facing the fact that each child is unique and be asking ourselves how we can compensate for the handicaps from which many children suffer. For example, many children living in high-rise

# 2. METHODOLOGY

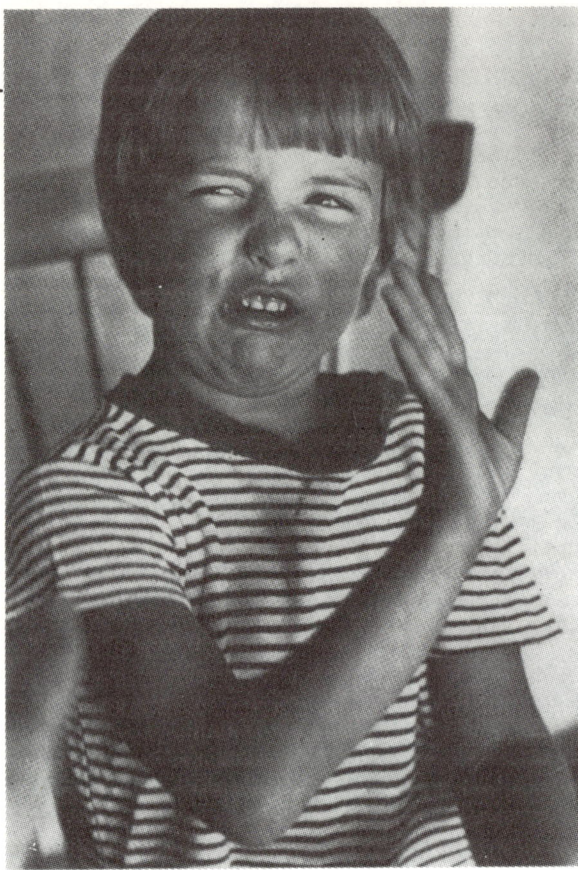

Photo © Denny Lorentzen, Stockholm

No words needed! This expressive gesture clearly means Ugh! Disgusting!

flats or overcrowded slums spend a great deal of their day playing in groups with other children on their balconies or in their yards. When their home background offers a low level of language stimulation, their needs are surely for more frequent contact with a responsive adult, an experience which a child from a more privileged social background might have in abundance whilst missing out on the experience of playing with children of his own age.

For the deaf child we have to examine our current programmes to ensure that they are bombarding the child from the earliest moment with symbols—spoken or manual—which he can experiment with and manipulate. However we must not make the error of assuming that language is something "out there" to be poured into a child so that it finishes up inside him. Rather the task is to give the child sufficient appropriate stimulation to trigger off his own latent language-forming skills.

And for the mentally handicapped child might not the task for our educators be to appreciate that a child's utterance, no matter how poorly expressed, is his own creation, his own unique assembly, to be fostered and cherished rather than to be corrected in accordance with adult standards? And for the blind child who is not lacking in linguistic competence, how can we ensure that the words he uses are not mere empty concepts, pseudo-words which lack the sighted child's richness of meaning?

Such are the questions we should pose in this International Year of the Child if we are to ensure that all our children have the best opportunities to develop fully.

# The Sexual Needs of the Handicapped

Warren L. McNab, PhD, FASHA

## ABSTRACT

*One of the basic needs of life to the handicapped, as well as to all individuals, is the understanding of one's own sexuality. Sex education can help handicapped individuals in finding sexual satisfaction and may foster self-responsibility, maturity and positive actions toward other rehabilitation goals.*

*Traditionally, the teachings of sexuality to handicapped persons have run into objections resulting from society's negative attitude toward the handicapped and parental apprehension regarding the decision-making skills of their children in relation to acceptable and unacceptable sexual behaviors. However, the Education for All Handicapped Children Act of 1975 has provided a way for parents and health professionals to put pressure on local, state and federal programs to allocate funds for the development of a sound sex education program. As professionals in health education it is our challenge and responsibility to see that the sexual needs of the handicapped are not forgotten.*

## INTRODUCTION

Developments in the training of teachers and in diagnostic and instructional procedure have advanced to the point that given appropriate funding, state and local educational agencies can and will provide effective special education and related services to meet the needs of handicapped children. [1]

This statement, with which we are all now familiar, comes from Public Law 94-142, The Education For All Handicapped Children Act, which states that because of our concern for human beings, we must attempt to place handicapped children in settings where they will receive the fullest measures of our educational resources. [2] The educational system must provide special instruction for the unique needs of handicapped children. One of the basic needs of life to the handicapped, as well as to all individuals, is the understanding of one's own sexuality. Sexuality is the ability to feel and give warmth and love, to develop a positive self concept, and the ability to make responsible decisions regarding the physical, mental, emotional, and social aspects of one's sexual health. In accepting one's self as a sexual being and knowing the positive aspects of sexuality, hopefully handicapped children will believe in themselves and attempt to deal with their existing circumstances in a positive way.

Sex education can help handicapped individuals understand their own responsibility in finding sexual satisfaction and may foster self-responsibility, maturity, and positive actions toward other rehabilitation goals. [3] Through this process, they can reject the idea that they are not capable of being loved or sexual and initiate the process of doing something about it. Sexual health is but one aspect of total health which is necessary in preparing all young people for life.

## REVIEW OF RELATED LITERATURE

The Sex Information and Education Council of the United States [4] believes that the sexual nature and needs of individuals with physical or mental handicapping conditions have rarely been considered in the past. Gordon [5] states that sex education is essential if we are ever to make significant headway toward the normalization of people who are disabled.

If handicapped people are kept out of sight, how can

*The Journal of School Health,* Vol. 48, No. 5, May, 1978, pp. 301-306. ©1978, American School Health Association, Kent, Ohio
44240

the able-bodied majority in our society ever learn that these citizens are human beings who have a right to information and full participation in our society? Under conditions of nearly complete repression and denial of the sexual drive, Gordon[5] believes the maturing mentally handicapped child becomes increasingly bewildered and anxious in our environment which is

---

**"One of the basic needs of life to the handicapped, as well as to all individuals, is the understanding of one's own sexuality."**

---

filled with concrete and symbolic stimuli. Certainly a mental, emotional or physical handicap does not reduce the sexual drives that are characteristics of everyone's environment. Each citizen has a right to an appropriate education, and this education certainly includes sex education for the exceptional child. Humanness takes precedence over the handicapped condition. Whether physically or mentally handicapped, they are first and foremost human beings who need to be valued and accepted as sexual individuals.

The positive teaching of sexuality traditionally runs into public objections. Few schools have comprehensive sex education for students in high school, let alone classes for the handicapped students. Johnson succinctly summarizes this dilemma in stating "one socially unacceptable phenomenon is difficult enough to deal with, but combine two socially unacceptable phenomena — in this case specialness and sexuality — and there is bound to be real trouble, including avoidance behavior."[6]

Traditionally, society has expected the handicapped to adopt sexually acceptable behavior even though society offers no programs on responsible sexual behavior. Gordon[5] believes the question is not "Should these young people be knowledgeable about sexuality?" but "Who are they receiving this information from — the media, movies, experience or educational programs?" He emphasizes that handicapped children have the same emotions and sexual drives as their normal counterparts, but with less knowledge; and they are therefore a most vulnerable seqment of our youth regarding sexual exploitation. Handicapped children must not only cope with their sexual conflicts as do other children, but they must also deal with additional problems created by their individual handicap.

One of the biggest barriers that must be overcome regarding sexuality and the handicapped is society's negative attitudes toward these people. These attitudes have been created because of isolation of the handicapped and the resultant negative conditioning ingrained in the minds of people because of a lack of understanding and association. The National Informa-

tion Center for the Handicapped states that for progress to be made, there has to be a change in societal attitude — "We have to really mean it when we say that to be different from the "norm" is not just okay — it's what being human is all about."[7]

Cole[8] believes society is beginning to understand that an individual's sexuality is not earned through material works, nor lost because of an accident or congenital handicap. Enby[9] reiterates this point in stating that if society were better informed about the abilities as well as the disabilities of the disabled, we would all benefit. The disabled would be less handicapped by real or perceived barriers and would therefore be able to participate more fully and productively in life.

Parents many times set the tempo as far as accepting their child as a person and an integrated, functional part of society. Gorham discusses this process as a positive or negative labeling process in stating, "Pragmatically speaking, 'good' labels are those a parent can use to open doors for his child and maximize the chances of marshalling resources in his behalf. 'Bad' labels are those that close doors to the child, which place him in inferior programs or subject him to unpleasant or humiliating experiences and attitudes."[10] Parents are many times apprehensive and worried about the decision-making skills of their children in relation to acceptable and unacceptable behaviors. This indicates a need for a certain amount of parental education and counseling regarding the sexuality of their children so that they will be able to help their handicapped child feel at ease with his/her sexuality and be as responsible as their handicap permits in making sexual decisions.

Johnson[6] states that sex education is usually not provided to "special groups" because (1) people have misconceptions about sex and are basically ignorant on the subject, (2) there is an uncertainty as to what constitutes good sex education for people generally, let alone special groups; and (3) people have mistaken attitudes that the special group member's label tells us about his

---

**"The initial objective is to help other class members accept the handicapped as individuals who are more like than different from other members of the class . . ."**

---

sexuality. Because of these factors, Johnson believes parents have three choices regarding their child's sexuality — try to eliminate the sexual expression, tolerate or accomodate it, or cultivate it. In the past, society has basically tried to repress or discourage sexuality in many segments of the handicapped population. Parents felt that the less their child knew about sex, the less overt behavior he would actually attempt.

We are just beginning to tolerate and accommodate the sexual needs of the special individual. Hopefully our efforts in this direction can and will positively influence the maturation process of the child. With these special efforts in mind, the basic question is how can our educational efforts help parents to help their children achieve a good gender and role identity given each of their handicaps; and how can we help the handicapped learn appropriate sexual behavior based upon their own maturational feelings and capabilities.

## MAINSTREAMING

In education, the mainstreaming philosophy maintains that as many physically, mentally, and emotionally handicapped children as possible should be included in regular classes with as much extra support from professional specialists as each requires. [7] As for sex education, it means breaking down sexual misconceptions and stereotypes that persist about the handicapped. It means finding out how to foster new attitudes and how to construct a sexuality curriculum that examines the needs of the handicapped and provides competent programs to meet these needs. Birzea and Dockrell [11] emphasize that as far as education is concerned, the important point is not the physical placement of the handicapped into the normal classroom; it is the provision of skills to interact with normal children and function in society.

---

**". . . the basic question is how can our educational efforts help parents to help their children achieve a good gender and role identity given each of their handicaps; . . ."**

---

The term "exceptional or handicapped children" in today's society covers a diverse variety of children who deviate from the norm and require some kind of special educational programming. Kirk's [12] definition states that the exceptional or handicapped child is the child who deviates from the normal or average child in (1) mental characteristics, (2) sensory abilities, (3) neuromuscular or physical characteristics, (4) social or emotional behavior, (5) communication abilities, or (6) multiple handicaps to such an extent that it requires a modification of school practices or special education services in order to develop his maximum capacities.

Regarding sexuality, Johnson [6] reiterates that emphasis should not be upon the handicapping condition, but upon individual human beings dealing knowledgeably with their sexuality, whatever their condition. The sexual adjustment of the handicapped does not differ much from everyone else's regarding sexuality; the behavior may be normal or abnormal depending on the context and viewpoint from which it is evaluated.

Incorporating Kirk's [12] broad interpretation of what is implied by handicapped or special children, the author would briefly like to review certain common handicaps in the physiological and mental categories.

## PHYSIOLOGICAL HANDICAPS

### Hearing

Few people realize that hearing impairment is the single most prevelant disability in the United States. Fitz-Gerald [13] states the handicap of deficits in hearing is one of the most severe because it strikes back at the basic human function of communication. In addition, this "invisible" handicap creates a communication problem as well as a language problem which may cause social isolation and reduce the amount of information on sexuality available to deaf children. Grossman [14] found that deaf students had less sex knowledge, were more susceptible to sexual myths, and engaged in more sexual activity than did freshmen and sophomore students in college who were not handicapped. Fitz-Gerald [15] suggests a reason why there is such a discrepancy by stating that the sex education offered at most deaf residential facilities are meager and crisis oriented. He also indicates that in 97% of the training centers for teachers, there was not one course provided to enhance the teacher's ability to teach sex education.

A major problem with deaf children is their dependence on reading materials. It is a problem because 50% of deaf students age 20 and below read less than mid-fourth grade level, and it is difficult to provide materials regarding sexuality. [16] This dependence on visual stimuli also makes it difficult for students to understand abstract ideas such as motherhood, relationships, and pregnancy. Once again, a lack of priorities and a negative attitude reduces the amount of education about sexuality that the deaf receive, even though their sexual needs are the same as everyone else's.

### Vision

The visually-impaired adolescents have the same interests regarding sexuality as do sighted individuals. They are interested in interpersonal relationships, self identity, heredity, and reproduction at the junior high level. At the senior high level, marriage, establishing a home, love, responsibility, contraception, and the possibility of genetically transmitting a handicap to offspring are all of primary importance. [3]

Problems related to sex education for the blind include how they learn, how concepts are formed, how to select content, how to select and train teachers, and how to help parents get involved. Proper attitude reinforcement and the development of a positive self concept are also a must in sex education for the visually handicapped.

### Paralysis

Physical paralysis may create a situation where individuals, because of the loss of movement, believe they have lost their sexuality. Although some physical disabilities directly affect sexuality by the disablement of genital function, most do not. [8] Many times, the physically handicapped must be convinced that they are sexual, that they can share love and affection with others, and that they can succeed in the sexual act.

In situations where a male cannot have an erection, there must be provided other ways to deal with his sexual needs. Paraplegics and quadriplegics must discuss and understand sexual options available to them that allow them to maintain their feelings of masculinity and femininity. There is a need at times to reduce the emphasis on performance of sex and facilitate and reinforce the communication of sexual feelings and the sharing of the basic concept of being a sexual human being.

Anderson perhaps best summarizes the importance of the handicapped who suffer from paralysis. "Absence of sensation does not mean absence of feeling. Inability to move does not mean inability to please. The presence of deformity does not mean the absence of desire, and the inability to perform does not mean inability to enjoy." [17]

### The Mentally Retarded

The sex education of the retarded should not begin with a dramatic description of the dangers of sex. Rather it should convey the beauty and self-fulfillment associated with one's own sexuality.

According to Fisher, [18] most mentally retarded are capable of learning the concepts of time and place and of confining their sexual activity to times and places in which they are not likely to run afoul of punitive persons or the law. Much of the sex education of the mentally retarded involves learning appropriate versus inappropriate behavior and/or basic public versus private behaviors which help them in their decision-making processes. This could range from meeting people and initiating conversation to knowing the basic differences between girls' and boys' anatomy.

Sol Gordon believes that the following basic principles regarding acceptable or unacceptable behavior must be emphasized to retarded individuals:

1. Masturbation is a normal expression of sex, regardless of how frequently it is done and at what age. It becomes a compulsive, punitive, self-destructive behavior largely as a result of guilt, suppression, and punishment.
2. All direct sexual behavior involving the genitals should be done in privacy.
3. Any time physically-mature people have sexual relations, they risk pregnancy.
4. Unless they are clear about wanting to have a baby and about the responsibility that goes with child rearing, both the male and female should use birth control.
5. Until you are, say, 18, society feels you should not have intercourse. After this, you decide for yourself, providing you use birth control.
6. Adults should not be able to use children sexually.
7. In the final analysis, sexual behavior between consenting adults (regardless of mental age and whether it is homo or hetero) should be no one else's business — providing there is little risk of bringing a child into this world. [19]

> **". . . the important point is not the physical placement of the handicapped into the normal classroom; it is the provision of skills to interact with normal children and to function in society."**

The mentally retarded are not exceptional in their sexual drives. Johnson describes the dilemma of the mentally retarded.

The mentally retarded do indeed tend to be mentally retarded with respect to sex education, and this is one of the characteristics that they share most fully with the brilliant and so-called normal. Nearly all of us are ignorant about sex; and many intelligent people are not even educable or trainable in this respect. Unfortunately, some of these sexually-uneducable people are supposed to instruct or otherwise manage the lives of the retarded concerning sex. [20]

Turchin's [21] research indicated that mothers of mentally retarded children wanted sex education taught in the schools, and they also desired the formation of parent groups to aid them in understanding the sexuality of their children. The parents felt ineffective in dealing with their children's sexuality and were confident that teachers were more qualified to give sex education to mentally retarded children than were parents, doctors, or social workers.

One of the major goals of sex education is to help parents reduce the negative connotations associated with the mentally retarded and help their children experience appropriate behavior at appropriate times regarding their own sexuality.

### EDUCATIONAL IMPLICATIONS

In attempting to establish an educational program in sexuality for handicapped individuals, it is imperative that one understand the overall needs of the students. One basic need is the ability to make decisions about self-image, responsibility, interpersonal relationships, possibly marriage, and how to express one's sexuality in a positive manner. This requires honest and comprehensive information that will help them decide which behavior is appropriate and acceptable in various situations.

Selznick [22] states that this process will help handicapped people develop attitudes, ideals, and behaviors enabling them to live wholesomely and effectively as individuals, as members of families, and as citizens of the community. To do this, educational programs must include the physical, mental-emotional, and social aspects which influence one's sexuality.

> **"There is a definite need to establish the goals and objectives of our sexuality programs and define parameters and limitations."**

Our profession must be cautious, however, in establishing sex education programs for various individuals with handicapping conditions. Scientific research in the area of sexuality is just beginning. Overall, there is a lack of empirical, scientifically-based information on the effectiveness of sex education. There is a definite need to establish the goals and objectives of our sexuality programs and define parameters and limitations. Likewise, a built-in assessment plan to show the validity and effectiveness of the program to parents and the community is imperative.

Precautions should be taken regarding the initial establishment of a sex education program. This implies recognizing the needs and feelings of the students, avoiding generalizations, knowing the group that one is working with, and not assuming that all handicapped persons need help regarding their sexuality. Each child is a unique individual, and all handicapped children obviously should not be exposed to the same sex education curriculum.

In implementing a sex education curriculum that includes handicapped children, the initial objective is to help other class members accept the handicapped as individuals who are more like than different from other members of the class, and to encourage participation in regular group activities.

---

**"We cannot afford to be naive about sex and the handicapped if we hope they will eventually become independent, functional members of the community."**

---

The actual implementation of an effective program that will help individuals feel at ease with their own sexuality and responsible for decision-making processes requires several factors. First is the need for competent teachers who are comfortable with their own sexuality and who understand the total meaning of sexuality. This competence comes from academic preparation and/or working with professionals in education who help teachers understand and meet the needs of special as well as overall class participants.

Second is the need for a sound curriculum that meets the needs of the students in the classroom. This includes a positive philosophy, educational guidelines and objectives, a means of evaluation, value clarification, and resource or educational materials. A curriculum which provides continuity and progression to meet the maturational levels of the students is essential.

Third, there is a need for a variety of teaching methodologies and materials. Different approaches are needed for different students. The task or information must be broken down, and the vernacular must be appropriate for comprehension to take place.

Fourth, parents must be included in the learning process. The need for the program must be justified, and parents should be helped to deal with and understand their own child's sexuality. Parents can be asked to help in educating their child about the positive aspects of sexuality. Likewise, it means providing the opportunity for parents to exclude their child from the program.

And finally, there is a need to have feedback from those involved in writing, teaching, and participating in the curriculum regarding revisions that are needed to make it more effective.

## CONCLUSION

Until society can accept the idea that the physically and mentally handicapped have the same educational rights as other children, we are on a hazardous avenue that can lead to the belief that only people without handicaps can become self-sufficient citizens. We cannot afford to be naive about sex and the handicapped if we hope they will eventually become independent, functional members of the community. As the literature indicates, the handicapped have the same sexual needs and desires as others; but a lack of exposure prevents them from obtaining the skills necessary to function in society.

There must be massive but cautious educational efforts — not only to instruct the handicapped, but also to share their feelings, to understand their fears, to give them assistance and materials, and to help them experience success regarding their own sexuality. Perhaps the 1970 Joint Commission on Mental Health of Children best summarizes our task:

Sex education should be included as one aspect of the comprehensive goals to deepen sensitivity to the emotional aspect of human interaction; it should be integrated with moral education as part of the total curriculum, not formalized as an isolated topic; factual information on sex should be integrated with health education aspects of the curriculum and with the consultation of parents. [23]

The task of teaching sexuality to the handicapped will not be an easy one. Our efforts must be carefully planned to meet specific objectives that will positively enhance the educability of our handicapped population. We will make mistakes, but our overall efforts to "life stream" the handicapped into our society can be achieved through competent programs.

The Education for All Handicapped Children Act of 1975 has opened the doors for parents and health professionals to put pressure on local, state, and federal programs to provide funds to develop sound sex education curricula. As professionals in health education, it is our challenge and responsibility to see that the sexual needs of the handicapped are not forgotten.

## 2. METHODOLOGY


### REFERENCES

1. Public Law 94-142: *The Educational for All Handicapped Children Act of 1975.*

2. Martin EW: Some thoughts on mainstreaming. *Excep Child* 41: 150-153, November 1974.

3. Holmes RV: A sex education program for the visually impaired in a residential school. *SIECUS Report* 4(5): May 3, 1976.

4. SIECUS Board of Directors: Position paper concerning sex and the handicapped. *SIECUS Report,* May 1974.

5. Gordon S: Missing in special education: sex. *J Spec Education* 5: 351-354, Winter 1971.

6. Johnson WR: *Sex Education and Counseling of Special Groups.* Springfield, IL, Charles C. Thomas, 1975.

7. Closer look: it's okay to be different. Report from *Closer Look* 1-3, Winter 1975.

8. Cole TM, Cole, SS: The handicapped and sexual health. *SIECUS Report* 4(5) 1-9, May 1976.

9. Enby G: *Let There Be Love; Sex and the Handicapped.* New York, Taplinger, 1975.

10. Gorham K, Des Jardins R, Page E, et al: The effect on the labeling of their children. In *Issues in the Classification of Children.* A Handbook on Categories, Labels, and their Consequences. Hobbs N (ed): San Francisco, Jossey-Boss, 1974.

11. Dockrell BW, Birzea C: Education of handicapped children, the social dimension. *Int R Educ* 20(3) 273-276, 1974.

12. Kirk S: *Educating Exceptional Children.* New York: Houghton-Mifflin, 1972.

13. Fitz-Gerald D, Fitz-Gerald M: Deaf people are sexual, too. *SIECUS Report* 6(2): 1-13, November 1977.

14. Grossman SK: *Sexual knowledge, attitudes and experiences of deaf college students.* Unpublished Master's Thesis, George Washington University, Washington, DC 1972.

15. Fitz-Gerald D, Fitz-Gerald M: Behind the times. *SIECUS Report* 6(2): 3-5, November 1977.

16. Trybus RJ, Karachmer, MA: School achievement scores of hearing impaired children: national data on achievement status and growth patterns. *American Annuals of the Deaf* 62-69, April 1977.

17. Anderson TP, Cole TM, Chilgren R: Sexual counseling of the physically disabled. *Post Grad Med* 117-123, July 1975.

18. Fischer HL, Krajieck MJ: Sexual development of the moderately retarded child. *Clin Pediatr* 13: 78-83, January 1974.

19. Gordon S: Okay, let's tell it like it is. *J Spec Educ* 5(4): 351-354, Winter 1971.

20. Johnson WR: Sex education of the mentally retarded. de la Cruz FF, LaVeck GD (ed): *Human Sexuality and the Mentally Retarded.* New York, Brummer-Mazel 1973.

21. Turchin G: Sex attitudes of mothers of retarded children. *J Sch Heath* 44 (9): 490-492, November 1974.

22. Selznick H: Sex education and the mentally retarded. *Excep Child* 640-643, May 1966.

23. Joint Commission on Mental Health of Children. *Crisis in Child Mental Health: Challenge for the 1970's.* New York, Harper & Row, 1973.



*Warren L. McNab, PhD, FASHA, is Assistant Professor of Health Education, University of Houston, 3801 Cullen Boulevard, Houston, TX 77004.*

**by Scout Lee Gunn and Carol Ann Peterson**

*Scout Lee Gunn is coordinator of therapeutic recreation for the Department of Leisure Studies at the Uiversity of Illinois. Carol Ann Peterson is a therapeutic recreation specialist for that university's Office of Recreation and Park Resources.*

# therapy and leisure education

*Leisure education extends far beyond the public school classroom into any setting in which learning leisure skills, values, and attitudes is important.  Leisure education must be considered a part of the total continuum of therapeutic recreation services.*

MARYLAND-NATIONAL CAPITAL PARKS AND PLANNING COMMISSION PHOTO BY KAREN LITTMAN

Therapy and Leisure Education, Scout Lee Gunn and Carol Ann Peterson, *Parks and Recreation,* Vol. 12, No. 11, November, 1977. ©1977 National Recreation and Park Association, 1601 North Kent Street, Arlington, Virginia 22209.

# 2. METHODOLOGY

EMERGING as a dominant focus of therapeutic recreation is the concept of leisure education for the handicapped. Though not actively implemented, education for leisure has long been conceptualized and supported in educational philosophy.

In a paper entitled ''What Knowledge Is of Most Worth,'' Herbert Spencer in 1860 cited as being significant ''miscellaneous activities which make up the leisure part of life devoted to the gratification of tastes and feeling.''

In 1918, the Commission on the Reorganization of Secondary Education identified ''worthy use of leisure'' as one of the seven ''Cardinal Principles of Education.''

In its list of ''Imperative Educational Needs of Youth,'' developed in 1944, the Educational Policies Commission included ''Good health and physical fitness, . . . opportunities to develop capacities to appreciate beauty in literature, art, music, and nature, . . . and ability to use leisure time well and budget it wisely, balancing activities that yield satisfactions with those that are socially useful.''[1]

In 1961, the Educational Policies Commission stated in the document *The Central Purpose of American Education*, ''The worthy use of leisure is related to the individual's knowledge, understanding, and capacity to choose, from among all the activities to which his time can be devoted, those which contribute to the achievement of his purposes and to the satisfaction of his needs. On these bases, the individual can become aware of the external pressures which compete for his attention, moderate the influence of those pressures, and make wise choices for himself.''[2]

In 1969, the American Association of School Administrators stated, ''As educators, we believe: that schools have opportunities for awakening in the minds of young people an awareness of the importance of leisure time and for cultivating values, habits, and practices that will lead them to effective use of leisure time.''[3]

Within the last few years leisure service professionals have joined with educational philosophers in purporting education for leisure. In a 1976 report, Hugh Brooks wrote:

''Within the past eighteen months, inauguration of The National Leisure Education Conference and the funding of the Leisure Education Advancement Project of the National Recreation and Park Association have given testimony to the concern of leisure specialists that education shall prepare students for more than just classroom and occupational calisthenics. Leisure specialists are saying that education, if it addresses itself to the totality of the human experience, can provide a framework on which time, activities, and attitudes may be manipulated so as to allow each individual to develop his/her full potential.''[4]

In her keynote address at the 1976 National Leisure Education Conference, Jean Mundy stated, ''With the changes occurring in our society in terms of more nonwork years than work years and even during our working lifetimes having more nonwork hours than work hours, education for leisure must become a major concern to which the leisure services profession and the American educational system in particular, should not only respond, but take action-oriented, futuristic leadership positions in jointly initiating and implementing.''[5]

The need for leisure education for the handicapped is even more critical. According to Jean R. Tague and Fred Humphrey:

> When an individual is ill or handicapped, the problem of leisure is compounded. Behavioral impairments, functional loss or social barriers have frequently caused limited exposure or participation in leisure experiences. The majority of handicapped individuals have an even greater abundance of free time than the average American and many are confined to institutional settings. The need for leisure education is imperative if these individuals are to reach their potential in independent living and thus achieve for themselves, as individuals, a meaningful and purposeful life.[6]

The inclusion of leisure education services as a component of total education has received strong support through the passage of Public Law 94-142, the purpose of which is to ''assure that all handicapped children have available to them . . . a free, appropriate public education which emphasizes special education and related services (including recreation) designed to meet their unique needs.''[7]

Though recent efforts have focused predominantly on the inclusion of leisure education within the structure of the public school system, it need not be assumed that leisure education is strictly a phenomenon of public education. To the therapeutic recreation professional, leisure education is and has been an integral part of recreation services in community and institutional settings.

Perhaps in the past leisure education did not demand the respect from recreation professionals that now seems apparent, due to the misconception that confined the phenomenon to the classroom. However, it is now accepted that leisure education extends far beyond the classroom into any setting in which learning leisure skills, values, and attitudes is important. Leisure education must be considered a part of the total continuum of therapeutic recreation services.

The three major components of therapeutic recreation services focus on therapy, education, and recreation (Figure 1).

The long-range goal of all therapeutic recreation services is to enable handicapped individuals to engage as independently as possible in meaningful socio-leisure life-styles.

In order to achieve independent, meaningful leisure functioning, some individuals must first acquire the basic functional skills of relating, communicating, associating, moving, and so on. Having acquired these skills through treatment, the individual is ready for leisure education.

The accompanying model portrays the basic content of any leisure education program for the handicapped regardless of the setting in which the service is rendered (Figure 2).

The purpose of leisure education is to enable the individual to acquire meaningful leisure skills and attitudes. The following components identify the four major content areas inherent in the leisure education process: (1) developing awareness of leisure values and attitudes, (2) developing social interaction skills, (3) developing leisure activity skills,

**Figure 1.**

COMPONENTS OF THERAPEUTIC RECREATION SERVICES

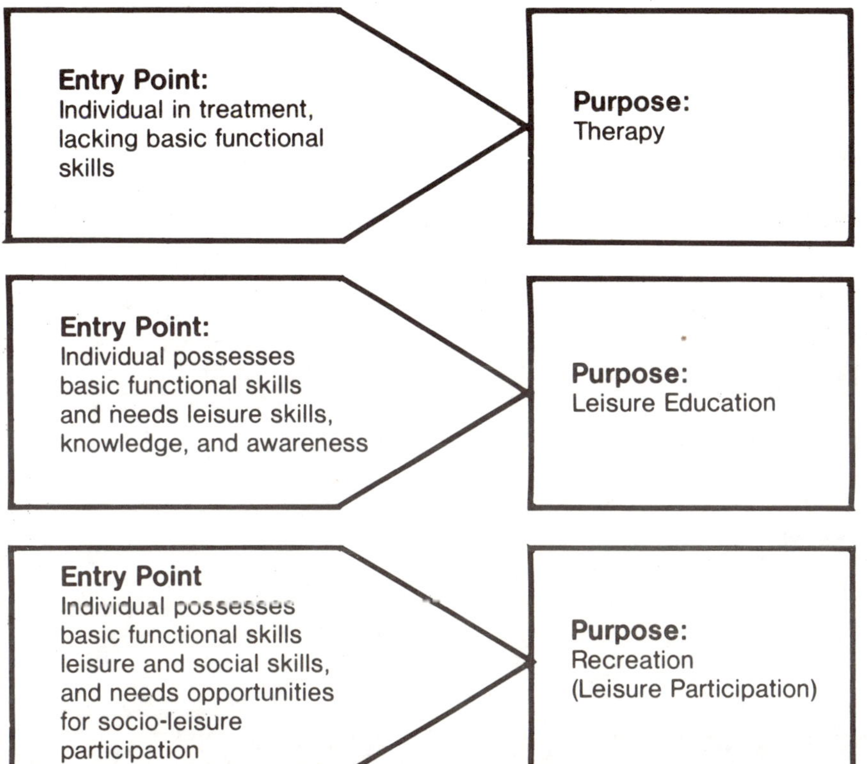



and (4) developing knowledge of leisure resources.

**Developing Awareness of Leisure Attitudes and Values.** Before individuals can successfully engage in meaningful leisure, they must first develop an understanding of the concept of leisure, and an awareness of personal attitudes and values regarding leisure and play behavior. They must become aware of their own play behavior and the process by which they make decisions regarding their leisure.

Reaching such understandings requires that certain questions be addressed, such as: What is leisure? What is the significance of leisure? How does leisure relate to me—my health and functioning? How do I feel about play? How do I keep myself from playing? What do I value most about play and leisure? How do I feel when I'm playing? What abilities and skills do I have? What limitations do I have? How

can I acquire playfulness—leisure abilities and skills? What problems do I have in play?

Developing an awareness of leisure attitudes and values is predominantly cognitive and utilizes skills of *leisure counseling*. All counseling basically deals with perceived problems and utilizes verbal facilitation techniques in the helping relationship.

Leisure counseling can therefore be defined as a process utilizing verbal facilitation techniques to promote self-awareness, awareness of leisure attitudes, values, and feelings, and the development of decision-making and problem-solving skills related to leisure participation.

Leisure counseling is the facilitation process used to develop awareness of leisure attitudes and values. This component of leisure education is usually followed by decision making and instructions or experiences

intended to facilitate play behavior.

**Developing Social Interaction Skills.** Most people play in a social context with friends, lovers, peers, and other groups. Meaningful leisure involvement therefore requires that players learn social interaction skills. Often overlooked is the importance of teaching individual ways of interacting in dyads, small groups, and large groups, either cooperatively or competitively.

Social interactional skills can easily be acquired through activity involvement. Inherent in activity participation are immediate opportunities for feedback and the availability of positive role models. Socially appropriate behavior can be immediately reinforced and problematic behavior can be dealt with on the spot. Again, leisure counseling techniques can be helpful in dealing with problematic behaviors, attitudes, and feelings.

**Developing Leisure Activity Skills.** Teaching specific activity skills appropriate to the interest, age, need, and limitation of the participant has long been a function of the therapeutic recreation professional. Unfortunately, it has sometimes been done in isolation, ignoring the need for the other major components of total leisure education. Only to the extent that the participant understands himself or herself at play and feels confident in the resulting social interactions, can he or she truly enjoy leisure activities.

Any attempt to successfully categorize the multiplicity of activities available to participants results in argument. The following list is therefore offered only as a generic guide to developing leisure activity categories: sports, aquatics, outdoor activities, fitness, expressive arts, home and family activities, mental activities, community service activities, appreciation activities, and spontaneous play activities.

**Developing Knowledge of Leisure Resources.** This component of leisure education is predominantly cognitive and purports to teach participants to identify, locate, and utilize available resources and leisure opportunities.

Assisting the handicapped individual in developing awareness of leisure attitudes and values, social in-

# 2. METHODOLOGY

KAREN LITTMAN PHOTO

## Figure 2.

### LEISURE EDUCATION CONTENT MODEL



teraction skills, and activity skills is not enough. In the total leisure education process the individual must be directed to available resources that he or she can use independently, including available activity opportunities, personal resources, family and home resources, community resources, and state and national resources.

When the individual has developed an awareness of leisure attitudes and values, social interaction skills, leisure activity skills, and knowledge of leisure resources, he or she is equipped to exercise independent choice in ongoing leisure pursuits.

For some, independent leisure involvement may continue to require a protective environment, offering assistance, supervision, and adaptation. For others, the world of leisure opportunities will be totally opened.

In either event, the leisure education process will have assisted the individual in understanding and evaluating his or her own leisure behavior in relation to personal goals for self-fulfillment.

FOOTNOTES

1. Ira G. Shapiro, "A Rationale as Revealed in Education Literature," *Leisure Today,* American Association for Leisure and Recreation, American Alliance for Health, Physical Education and Recreation, Washington, D.C., 1976, p. 5.
2. Linda L. Odum and Roger Lancaster, "Leisure Education Advancement Project: Rationale II," preliminary draft and unpublished paper, January 28, 1976, p. 2.
3. Ibid.
4. Hugh Brooks, "Leisure Education: The Practical Process," unpublished paper, National Leisure Education Conference, New York City, February 1976, p. 1.
5. Jean Mundy, "Leisure Education: Current and Future Perspectives," keynote address, National Leisure Education Conference, New York City, February 1976.
6. Jean R. Tague and Fred Humphrey, "Leisure Education/Leisure Counseling: A Continuum in Therapeutic Recreation Services," unpublished paper, National Leisure Education Conference, New York City, February 1976, p. 1.
7. Public Law 94-142, 94th Congress, S.6, November 29, 1975, p. 3.

# Critical Issues in Career Education for Handicapped Students

DONN E. BROLIN
BRUNO J. D' ALONZO

Abstract: This article discusses the career education concept and its need, significant events, critical issues, and recommendations to make it a viable educational thrust for handicapped students. The authors contend that career education should encompass the knowledges, skills, and attitudes needed for the various life roles and settings that comprise an individual's life, including employment. This will require curriculum efforts to be more extensively directed toward teaching daily living, personal-social, and occupational competencies, as well as basic subject skills. Career education includes the academic/work study curriculum design, but it goes one more step by requiring all teachers to relate their subject matter to its career implications. In addition, it requires a shared responsibility and cooperative relationship among all school disciplines and substantial involvement of parents and community agencies and industries in all phases of education.

DONN E. BROLIN is Professor of Education, Department of Counseling and Personnel Services, University of Missouri-Columbia; and BRUNO J. D'ALONZO is Associate Professor, Department of Special Education, Arizona State University, Tempe.

CAREER education was formally introduced at the national level in 1971 by former US Commissioner of Education Sidney Marland, because of what he and many other education leaders considered a pervasive lack of curriculum relevance for a great majority of youth, including handicapped and deprived individuals (Marland, 1971). Since that time, many efforts have been made by federal, state, and local educators to conceptualize and implement career education in schools throughout this country. Some individuals and groups have endorsed the concept wholeheartedly, others have taken a wait and see attitude, and still others have resisted changing their educational orientation and practices.

These differences of opinion concerning the nature and structure of career education are substantial. They result in part from the different perspectives individuals and groups have about human growth and development and their social institutions (Gysbers & West, 1975). These differences form the basis for a number of critical issues in career education that must be resolved if its full potential is to be realized and if handicapped students are to receive the type of career preparation needed for successful living and working in today's complex and rapidly changing society.

This article will discuss the need for career education for handicapped individuals; significant events that have occurred in recent years to meet the need; critical issues that exist and that must be resolved before career education can be fully realized; and recommendations for solving the issues and meeting the career education needs of handicapped citizens.

Reprinted from *Exceptional Children* by Donn E. Brolin and Bruno J. D'Alonzo by permission of The Council for Exceptional Children. ©1979 The Council for Exceptional Children, 1920 Association Drive, Reston, Virginia 22091.

## 2. METHODOLOGY

### The Need for Career Education

The career development of handicapped students has been an area of concern among many special educators for a great number of years. In the 1950's and 1960's work-study programs were initiated in many schools because it was apparent that academically oriented curricula were not adequately meeting the vocational and community adjustment needs of most handicapped students leaving the school system. For example, research on the community adjustment of educable retarded students (Brolin, 1972; Brolin, Durand, Kromer, & Muller, 1975; Tobias, 1970) revealed that a majority had major problems after leaving the school. However, a number of other studies (Brolin et al., 1975; Chaffin, Davison, Regan, & Spellman 1971; Halpern, Raffeld, & Littman, 1972; Kidd, Cross, & Higginbotham, 1967; Kokaska, 1968; Strickland & Arrell, 1967) revealed that vocational adjustment improved markedly if handicapped students were provided with a more occupationally oriented program.

Followup studies of the adjustment of handicapped students have found that personal-social and daily living skills are also inextricably related to the vocational success of these individuals (e.g., Beedy, 1971; Burger, Collins, & Doherty, 1970; Kolstoe, 1961; Sali & Amir, 1971; Stephens & Peck, 1968). These studies have revealed that personality characteristics, social skills, and management of daily living affairs are critical to vocational and community adjustment. Brolin and Thomas (1972) found that secondary special education teachers felt that more attention should be given to occupational instruction and less to academic skills, that more involvement by other school personnel was necessary, and that such competencies as personal care, home management, social interactions, manual skills, home mechanics, transportation, and occupational skills are priority competencies for mildly retarded students to acquire.

In the last few years considerable national attention has been directed to the problems handicapped individuals are encountering in securing adequate vocational training and employment. Speaking at the annual meeting of the President's Committee on Employment of the Handicapped, Viscardi (1976) reported that only 4 million of the 11 million handicapped adults capable of competitive employment are actually working. He cited education in the schools and postschool services as major reasons for the problems of the handicapped. Delegates at the 1977 White House Conference on Handicapped Individuals identified prevocational and vocational training programs, including counseling, placement, and exposure to different jobs, as the most important need for school age handicapped children. But, although vocational preparation is recognized as a major need of handicapped citizens, less than 2% of the estimated 10% handicapped school age population is served by vocational education (Stacts, 1976).

As the preceding discussion reflects, meeting the career development needs of handicapped individuals is still a major problem in this country. There obviously is a need to go beyond the academic and work-study approach that has characterized the 1960's and 1970's. The career education approach adds additional components that have been missing in educational efforts for these students.

### Responses to the Need for Career Education

A number of major significant events have occurred since the introduction of the career education concept in 1971. The US Office of Education's Bureau of Education for the Handicapped (BEH) has become interested in career education and has identified it as a major educational priority. In fact, BEH proclaimed that by 1977 every handicapped child who leaves school would have career education training relevant to the job market, meaningful to the child's career aspiration, and realistic to the child's fullest potential. Edwin Martin (1973), BEH Director, called for a redefinition of the basic educational programs for handicapped students, including the opportunity for career education experiences. In 1975 BEH sponsored a special Conference on Research Needs Related to Career Education for the Handicapped to help guide them in determining funding priorities for special research and demonstration projects that are submitted to their agency.

Second, an Office of Career Education was established in the US Office of Education in 1974. This office, under the direction of Kenneth Hoyt, has assumed leadership in promoting the career education concept and has funded several projects relative to developing effective methods and techniques for handicapped students. The agency has released several monographs on career education and has been extensively involved in conducting a large number of miniconferences with business and industry leaders as well as with professional associations and organizations such as The Council for Exceptional Children.

Third, recent legislation has provided impetus to the career education concept. The Rehabilitation Act of 1973, the Education for All Handicapped Children Act of 1975, and the Vocational Education Amendments of 1976 have resulted in a movement toward more cooperative efforts among vocational education, special education, and vocational rehabilitation. In 1977 BEH and the Rehabilitation Services Administration (RSA) formed a joint work group to specify guidelines on how school districts can better coordinate services to handicapped children under the three pieces of legislation.

Fourth, new divisions within the American Vocational Association (AVA) and The Council for Exceptional Children (CEC) have been established to focus on the career development needs of exceptional individuals. AVA formed a National Association of Vocational Education Special Needs Personnel (NAVESNP) in 1975, which has over 1,000 members from vocational education, special education, and other types of disciplines. The CEC Division on Career development (DCD) was formed in 1976 and has almost 1,000 members with the goal of promoting the career education concept within CEC and other related organizations. These two organizations reflect the high degree of interest and concern that is mounting for the career education concept.

Fifth, a number of career education instructional materials have been developed through the efforts of federal, state, and local projects, agencies, and commercial publishers. Several excellent sources of information such as The Educational Products Information Exchange (EPIE, 1975) Career Education Selection and Evaluation Tools, the ERIC Clearinghouse on Career Education at the Ohio State University, and the ERIC Clearinghouse on Handicapped and Gifted Children at CEC are now available to meet this need.

Sixth, several major conferences and workshops have been conducted on career education for handicapped individuals. In 1973 CEC and AVA cosponsored a National Topical Conference on Career Education for Exceptional Children and Youth. In 1975 BEH sponsored the Conference on Research Needs mentioned previously. In 1976 and 1977 the University of Illinois and the University of Kentucky sponsored national workshops for vocational and special educators relative to implementing career/vocational education in university and local programs. Through the Project RETOOL grant at the University of Alabama, the University of Kansas developed a five state Midwestern Consortium to train university faculty and others in career education concepts. And, in February 1979, CEC will sponsor a major National Topical Conference and Training Institutes on Career Education for Exceptional Individuals in St. Louis. Many state and local workshops on career education are also being conducted throughout the country.

Seventh, new scientific inventions and breakthroughs are now making it possible for handicapped individuals to be more mobile and to interact and communicate more effectively within their environment. Some examples of new technology include the following:

- A light sensor attached to a garment-snap machine assists a blind operator by emitting a squeal when the hole and the snap have been aligned.
- Deaf and hearing impaired individuals may now converse through the printed word with teletypewriters or through the use of small portable communication modules, a hearing aid adapter, a volume control handset, or an artificial larynx.
- Reading machines and low vision aids for blind and visually impaired individuals magnify the printed word or convert the printed word to a tactual form. Accessories such as typewriter, calculator, and computer attachments enable a blind typist or programmer to read what is being typed and type preprinted forms.
- Electronic aids assist handicapped individuals to manipulate and function within their environment through various switches activated by movement of body parts or by mouth operated suction or pressure. Tape recording, typing, using the telephone, turning pages of printed materials, or opening door locks enable handicapped individuals to function more independently.
- A brace developed for quadriplegic individuals is electrically controlled by a tongue operated switch. It provides finger, wrist, elbow, and shoulder motion and can be used to control an electrically powered wheelchair.
- Power assisted wheelchairs and vehicles to accommodate wheelchairs are available. Special controls are used to operate the vehicle and enable handicapped individuals to function more independently (Carmel & Renzullo, 1977).
- Computers with capacity to store, instantaneously retrieve, and update masses of data related to public and proprietary schools and 21,741 occupations identified in the *Dictionary of Occupational Titles* provide feedback, review, and personalized assistance to counselors or handicapped individuals (Harris & Tiedeman, 1974).
- Computer involved career guidance systems have been developed, such as The Guidance Information System (GIS), The Oregon Information Access System (OIAS), The Computerized Vocational Information System (CVIS), The System for Interactive Guidance and Information (SIGI), and Project Discover.

Unquestionably, many significant events have occurred in the last several years to make

# 2. METHODOLOGY

career education a viable reality in American education. However, as the career education movement goes forward, there are a number of issues that need to be resolved. These issues relate to the nature, purposes, and structure of career education.

## Critical Issues in Career Education for the Handicapped

The following are some of the major issues that need to be resolved if career education is to be effectively implemented and conducted in American schools.

One issue relates to the nature of career education. Should it be primarily job centered or life centered? When the official US Office of Education definition was released in 1975 (Hoyt, 1975), career education was defined as "the totality of experiences through which one learns about and prepares to engage in *work* as part of her or his way of living" (p. 4, emphasis added). Many people interpreted this definition as a focus on job preparation, even though *unpaid work* (volunteerism, homemaking, and productive leisure and recreational time) was considered as part of one's productive work life. But the prime emphasis of this definition was preparation for paid employment.

Other definers of career education have taken a more expanded view of career education (e.g., Gysbers & Moore, 1975; Hansen, 1977; Super, 1976). They believe one's career is multifaceted and consists of many different roles: occupational, social, leisure, and interpersonal. They believe a job is only one part of an individual's career. Goldhammer (1972) identified several "life careers" in which individuals engage as members of society: "1) producer of goods and renderer of services; 2) member of a family group; 3) participant in social and political life; 4) participant in avocational pursuits; and 5) participant in the regulatory functions involved in aesthetic, moral and religious concerns" (p. 129).

In a more recent publication, Hoyt (1977) defined career education as "an effort aimed at refocusing American education and the actions of the broader community in ways that will help individuals acquire and utilize the knowledge, skills, and attitudes necessary for each to make a meaningful, productive, and satisfying part of his or her way of living" (p. 5). In this publication he defined *work* as paid employment for some and for others the productive use of leisure time, volunteerism, or homemaking. Thus, it appears that Hoyt's position, though still emphasizing paid employment, recognizes more clearly the other roles that constitute one's total career pattern.

It is time for consensus to be reached about a universal and operational definition of career education so that programs can be developed and conducted in a systematic manner. Otherwise, confusion will continue to exist in the profession regarding whether career education refers to vocational education, an expanded view of vocational education, or a more complete educational approach that focuses on all the various roles, settings, and events that comprise an individual's career. At the present time it is impossible to know what is meant when career education is discussed.

Whether career education is a separate program or whether it permeates the educational process is a second major issue. There appear to be many who believe that career education is a course that can be taught in one or two hours each day, with remaining time devoted to general and vocational education. The other position is that this perspective is too narrow and that career education concepts and materials are to be infused throughout the curriculum, requiring *all* school personnel to modify their courses so that career education concepts can be totally inculcated. These advocates believe that education cannot be divided into segments such as career education, health education, and aesthetic education. In addition, they believe that the counselors, parents, and community representatives must join forces with teachers to assist students in their personal and career development.

If career education is perceived as a separate program, then a narrow focus will occur in those schools that adopt this viewpoint. It obviously is much easier to develop a separate course of this nature than to attempt a wholesale infusion attempt, which permeates the entire curriculum and its courses. Most career education proponents, however, would not consider this an appropriate approach.

A third major issue concerns ultimate responsibility. Is the special education teacher still primarily responsible for the handicapped student? Many special education personnel will find it difficult to release this responsibility, and many general educators will probably not permit it. Most likely, special educators will need to continue assuming this responsibility, even though the career education approach advocates a shared responsibility among all school personnel. With the advent of the individualized education program (IEP), other school personnel and the child's parents have to collaborate in planning and monitoring each handicapped student's program. With other school personnel becoming more involved and responsible, the job of the special educator could be expanded to include other roles that have been neglected because of direct service responsibilities. The special educator needs to have a thorough knowledge of career education to assume this reponsibility.

Ideally, the responsibility for handicapped students should be the same as for all other students—everyone's. Whether this concept can be put into practice after so many years of abrogation remains to be seen. Both career education and mainstreaming may be too much for many school personnel to undertake, unless the special educator is available to assure that the curriculum and learning experiences of handicapped students are appropriate.

A fourth major issue relates to the mainstreaming movement. Does career education aid or abet the mainstreaming process? Many teachers fail to implement career education because they are concerned about individualized education programs and how they can accommodate handicapped students within their regular classes and services. They may not realize that implementing career education can enhance the assimilation and achievement of handicapped students in their classrooms. Since handicapped students often learn best by relating instructional material and information to the real world and hands-on experiences, career education can greatly enhance mainstreaming efforts.

Administrators and educators need to be apprised of the potential of career education for accommodating handicapped students in the mainstream. Although there is yet no definitive research that clearly supports this view, the present authors can only strongly suggest that it will.

What to do with former courses, materials, and teaching approaches is another issue. Is everything accomplished by teachers prior to career education worthless? The answer to such a question is an unequivocal no. Career education does not mean abandoning present practices and materials. Rather it requires adaptations to previous courses and experiences so that career awareness, exploration, decision making, and preparation can be appropriately provided for each student. It will also require a more democratic school environment that focuses attention on each student's personal development. But, it does not abandon basic education, citizenship, family responsibilities, and other important education objectives.

Career education does require school personnel to take a hard look at what they are doing and why. It will require modification of courses, elimination and addition of some materials, and new teaching approaches. But, it does not de-emphasize the fundamentals. It adds to the curriculum and seeks more relevance in the educational program.

A sixth major issue revolves around the important area of personnel preparation. How can career education become more acceptable to teacher educators so that its concepts are infused into university training programs? Not only do special education departments have to respond appropriately, but so do other college of education departments that train regular teachers, counselors, and administrators. If teacher training institutions are not responsive, new personnel entering the schools will be inadequately prepared to meet the career development needs of handicapped students. Inservice training is also a major area of need. What constitutes an effective inservice delivery system and approach? How can school personnel get enough release time when there are so many changes and priorities for educators to respond to today?

Much remains to be done in this area, although some universities are beginning to respond to the need for career education. But, many more universities must initiate programs and courses that are responsive to the needs of the field and the national scene if career education is to become a reality for handicapped citizens.

While several other pressing issues currently exist, few can reject the premise upon which career education is built. But, as with many new educational interventions, resistance and apathy continue. This is unfortunate because a considerable number of handicapped students suffer not only social and academic lag but also career development discontinuity. Unlike the average student who is enrolled in general or vocational programs, handicapped students are often excluded from programs because of their condition. The longer the interruption in career education and career development experience, the more critical will be the long range educational and occupational problems facing the student. Consequently, the development of an integrated program of career education for handicapped individuals must be viewed as an effective mechanism to accelerate the student's lagging program (D'Alonzo & Barrett, 1977).

## Conclusions and Recommendations

Career education is a total educational concept. It is not intended to replace present educational practices, as some seem to believe, but rather to help make all instructional material personally relevant by restructuring it around a career development theme. It encourages open communication among students, teachers, parents, and the community and provides for career awareness, exploration, decision making, and skills development at all ages and levels. Career education brings meaning to the curriculum by making individuals more aware of themselves, their potentials, and their educational needs. Every teacher can incorporate

# 2. METHODOLOGY

career education concepts into his or her classroom.

In the authors' opinion, the definition of career education should include the many roles and positions occupied by handicapped individuals during their lifetime. Career education can then be clearly distinguished from vocational education so that educational efforts can be directed to the important knowledges, skills, and attitudes students need for the various life roles and settings that comprise one's life, including paid work. For the majority of handicapped individuals paid employment will be a major part of their career, if they can receive the occupational guidance and preparation that will permit them to earn a living in a job commensurate with their potentials. For many other handicapped individuals paid employment will not necessarily be a major part of their career. These individuals will need to know how to function adequately in avocational, family, and civic pursuits in order to lead a satisfying, meaningful, and productive life. This in essence is their career. Thus, career education is for everyone, the focus depending on each individual's unique set of abilities, needs, and interests.

Second, we believe that career education is everyone's responsibility and that it must be infused throughout the school curriculum and in home and community settings. It is not the only education students should receive, but it should be a very significant and pervasive part of what is taught. Thus, we recommend that special educators actively seek to involve school and community resources to the greatest extent possible so that their students are provided with the least restrictive career development experiences. Because of the wide range of learning styles, ability levels, sensory motor development, and social-emotional development of handicapped students, career education experiences will need to be personalized and tailored to meet their special needs.

Third, we suggest that special educators not abandon too readily their responsibilities for the education of handicapped students. Although handicapped students are being integrated into regular classes, someone knowledgeable about handicapping conditions and educational needs must monitor each student's progress and special needs and recommend necessary changes. It may be more deleterious for students to be in a regular class where they learn nothing and become frustrated and depressed than in a special class where learning and personal development can occur.

Fourth, we recommend career education as the vehicle by which successful mainstreaming can take place. We suggest shifting from the traditional content oriented curriculum to one that is more process based. The development of skills needed in the outside world must be emphasized, in addition to the acquisition of information. We suggest a competency based curriculum approach with a greater emphasis on learning daily living, personal-social, and occupational skills; a partnership between school personnel, family, and community representatives; and incorporation of substantial career awareness, exploration, preparation, and placement experiences into curriculum design at all grade levels. Career education provides the opportunity to put it all together.

Fifth, we recommend that school districts develop systematic and comprehensive career education plans so that modification of courses, more appropriate materials, effective teaching strategies, and instructional responsibilities and commitments can be determined in an effective scope and sequence. This will require administrative support for the career education concept, extensive opportunity for faculty input, and sufficient funds and time to "retool."

Sixth, considerable changes in staff development training, both at the inservice and preservice levels, are needed. Local school districts must identify a cadre of inservice trainers who are familiar with career education methods and materials and can teach other faculty while they work together to develop career education plans for their schools. State and local administrators must convince universities to respond to the career education needs of handicapped students so that their graduates are prepared sufficiently with skills in this area. Trained personnel and support systems are badly needed. Inservice training programs must be given sufficient time for personnel to learn enough about career education and handicapped students to respond to their educational needs.

Career education adds a much needed dimension to the rejuvenation of educational services for handicapped individuals. Educators can no longer neglect the fact that a majority of handicapped individuals are not adjusting satisfactorily in employment and community living. Special education has responded many times to the changing needs of handicapped individuals as our society has grown more complex and demanding. The time has come again to redirect our efforts so that the total needs of these citizens are really fulfilled.

# handicap

By Ethel Huttar

*What happens when a special kind of teacher and a special kind of composer work together to prepare a class for mainstreaming? Why, just about anything*

Which came first, the music or the lyrics? Neither. It was a phone call from EARLY YEARS to Carmino Ravosa, one of EY's frequent contributors and a regular song writer for the "Captain Kangaroo" television show. EY's request: Would Carmino write a song on handicaps for their April issue?

Carmino wasn't quite sure how he'd go about it, but, luckily for all of us, he accepted the challenge. Before the receiver was even back in the cradle, his creative thought processes were ticking away. The idea of a cap . . . that's it. A real cap. A blind cap? A deaf cap? Caps to wear and do some roleplaying with?

The author teaches kindergarten at Fox Meadow Elementary School in Scarsdale, N.Y.

Quite used to Carmino's spontaneity, it came as no surprise when one day he came bursting into my kindergarten room. "I have an idea about a song," he said. "Put on a handicap and see just what it's like to be . . . blind, deaf, lame." More fast-flying thoughts: "What do you think of this? Do you think that will work? Will you try it out?" There's really only one answer to such enthusiasm: Of course!

Roleplaying what it would be like to have a handicap is a "natural" for five-year-olds. It fits their innate interests, curiosity and sensory exploration to a tee. And so our musician-kindergarten teacher was born. We

had one big plus going for us—we shared common goals: To create an awareness, understanding and appreciation of handicapped people; and, along the way, to develop some positive attitudes at early childhood age.

**Who Wears a Cap?** How does one go about introducing such a sensitive subject in the classroom? This was a problem easily solved by reading the class two storybooks: Dr. Seuss' *The Five Hundred Hats of Bartholomew Cubbins* (Vanguard Press, 424 Madison Ave., New York 10017) and Esphyr Slobodkina's *Caps for Sale* (Childrens Press, 1224 W. Van

Reprinted with permission of the publishers Allen Raymond, Inc., Darien, Conn. 06820. From the April 1978 issue of *Early Years*.

# 2. METHODOLOGY

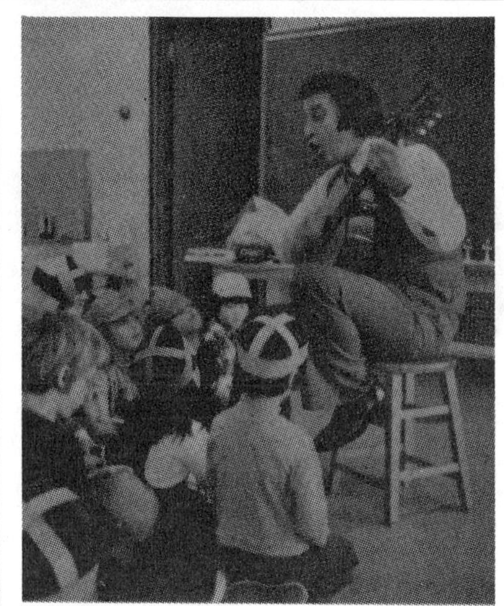

Buren St., Chicago 60607). Both tales are delightful and were a perfect way to launch our "Handicap" cap idea.

Since we wanted the children to start thinking, we asked, "What is a cap? How is it different from a hat? Who wears a cap?" The answers poured forth: kids, policemen, mailmen, painters and baseball players being just a few of the ones we got. While this was going on, the children were also involved in making their "Handicap" caps (see the accompanying diagram). The youngsters still didn't have an inkling about what Carmino and I were leading up to and their five-year-old curiosities were growing by leaps and bounds.

Finally, it was time to explain what we were doing. We named deafness, blindness, dumbness, lameness, physical deformity and mental retardation as the handicaps we'd be focusing on. Carmino's title song was introduced at this point, too. It immediately became our theme, as the kids "put on a handicap to see just what it's like to be . . . " (By the way, that's Carmino you see in the picture, strumming his guitar and singing along with the children.)

**Roleplaying.** Singing about handicaps, and talking about them, is a far cry from actually experiencing them—and we wanted the kindergartners to have an idea of what it was like to be handicapped. So we turned to roleplaying. For example, we simulated visual impairment by playing games of Blindman's Buff and by letting the children touch and describe a bag of objects while wearing an eye mask. Also, we had them make dark eyeglasses out of construction paper, colored cellophane and pipe cleaners.

To help the children understand what it would be like to have a hearing impairment, we played a lip-reading and body-actions-only variation of "Simon Says." We also showed filmstrips and TV programs without sound and followed them up with class discussions of what had been observed.

Since there are varying degrees of deafness, the children were instructed to put fingers in both ears, then a finger in one ear, then in the other ear. To culminate these activities, the children made "Finger Talk" booklets, using the same pictorial alphabet that the deaf use to spell words.

Physical impairments were simulated by staging three-legged races and by giving the children opportunities to walk with crutches and ride (or push another child) in a wheelchair. They engaged in a work project while wearing an arm sling. And to feel what it would be like to have uneven footing, they put a small, wooden building block in the heel of one of their boots or tied a block to the bottom of a shoe.

Other handicaps were more easily presented through books. Hans Christian Andersen's tales (especially "The Ugly Duckling") provided examples of physical deformities, while Harriet Sobol's *My Brother Steven Is Retarded* (Macmillan, 866 Third Ave., New York 10022) and Joan Fassler's *One Little Girl* (Human Sciences Press, 72 Fifth Ave., New York 10011) dealt with mental retardation. To familiarize the children with speech problems—and how they could be overcome—we read biographies of Helen Keller and even brought in a recording of Sir Winston Churchill (who stuttered and had a cleft palate) as an accomplished speaker.

**Hall of Fame.** Really, there are so many famous people who have made large contributions to society despite being handicapped. We talked about these people and, whenever possible, put poster pictures of them (or art reproductions of their work) on our classroom wall. Our Hall of Fame included pictures of Franklin D. Roosevelt (crippled legs), Thomas Edison (deaf) and Sir Winston Churchill (speech) and reproductions of paintings by Goya (deaf), Dufy (crippled hands) and Degas (blind during his later working years). We also let the children listen to a recording of music by Beethoven (deaf) and look at books of collected art works by Matisse (crippled hands).

While all of this is a natural subject to present to young children, it's not without certain difficulties. Actually, there are three main problems a teacher must deal with when presenting a unit on handicaps. First, the teacher must be prepared to reassure children who ask, "Could this happen to me?" Second, there's a need to guard the respectability of handicaps; it's easy enough for children to think of them as "funny" during simulation activities. Finally, there is a great deal of difficulty

involved in researching the topic and preparing lessons for proper presentation.

Since the commercial market is just beginning to supply usable materials on a young child's learning level, teachers must look elsewhere for help if they wish to achieve their goal. Our project, for example, involved a music teacher (with additional songs relating to feelings and self-image), school nurses, the librarian, an art teacher, a gym teacher, the principal (who had the newest bibliographical releases on the subject), public libraries, the Board of Cooperative Educa-

tional Services Library, the Lighthouse for the Blind, the School for the Deaf, hospital supply agencies, ambulance corps, occupational therapists and, above all, parents.

This, of course, is a lengthy resource list for any subject; and, needless to say, it meant a lot of running back and forth from one resource to another. But it was worth it. In the final analysis, it was an opportunity for us to help children understand a concept naturally, simply and comfortably on a subject that touches all mankind. Just being able to do that was its own reward.

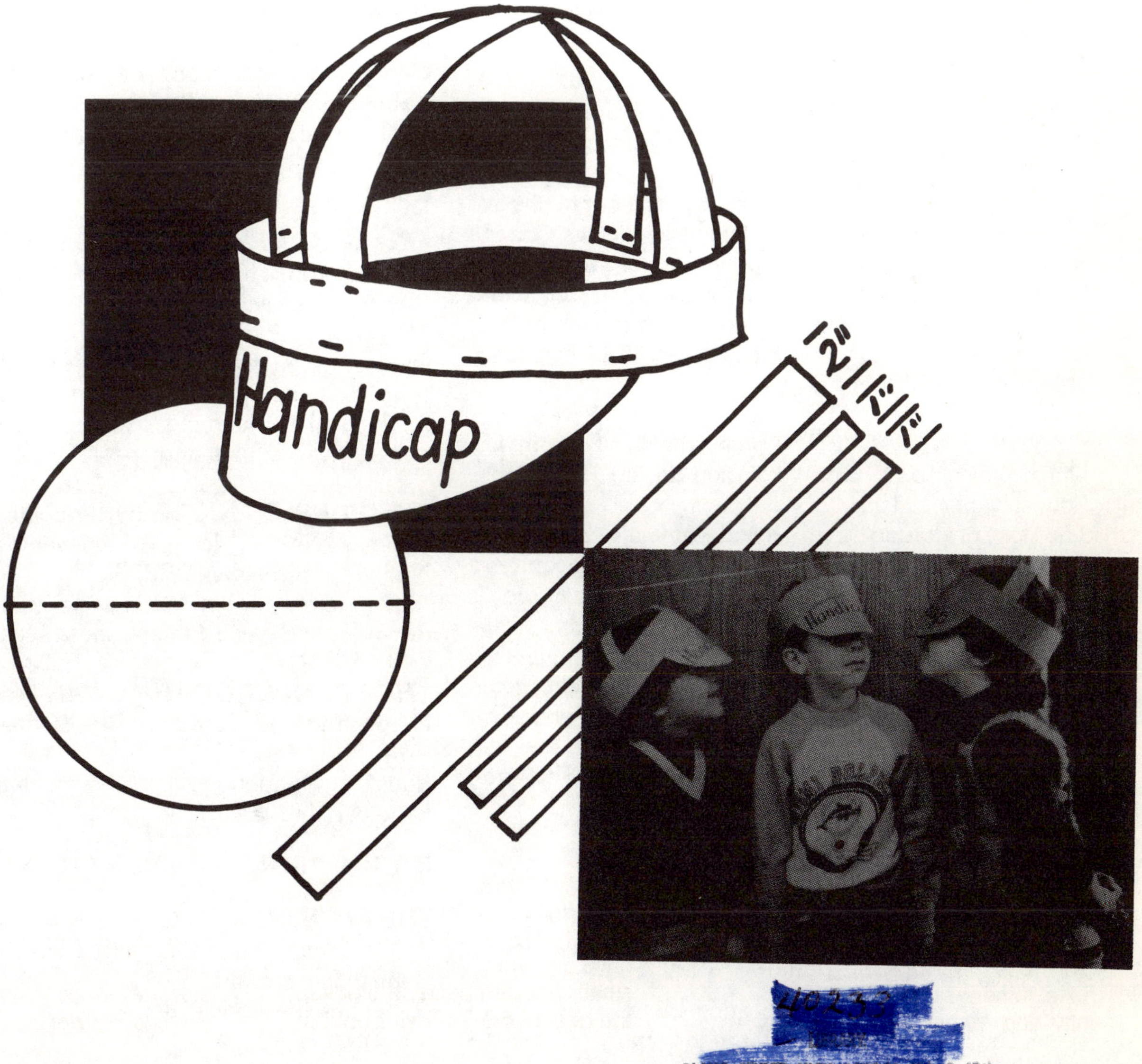

# FOCUS. . .

## CHILDREN'S LITERATURE: AN AID TO MAINSTREAMING

Books can help children understand handicaps. The following list can be used in two ways. First, it can be used with handicapped children to help them see that there are other children who have the same problems as they have. This can assist the children in understanding themselves and build a better self image.

Secondly, the books are useful for non-handicapped children in the regular classroom. They can introduce handicaps to the children who may soon have a handicapped child in class for the first time.

### BOOKS ABOUT BLINDNESS

*A BOWL OF SUN* by Frances Wosmek. From Children's Press, 1224 West Van Buren Street, Chicago, Illinois 60607.
A little girl, named Megan who is blind, and her family live together and are very happy. Her father decides to move so that Megan can attend a special school for the blind. Megan has difficulty adapting to her new environment and is befriended by a woman who teaches her to use a pottery wheel. Megan makes a bowl for her father and is eventually able to cope with her new life.

*CONNIE'S NEW EYES* by Bernard J. Wolf. From J.B. Lippincott Company, East Washington Square, Philadelphia, Pennsylvania 19105.
The story of Connie David, a blind woman from birth who is about to begin her teaching career. Connie acquires a seeing eye dog. The text describes how a seeing eye dog is raised and trained.

*FOLLOW MY LEADER* by James B. Garfield. From Viking Press, 625 Madison Avenue, New York, New York 10022.
A boy is accidentally blinded by firecrackers. The book describes how he adjusts to his now sightless world.

### BOOKS ABOUT DEAFNESS

*ANNA'S SILENT WORLD* by Bernard Wolf. From J.B. Lippincott Company, East Washington Square, Philadelphia, Pennsylvania 19105.
Anna, a girl with profound hearing loss, is now able to speak and understand others through therapy. Anna, as a result of this therapy, can go to a "regular" school with normal hearing children.

*CHILD OF THE SILENT NIGHT: THE STORY OF LAURA BRIDGMAN* by Edith F. Hunter. From Houghton Mifflin Company, 1 Beacon Street, Boston Massachusetts 02107.
The story of the life and accomplishments of Laura Bridgman who became a deaf-blind mute at the age of two. The story takes place in the 1800's.

*HANDTALK: AN ABC OF FINGER SPELLING AND SIGN LANGUAGE* by Remy Charlip, Mary Beth, and George Ancona. From Parents Magazine Press, 52 Vanderbilt Avenue, New York, New York 10017.
An illustrated book giving examples of finger spelling and sign language methods for several words and letters of the alphabet.

*LISA AND HER SOUNDLESS WORLD* by Edna S. Levine. From Human Sciences Press, 72 Fifth Avenue, New York, New York 10011.
The book, designed to help other children understand what it is to be deaf, deals with a deaf child who is outcast from the neighborhood children. After attending school for the deaf and learning to use a hearing aid, Lisa is finally able to hear sounds and speak.

*THE PURPLE MOUSE* by Elisabeth MacIntyre. From Thomas Nelson, Inc. 405 Seventh Avenue, South, Nashville, Tennessee 37203.
A story told by a deaf girl, it describes a teenage girl who discovers she has art talent and a sense of color.

*THE TRUMPET OF THE SWAN* by E.B. White. From Harper and Row, Publishers Inc., 10 East 53rd Street, New York, New York 10022.
Louis, a trumpeter swan who is mute, overcomes his handicap and leads a full life.

### BOOKS ABOUT THE MENTALLY HANDICAPPED

*THE BLUE ROSE* by Gerda Klein. From Lawrence Hill & Company, Inc., 24 Burr Farms Road, Westport, Connecticut 06880.
A look into the world of Jenny, a retarded child who is very unique.

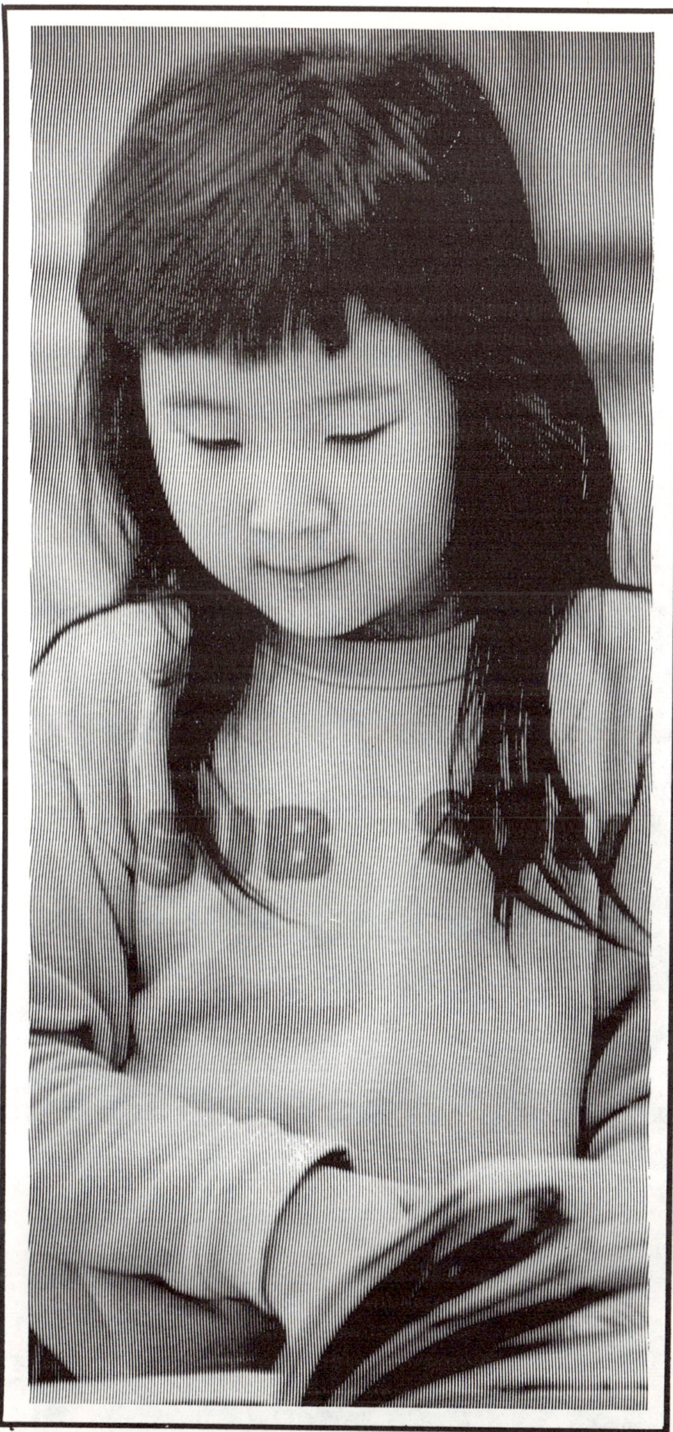

*ESCAPE THE RIVER* by Roy Brown. From Seabury Press, Inc., 815 Second Avenue, New York, New York 10017.
A 12-year old boy, upset when it is learned he is adopted, takes his retarded brother away from home and escapes down the river on a boat.

*LIKE ME* by Alan Brightman. From Little, Brown and Company, 34 Beacon Street, Boston, Massachusetts 02106. The thoughts of a retarded boy are examined. Fully illustrated, the book reveals how the boy feels about himself as compared to other children.

*TAKE WING* by Jean Little. From Little, Brown and Company, 34 Beacon Street, Boston, Massachusetts 02106. The book gives the example of a girl who cares for her retarded brother and helps to give a good feeling to him through love and caring.

## BOOKS ABOUT THE PHYSICALLY HANDICAPPED

*ABOUT HANDICAPS* by Sara Bonnet Stein. From Walker and Company, 1720 Fifth Avenue, New York, New York 10019.
This book describes the feelings of a little boy who has a disabled friend. The boy must sort out his feelings about this friend and dispell any imaginings which he has about handicaps. It is illustrated with photographs and is in easy to read type, making it useful for younger children.

*BEN AND ANNIE* by Joan Tate. From Doubleday and Company, Inc., 245 Park Avenue, New York, New York 10017.
A story about a boy and his handicapped neighbor who he befriends. He talks with her, plays with her and takes her places, until one day, he and some other friends, accidently roll her chair down a hill. The handicapped girl's family forbids her to play with her again. The girl is again lonely.

*DON'T FEEL SORRY FOR PAUL* by Bernard J. Wolf. From J.B. Lipponcott Company, E. Washington Square, Philadelphia, Pennsylvania 19105.
The story of a physically handicapped boy and his everyday life. It is illustrated and shows how the boy manages in school and the day to day living.

*HOWIE HELPS HIMSELF* by Joan Fassler. From Albert Whitman and Company, 560 West Lake Street, Chicago, Illinois 60606.
The description of a boy with cerebral palsy, confined to a wheel chair, and how he manages in life, at home and school. This boy finally achieves his greatest desire when he is able to push his own wheelchair.

## BOOKS ABOUT LEARNING DISABILITIES

*KEEP STOMPIN TILL THE MUSIC STOPS* by Stella Pevsner. From the Seabury Press, Somers, Connecticut 06071.
A book for older children, the story revolves around a boy who has a learning disability. It describes his feelings, compassion, and understanding and how these traits set an example for his fellow classmates.

*A RACECOURSE FOR ANDY* by Patricia Wrightson. From Harcourt Brace Jovanovich, Inc. 757 Third Avenue, New York, NY 10017.
The book describes the adventure of a slow learning boy and his friends.

photo: Office of Human Development Services, DHEW

# MENTALLY HANDICAPPED

Historically the definition of mental handicaps was based solely on I.Q. The category or label was determined by finding the number of standard deviations from the norm on a given I.Q. test. It is now common practice to assess the adaptive behavior, along with the I.Q., looking at the entire mental and physical framework of the child when testing for the possibility or severity of mental handicaps.

The opening article "What is Mental Retardation," examines the various methods of assessment and also explores the various issues surrounding this handicap. "Teaching the Invisible Retarded" then looks at the problems that exist in recognizing a mildly handicapped retarded child from his normal peers. Finally, it is noted that the definition for severely retardation is also a difficult task. This is shown in the article which is the result of a survey taken of state departments of education, many of which do not have a definition available.

The section concludes with several articles on preparing curriculum for the mildly and profoundly handicapped individual. The concluding article examines the role of the community in preparing a severely handicapped person for active participation in the community. It is suggested in this article that with help, the severely handicapped can and should become an asset to the community.

# WHAT IS MENTAL RETARDATION?

 What is Mental Retardation? President's Committee on Mental Retardation, *Mental Retardation: Past and Present*, 1977.

Mental retardation presents itself in so many forms, degrees, and conditions, from so many known and unknown causes, with so many questions unanswered, that it is difficult to say clearly: these are the people who are retarded and this is what they can do, and this what we can do for them, and this is how we can eliminate the problem.

To reach into the problem we have to know what it is.

To reach the people who have the problem we have to know who they are, how to understand them and how to help them.

## Who Are They?

Mental retardation refers to significantly subaverage general intellectual functioning existing concurrently with deficits in adaptive behavior, and manifested during the developmental period.

This is the formal definition published by the American Association on Mental Deficiency in 1973 and widely accepted today. It identifies mental retardation with subnormality in two behavioral dimensions—intelligence and social adaptation—occurring before age 18. The definition is a culmination of long debate and revision, and may well be modified in the future.

The severely retarded person has an obvious incapacity to exercise the expected controls of reason and of personal management necessary for normal living in any human culture. Left to himself, anyone so impaired cannot easily survive. The great majority of severely retarded individuals also have physical characteristics which suggest a central nervous system defect as the basis of the developmentally retarded behavior.

In many cases no detectable physical pathology accompanies the deficiency of intelligence and adaptation. The limited ability to learn, to reason and to use "common sense" is often unexplainable. Can undetected physical pathology be assumed?

Further questions arise when we discover that milder degrees of intellectual and adaptive deficit are commonly associated with particular families who have serious social and economic problems. Do poor living conditions produce mental retardation, or is it the reverse? Or does each condition compound the other? Still further, members of certain minority groups tend to be highly represented among those identified as having intellectual and adaptive problems, especially in the school-age years. Is such overrepresentation of certain groups a product of racial inferiority or of racial and ethnic discrimination and disadvantage?

For a long time, mental retardation (or its earlier terms idiocy, feeblemindedness and the like), was thought to have much in common with insanity, epilepsy, pauperism and social depravity, all of which were lumped together. And so, a concept of mental deficiency in terms of social deviance developed.

Then, as knowledge advanced, retardation was identified with congenital brain defect or damage, and assigned to heredity. This approach led to redefining mental deficiency in medical terms as an organic defect producing inadequate behavior. Mild forms of intellectual "weakness" became associated with forms of immoral behavior and social disturbance (the "moral imbecile"), and ascribed to more subtle defects of inherited character. Legal definitions in terms of social behavior began to appear.

During the 19th and early 20th century what we now call "mild" retardation was not recognized except as associated with disturbed or delinquent behavior. There was no simple way of diagnosing the more mild or incipient forms of mental retardation until the development of psychometrics around 1910. Then the "IQ" rapidly became a universal means, not only of identifying mental deficiency, but also of measuring its severity.

Goddard, in 1910, in applying the new techniques of Binet and Simon in the public schools, discovered there were ten times as many feebleminded as anyone had suspected, and promptly coined the term "moron" to cover them! Thus a psychometric definition of retardation came into being.

The intelligence test actually measured behavioral performance on tasks assumed to be characteristic of the growth of children's ability at successive ages, but it was interpreted as a measure of capacity for intellectual growth and therefore as a predictor of future mental status. It was assumed to represent an inherent and usually inherited condition of the brain with a fixed developmental potential.

Persistent debate over the nature and composition of intelligence finally led to an operational definition that it is "whatever an intelligence test measures." Since intelligence measurements are scalar, and degrees on the scale were found to correlate rather well with other clinical and social evidences of mental proficiency, low IQ became virtually the sole basis for a diagnosis of mental retardation and for its classification at levels of severity from "borderline" to "idiot."

This measurement was especially important in schools for which, in fact, the first tests were devised by Binet and Simon. IQ tests became the standard means of determining school eligibility and classification. Intelligence tests also were used extensively as sole evidence for determining legal competency and institutional commitment, as well as the subclassifications of institutional populations. The leading authorities, Tredgold, Goddard, Porteus, Penrose, Doll, Clarke and Clarke, all rejected a strictly psychometric definition, but it nevertheless became standard practice in diagnosis and classification.

In the meantime, research in twins, siblings and unrelated children had shown that general intelligence (i.e., measured IQ) is strongly inherited as a polygenic characteristic, following a normal Gaussian curve of frequency distribution in the general population. A slight negative skew was attributable to brain damage or genetic mutation. This deviation led to a theory of mental retardation which divided it into two major groups on the basis of presumed causation. One group consisted of the more severely deficient type with brain damage or gross genetic anomaly characterized by various physical abnormalities and IQ generally of 55 or less. The other group consisted of the lower portion of the negative tail on the normal curve of distribution of polygenic intelligence with IQ between 50 or 55 and 70 or 80 and not otherwise abnormal (Kanner, 1957, Zigler, 1967). This theory could explain the association of milder forms of low intelligence with low socio-economic

status and its concomitants. In other words, the less competent tend to sink to the bottom of the social scale in a competitive society. The issue of cultural bias was raised immediately, however, with respect to racial and ethnic groups who scored consistently lower on the standard tests.

Evidence began to accumulate which generated a variety of additional controversial issues. The "constancy of the IQ" was questioned on both statistical and experimental grounds. The pioneering work of Skeels, Skodak, Wellman, and others, in the 1930's (e.g., Skeels, et al., 1938) had indicated that measured intelligence as well as other observable behavior could be substantially modified by drastic changes in the social environment of young children. The quality of the infant's nurture was found to have enduring effects of intellectual functioning, especially in the absence of detectable brain pathology.

Follow-up studies of persons released from institutional care and of those who had been identified in school as retarded showed high rates of social adaptation, upward mobility and even substantial increases in measured intelligence in adult years (Cobb, 1972). Epidemiological studies have consistently shown a "disappearance" of mildly retarded persons in the adult years.

Explanations for these findings could be offered without abandoning previous assumptions: Improvement in low IQ scores over several repetitions simply exemplifies the statistical regression toward the mean, inherent in errors of measurement: those who improve with stimulation and environmental change were never "really" retarded, but exhibit "pseudo-retardation" which masks true capacity.

Eventually, evidence converged to show that measured intelligence is modifiable within limits, that it is not in any case a measure of fixed capacity, but of the continuity of a developing intellectual and social competence in which "nature" and "nurture" are inseparable components and individual "growth curves" may take a variety of forms and may be influenced by many factors.

A gradual trend developed toward the

definition of mental retardation in functional rather than in structural terms and not tied either to specific cause or to unchangeable status. There were those, however, who continued to find a dual view of retardation more credible than a single continuum.

The Stanford-Binet and similar measures of intelligence came to be recognized as primarily predictive of school performance of an academic or abstract nature requiring language skills, and less predictive of other non-verbal types of behavior. Consequently, the need developed to measure other dimensions of behavior. The Army "Beta" test of World War I anticipated this development. New tests, such as the Wechsler series, combined linguistic with non-linguistic performance or quantitative elements and yielded a "profile" of distinguishable mental traits. Factor analysis of measures of intellectual behavior had demonstrated that "intelligence" is not a single trait but a composite of many distinguishable functions.

The measurement of adaptive behavior presented even greater difficulty. Such measures as the Vineland Social Maturity Scale were extensively used but had only a limited validity. The Gesell Infant Development Scale, the Gunzburg Progress Assessment Chart, and subsequently, the AAMD Adaptive Behavior Scale all attempted to measure the non-intellectual dimensions of developmental adaptation but they lacked the precision and reliability of the intelligence measures. Consequently, there has been a continuing reliance, especially in the schools, on measures of IQ alone as the criterion for mental retardation. This practice is defended by some authorities as legitimate in the absence of better measures of adaptive behavior (Conley, 1973.)

In the meantime the issue of cultural bias became an increasingly serious problem. All measures of either intelligence or of adaptive behavior reflect social learning, hence tend to be culture-bound. Their validity, therefore, is dependent on the cultural population on which the norms have been standardized. No one has succeeded in developing a universally applicable "culture-free" test of behavior. Attempts to devise "culture-fair" tests which employ comparable but culturally different elements have as yet failed to yield valid bases of comparison.

Recent studies by Mercer (1973 and 1974) and others have shown the extent to which cultural bias affects the frequency with which members of minority cultures are labeled "retarded" and assigned to special education classes. This is especially true when only measures of IQ are used; representatives of lower socio-economic and of Black, Mexican-American, Puerto Rican, Indian and other ethnic groups are identified as retarded far out of proportion to their numbers in comparison with middle-class Anglo children. Social evaluations of such children show that a high proportion are not significantly impaired in their adaptation in non-school environments.

This discovery has led to a coining of the term "Six-Hour Retarded Child," meaning a child who is "retarded" during the hours in school, but otherwise functions adequately (PCMR: *The Six-Hour Retarded Child,* 1970).

Mercer has called such persons who are identified in one or two contexts but not in others the "situationally retarded," in contrast to the "comprehensively retarded," who are identified as such in all the contexts in which they are evaluated. "Situational retardation" occurs by far most frequently in school settings, and next most frequently in medical settings, and much less frequently in ratings by families or neighbors or in settings officially responsible for the comprehensively retarded. "We conclude," Mercer says, ". . . that the situational retardate is primarily the product of the labeling process in formal organizations in the community, especially the Public Schools" (Mercer, 1973).

The work of Mercer and others has led to litigation and legislative action, especially in California, limiting the use of IQ tests as the sole criterion for labeling and special class placement, on the ground that such practices systematically penalize minority groups and violate their rights to equal educational opportunity (Mercer, 1974).

## 3. MENTALLY HANDICAPPED

The present tendency is to accept the 1973 AAMD formulation by Grossman which requires *both* an IQ of less than 70 *and* substantial failure on a measure of adaptive behavior. The requirement of age of onset prior to 18 is more open to question and not always regarded as critical. The Grossman formulation differed from the AAMD definition of Heber (1961) principally in requiring a criterion of more than two standard deviations below the mean, rather than more than one s.d., as Heber had proposed. This was an extremely important difference because it excluded the "borderline" category which accounted for about 13% of the school age population!

Mental retardation, by any of the proposed criteria, occurs with varying degrees of severity. Many attempts were made in the past to classify differences of severity, usually on the basis of social adaptation or academic learning criteria. Social adaptation criteria distinguished borderline feebleminded, moron, imbecile and idiot. Academic Criteria distinguished slow learner, educable, trainable (with no term suggesting learning capability for the still lower category). Heber (1958) proposed using neutral terms to indicate standard deviation units on the continuum of the IQ and any other scales employed. This is continued in the Grossman (1973) AAMD system to categorize levels of intellectual functioning, thus:

| Level of Function | Upper S.D. Limit | Stanford Binet IQ/ (S.D. = 16) | Wechsler IQ (S.D. = 15) |
|---|---|---|---|
| Mild | − 2.0 | 67–52 | 69–55 |
| Moderate | − 3.0 | 51–36 | 54–40 |
| Severe | − 4.0 | 35–20 | 39–25 (extrap.) |
| Profound | − 5.0 | 19 and below | 24 and below (extrap.) |

Note that the borderline category (− 1.0 to − 2.0 s.d.) is not included under the definition.

Mercer has identified still another variable of a significant sociological nature. A majority of children who rated low on both IQ and adaptive measures by the Grossman criteria, and therefore technically "retarded," came from homes that did not conform to the prevailing cultural pattern of the community (socio-culturally nonmodal). This group appeared to be identified as retarded more because of cultural difference than because of inadequate developmental adaptation. Further evidence showed that members of this group who were identified as retarded children tended more than the socio-cultural modal group to "disappear" as identifiably retarded on leaving school.

Mental retardation, as an inclusive concept, is currently defined in *behavioral* terms involving these essential components: *intellectual functioning, adaptive behavior* and *age of onset*. The causes of retardation are irrelevant to the definition, whether they be organic, genetic, or environmental. What is indicated is that at a given time a person is unable to conform to the intellectual and adaptive expectations which society sets for an individual in relation to his peers. In this sense, mental retardation is a reflection of social perception aided by a variety of clinical and nonclinical techniques of identification.

Within this broad functional definition, the deficits indicated in a diagnosis of mental retardation may or may not be permanent and irreversible. They may or may not be responsive to intervention. They may persist only so long as the person remains in a culturally ambiguous situation, or at the other extreme, they may be of life-long duration. Or perhaps only their consequences may be ameliorated in greater or lesser degree, not the condition itself.

Consequently, it is difficult to estimate how frequently mental retardation occurs and how many retarded people there are.

### How Big Is the Problem?

The *incidence* of a disorder refers to the frequency of occurrence within a given period of time. For example, the incidence of smallpox in the United States might be expressed as the number of cases in a specific year per 100,000 population; the incidence of Down's syndrome might be expressed as the average number of cases per year per 1,000 live births. The purpose of determining incidence is to yield information as to the magnitude of the problem with a view to its prevention and to measure the success of preventive programs.

The *prevalence* of a disorder refers to the number of cases existing at a specified time in a specified population and is usually expressed as a percentage of that population or as a whole number. Thus, the prevalence of *diabetes mellitus* in the United States might be expressed either as the percent or as a whole number of the total population known or estimated to have the disease in a designated year. The prevalence of people crippled from poliomyelitis can be expressed as a gradually decreasing figure as the result of the greatly reduced incidence of the disease following the discovery of the vaccines. This shows that prevalence is derived from incidence, but modified by the extent to which cases disappear by death, recovery or inaccessibility. The value of prevalence rates is in determining the magnitude of the need for care, treatment, protection or other services.

*Incidence*

By definition mental retardation can be diagnosed only after birth when appropriate behavioral indices have developed sufficiently for measurement. During gestation the identification of certain conditions usually or invariably associated with mental retardation may be detected and *potential* retardation inferred.

From the examination of spontaneously aborted fetuses, it is estimated that probably 30 to 50 percent are developmentally abnormal and that if they had survived many would have been mentally deficient; but this information gives us only an incidence of fetal mortality and morbidity, with an estimate of some types of developmental deviation, not an incidence of mental retardation itself.

The mortality rates of the potentially or actually retarded vary with severity of defect, which means that many developmentally impaired infants die before retardation has been, or even can be, determined. Anencephaly, for example, is complete failure of brain cortex to develop; the infant may be born living and exhibit a few responses typical of the neonate, but survival is brief. Is such a case to be counted as an instance of incipient mental retardation or only of anencephaly in particular or birth defect in general?

Since mental retardation manifests itself at different ages and under different conditions, there is no single time—e.g., at birth or at one year of age—when it can be determined of every child that he is or *ever will be* identified as mentally retarded.

Mildly mentally retarded persons are most frequently identified, if at all, during school years, and frequently disappear as recognizably retarded after leaving school.

The methods of identifying retardation are still highly varied; consequently, surveys of incidence or prevalence are frequently not comparable.

The degree of subnormality employed as criterion for identification as retarded greatly affects the count of incidence. For example, the 1961 AAMD definition used a criterion of standard deviation greater than one (S.B. IQ$<$85). The 1973 version uses a more restricted criterion of more than two standard deviations (S.B. IQ$<$68). This change in criterion reduces the incidence of mild mental retardation automatically by 80%!

A similar problem is created by the use of multiple dimensions rather than a single dimension. If only IQ is employed, say at two standard deviations (IQ$<$68 or 70), a global incidence of about 3% of school-age population will be found (cf. Conley 1973). But if a second dimension of impaired adaptive behavior is also required, then some with IQ below 70 will not be classified mentally retarded, and some with low adaptive scores, but IQ above 70, will not be classified as retarded. This reduces the obtained prevalence rate to more nearly 1%. If, following Mercer, a still further determination is made on the basis of "socio-cultural modality" the rate may be still further reduced in some heterogeneous communities.

Taking many such considerations into account, Tarjan and others (1973) estimate that approximately 3 percent of annual births may be expected to "acquire" mental retardation at some time in their lives, of which 1.5% would be profoundly, 3.5% severely, 6.0% moderately and 89% mildly retarded. Currently, however, in view of the problems of arriving at truly meaningful estimates of the incidence of mental retardation on a global basis, emphasis for purposes of prevention is placed on the incidence from specific known causes. Unfortunately, these comprise only a small proportion of the total identified as retarded (Penrose, 1963; Holmes et al, 1965). The following are examples.

One of the earliest success stories in the reduction of the incidence of mental retardation was in the case of endemic cretinism. This condition occurred rather frequently in certain localities, notably some of the Swiss alpine valleys. The problem was attacked in the second half of the 19th century. The first step was to identify the condition with the occurrence of goiter, an enlargement of the thyroid gland. The next step was to relate this condition to the people's diet, and finally to the absence of trace iodine in the soil and water supply. Iodine was found to be necessary to the functioning of the thyroid gland in its production of the hormone thyroxin, the absence of which can cause cretinism.

The addition of iodine to table salt resulted in reducing mental retardation caused by endemic cretinism to near zero. It also led to the preventive and therapeutic use of extract of thyroxin in the treatment of myxoedema or hypothyroidism from other causes (Kanner, 1957).

The incidence of Down's syndrome is well-documented. It has been identified with a specific chromosomal abnormality which occurs most frequently as an unpredictable non-disjunction of autosome 21, but infrequently also as the Mendelian transmission of a translocated portion of autosome 21. The former type is definitely related to maternal age, occurring at about .33 per thousand live births to mothers under age 29 but rising sharply after age 35 to a rate of about 25 per thousand to women over age 45.

Overall, the incidence of Down's syndrome is 1 in 600 to 700 live births, with over half occurring to women over 35 (Begab, 1974). The overall incidence of gross chromosomal malformation of children born to women over 35 is 1 to 2 percent (Lubs and Ruddle, 1970; Begab, 1974). The existence of the condition is detectable by amniocentesis (analysis of a sample of amniotic fluid) during pregnancy.

This knowledge creates the possibility of reducing the incidence of Down's syndrome substantially by: a) limiting pregnancy after age 35; b) detecting the transmissable karyotype of translocation in either the male or female and limiting reproduction; c) identifying the condition early in gestation and terminating pregnancy.

A third example of incidence is more problematic, but nevertheless significant. From prevalence studies, it is known that mild retardation is more frequently found in families of low socio-economic status, especially in families in which the mother is mildly retarded. Heber and others have determined that the incidence of retardation in such families can be reduced by early intervention in providing stimulation to the child and home assistance to the mother.

These examples are sufficient to illustrate the values of pursuing the study of incidence to identifiable causes or correlative conditions as a means of identifying preventive measures (see Stein and Susser, 1974; Begab, 1974). Further discussion of currently known preventive measures appear in later chapters on prevention.

*Prevalence*

The principal problems of obtaining reliable prevalence estimates relate to definitions, criteria and administrative procedures on the one hand, and to the absence of uniform and centralized data collection, on the other. The former problems are gradually becoming resolved. The latter requires vigorous and sustained efforts by Federal and State governments to establish an effective data bank.

Prevalence is a product of cumulative incidence modified by loss. Loss may be the result of death or cure or unaccounted disappearance. Whereas measures of incidence are important to the problem of prevention, measures of prevalence are important to the provision of service resources. As prevention requires differential classification by identifiable cause, so service provision requires differential classification by types of need.

Overall estimates of prevalence of mental retardation have been made by two methods: by empirical surveys and by selection of a cut-off point on a Gaussian curve for the distribution of intelligence scores. The latter has led to a widely used estimate of 3%, ambiguously referring to either incidence or prevalence. This would correspond to an IQ level of approximately 70 and is, in fact, an average general prevalence found in some surveys of children (Conley, 1973; Birch et al, 1970).

However, it possible to select a 9% cut-off at about IQ 80 or 16% at IQ 85, the 1961 AAMD criterion. All surveys, however, show that mental retardation does not represent a simple portion of the lower tail on a general Gaussian curve. It is far from being normally distributed, varying widely by age, by socio-economic and ethnic factors. The use of an IQ cut-off alone also assumes a one-dimensional definition of mental retardation, contrary to the AAMD formula and other leading authorities (Tarjan, 1973; Mercer, 1973).

Tarjan (1973, p. 370) points out that the estimate of 3% prevalence, or 6 million persons in the United States, makes four dubious assumptions: "a) the diagnosis of mental retardation is based essentially on an IQ below 70; b) mental retardation is identified in infancy; c) the diagnosis does not change; and d) the mortality of retarded individuals is similar to that of the general population." The first assumption ignores the adaptive behavior component; the second holds only for a small portion, nearly always organically and severely impaired; the third holds only as a generality for those of IQ below 55, and the fourth holds only for the mildly retarded.

As a statement of potential incidence, Tarjan (1973) is probably quite conservative in estimating that 3% of all infants who survive birth will at some time in their lives be identified as mentally retarded in some context—most probably in the public schools.

Epidemiological surveys conducted in various parts of the United States and abroad show comparable prevalence rates for the more seriously retarded—i.e., moderate, severe and profound levels on the AAMD classifications or IQ below 50. Fifteen such studies converge on an average rate of approximately .46% or 4.6 cases per thousand population (Stein and Susser, 1974). These surveys generally covered ages roughly 10 to 20, obscuring

the high mortality rate in early childhood. When the surveys are divided between general and rural populations, the three rural studies average at more than double the general rate, or 9.84 per thousand, while the remaining twelve cluster quite closely around 3.6.

Penrose (1963) suggests that prevalence of malformation predictive of profound retardation at birth might be as much as 1 percent, Conley (1973) suggests 1.5 to 1.7 percent, including severe and moderate levels. The rate among prematurely born infants is much higher than among full-term babies. The rate among lower-class nonwhites is higher than among middle-class whites, but the differences are not so striking as is the case in mild retardation levels. Higher rates of prematurity, higher health risk and inferior maternal and child health care could account for the difference at the more severe levels.

In any case, the presumption of actual prevalence of the severe forms of defect predictive of mental retardation would be highest at birth, declining rapidly by mortality to a relatively low rate of .2% in adult life.

Prevalence rates of the severely retarded have been affected by a number of tendencies in the past 20 years. On the one hand, modern medicine has made enormous strides in its ability to preserve life. Infant mortality rates have fallen markedly; survival of prematures at progressively younger ages has become possible, with correspondingly increased risk of developmental damage; recovery from infectious diseases by use of antibiotics has become commonplace. Consequently, along with other infants and young children, severely and profoundly retarded children now have a better chance of prolonged survival.

On the other hand, improved health care, especially for mothers at risk, immunization, protection from radiation exposure, improved obstetrics, control of Rh isoimmunization and other measures have prevented the occurrence of some abnormalities and reduced the complications which formerly added to the incidence and prevalence of retardation. New hazards appear, however, in environmental toxic substances, strains of microorganisms more resistant to antibiotics, new addictive and nonaddictive drugs, new sources of radiation, environmental stress, all of which are potential producers of biological damage and mental retardation (Begab, 1974).

On balance, it is possible that incidence of severe retardation is falling while prevalence is continuing to rise.

The high birth rate of the post World War II period produced a record number of severely retarded children who are surviving longer than ever before. The future, envisioning more control of the causes with a lower birth rate more limited to optimal conditions of reproduction may in time yield lower prevalence rates of the moderate, severely and profound retarded. Currently, a very conservative estimate of their number in the United States is approximately 500,000 (Tarjan, et al, 1973) but may actually be nearer a .3% level or 660,000 surviving beyond the first year of life.

The prevalence of mild retardation is quite a different matter. Where the severely retarded show a declining prevalence by age, based wholly on mortality, the mildly retarded show a sharply peaked prevalence in the school years (6–19) and a rapid falling off in the adult years. This phenomenon cannot be a product of mortality, because the mildly retarded have shown longevity very nearly that of the general population. There are two possible alternatives, both of which may be the case. Large numbers remain retarded but cease to be the objects of attention; or they in fact cease to be retarded. In any case, no survey has yet found prevalence rates of mild retardation remotely approaching a constant across ages, such as would be expected on the assumption of unchanged relative mental status. Tarjan suggests that the rate of 3% traditionally projected as a constant across all ages, actually holds only for the school-age, with rated prevalence in selected age groups of .25% in the 0–5 group, 3.0% from 9–16, .4% from 20 to 24, sinking to .2% in the population over 25; the overall prevalence being approximately 1% (Tarjan, et al, 1973, p. 370). This would yield a total of approximately 2.2 million retarded persons in the United States, as against 6.6 million if an overall 3% is assumed.

In studies of the Riverside, California, population, Mercer (1974) showed that the prevalence and social distribution of mild mental retardation differed markedly according to the definition and methods of identification employed. She compared the application of a "social system" definition ("mental retardate" is an achieved status, and mental retardation is the role associated with the status) with a "clinical" definition (mental retardation is an individual pathology with characteristic symptoms which can be identified by standard diagnostic procedures).

It was found that the use of a one-dimensional clinical definition (IQ less than 69) yielded an overall rate of 2.14% retarded, with Blacks showing a rate 10 times and Mexican-Americans 34 times the rate of Anglos. When a two-dimensional definition is used (IQ less than 69 *plus* deficient adaptive score) the overall rate shrank to .9% which is the "clinical" rate predicted by Tarjan. The distribution now showed Blacks approximately at the same rate as Anglos, but Mexican-Americans still 15 times greater. When pluralistic, culturally adjusted norms were used for both IQ and adaptive behavior, the overall rate reduced still further to .54% but the total shrinkage in this case was accounted for in the Mexican-American group where sociocultural nonmodality (a cultural pattern distinctly different from the predominant mode) and bilingual background were most prominent. Furthermore, when higher criteria for IQ and adaptive behavior were used, the disadvantage to both Blacks and Mexican-Americans, as compared with Anglos, was markedly increased.

The social distribution of mild mental retardation has been found by all investigators to be inversely related to socioeconomic status. It is, according to Conley (1973) 13 times more prevalent among poor than among middle and upper income groups and found most frequently among rural, isolated or ghetto populations. Controversy persists concerning the contribution of constitutional and social learning factors to this distribution, but it is a question of the relative wieght rather than an exclusive alternative. No one doubts the multiple effects of environmental deprivation on both physical and psychological development. Nor is there much doubt that social learning enables the great majority of those with mild intellectual limitations to assume normal social roles in adult life. It is evident that what might appear to be a manifestation of the normal distribution of polygenic general intelligence is really a complex product in which the genetic component is only one among many factors yielding varying degrees and rates of retarded behavior, among varying populations at varying ages.

There is little point, then, in arguing who is "really" retarded. There is great point in determining who is in need of developmental and supportive assistance in achieving a reasonably adequate adult life, in determining the relationships between identifiable characteristics and the kinds of services that will be profitable, and in employing terminology that will aid rather than obscure these relationships. A critical issue is the degree to which cultural pluralism is reflected in the educational process.

The classification suggested by Mercer (1973) involves a four-dimensional matrix in which potentially handicapping conditions, including mental retardation defined in either "clinical" or "social system" terms, may be identified:

a) The dimension of *intellectual functioning,* measurable on a continuous scale represented by IQ. On this scale, following the 1973 AAMD standard, an IQ of 69 or less is regarded as potentially handicapping and is one clinically defining characteristic of mental retardation. Mercer terms the person with *only* this dimension of disability as *quasi-retarded.* Ordinarily this will be reflected in learning difficulties in the school setting and justifies individually prescriptive educational assistance.

b) The dimension of *adaptive behavior,* measurable on a developmental scale of behavioral controls accommodating the person to his environment. On this dimension a person falling substantially below age norms (perhaps in the lowest 3% of a normative distribution) is regarded as potentially handicapped. This constitutes a second clinically defining characteristic of mental retardation of the 1973 AAMD standard. Mercer terms the person who

has *only* this dimension of disability as *behaviorally maladjusted,* but she identifies the person with disability in both a) and b) as *clinically mentally retarded,* requiring services in both school and non-school settings.

c) The dimension of *physical constitution,* describable in terms of the health or pathology of the various organ systems of the body. While not a defining characteristic of mental retardation, physical impairment may be in itself potentially handicapping and may be the cause of or magnify the handicapping limitations of a) and b). The probability of organic impairments being present increases with the severity of mental retardation, from 3% at mild retardation levels to 78% at moderate levels and 95% at severe and profound levels (Conley, 1973, pp. 46–7). Individuals characterized by only c) may be termed generically as *physically impaired,* and in combination with a) and b) as *organic mentally retarded.* The term "multiply handicapped" is commonly used, but this would apply equally to persons with more than one substantial physical impairment.

d) *Sociocultural modality* is a fourth dimension which is distinguishable from the other three. It refers to the extent to which sociocultural variables of family background conform or do not conform to the modal culture in which the individual is assessed. When the family background is substantially non-modal, in this sense, the individual may be potentially handicapped in relation to the prevailing cultural expectations because of lack of opportunity for the appropriate learning. Such a person may be termed *culturally disadvantaged.* Mercer found that non-modality yielded effects which, to the dominant culture, appeared as low IQ, low adaptive behavior, or both when measured by the norms of the dominant culture. Utilizing a pluralistic model of mental retardation, sensitive to socio-cultural differences, Mercer found a substantial reduction in the prevalence of mental retardation in the Mexican-American as compared to the Anglo population of Riverside. Throughout the investigation, the Anglo sample yielded a constant rate of 4.4 per thousand identified as mentally retarded (i.e. no Anglos in this sample were judged either quasi-retarded or non-modal culturally). The Mexican-

## 3. MENTALLY HANDICAPPED

American population yielded the following succession of rates per 1,000:

a) One dimensional—only standard IQ norms, 149.0

b) Two dimensional—standard IQ + standard adaptive behavior norms, 60.0

c) Partial pluralistic two dimensional—standard IQ, pluralistic adaptive behavior norms, 30.4

d) Pluralistic two dimensional—pluralistic norms for both IQ and adaptive behavior, 15.3

(Mercer, 1973, pp. 235–254)

The residual differences between the rate of 4.4 for Anglos and the 15.3 rate for culturally adapted assessment of Mexican-Americans may be attributable to the pervasive effects of their bilingual status.

Granted that Mercer's research is based on a single local population sampling and is a first approach to a "social systems" definition of mental retardation, it suggests the need for much more highly refined procedures in the definition and epidemiology of mental retardation as a basis for the adequate and appropriate delivery of developmental and supportive services where they are needed.

There is complete agreement that it is impossible, at our present state of knowledge, to determine accurately either the incidence or the prevalence of mental retardation. There is far less agreement on what we can do to remedy this situation. Among the most urgent issues in classification:

1. **Definition.** The formulation adopted by the American Association on Mental Deficiency involving two-dimensional deficit in the level of behavioral performance unquestionably is responsive to many problems arising from older definitions. But a number of issues remain:

a) The two dimensions are not independent, but are, in fact, highly correlated, the degree of correlation being related to severity of deficit, suggesting the distinction of intellectual and adaptive measures has not been sufficiently refined. In practice, more reliance is frequently placed on IQ measures than on measures of adaptation or other bases of clinical judgment.

b) The cultural contamination of standardized tests as currently used makes their findings suspect. Mercer and others require a corrective for cultural insensitivity of the instruments employed.

c) The use of a global IQ measure which may be adequate for epidemiological purposes obscures the complexity of intellectual functioning and the variability of individual profiles which is the basis of service provision. Global IQ measures are rapidly losing favor among professional pro-

viders of service but are maintained for administrative convenience and ease of determination.

d) Differences in the conditions associated with mild retardation as compared to the more severe forms in terms of organicity, comprehensiveness of impairment, resistance to modification, relatedness to cultural norms, etc., suggest to some that the two types are sufficiently different as to require separate classification, probably based on organic (or presumed organic) versus psychosocial etiology.

2. **Services.** Since the instruments for the measurement of intelligence and adaptive behavior are scalar, with continuous variation on both sides of central norms, the relationship between a specific level of deficit and the need for specific types of service and treatment may be highly artificial. This appears to be the central question underlying the controversy over the criterion level in the AAMD definition which now excludes persons with IQs from 70 to 85 who formerly were included. The fact that relatively few scoring above 69 IQ manifest significant deficits in adaptive behavior may miss the point. Adaptive behavior may be quite specific and situational, especially where culture modality may also be in question. The real issue is to determine individual need, which cannot be derived from the IQ or adaptive behavior. This issue has been exacerbated by legislation which requires categorical classification as a condition of eligibility for service.

3. **Labeling.** Titles are necessary for any scientific system of classification, and may be useful for certain administrative purposes; but their use in human service systems is a different matter. The attachment of a label to a species of plant or a type of rock makes no difference to the plant or the rock. The label assigned to classify a human being does make a difference. To label a person mentally retarded has consequences of a psychological nature if the person is cognizant of it and can assign a meaning to it; it has consequences of a social nature insofar as other persons assign meaning and respond in terms of that meaning. This is especially the case with the label of "mentally retarded" because all terms associated with deficiency of intelligence are, in our culture, highly charged with negative values.

There have been many attempts to use systems of intellect classification as a means of adapting school and other programs to individual differences without making those differences appear invidious. These have not been entirely successful because value systems, even for children, tend to filter through the most subtle of euphemistic terminology.

This is a difficult issue to resolve. Success is possible only if: a) classification for epidemiological purposes is entirely separated from need-evaluation for purposes of social grouping and prescriptive treatment, b) all treatment is person-centered rather than system-centered, c) cultural value systems are recognized and respected, and d) eligibility for categorical assistance is based, not on global statistical criteria, but on the individual's need.

4. **Recording, Registering and Information Control** (corollary to labeling). Obviously, the best data base for the epidemiologist would be a computerized data bank including all information on every case. This has, in effect, been advocated since Samuel Howe's first attempt to catalogue the "idiotic" population of Massachusetts in 1848, long before modern systems of information storage and retrieval were dreamed of. However, rights of privacy and confidentiality have become a critical issue. The problem is one of reconciling the needs of the service delivery system and the individual recipient, so that he will neither be "lost" as an anonymous number nor stigmatized for having his needs recognized.

5. **"Negativism."** The nature of retardation lends itself to definition and assessment in the negative terms of deficit from desirable norms. The individual person, however, is not made up of deficits but of asset characteristics, however meager or distorted some of them may be. All treatment rests on the positive capacity of the person to respond, whether physiologically or psychologically. The issue of negatively versus positively defined traits and classifications is a basic one between the purposes of epidemiology and the purposes of service assistance.

Who are the people who are mentally retarded? They are individuals whose assets for effective living in their cultural and physical environments are insufficient without assistance. The screen by which they are brought into view to be identified and counted is composed of a mesh of intellectual and adaptive behavior norms. But the screen is a somewhat crude and abrasive instrument and requires to be refined and softened by concern for the individuals it exposes.

How many mentally retarded people are there? The loss of potential for normal development and even survival affects a high proportion of those who are conceived, and probably 3% of those who survive birth. In addition to those hundreds of thousands who are not well-born, there are millions who are not well-nurtured by the world in which they live. How we sort out these millions, how many will be called "mentally retarded" will depend on our definitions and our perceptions of need. The roots of these needs are not yet under control, nor have we sufficiently provided for their assuagement.

Plate I

Sketch from the colored illustration of the simplest picture in the series, the demonstration picture, with the inserts which particularly relate to this picture. Of course only one is quite correct, but the others can be inserted with some show of reasonableness.

# teaching the
# *invisible*
## retarded

**Barbara Moller**

Mrs. Moller, a resident of Coral Gables, Fla., teaches in a public school center for exceptional children.

*One of the real tragedies of mildly retarded children is that they often appear so normal, except for their learning difficulties in school*

Imagine what it would be like to be retarded from nine till three. The mildly retarded child wakes up, prepares for school and rides the bus like any other kid, but a change occurs once he reaches the school. Assignments that are easy for friends seem impossible, and much of what happens in his regular classroom is a confusion of unasked, unanswered questions. Help is available, but to get it, he must leave his friends and go to a special class.

When school is over, he returns home to his family and friends. Out of school, he probably does not feel any different from his peers or siblings unless someone mentions ''that word.''

''That word'' may have haunted him for a long time. Maybe he knew, even before he started school, that other children were not having so much trouble learning and that other children didn't see so many doctors and take so many tests. And then someone said *retarded . . . mentally retarded*. But he didn't feel retarded. He could do things that other people could do. Not all of them, maybe, but so what if a kid needs a little extra help?

What's a kid supposed to say when he's asked what's wrong or why he's in a special class? Should he admit to being mentally retarded? What about those fights his brothers and sisters get into when someone calls him retarded? And what are they saying about him when they aren't fighting?

The mildly retarded child may have a self-concept that is confused by conflicting reactions to his handicap. He may have been directly confronted with the label of mental retardation or simply have overheard it during the process of diagnosis and special placement. Without a sympathetic explanation, he may feel that he has been labeled inferior.

For these reasons, modern educators generally try to avoid labeling, but such descriptive terms are tied to the funding for the special services these children require. A precise definition of mental retardation is also necessary to assure that programs for children with limited ability are not assigned to just any child who has trouble in school.

But what should the mentally retarded child do or say to a stranger who does not perceive his limitations? While the goal of his education is integration into normal society, he may not have the words to explain the many

Reprinted with permission of the publishers Allen Raymond, Inc., Darien, Conn. 06820. From the April, 1977 issue of *Early Years.*

awkward situations he encounters where he needs help with simple tasks or when he requires additional time to finish what others have completed rapidly. He needs help, but what can he say to get it and still maintain his pride?

**Difficult Diagnosis.** Identification as mentally retarded may be the only way a child will ever obtain special instruction. The diagnosis of subnormal mental ability, however, is often difficult for the child and his family to accept. While the classroom teacher may seldom be involved in the actual testing or diagnosis, she may be one of the first to experience an adverse reaction by the family or the child.

Occasionally, the discovery that a child is mentally retarded may be a relief to a family unable to understand or manage his behavior. Retarded children are often described as "stubborn," "un-cooperative," or "forgetful" when they are unable to perform simple tasks their peers have easily mastered. Some mentally retarded children have a history of disrupting classes when they abandon frustrating academic tasks and try to gain the attention of their instructor and peers with inappropriate behavior.

In such cases, finally pinpointing a child's problem and finding ways to help him may alleviate many difficulties. But not all parents perceive their mentally retarded child as having a problem. The news that testing performed at the school has revealed that a happy, seemingly well-adjusted child is mentally retarded and requires special education may be a shocking diagnosis that some parents will reject. Academic problems may be viewed as much less of a crisis than the stigma for family and child of having the youngster in a group that is considered to be mentally subnormal.

The classroom teacher should be both cautious and sympathetic in her communica-tions with parents when discussing the possibility of a child's mental retardation. Several suggestions offered here may help to begin parent conferences on this difficult subject.

**1.** Begin with a few questions. For example: How do you think your child is adjusting to school? Do you think he might have learning problems? What do you suspect these learning problems might be? Does your child have difficulty doing some things at home? How do you help him when he needs adult assistance? Is his behavior a problem? Do you think he's aware of his problems? Do you think this child is different from your other children? The parents' answers may provide insight into their perception of their child's problem and give you clues as to how they may react to a discussion of this child's performance in school.

**2.** Avoid labels, such as hyperactive, which may cause objections or create misunderstandings. Instead, describe the child's performance and behavior in school with specific examples; and enumerate the techniques which have been tried in an effort to change his classroom behavior. The parents may relate other examples of the kinds of behaviors you describe. By comparing behavior at home and in school, consistencies may be found even in unusual behavior.

**3.** Be sure to point out the child's positive qualities as well as his problem areas. Parents may be overwhelmed by the child's disabilities. It's important that they do not give up on their mentally retarded child or communicate a negative attitude to him as a result of their own frustration in dealing with his problems.

**4.** Explain what is meant by the label "mental retardation." Some parents may become so upset when the school gives their child this label that they'll visit one specialist after another, shopping for a more acceptable description of their child's dis-ability. The label may also be considered such a stigma that some parents will deny it or refuse to discuss the subject. Mental retardation can be explained as meaning that a child may have difficulty with tasks that come easily to most children. The learning rate of the mildly mentally retarded child may be slower, but he'll probably achieve basic academic skills, even though he can't keep pace with his, chronological peers.

**5.** Discuss the various sources of help for the child. Encourage the parents to seek accurate professional help for their child's problems, rather than rely on the hearsay opinions of well-meaning friends and relatives. A competent medical doctor can calm the fears of many parents with a thorough explanation accompanying his diagnosis.

**6.** Help the parents set realistic goals for their child. Discourage them from seeking miracle cures for mental retardation through unusual diets or fad exercise programs. State goals that you hope to achieve with the child. Suggest ways that the parents might help the child when they are ready to work with him at home. Caution them that they may become frustrated in attempting to teach their own child; and if they do, the child should not be punished for failure to master a task. Rather, the parents should praise their child for his effort.

**7.** Suggest membership in organizations such as the National Association for Retarded Citizens. Such an organization can guide parents to counseling or introduce them to other parents who have had similar problems. Often this provides the reassurance that a mentally retarded child is not the result of errors as parents.

**8.** Encourage the parents to support their child's participation in social activities with normal peers such as the Y.M.C.A. or sports teams. Parents can discreetly inform adult organization leaders of their child's handicap so that appropriate expectations will be formed for him.

**9.** Let the parents know that you are concerned about the child's adjustment at home as well as in school. If the parents indicate they are having difficulty managing his behavior, a program of behavior modification or counseling might be recommended. Discourage the parents from comparing the retarded child to others with normal ability. Stress the importance of establishing independence in the child—especially if the parents seem overprotective.

**10.** Let the parents know that you can accept their child—or any child—despite his handicaps. The knowledge that a classroom teacher is working to make the child an important member of his class will probably help keep communication channels open with the parents.

**Self Image.** Soon after a mental handicap is diagnosed, a child may begin to receive subtle and sometimes direct communications that he's different from other children. Many mentally retarded children seek assurance from parents and teachers with such questions as "Why am I retarded?", "I'm not dumb, am I?" or "I can learn, so why am I in a special class?"

A child's fear of being different may be further compounded by bits of information overheard in discussions of his problems. Children with apparent physical handicaps such as those associated with genetic syndromes may also experience the stares of strangers or be imitated by other children. Such children may become self-conscious and fearful of any contact with strangers.

Children who have both physical handicaps and mental retardation may have visited numerous physicians and diagnosticians, even by the time they enter school. As a result they may be fearful of any type of examination or testing. A child who has a handicap such

as a deformed hand, for example, may try to conceal the hand and refuse to use it even in the ways it can function. A child with a speech defect may lapse into complete silence if he believes his problem has been noticed. Retarded children may simply say "I can't" rather than risk failure.

The retarded child who is aware of his problems may be an unhappy youngster with tremendous feelings of inferiority. As a result of his poor self-concept, he may wish to avoid unfamiliar situations. A history of failure may also cause the child to have a very low tolerance for frustration and emotional immaturity.

The problem may compound itself since a child who believes he is different may not attempt to conform to accepted behavior for his peer group. Some retarded children are also limited in their social perceptions and need the guidance of parents and teachers to become aware of proper social behavior.

**Classroom Strategies.** The teacher with a mentally retarded child in the classroom might try some of these strategies to aid the child's adjustment and overall development.

**1.** Let the child know that you like him. His adjustment to your class will be easier if he feels welcome. However, he may not perceive the subtle social cues which communicate acceptance, so you may wish to simply tell the child privately that you like him.

**2.** Stress the similarities between the retarded child and your other students. The other children may be aware of the ways in which a mentally retarded child is different, especially if he is unable to do the same assignments, leaves the classroom for special instruction or has unusual physical characteristics. Occasional intervention at a critical moment to point out similarities may help all the children understand the commonality of feelings, likes

and dislikes, and the need to be recognized and loved.

**3.** Encourage him to make his unique contribution to your class. His ability to participate may be limited, but try to praise his efforts to become involved in group activities.

**4.** Retarded children learn much of their behavior through imitation. It's important that they be exposed to positive behavior models that will help them develop appropriate social behavior. The mentally retarded child should be seated and grouped with children who are able to accept him and provide appropriate language and behavior models.

**5.** Help him set realistic goals. (He may sometimes ask the teacher to give him the most difficult assignment he observes in his class.) The teacher should help him understand that academic mastery is a series of sequential steps and that when one is completed, the next will follow. Avoid describing the mentally retarded child's assignments as "easy" and stress instead that he's able to complete the same steps in learning that all children follow.

**6.** If he displays very immature or inappropriate behavior in the classroom, talk with him privately. Explain exactly what is undesirable in his behavior and specify how he's expected to act. If the problem persists, the parents and the specialist may become involved in starting a behavior modification program to extinguish undesirable behavior and reinforce appropriate actions.

**7.** Note any changes or unusual developments in his behavior. Medication, epilepsy and physical handicaps sometimes cause changes in the child as he matures. The classroom teacher who sees the child daily in a room full of normal youngsters may often be the first to detect a problem requiring medical attention.

**8.** Try to establish a regular channel of communication with his special instructors.

Classroom activities are the best place to reinforce skills patiently developed on a one-to-one basis. Periodically check the skill level of the child with his special ed teacher.

**9.** Reward effort as well as achievement. The child with limited mental ability who progresses at a slow but steady rate may well be working to the best of his ability, even though his achievement is well below his peers. Often, a mentally retarded child may feel that his best is never good enough because of the gap between his own achievement and that of other children his age. His work can be recognized through awards for effort when other children are receiving distinctions for achievement.

**10.** Think about how you'll answer him when he tries to confront his problem. Such questions as ''What is wrong with me?'' ''Am I retarded?'' or ''Can I ever be like other kids?'' are very likely to occur when he sees himself in sharp contrast to his peers in the regular classroom. To avoid the issue after a child has sought your answers will only compound the fears that caused him to state the original question. He wants assurance, not a sermon on the worth of the mentally retarded. Point out his strengths and tell him that he's special.

**The Other Kids.** Now what about the rest of the class? The other students may well resent the intrusion of a mentally retarded youngster who seems to receive teacher's special love and attention for doing work that's too easy to be assigned to anyone else. Children who are suddenly called upon to befriend a child who is perceptibly different may be hostile. Young, uninhibited children may openly stare or ask the retarded child questions about what is wrong.

In the complexity of children's play, the retarded child may often be excluded from the games of his peers when he's unable to understand rules or cannot compete without special consideration. He may seek the companionship of children who are several years younger but who share more immature interests and have a similiar mental age. Even with such companions, the retarded child's gullibility may cause him to be the victim of cruel jokes. A mentally retarded child may only be allowed to join other children's play when he agreed to follow their directions or take the least desired role.

No one can shelter the retarded child from all these unhappy moments, but there are ways the teacher can work to create an atmosphere where he's accepted into a peer group in which he can grow through interaction with his classmates. For example:

**1.** Encourage an atmosphere of acceptance. Children can perceive differences in a classmate without using him as a vehicle for abuse. The unattractive child may also need the special support of a classroom teacher who is able to emphasize the similiarities of all children.

**2.** Help the children organize group play that is inclusive. Divide them into teams, using systems such as odd-even numbers rather than letting children be picked by popular leaders.

**3.** Rotate classroom responsibilities so that all children will have a turn.

**4.** Discuss ways in which all children are similiar. Note a few differences, too; but discourage the use of such words as ''good'' and ''bad'' when personal characteristics are the subject.

**5.** Initiate a special day for each child in class. Each day a different child might wear a button which says ''I am special today.'' When the mentally retarded child is given his special day, allow him to explain his special program and help him field classmates' questions about his disability.

**6.** Emphasize that there are individual expectations for every child in class. Let the children compare their effort on a task rather than its degree of difficulty.

**7.** If your classroom has charts that record progress, prepare a separate scale to measure the work of your slower and mentally retarded students.

**8.** The mentally retarded child's work may frequently have as many errors as correct responses. Try marking the correct answers with a check and circling the wrong answers. This gives the child the opportunity to learn through correcting his errors, rather than accepting a paper filled with failure.

**9.** If you must make exceptions to classroom rules and procedures to accommodate your mentally retarded student, explain decisions that may cause jealousy or resentment. Children can understand that rules should be sensibly applied. Assure them that the well being of each individual child is always the primary consideration in any decision regarding behavior standards.

**10.** Be ready to answer frank inquiries from the retarded child's classmates. When asked ''What is wrong with him?'', try to use terms and concepts that the children can accept and use to explain a retarded child's problem to others. Avoid labeling the child ''mentally retarded.'' Explain that some work is difficult for the child and that he may need more time and special help with his assignments.

Physical handicaps or motor problems may be discussed as disabilities that a child must learn to overcome. Classmates can be encouraged to be patient and to offer assistance when they see any child confronted by a situation he cannot master.

Finally, enjoy the mentally retarded child in your class just as you enjoy any child. Remember the educational goals for the mentally retarded are the same as for any child. You are working to help the child develop to his fullest potential.

# Mainstreaming the Mildly Handicapped Secondary Student — Another View

**LEE A. WITTERS**
*The University of Nebraska*

Lloyd Dunn's 1968 pronouncement that a better education than special class placement ought to be provided for the mildly handicapped student resulted in a widespread debate in American education and in the "mainstreaming" movement. Mainstreaming has caused more than a ripple in the elementary grades where the bulk of the special education pupils were schooled at that time. But at the secondary level, it has become a particularly difficult issue to deal with since most junior high and senior high schools struggle with subject-centered curricula, departmental organization, honor rolls and scholastic grades, diplomas, college preparatory requirements, academic achievement esteem, and a host of barriers to change. Previously, mainstreaming was no problem since by the time the handicapped pupil reached the secondary level, he/she usually dropped out.

With minor exceptions, secondary education has not dealt with mainstreaming or the training of teachers to cope with the handicapped youngsters who, by virtue of federal and state laws, will soon find themselves in the regular classroom if they haven't been there already. It is not necessarily implied here that all special students are expected to return to the mainstream of education, but for those who do, secondary teachers ought to be prepared.

The handicapped that Dunn referred to were classified as the retarded. Within the past five years, the mildly handicapped have come to include the multi-sensori and physically disabled, the learning disabled and the behaviorally disordered as well.

## Mainstreaming

The most commonly accepted definition of mainstreaming today is the integration of eligible handicapped youngsters with normal peers, based upon individually determined educational needs and necessitating "share responsibility" for planning and programming by regular and special educators. Associated with mainstreaming is the "Zero Reject" model, advocated by Stephen Lilly (1971), which means that once a child enrolls in a regular program it is next to impossible to remove the child from that program for any reason, i.e., access to free public education for all handicapped youngsters. These two popular concepts are based upon a number of assumptions, among which are: 1) Labeling and classifications do more harm than good, 2) Efficacy studies do not support the continuation of special classes, 3) Regular education can better meet the needs of individual learners, and 4) Psychological testing for diagnosis and placement can be unreliable and unfair (Birch, 1974).

The question, of course, is the regular secondary classroom the most viable option for the education of the mildly handicapped? Obviously, not all educators can agree (Clark, 1975). Nevertheless, mainstreaming provides a means by which individualized instruction can be used effectively.

## Legal Basis

Trends in secondary education suggest an urgent need to rethink the traditional normal and handicapped dichotomy which has characterized our views of youngsters. Recent court decisions, such as the Pennsylvania Association for Retarded Children vs. the State of Pennsylvania (1971-72) and Mills vs. District of Columbia Board of Education (1972) have affirmed the requirements for equal opportunities for all handicapped youngsters by public education. Practically all states within the past two to three years mandated that a significant portion of the mildly handicapped pupils will be enrolled in regular class programs in the schools.

Prior to these court decisions and state mandatory laws, education of the handicapped had been largely restricted to special education programs separate from the normal school activities. Thus, secondary teachers have received little instruction either in the identification of the special needs or in the teaching of the handicapped student within the regular class setting. Regular secondary teachers now have a legal and professional commitment to the education of the handicapped. Secondary schools must be reconceptualized to provide a more adequate education for handicapped and non-handicapped.

### Focus at Secondary Level

It is not the intent of this paper to deal with a delivery system for mainstreaming in secondary schools, but to suggest some skills that would be helpful to regular teachers who must teach the handicapped pupils. However, in dealing with some practical ideas for class management, one must instruct from some kind of school organizational model that is designed to meet the needs of the handicapped.

The accompanying chart may serve as a model for reconceptualizing the school for mainstreaming. In the early elementary years where differences in performances in scholastic achievement and functioning academic skills are not so acute, the degree of integration of handicapped with non-handicapped would be high, say 90% of the time. There are noticeable differences in adaptive behavior, however, and it appears advantageous for integration to occur only about one-fourth of the time so that in segregated settings the maladjusted child could be given special help in developing more appropriate social skills.

At the secondary level there are marked differences in the performances and teacher expectations of handicapped and non-handicapped in the basic studies, and it would be extremely difficult for the high school handicapped student to cope in the traditional math, history, English, and science classes. Mainstreaming in the so-called academics would occur only about 10% of the student's time. What seems the most reasonable approach are life-application activities in the basic tool subjects in a special or vocational setting (*Thresholds*, Fall, 1976).

The issue, however, is not really a question of integration or segregation but that of providing the best opportunities to help the mildly handicapped to develop those skills that will enable them to cope independently in the community. The vehi-

cle to achieve this goal could very well be Career Education, the development of knowledge and skills by which each individual may fulfill unique needs for occupational choice, social responsibility and personal growth. Work experiences facilitate decision-making abilities and help develop social skills (Hoyt, 1975).

### Suggested Skills for Secondary Teachers

What do regular secondary teachers need to know, and what skills do they need to possess to meet the needs of all mildly handicapped at the secondary level? Basically, there are two kinds: 1) diagnostic skills and 2) prescriptive skills. Stellern, Vasa, and Little (1976) provide us an intervention model worth trying.

Diagnostic skills help the regular teacher to assess the entry level of the student, and thus do a better job of planning instruction. Teachers basically need to know five things about handicapped learners: intellectual potential, adaptive behavior, achievement level, style of learning, and what is reinforcing to them.

The learner's intellectual potential, i.e., the strengths and weaknesses in problem solving abilities, is obtained from formal intelligence tests. Whatever the limitations of intelligence tests, some idea of general classroom learning potential makes for realistic goal setting for the learner.

Although there are formal instruments that provide data about adaptive behavior, some teacher-made informal checklists, sociometric techniques, and group participation charts are easy and convenient methods to obtain learner social-performance levels.

Standard achievement tests provide the teacher with information about the learner's school performance in relation to others. These data help teachers decide what instructional materials are appropriate.

Information from interest and reinforcement inventories can be used in programming a reward schedule for desirable academic and social behavior. Styles of Learning questionnaires (Dunn & Dunn, 1973) are informal techniques that teachers can use to discover how the learner learns best. Teaching to learning strengths (rather than remediating weaknesses) most of the time is recommended.

Prescriptive skills enable the teacher to make instruction both individualized and successful for the handicapped student. Instruction in the regular classroom needs to be improved through increased individualization.

**CHART NO. 1**

*Delivery Model for Secondary
Mainstreamed Handicapped Pupils*

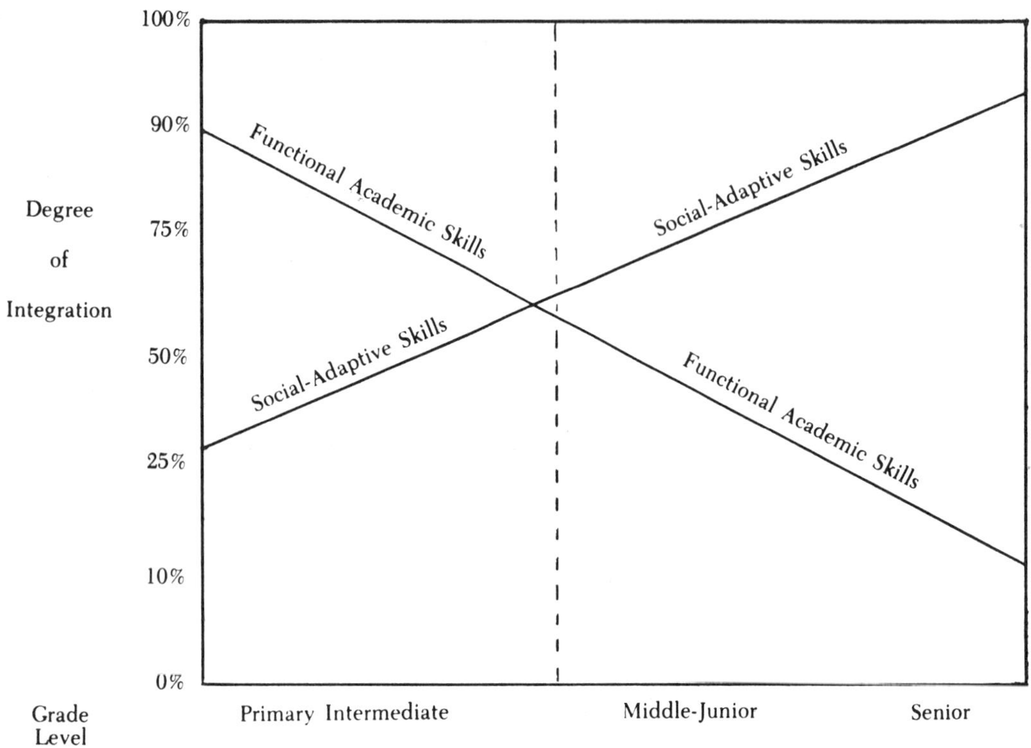


Based upon all the information obtained from the diagnostic procedures, the teacher prepares a prescriptive program. Most prescriptive programs include behavioral-instructional objectives, a task analysis, a reinforcement schedule and behavior modification system, a curriculum analysis model, and the continuous collection of data about behavioral change.

A behavioral-instructional objective is a prescriptive plan-of-action that defines precisely the desired academic or social behavior. The selection of appropriate and realistic learning materials and activities depends upon how precise the target behavior can be explained. For example, "Student X cannot read" will not help us design effective instruction. Pairing the diagnostic data with a precise, presenting problem leads to successful intervention.

A task analysis is simply sequencing the learning that is necessary for the learner to get from the observed behavior (presenting problem) to the terminal behavior (objective). Systematically applying behavior modification such as the various mechanics of positive reinforcement, contigency management, contract learning, high interest activities and materials, and token economies increase the chances of intervention success. Curriculum analysis enables the teacher to match commercial and teacher-constructed materials and activities with sequential learning.

Finally, the teacher should collect data about the occurrence of the target behavior by means of baseline measurement. Continuous baseline measurement is the accountability system to assess the learner's progress and the success of the teacher's prescriptive program.

# Definitions of severely handicapped: A survey of state departments of education

Joseph E. Justen III
Gregory E. Brown

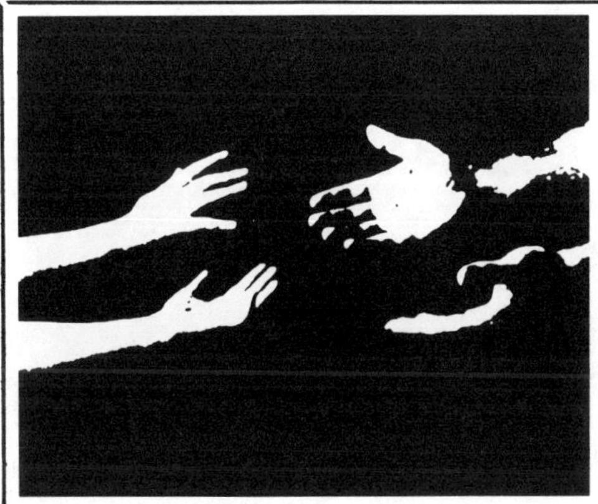

*State departments of education were surveyed to determine the definitions of severely handicapped currently in use and also to determine whether the provision of education services to this population was mandatory or permissive. It was found that while the majority of states required that education services be provided to all children, fewer than half had a definition of the severely handicapped. Of the states surveyed which had definitions, the majority referred to either the mentally retarded or the multiply handicapped.*

Because of recent litigation and legislation, more and more states have begun to recognize and provide services for a group of children loosely referred to as the "severely handicapped." However, the exact composition of this group is often difficult to ascertain. In viewing programs across the nation supposedly designed specifically for the "severely handicapped," one can readily conclude that there is little consensus regarding the parameters of this population.

Undoubtedly, various administrative and political constraints contribute to the lack of consistency in the populations served by these programs. For example, the patterns and sources of funding, or the difficulty of serving low incidence populations in a low density population area, may determine what services are provided to whom. However, this lack of consensus about who should be included in the *severely handicapped* population undoubtedly goes beyond mere administrative concerns to reflect some basic philosophical differences.

The lack of consensus reflected in the programs for the severely handicapped across the nation is also reflected in the positions taken by leading professionals in the field. While most of these individuals have not provided operational definitions of the population to which they are referring, it is clear in their writings and presentations that many are using the term *severely handicapped* in quite different contexts (AAESPH, Note 1; NARC, Note 2). While some have used the term in a rather restricted context to refer to individuals with the most profound forms of retardation, others have used it quite loosely to refer to a wide range of debilitating conditions, often including individuals some might contend are more moderately handicapped. At the most general level, the term *severely handicapped* has probably been most used to refer to any and all children excluded from public schools in the past because of a handicapping condition. Thus, in a real sense, for many states and professionals the term *severely handicapped* is synonymous with *unserved handicapped*.

While the designation *unserved* may be useful in identifying a population in need of special services, it probably is not very useful as a construct for service delivery. In addition, as more and more services become available it will probably not continue to serve as a useful diagnostic construct. As states develop and implement service delivery models for individuals previously denied services, it apparently will be necessary to more adequately describe the population for whom these services are intended and, thus, to resolve definitional problems. The purpose of this study was to ascertain the definitions in current use by state departments

"

across the nation, in order to find viable directions for future efforts to define this population.

## PROCEDURE

In October, 1975, letters were mailed to the directors of special education in the 50 state departments of education. Information regarding the following questions was requested in these letters.

1) Does your state have legislation pertaining specifically to the education of the severely handicapped? If yes, are services mandatory or permissive?
2) Does your state have a definition(s) of the severely handicapped for educational purposes? (You may have more than one categorical definition.) If you do, what is that definition? Is it statutory or provided through administrative regulations?

It was also requested in these letters that, if a state had neither a definition nor legislation, this fact be indicated since this information was also important.

In January, a second letter requesting the same information was mailed to those who did not respond to the first letter. A total of 45 states (90%) replied.

In analyzing the information received from the states, the authors attempted to answer the following questions:

1) How many of the states have definitions of the severely handicapped?
2) How many of the states have legislation pertaining to services for the severely handicapped?
3) Is there a relationship between a state having a definition and the mandatory provision of services?
4) What elements do the definitions used by the various states have in common? What are the major differences?

## RESULTS

Of the 45 states responding to the survey, 29 (64.4%) indicated that the provision of educational services to the severely handicapped is mandatory in their state. On the basis of the information available, an attempt was made to distinguish between mandatory educational services provided by the local school board or comparable agency and those services provided through the traditional state institutions. Only the former were included in the category of mandatory services.

All but one of these 29 states have legislation which mandates the provision of educational services; the exception, Pennsylvania, is required by U.S. District Court order to provide educational services. With few exceptions, the state laws requiring educational services are general in nature and refer to "all children" or "all handicapped children." Only nine of the 29 states mandating services make specific reference to the *severely handicapped*.

Less than one-half of the states responding (22 of 45) have some sort of definition of the severely handicapped. Of these, only three are statutory and 19 are part of administrative rules, regulations, and guidelines. Two states indicated that the definition provided was only proposed and had yet to be formally adopted.

A fourfold point correlation or phi correlation was computed to determine the relationship between a state having mandatory services and a definition. This relationship is represented graphically in Table 1. A weak positive correlation was found ($r = .17$). Thus, states which have mandatory legislation are somewhat more likely to have a definition as well. However, when tested for statistical significance, this correlation was not found to be significant ($t = 1.12$, $p < .05$).

The insignificance of this correlation and the general lack of consensus in the field regarding the definition of the severely handicapped is reflected in the fact that 13 of 45 states (28.9%) report the mandatory provision of services but lack a definition. Another six (13.3%) have a definition but do not report mandatory services.

The types of definitions used by the various states were categorized on the basis of their main features and emphasis. The categories and the number of states using these definitions are reported in Figure 1. Two types of definitions are used most frequently by those 22 states which have definitions. Nine states refer primarily

**Table 1** *States with permissive or mandatory services and with or without a definition*

|  | Permissive services | Mandatory services | Total |
|---|---|---|---|
| Definition | 6 | 16 | 22 |
| No definition | 10 | 13 | 23 |
| Total | 16 | 29 | 45 |

to the *mentally retarded,* usually to the *severely* and/or *profoundly retarded*; another nine refer to the *multi-* or *multiply handicapped*; three states use both of these definitions. Therefore, while only 22 states indicate that they have definitions, 25 different definitions of the *severely handicapped* are presently in use in those states.

Three states take an open-ended approach and attempt to focus on those children not currently receiving services. Two take a categorical approach, referring to traditional diagnostic labels, e.g., *deaf-blind, autistic*. And another two attempt to define the *severely handicapped* by referring to the intensity of services required, e.g., staffing patterns.

In order to provide the reader with a feel for the type and range of definitions used by states in working with the severely handicapped, an example of each type is provided.

1) Definitions which focus primarily on the *severely* and *profoundly retarded* (nine states)·
   **Rhode Island** (proposed)—"The severe and profound mentally retarded [includes] a child who, at the time of school evaluation, obtains a score on an individually administered test of intelligence 4 or more standard deviations below the mean . . . and who manifests a pervasive severe or profound impairment in adaptive behavior." (Rhode Island State Board of Regents, Note 3). Some states use the AAMD levels of *mild, moderate, severe,* and *profound* retardation while others use the traditional educational categories, *educable, trainable,* and *custodial*. Although some states indicated that some severely handicapped children are being served in existing programs for the trainable retarded, a definition which referred solely to the *TMR* was *not* considered as constituting a definition of the *severely handicapped*.

**Figure 1** *Number of reporting states using each type of definition*

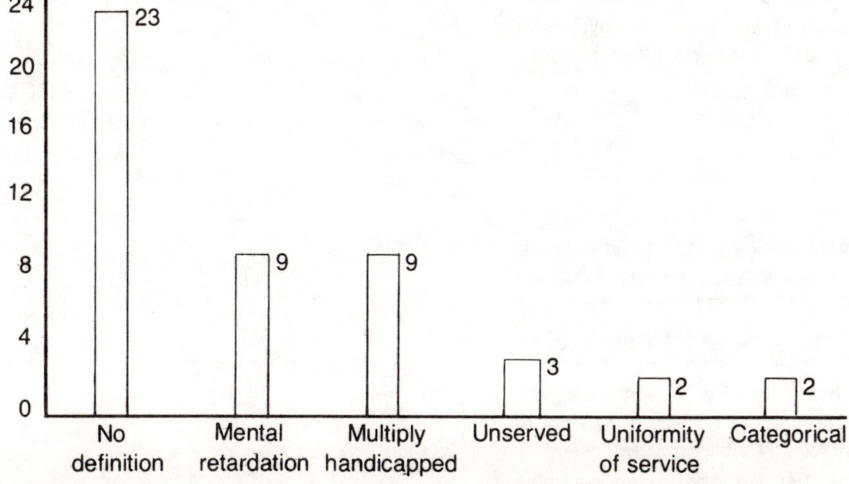


*Totals to 48 because some states had more than one definition; 45 states reported.

# 3. MENTALLY HANDICAPPED

2) Definitions focusing primarily on the *multi-* or *multiply handicapped* (nine states):

    **New York**—"Multiply handicapped: a child who, because of the multiplicity of his handicapping conditions, requires intervention by more than one certified specialist in the area of education of the handicapped. For purposes of the section, visually impaired children shall be included, but those children whose second handicap is solely in the area of speech shall not be included" (New York State Education Department, Note 4).

3) Definitions which focus on those who are not currently being served by any existing educational program (three states):

    **Missouri**—"'Severely handicapped children,' handicapped children under the age of twenty-one years who, because of the extent of the handicapping condition or conditions . . . are unable to benefit from or meaningfully participate in, programs in the public schools of a regular or special nature" (Vernon's Annotated Missouri Statutes, Note 5).

4) Definitions which did not fit one of the preceding categories and which refer primarily to the intensity and/or extent of service(s) required by the severely handicapped (two states):

    **Iowa**—"The severely handicapped are those pupils also termed 'profoundly handicapped' who have special education needs which require intensive special education programs and services" (Iowa Department of Public Instruction, Note 6).

5) Definitions which define the severely handicapped by enumeration of a number of traditional categories (two states):

    **Idaho**—"The severely handicapped are those children who are profoundly retarded, seriously emotionally disturbed, deaf, blind, and deaf-blind" (Idaho Department of Education, Note 7).

While none of the states surveyed had adopted the BEH definitions of the severely handicapped, programs with federal funding will undoubtedly take this definition into account. It is included as an example in this discussion for two reasons: (1) it cuts across and includes a number of the different types of definitions discussed earlier, and (2) it is likely to have nationwide impact. This definition states:

> A severely handicapped child is one who because of the intensity of his physical, mental, or emotional problems, or a combination of such problems, needs educational, social, psychological, and medical services beyond those which have been offered by traditional regular and special education programs, in order to maximize his full potential for useful and meaningful participation in society and for self-fulfillment. Such children include those classified as seriously emotionally disturbed (schizophrenic and autistic), profoundly and severely mentally retarded, and those with two or more serious handicapping conditions such as the mentally retarded-deaf, and the mentally retarded-blind.
>
> Such children may possess severe language and/or perceptual-cognitive deprivations, and evidence a number of abnormal behaviors including: a failure to attend to even the most pronounced social stimuli, self-mutilization, self-stimulation, durable and intense temper tantrums, absence of even the most rudimentary forms of verbal control, and may also have an extremely fragile physiological condition. (United States Office of Education, Bureau for Education of the Handicapped, 1974).

## DISCUSSION

As evidenced by this survey, relatively few states have attempted to develop a definition(s) of the *severely handicapped* in both functional and operational terms. Even more surprising was the finding that over half of the states surveyed said they had no definition of the *severely handicapped* and yet 56.5% of these same states claimed to have legislation mandating services to all exceptional children. Thus, several states are in the process of serving children they have not even defined.

With the recent passage of PL 94-142, The Education For All Handicapped Children Act (Senate Bill 6), states soon will be required to provide educational services to all children. This national educational mandate will insure that no more children will fall between the cracks of the traditional educational categories and thus be excluded from educational services. This law will not, however, determine what types of educational services are provided to whom.

If appropriate educational programs are to be developed for the severely handicapped, it is necessary to examine systematically what is known about this population. In order to accomplish this, it is important to define clearly the population in question so that all those concerned can communicate with a minimum of confusion and misunderstanding. Thus, as Kolstoe (1972) has noted, at the most elementary level it is important to develop or to accept some definition in order that a common conceptual basis exists for further discussion, research, and program implementation. Without this common frame of reference, it is possible that many professionals within the same state will hold widely divergent views about who should be included in which program.

Undoubtedly, the lack of state definitions observed to date is due to the relative newness of mandatory legislation and the lack of previous programs for the severely handicapped. Hopefully, states will not be complacent in reacting to the new legislative mandates for the severely handicapped but will rather take leadership roles in formulating and implementing effective plans. While they may seem a small issue, initial definitions established by the various state departments may well set the stage for the effectiveness and efficiency of future service delivery models.

## REFERENCE NOTES

1. American Association for the Education of the Severely/Profoundly Handicapped. *Second annual conference.* Kansas City, Mo., November 12-14, 1975.

2. National Association of Retarded Citizens. *Proceedings: National training meeting on the education of the severely and profoundly mentally retarded.* New Orleans, La., April 1975.

3. State of Rhode Island, State Board of Regents. *General regulations of the state board of regents governing the special education of handicapped children.* Providence, R.I., 1975.

4. State of New York, State Education Department. *Commissioner's regulations.* Albany, N.Y., 1974.

5. *Vernon's Annotated Missouri Statutes,* 162.670 (Supp. 1975).

6. State of Iowa, Department of Public Instruction. *Rules of special education.* Des Moines, Ia., 1974.

7. State of Idaho, Department of Education. *Administrative rules and regulations: Handbook for special education.* Boise, Idaho, 1975.

## REFERENCES

Kolstoe, O. P. *Mental retardation: an educational viewpoint.* New York: Holt, Rinehart and Winston, 1972.

United States Office of Education, Bureau for Education of the Handicapped. *Definition of severely handicapped children.* (45 CFR 121.2), 1974.

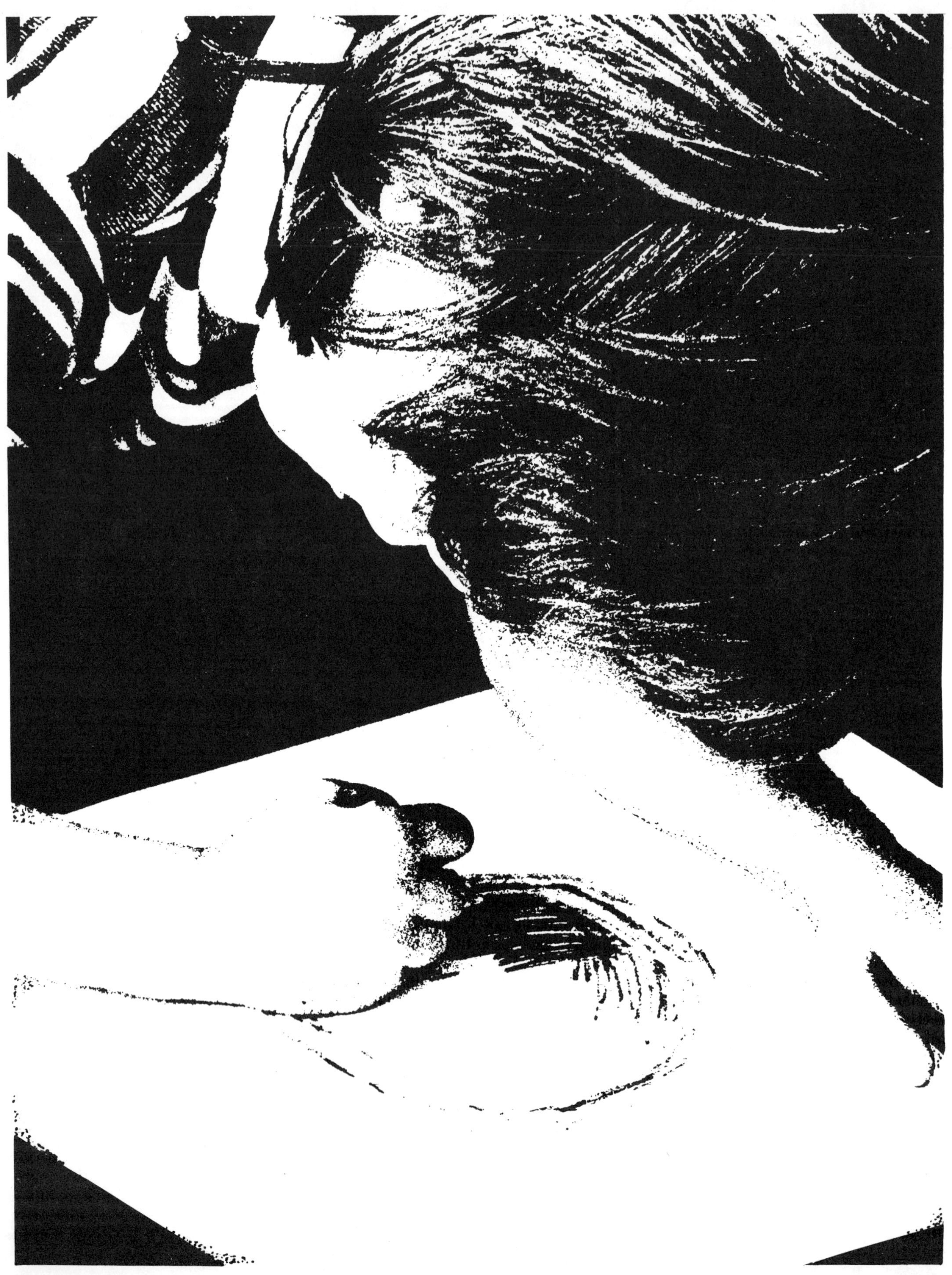

# Toward a Curriculum for the Profoundly Retarded, Multiply Handicapped Child

Chris Kiernan

Deputy Director, Thomas Coram Researchn Unit, University of
London, Institute of Education, 41 Brunswick Square, London WC1

*Summary*    An approach to formulating programmes for the profoundly retarded child is described. It is suggested that the basis for programming should be an analysis of the child's ability to operate on, and find
out about, his environment. This analysis can be approached by asking
questions about blocks to development, needs and preferences, socialization and communication and play and sensori-motor coordination.

## INTRODUCTION

In this paper I want to describe an approach to the curriculum for the
more severely mentally and multiply handicapped child. Following the
World Health Organisation convention I will refer to these children as
profoundly retarded, in other words having measured intelligence of
less than 20 IQ points. Our approach to this group can be summarized
very briefly. It is a child-centred approach in which the objectives and
methods stem from a consideration of the needs of the child in his
broad environment. Objectives for teaching are drawn from his environment and from a consideration of the development of normal and
handicapped children. The stress is on the elimination of problem behaviours and on the development of skills, especially cognitive skills,
which will allow the child to meet his environment in a more flexible
way. The teaching methods are designed to fit the child. Highly structured teaching techniques are seen as necessary when the child lacks
skills, but when he acquires skills structure may be relaxed. Throughout,
the appropriate use of rewards is seen as central.

Toward a Curriculum for the Profoundly Retarded, Multiply Handicapped Child, Chris Keirnan, *Child Care, Health &
Development*, Vol. 3, No. 4, July/August 1977. ©1977 Blackwell Scientific Publications Ltd., Osney Mead, Oxford, England 0X2
oEL.

# 3. MENTALLY HANDICAPPED



FOCUSSING ON THE CHILD

I have described our approach as child-centred. Too often in dealing with special children different professions tend to impose their system of priorities on teaching the child. For example a teacher may see the development of concepts in play settings as crucial in language development whereas the parent may find that the child's life is continuously in danger because he has not learned to respond when told to 'stop' on a busy high road. Or the physiotherapist may try to insist that a child holds a posture which effectively precludes his being taught. Often this results from a so-called multi-disciplinary team approach which, sadly, boils down to a situation where each profession has a bite at the child without any proper coordination of a programme for the child. Patchworks are not programmes.

We would make a plea for giving more say in what is taught to people who deal with the child for most of the day, the parents or nurses and the teachers. In practice these people do have effective control. What needs to be recognized more explicitly is that specialist professions need to share their skills with these groups and work through them, acknowledging that the people closest to the child do make the effective decisions on objectives and methods. This would suggest that there is a need for more equal status to be given to parents wishes than is currently common and more help given to them in allowing them to achieve goals which are especially relevant to the child in the home setting.

FOUR QUESTIONS

The central purpose of education is to allow the individual to meet and deal with his social and material environment in a more effective way (Kiernan, 1974). Given this assumption we can ask four questions in building up a programme for the child.

These questions are designed to give a basis for deciding on urgent priorities in teaching whether it be in the home or the school. The four questions are interrelated and represent areas for discussion rather than an attempt at a checklist. The solution to a problem in one area may well lie in the development of a programme in another.

## 1. Developmental blocks

Are there any behaviours or problems which represent blocks to development? Blocks may include sensory or motor deficits, blindness or cerebral palsy, or behaviour problems such as aggressive behaviour which prevents the child from benefiting from his environment in a way which would otherwise be possible given his intellectual abilities. Blocks may be dealt with in different ways. Some can be dealt with directly. Problem behaviour can often be extinguished by withdrawing reward for the unacceptable behaviour and teaching an alternate way of achieving the same goal. Shouting for attention can be replaced by simply asking for help. Other problem behaviours may take longer to eliminate and whilst competing behaviour is being taught crude coping techniques may have to be used. Wandering out of the classroom can be eliminated by saying 'no' and bringing the wanderer back at the same time as teaching the child to do all sorts of rewarded things in the classroom, but developing a range of rewarded and rewarding activities will take time. Meanwhile a 'coping' mechanism of putting a bolt on the classroom door may be necessary to prevent disruption of the classroom and souring of relationships.

Sensory and motor deficits have to be dealt with either by use of ameliorating techniques, the use of glasses, hearing aids, etc., or special aids to mobility, or through developing programmes to capitalize on the child's remaining ability, thereby outflanking the deficit.

Having some strategy for dealing with educational blocks is a central priority in developing a programme for a child. We cannot simply ignore them, we must evolve a method of dealing with them. However the method may involve other areas of development.

## 2. *Needs and preferences*

Does the child have things he likes and dislikes, can we reward him? The most difficult type of child to teach is the child who appears to have nothing he likes or dislikes, either in terms of material or social events. One problem here is that one cannot see how to reward desirable behaviour. Although we have found that it is usually possible to find *something* the child likes or prefers to do, a programme for such a child must focus on development of needs and preferences.

Sometimes the difficulty emerges that the child has preferences but because he has never been given a choice has not learned to express them. In other cases, the child has had very limited experience and has therefore not learned to like or dislike things. In both types of situation teaching which focusses on broadening the childs experience and requiring him to show preference, even initially by just a slight movement of the lips, is necessary as a first step.

If the child fails to show needs and preferences this must become a central area of concern both in terms of material and social rewards. If the child has an adequate range of needs and preferences allowing rewards to be readily isolated other areas may take prior claim on teaching time.

## 3. *Socialization and communication*

Does the child have means whereby he can relate to adults or other children and communicate with them? If the answer to this question is 'no' then getting some way of developing appropriate behaviour should be given equal priority to the removal of developmental blocks. In our society most learning and satisfaction of need comes from interaction with other human beings. Especially for the child who is only partially mobile the development of social responsiveness and communication will be crucial.

How do we evaluate social responsiveness and communication? Clearly normal development can be used as a model. We can ask, 'where does the child stand in relation to normal development', and then take as our objective the next stage of development. This model has been widely advocated and can prove very useful, but its drawbacks are equally clear. We really know relatively little about the development of children before the age of 2. And yet it is this level which is likely to be important. Secondly, the 12 year old, profoundly retarded child is *not* a one year old, normal child. Only some of his behaviours will be similar. His overall pattern of behaviour will be different and this will need to be taken into account. Finally the fact that normal development occurs in a particular way does not mean that our teaching should be based on this. Normal children learn speech informally around the family home. The fact that the mentally handicapped child does not, suggests that he needs a different approach rather than the same one in a different context.

*Imitation* Let me give you two examples which will help to make these points. Within the last few years there has been an increase in interest in imitation in the mentally handicapped. The willingness and ability to imitate is significant in several ways. If the child imitates it means that he sees the other person as similar to him, it suggests that he has a positive attitude to the other person, and this can certainly be developed if, as a result of imitating, interesting and rewarding things happen. The ability to imitate is clearly useful. The child can learn new motor responses very economically, including ways of solving problems. At a later stage verbal imitation can lead to language learning. However, the place of imitation in normal development is a source of controversy. In particular imitation is not felt to play a very significant part in the learning of speech and language. This is a point at which normal development and teaching of the retarded may part company and in which the normal model may be misleading.

In our own work, and that of many others, it has now been shown that non-imitating profoundly retarded children can be taught to imitate and to use this ability in learning new responses.

The basic strategy in teaching involves as a first step the testing of children on a range of simple imitation tasks, eg. hands on head, picking up a cup, etc. If the child does not imitate, then two simple responses are taught. These are selected to be different from the test set. The child is physically prompted and rewarded for correct performance. Prompts are faded over trials. Two responses are used so that the child has to look at the teacher rather than responding automatically to the request 'John, do this'. Once the two responses have been learned the child is tested again on the range of tasks. If he has learned to imitate then he will try to imitate each model, if not then we select and teach two more responses, test again, and so on.

In our experience the rate of learning is variable. Some children learn the generalized tendency to imitate after two or three pairs of tasks, others take very much longer. Some children appear to have particular difficulty with responses which do not involve objects (Kiernan & Saunders 1976).

Once the tendency to imitate has been learned imitation can be used as a means of teaching new responses, and is likely to be used by the child to his own ends in imitation of things which other children or adults do which achieve ends he wants to achieve. So the ability to imitate can be used by the child thereby partly freeing him from the constraints of his handicap.

*Communication* My second example concerns communication. Here the relevance of normal development can be examined in several ways. First of all it is worth noting that it is only within the very recent past that attention has been directed at the very early stages of development of communication. There are still only very few studies of one word communication and none of pre-verbal communication (Greenfield & Smith 1976, Rodgon 1976). The studies suggest that the first words learned by the child express wants, or named objects or events, thereby drawing the adults attention to them. So the child might say 'drink' meaning 'I want a drink' or 'noise' drawing attention to a noise. In our work with mentally handicapped children we have used as a first step in language training words or signs to represent the child's wants. The other type of response, naming, is more difficult to establish if the child is not well motivated.

We can relate this to the logical theoretical basis of normal communication. In order to communicate the child must have (a) the idea of communication, the idea that he can affect the environment by what he does; (b) something to say, in other words some need to express or a comment to make, and (c) a means of communicating. In the case of profoundly retarded children their problems may lie at all levels.

Quite often children emerge who do not appear to have the basic idea that what they do can affect others. For example, a child in the F6 Study (Kiernan, Wright & Hawks 1973) would often have her hair pulled by another child. She would cry at this, but cry silently, and not go for help to an adult. She had not learned that crying or approaching an adult had a communicative function.

With a child in another study we noticed that he never 'asked' for anything. Even if something he liked playing with was taken away he would not cry or try to get it back. We decided to teach him to 'ask' by pulling the teacher and later pointing to what he wanted. We began by taking away a Galt aeroplane on which he liked scudding around. When he was playing we took it away and put it high up. He was then prompted to touch the teacher, who then returned it. The prompts were faded quickly as he learned to touch the teacher spontaneously and then to push or pull her to the plane from other parts of the room. The new response quickly generalized to other people, other situations and other needs, giving him his first way of systematically communicating with other people.

Some mentally handicapped children appear to have very little which they want to say. They will express needs or wants but appear not to derive satisfaction from communication for its own sake in the form of commenting or sharing experience. In this they differ from the general run of normal children. This should represent a challenge to teaching.

It would seem likely that the child will only develop this type of response if pleasurable interaction with adults or others follows from it. This may be in terms of attention or because adults can make interesting things happen, like showing the child how something works or lifting him up to see a car or train, and that this is more likely to happen if he names things.

Finally, the profoundly handicapped child often requires different means of communication from that open to the normal child. He may use more pulling and pushing to direct you to what he wants, or have to squeal or bounce if he is physically incapable of this.

Just exactly how different the means of communication may be has been seen in recent studies of the use of manual and representational communication with the mentally handicapped.

## 3. MENTALLY HANDICAPPED

Over the last few years, mime systems (Levett 1969), deaf sign languages or systems (Cornforth, Johnson & Walker 1974, Fenn & Rowe 1975) communication boards, and Bliss & Rebus systems have all been used with the mentally handicapped (Vanderheiden & Grilley 1976) (see Kiernan 1977 for review). Very substantial successes have been claimed in some studies where it seems unlikely that speech training would have been successful. In some cases the reasons are clear, the students were deaf or had problems with speech musculature in addition to mental handicap. But in an increasing number of instances this explanation is not enough. The students are not sufficiently deaf or physically handicapped. Here we have to look for other explanations. One which offers itself is that the mentally handicapped may find it actually easier to understand and use visually presented information rather than information from sound. Several experimental studies have suggested this possibility (O'Connor 1975). If this is true then it would explain much of the difficulty experienced with language learning and would suggest that we should be either using a visual medium for communication with the mentally handicapped or at least using signs or similar methods as a first stage in the learning of the use of speech.

One tail-piece is in order. We can look back at normal development armed with the idea that gestures or manual signs may be crucial in development. When we do we find that a few authors have picked up this point in *normal* development (Piaget 1952, Werner & Kaplan 1963). Again we are reminded that we really know little about the dynamics of normal development. The theory of infant language development is itself in its infancy.

Let us return to our general theme of priorities in formulating the curriculum. As with previous areas, socialization and communication must be considered in the initial survey of priorities. If the child has no means of communication and shows little responsiveness, central focus needs to be placed on development in this area.

### 4. Play and sensori-motor coordination

We can ask the question, 'can the child play with objects in his environment in such a way that he can find out about their properties?' Again if the answer is 'no' we would suggest that high priority needs to be placed on development in this area. If the answer is 'yes' we may be able to rely on the child to develop in a good educational environment without special programming.

Normal play involves as a fundamental feature the child reaching grasping and then manipulating objects. If the child does not show the basic sensori-motor coordination involved in reaching and grasping we need to focus attention on this response. The attainment of this stage is a crucial watershed in normal development. Self-help skills and cognitive development are all dependent on it.

Even with an effective reach and grasp many profoundly retarded children show little or no effective play behaviour.

In one study which we did, 25 physically able, but profoundly retarded, children were observed in a setting in which they were given a selection of toys to play with. These included balls, rattles, a tambourine, cars and dolls. The vast majority of children banged, mouthed or simply held the toys. Responses like turning the toys over whilst looking at them, squeezing them to see if they squeaked, pushing them along or examining parts of the toys scarcely ever occurred. Yet it is these responses which allow the child to learn about the toys and, in different contexts, about his environment in general (Kiernan 1974).

Again, as with imitation and communication, the child lacks critical skills with which he could exploit his environment.

In our work we have taken a similar line to that on imitation. In a series of studies we have tried to teach the child new responses which he can then use with new toys. This approach has been fairly successful with responses like pushing objects, rolling objects, squeezing, pressing buttons and turning handles on toys (Kiernan 1974, Saunders 1977).

Many profoundly handicapped children have physical problems which prevent their exploiting the environment in this way. With these children it seems crucial that we devise mechanical or electronic means whereby they can learn from their own efforts for development of ideas of space and ideas about the constancy of size and shape of objects regardless of their position in space (Wedell 1973). Responsiveness of the environment to particular responses may be essential to the development of simple concepts of cause and effect and later to the understanding of choice.

One final word about play. It is often suggested that through observing the child's play we can find out how he sees his world. This is certainly true in some situations, but a proportion of the behaviour of some profoundly handicapped children can be seen as 'garbage', stereotyped behaviour which has no clear function and which fails to develop over time. This type of behaviour can be seen as analogous to smoking, or nail biting; something the person finds satisfying, but which has no function beyond filling the time or possibly reducing tension. This type of behaviour often develops in situations in which the child can make no contact with the environment, as in many hospital wards, or because the environment is unsuitable. Many handicapped children in normal playgroups fail to make effective contact with their environment. I would suggest that one needs to be sceptical about existing play behaviour and, rather than saying that it is intrinsically meaningful and that the child needs to grow through it, ask the question whether or not the child 'plays' in this way because he does not know an alternative means. Tragically, we can find people who 'judge' the child as being too handicapped to benefit from a 'good' environment. This approach places too much confidence in the effectiveness of the environment in bringing out behaviour and too little on the need to teach. It is the kind of thinking which has been used as a justification for desert-like hospital environments which effectively prevent development.

CONCLUSION

In this paper I have suggested an approach to a child-centred curriculum. This involves asking four questions. Is there anything holding the child back from realizing his intellectual potential? Does the child have developed needs and preferences? Does the child show social responsiveness and has he a means of communication? And does he have a functioning level of sensori-motor coordination and play behaviour? The central focus of each of these questions is the child's ability to operate on and find out about his environment. In each case the child who lacks competence is limited, the child who has some competence can advance in the context of a good educational environment. Consequently, if an examination of the child's behaviour suggests basic deficits priority needs to be placed in that area.

In this account we have stressed also the need to examine these areas in relation to the whole life pattern of the child, his functioning at home and at school. The profoundly retarded have difficulty in transferring responses from one setting to another and so cross-environment planning is necessary. Moreover, the parents and other caretakers of the child must be allowed a strong voice in curriculum objectives. Given this comment it is possibly surprising that self-help skills have been given scant mention. The reasons, however, are simple. First of all they may represent blocks and so be seen as constant. A child may be excluded from a playgroup because he is incontinent or aggressive. Secondly sensori-motor coordination is fundamental to most self-help skills and development of needs and preferences to all. The third and most important reason is that concentration on self-help skills may distract us from what we would see as more fundamental human needs in education. The 'difficult' feeding behaviour of a child must be seen within the context of the fact that the only individual attention the child gets during the day is at meal times. To take that away may lead to increased isolation and be counterdevelopmental.

The profoundly handicapped child is a developing human being. It is our job to help him develop as a human being. For this reason it is the human needs, preferences, communication and abilities which we must pay central attention to in order to lead him to growth.

REFERENCES

Cornforth A.R.T., Johnson K. & Walker M. (1974) Teaching sign language to the deaf mentally handicapped. *Apex* 2

Fenn G. & Rowe J.A. (1975) An experiment in manual communication. *British Journal of Disorders of Communication* **10**, 3

Greenfield P.M. & Smith J.H. (1976) *The Structure of Communication in Early Language Development.* Academic Press, New York

Kiernan C.C. (1974) Experimental investigation of the curriculum for the profoundly retarded. In *Mental Retardation Concepts of Education and Research*, Tizard J. (ed). Butterworths, London

Kiernan C.C. (1977) Alternatives to speech: a review of research on manual and other alternative forms of communication with the mentally handicapped and other non-communicating populations. *British Journal of Mental Subnormality*, 23, 6

Kiernan C.C. & Saunders C.A. (1976) *Generalised Imitation.* Unpublished manuscript

Kiernan C.C., Wright E.C. & Hawks G. (1973) The ward wide application of operant training techniques. In *Proceedings of the Third International Congress of the IASSMD*, Primrose D. (ed). The Hague

Levett L.M. (1969) A method of communication for non-speaking, severely subnormal children. *British Journal of Disorders of Communication* 4, 64–66

O'Connor N. (1975) *Language, Cognitive Deficits and Retardation.* Butterworths, London

**Piaget J. (1952)** *The Origins of Intelligence in Children.* **Norton, New York**

Rodgon M.M. (1976) *Single-Word Usage, Cognitive Development and the Beginnings of Combinational Speech.* Cambridge University Press

Saunders C.A. (1977) Shaping play behaviour in severely mentally handicapped children. Unpublished manuscript

Vanderheiden G.C. & Grilley K. (1976) *Non-Vocal Communication Techniques and Aids for the Severely Physically Handicapped.* University Park Press, Baltimore

Wedell K. (1973) *Learning and Perceptuo-Motor Disabilities in Children.* Wiley, London

# THE EDUCATION AND COMMUNITY SUPPORT OF SEVERELY HANDICAPPED PEOPLE

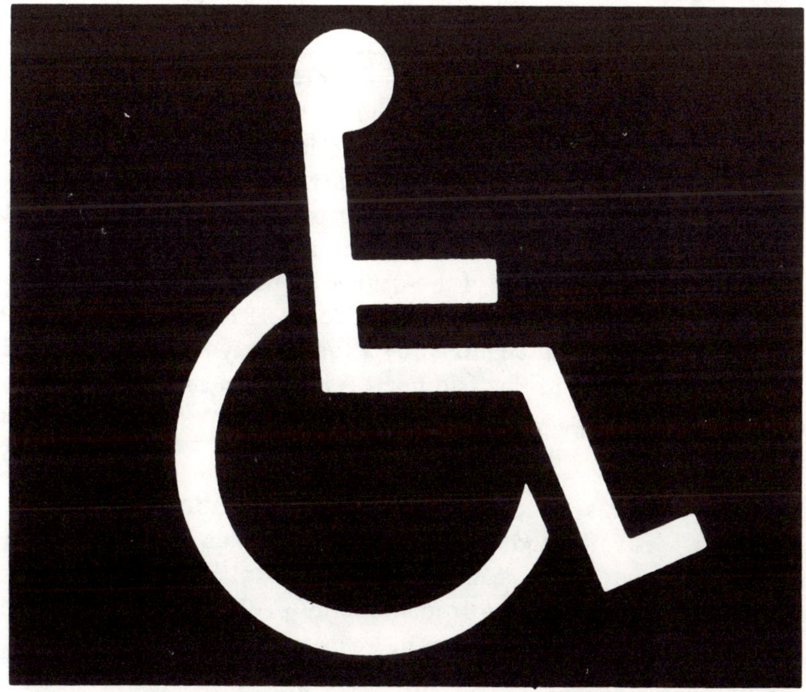

EDWARD W. SONTAG, NANCY DODD,
and JAMES E. BUTTON

Dramatic changes have occurred over the last five years in the education of severely handicapped people. Educators who are working with them have developed a wide range of efficacious teaching procedures that have had a major impact on the performance of handicapped people. The increases in adaptive skills that have resulted from these instructional procedures have enabled severely handicapped individuals to perform at levels previously thought unattainable. Because of these increased levels of performance, it is now possible to argue that severely handicapped citizens should be helped to become active and accepted members of the community.

But the process of becoming active, useful citizens goes far beyond the traditional domain of the classroom educator. Therefore, the purpose of this paper is to develop the notion that the education of severely retarded or handicapped citizens is a joint venture. It is a joint venture that entails the close cooperation of

©1977. Reprinted from *International Journal of Mental Health* by permission of M.E. Sharpe, Inc., White Plains, NY 10603.

a number of professionals, across a variety of disciplines, whose major work is concerned with both the individual and the social system within which the individual resides. If the integration of severely handicapped citizens into full community participation is to be achieved, it seems that professionals in a variety of positions should become active facilitators of this move. This paper is directed toward explicating these facilitating roles, within the context of a joint cooperative structure.

# The Education of the Severely Handicapped

A number of the traditional assumptions underlying instructional programs for severely handicapped children have been challenged by those who believe that acquisition of skills may be more a function of instructional programming than a question of limited mental ability (Entrikin, York, & Brown, 1975). A crucial difference in the teaching procedures utilized with the severely handicapped, as differentiated from the normal or the mildly handicapped, is the degree of precision required in instructional programming (Brown & York, 1974). As a result, the disciplined precision required by a task-analysis approach to instructional programming has been relied upon in an increasing number of successful educational programs for the severely handicapped (Williams, Brown, & Certo, 1975).

In addition to advances in instructional technology with the severely handicapped, there have been a number of court decisions and, more recently, federal legislation that have provided additional impetus to community programming. Beginning with the landmark decision in Pennsylvania (Pennsylvania Association for Retarded Children v. Pennsylvania, 1972), a free public education was guaranteed for all retarded children, regardless of the degree of retardation or associated handicaps. This concept of zero-reject was extended to all handicapped children by Mills v. Board of Education of the District of Columbia (1972). The basic concepts of these court decisions have been combined into federal legislation as PL 93-380 and, as amended, PL 94-142. Although the initial thrust of the court decisions and early legislation supported the idea of zero-reject as it pertained to mildly or moderately handicapped students, the current emphasis is clearly on a zero-exclusion model that applies also to the severely handicapped, who have traditionally been excluded from a public-school education.

Associated with this trend of allowing the severely handicapped into the mainstream of public education has been a growing disenchantment with institutionalization. The move toward a more normal educational experience, allied with the increase in the efficacy of educational technology, has produced a trend toward deinstitutionalization. This trend is an attempt to generalize the initial gains in skill development that have resulted from a more normal educational experience, through integration of the handicapped into the public school, to the more pervasive idea of the "normalizing" experience of community living.

# The Need of Community Action Networks



Thanks to the advances in educational programming, the pressures exerted by "right to education" legislation, and the growing movement toward decentralization, increasing numbers of severely handicapped individuals are now remaining in their communities or returning to their communities from institutions. It is vital that we provide these community-based handicapped individuals with a range of educational and community services in order to assist them in learning to adjust to the demands of community living.

We know that, from an educational standpoint, severely handicapped children can learn the skills necessary for community living (Brown, Certo, Belmore, & Crowner, 1976; Brown, Crowner, Williams, & York, 1975). In addition, we have available a variety of effective and efficient methods and techniques for teaching the required living skills (see Fredericks et al., 1976; White & Haring, 1976; Williams, Brown, & Certo, 1975).

Although we have made substantial progress in teaching severely handicapped people living skills and in helping them develop proficiency in these skills, one of our most pressing concerns is to find ways in which to maintain and generalize these learned skills to the handicapped person's natural environment. Even in this most difficult area, technological advances are beginning to surface. Instruction techniques that vary the physical setting, teacher, language cues, and/or materials during initial skill acquisition have been demonstrated to facilitate generalization (Barrett & McCormack, 1973; Corte, Wolf, & Locke, 1971; Garcia, 1974; Johnson & Johnson, 1972; Kale, Kaye, Whelan, & Hopkins, 1968; Martin, 1975; Stokes, Baer, & Jackson, 1974).[1] It is our belief, however, that attainment of the total goal of both maintaining and generalizing classroom learning to the community will necessitate the involvement of professionals from areas other than education.

Successful adaption of severely handicapped children to a community living situation is a reciprocal process. It involves, on the one hand, the education of the handicapped individual to the point of maximum normalcy and, on the other hand, the adjustment of community service facilities to the needs of the handicapped individual and his family.

A variety of community living skills has been developed and taught to severely handicapped students. Aside from the more traditional programs emphasizing the self-care skills of dressing, toilet training, and eating, much more complex programs have been initiated. Certo, Schwartz, & Brown (1975) have taught severely handicapped children to ride a public bus system. Williams (1975) has taught severely handicapped students to respond differentially to individual components of language cues and has developed a mathematics skill sequence for the severely retarded.

Nietupski, Certo, Pumpian, & Belmore (1976) have taught severely handicapped students to draw up a shopping list and purchase groceries. Certo & Swetlik (1976) have taught severely handicapped students to make general purchases based on simple decisions of enough or not enough money. Williams, Pumpian, McDaniel, Hamre-Nietupski, & Wheeler (1975) have developed a procedure to teach social interaction skills to severely handicapped students.

It is, however, of little social value to the severely handicapped to possess skills that they cannot utilize and further expand. It is therefore necessary to develop a network of services that will allow for the maintenance and generalization of these learned skills within the community. Kenowitz, Gallaher, & Edgar (1977) have proposed such a system, which they term a community action network. The purpose of such a system would be to sensitize community services to the needs of the severely handicapped and their families. According to these authors, such a network would serve in a linkage capacity to bring together families of the severely handicapped and all agencies that traditionally deliver a service these families could utilize.

Regardless of what term is used or how intensive a network is proposed, some attempt to develop a total service delivery system to families of the severely handicapped is necessary. If the initial promise of educational procedures is to be turned into the reality of community living, cooperation between educators and other professionals involved in community programming is essential. The remainder of this paper will outline a cooperative venture involving a variety of professionals in the areas of vocational training, social development, and recreational programming.

# Vocational Opportunities

Now that it has been established that severely handicapped persons can acquire a wide variety of skills that were previously considered to be unattainable, it becomes important to attempt to apply these learned behaviors to areas other than the classroom. A prime target for this transfer process is the vocational area. Training of severely handicapped people in vocational skill acquisition and proficiency in highly complex tasks has already been demonstrated (Gold, 1972), but transfer of these work skills from structured, closed settings to the community has rarely been attempted.

Sheltered workshops and activity centers have been the most common response to the vocational needs of the severely handicapped. These alternatives to competitive, community employment have often been self-limiting, and certainly ineffective in providing the normalizing experiences necessary for employment in the community. Such alternatives may be, in part, the result of long-held beliefs concerning the limited capacity of severely handicapped people to function in a vocational setting. Even the most advanced programs of vocational training still involve some educational or sheltered workshop support.

Recently, Gold & Torner[2] have proposed an integrated plant employing both handicapped and nonhandicapped workers. DuRand[3] has successfully piloted a project utilizing a work-station and a work-team concept to establish a degree of normalization for the handicapped. The work station consists of approximately eight severely handicapped people working under a separate supervisor in a small group, but placed in a regular, much larger, industrial setting. In this way they blend into the normal work environment. The work team consists of a small group of severely handicapped employees, together with a supervisor, who contracts for special jobs. This approach is most often used with such tasks as janitorial work or yard work.

The utilization of such approaches as work stations and work teams is an improvement over institutional settings, but there is potential for even more normal work environments for severely handicapped people. Schwartz,[4] utilizing a work assessment model developed by Belmore & Brown (1976), has demonstrated the transfer of dishwashing skills acquired by severely handicapped individuals in a structured work environment to paid jobs under normal employment conditions.

Once again, the technology required to teach severely handicapped persons viable vocational skills seems to be available. But the maintenance of a severely handicapped worker on a non-sheltered job requires the cooperation of employer, employees, the training agent, and allied services. If extensive transfer of vocational skills acquired by severely handicapped workers is to be effected, a cooperative network of community-based professionals is obviously needed. Forming such a cooperative alliance on an individual basis for each worker does not seem to be the most efficient approach when one balances the time and effort expended against the number of positions required. Only through the joint efforts of a variety of knowledgeable professionals can we hope to capitalize on the results of the severely handicapped individual's rising potential and allow for the maintenance and generalization of his/her newly developed vocational skills.

Vocational competence is an important economic consideration in society. Productive work that contributes to the general well-being greatly affects people's attitude toward their peers. As severely handicapped workers demonstrate their vocational competence in the open job market, their perceived value to society will be enhanced.

# Social Skills

Educational programs that enable the severely handicapped to acquire and become proficient in the skills necessary for social living have been demonstrated (Brown, Crowner, Williams, & York, 1975). Educational research has clearly established that severely handicapped people can develop competency in social skills that will enable them to blend successfully into the community (Neisworth & Smith, 1973). The implementation of programs emphasizing maintenance and generalization of social skills has, however, been less prevalent than programs for the acquisition of skills and the development of proficiency.

Social acceptance is a vital component in any attempt at community integration.  It is often influenced by the number of problems the person presents to community members.  To the extent that the presence of a handicapped person does not make others uncomfortable or compel them to perform activities they would not otherwise perform, the probability of community acceptance is enhanced.

The development of control over social behaviors has been a two-part process.  First, a variety of procedures has been developed to modify or extinguish bizarre or inappropriate behaviors that interfere with social acceptance (Fox & Azrin, 1973; Koegel, Firestone, & Kramme, 1974; Weisberg, Passman, & Russell, 1973).  Second, procedures have been utilized to develop more appropriate or nonexistent social behaviors in severely handicapped people (Morris & Dolker, 1974; Paloutzian, Hasizi, Streifel, & Edgar, 1971).[5]  Again, as in the area of vocational integration, the maintenance and application of these learned social skills in a community setting will involve cooperative effort from a community service network.

Community-based severely handicapped people and their families will need help with communication, housing, transportation, shopping, food preparation, economic transactions, selection and care of clothing, medical care, dental attention, babysitting needs, and a variety of other activities associated with community living.  The provision of services to meet these needs will call for the active participation of mental health workers, medical workers, housing specialists, nutritionists, and family service professionals.  These individual professionals, acting in concert, will be able to link individuals to services, modify existing services to meet pressing needs, and act to establish necessary services that do not exist.

Since social skills of either a verbal or nonverbal nature pervade most situations of human interaction, the development, maintenance, and generalization of these skills need to be incorporated as a subgoal in the services provided by all professional agencies that focus on the severely handicapped.  As professionals we can be satisfied only when a severely handicapped person can, for example, go undetected into a store and buy some toothpaste without continual support.

# Recreational Skills

Vocational skills and competency in social functioning are recognized as essential components of a normal lifestyle; but the handicapped also need recreational skills and interests (Brown, Bellamy, & Sontag, 1971), and this area has received little attention in the literature.  There seems to be ample reason to conclude that the same basic methods and techniques used to teach other skills can be used to teach recreational skills as well.

One explanation for recreational skills' receiving less attention from educators may be related to the somewhat artificial distinction between academic concerns and play.  It is likely that educators look upon recreation as more properly the function of the community and family.  Although this may well be the case with the education of the less seriously handicapped, it cannot be justified with the severely handicapped.

The literature on the motor characteristics of the retarded points out that the retarded are markedly inferior to normal children on all motor tests (Francis & Rarick, 1959). Malpass (1960) has summarized the research on motor skills in retarded children and indicated that as a group they demonstrate less motor competence than normal children, and that the severely retarded are less physically capable than the moderately retarded.

But the problems in the area of motor skills of the severely handicapped cannot be explained simply as a lack of proficiency. Many older, severely handicapped people function physically at very rudimentary developmental levels. For example, before a severely handicapped person might be able to participate in a game that required movement across a rough or uneven surface, he or she might need to learn to inhibit primitive reflex reactions to the tactile sensation of the uneven surface on the feet. By arranging for minor adaptations in a running game, such as running barefoot across a carefully designed surface, the benefits from a carefully planned recreation activity can be extended. Through the cooperative efforts of occupational therapists, physical therapists, and educators, recreational programs for the severely handicapped can become a very useful area of learning.

Aside from motor ability, three other considerations are relevant to the learning of recreational skills by the severely retarded. First, they do not usually spontaneously engage in play through association: they must be taught (Frye & Peters, 1972). Second, they must be taught any physical activity step by step, through a task-analysis procedure similar to academic programming. Finally, many recreational skills provide an excellent means of extending, maintaining, or generalizing social skills.

Fortunately, therapeutic and community recreation personnel have realized the extensive need for recreation for the retarded, and a variety of therapeutic programs has been developed for handicapped children (Frye & Peters, 1972). Unfortunately, little work has been carried out with the severely handicapped; but therapeutic and community recreation professionals have a strong background and commitment to the integration of the handicapped into more normal environments through the provision of recreational activities.

# The Family as Catalyst

Educators now realize that the family is an important component in providing for the education of severely handicapped children. Home-school cooperation is a growing reality (Sontag, 1976), as both parents and educators recognize the child's need for a 24-hour environment conducive to learning. Educators have recognized that parents can learn to teach their children skills at home and to reinforce the skills taught at school through appropriate practice. This cooperative effort has led to increased acquisition and proficiency of skills. In addition, this cooperative effort has had a pronounced impact on the maintenance and generalization of skills through the provision of opportunities to practice in situations offering a variety of persons, places, and language cues (Barrett & McCormack, 1973; Corte, Wolfe, & Lock, 1971; Garcia, 1974; Johnson & Johnson, 1972; Kale, Kaye, Whelan, & Hopkins, 1968; Martin, 1975; Stokes, Baer, & Jackson, 1974; Williams, 1975).[6] If effective community services can be instituted so that they become an integral part of this home-based partnership, opportunities for appropriate practice will increase, which will, in turn, lead to even greater opportunities for the maintenance and generalization of academic, vocational, and social skills.

The positive benefits that accrue to severely handicapped people through the ability to utilize skills in a number of community settings is but one of the benefits of community programming. An equally important function of a community service network is to lend support when people are experiencing stress. It is generally agreed that the presence of a severely handicapped member within the family group produces stress. Not only are extensive adjustments demanded in family routines but family members must respond in unusual ways to even the most commonplace needs. Such services as babysitting, dental work, and transportation, which the nonhandicapped population may take for granted, are exceptionally difficult for families of the handicapped to obtain (Kenowitz, Gallagher, & Edgar, 1977).

The provision of services to help these families circumvent common areas of stress or to help them cope more effectively with unavoidable stress-producing situations would be an appropriate activity for a community service network. Mental health professionals have traditionally been involved in providing such supportive services to a variety of client populations, and their services would be a useful and effective addition to any community service system organized to work with the severely handicapped.

A common source of stress in families with a severely handicapped member is change. Community service personnel, mainly mental health workers and medical personnel, have typically provided either services of an informational nature, relating to placement possibilities for a severely handicapped person, or services of a supportive nature, relating to the adjustments necessary to maintain the person in the home. The focus on placement or adjustment has usually been based on the assumption that the handicapping condition would persist in its present form over time. This assumption of stability has proved to be erroneous, for it fails to take into account the impact of educational programs that have produced levels of functioning that were previously thought unattainable.

Learning to cope with changes in performance will have a major impact on the families of the severely handicapped. In some ways, acceptance of and adjustment to the handicapping conditions may be easier than dealing with the stress generated by uneven and sporadic change. The demands of a rigorous home learning program, coupled with the unknowns associated with individually specific anticipated performance estimates, are bound to produce conditions of stress and uncertainty within the family.

In summarizing this section on the family, we might well look at the family group as a central agent that mediates the provision of services to the severely handicapped. These services can be looked upon as a combination of direct services to meet immediate needs and social action to influence future interactions. Community service professionals must constantly remind themselves of the reciprocal nature of social change. Community programming must attend not only to the adjustment needs of the handicapped vis-à-vis the larger society but also to the corresponding need to influence the larger society to adjust to the handicapped.

# Conclusion

Increasing numbers of severely handicapped people are becoming members of our communities. They have the legal and the moral right to an appropriate education and to adjunct community services to prepare them for independent functioning as participating members in the daily activities of their communities. Educators have made a solid beginning in showing the way to teach skills that were previously thought to be unattainable. Now, through the cooperative efforts of a larger community service network, educators and other community service professionals can work together on maintaining and generalizing these essential skills. Community service professionals have the opportunity and the responsibility to adapt their traditional expertise to ways of providing for the needs of the severely handicapped. These needs are urgent, and the potential for meeting them through cooperative effort is but a handshake away.

NOTES

[1] N. Certo (1976) A systematic comparison of the relative effectiveness of inducing generalization through the utilization of a concurrent versus successive procedure during initial skill acquisition with handicapped students. Unpublished doctoral dissertation, University of Wisconsin, Madison.

[2] M. Gold & R. Torner (1974) A request for a program-related investment. Unpublished report, Macron, Inc., Champaign, Ill.

[3] J. DuRand (1976) Year-end report. Unpublished report, Minnesota Diversified Industries Plant #1, Minneapolis, Minn., May 6, 1976.

[4] R. Schwartz (1976) Teaching severely handicapped workers to function as dishwashers in simulated and natural settings. Unpublished Master's thesis, University of Wisconsin, Madison.

[5] A. Kazdin & B. Erickson (1974) Development of play responses in the severely and profoundly retarded. Paper read at Association for Advancement of Behavior Therapy Convention, Chicago.

[6] Certo, op. cit.

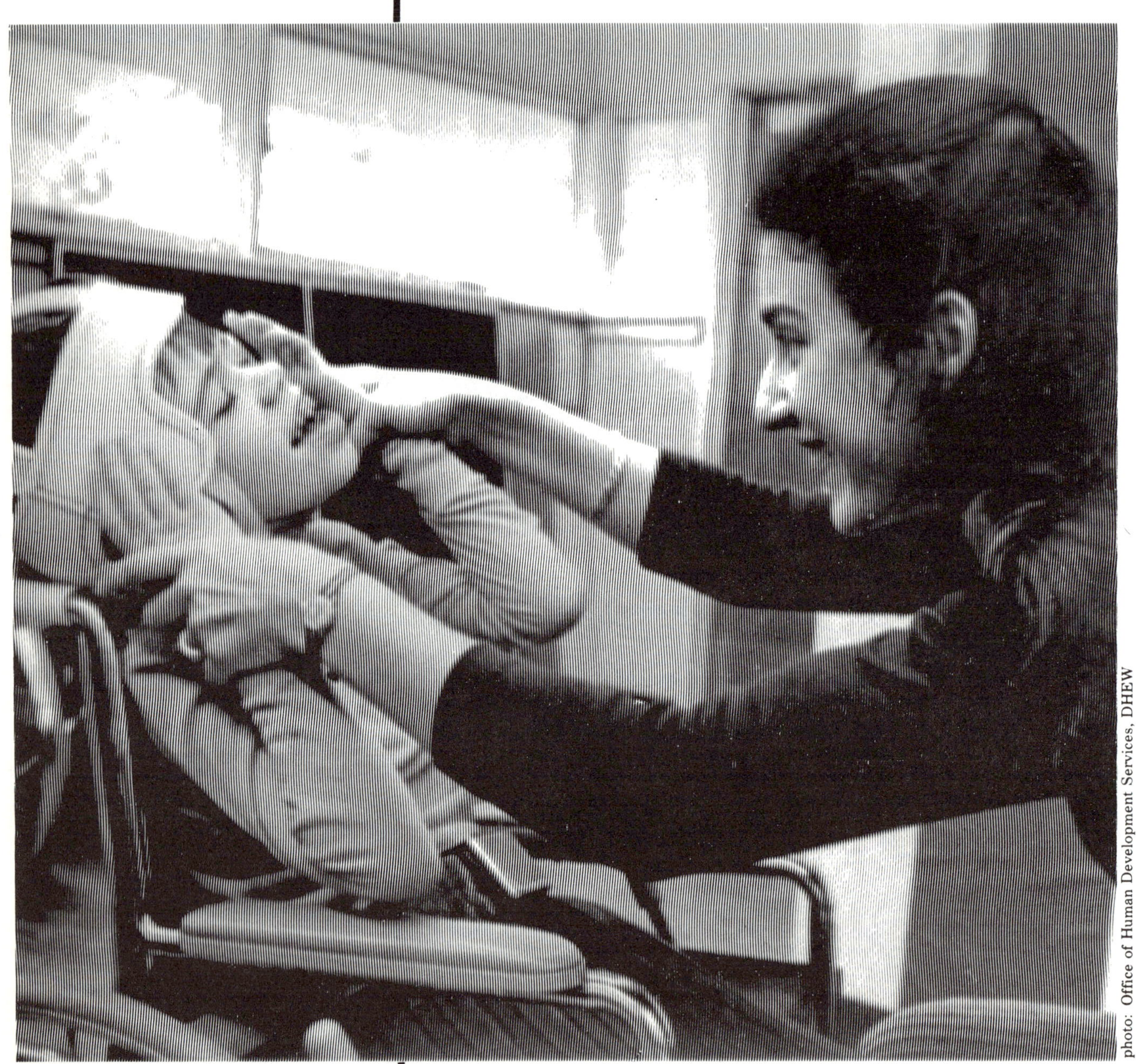

photo: Office of Human Development Services, DHEW

# EMOTIONAL AND BEHAVIORAL DISORDERS

Emotional and Behavioral Disorders is a very broad topic. In choosing the articles for this section, an attempt has been made to find articles which first, give the educator an overview into the causes of various emotional and behavioral disorders. Secondly, articles were chosen which give examples of techniques or treatments used for these various disorders.

The section opens with an article which presents ideas for why adolescents have emotional problems. Erikson and Friedman suggest that one must look at the developmental cycle of the child from infancy on to find where the deficit lies.

The articles discussing hyperactivity were selected because they give an idea where the problems with this disorder lie. Diagnosis is a major problem. It has been noted in the past that many children were falsely identified as hyperactive because of some other disruptive behavior. After thorough diagnosis a problem also arises. This being how to treat the disorder. Dr. Kinsbourne suggests that with careful use, drugs can control the hyperactive child. Mr. Box, on the other hand, feels there are other, more suitable methods of treatment. These are presented in his article., "Hyperactivity: The Scandalous Silence."

This section concludes with articles examining various remediation techniques. One article looks at how art therapy helped mend the broken self-image of several children. Following, Dr. Carberry gives examples of how to control behavior specific problems in the classroom. And finally the section looks at the work being done at a center in Georgia with emotionally disturbed children.

# Understanding and Evaluating Adolescent Behavior Problems


Candace J. Erickson, MD

Stanford B. Friedman, MD



## ABSTRACT

*A knowledge of normal adolescent development and the adolescent's own stage of psychosocial development is necessary in evaluating the significance of his behavior. Understanding the youngster's previous development is useful as those experiences will influence how well he will master the adolescent task of identity formation. Issues which directly impact on this developmental task include separation from parents, peer support, changes in body and body image, sexuality, development of abstract reasoning, and career choice. Difficulty in resolving any of these issues may result in a behavior disturbance. The evaluation of the adolescent's functioning in various life spheres at school, with peers, and at home should enable the professional to better determine whether a teenager's behavior is normal or a symptom of an emotional problem. Professionals, particularly those in schools, should take advantage of their interaction with adolescents in order to asssess behavior and identify the presence of underlying problems.*


To evaluate an adolescent behavior problem, it is essential to examine the meaning and chronicity of the youngster's actions. Many adolescent behaviors are viewed as "problems" by adults. These behaviors may include "rejecting" parental values, sexual experimentation, mood swings, depression, drug use, and school "under-achievement." Some of these behaviors — such as separation from parents, sexual experimentation, and mood swings — may be normal aspects of adolescent development. However, because they may conflict with adult expectations, they may erroneously be considered deviant or abnormal. On the other hand, other behaviors such as running away and drug abuse are not "normal" and may identify a need for mental health intervention. Even some "normal" behaviors, if exaggerated or present for a prolonged period of time, may represent an emotional disorder. It is therefore useful to regard certain behaviors as "symptoms" and to investigate their cause and duration. It is only by doing this that true behavior problems can be distinguished from normal adolescent behaviors.

The question then arises as to who is to evaluate the teenager's behavior. Parents do, but they are often too involved in the situation or lack the necessary understanding of adolescent development to make an objective, rational assessment. It is, therefore, usually helpful for a professional to aid the parent in deciding whether or not the teenager's behavior represents a "normal phase," a reaction to a specific situation, or a symptom of a more serious underlying emotional problem. Because of the large number of adolescents in high schools and colleges, the majority of professionals interacting with teenagers are those in educational systems. It is therefore important that educators and school health personnel, as well as mental health professionals, have a base of knowledge from which they can judge the significance of an adolescent's behavior.

To understand the meaning of a teenager's behavior, it is necessary to understand normal adolescent development and then to assess and compare to normal the youngster's own psychosocial growth. Throughout life, development occurs by building on what came before and adding to and changing what is already there. Therefore, understanding what happened in early life is essential to understanding what is happening during adolescence.

Erik Erikson developed a theory of psychosocial development which is comprised of eight stages.[1] These stages follow in order, and each builds on the previous one. An individual must pass through each stage and master it to a greater or lesser degree before proceeding to the next. The success one has in mastering the task at each level depends on how well earlier tasks have been mastered. The Erikson's eight stages are shown in Table 1.




*The Journal of School Health*, Vol. 48, No. 5, May 1978, pp. 293-297. ©1978 American School Health Association, Kent, Ohio 44240.

### TABLE 1
### Life Stages

| I.<br>INFANCY | TRUST<br>vs.<br>MISTRUST |
| --- | --- |
| II.<br>EARLY<br>CHILDHOOD | AUTONOMY<br>vs.<br>SHAME, DOUBT |
| II.<br>PLAY AGE | INITIATIVE<br>vs.<br>GUILT |
| IV.<br>SCHOOL AGE | INDUSTRY<br>vs.<br>INFERIORITY |
| V.<br>ADOLESCENCE | IDENTITY<br>vs.<br>IDENTITY<br>DIFFUSION |
| VI.<br>YOUNG ADULT | INTIMACY<br>vs.<br>ISOLATION |
| VII.<br>ADULTHOOD | GENERATIVITY<br>vs.<br>SELF-ABSORPTION |
| VIII.<br>MATURE AGE | INTEGRITY<br>vs.<br>DISGUST, DESPAIR |

Table of Life Stages modified from: Erikson EH: Identity and the life cycle, in *Psychological Issues,* Klein GS (ed), New York, International Universities Press, Inc. (Monograph 1) 1: 101-164, 1959.

During the first stage, the infant must develop a sense of trust. Erikson explains that the child must learn ''to rely on the sameness and continuity of the outer providers.'' In the next stage, the toddler develops a sense of autonomy — that is, an idea that he can assert himself and ''stand on his own feet'' without losing the love and support of the adults in his life. In the pre-school child, ''initiative adds to autonomy the quality of undertaking, planning, and attacking a task for the sake of being active and on the move, where before self-will, more often than not, inspired acts of defiance or, at any rate, protested independence.'' In the fourth stage, industry, ''bringing a productive situation to completion is an aim which gradually supersedes the whims and wishes of play'' for the school-age child. ''The work principle teaches him the pleasure of work completion by steady attention and perservering diligence.'' The adolescent's task is that of forming an identity. The teenager needs to compare and integrate the way others see him with how he sees himself. He must also decide ''how to connect the roles and skills cultivated earlier with the occupational prototypes of the day.'' The young adult is faced with developing intimacy or ''the capacity to commit himself to concrete affiliations and partnerships and to develop the ethical strength to abide by such commitments, even though they may call for significant sacrifices and compromises.'' Once able to be truly intimate, the individual proceeds to the stage of generativity where he is ''primarily concerned with establishing and guiding the next generation.'' The final stage of ''Integrity vs. Despair'' is characterized by acceptance of one's life as it has been and a sense of peace which accompanies this acceptance. [1]

As noted before, each of these stages follows in order, and the mastery of each developmental task depends on how previous tasks were mastered. So, with adolescents, the success in forming an identity depends, at least to some extent, on how the youngster mastered the previous four stages. A child having difficulty attaining a sense of autonomy may well have later problems separating from his parents during his teenage years. In fact, adolescence is viewed by some as a reliving and re-working of the task of autonomy. How well the individual can consolidate his identity will in turn influence his capacity to later form intimate relationships. Without being secure in one's identity, it is impossible to risk losing one's self by intimate association with others.

In addition to relating an adolescent's stage of development to his previous life experience, it is important to consider the various issues which directly impact on the teenager's present task of identity formation. The adolescent needs to separate from his parents so that he can see himself as having values of his own. In order to do this, he relies heavily on his peer group for support. The teenager's body is changing, and he needs to assimilate these changes into his self-image. The issue of sexuality must be explored. Increasing intellectual ability and the use of abstract reasoning needs to be integrated into the youngster's idea of himself. Career choice and plans for the future must also be considered. Each of these aspects of identity formation is important and will be discussed separately. However, it is also important to remember that they are all closely inter-related and influence each other.

### Separation From Parents

Throughout childhood, the individual has been dependent both physically and emotionally on his parents. He has become progressively less dependent as he matures. However, his major identification has been with his family. With the advent of adolescence, the child begins to separate from his family to assume his role as an adult in society. This separation is not easy. The adolescent risks leaving the security and stability of his structured life within the family, where expectations, rewards, and punishments are known. He ventures into an unknown world where expectations and values may not be predictable. The adult world is interesting, exciting, and waiting to be mastered; but fear of the unknown and insecurity regarding his ability to master it draw the teenager back. This process is reminiscent of the stage of autonomy when the toddler runs to explore his rapidly-expanding world, realizes that he has run away from his mother, and then must come running back. The teenager exerts his independence, and then, insecure in his abilities, retreats to the comfort of dependency. Then, angered and frightened by his need to be dependent, he surges forward again on his own. This swing back and forth accounts for much of the mood swing observed in adolescence.

The tie between parent and child can be too strong or too weak. If it is too strong, the teenager may have trouble separating, and therefore stay with his parents, making no attempt to grow up. This problem of separation may also make it difficult for the youngster to move into social interaction with his peers who are "rejecting" adult society. Such separation problems may show up as social withdrawal or school phobia. Another common reaction to extreme parental control is to rebel against the parents, thereby denying the strength of their influence. It is not unusual for normal adolescents to "test" limits set on them. This may manifest itself by staying out past curfews, neglecting assigned chores and the like. However, when parents attempt to impose their will on a teenager to an extent that the teenager is unable to begin testing his independence and responsibility, a power struggle is set up in which the youngster continually attempts to overcome his parents' will. He becomes progressively more hostile and more extreme in the behavior he exhibits. This may lead to a wide range of behaviors including running away, delinquency, sexual promiscuity, and school failure. The same reaction can be seen in a child who feels overly dependent on his parents, and fearing that dependence, exhibits his "bravado" by extreme behavior.

A "too weak" relationship between the teenager and parents can also lead to problems. The youngster may participate in negative behavior merely to attract attention from his parents. In addition, a lack of role models for the adolescent may be a significant problem when parental or adult influence is weak. Even though adolescents pull away from adults, they nevertheless view them as models for their behavior. Teachers often serve as role models in this sense. Parents do to some degree. Heroes, be they rock musicians or athletic stars, may also fill this need. A lack of strong, effective adults in his environment may leave the adolescent without an adequate model for adult behavior.

One other problem meriting consideration while discussing adolescent-parental ties is that of exploitation of the teenager by adults. The exploitation takes the form of adults expecting the youngster to perform — either scholastically or in other endeavors — in order to provide the parents with an "ego boost." This is done without regard as to whether or not the performance is meaningful or ultimately beneficial for the adolescent. This kind of exploitation can lead to excessive expectations which the teenager cannot meet. He may then experience a sense of failure and develop a poor self-concept. The exploitation can also lead to the alienation and rebellious behaviors mentioned before.

### Need For Peer Support

Influence of the peer group is also very important to the adolescent. During this time when the adolescent is trying to discover who he is, he must at least temporarily reject some adult values so that he can begin to see himself as having values of his own. These values will be based not only on his interaction with his parents, but on his total contact with society. To break away, the teenager must have some support system other than his family, and he finds this in his peers. It is obvious that too little peer support can be devastating to the youngster's attempt to pull away from his parents. On the other hand, too much dependence on peer acceptance can lead to "following the crowd" and involvement in unacceptable behavior merely because it is necessary to win approval.

This need for peer approval strongly interacts with the adolescent's overwhelming need to perceive himself as "normal." Adolescents have great difficulty tolerating differences. This intolerance operates as a "defense against a sense of identity confusion."[1] When separating from parents, the teenager uses his sameness, and therefore his identification, with his peers as a support of his identity. In other words, he shifts his identification away from his parents to his peers. However, being "different" from peers threatens this identification, leaving the unsupported, newly forming identity of the adolescent vulnerable. The youngster may decide to return to the safety of identification with his parents, or he may strive harder to be more like his peers. The need for sameness among adolescents is easily seen in the fads that are so common among teenagers. It is also the reason for the extreme popularity of "cliques" among this age group.

Children with chronic illness or physical disability have a particular problem with peer acceptance. Because they are different, the chronically ill child points out to his peer group that they, the normal peers, may be physically vulnerable. The normal adolescents may have difficulty coping with this, and therefore are unwilling to accept the chronically ill child's attempt to identify with them. The decreased peer acceptance may lead to such things as increased dependence on parents, social immaturity, poor self-image, decreased confidence, and a fear of failure. This may in turn lead to feelings of anger, frustration, and depression, and failure to proceed through adolescence. It must be noted, however, that not all handicapped children have this problem with peer acceptance and many do proceed through adolescence normally.

## Physical Changes of Adolescence

Normal children may also have difficulties during adolescence. Youngsters may be early or late maturers. This means that they develop their sexual characteristics, such as beards, deep voices and body hair in boys, and breasts, pubic hair, and menstruation in girls, either earlier or later than their peers.[2] Despite the fact that these youngsters are normal, their difference may cause problems with peer acceptance. Even if they do not experience rejection by their peers, their awareness of the difference may cause anxiety about their acceptance and about their identities.

Similar problems can develop in youngsters who do not experience their adolescent growth spurt at the same time as their peers. At puberty — that is, at the time when hormonal changes cause physical sexual maturation — there are hormonal changes which cause an increase in the rate of growth. This means that the youngster grows faster around puberty. This accounts for the marked increased in height seen during the teenage years. Like sexual maturation, the growth spurt does not occur at the same chronological age in every youngster. Because of this, some children may have their growth spurt at 12 and be taller than everyone else until the others have grown, too. On the other extreme, there are youngsters who do not have their growth spurt until age 16; and until that time, they may be shorter than everyone else their age. This can happen among children who, as adults, will be approximately the same height.[2,3] There are, in addition, those individuals who will always be shorter or taller than their peers. These differences in height can cause difficulties in peer acceptance merely because the youngster is different. This problem may be compounded if it is a boy who is short or a girl who is tall. The youngster will then have to contend with the societal prejudice that boys should be taller than girls. This prejudice may seem silly to some adults; but to the adolescent who is trying very hard to be like his peers, it not only may accentuate his difference, but it may also make him feel inadequate in his relationship with the opposite sex.

The physical changes in sexual characteristics and height experienced by adolescents may cause difficulties if they do not occur at the same time and in the same way as in peers. However, they often occur in a way that enhances the teenager's peer identification because the changes are being experienced by his peers at the same time. Even then, the adolescent needs to integrate these changes into his previous body image so that this image actually reflects the change in his body.[4] The rapidity of changes in the teenager's body make it difficult for the body image to keep pace. The teenager may therefore have a body image which does not accurately reflect how his body appears. He may at some level be aware of this disparity and therefore be very confused and insecure about how his body looks. A discordance between body image and reality may also relate to the awkwardness often experienced by adolescents. This clumsiness can be another embarrassing change for the teenager who previously had good motor control.

## Sexuality

The pubertal hormonal changes which lead to physical-sexual maturation also lead to an increase in sexual arousal. The teenager may experience this arousal and be both pleased by its sensation and embarrassed by its presence. He may also experience conflict over whether or not to act on his sexual feelings. It is during adolescence that an individual explores his own sexuality. This is done by sexual experimentation. The teenager may engage in various types of sexual activity ranging from masturbation to "necking," "petting," and actual intercourse. He may try homosexual as well as heterosexual encounters. It is not unusual for the adolescent to have sexual relationships with more than one individual, and the sexual activity may be the sole purpose of the interaction; or it may be a part of a more complete relationship. It is through this exploration and experimentation that the adolescent establishes the values he will use to guide his adult sexual behavior. It is important to remember that this experimentation may be normal; but if it is excessive, either in quantity or duration, it may represent a problem in the adolescent's development.

## Intellectual Functioning

During adolescence, the individual's cognitive functioning develops to include abstract reasoning. This corresponds to Piaget's level of "formal operations."[5] During adolescence, the child becomes able to detach "the concrete logic from the objects themselves so that they can function on a verbal or symbolic statement without support . . . The great novelty that results consists in the possibility of manipulating ideas in themselves and no longer in merely manipulating objects. The adolescent is an individual who is capable (and this is where he reaches the level of adult) of building or understanding ideas, or abstract theories or concepts."[6] The adolescent is capable of thinking of the future and making plans for it.

## Career Choice

Concomitant with the expansion of cognitive functioning to include planning for the future comes the expectation that the adolescent will choose a career or life work. This does not mean that the adolescent is necessarily clear that he would like to become, for example, a certified public accountant, but only that he has some broad views of where he would like to go in terms of his career or his overall interest in life. Inability to choose a life work or at least focus on a general area of interest represents identity diffusion.[1] "Trying on" various roles as experimentation in order to make a choice is a normal and necessary part of adolescent development. However, inability to finally focus on some specific area reflects uncertainty in the teenager about who he is and what he can become. This results in a lack of direction for the future. Teenagers who do not demonstrate development in this area are, often incorrectly, described as being lazy, unambitious, or shiftless. It is seen not so much as a problem of development, but as a voluntary uncooperation. This evokes from adult society — including those in education — feelings of anger, which may lead to the rejection of the teenager.

Even when the youngster has a sense of who he is and what he is to become, he has to fit those views into the perceptions and expectations of society. This is of particular importance in certain underprivileged groups because a youngster may have a fairly good or even excellent idea of what he is and what he is to become, but unfortunately his view does not fit the overall expectation of society. This inability to fit one's identity into the expectation of society is called ego diffusion and can result in the adolescent becoming a misfit in society.

Understanding overall psychological development and the particular issues that impact most directly on adolescents is essential in understanding adolescent behavior. This knowledge can help one evaluate whether or not a specific behavior represents a normal behavior or a symptom of an emotional problem. Professionals who counsel adolescents can do a great deal of harm to the teenagers and their families by saying that rebellion, indiscriminate sexual activity, shoplifting and other problems of adolescence are "normal phases" and that the teenager will "outgrow them." It is imperative to differentiate the normal "pulling away" necessary for the teenager to separate from adult society from the angry, hostile, rebellious behavior that may include vandalism, shoplifting, and delinquency. It is necessary to discriminate normal sexual experimentation from the sexual activity with many partners and without meaningful relationship that is seen in promiscuity. One needs also to distinguish between the more common experimentation with drugs like marijuana and alcohol and the abuse of these and other drugs as an escape from the stresses with which the teenager cannot cope.

Investigating functioning in various life spheres should enable the professional to better evaluate whether a problem behavior is an isolated incident, a situational reaction, or a symptom of a more clinically-significant psychological problem. A teenager should be evaluated in terms of the three major spheres of his life — namely, his functioning at school or on the job, his functioning with his peers, and his functioning at home with his family. Without investigating all three of these areas, one is apt to miss the source of the adolescent's conflict. One rule of thumb is that if an adolescent is functioning well in two of these three areas, he probably does not have a clinically-significant psychological problem needing professional intervention. If, for instance, he is having a school problem but is functioning well with his peers and at home with his family, the problem is probably largely situational to school and not a reflection of a severe underlying problem in the child. On the other hand, if he is having significant difficulties in two of these three areas, the teenager may well have a psychological problem and be in need of help. If the youngster is having difficulty in all three areas, it is certain that he or his family needs some type of mental health intervention.

One of the important matters in dealing with teenagers is that this may be, in a sense, the last chance to help them with their tasks of childhood and adolescence. If they are successful with these tasks, they can move on to the tasks of adulthood. It behooves all professionals, particularly those in schools, to take advantage of the opportunity to systematically assist adolescents in moving into adulthood.


### REFERENCES

1. Erickson EH: *Childhood and Society,* New York, W.W. Norton and Company, Inc, 1963, pp 247-274.

2. Tanner JM: *Growth At Adolescence.* Springfield, IL, 1962.

3. Tanner JM, Whitehouse RH: Clinical longitudinal standards for height, weight, height velocity and stages of puberty. *Arch Dis Child* 51: 170-179, 1976.

4. Schonfield WA: The body and the body image in adolescents, in *Adolescence: Psychosocial Perspectives,* Caplan J, Lebovici S (eds). New York, Basic Books, Inc, 1958.

5. Inhelder B, Piaget J: *The Growth of Logical Thinking From Childhood to Adolescence.* New York, Basic Books, Inc, 1958.

6. Piaget J: The intellectual development of the adolescent, In *Adolescence: Psychosocial Perspectives,* Caplan J, Lebovici S (eds). New York, Basic Books, 1969, pp 22-26.

# Educating Adolescents with Emotional and Delinquency Problems

D. MAINPRIZE and P. MANN

*Dr. Mainprize is Supervisor of Adolescent Education and Mr. Mann is co-ordinator of Education for emotionally disturbed hospitalized children at Windsor Western Hospital, Windsor, Ontario, Canada.*

Almost every classroom today is faced with handling some form of learning disability or delinquency evidenced by negative self-concepts and low frustration tolerances in students (Miller and Windhauser, 1971).

According to the Canadian Government Ministry of Education 1973 programs report, three-quarters of all youth with emotional disturbances are housed in regular school classes (Gill and Silversman, 1973).

The approaches to educating these young people are varied in terms of techniques and successes. Teachers face three basic behavior problems in dealing with these emotionally troubled students. The majority stem from anxiety displayed in the form of defiance, low self-concepts and inappropriate social behaviors; the second problem is inattentiveness exhibiting short attention spans with minimal work output; and the third is hyperactivity and attention-seeking behaviors (Ragor, 1970; Swift, *et al.*, 1973, 1974; Vital Health Statistics, 1972).

The Education Department of the Regional Children's Centre at Windsor Western Hospital has found several classroom techniques to be extremely effective in handling the school-related problems of adolescents with emotional handicaps.

Adolescent students at the Centre keep school records on their daily behavior and academic output, forego initial feedback on academics until they are functionally ready for a consistently positive modality of feedback, and also keep a teacher-rating sheet of each lesson they are taught.

## Self-Kept Student Records (inattentiveness and hyperactivity controls)

Having students keep records on themselves is not a new practice in educational settings. Kroth (1968) had his students record the time it took to complete their work, and Broden *et al.* (1971) allowed his children to keep records on their own behavior. Self-kept student records have also been maintained in after-school remedial programs (Drabman *et al.*, 1973), and special research rooms (Felixbrod and O'Leary, 1973, 1974).

McLaughlin (1976) reviewed over 20 recent studies dealing with student groups practicing self-control procedures by recording their own behaviors, consequences and reinforcers. The student record sheets at the Centre did not have the self-control status found in McLaughlin's review because the teacher monitored the reports of the students to insure supportive control.

According to a study by Sanlogrossi *et al.* (1973), hospitalized adolescents under psychiatric care in a setting similar to the Centre, tried student self-recording procedures but failed to control disruptive behaviors with them. The differences in the Santogrossi study and the experimental class at the Centre were in the reinforcers and monitoring. The Centre had no highly prized external back-up reinforcers for students to justify their extra recording labors. The Centre merely allowed the students a personal record to match or refute the teacher's monitoring records.

## 4. EMOTIONAL

Along with the teacher, the students at the Centre recorded all academic work completed, subject by subject, and kept an accurate account of the the type and number of warnings given for inappropriate behaviors, as well as consequences of those behaviors.

Besides allowing for a concrete reminder of where the student was academically and behaviorally at any given point in the day, students kept the records to verify progress and output over indefinite time periods.

The records provided a needed structure (Newman 1959) by simplifying and laying out the academic day. They provided clear directions, firm expectations and consistent follow-through which reduced external stimulation, established limits and maintained the consistent, clear ground rules prescribed by Haring *et al.* (1962) and Cruickshank *et al.* (1968) in controlling emotional stress.

### Lack of Initial Academic Feedback (anxiety control)

Feedback has always played a pertinent role in the educational experience. Hall *et al.* (1968a, 1972) reported on verbal and checkmark feedback in class, Quay *et al.* (1966) flashed a light as feedback to children's output, and Willis and Crowder (1972) used a start-and-stop clock system in the classroom. As Hull-Skinner behavior modification programs have infiltrated education, the contention has existed that feedback of a positive vein (reinforcement) is paramount to learning. However, because of the inconsistency involved in providing both positive feedback to motivate and accurate feedback to increase learning rate in academic subjects, it was felt that an absence of feedback would facilate in-class work sessions in their initial stages.

Depending on the academic level, a student was given specific curriculum material to learn. If the student functioned appropriately with this material, he was moved on to new material. If the student was not learning in an appropriate fashion, he was tutored until he could incorporate the material on a functional basis. During the tutoring the student was coached with immediate verbal and concrete feedback (checkmarks), but at the day's end no corrected material was returned to the student.

This procedure of not returning corrected material to the students initially allowed them to function in class without the negative self-concept most learning problem children contend with due to concrete examples of errors.

It was found that the students became more willing to try new material simply because it was no threat to them. The lack of feedback, however, did not impede the learning process, because individual tutoring accompanied the procedure of repeated curriculum until the student mastered his work and was ready to try new material.

### Teacher Rating Sheets (anxiety control)

Rating sheets patterned after Corcoran (1976) were given to each student to evaluate each class on the basis of appropriate learning for future use, difficulty and timing, the teacher's effectiveness in meeting academic needs and controlling individual and class behavior.

The rationale for providing student-to-teacher feedback was to give a motivational lift to the student by making him believe he was a part of the control process and allowing him to share indirectly the classroom responsibility with the teacher.

Most students were able to make meaningful connections between their academic work, their nonacademic future and their self-image.

The rating sheet was also used to decrease school-rated anxiety similar to Bruner's (1966) concept activities of having students role play teachers and Dickinson's (1968) concept of allowing students to take responsibility in punishment decision making.

### A Final Comment

The classroom at the Centre which incorporated these techniques for managing emotionally troubled children handled residential students under psychiatric care and community students displaying various forms of behavior problems in regular school classes.

The classroom size rarely exceeded ten adolescents and child care support was provided on a consistent basis to aid in behavioral and remedial management.

The success with these behaviorally unmanageable students was twofold: (1) Students were returned to former school programs without extended hospital care and (2) transferable limits were established to take community students back into regular school boundaries as an attempt to deal with emotional problems before psychiatric intervention was perscribed.

Although these procedures were initially investigated within a special classroom setting under a special student-teacher ratio with complementary staffing, the success of the program (Mainprize, Mann and Bain, 1976) has been so overwhelming as to warrant incorporation of some of these ideas into the reuglar classroom for use with the emotionally handicapped adolescent.

# New Light on Autism and Other Puzzling Disorders of Childhood

Herbert Yahraes

Micky at birth weighed almost 8 pounds and appeared to be perfectly healthy, yet he showed no pleasure when held by his parents and did not respond to their smiles or other shows of affection. His motor development was normal, and he walked when he was 16 months old. But he never babbled. When he was 18 months old, he said something that sounded like "no"; it was his first and last word. By the time he was 2½ years old, he was completely uninterested in social relations and totally unconcerned by separation from his parents. During the next few years he remained easily distracted and very hyperactive. He was either extremely anxious or extremely lethargic. He also swung between periods of aggression directed at himself and periods of aggression directed at others.

At 7½, Micky was attractive and bright eyed, but his only attempts at communication were aggressive lunges toward the medical staff of the hospital where he had been taken for treatment and "whining to his mother to indicate hunger." The doctors could find no specific neurological or biochemical abnormalities. They prescribed one of the phenothiazine drugs commonly used against schizophrenia. For a while he improved, showing decreased activity and increased social relations, "and for the first time he was able to follow simple instructions." After 4 months, though, he lost these gains, and "even with manipulation of the medication, there was no way of reducing his activity and destructiveness." Because life was becoming harder and harder for his family, Micky was admitted to a residential treatment institution.

## 4. EMOTIONAL

During the first four months in the school, he made educational
and social gains. Then, again, at age 8½ years, he had another
radical mood shift, which left him uncontrollable, banging his
head all day, and bruising himself. During this time, he seemed
uncontrollable, and at times he required restraints to prevent
him from hurting himself. He then had another shift, and he
would sit for hours, holding a nurse's hand, apparently in great
distress and muttering 'un, uh.' He pulled his hair, leaving wide
areas of baldness. A detailed neurological and metabolic evaluation was performed, revealing him to be thinner, more dis-
tressed, and even more socially unresponsive than he had been
one year before, but otherwise with no indications of any central
nervous system disturbance.

Micky suffers from *primary childhood autism.* His story is
told by child psychiatrist Donald J. Cohen, Associate Professor of Pediatrics, Psychiatry, and Psychology at the Yale
University School of Medicine and Child Study Center.
Cohen, who is also Psychiatric Director of the Children's
Clinical Research Center, Yale University School of Medicine, is one of the country's leading authorities on autism
and several other neuropsychiatric disorders of children
which are discussed in this article. Although these disorders
still have many puzzling aspects, authorities such as Cohen
are making progress in distinguishing one from the other,
elucidating subgroups, getting at the basic causes, and testing drugs and other forms of treatment.

In addition to Micky's classical or primary autism, there is
a condition known as *secondary childhood autism.* Development and behavior in this type may be almost the same as in
the other, but the trouble seems to be secondary to recognized disturbances, such as brain damage associated with
measles or with lead poisoning, inborn errors of metabolism,
and a type of blindness (retrolental fibroplasia) sometimes
following the administration of too much oxygen to premature infants at birth.

"The universal symptom of autism," Cohen points out, "is
the inability to relate to people and social situations in a
normal way." This inability is accompanied by aloofness,
inaccessibility, and lack of interest "which superficially may
resemble the picture presented by the most severely mentally
retarded child. However, the autistic child's usually normal
developmental landmarks and relatively normal physical
development differentiate this type of disorder from mental
subnormality."

One child out of every 3,000 has autism. The condition may
be noticeable from the very start. The child's attention may
fade in and out. He is likely to be uncomfortable when held.
He may cry almost without letup, or he may seem unusually
quiet. Around the age of 1, his main occupation may be looking at his fingers or banging his head against the crib—for
hours—or he may become occupied with one toy and reject
everything else.

Research concerning autistic and other developmentally
disabled children requires an integrated team of experts
with special competencies and interests. The core research
team at the Yale Child Study Center working with Cohen
includes a developmental psychologist and educator, Barbara Caparulo; a research child psychiatrist, Dr. J. Gerald
Young; and other research associates. They work in collaboration with other clinical investigators—Dr. Bennett Shay-
witz, a pediatric neurologist who heads the section on pediatric neurology at Yale; Dr. Myron Genel, the chief of the section on pediatric endocrinology; and Dr. Julian Ferholt, a

child psychiatrist who specializes in psychosomatic disorders of early childhood. In addition, neuroradiologists, pharmacologists, psychologists, and human geneticists join in collaborative research projects which no one could undertake alone.

Biologically oriented clinical research with children is expensive. During research hospitalization, disturbed children require private nursing care and the almost full-time attention of a researcher. Specialized tests and laboratory procedures may cost hundreds of dollars. Thus, a several-day research study of one autistic child may cost over $1,500 in time, laboratory studies, and hospital costs. The research of the Cohen group is funded by several sources, both public and private. The Children's Clinical Research Center is supported by the Division of Research Resources, National Institutes of Health. A special Mental Health Clinical Research Center will be opened as the result of a 1977 award from the National Institute of Mental Health; co-directors will be Cohen and psychiatrist Malcolm Bowers. Private foundations, such as the William T. Grant Foundation and the Ford Foundation, have funded certain aspects of the research. Most gratifying, according to Cohen, has been the support of private donors whose involvement in the research stems from being parents of children who have the disabilities being investigated.

## The Saddest Disease

Of all the afflictions of childhood, primary autism may well be the saddest because its core symptom, in Cohen's words, is "the inability to relate to people and social situations in a normal way." Even to the mother, the autistic infant may respond no more warmly than to a piece of string or a flashlight.

Yet some autistic children display amazing word recognition skills. They can read very well, and they can also repeat complex sentences read to them. They cannot explain, however, what they have read or heard. "Autistic children," Caparulo and Cohen report, "are notorious for their abilities to repeat strings of sentences, to remember routes to places months or years after first being exposed to them, to notice changes in the placement of furniture or the presence or absence of toys in an office, and to remember dates and numbers...." What seems to be impaired "is the *significance* or *meaning* of the objects, events, and people, and relations among them, reflected in the written word or aural communication." Examination usually uncovers nothing neurologically wrong.

For many years, as even occasionally today, autism was laid at the parents' feet. Fathers and mothers were judged to be cold, to show little more than a polite interest in their child, to be incapable of extending love. Many parents—in particular, many mothers—grieved for years because of the surmises of child experts.

Cohen puts it this way: "The hope during the 1940's and 1950's that one would find parents to blame was both mean and, yet, optimistic. If autism could be caused by parental feelings and action, we would have a much greater sense of conviction in the power of environmental provision and optimism about what could be potentially undone. Today, however, parents of autistic children are considered to be like the parents of other handicapped children whose care poses inhuman burdens. Parents are usually unhappy, worried, angry, discouraged, and exhausted. But they are not, as a group, unconcerned or unloving." Many of the parents of the autistic children studied by Cohen keep their children home rather than send them to a residential treatment facility. And for these parents, "marital strife, separation, and divorce are almost expected outcomes," because an autistic child places an "impossible stress" on a marriage.

Instead of environment, congenital endowment may somehow be playing a hand. A number of investigators, including Cohen's group, have found a "relatively high incidence of depression, language difficulties, severe psychological disturbances, and anxiety of eccentricity in the blood relatives of autistic children."

Notions about the root of the trouble are beginning to accumulate, and these have nothing to do with relationships within the family. One basic problem appears to be the autistic child's inability to generate rules for dealing with information received through the senses—or even to understand these rules when they are explained. Caparulo and Cohen, for example, have studied a bright, autistic 10-year-old who liked to draw a popular restaurant over and over again. His drawings were accurate; obviously he had a sense of size. Yet, when he was asked to arrange eight geometric shapes according to size, he was baffled. In other words, he could draw a building according to scale, but he could not understand the concept of smaller and larger.

In some autistic children, another problem seems to be an abnormality or dysfunction in the body's system for regulating the state of arousal and attention. For example, the rate at which the heart works and the blood flows usually changes as states of attention change. But Cohen and an associate found that in the most disturbed children such rates did not follow the normal pattern. Such children apparently were actually rejecting sensory messages that in other children led to higher levels of arousal. Cohen believes that such rejection is not voluntary but is caused by some abnormality in the ability to process external stimuli. Recent work in the laboratories of Cohen and other investigators suggests that the most disturbed of the children may be almost habitually in a state of hypervigilance. Such a state "may be associated with recurrent cognitive confusion and a compensatory withdrawal and turning inward of attention to avoid environmental bombardment."

Far from trying to be contrary or to cause pain and grief, the autistic child, impaired cognitively and attentionally, may be simply trying "to impose order on his world." Many of his symptoms, the Yale investigators point out, "may be seen as compensatory mechanisms." As one 16-year-old movingly explained: "I am sad about my body, but it's no good to be sad. You should try to make jokes when you're feeling sad."

Some aspects of autism, Cohen speculates, may be associated with overactivity of the dopamine system. Dopamine is one of the so-called "biogenic amines" essential for proper brain functioning. It is, in fact, a neurotransmitter. Like other neurotransmitters, each apparently acting in its own portion or portions of the central nervous system, it carries from one nerve cell to another, at an unbelievable speed, the electrical signals propagated in the brain. A transmitter serves in effect as a bridge over the synapses, or the tiny clefts between nerve cells.

Cohen notes that drugs, such as Haloperidol and the phenothiazines, which inhibit dopamine action have therapeutic value in some cases of autism, while drugs, such as the stimulant, dextroamphetamine, which increases that action, exacerbate the symptons. Moreover, in the cerebrospinal fluid of severely autistic children, he has found greater quantities of dopamine breakdown products. This discovery suggests that in these children an excess amount of this brain chemical is being manufactured and broken down. Its release and catabolism have been shown to be greatly affected by stress. It may well be that, as seems to be the case in schizophrenia and depression, in autism a disturbance in the neurotransmission system may help cause the stress, instead of the other way around. However, as Cohen is the first to point out, a great deal of research by a number of investigators will be needed to establish the truth or falsity of these and related ideas.

Nonetheless, the recent discovery by other scientists of two groups of neurotransmitters quite different from those found earlier seems only to strengthen the transmitters' importance to mental health. The new groups have been named the enkephalins and the endorphins. Chemically, they are peptides, or combinations of amino acids, which in turn are the building blocks of protein. Cohen and J. Gerald Young point out that the newly found compounds affect the processing of sensory and emotional signals and "may be involved in modulating pain and pleasure." They have wide implications for understanding and treating a variety of mental illnesses. Among the subjects to be investigated, or re-investigated, as the result of the new findings, these researchers list "the turning away from sensory stimulation and the unusual sensitivities of some autistic children," the hypervigilance of psychotics, the inability of clinically depressed persons to experience pleasure, and the nature of drug dependency.

Other investigators have found that one of the main hormones, triiodothyronine, produced by the thyroid gland, makes for improvement in some cases of autism. Cohen's group, in turn, finds that some autistic children show marked swings—ranging from the *hypo*thyroid to the *hyper*thyroid level in a few days—in the amount of thyroxine, another principal thyroid hormone. Because of these and the earlier findings, Cohen and other researchers are studying the way in which thyroid hormones affect the metabolism of brain neurotransmitters.

One role of thyroid hormone, Cohen suggests, may be to sensitize neurons to the effect of the various transmitting agents. When the flow of thyroid hormones is reduced for some reason, the brain tries to maintain a steady state by increasing their production and use. On the other hand, when these compounds are produced too rapidly, the brain signals the thyroid to ease up.

The marked swings of a thyroid hormone noted in severely autistic children may go hand in hand, under this hypothesis, with broad swings in behavior. Thus the effectiveness of thyroid medication may be related to its "dampening of fluctuations."

Another factor apparently at work in at least some cases of autism is a higher-than-average amount of lead in the blood, which even in normal children can lead to disordered behavior such as irritability and lessened attention. The Yale investigators found these higher levels—in some cases well above the toxic mark—among autistic children as a group. Presumably they arise because many such children, besides having peculiar eating habits, swallow or at least take into their mouths a wide variety of inedible material, some of it containing lead. The lesson is that autistic children should be tested for the presence of lead in the bloodstream though they rarely are. Lead does not cause autism, but it can add to the problems.

What happens to autistic children as they grow into adolescence and then adulthood? Most of them remain in institutions or are placed there. Cohen and his fellow workers report the feelings of a devoted mother, who had spent every day with her son during his first 17 years, when she first brought him to a residential center. "I knew that as soon as I brought him there," she said, "he would be as happy as he was at home. He didn't seem to miss me for a minute." But Cohen estimates that there are a "fortunate 10 to 15 percent of older autistic individuals with language abilities and improved social relations who may seem merely "odd, eccentric, or very immature." In social situations, their behavior "usually lacks spontaneity and reflects the hard work they and their parents and teachers have put into education. They must be taught social conventions, for example, how to say 'fine, thank you,' instead of honestly responding with a discussion of their daily lives when they are asked how they are doing."

> In school, such autistic individuals may show areas of high intellectual ability and may learn to read well, yet their comprehension may be relatively limited, and the information they acquire may be of very questionable value. The older autistic individual's speech usually remains deliberate and stiff.... In spite of major improvements, these older individuals remain anxious and perhaps depressed as they recognize their limitations; they may have odd mannerisms or flapping behavior, especially when they are upset or excited, and they may be unable to engage in imaginative activities or work or play in a mutually meaningful way with others.
>
> For the less fortunate autistic child whose language does not progress, behavior during the school age and adolescent years remains clearly continuous with that of the preschool years. His overactive behavior may decrease with training but his ability to communicate. . . or relate with peers or adults may be extremely limited.

# Hyperactivity: Diagnosis

By Marcel Kinsbourne, M.D., Ph.D.

*In October and December 1977, we presented Dr. Kinsbourne's two-part article entitled* **Learning Disabilities: Diagnosis and Management.**

*In this article, Dr. Kinsbourne describes the characteristics of the hyperactive child. In recent years children who seemed to be overly fidgety or too active have been mislabeled hyperactive. Dr. Kinsbourne sets out some specific characteristics that can lead us to an appropriate diagnosis of a child who is hyperactive.*

*In the learning disability article Dr. Kinsbourne noted that "Two types of ability are important for learning. One is attention, or concentration – what one might call 'task orientation.' The other is processing or mental capacity – the ability to solve the problem once the individual is trying to do so and is concentrating on it. If a person has the necessary mental power but does not focus it on the task, his processing power is not being used. It might as well not be there. That is the case with 'hyperactive' children, who have a deficit of attention."*

---

Problems in the three areas of movement, attention and social interaction are not equally important at every age.

---

**I**n order to make a diagnosis of hyperactivity three areas of a child's behavior must be observed: movement, attention and social interaction. Without considering all three facets, it is impossible to obtain a proper picture of what one is up against in trying to help these children.

Problems in the three areas of movement, attention and social interaction are not equally important at every age. The abnormal movement is most prominent in infancy and less important as the child grows older. The problem of paying attention is least important in early childhood, very important during school age. The social problem becomes increasingly important as the child grows up. Anyone who does not look at the social side may be deluded into thinking that a hyperactive child has recovered just because he is no longer moving excessively. This mistake is commonly made.

The rest of this article presents a description of children who are called hyperactive. No one child will show all the manifestations of hyperactivity. Nor does a child need to show them all to justify a positive diagnosis.

### Infancy

Hyperactive children already stand out from other children in the first year of life. Excessive motor behavior — almost constant movement — is the first clue to the disorder in babies. Nobody expects sustained attention or social interaction from very small children. Parents frequently describe the hyperactive child as remarkably wiggly and active in the first few weeks of life. They usually do not complain, because a restless baby inside the crib is not breaking anything. So no one worries. At this early stage, people may think the baby's motion is cute.

Eating and sleeping problems sometimes bring parents to the doctor during the baby's first year of life. Children with eating problems are often called colicky. The mechanism of colic is not known, but some assumptions are made — that the child is full of gas because he gobbles greedily and swallows air, or that he is tense and irritable, upset by feelings that interfere with eating. In any case, hyperactive children often have early eating problems.

They also have early sleeping problems. Actually, the hyperactive infant's trouble sleeping is not really *his* problem. The child experiences no discomfort when he wakes up at 2 a.m. He has slept and is ready to play. His parents are the ones who are unhappy being awakened at that hour. They will complain that their child does not sleep enough, but it may not be clear whether he needs to sleep more. Sometimes the child will seem fully energetic after only a few hours of sleep, and sometimes he will seem sleepy but on the go. The particular sleeping "problem" probably differs from child to child. Nonetheless, there is typically a sleep pattern that disrupts the parents' life more than the child's.

The interruption of sleep reflects the hyperactive child's generally great sensitivity to external change. He may even feel a need to generate change. This reaction has been called stimulus sensitivity, stimulus hunger or stimulus-seeking behavior. The child seems avid for more and more experience. He moves around, gobbles food and is up at night — ready, awake and wanting to explore.

The urge to explore becomes more evident during the second and third years of life. A hyperactive child may dive into everything. He explores the various crevices of the house; he may find and eat poisons or medicines, and he often shows up in the hospital emergency room with poisoning or broken bones. When parents expect order and structure in their home and are concerned about having possessions broken, they consider this urge to explore a problem. Parents from the middle class are more likely than parents from lower socioeconomic groups to complain about hyperactivity in the second or third year of the child's life.

### Preschool

Complaints are more likely when a child enters preschool or a day care center. Two aspects of the socialization style of hyperactive children are already apparent at this stage and become increasingly important as time passes. One is an impulsive style of personal interaction; the other is an attention-seeking style. Hyperactive children are

remarkably unpopular for both reasons.

Hyperactive children have an impulsive, overbearing, apparently dominating way of approaching others. These children come on too strong, they approach too briskly, they do not go through customary patterns of hesitation and tentative "courtship" when meeting a new person or joining a new group. Quite often the group rejects the child. This kind of impulsive advance, met by rejection, followed by the same advance met again by more rejection, is a typical hyperactive pattern.

These children are not oblivious of unpleasant experiences. They do not like being rejected or hurt any more than anyone else. But somehow they do not seem to be able to change their behavior on the basis of such experiences. So they continue to do the thing for which they are rejected or, at home, perhaps punished. This pattern presents a difficult challenge to parents, since the usual punishments for children's misbehavior do not result in changes of behavior.

The second problem is the child's need for personal attention. This will cause problems in the grade-school classroom and adjustment difficulties in adolescence. Usually he is quite capable of learning if the teacher stands over him, but in a group he either does nothing or else acts disruptively so that the teacher must constantly attend to him. This behavior creates resentment in the teacher and in the other children.

---

Parents, teachers and physicians often have conflicting observations of the child's behavior.

---

### Kindergarten and Grade School

An inability to focus or concentrate on a task becomes a serious concern when the child is in kindergarten and grade school. Such children tend to fall behind not just in one or two subjects but in anything that requires concentration for an appreciable time. Hyperactive children do not have difficulty in turning to the subject but rather in maintaining their focus. They are not so much unwilling as unable — or able only with great effort — to exclude competing stimulation. The child focuses on a task but has to break off to see who is coming through the door, check on the jacket the child next to him is wearing, or wonder what is happening outside the window. These children do begin tasks. In fact they constantly begin tasks. But they abandon them prematurely and do not finish them unless the project takes little time or the child is very bright, so that brief attention to a task may be sufficient. Thus a bright hyperactive child may not have a learning problem. In other words, he may not be underachieving because much of what happens in a classroom is repetitious and a bright person can pick up the gist in just a few moments.

But the "average" hyperactive child loses concentration before he has fully understood or practiced the material. The next time he approaches the material, the same thing happens again. Over a period of time the hyperactive child of average intelligence falls behind academically because his difficulty in concentrating curtails his learning time.

These children do seem to learn things for which concentration is not required, such as language. Thus they usually have normal language development and a reasonably large vocabulary.

## Conflicting Observations

Parents, teachers and physicians often have conflicting observations of the child's behavior. When teachers and parents disagree, the clinician should find out something about the teacher's and parents' expectations of the child, because they are very often quite different. A child who is agreeably reflective in class may seem unnaturally subdued to parents who are accustomed to more vivid behavior. And a child who appears merely normally energetic to his parents may seem edgy and restless in school.

Hyperactive children often make a special effort to behave when they are in a doctor's office. The doctor may say, "The child kept perfectly still for me" — implying that if the parents only had his personality and character they would have no problem. But that is not true. Once the children have made a supreme effort for the few minutes, they leave the intimidating situation and go wild with pent-up energy. So observations like "He can watch his favorite television program" or "He sits still in the office" do not invalidate what parents and teachers observe. What parents and teachers report is crucial. It is more important than what occurs in a physician's or psychologist's office.

Dr. Kinsbourne is a pediatric neurologist and child psychologist. He is currently Professor of Pediatrics at the University of Toronto Medical School and Professor of Psychology at the University of Toronto. He heads the hospital's Neuropsychology Research Unit. Dr. Kinsbourne's research deals with brain-behavior relationships in adults and children, with emphasis on learning disability and hyperactivity, both from the point of view of the basic mechanisms involved in these disorders and of common sense ways of helping the children overcome them.

# Hyperactivity: Treatment

By Marcel Kinsbourne, M.D., Ph.D.

*In the following article Dr. Kinsbourne, an expert in the field of stimulant therapy, discusses a controversial topic — the use of drugs in the treatment of hyperactivity.*

> Impulsive children need to be given control over their own impulses; only a treatment that will give them this additional control is acceptable.

**S**timulant medication for hyperactivity has been around for nearly 40 years and has been thoroughly investigated scientifically. Stimulant therapy has been proved to be effective, but it only works when used correctly and in appropriate cases — not when used incorrectly or with the wrong children. With correctly diagnosed hyperactive youngsters, the question "Should drugs be used or not?" never arises. Instead, the question is "How much of what drug should be used?" The answer will be different for each child.

The so-called paradoxical effects of stimulant medications such as Dexedrine and Ritalin on hyperactive children are sometimes mentioned.

However, the effects of these medications on hyperactive children are similar to those they would have on anyone else. What is different is not the effect of the drug but the condition of the individual before taking the drug.

**Behavior of Hyperactive Children**

Human beings' personalities differ in a variety of ways. One difference is the extent to which they are impulsive or reflective. One person may typically launch himself impulsively toward a goal; another may be more apt to think hard and hesitate (appropriately or excessively) before moving. Hyperactive children are extreme impulsives. They do not think before they act, so they need help to pause for a moment before acting.

If they could stop and think, their behavior would be more efficient, selective and appropriate. But it takes a tremendous effort for them to think before acting; they can only control their impulsiveness temporarily. At the other end of the scale are people who hesitate so long that every opportunity passes before they move; they like to have everything around them very structured.

**How Stimulant Therapy Works**

Impulsive children need to be given control over their own impulses; only a treatment that will give them this additional control is acceptable. The goal is not to change or drug them but rather to give them more control over their own behavior. Then, like everyone else, they can use their control for better or worse. In other words, stimulant medication does not subdue a person into obedience. It is not an infringement of individual freedom. In fact, it is just the opposite: it extends the child's freedom.

Its effect is the same as in students who take Dexedrine before examinations — not because they

 Hyperactivity--Treatment, Marcel Kinsbourne, MD, Ph.D., *Exceptional Parent* Vol. 8, No. 5, October, 1978. ©1978 Psy-Ed Corporation, Boston, Mass.

wish to be stimulated but because they want help in keeping their attention focused on a task. When properly treated with stimulants, hyperactive children are better able to focus attention. The effect of stimulants both on normal people and on hyperactive children is the same. Since hyperactive children are particularly impulsive, however, the stimulant shifts them toward the normal range of behavior. That is, it allows them to act in the same way as nonhyperactive people do without medication.

## Which Children Need Medication

One can find out whether a stimulant should or should not be prescribed for a particular child only by trying the drug to see if it is effective. If the child's history shows him to be impulsive or easily distracted, the use of stimulants is a viable option. If he has difficulty in focusing or is impulsive in social situations at any age, it is worthwhile to try out the medication. It is never valid to make a commitment in advance to any form of long-term treatment.

The important thing is to be liberal about trying out stimulants and conservative about continuing them beyond the trial period. That way the child's safety is ensured. The medication acts quickly and does not accumulate. Therefore a trial of no more than a week or two should clarify whether the child is being helped substantially or not helped at all. Before the trial period is up, it is best not to be overly concerned with the details of long-term maintenance.

The physician should explain the situation to the parents. "First we test whether your child is likely to respond to these drugs. If the answer is no, we have learned something and no harm has been done. If the answer is yes, then we can discuss the implications in detail." Of course, the clinician has an obligation to get frequent reports from parents and teachers while the medication is being tried out; otherwise he should not be handing out pills.

At the Hospital for Sick Children in Toronto, we test the effect of stimulants in the clinic by repeating the same test with and without medication. This way we can compare the child's performance exactly and see how different amounts of medication work. Even if the clinician cannot make such careful tests, observations by parents and teachers will give the answer clearly in almost every case. Ultimately, unless there is clear-cut improvement with the medication, it should not be used. Medication should especially not be used to achieve dubious or marginal results. Management with stimulants is an important commitment and should only be made if it is really justified. If this is the case, then it is worth sticking to the medication program.

## Consistent Use of Medication

In the case of a particular child, the clinician should either not use stimulants at all or use them thoroughly. It is not helpful for a child to flip-flop in personality every day, going from a reflective morning to a hyperactive night. Instead, he should be covered right through his waking day. This means a minimum of three tablets a day of Ritalin or one daily spansule of Dexedrine. If the medication works in school, it is also needed at home. It should be taken seven days a week, not just five. If it works for school time, it is needed during vacation time.

It is harmful to set up a Jekyll and Hyde situation in which reflective and impulsive behavior alternate. Stimulant therapy gives the child an important degree of control over his behavior. It is cruel to deprive him of this control just to ease the clinician's or parents' anxieties about continuous medication. If parents or clinicians want to use an effective measure only intermittently, they should examine their own motives.

Hyperactivity affects not only classroom learning but also everyday living. The child should be helped to live consistently and sensibly every day. By extension, this logic applies to people of all ages. The mistaken notion that hyperactive children improve in adolescence, because their physical restlessness decreases, is common. In fact, an impulsive style can be harmful right through life. The age of the child neither indicates nor contraindicates stimulant therapy.

## How Medication Helps

Hyperactive children tend to have poor relationships with peers and often with their parents. The child's attention is jumping all over, which is not comfortable for the person talking to him. As a result children of his own age probably do not want to spend much time with him. The hyperactive child also tends to hop from one activity to another on the playground, so he has a great deal of trouble establishing good relationships with peers. He tends to fight a lot with other children. These problems do not arise so often when medication is prescribed and taken regularly.

Parents generally observe that a hyperactive child who is not taking medication tends to deal with stress by denial. They often find the child becoming anxious or depressed but denying any distress. When a child is taking medication his problems do not disappear, but he becomes accessible to adults' expressions of concern. In addition, he becomes accessible to peers.

Hyperactive children who are not taking stimulant medication tend to play with younger children, whose level of impulsiveness is close to

Hyperactive children need structure; they need to have limits firmly and clearly set so that they will have some chance of stability and of functioning normally.

their own. When they are taking medication, they are more likely to play with children of their own age. Therefore taking a child on and off medication varies an essential part of the way he interacts with other children and with his parents.

Although the disappearance of excessive movement is not an indication for stopping medication in older children, the disappearance of impulsive behavior is. Many hyperactive children may eventually cease to need medication. We should make no preconceived assumptions about how long the need for medication will last.

Instead, we need to observe when various behaviors occur. For instance, a child may take a stimulant at 8, 12 and 4 o'clock — a customary pattern. The parents may report that the child was generally better but that yesterday he had a terrible tantrum. The clinician notes that this outburst happened just before lunch, when the child was due for his next pill. The stimulant had worn off, and the child had once again become impulsive.

Parents should be aware, incidentally, that Ritalin taken with meals is effectively no Ritalin at all. This medication must be taken half an hour before each meal, since alkaline digestive juices in the stomach neutralize its effect. The same is not true of Dexedrine.

### The Risks of Stimulant Therapy

Stimulant therapy may have two types of adverse effect: the ordinary side effects that may occur with any drug, and effects that stem from overdosage. Too much reflectiveness may be an effect of overdosage. Rather than being wide open to the environment, the child becomes locked in, anxious, whiny, suspicious or withdrawn.

One mother complained that her son was reacting badly to the medication. "The teachers think he is wonderful," she said, "but he comes home from school, takes a book and goes straight upstairs to read it. His friends want to play, but he sends them away and would rather read." In this case the dosage was reduced because so much reading was maladaptive for the child. When too high a dosage makes a child withdrawn, the answer is not to stop medication altogether but rather to cut it back; the dosage should be just enough but not too much.

Side effects of stimulant therapy may be real or imaginary. Actual side effects that sometimes occur

are depression in appetite and sleep disturbances. The reduced appetite usually lasts only a few weeks. Over the long term it is not serious enough to cause any problems, given a nutritious diet. Sleep problems may be caused by either too much medication or too little. If the cause is too much medication, the child is preoccupied with his own ideas; he has recurrent thoughts that he cannot share and that produces insomnia. If he is not getting enough medication, the drug wears off too rapidly; the child is wildly hyperactive and may not even get into bed, let alone sleep. Once again the challenge is to adjust the timing and dosage of the drug.

A report has claimed that hyperactive children taking large doses of stimulants showed slower physical growth than hyperactive children who received smaller doses or no stimulant. The study was only exploratory and was poorly controlled. It has not been confirmed. Normally such a study would not be quoted until its results were verified. But because many people are anxious about these medications, most pediatricians have heard of it.

The most important cause of adverse attitudes toward these particular medications (as opposed to a drug like insulin, which nearly everyone accepts) is the fear of a relationship between stimulant therapy and drug addiction. The question should be brought into the open: "Does the child who is taking stimulant therapy for hyperactivity incur a greater-than-average risk of drug addiction later on?" Surprisingly, the answer to this question is no. Such a child seems to face a smaller-than-average risk.

We have been unable to find a hyperactive child who has taken this medication and has later become addicted. In Toronto, my associates and I have been investigating why hyperactive children do not become addicted to stimulants. These are some of our preliminary conclusions:

- People do not usually become addicted to medicines they have used for therapy.
- The amount of stimulant given therapeutically to hyperactive children is only a small fraction of the amount that people take to achieve a "high."
- Hyperactive children usually do not associate differences in their feelings with taking or not taking the medication; they cannot tell whether they have taken a stimulant or a placebo.

This issue must be discussed with parents whenever a commitment to stimulant therapy is considered.

### What Parents and Teachers Can Do

Teachers and parents usually wonder whether they can help the impulsive child modify his behavior at home and in school. One method that has been tried is called "speech for self," which trains the child to ask himself questions about what he is going to do before doing it. In the less severe cases, a certain amount of such look-before-you-leap training can be helpful. But a seriously hyperactive child will find it difficult to persist in carrying out this method.

One thing adults can do is to keep hyperactive children out of the open classroom. Such learning situations are wonderful for many children — but not for this group. Hyperactive children need structure; they need to have limits firmly and clearly set so that they will have some chance of stability and of functioning normally.

What can be done when a hyperactive child oversteps such a limit? This is a difficult question, for which there is no good answer. It is clear that punishment or depriving the child of future privileges does not do the trick. The whole point about the hyperactive child is that he acts on short-term needs. Not watching television tonight or not going to the zoo tomorrow will not change his behavior because he does not think about tonight or tomorrow when misbehaving; he only thinks about the here and now. Another reason why punishment does not work is that the hyperactive child is too impulsive to stop and recognize that he is about to repeat the act for which he was punished earlier.

The only solution I can recommend is to send the child to another room when he throws a tantrum or acts dependent and whines, until he can cool down and behave in a mature way. Of course, it is even better to give him the right medical treatment, since a hyperactive child who is taking stimulants is better able to learn from discipline. From the behavioral point of view, a reasonably well structured situation with definable, consistent limits (and isolation when the child oversteps them) is the best parents can manage.

## The Limits of Therapy

Stimulants, when properly used, help hyperactive children. They do not cure all their problems. Medication is not a substitute for human insight and relationships that may include a variety of other aids — from behavior-modification therapy through counseling. These other possibilities should be left open. Once a program of stimulant medication has been established for the child, it is up to parents and professionals to assess the new situation and see what additional needs the child now has for guidance.

Dr. Kinsbourne is a pediatric neurologist and child psychologist. He is currently Professor of Pediatrics at the University of Toronto Medical School and Professor of Psychology at the University of Toronto. He heads the hospital's Neuropsychology Research Unit.

# Hyperactivity: The scandalous silence

By Steven Box

*Steven Box is a lecturer in sociology at the University of Kent, Canterbury, Kent, England. This article first appeared in* New Society, London, *the weekly review of the social sciences. It is reprinted here by permission.*

 Reprinted from *Arise Magazine*, 1978, Vol. 1, No. 9 by permission of the publisher.

There is a scandalous silence about a form of violence going on in schools. It is of a kind that is far more psychologically and socially damaging than the violence against people and property that has recently had widespread publicity and has led to an outcry for more punitive measures against the culprits. This pernicious silence is understandable when you realize the villains are educational and medical authorities.

The violence I mean is the increasing employment of "medical solutions" to school problems which are *essentially* moral, legal, and social. There are good reasons, from the viewpoint of those in authority, why moral, legal, and social problems should be transformed into medical problems requiring medical intervention. But first let us look at the case of one so-called schoolchild psychiatric behavioral disorder—namely, "hyperactivity."

There are two reasons why hyperactivity has become a disease of extreme national and international importance since its "discovery" in 1957. First, like diphtheria nearly seventy years ago, it is a disease which has now reached epidemic proportions; second, if untreated, its prognosis is disastrous for the individual and catastrophic for the community.

In America, anywhere between five hundred thousand and a million schoolchildren are currently diagnosed as hyperactive. This makes it, according to a recent book, "One of the major childhood behavior disorders of our time. It is the single most common behavior disorder seen by child psychiatrists, a problem frequently presented to pediatricians and a major problem in the school system." Even more alarming to educational and medical authorities, the epidemic is apparently becoming more extensive. It is reported that "already specialists...state that at least 30 percent of ghetto children are candidates "for being treated as hyperactive" and this figure could run as high as four to six million of the general school population."

In the United Kingdom, synonymous or overlapping disorders of hyperactivity are less well documented, relatively unanalyzed, and underdiscussed. Furthermore, differences in disorder classification and diagnostic procedures make strict comparison difficult

and open to numerous criticisms. Nonetheless, an epidemic of schoolchild psychiatric disorders is clearly taking place, on a pattern similar to the United States, though on a much smaller scale. For example, if we take the diagnostic category of *maladjusted,* of which according to the Department of Education and Science, hyperactivity is a major symptom, there were in 1950 only 587 so classified full-time pupils in special schools. In the next 20 years, this figure had risen to over five thousand, and only five years later had leaped again to nearly fourteen thousand. This increase of nearly 2,500 percent is far, far in excess of the 50 percent increase in the total school population. In addition, in the last ten years, the number of so-called maladjusted children who are not in special schools has doubled.

A second reason for its importance is that experts now believe hyperactivity indicates there are worse things to come. Originally viewed as a problem of middle childhood and early adolescence, it is now clear to officials that it can be detected in the last three months of pregnancy. It also continues well into adulthood where it shows itself in other forms of deviant behavior. A letter published by Dr. Carham and Dr. Tucker in the *Lancet* argues that by studying the neurochemical determinants of hyperactivity, more insight may be gained into sociopathy, alcoholism, and hysteria. This is because all four are "characterized by cognitive or attentional defects and aggressive impulsivity of varying severity." If this theory is correct, in the victory over hyperactivity lies the potential for conquering any of our most serious forms of disruptive and injurious mental illness, especially psychopathy. Indeed, for every hyperactive schoolchild cured, we will be spared the murderous villainy of a later grown-up psychopath.

Let us take a closer, more critical look at hyperactivity, the disease said to be debilitating so many schoolchildren.

Why do both hyperactivity and maladjustment afflict boys much more than girls? In most reports, the ratio is rarely less than four to one and sometimes reaches nine to one. Furthermore, once we consider its incidence by geographical location, ethnicity, or social class, we find it is not evenly spread through the population. Hyperactivity is diagnosed more frequently among the urban ethnically and econoically disadvantaged. But why should it affect only some and not others: is its identification a medical or a social process?

The efforts of hundreds of research workers have not managed to demonstrate that hyperactivity is the result of any genuine histopathological lesion or pathophysiological process. There has been a complete failure to prove that hyperactivity is a genuine disease.

## Diagnoses of deviance

The typical procedures for diagnosing hyperactivity are also disturbing. As there is no valid physical sign of disease, the official favorite procedure is to evaluate the child's behavior. This is often accomplished by teachers completing the Conners rating scale. This includes, first, items like classroom behavior (a child fidgets, hums or makes odd noises, is easily frustrated, restless, excitable, inattentive, overly sensitive, serious or sad, daydreams, sulks, cries, disturbs other children, quarrels, acts "smart," is destructive, steals, lies or loses temper). Secondly, group participation (a child is isolated from others or unacceptable to them, is easily led and lacks leadership, does not get along with same or opposite sex, teases others, and has no sense of fair play). Thirdly, the attitude toward authority (defiant, stubborn, uncooperative, plays truant).

What is disturbing about these typical diagnoses is that they have nothing to do with disease, but everything to do with deviance. Such behavior violates important school norms about paying attention to teacher, obeying teacher, and being responsive to teacher's wishes, instructions, or commands; not interfering with other children; not answering teacher back or threatening or actually assaulting teacher; not mistreating or damaging school property; being orderly and disciplined.

When most of us were at school, children who behaved in these ways were called disruptive, disobedient, rebellious, anti-social, a bloody nuisance, and naughty; they were clipped round the ear, caned on the hand, or in my school slapped on the backside. Apparently, there has been much medical progress from those uncivilized times. Children are no longer naughty, they are medical cases. With this conceptualization of the problem, American schools, particularly in poor Negro ghettoes, and English schools in urban slums and ethnically mixed areas are being transformed from places where children attended educational courses to places where they receive courses in medical treatment.

The form this treatment takes can be alarming. Some children diagnosed as hyperactive have had individual psychotherapy, others behavior therapy, and still others brain surgery, but by far the most favored and widely practiced treatment is drug therapy. Schoolchildren, by the millions in America, and the tens of thousands in this country, are being put on long-term programs of drug therapy simply because their behavior does not fit in with the requirements of school . . .

When we consider what kind of behavior constitutes hyperactivity, and who is involved, we might see this behavior as reflecting social rather than medical problems. During rising and often chronic unemployment, many schoolchildren, particularly lower-class and ethnically under-privileged boys, naturally cause problems. A lot of the frustration, rejection, humiliation, and oppression they experience shows itself in delinquency, truancy, disobedience, and other behavior which upsets figures of authority, including parents and especially teachers. The state, as a custodian of moral and legal boundaries, tries to contain and control such behavior. It naturally gives support to those groups of professions who come up with viable solutions.

During the 1950s and 1960s, it looked as though criminology and sociology would solve the growing problem of disobedient youth, but their programs were either counter-productive or too utopian. Even while lip service was still being paid to criminology-based programs, alternative solutions were being sought to the delinquent-disobedient youth problem. One of these was already under way and only required more funds and official certification to mushroom. This was a new version of *biological determinism*— the conception that delinquents and pre-delinquents were essentially either mentally ill, or, in the case of hyperactivity and maladjustment, physically and organically ill, and required treatment, especially drug therapy.

This view of the problem creates an entirely new and frightening conception of school health care. Under the guidance or dominance of a therapeutic system of social control, the school medical system has shifted from screening, preventing, and treating real diseases (that is, diseases of an organic kind that refer to cellular pathology). Instead, it screens, prevents, and treats *non-organic behavior disagreements*. It has shifted in such a way that it deliberately confuses curing diseases with controlling deviants.

D.M. and S.A. Ross write in *Hyperactivity: Research, Theory and Action* (New York: Wiley, 1976): "Having always professed concern about the whole child, the school system is for the first time now assuming its rightful responsibility in this area." This, they say, has "the potential to be the most important of all major advances in the 1970s." But they fail completely to spell out from whose vantage point, and with whose interests in mind, this is a major advance. Surely not those millions of schoolchildren who suffer only from a desire to rebel at school, from boredom, from a sense of failure (due to an educational environment aimed at achievement), who are fearful of future unemployment and the welfare, and who demand more of school than teachers can possibly give.

It is on this ever-expanding number of frustrated and disillusioned schoolchildren that violence is being committed. Instead of recognizing their inarticulate cries of rage and despair and examining the very serious problems they face, there is an intense drive to individualize their problems, and blame them on an organic impairment. Drugs are then administered

to dampen and confuse the child's scarcely-heard protests. In this way, the minds of a generation of the ethnically and economically deprived are being hollowed out, and the revolt of a potentially delinquent population avoided.

## Medicine unbounded

All this might seem very unfair comment on a profession which has undoubtedly saved the lives of millions from crippling and fatal diseases; but the history of medicine reveals that it does not confine its boundaries to real diseases. It has always been prepared to involve itself in transforming moral and political issues into medical conditions. This was massively enhanced when it acquired a legal monopoly of the mind as well as the body, for this allowed the discovery of diseases without the need to establish any observable or detectable organic impairment or malfunction. When the demonstrable organic basis for a disease was removed, the "tinkering" medical profession was able to discover a whole spectrum of so-called mental illnesses to cover an ever-growing proportion of human behavior. This wave of medical expansion, including the recent "epidemics" of hyperactivity and maladjustment, has had dramatic shot in the arm by the pharmacological revolution over the last three decades, as it now has more technological control over the "symptoms" (behavior) or diseases.

To do justice to the rising generation, particularly those males from ethnically and/or economically impoverished backgrounds, their disturbing behavior must not be explained away as symptomatic of a disease. Admittedly, surrendering to this temptation has many advantages: it justifies actions, particularly therapeutic interventions, not allowed if the problem were not medical; it justifies intervention before any offense has been committed, as medicine advocates prevention being better than cure; it takes the issues out of public moral debate and places them into the secretive and impenetrable hands of educational and medical professionals; it avoids issues of legal rights or the complicated protections afforded to the "accused" by due process; and it de-politicizes the issue. Finally, it justifies continuing treatment far beyond alteration of any deviant behavior.

It may be difficult to turn away such a gift-horse, and clearly government officials have not been able to do so. But if we are to stem the steady slide not towards *1984* but *Brave New World*, then we must end the psychological violence many schoolchildren are suffering due to the educational authorities' direct refusal to come to grips with the problems faced by many of their pupils. What they need is not drug therapy, but the opportunities to live their lives more fully. That requires a rethinking of the entire purposes and functions of compulsory education and the place of medical and psychiatric care within it.

# The medicine pots—
# a motivation operation

Letti L. Clark

"It's nice that kids get to make so many things in art these days. We didn't have these opportunities when I was in school."

Art teachers across the country hear echoes of this thinking. Ironically, though, the *making of things* in an art class is *not* the most important happening or the greatest humanizing opportunity which is presented.

So often, by the time many students reach the upper elementary grades, they are experiencing central school system dysfunction. They have been put down, shut up, forced into, bawled out, embarrassed in-front-of and held behind so often that they are exhibiting symptoms of ego-collapse and educational shutdown. The art interval offers an anecdotal opportunity to recondition the broken spirit and medicate the ill-functioning self concept. Here a child has the chance to be an individual. A bruised self-image can be treated.

What do you do with a child who has an established record of failure and comes to you in a condition of ego arrest? How do you motivate a child who already has ceased his academic breathing? The problem is common. The solution is not simple.

At our school during a recent unit on ceramics, I witnessed the return to life of several students, non-achievers, who were led to believe that they could succeed instead of fail in a pot-building assignment. The believing did not come easy. The resistance was strong. When you have experienced failure so many times it is very dangerous and threatening to show your feelings and extend your hopes with the possibility of again meeting defeat. A believing environment had to be carefully and slowly created for the patients in this operation.

Before actually beginning work with the clay, the students were given a contract which clearly set forth the A, B and C grade requirements. To help the formation of a believable plan, a chart was furnished which listed all the possible combinations of pot building methods and decorating techniques

along with the number of firings required for each. Using this information the students attempted to estimate the amount of time necessary for each step of the work. Their expected rate of progress was then plotted on their personal project calendar, which showed the number of working days available. Vacation days were designated as well as the days on which the kiln would be fired. At first this process, which admittedly was very complicated, confused even the quickest students. Very soon, however, the confusion cleared and the students began working with a directed purpose which had not been in evidence previously. The plan that each student made was kept in the

room and was available during each working period. Most students consulted their plan daily.

Initially the non-achievers required a good deal of individual attention. Noticeably though, before long, they began realizing that they were making it. The idea even occurred to some that if they could work a little faster they would be able to earn the next higher grade. All of the students were encouraged during their routine consultation with the teacher. The students who were less secure about their ability to succeed were given more attention and positively reinforced more often. The initial horseplay which was paraded to mask feelings of inadequacy and pos-

The Medicine Pots--A Motivation Operation, Lettie L. Clark, *School Arts,* Vol. 76, No. 6, February, 1977. ©1977 Davis Publications, Inc., Worcester, MA.

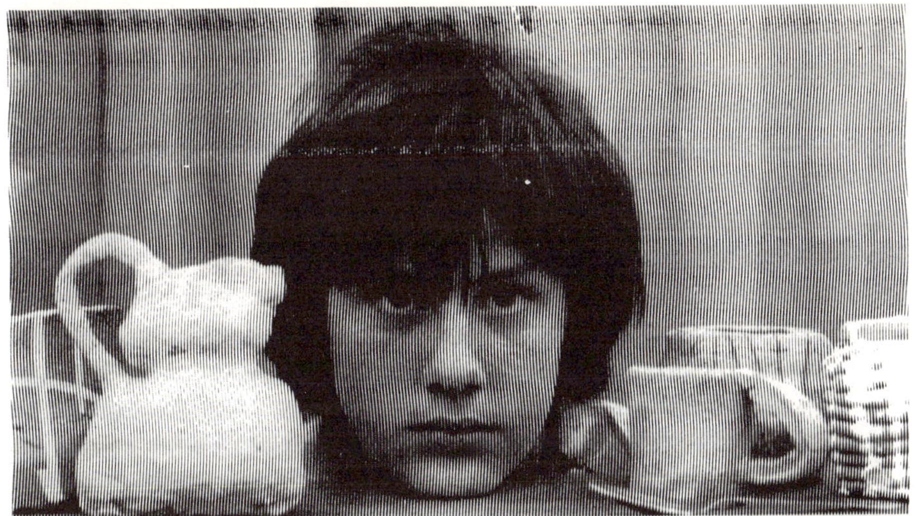

sible defeat, were ignored. The social interactions between students and teacher were carefully limited to positive exchanges concerning the student's work progress.

In a very short time ceramic engineers began to dominate the room. Small successes began to be realized. These small successes fostered larger ones and damaged concepts of self experienced recovery as the students worked with confidence guided by their calendars.

The pot making operation was successful for this eighth grade group which consisted of students who were performing with an extremely varied amount of success academically. The achievers continue to achieve and the non-achievers blossomed under the therapeutic encouragement which enabled them first to trust, next to believe success a possibility and finally to succeed. Our ceramic pots truly were *medicine pots*.

Letti L. Clark is an art teacher, State Street Middle School, Alliance, Ohio.

# Behavioral Blockbusters!

Do you have trouble with negativistic, impulsive, passive-dependent, or anxious kids? In this four-part article, noted psychologist Dr. Hugh Carberry tells you how to handle and help them.

THE children we will be talking about here are not learning disabled or mentally handicapped. But they do have problems, or blocks, which create situations the teacher must resolve if the learning process is going to be effective. And these problems, if not properly dealt with now, can become serious adult deficiencies. So it behooves the teacher to help these troubled children—for their own sakes and for the sake of all around them.

## The negativistic child

The youngster who is negativistic typically seems sullen or antagonistic. He refuses to do what is asked, even when the request is reasonable. When he experiences failure or perceives that things are going against him, he may pout or quit. In more extreme instances, he may even become violent, sometimes inflicting punishment on himself or others.

This youngster can be a dramatic underachiever in spite of good intellectual ability. His negativism can get in the way of using his intelligence in a productive, efficient way. This tendency toward negativism can, of course, be coupled with an impulsive or anxious approach to learning, further decreasing efficiency.

The negativistic youngster is one of the most difficult to deal with and one of the easier children to get involved with in a very negative relationship. At the same time he can be a very challenging youngster. It is important to realize that the child's negativism is learned behavior and can be unlearned. Here are some things you can do.

1. Focus initially on those situations in which the child is usually cooperative; concentrate and reinforce that behavior. Usually, this will be something in which the child is interested.

2. Ignore in a very matter-of-fact way any confrontations with the child. The negativistic child has discovered that negativism very often is a sure way to gain attention.

3. Gradually introduce situations in which the child is usually negativistic, working for change. Tell the child that you appreciate that he is changing his behavior and discuss briefly with him the fact that you are working with him toward certain goals.

4. Reduce the criterion for the correctness of a task while you're working with his negativism. Reduce expectations; settle for small gains and resist constant preoccupation with success.

5. Create a predictable environment for the child in which he is rewarded for accomplishments, nonrewarded if he fails to meet reasonable demands.

6. Be prepared to modify tasks and reset expectations if the child fails or becomes negative.

The avoidance of confrontations with the youngster while rewarding cooperative behavior is the basic key to success. If you find that it is very difficult to be positive with this child, this is a good cue that you are involved in a vicious circle of will struggles and the unhappiness that goes with it.

Quite often the negativistic child will be supersensitive to any perceived "unfairness" by the teacher, and while he may not express his anger directly, he may sulk and brood. Typically, the youngster catastrophizes in an irrational way about perceived injustices. Discussions around these themes (e.g., teacher's unfairness, favoritism in the classroom, always being picked on, and so on) can help reduce angry, hostile feelings. Listening to the child discuss these feelings can help alleviate some of the guilt and angry feelings that the child may have. Help the child to understand that it is not the end of the world if he is treated unfairly, that teachers and parents make mistakes, too. That can go a long way in helping him become better equipped for life.

## The impulsive child

The youngster who is impulsive is also a very difficult child to handle. Very often he will rush into a situation without thinking. Thought and planning usually follow rather than precede his actions. The impulsive child has not learned to control some of his behavior, and that often gets him in trouble. He often falls behind

Reprinted from *Instructor* © March 1979 by the Instructor Publications, Inc. Used by permission.

because his learning efficiency is significantly lowered by his impulsivity. How can this youngster be helped?

1. The child needs a great deal of *structure*. Take time to talk with him, to help him develop the habit of listening. For example, preface conversation with such statements as: "I am going to say something. I want you to listen, then say it back to me." Start with short phrases and graduate to sentences and later brief paragraphs. Also, give only one or two instructions at a time. Frequently the impulsive child learns best and increases his attention by being shown what to do rather than by being told.

2. Decrease permissiveness and choice making. The impulsive child typically has difficulty when faced with too many alternatives. He also needs to know clearly the rules and limits of the classroom. When he is faced with too many choices, he gets frustrated. It is better to reduce the choices. Move slowly toward helping him learn decision making.

3. Train the child in organizational skills. Impulsive children usually need help in approaching a task. Go through the process with the child in a step-by-step manner and then check the child as he accomplishes each step. For example, if the youngster needs to learn how to add a column of double figures and to understand the concept of carrying, this should be shown in detail in a concrete way.

4. Reduce stimulation in the environment. The impulsive child is often distractible. His attention is drawn quickly to other stimuli around him. It is important to reduce the possible sources of stimulation. A quiet place is difficult to find in many schools, but it's worth the effort.

5. Reduce pressure. The impulsive child has many new behaviors to learn to increase his efficiency. But you need to work on a continuum of change, giving rewards initially for very small steps. If a child can only attend for one minute, he needs to be praised for this and then moved to the next step. In our culture, we tend to value the final product more than the process, but if one of your goals is for your youngster to concentrate for 15 minutes on a project, it is important to realize that being able to do that three out of five days a week is an im-

provement which needs to be communicated to the child.

Finally, you should provide a model that is organized, nonimpulsive, and structured. Before you can help the youngster you have to look at your own behavior and work toward desired change. Teachers may fear that these suggestions, which decrease impulsivity, could produce side effects that decrease spontaneity. However, there is a real difference between freedom of expression that is sensitive, disciplined, and organized and the impulsive approach that at times creates problems through insensitive chaos and disorder. Structure and organization do not necessarily mean repression of impulses or a climate of fear.

## The passive-dependent child

The passive-dependent child simply does not take the initiative in most situations and is a problem because he is not utilizing his full potential and quite often dramatically under-achieves. Teachers often describe this child as "immature" or "not aggressive enough."

If a child continues to have this passive-dependent stance reinforced, he may develop a life-style marked by a lack of healthy assertiveness. This can be very handicapping as an adult. Reinforcement of the child's passivity and dependence breeds anger for both teacher and child. This type of child typically expresses his anger indirectly by stubborn resistance, dawdling, procrastinating, and sometimes lying and petty stealing.

Behaviorally, this is a child who rarely asks questions when he does not understand or who is always asking questions when, in fact, he probably does understand. In the latter instance, the teacher eventually finds herself getting irritated at the child because of the excessive dependency and his constant demand for attention. Identifying such a child is the first task of the teacher. It is important to remember that this may be the child's basic approach in many life situations and that change in the learning style is necessary before gains can be made. This child may be fairly good in rote memory tasks like spelling or memorizing the multiplication tables but has difficulty in tasks demanding more

assertiveness like solving arithmetic problems, logical reasoning, or social interaction with peers. The goal for the teacher is two-fold: to decrease the frequency of passive-dependent behavior; and increase the frequency of assertive, risk-taking behavior.

The teacher should make a profile of the child's behavior to know what to ignore and what to reinforce. This is an essential first step. This profile should consist of actual descriptions of behavior, not attitudes. Knowing what you want is as important as knowing what you do not want. One way is to make a list of negative statements and convert them to positive statements, which then become specific behavioral goals for the child. For example, "Laura is constantly seeking reassurance for understanding simple instructions from the teacher," can be converted to, "Laura attempts assignments independently without asking unnecessary questions." Also, reward in a meaningful way any behavior that approximates assertive, risk-taking behavior. A child cannot go from one style to another in one jump.

The critical element in the success of any such plan is the teacher-child relationship. Involve the child right from the beginning directly in the change process. What is really a reward for the child can only be discovered by talking to the youngster about it. Once desirable behavior is established the teacher can then reinforce on an intermittent basis.

A child who is passive in his approach to others has a negative self-image. A teacher can be helpful by having the child write five things about himself which he sees as good. Teaching the child how to handle a compliment or to give compliments is one way of increasing assertiveness.

Again, the idea of providing a model to the child of assertive behavior is critical because so much of children's learning occurs through imitation. As teachers we find passive and conforming behavior easier to deal with than assertive or aggressive. However, the passive child tends to become the passive adult and this can complicate his life.

## The anxious child

This is the child who sets about most tasks by being frightened. He decides in advance that a situation may be too difficult, and he's petrified at attempts to get him to try something new. Typically, he freezes or blocks, and if you are not aware of his fear he may come across as being intellectually dull. Memory and attention are also affected. As adults, we can all identify with this state of mind, for at some point in our lives we have experienced it. It is a very human phenomenon and occurs most often when we are threatened or feel inadequate in some way. This is especially true in new learning situations. If a child is allowed to withdraw and retreat from stress, he will have fewer and fewer experiences and less growth will take place. The more situations that are avoided out of fear, the more fearful the child becomes.

Obviously, the child who is fearful and anxious cannot be thrust directly into those situations which he fears. This would be too traumatizing and not effective. Teachers, however, can help in a variety of ways.

1. Reduce the criterion for success or correctness. Initially, lower standards and "settle for less." Give praise for every small effort that is made. If a child is fearful of talking in front of friends or classmates, praise him for talking to one or two individually.

2. Guarantee the child success in learning. If a youngster is fearful of reading aloud in class, for example, have him tape his reading at home and play it back to him as a way of instilling confidence. Movement along a continuum of geared activity can also be rewarding.

3. Structure any new learning situation for the child so that he fully understands the process. An anxious child will worry about what might happen, what could go wrong, and how he might make mistakes. It is important not to assume that the child knows what is to take place.

4. Reduce any sense of group competitiveness by helping the child see that he only needs to compete with his own record. In our society, we seem to be conditioned to compete with our peers. For a child who already feels inadequate this can be overwhelming. Helping him develop an attitude of self-competition can be much more realistic. Instead of letting him compare himself with the other children on a test, ask, "How does this compare with what you expected, or how you did last time?"

A child develops the attitude of "what if" this happens or that happens. This can be immobilizing and we need to help him see that usually the worst thing that happens is that we make a mistake and this only proves we are human beings.

The children we have discussed here are not exceptional, but they do have problems. And it's important you help them alleviate those problems. Make the above methods work for you and for your anxious or impulsive child.

# Georgia's Rutland Center

In an antebellum house in Athens, teachers with a special kind of patience and love are having unusual success guiding emotionally disturbed children from turbulence into life's mainstream

By Jane Hauser Hoyt

Trying to enter the shadowy and sometimes turbulent world of an emotionally disturbed child can be a difficult, frustrating experience. To turn that child toward learning and acceptable behavior requires a special kind of patience and love—and a certain sense of personal security.

In Athens, Georgia, teachers at the Rutland Center regularly venture into the private preserves of children in emotional crisis. Their success in dispersing some of the shadows and orienting the children toward reality is statistically documented: 90 percent of those who leave Rutland's classrooms do not have to return for more help. A further indicator of success is that 53 other places in the country are trying the techniques used by Rutland, itself recognized as a model for what is now the Georgia Psychoeducational Center Network, with 24 such centers serving the entire state.

Rutland serves children from infancy to 14 years of age who have one or maybe a variety of problems but who all have some serious emotional difficulty which somehow impairs their day-to-day activities. As with all handicapped children, the earlier these youngsters begin getting help, the better, a point and one of the few—on which practitioners in the field would probably agree. Ask five of them what causes a child, particularly a very young one, to be emotionally disturbed, and you will most likely get five different answers. Depending on whom you question, the causes will range from neurological to environmental factors, with many qualifiers in between. And the variety of views about what causes emotional disturbance is further complicated by natural differences in the children themselves.

Ms. Hoyt is on the staff of OE's Office of Public Affairs.

Consider four children recently enrolled in Rutland. One would take only soup and milk, another sat and stared, another had the additional complications of cerebral palsy. The fourth child spent his first week in class whirling in circles, flapping his arms and slapping himself, and ended each class period by throwing up. His doctor called him a "ten-acre child," meaning that it was clear a classroom could never contain him.

On a warm, muggy day not too long ago, these same four children were sitting together at a child-sized table, bulldozing their way through an energetic yum-yum time of yogurt and cookies. Later, all were gently swaying to the taped soft sounds of violins during music time.

There were still occasional cracklings of tension as one child or another became alarmed when it came time to change activities. But the point to be noted was that this small group did not differ greatly from any

*"Hello time is almost over. Now it's yum-yum time." When a child desperately needs a consistent, secure environment, all activities are carefully organized and done at the same time each day.*

four children one might expect to find together in a preschool classroom. In fact, the teachers sometimes joke that unless a child begins acting up, some observers find it hard to believe that the Rutland Center is working with children who have very deep emotional problems.

In that paradox is a key to the way Rutland deals with its children. "We focus on normal growth and development, not on pathology. We look at what the youngsters can do as opposed to what they can't do," says Anthony Beardsley, who has been with Rutland since it began in 1972 and has done everything from driving the bus to training other teachers. Beardsley is in charge of Rutland's National Technical Assistance Office, funded by OE's Bureau of Education for the Handicapped to show educators in other schools around the country how to use the model. "The term 'emotional disturbance' focuses on pathology. I think a label is a deterrent to child and teacher alike. Take away that label and look at the child," he suggests. "All the same things are going on that go on with any child. What he does, what he feels, what he likes, what he is. All the neat things and the not so neat things. But we are working with this child because he has a problem. Something is interfering with all of his feelings—with his good feelings, with his bad feelings—interfering with him. What we try to do is help him to a point where he can function within his own normal range without these emotional problems interfering."

To accomplish this, Rutland follows an approach called "Developmental Therapy." Children learn and develop in a well-documented step-by-step order. Program work is matched to a child's particular stage of physical, emotional, cognitive, and social development. This sounds complicated but is accomplished in a straightforward manner. The Rutland Center Developmental Therapy Model uses 146 objectives as a guide for the mental health and special education personnel it brings together to work with the children.

The Developmental Therapy curriculum deals with behavior, communication, socialization, and academics or preacademics. Since children go through certain stages of development in a certain order, Rutland has set up specific techniques and materials for four stages corresponding to levels of development and adjustment. If a child exhibits inappropriate behavior at a certain stage of development, teachers immediately help the child learn more constructive ways to deal with whatever is causing the difficulty. As certain objectives are achieved, the child moves up into another stage.

In the earliest stages, an objective may mean simply trusting an adult enough to respond to him or her. Or in academics, putting puzzle blocks into a box. In later stages, a child's socialization would extend to being sufficiently self-confident to help another child. And what was learned earlier about shape discrimination by putting blocks into slots would be refined to the point where a child could recognize numbers and letters.

Of course, it's not quite that easy. For one thing, Rutland believes that a young child's emotional and behavioral disturbances are subtly interwoven with his or her normal behavior. Therapy must deal with both the normal and the disturbed elements. Probably nowhere is this more evident than at the first level or stage I classroom. Here the children's world is frustrating, painful, and confusing. The children's actions anger those around them. People have a hard time understanding them, and they themselves cannot understand. Many just stopped responding at some point. Others never began to respond.

According to Mary M. Wood, who started the program and is project director of the Developmental Therapy Institute in the Division for Exceptional Children at the University of Georgia, these are children who might ordinarily be placed in an institution. "Often the children will have a significant delay in speech and language with no demonstrable—that is, organic—cause. This usually results in a breakdown in interpersonal relationships."

Wood points out that these stage I children can't respond to certain given stimuli. Or they may have processing disorders—they can't make sense of their environment. They didn't trust adults initially and, until their admission to Rutland, faced experiences daily that reinforced their distrust.

To combat this, says Faye Swindle, director of Rutland's program for the autistic, "we make the environment so pleasurable and so alluring, that the children can't resist." As she explains it, how a child feels about himself and how much he is willing to risk in a new situation comes out of significantly pleasurable experiences.

teachers. It is a place which is so luring [sic] that they are enticed into responding. They find that old behaviors, infuriating and pain-producing to themselves and others, are no longer useful. They are not rejected for these behaviors but are reorganized and redirected to new responses which bring them pleasure."

At this stage, when a child so desperately needs a consistent, secure environment, all activities are carefully organized and done at the same time each day. Even the language the teachers use is structured, that is, limited at first to words that directly refer to classroom and home activities (milk, cookies, play, work). This provides key words to learn as a beginning for the children's later forays into language.

The stage I classroom itself is about the size of a large living room. Part of the floor is carpeted, part is bare wood—important for children who will begin to distinguish differences in how things feel and look. Two sets of cabinets, one near the play area and another near the table used for snack time and art time, have counters, but there is nothing on top of them. All doors—to the cabinets, to the two exits to the bathroom—are closed. Materials are quickly brought out for activities and just as quickly put away after use. All of this keeps distractions to a minimum.

Today is one of those difficult days. During play time, Cindy gets very angry and cries and tries to bite herself and Rey, the support teacher. He holds her while trying to direct her activities to those of the group. Then, in a bright, upbeat voice, Amy, the lead teacher, announces, "Hello time is almost over. Now it's yum-yum time." In this way she prepares the children for the next activity. This is essential; as Lomax explains, "Transition times are difficult because the children worry they won't succeed in the next activity." But this transition goes smoothly, and during yum-yum time, Cindy calms down and turns her considerable energy to a bowl of yogurt.

The table is positioned directly in front of the observation window. "You really have to know the children to understand some of the things that are going on," says Swindle. Just before everyone sits down, Bobby takes off on a dash across the room—inappropriate behavior for him. Meanwhile Ned is drinking his juice, smiling occasionally. He weighed one pound when he was born. When he came to the program he could not tolerate anything coming into his world and particularly near his mouth. For a moment, his eyes glaze over and he is somewhere else. Amy, who is sitting next to him, touches his arms and says, "Juice, Ned?" He starts to form the word with his lips but never quite gets it out. Even a sound will go on the word chart that shows each child's daily language progress.

The ten-acre child meanwhile is alert to everything. His mother, who is visiting the project today, says, "He's an entirely different child from the one he was six months ago. He's paying attention. He's more observant of other children. Outside he sees trees and flowers. A bee is fascinating to him." In class he has even begun to anticipate activities before they start, another sign of advancing development. And later that day, he will delight everyone by picking himself up from an outside spill and announcing, "I fell down." A complete sentence.

"We work a lot for language," says Swindle. What may start as babbling, gibberish, or repetition of sounds can be shaped in time into a coherent language structure. To help this development, both Amy and Rey use

---

## "The term 'emotional disturbance' focuses on pathology. I think a label is a deterrent to child and teacher alike. Take away that label and look at the child."

---

At the same time, Andrea Lomax, a teacher trainer with the Developmental Therapy Institute, points out, "As the children begin to trust us, they find more pleasure in the environment."

"At first," says Swindle, "most messages these children can receive are through touch because they aren't making any sense out of the spoken word. A child learns from experience more than from words, so at first, he learns more from the actions and body language of the teacher."

According to the teachers' text *Developmental Therapy*, edited by Mary Wood, children entering the stage I class . . . "are dealt with so consistently, but so warmly, that they begin to trust this class and these

On the wall is a list of activities: play time, hello time, yum-yum time, work time, dance time, art time, juice and cookies time, music time, goodbye time. Two adults are present, a lead teacher and a support teacher. Often one of them is a student in the Division for Exceptional Children at the University of Georgia doing an internship or practicum at Rutland. Music, recreation, and art therapists also work directly with the children.

Behind a one-way glass, a parent and a team social worker observe and make notes that will indicate whether a child is moving toward or away from objectives set for him or her. There are three children, joined later by a fourth. Age range in this class is three-and-a-half to seven years.

sign language in conjunction with their own carefully constructed sentences. It gives the children a more complete field of information and may help them verbalize. It also can help dissipate anger to have a child physically sign.

"Yum-yum time is over," announces

The next activity is dance time, which is in some ways, says Swindle, "another name for nurturing time." With the sound of violins on the tape recorder, the teachers take the chil-

(which the program people call debriefing) or analyzing what is going on. This can range from such subtleties as deciding who should sit closest to the teacher in a given activity to more direct matters like taking

*A "ten-acre" child spent his first week at Rutland whirling in circles, flapping his arms, and slapping himself.*

Amy, quickly putting all the bowls and spoons into the cupboard behind her. "It's work time." Usually a class works together, but right now these children are working on individual preacademic tasks. So while Amy takes out a peg board for one child and a board with holes in the side to be laced for another, Rey is in the corner with Peter and Ned starting a learning game called "Pictures and Objects." Rey holds up a picture of an orange, says its name, and then, from a box behind him, pulls out an orange for the child to hold.

dren by the arms and sway back and forth to the music.

And so the day continues. Each activity announced as it begins and ends. All children expected to be in the same place before another activity begins. Built-in expectations. Adults they learn to trust. A world that grows a little more secure each day. Finally, it's goodbye time. Total time elapsed —two exhausting hours.

It is possible to see constructive things going on, although sometimes it takes a practiced eye. Says one parent, "It's almost like looking through a microscope." And it is reassuring to see how very little Rutland leaves to chance. About a third of a teacher's time is spent planning or determining

*During music time the children listen to the taped soft sounds of violins.*

a dramatic step to improve language development in a child whose progress has stopped. The teacher's text makes clear the importance of details: "By sitting next to the most impulsive children in a group you can prevent much acting out because you are in a better position to react quickly before things get out of hand." Thus Rey kept a close watch and sometimes a protective hand on Cindy. During the morning class when she was fussy, a teacher was never far from her side.

Later during the debriefing session —the time that teachers and team social workers share their observations—

the social worker mentioned that Bobby was following and imitating Peter, a behavior change for both since it was usually the other way around. And Cindy? After a preliminary check by Amy to make sure Cindy's diaper didn't need changing (wet pants always upset Cindy), a weekend visit to a grandparent was pegged as part of the reason for her outburst. It was a big change in the pattern of her life and apparently was making her anxious and angry.

Following the two hours of intensive therapy in the class and the debriefing, the child either goes home or to some special placement, often accompanied by the teacher, who continues to work with the child in the other settings. As they progress, the children will go on outside trips—to the grocery store or the park. "As much as we can, we want the child out having normal experiences," says Wood.

Because so many factors affect a child's life, the center tries to know as many sides of its children as possible. When a child first comes to the center, needed information is gathered through a series of what are called "intake interviews." To cut down on distractions, these are conducted in "the little house," a place about half a block from the main center where a social worker asks a parent about the family situation—who's who in the family, how many other children there are, the extent and nature of the child's problem. A staff member will do an educational assessment of the child to get information about his or her development. Depending on the child's reaction to being tested, this can be done with or without the parent present. Psychological and psychiatric assessments are also done. The

other parents. Or a parent can simply walk right in for help.

Once a child begins a program, notes are kept on his or her activities and behavior. To help with recording, the Developmental Therapy Objectives Rating Form is used for each child every five weeks. Every ten weeks, all classes are regrouped and the children moved to their newly determined de-

the cause of the problem. So their reactions vary. Some tend to shy away and come only to a few required meetings; others get into the thick of it and even help in class.

No matter how far they go, parents are "the strength of any program," says Geter. "They have something to offer the child that no one else can. We pool our expertise with what the

---

**"Most messages these children can receive are through touch because they aren't making any sense out of the spoken word. A child learns more from the actions and body language of a teacher."**

---

velopmental level. Lomax says that this procedure, besides making sure each child is at the proper developmental level, exposes the individual to other teachers and "helps the child develop a feeling for the place as a whole."

Another reason for regrouping, according to Wood, is to avoid generating in the children an "undue dependence or attachment" toward their teachers. In more traditional forms of therapy, a close relationship between the therapist and the client is usually desirable. But Rutland doesn't want its teachers to supplant the parent relationship.

"Our job is to involve parents as much as possible. This is particularly important because of the provisions of the new public law 94-142. We want to get them into a better position to help their children grow," says Barbara Geter, who worked with Rutland's first parent group and now gives other centers the benefit of her experience. "We are helping parents to help their children," she says. Ideally, center staff likes to meet on a regular basis with parents and have them

parents know of the child and then discuss possible ways the child may be helped." Rewards come when, after such discussions, parents "start doing some individual thinking and come up with ways of their own to deal with a particular situation."

What is an ideal parent? After working with 20 different family groups for six years, Geter thinks it is "somebody compassionate, warm, loving, and nurturing who thinks her child or his child is the neatest child ever." In many parents, she says, "All that is there naturally. It just needs to be identified and directed."

And what of the teachers who deal with these kinds of children? What makes a good one? Here are three expert opinions:
☐ Andrea Lomax—"Teachers must be emotionally mature. They're on the line with these children, many of whom have been abused by adults and don't trust any of them. So a teacher starts out with two strikes. A strong ego helps."
☐ Tony Beardsley—"There is a thin line between the professional attachment as a therapist and becoming so involved that if a child makes a mistake and regresses, it reflects on the teacher. Teachers must be sensitive, but must also be able sometimes to put their emotions in a closet for a moment to evaluate a situation."
☐ Mary M. Wood—"A good teacher in this field believes in the basic integrity of the child and the child's ability, with help, to get it together. That teacher also has an ability to tolerate ambiguity. He or she has a sensitivity to the feelings of others as well as an openness to share feelings with others. But at the same time good teachers

---

**Teachers burn out faster in this field of special education than in any other. Yet Rutland has staff members who have been there nearly seven years and are still going strong.**

---

center, working closely with other community agencies, has access to many other support services a child may need.

Children do not have to be referred to the center. Some are discovered through the program's preschool screening work. Parents of children already at the center sometimes refer

observe what is going on in class and see how they can carry it over and do some of the things at home. The staff also helps teachers rate their children developmentally.

When the handicap is rooted in emotional problems, working with parents can be hard. Parents have natural anxieties that *they* might be

*A child learns more from experience than from words.*

must also have the ability to regulate their own emotions."

It is said that teachers burn out faster in this field of special education than in any other. Yet Rutland has staff members who have been there nearly seven years and are still going strong. "The administration tries to meet the needs of the teacher just as the teacher meets those of the child," says Wood. This is done in a couple of ways. One is the team approach—in the classroom, one person always supporting another, and outside, other specialists and the community lending a hand. If a teacher is under personal stress, the workload can be modified. Says Wood, "A teacher in crisis is no teacher at all. And certainly personal needs should never be allowed to interfere with therapy given a child. At the same time teachers need protection too."

Looking out for her teachers is not the only thing that has made Wood a major force in the program. In the beginning, her persistence paid off as she forged what she considers an unbeatable team—special educators working with mental health personnel. Of course, in the beginning, such persistence was requisite as there was little help for a child in emotional trouble.

It was during the late 1960s when a number of changes occurred to prepare the way for Rutland. The establishment of community mental health centers encouraged the movement of clients back to the community. And Georgia's large hospital was broken up into six or seven regional hospitals. According to Wood, "The community was being educated to keep its children at home."

Less than ten percent of Georgia's emotionally disturbed children were being cared for in 1960. And no teachers were being specifically trained to serve them. The University of Georgia became one of the first schools to offer training in this area, but there were still problems. The university needed a practicum site. "The only place we had to train teachers then was the state hospital where they were putting the youngsters in with adults. We weren't training good teacher-therapists because they were seeing an inadequate model," says Wood.

The solution? Start a community-based program. Wood went to the local health department with her dilemma and began what has been a successful and, she stresses, essential partnership. The department provided a room in what is now "the little house," and later the center moved its classes up the street to the pillared antebellum house it now occupies.

This model project was set up as a community-based program of psychological and educational services to children with severe emotional disturbances. Called the Rutland Center after Donna K. Rutland, a teacher in Clarke County who specialized in teaching deaf children and who also worked with emotionally disturbed children, the center was designed to serve children from birth to age 14 in a 13-county area. Simultaneously, the program received state and federal funding, the preschool component being funded by OE's Bureau of Education for the Handicapped (BEH) under its Handicapped Children's Early Education program. In five years it became a validated model for national dissemination. The school-age component was funded by the Georgia General Assembly with state funds made available through the Georgia Department of Education.

During those three years of model development BEH granted $307,460 for the preschool component and the State of Georgia $750,000 for the school-age component. Today, the state provides support for 24 such centers which make up the Georgia Psychoeducational Center Network. The past year the network served some 7,500 seriously emotionally disturbed children and their families.

That others believe in the program is convincingly demonstrated by the projects outside the state which the National Technical Assistance Project helps set up. On the average, for every dollar of discretionary money supplied through federal funding, states or local school districts using the model added $3.25 of their own money.

Today Georgia's network serves 100 percent of its own emotionally disturbed young children, Wood recently told the House of Representatives Subcommittee on Select Education. For Georgia, reaching out has been worth the effort—not only in dollars, but in lives.

photo: Office of Human Development Services, DHEW

# LEARNING DISABILITIES

Learning disabilities are a wide spread problem among the school age population.  Learning disabled children can be found throughout society, in every economic and social class and in every race or religion. Until recently, one could find many ideas explaining or defining learning disabilities. The federal government has passed regulations defining learning disabilities. These regulations became effective in February, 1978 and reads as follows:

> " 'Specific learning disability' means a disorder in one or more of the basic psychological processes involved in understanding or in using language, spoken or written, which may manifest itself in an imperfect ability to listen, think, speak, read, write, spell, or to do mathematical calculations. The term includes such conditions as perceptual handicaps, brain injury, minimal brain dysfunction, dyslexia, and developmental aphasia. The term does not include children who have learning problems which are primarily the result of visual, hearing, or motor handicaps, of mental retardation, of emotional disturbance, or of environmental, cultural, or economic disadvantage."

According to this definition, there are seven main categories where discrepancies between achievement and intellectual ability can occur.  These areas are oral expression, listening comprehension, written expression, basic reading skill, reading comprehension, mathematical calculation or mathematics reasoning.  For a child to be classified as learning disabled, he/she must be tested and found to have a deficit in one or more of the above categories.

The section opens with several articles which look at the characteristics of learning disabilities. "Why?" explores the idea that there are no clear cut answers to why a child becomes learning disabled. Definition and labelling issues are discussed in the article, "A Community Alert for Children with Learning Problems." Following several articles which examine identification and early treatment, the section ends with a look at how instructional materials can be made for the learning disabled child.

# No Easy Answers
## the Learning Disabled Child

SALLY L. SMITH

Associate Professor, American University,
in charge of the Learning Disabilities Program

Founder and Director,
The Lab School of The Kingsbury Center,
Washington, D.C.

# Why ?

*It is not because the parents haven't tried.*

*It is not because the parents don't care.*

*It is not because the child is stubborn.*

*It is not because the child is dull.*

*It is not because the child is lazy.*

*It is not because the child is spoiled.*

*Why does a child have learning disabilities?*

*They do not occur for these reasons. There is no known simple explanation.*

*. . . there is no one cause*

*. . . there seem to be many that are held responsible for learning disabilities*

**BEFORE BIRTH**

*maternal malnutrition*

*bleeding in pregnancy*

*poor placental attachment to the uterus*

*toxemia in pregnancy*

*infectious disease of pregnant mother—German measles, a virus disease, influenza or a chronic disease*

*alcoholism during pregnancy*

*the taking of certain drugs during pregnancy*

*RH incompatibility*



Why? Sally L. Smith, *No Easy Answers: The Learning Disabled Child*, DHEW Publication, 1978.

## DURING BIRTH

*long or difficult delivery producing anoxia (not enough oxygen in the brain)*

*prematurity*

*cord around neck or breech delivery*

*poor position in the uterus*

*dry birth where the water broke prematurely*

*intracranial pressure at the time of birth due to forceps delivery or a narrow pelvic arch in the mother*

*rapid delivery exposing the infant too quickly to a new air pressure*

## AFTER BIRTH

*length of time to produce breathing after birth (often with prematurity, difficult delivery or twins)*

*high fever at an early age*

*sharp blow to head from fall or accident*

*meningitis or encephalitis*

*lead poisoning*

*drug intoxication*

*oxygen deprivation due to suffocation, respiratory distress, breath holding*

*severe nutritional deficiencies*

## HEREDITY

*There are many families in which reading disabilities can be traced through several generations. Usually the father, an uncle or other relatives had the problem.*

It is not worth agonizing over which of these factors produced the problems of a particular child. It might be something else not even mentioned here, not known yet! Placing blame, pointing an accusing finger, feeling overwhelmed with guilt, giving way to fear that some thoughtless action produced a child's learning problems have never been found to help parents help children with the problem. Sometimes it temporarily helps teachers (who feel totally frustrated by the learning disabled child) to blame parents but that doesn't help the children either. Teachers, like parents, usually wish to do the best they can for each child and often seek an easy cause that can be remedied fast. The causes of learning disability are beyond teacher control as they are beyond parental control.

All races, religions, economic classes . . . fat, thin, tall, small . . . youthful parents, older parents . . . have produced children with learning disorders.

In proportionately very few cases have doctors found evidence of actual brain damage. In fact there are many brain-damaged children who do not have learning disabilities. There are scientists who are working in the area of medical computer science to detect signs of brain damage or dysfunction which previously could not be monitored; these clinicians hope that, by locating exact areas and types of dysfunction in the brain, more precise treatments will be possible. The Quantitative Electro-physiological Battery (QB), currently being used at the Brain Research Laboratory of New York Medical College, holds out many interesting possibilities, but it does not yet provide any total answers. Some neurologists point out that stroke victims, adults who have suffered damage to their brains, those with cerebral palsy, show many impairments of language and thought similar to those of children with learning disorders. There is a theory that learning disability is simply "an extremely mild and narrowly selective form of cerebral palsy." In a special school educating only intelligent children with learning disabilities, there were 56 children. Four of them had known brain damage. But there were 36 who acted just like them; the other 20 simply seemed immature and needed more time to grow up.

We don't know much except that there is a lag in the development of learning disabled children, that their central nervous systems are delayed in maturing. Neurological examinations most often fail to reveal any medical evidence that would support a diagnosis of brain injury. The absence of "hard signs" of brain injury led the medical world to believe that the constellation of "soft neurological signs" had to be noted. This is what led up to such medical terms as "minimal cerebral dysfunction," "minimal brain injury," "minimal brain dysfunction," (MBD).

**The soft signs are such conditions as:**

*persistence of some primitive reflexes of central nervous system which should no longer be present after certain ages*

*distractibility (lack of concentration)*

*hyperactivity*

*impulsivity*

*perseveration*
*inconsistency*

*left-right confusion*

*irritability*

*talkativeness*

*awkwardness*

*poor speech*

*social immaturity*

Scientists, neurologists, neurophysiologists are right now seeking answers to the causes of neurological immaturity, what's responsible for this maturational lag that we currently call "learning disabilities."

There are those specialists who say that the cause doesn't matter; we must focus on educating the child. True, we must reach the child early and give him readiness. We must find ways to teach him to do the things he cannot do. There are those specialists who say that the cause *does* matter for then we will be able to treat the child faster and more efficiently. It is possible within the next 5 to 10 years that advances in neurochemistry and neurophysiology will pinpoint the dysfunctioning parts of the brain. When more precise localization of brain anatomy is correlated with various thinking processes, masses of research will have to be done to determine which part of the brain responds best to what type of education. At this point, there are no sudden cures, no easy answers.

The learning disabled child needs more time to grow, more time to do his work, more time to learn. He must work hard. His parents and teachers must work hard with him and provide him with the supports he needs in order to learn properly and to behave appropriately. Those are the only reliable cures at this point.

The field of learning disabilities, which did not become a recognized field that received Government grants until the late nineteen sixties and early seventies, faces many unanswered questions about causes.

Why is there so much learning disability today when there was not 10, 20, 30, 50 years ago? Part of the explanation may lie in the fact that these children were dumped into already established categories of "mentally retarded" or "emotionally disturbed." Many learning disabled children are still being written off as "culturally deprived." Disadvantaged conditions and poor schooling are cited as the causes of learning disabilities in inner-city children. Sometimes they are. However, insufficient account has been taken of the effect of high fevers, malnutrition, lead poisoning, maternal malnutrition, lack of proper prenatal care, and similar factors which may contribute to learning disabilities, causing poor performance at school.

In fact, there may not be more cases today, but more recognition of the problem. There are some specialists who claim that, until the advent of miracle drugs and the widespread use of antibiotics, many learning disabled youngsters died of respiratory ailments before they ever reached school age.

It is also possible that the one-room schoolhouse of yesteryear allowed for slow maturing. There were heterogeneous groupings which allowed a child to proceed at his own pace. In the early years of this century, as the frontier disappeared and Americans moved toward the cities, mass education took on a vast, new importance. Public school systems burgeoned, paralleled by the growth of public libraries, and standardization of education at all levels became the new order. No longer could parents direct their children's education as they saw fit. The rise of modern industry required standardized human components in its management, and our upwardly mobile society came to see education as a measurable step to individual success and to a prosperous, enlightened Nation. Only in a culture obsessed with education would the failures at school be considered as disabled people.

Our national panic when Russia launched "Sputnik" in 1957 was merely the latest phenomenon in the trend to standardization, now seen on a worldwide scale. The American public, worried that the Russians were smarter, more educated, more efficient than we, exerted pressure on the educators to hurry up. Out went a lot of the "play" in nursery schools and kindergartens; letters and numbers replaced motor activities in many preschools. It is possible that the child who needed more time, more sensory-motor activities, was deprived of them, and his development lagged further. As our population becomes more concentrated in cities and suburbs, our schoolrooms have become more crowded. We are surrounded by BIGNESS—the bigness of Government, of cities, of buildings, of business, of supermarkets, of jumbo eggs and giant-size aspirin. The standardization of quantity rather than quality often determines our values: how much we own, how many high grades we have, how many correct answers.

A child cannot always conform within the given time period and, too often, is then classed as a failure. Perhaps because of the uncertainty of our times, the rapid changes in lifestyles, the vanquishing of accepted traditions, we have become more dependent on "the right answer" than before and less tolerant of individual differences. The child with a learning disability, under this pressure, may become so burdened with defeat and failure that he doesn't even learn at his own pace and thus widens the gap.

There are those who subscribe to the theory that our polluted air and rivers— noise—our unclean environment—have contributed to the increase in delayed development in our children. Some believe that insecticides and pesticides pollute our children's brains.

Are there more children with immature brains today? We don't know. If so, there is no easy answer as to why.

Why are boys affected so much more frequently than girls? The ratio is seven to one nationally, and some believe that it is ten to one. There are theories that the male organism is more vulnerable at birth, more prone to injury since the infant mortality rate is much higher among boys than girls. Some theorists claim that the male fetus is somewhat larger than the female and thus is more susceptible to injury at birth. One researcher claims that male heads are larger and so have more trouble exiting at the time of birth. We don't really know.

Why is the learning disabled child much harder to manage and teach in hot, humid weather, before storms, on very hazy days and, some say, when there is a full moon? Educators have noted that weather and seasons affect their performance, but nobody yet knows why.

Is there a connection between hypoglycemia (low blood sugar) and learning disabilities? So far, no substantive connection has been proven.

Doctors have noticed a significant relationship among allergic reactions and hyperactivity and learning disabilities. Some of them have treated the children with antihistamines, corticosteroids, and megavitamins, and some of the children experienced relief from allergies which decreased hyperactivity and improved learning; some did not. This did not provide any general answer.

A few years ago, there were doctors who felt that these children had a vitamin B deficiency or some other kind of vitamin deficiency, and many of the children were pumped full of vitamins with no significant success. There are always a few children who improve dramatically, but, for any cure to be more than a panacea, it has to cure many. So far, it hasn't.

There are a few specialists, convinced that the learning disabled children are lacking in protein, who recommend a high protein diet (much red meat, eggs, soybeans, etc.) Although some youngsters have demonstrated more energy to learn as a result of this, no known instant school successes have resulted from this treatment. Some doctors state that high protein diets are dangerous and can cause metabolic imbalance.

A current theory is that food additives cause hyperactivity and therefore many cases of learning disability. The child is put on a special diet, monitored constantly, and, in a number of cases, has improved. Still, there is no definite proof of this connection and no clear evidence that food additives cause learning disabilities.

There are some educators who believe that learning disabilities do not exist, that there are simply unmotivated children. Others believe there are merely undisciplined students. Their remedies follow their interpretation of the causes. Every once in a while a child improves under their care, but these "hard-liners" do not have the answer for children with learning disabilities in general.

Today, big money can be made by taking advantage of the prevalence and seriousness of learning disabilities. Along with excellent schools and treatment centers, a number of "instant remediation" parlors have opened. From pinching ears, to systematic yelling, to acupuncture, to transcendental meditation, to tactile treatments, to patterning of one sort or another, to helium experiences, parents are being promised substantive help by fly-by-night groups. All kinds of causes are enumerated, and these entrepreneurs usually make parents feel responsible for the problem as well as for the success of the treatment.

In our culture, where speed is a supreme value and where we prize the frozen dinners, the freeze-dried coffee, the soup can, we grab for the instant answer. Unfortunately there is no one way. There is no easy answer.

# A COMMUNITY ALERT FOR CHILDREN WITH LEARNING PROBLEMS

PAUL A. SOMMERS
*Marshfield Clinic and Medical Foundation*

Assessing and developing community-oriented programs for children with learning problems has been a complex and confusing task. Incumbent within such a process lies the problem of involving professionals from the domains of health, education, and the social services in addition to the parents. Given the polemic of trying to agree upon a similar definition of the problem, identifying interdisciplinary variations for similar symptoms, and conjointly interfacing services for purposes of solving the learning problem, it may take a magic act to get the job done! The vague learning disability (LD) syndrome could not have survived if it had not become popular with educators, physicians, and psychologists. LD as a diagnosis and assessment promotes confusion for those professionals who must constructively deal with the problem and for the child referred as LD, it invites a self-fulfilling prophecy of frustration and nonlearning.

Learning Disability (LD) has been used as a convenient diagnostic label, a categorical referent point, and an administrative label to facilitate program-accounting procedures. It also enables professionals to apply for State and Federal financial aid.

Wepman, Cruickshank, Deutsch, Morency, and Strother (1975) indicated that attempts to identify, assess, and develop programs for children with learning disabilities have been quite common within the disciplines of medicine, psychology, and education. They noted little agreement either between or among professionals in these areas on criteria to be used for identifying these children. Because the disabilities presented are extremely heterogeneous, the search for any commonality of symptoms, pathology, or etiology has so far been fruitless.

Medical studies have been able to delineate, with some degree of accuracy, reliable criteria for identifying as brain injured those children who show clearcut signs of central nervous system pathology. However, much confusion, discussion, and disagreement has developed over the observation and interpretation of vague, "soft neurological" indicators (Adams, 1973). On a similar note in the domains of education and psychology, procedures for the classification of children with learning disabilities are equally unsatisfactory. Great diversity exists in terminology on a national level as the following examples indicate: Special Learning and Behavior Problems (SLBP-Minnesota); Learning Disabilities (LD-Delaware and Wisconsin); Educational Handicapped (EH-California); Specific Learning Disabilities (SLD-Florida); Extreme Learning Problems (ELP-Oregon); Communicative and Intellectual Deviations (CID-West Virginia); Neurological Handicapped (NH-Connecticut, Nevada, and Oklahoma); Perceptually Handicapped (PH-Colorado, Indiana, New Jersey, and Washington); Brain Damage (BD-Pennsylvania). There has been little uniformity from discipline to discipline or from state to state regarding some communality upon which an understanding of learning disabled children could be based.

Generally incorporated within previous definitions, the term refers to children, youth, and adults who deviate from standards expected of them (McCarthy & McCarthy, 1969). McCarthy and McCarthy indicated that no other single label connotes

Reprinted by permission of author and publisher, Clinical Psychology Publishing Company.

a greater variety of unrelated conditions than the term *Learning Disabilities*. There is no clear professional unanimity for the meaning of the term, although the Bureau of Education for the Handicapped has offered a nationwide definition of learning disabilities. It was reported by Governmental Affairs Consultants in the Morris Associates Report in 1976 as part of the proposed regulations relating to the Education for All Handicapped Childrens Act of 1975 (Public Law 94-142): "Specific Learning Disabilities — Specific learning disabilities is a category of mental disorders that include minimal brain dysfunction, dyslexia and other handicaps that are manifested in an individual's inability to listen, think, speak, read, write, spell or do mathematical calculations not caused by identifiable conditions of mental retardation or physical deformity."

To settle the controversy caused by the ambiguous nature of the category and the great variation in diagnosis and application of the term, Congress has specified that the Department of Health, Education, and Welfare develop regulations that would establish a precise description that could be uniformly applied. [1]

POLEMICAL IMPLICATIONS

The most usual interpretation of Learning Disabilities (LD), as it is applied to children, is that it has become an all-encompassing, wastebasket term for any child who does not quite conform to society's stereotyped expectations of normal children. Almost any learning-related deficiency can be affirmed as LD (Schmitt, 1975). Children are labelled as such by school psychologists who find discrepancies on psychological testing, by teachers who find vague symptoms in the classroom that they relate to LD, and physicians who routinely relate aggressive and overactive behavior in children to LD.

However, the LD label could not have survived if it had not become popular with teachers, physicians, and psychologists who routinely deal with children (Sommers, 1977). In addition, as a support to the labelling fad are state and federal laws requiring such specifications (Public Laws 94-142 and 94-103). Most states reward schools and mental health programs with financial aids and a variety of other funding incentives in proportion to the number of children who have been labelled and provided services (i.e., Wisconsin Statutes, Chapter 115 and 51.42/51.437, and similar laws in other states). Such a dilemma has complicated the level and degree of service to be provided to those children who are in need of specialized services. The range and nature of confusion produced by this matter reflects upon the critical task of program development. Essential variables to consider include age requirements mandated by law, the type and extent of handicapping conditions, who should pay the bill, one county or city providing better services than another, and many more considerations. Nevertheless, the fact still remains that the child must be provided appropriate service and as soon as possible (hopefully at the same time the handicap is identified). To further complicate the issue, many agencies throughout the community may need to be involved, such as the public schools, day care programs, developmental disability programs, clinics, and private schools. Given current legislation, all needed child-oriented services should be available, but it may take a magic act to pull such services together.

*The Community At Large*

The child with learning problems can be found in any community. Services used to identify these children are available but must be sought out and coordinated to be most effective. Since children spend a majority of their early years in school, a reasonable approach to see that necessary services are provided would appear to be the responsibility of school staff. Both federal and state laws previously cited agree with this position and procedures for coordinating related activities have been developed (or are quickly developing) by each state. A school program coordinator represents each LD child and is responsible for planning, implementing, and evaluating daily activities aimed at alleviating learning problems. In addition to coordinating available school activities (i.e., school psychology, school social work, speech therapy, counselling, reading, and other services), the coordinator must recognize and utilize essential expertise often existing outside the school boundaries, i.e., medical, clinical psychology (neuropsychology) seem to be those most frequently associated with LD.

---

1   Since the writing of this article, Congress has passed regulations defining the term specific learning disabilities. These regulations became effective in February, 1978 as part of PL 94-142.

*Medical Services*

What should an LD program coordinator know about medical and psychological outside support? Many learning disability correlates have physical connotations, so the physician is often called upon for diagnosis and treatment services. The physician's primary role is basically one of determining whether a medical problem exists. This search for an etiology leaves little choice but to assume that the physician will become essential to the diagnosis and management of the child's problems. Unless the very reliability and validity of the learning problem is established, the physician is trapped in the ritual of hunting for the elusive diagnostic factors behind the learning disability label.

Evidence accepted by various experts as documentation of a learning disability is quite variable, since no test or neurologic sign has yet been proved to differentiate children with learning disabilities from normal children (Schmitt, 1975). Schmitt reviewed neurological screening as a guide to assist in the determination of learning problems. Schmitt further indicated that soft neurological signs are not helpful findings. Most of them represent transient phenomena and disappear with age. At best, they are evidence for neurological immaturity. The point at which they become abnormal is not well-standardized. They are so common under age seven that they should never be considered abnormal before that age (Hart, 1974; Kinsbourne, 1973). Even when they persist beyond age seven their etiological importance is highly speculative (Touwen, 1970). By and large, soft signs lead to additional confusion rather than clarification. Amphetamines and other behavior modification drugs have been given to school children for purposes of improving learning. There is a great deal of inconclusive evidence about the etiology, cure, and the nature of the disorder, which complicates a standardized approach to treatment (Lesser, 1970).

*Psychological Services*

Psychological findings form a major base upon which a judgment of LD is made. If a school is without psychological services or if an outside opinion is deemed relevant to the diagnosis and development of a program plan, then a psychologist from an outside health service system is engaged to help determine learning needs. Some discussion about the interpretation of psychological data indicates that abnormalities on visual-motor perceptual tests (Bender-Gestalt) and verbal-performance discrepancies on intelligence tests (Wechsler) have been used as diagnostic of learning disabilities. Less well-known is the fact that these same test discrepancies are equally characteristic of other groups of children, especially those with psychiatric disorders (Adams, 1973; Schmitt, 1973). It is quite common to find some overlap between scores derived on these visual-motor-perceptual and verbal-performance estimates between children with a specific learning disability and children meeting standard expectations. In fact, according to Weiner (1974), Bender-Gestalt test errors due to maturational delay are so common that this test is of limited value diagnostically prior to age seven. Even after age seven, one must be careful in interpreting such results.

There is also an hypothesis that a 20-point discrepancy between scores on the verbal and performance scales is diagnostic of learning disabilities and, in some cases, of central nervous system impairment. Schafer (1948) indicated that several other findings are more likely. For instance, high performance-low verbal is often found in children from verbally deprived environments (e.g., from inner cities and some rural areas), in children with auditory-perceptual problems, and in children who "act out" rather than think (e.g., juvenile delinquents). Two fairly common interpretations of individuals with high verbal-low performance test score discrepancies are (1) neurotics, especially those with obsessive, compulsive tendencies, and (2) children with visual-motor-perceptual problems (Anastasi, 1968).

*A Guide to Program Development*

Labelling and the interpretation of findings have much to do with the development of an effective program.

*Labelling.* The labelling of a child as anything but normal sets in motion those processes that discriminate inferiority (Rains, Kitsuse, Duster, & Freidson, 1975). Labelling tends to influence the parent's, school's, and community's expectations of the child. After being labelled as Learning Disabled, the child begins to be treated as a nonlearner rather than a "normal" individual. Over time, the child begins to live and play the expected role of a nonlearner. The label may develop into a self-fulfilling prophecy (Rosenthal & Jacobson, 1968).[1] Once a label has been attached to the child, it becomes very hard to change. To the parent it can represent a hopeless, irreversible situation. Other than for accounting and classifying purposes, labelling does not appear to add much to a child's program. It is a convenient referent point for administrators and planners, but lacks a good reason to be attached to any child (Aldrich, 1971; Mercer, 1975).

*Interpretation*. Perhaps we should arrive at a more flexible interpretation of normal. A paucity of data exists which fails to confirm a generalized learning disability. The term LD is an overworked, nonspecific, uninterpretable assessment. A discrepancy in incidence exists between different communities, countries, and states which points to observer and identifier bias (Huessy, 1970; Kenny, 1971).

Children can be vastly different without being diseased or having a learning disability. Abrams (1968) described an immense individual variation in behavior, emotion, intellect, and cognitive ability. He indicated that it is incumbent upon those who provide services and/or programs to children with specialized needs to completely search out all relevant data prior to the development and implementation of an intervention effort. The LD population is not a homogeneous group and each individual would be best looked at in terms of specific strengths and weaknesses for planning purposes.

*Implementation*. The implementation of an effective learning disability program can be facilitated through a community effort which is based on a mutual understanding of LD, frequent discussion between and among different agency staff dealing with similar children, and knowledge of current federal and state laws affecting LD children. Effective program implementation begins with an accurate and complete evaluation to screen and identify specific learning problems. A search for necessary individualized data is accomplished through a comprehensive multidisciplinary assessment (Jones & Sommers, 1975; McCormack, 1976; Sommers, 1973).

Public Law 94-142 mandates that Individual Education Plans (IEPs) be developed for each child having confirmed specific learning disabilities. The IEP is the responsibility of the child's school district of residence. However, a community-based multidisciplinary team is often called for to reflect each child's individualized needs most appropriately. Such a team could include the child's doctor, clinical psychologist and/or social worker, the regular classroom teacher(s), school psychologist, speech and language clinician, and learning disability specialist. In total, a community-based multidisciplinary team procedure brings together each necessary specialist from a variety of disciplines, in addition to the child's parents, to assess and develop a complete program plan organized to alleviate the discrepancy existing between the child's expected and actual achievement level.

Community-based multidisciplinary teams are mandated by PL 94-142. It is the responsibility of the child's public school district of residence to see to it that the "multidisciplinary team" procedure be established. Primary membership on the team includes those learning specialists from the local school district who are trained to assess and program for each child's individualized learning needs. In addition, it is up to the school district to see that the community specialists outside of the school staff (i.e., the doctor, clinical psychologist, and/or social worker) are actively involved in the multidisciplinary team even if on an ex-officio basis.

### CONSIDERATIONS

*Avoid using the LD label*. If one must use labels, it is better to use those that describe a specialized need in terms of some measurable functioning, i.e., the number of letter or word reversals contained in a written sentence. A specific assessment can help to plan a remedial program (McCormack, 1976), i.e., decreasing 25% of letter and word reversals contained in a written sentence.

*Be aware of false hope merchants*. Unwarranted programming for children with learning problems has been erupting on a nationwide basis ever since the area of learning

---

[1]There is a current controversy about the labelling issue. For other points of view on this subject, the reader is referred to Goffman (1961), Kitsuse & Cicourel (1963), and Paul (1969).

disabilities began receiving widespread publicity. Parents and educators must be cautioned of the false hope merchants who are trying to sell expensive remediation/treatment packages for children whom they describe as having learning disabilities. Many of these solicitors advocate relearning motor development, thus inducing the remediation of specific learning disabilities through patterning by crawling; performing body coordination exercises; using laterality training or walking on balance beams; and the like. There is no evidence that these techniques improve learning or ameliorate a specific learning disability. In addition, many health-related programs have also been acclaimed to remediate learning problems. They have included megavitamin and trace element approaches, hyposensitization, food allergy experimentation, and special visual training activities including muscle exercises and ocular pursuit activities. Even eyeglasses have been advocated for helping to remediate reading-related learning problems in children. Although these specific activities, techniques, and appliances may lead to specific improvement in body coordination or allow the individual to see what they are looking at, they do not lead to improvement in learning or reading. Allington (1975) suggested that if one wants to improve reading, reading activities should be taught.

*Keep medical evaluations reasonable.* Unwarranted diagnostic procedures should be avoided wherever possible. A specific request must be made of the clinicians to answer questions about learning problems in such a way that their data are effective and meaningful to the learning situation. It is often very helpful and appropriate for educators and parents to briefly outline their major points of medical concern and send this information, in advance of the clinic visit, to the primary physician, clinician, or coordinator who can incorporate it into the evaluation and treatment plan.

*Drugs are not essential to solve learning problems.* Drugs represent a very simplistic approach to a complex problem that involves the manipulation of affective, cognitive, and psychomotor variables in addition to the basic physiologic mechanism affected by drugs. Only a physician can prescribe drugs and such utilization should reflect one alternative to resolve a medical-based problem. It is unfortunate that some physicians have joined some educators and psychologists in advocating large-scale drugging of noncompliant children who may be representing problems because of their behavioral, physical, and attitudinal challenges that confront educators in the process of providing instruction for remediation of the learning problems (Schmitt, 1973).

*Psychological findings are extremely helpful to both LD assessment and program planning.* The LD program coordinator must know how to use this type of information in support of (not in place of) each child's daily program.

*Keep psychological evaluations reasonable.* It is essential to specify learning questions of psychological importance prior to psychological evaluation. In this manner the psychologist will have an opportunity to address the specific areas in question as the psychological examination proceeds. It is often very helpful and appropriate for educators and parents to briefly outline their expectation(s) of this assessment and send it to the psychologist before testing is initiated which will assure that a main focus of the testing will reflect on the important questions.

*Look into the environmental and family background of each child.* Perhaps what is appearing as a significant learning deviation can be explained by understanding the child's world outside of school. To insure that each child is properly served, a review of the current local practice of working with children who have learning problems must be initiated to determine the appropriateness of assessment prior to placement and, the longitudinal success of programming efforts after each child has been placed (Hobbs, 1975).

REFERENCES

ABRAMS, A. L.   Delayed and irregular maturation versus minimal brain injury. *Clinical Pediatrics*, 1968, *7*, 344-349.

ADAMS, J.   Clinical neuropsychology and the study of learning disorders. *Pediatric Clinics of North America*, 1973, *20*, 587-598.

ALDRICH, C. K.   Thief. *Psychology Today*, 1971, *4* (10), 66-69.

ALLINGTON, R.   Attention and application: The oft forgotten steps in teaching reading. *Journal of Learning Disabilities*, 1975, *8* (4), 22-25.

## 5. LEARNING DISABLED


ALLMOND, B. W.   Psychological testing of children: Review and commentary. *Pediatric Clinics of North America*, 1974, *21*, 187-194.

ANASTASI, A.   *Psychological testing* (3rd ed.) New York: Macmillan, 1968.

FURTH, H. G.   *Piaget and knowledge: Theoretical foundations*. Englewood Cliffs, New Jersey: Prentice-Hall, 1969.

GOFFMAN, E.   *Asylums*. New York: Anchor Books, 1961.

GOVERNMENTAL AFFAIRS CONSULTANTS. MORRIS ASSOCIATES REPORT. *Developmental Disabilities*, 1976, *4*, 8.

HART, Z., RENNICK, P. M., & KLINGE, V.   A pediatric neurologist's contribution to evaluations of school underachievers. *American Journal for Disabled Children*, 1974, *128*, 319-323.

HOBBS, N.   *The futures of children*. San Francisco-Washington: Jossey-Bass, 1975.

HUESSY, H. R., & GENDRON, R. M.   Prevalence of the so-called hyperkinetic syndrome in public school children of Vermont. *Acta Paedopsychiatrica*, 1970, *37*, 243-248.

JONES, W. A., & SOMMERS, P. A.   Comprehensive needs assessment: An inferential approach. *The Journal of Educational Technology*, 1975, *15*, 54-57.

KENNY, T. J., CLEMMENS, R. L., HUDSON, B. W., LENTZ, G. A., CICCI, R., & NAIR, P.   Characteristics of children referred because of hyperactivity. *Journal of Pediatrics*, 1971, *79*, 618-622.

KENNY, T. J., & CLEMMENS, R. L.   Medical and psychological correlates in children with learning disabilities. *Journal of Pediatrics*, 1971, *78*, 273-277.

KINSBOURNE, M.   School problems. *Journal of Pediatrics*, 1973, *52*, 697-710.

KIRK, S. A., & BATEMAN, B.   Diagnosis and remediation of learning disabilities, *Exceptional Children*, 1962, *29* (2), 73.

KITSUSE, J. I., & CICOUREL, A. V.   A note on the uses of official statistics. *Social Problems*, 1963, *11*, 131-139.

LESSER, L. L.   Hyperkinesis in children: Operational approach to management. *Clinical Pediatrics*, 1970, *9*, 548-552.

McCARTHY, J. J., & McCARTHY, J. F.   *Learning disabilities*. Boston: Allyn & Bacon, 1969.

McCORMACK, J. E.   The assessment tool that meets your needs: The one you construct. *Teaching Exceptional Children*, 1976, *8*, 3.

MERCER, J. R.   Psychological assessment and the rights of children. In N. Hobbs (Ed.), *Issues in the classification of children* (vol. 1). San Francisco: Jossey-Bass, 1975.

PAUL, G. L.   Chronic mental patient: Current status, future directions. *Psychological Bulletin*, 1969, *71*, 81-94.

RAINS, P. M., KITSUSE, J. I., DUSTER, T., & FREIDSON, E.   The labelling approach to deviance. In N. Hobbs (Ed.), *Issues in the classification of children* (vol. 1). San Francisco: Jossey-Bass, 1975.

ROSENTHAL, R., & JACOBSON, J.   *Pygmalion in the classroom: Teacher expectations and pupils' intellectual development*. New York: Holt, 1968.

SCHAFER, R.   *The clinical application of psychological tests*. New York: International Universities Press, 1948.

SCHMITT, B. D.   Responsibility for school problems: An objection to pediatric globalism. *Journal of Pediatrics*, 1969, *44*, 771-773.

SCHMITT, B. D., MARTIN, H. P., NELLHAUS, G., CRAVENS, J., CAMP, B. W., & JORDAN, K.   The hyperactive child. *Clinical Pediatrics*, 1973, *12*, 154-169.

SCHMITT, B. D.   The minimal brain dysfunction myth. *American Journal for Disabled Children*, 1975, *129*, 1313-1315.

SOMMERS, P. A.   An inferential evaluation model. *Journal of Educational Technology*, 1973, May (3), 65-67.

SOMMERS, P. A.   A prospective on exceptional children: Focus on mental retardation and learning disabilities. *The Bureau Memorandum*, 1977, *18* (2), 28-31.

TOUWEN, B., & PRECHTL, H. F.   *The neurological examination of the child with minor nervous dysfunction*. (Clinics in Developmental Medicine.) London: Spastics International Medical Publications, 1970.

WEINER, I. B., & GOLDBERG, R. W.   Psychological testing of children. *Pediatric Clinics of North America*, 1974, *21*, 175-186.

WEPMAN, J. M., CRUICKSHANK, W. M., DEUTSCH, C. P., MORENCY, A., & STROTHER, C.   Learning disabilities. In N. Hobbs (Ed.), *Issues in the classification of children* (vol. 1). San Francisco: Jossey-Bass, 1975.

# THE ABC'S OF LEARNING DISABILITIES

## Evelyn Cappell Rubin and Ron Rubin

*Evelyn Cappell Rubin is a private therapist and a fellow at Teachers College Institute of Learning Disabilities. Ron Rubin is a professor of social science at CUNY.*

**"…Learning disabilities mar the school careers of thousands of city students; boys with L.D. outnumber girls four to one…"**

Eight-year-old Paul is a puzzle to his parents. Although the sandy-haired third-grader is an accomplished swimmer, bike rider, and skater, he has problems in school which have lately reached a crisis.

At a meeting set up by the school psychologist, Paul's parents were told that he is reading like a beginning first-grader, his spelling is erratic, and his attention drifts in class. Previously popular, Paul is now having daily scraps with his classmates.

Paul's mother, a career woman, has difficulty understanding the causes of her son's growing problems in school: "Paul," she says, "was an unusually alert and curious child. True, he was always hyperactive—darting from the TV set to his baseball cards and back again—but we figured he would outgrow this behavior."

Paul's father, a successful businessman, has his own theories: "Paul's been indulged too much and he refuses to work at school. He has the ability —he's just plain lazy."

What Paul's parents have yet to discover is that Paul is a learning-disabled child. He is one of a group that comprises anywhere from 2 to 15 percent of the healthy school-age population. Depending on which estimate you accept, this means that L.D. (learning disability) mars the school careers of between 30,000 and 225,000 New York

Illustrated by Tudor Banus

City students, including four times as many boys as girls.

Many educational theorists see L.D. as the main reason why Johnny can't read, write, speak clearly, spell, add, or subtract. In 1975, the United States Congress, driven by the anguish of constituent parents, passed the Education for All Handicapped Children Act, which defined the L.D. child as follows: a student of at least average intelligence who performs 50 percent below expectation in the school staples of reading, spelling, speaking, and math. Congress's definition specifically differentiates L.D. from other educa-

tional disorders, such as mental retardation, emotional disturbance, cultural disadvantage, and school problems based on poor hearing and vision, because these require treatment different from that given the L.D. child.

The causes of L.D. are subject to wide debate and essentially remain a mystery to neurologists, psychologists, audiologists, pediatricians, speech pathologists, teachers, and therapists alike. Possible causes are birth trauma, injury to the head, family history of L.D., and the mother's illness during pregnancy. There is, however, general agreement among specialists that these disabilities, whatever their cause, have to do with the way the brain processes information.

A major psychological clue in detecting L.D. is the presence of uneven developmental signs—in Paul's case, he showed excellent motor control in bike riding but scribbled his class lessons with the awkwardness of a four-year-old. Another instance of L.D. might express itself in a child's difficulty in mastering such environmental trappings as the order of the days of the week, telling time, or the layout of neighborhood streets.

But parents should not needlessly alarm themselves by imagining that their child has L.D. simply because he exhibits a standard L.D. symptom. Every child's rate of development is unique—one buttons his shirt before

©1978 by the *New York* Magazine Company, Inc. Reprinted with the permission of New York Magazine.

age three, and another not until four and a half. Neither does slowness in spelling or reading automatically indicate L.D. This uneven growth and learning rate is part of the normal process of development. "We look for a cluster of symptoms," says Dr. Ruth Gottesman, chief of psychoeducational services at Albert Einstein College of Medicine in the Bronx. "One sign alone doesn't confirm L.D."

"The first step for a parent who suspects that an otherwise normal child has a learning disability is a visit to the family pediatrician," advises Dr. Nola Marx, a fellow in developmental pediatrics at the University of Rochester. An office exam will rule out physical problems such as a hearing loss, impaired vision, and poor food and sleep habits. If the diagnosis turns up subtle neurological disorders, the outward manifestations of which might be awkward gait, articulation difficulties, or poor eye-hand coordination involving writing or cutting, for instance, suspicions of L.D. are heightened. The next step on the L.D. checklist might be a referral to a neurologist.

Real confirmation of L.D. rests on weak performance in specific academic areas where a discrepancy is found between a child's ability and achievement. The chief area of difficulty encountered by L.D. children is reading. Paul, for example, could not remember the sounds corresponding to certain letters of the alphabet. Vowel sounds in particular seemed to perplex him. "Men," his teacher reported, might just as likely be read by Paul as "mun" or "man."

This reading problem is called dyslexia, other symptoms of which include letter and word reversals. A dyslexic child will often substitute a *b* for a *d*, or confuse "was" with "saw." Some of these children are stumped by the seemingly natural process of combining letter sounds when they occur together in a word—"glad" emerges as "guhlad" or "gad."

"In the early grades, problems with such reading-deciphering skills might be camouflaged by a child with a sharp memory for the configurational picture that words present, skirting the problem of sounding out the word," says Professor N. Dale Bryant, director of the Research Institute for the Study of Learning Disabilities at Columbia's Teachers College. But the child's basic reading deficiency will become evident by the third or fourth grade, when he will be expected to make out unfamiliar words. A dyslexic child's oral reading, according to Columbia-Presbyterian's Dr. Jeannette Jansky, is marked by a slow, disfluent, word-by-word approach.

In addition to the roadblocks presented by reading individual words, the dyslexic child often finds comprehending written or spoken language a chore, and has difficulty in spelling even the simplest of words.

Henry, a Bronx elementary-school student, has another type of learning disability: dyscalculia, difficulty in managing mathematical symbols and computations. In the stamp album he received for his tenth birthday, Henry placed his large commemoratives in spaces outlined for smaller ones. This difficulty in grasping size relationships underlies his trouble in mastering numerical concepts.

Another sign of dyscalculia is difficulty with spatial relationships, such as the inability to learn the concepts of up and down, right and left. When Henry's gym teacher calls out, "Right turn," Henry furtively glances over his shoulder and follows the lead of his neighbor. On his math work sheet, Henry's problem translates into adding two columns diagonally instead of vertically. But most socially embarrassing for Henry are trips to the store with his friends, when he fumblingly hands over a dollar bill to the cashier rather than the appropriate small change, thereby avoiding the money calculations which baffle him.

Perhaps most bewildering to a parent is something called dysgraphia—the inability to print even one's own name clearly on a lined piece of paper.

Dr. Laura Ann Wilber, president of the New York State Speech and Hearing Association, emphasizes that the origins of L.D. go beyond their specific manifestations in reading and writing skills and lie in a deficiency in mastering language. According to Dr. Wilber, words as a means for clearly expressing thought patterns elude these children.

Speech disorders, which can be detected in children aged three to five, are a potential red flag that L.D. may be in the offing. Dr. Marx stresses that the learning problems later on can sometimes be circumvented through early intervention. "If I see a four-year-old whose speech is decipherable to no adult other than the parent, I consider that child to have communication difficulties," she says. There are other early warning signs: if the names of familiar objects, such as parts of the body, escape his memory; if following the simple directions of his nursery-school teacher is beyond him; if a short attention span and impatience distinguish him in group activities.

If unattended, such language problems will intensify with age. The second-grader with this handicap will be unable to sequence a story coherently. Questions in school on the whys, whens, or wheres of study topics will confuse him. But with therapy, remarkable success has been achieved in raising the level of academic achievement in these children.

While each L.D. child has an individual cluster of problems to which the therapy should be tailored, the following rules of remediation are always applicable, according to Columbia's Professor Bryant, former president of the Orton Society, the professional group specializing in L.D. problems:

☐ *Break the problem down to its simplest level.* Teach only one element at a time. For example, don't teach the whole area of reading, but emphasize the "short *a*" sound (the *a* in apple).

☐ *Simplify the presentation.* Be clear. Many L.D. children can't differentiate between essential and unessential detail, so use explicit instructions and educational material.

☐ *Focus on the text.* Children with learning disabilities are easily distracted. The therapy session should take place in a quiet area where nothing else competes for the child's attention.

☐ *Be patient and repetitive.* These children are slow to absorb new skills, so don't expect quick success. Frequent reviews and drills ensure that whatever knowledge is gained will be maintained, so sessions with a therapist should be held two to four times weekly. Summers can't be considered time off.

☐ *Teach a specific application.* Since L.D. children find it hard to apply a skill to a novel context, specific skills must be taught in different contexts.

In the school years, parents should minimize the emotional scars wrought by L.D. and remind the child that he is bright. Since areas of weakness tend to be stressed, areas of strength should be pointed out and praised.

What does the future hold for the L.D. child? In the classroom, progress can be expected provided that the child receives proper remediation. Not unusual is the case of Fred, now eleven, a sixth-grader who at nine years of age lagged two years behind his classmates in reading. With the benefit of weekly remediation sessions, he is no longer in the lowest reading group.

Because L.D. is most glaring in a school setting, it takes on less significance in adulthood. Naturally, youths handicapped by L.D. will automatically select careers which avoid their disability, but they will still function as normal adults—as does Nelson Rockefeller, who has dyslexia.

## Where to Get Help

Both parents and school officials often confuse the indications of L.D. with a lack of motivation on the child's part. And because L.D.'s outward manifestations are not as severe as those of, say, mental retardation or emotional disturbance, schools are less likely to focus their limited resources on helping children with this handicap.

For these reasons, discovering the proper course of remediation amounts to a "sleuthing process," as Mark Usdane of Long Island College Hospital puts it. "Parents have to push to get an L.D. child accurately diagnosed and treated." Parents who suspect that their child may have L.D. should check out their suspicions with school authorities.

**Private schools:** Most New York City private schools are equipped to diagnose signs of L.D., although remediation may require help from the outside. Parents should get in touch with the school's principal, who will probably set up an appointment with the school psychologist and the child's teacher. The school psychologist may be trained to spot L.D., or may refer the parents to the learning-disabilities teacher, a position increasingly common among private-school faculties.

**Public schools:** While the New York City Board of Education provides a host of services for students with severe handicaps, such as brain damage, mental retardation, deafness, and blindness, there is no one bureau that deals specifically with the L.D. child. Parents with initiative, however, can get their child professionally evaluated by the board's Evaluation Unit (852-7952), al-

though it has a long waiting list. The board also operates a Readiness Program (876-0260)—for five- and six-year-olds with "severe" learning disabilities—in 30 diagnostic-therapeutic classrooms in all boroughs.

**Hospitals:** Because of the medical, psychiatric, and neurological aspects of L.D., hospitals are becoming increasingly involved in this area, and the number of hospital-operated clinics for L.D. children is growing. Pediatric training programs in the last ten years have given steadily increasing attention to L.D. and other educational disorders, and pediatricians report that children with learning problems make up a significant percentage of their patients.

While the guide to hospital facilities below aims at being comprehensive, it should be noted that the picture is fluid. Depending on government funding, private resources, personnel, and community needs, an L.D. program may live or die.

**Universities:** University-sponsored L.D. facilities (see guide, page 66) serve the dual role of training professionals in these areas and treating actual patients. At a university clinic, a child is often examined by a graduate student whose performance in turn is supervised by a faculty member. Treatment fees are generally lower than those at hospitals.

**Private sources:** While there are many private agencies and individual therapists in practice in the city, the quality and training vary widely. For guidance, parents should consult school officials, medical personnel, and the parent grapevine.

Parents considering private sources should be wary of therapists promising miracles—treating the L.D. child is a slow process and the competent specialist focuses on specific problems—and find one who is willing to hold periodic conferences with them. Because the L.D. child is intelligent and up to par in areas other than his particular disability, he's generally mature enough to sense whether or not his tutoring is helpful.

# "...An L.D. child is intelligent and up to par in areas other than his disability..."

# When a child has a learning problem...

**E**IGHT-YEAR-OLD Billy is a bright child, and most of his schoolwork shows it. But he can just barely read. "Tar" looks to him like "rat," "dud" transforms to "bub" or even "pup." He easily loses his place while reading and his handwriting is atrocious.

Jeffrey, age 6, is a perpetual motion machine, constantly revved up. He rarely sleeps through the night, taking his rest in short naps. His rambunctious behavior often makes normal activity in his first-grade classroom impossible.

Sally, 10, regularly trips over her own feet and bumps into things. Her coordination is so poor that she can't play jump rope with her friends. In school she is having great difficulty because she writes so poorly.

Each of these children is suffering a recognized educational handicap. Billy has a condition known as dyslexia. Jeffrey you may recognize as hyperactive. Sally's affliction is something called ataxia. As diverse as their symptoms are, though, you could lump their difficulties together under one label: learning disabilities.

"Learning disability" describes a variety of conditions that make it difficult or impossible for normally intelligent children to master one or more of the skills essential to learning in their early school years. Though it is an educational concept, the roots of its various manifestations are physiological, and most cases are thought to be due to malfunctions of the central nervous system.

Children with learning disabilities may have visual-perceptual problems that prevent them from judging accurately the relationship between objects and themselves. They may have poor eye-hand coordination that makes it extremely difficult for them to draw and write. They may not be able to convert information received by one of their senses into a form usable by another—they can't associate objects with printed words, for instance. They may have auditory perceptual problems that make them hear jumbled-up versions of other people's speech. They may have trouble remembering what they hear and find it difficult to follow instructions.

The list of identifiable symptoms is long, and



Reprinted with permission from *Changing Times Magazine,* ©1978 Kiplinger Washington Editors, Inc., 1729 H Street, NW, Washington, DC 20006.

most learning disabled children display not one but several. Some observers contend that the term "learning disabled" is overused, freely applied by educators to learning problems that don't respond to their particular way of teaching.

But there is no doubt that these conditions exist. A common estimate attributes some form of learning disability to about 10% of the school-age population, though individual estimates have ranged between 2% and 40%. Whichever estimate you take, it translates to millions of children. Left untreated they face failure and frustration. The resulting emotional conflict can lead to withdrawal, alienation, misbehavior. As emotional problems grow, there is the danger that they may be interpreted as the primary cause, rather than a result, of the child's learning difficulties.

### Finding the problem

Sometimes, of course, a child's problems in school are the result of emotional upheavals that have nothing to do with neurological disorders; sometimes a hearing aid or pair of eyeglasses can correct what appears to be a perceptual problem. These children are not learning disabled, and an important but often difficult task is telling them apart from those who are.

Ideally, a child should not be declared learning disabled until he or she has undergone careful psychological evaluation, a complete educational assessment and a medical diagnosis. Some school systems have teachers especially trained to deal with learning disabled students. They know which tests to administer to uncover telltale characteristics, they know when to refer to doctors and psychologists, and they are familiar with several different approaches to alleviating the problems they find. Federal money is available to beef up such services.

Unfortunately, many schools are too poorly equipped to provide screening, and many family physicians and pediatricians are relatively unschooled in the diagnostic procedures used to track down learning disabilities.

University-affiliated clinics and child development centers may be equipped to make a diagnosis. Privately owned schools and clinics can often help, but they tend to be expensive and hard to find. At the nonprofit New York Institute for Child Development, Inc., which has seen thousands of learning disabled children in the past ten years, the basic diagnostic fee is $500 with additional charges for therapy. On the West Coast the Southern California Neuropsychiatric Institute in La Jolla charges similar fees.

### Treatment and success

Once the diagnosis has been made, treatment will depend on which disability or cluster of disabilities has been found. In cases of hyperactivity stimulant drugs, chiefly Ritalin and Dexedrine, are often prescribed because they tend to have a calming effect on hyperactive children. But the possible side effects—nervousness, loss of appetite, insomnia and, in extreme cases, hypertension—make this course of treatment somewhat controversial. Dr. Sydney Walker III, director of the Southern California Neuropsychiatric Institute and author of *Help for the Hyperactive Child* (Houghton Mifflin; $8.95), condemns the use of Ritalin on the grounds that it merely masks symptoms without curing them and makes an accurate diagnosis very difficult. Others, however, including the American Medical Association, endorse careful use of the drug.

For various learning disabilities a combination of special teaching methods and exercises can often help. Problems with muscle coordination may be eased by such activities as bouncing, throwing and catching a ball. Troubles with color and shape differentiation can be approached through sorting games in which parents can participate. Children who have trouble identifying letters may be guided through exercises in which they write them, say them, cut them out of cardboard or sandpaper and hold them in their hands.

These are approaches that are generally accepted. Less accepted are programs involving special diets (mainly additive-free diets), megavitamin therapy and biofeedback. Many doctors and educators familiar with learning disabilities believe that proof of the effectiveness of these techniques is unconvincing.

### Where to get help

Parents of children with actual or suspected learning disabilities must contend with a lot of well-intentioned but often conflicting advice. Even experts may disagree on the proper kind of treatment. Your best course is to obtain the most thorough diagnosis you can through schools, doctors and clinics and to consult the following organizations and publications for guidance.

▶ Association for Children With Learning Disabilities, 4156 Library Rd., Pittsburgh, Pa. 15234. Can direct you to state and local affiliates set up to share information and assist in obtaining help.

▶ Orton Society, 8415 Bellona La., Towson, Md. 21204. Devoted to the study and treatment of dyslexia.

# BRIGHT CHILD, SCHOOL FAILURE

**An all-too-frequent combination that need not occur if parents pay attention to the early-warning signs of physically-based learning disability.**

by Morris A. Wessel, M.D.
Clinical Professor of Pediatrics, Yale School of Medicine

■ All parents hope that their children will be successful in school. And yet, educators and pediatricians believe that between ten and fifteen percent of perfectly bright children have special problems which make learning more difficult for them than for their classmates.

What are the kinds of problems that cause some youngsters to become learning-disabled? An exact definition is difficult, since many conditions may interfere with a child's capacity to learn. The Bureau of Education for the Handicapped of the Department of Health, Education and Welfare suggests the following broad definition:

"Children with learning disabilities are those who exhibit a disorder in one or more of the basic psychological processes involved in understanding or in using spoken or written language. These children may have difficulty in listening, thinking, talking, reading, writing, spelling or arithmetic. They are those children often referred to as suffering from perceptual handicaps, minimal brain dysfunction, dyslexia or developmental aphasia."

Such youngsters can—and should be—identified early in life so they can get special attention before school. If their difficulties go unrecognized during their preschool years, they're almost certain to fall behind their classmates, and to develop feelings of inadequacy which add to their difficulties, and which can last a lifetime. The need for early intervention, and the success that can be achieved with very young children, is discussed more fully in the accompanying article, "School Before School Can Be the Answer."

Pediatricians and other specialists know that certain kinds of stress early in life may produce learning disabilities later on. Premature rupture of the membranes prior to delivery, for example, infection of the amniotic fluid, prolonged labor or slowing of the fetal heart rate during delivery are significant stresses which often leave a deficit in the child, and result in learning disabilities later on. An infant who experiences a delay in taking his first breath, or who suffers respiratory difficulties during the early hours of life or who has an infection in his lungs or elsewhere is also considered to be in the "high risk" category; he has a slightly higher chance of developing a neurologically-based learning problem than if he had not undergone these stressful experiences.

Another condition which concerns pediatricians is the "small for date infant," that is, a baby born close to his anticipated date of arrival who weighs less than five-and-one-half

---

### RESOURCES AND DIAGNOSTIC FACILITIES

**The following books on Delayed Development and Learning Disabilities, geared for parents, are available at most large libraries and bookstores.**

*Speaking of Children, Their Learning Abilities/Disabilities,* Careth Ellingson, Harper & Row, 1975

*Helping Children Overcome Learning Difficulties,* Jerome Rosner, Walker and Company, 1975

*Square Pegs, Round Holes,* Harold B. Levy, M.D., Little, Brown and Company, 1973

*Living With Our Hyperactive Children,* edited by Marvin L. Bittinger, BPS Books, Inc., 1977

**The following organizations will send literature on the subject.**

Association for Children with Learning Disabilities (ACLD), 5225 Grace Street, Lower Level, Pittsburgh, PA 15236

California Association for Neurologically Handicapped Children (CANHC), Literature Distribution Division, P.O. Box 1526, Vista, CA 92083

Closer Look, P.O. Box 1492, Washington, D.C. 20013

Council for Exceptional Children, Division for Children with Learning Disabilities (DCLD), 1920 Association Drive, Reston, VA 22091

#### Where to go for diagnosis:

1. *Directory of Facilities for the Learning Disabled and Handicapped,* Careth Ellingson and James Cass, Harper & Row, 1972. This is a comprehensive directory giving state by state listings with information on diagnostic procedures, remedial, developmental and therapy programs, fees, faculty, funding and enrollment requirements.

2. University child development programs and special education clinics.

3. University medical centers.

4. Local school districts.

5. Local child guidance and health screening clinics.

6. Major hospitals with child development programs.

7. Local offices of the National Easter Seal Society for Crippled Children and Adults. The national office is located at 2023 West Ogden Avenue, Chicago, IL 60612.



Bright Child School Failure, Morris A. Wessel, M.D., *Parents Magazine*, Vol. LIII, No. 1, January, 1978. ©1978 Psy-Ed Corporation, Boston, Mass.

pounds. This baby may be small because his mother was malnourished, or he may have been deprived of nourishment due to a malfunction of the placenta. Other small babies suffer metabolic stress because of a mother's thyroid dysfunction or other endocrine abnormality. A viral infection early in the mother's pregnancy may affect a baby's neurological development adversely. The effects of these occurrences may be quite subtle and appear only when a child begins to face educational tasks requiring fully developed motor, visual and other perceptual skills.

As we consider our current knowledge of what causes many children to have learning disabilities, there is one important conclusion: any child with a history of unusual stress during fetal life, delivery or infancy may have suffered an injury to his nervous system which can affect his capacity to learn. A careful, thorough physical and psychological evaluation is imperative.

Medical examination often alerts a physician to the possibility that a potential learning problem may have a physical basis. First of all, a child should be growing normally. Any significant deviation, particularly of recent onset, suggests the need to investigate metabolic, gastrointestinal, neurologic and kidney functions. If any one of these is abnormal, it can seriously interfere with the child's ability to absorb food. A child may thus be starved, even though he may have an adequate, even at times enormous, food intake.

Anemia, too, can slow up a child's ability to learn. Unrecognized seizures, often detected only by electroencephalographic studies, may cause a child to "fade in and out" of classroom activities. Kidney infections or other disturbances of kidney function, detectable by an examination of the urine, are conditions which often hamper a child's ability to concentrate in the classroom.

Recent studies by the New York City Health Department suggest that even moderate elevations in the concentration of lead in the body, to a degree previously assumed to be harmless, may seriously interfere with development of the nervous system and alter a child's ability to learn. Whenever parents seek my advice about a child's difficulties in school, I begin by taking a careful family history. I pay attention to the educational experiences and reading habits of close relatives. Often, I discover that a parent, aunt, uncle or sibling of the child in trouble also had difficulty in learning to read during the early years in school. One or more adults in the family often fail to experience any enjoyment in reading; they read only when they "have to." This bit of family history suggests that a child may suffer from an inherited form of specific language or reading disability.

There are many variations of this condition. Even in adult life some people are utterly confused as to right and left. They have difficulty putting their shoes on the correct foot; they often cannot set the table properly. Writing and spelling may be impaired. The tendency to reverse and interchange letters—normal in the early primary grades—may continue to be a lifelong pattern for these individuals.

Other school-age children with learning disabilities read well, yet they fail to comprehend what they are reading. They cannot process what they read into a plan for action. Instructions such as "Put the ball on the table" are read easily, but these children possess limited ability to follow the instructions which they have read with ease.

More than 50 years ago, Dr. Samuel T. Orton, a pioneer clinician in the field of learning disability, postulated that while normal children develop a dominance of one side of the brain, children having difficulty learning often fail to develop this dominance. These children suffer from dyslexia, a condition in which there is a marked tendency to reverse letters. They confuse "b" and "d," "p" and "q," and "m" and "w." They confuse left and right. They may be ambidextrous, writing equally well or badly with either hand. Dyslexic children work doubly hard to achieve success in reading and writing. They are often exhausted because of the unusual amount of energy they put forth to achieve even small successes.

Other children have difficulties in visual motor functions (which also may be present in their relatives). They find it difficult to distinguish a triangle, a diamond, a square and a rectangle. They cannot reproduce accurately on paper what they see on the blackboard.

Careful evaluation of visual functioning is important. A school-age child needs to be able to do more than read the appropriate size letters from an "E" chart twenty feet away. Eye movements must be smooth and brisk. A child who has difficulty in focusing his eyes on his reading material uses an enormous amount of energy performing daily tasks at his desk, and becomes exhausted long before his classmates do. He needs careful evaluation by an ophthalmologist or other doctor, experienced in evaluating visual problems in children.

Clumsiness as a child climbs onto the examining table or an appearance of being "all thumbs" suggests difficulty in integrating neurologic function. The child's mother may mention that her son or daughter is the last one chosen to join a team on the playground and, as I watch the child, I can well understand why this happens. He or she often has a limited capacity to coordinate body move-

ments into the smooth effective manner so necessary for successful participation in sports. A child exhibiting clumsiness often has accompanying deficits in visual and motor function which interfere with his capacity to copy, read and write.

Any consideration of children with learning disabilities inevitably raises the question of administering medications, such as amphetamines or methylphenidate, as a means of decreasing restlessness. Many children, with or without learning dysfunction, are very restless in a classroom. Their inability to concentrate for more than a few seconds makes life difficult for everyone around them. Teachers, parents and even classmates are exasperated by these children. However, to medicate a restless child without first evaluating his physical and psychological status is poor medical practice.

Even when medication does help a child to "settle in," it is imperative that his teachers have a clear understanding of his capacities in all areas. Children are restless for many different reasons. Some may be emotionally upset. Some are hungry. Many children have little or no breakfast before coming to school. Low blood sugar, allergic reactions to foods or food additives, unrecognized seizures, deficits in the ability to comprehend spoken or written words—all of these conditions are bound to make a child restless. A poor and deprived background, family turmoil, divorce or the severe illness or death of a loved one are stressful events which can markedly impede a child's ability to meet school demands. Restlessness associated with these conditions should not be treated with medication without a careful consideration of ways and means to alleviate these serious medical, social and emotional stresses. Medicine is a poor substitute for proper "whole child" care.

True hyperactivity—or hyperkinesis, as it is often called—is a relatively rare condition. Nevertheless, vast numbers of children are all too often casually diagnosed as being hyperkinetic. When the condition does exist, the use of appropriate medication can produce dramatic improvement. However, most physicians prescribe medication with caution, insisting that a concerted effort be made to discover a child's level of psychological functioning before taking this step.

How does one recognize a child suffering from true hyperkinesis? A parent of such a child usually describes the youngster's infancy with comments such as, "He was never still from the moment he was born; he was a terrible eater; he was never satisfied; he used to vomit a lot; the nights were terrible." Teachers report that it is impossible for the truly hyperkinetic child to concentrate for more than a few seconds. As one teacher described such a child, "He can't settle down to any one task. As soon as I get him settled with pencil and paper, he's out of his seat and off to something else. The worst of it is that he's not stupid. When he does manage to sit still he performs quite well. But he is so easily diverted he can't concentrate on any one task long enough to do the work I know he can do. Even his own thoughts set him off in a dozen different directions."

Another teacher described a child in these terms, "When I sit by his desk with my hand on his shoulder, he struggles to control himself. I can feel his entire body tighten up as he tries to concentrate on his work. But the moment I move away, he explodes. He's out of his seat and off to another part of the room."

Dr. Alan Ross, Professor of Psychology at Stony Brook College, Long Island, New York, and the author of *Psychological Aspects of Learning Disabilities and Reading Disorders*, believes that hyperkinetic children experience a delay in developing the capacity to achieve "selective attention." Just as some normal children walk or talk later than other children, some are late in developing the capacity to set a priority for a specific task. The hyperkinetic child's attention is captured by everything he sees and hears. An ordinary classroom with pictures, books, educational equipment and classmates presents itself to him as a veritable whirlwind of exciting stimuli. Hyperkinetic children respond to all of these stimuli, often like a chain of firecrackers exploding.

Hyperkinetic children seem to do well on medication such as amphetamine or methylphenidate. Although why these drugs work is still poorly understood, it can be seen that they do increase the child's ability to concentrate on the task which is most important at any given moment. Occasionally children experience undesirable side effects from these medications, such as an increase in blood pressure or a decrease in appetite and growth. Any child receiving these substances should have careful, periodic medical supervision. Many children who benefit from the use of such medication can dispense with it after a while. This well-documented experience supports Dr. Ross's concept that hyperkinesis is in many instances only a delay in the development of the capacity to pay attention to one stimulus at a time.

Once a child has been evaluated and diagnosed as having a specific learning disability, parents are often at a loss as to how to proceed in order to provide an appropriate educational experience for their child. No wonder there is confusion. Physicians in all sincerity may suggest that the next step is up to the school, since the child does need special educational help. Teachers, on the other hand, recognizing the presence of a medical problem need a physician's advice to plan a child's program.

My experience as a practicing pediatrician is that a conference of school personnel, parents and physician to consider a child's strengths and weaknesses usually results in the development of an appropriate program either in the child's school, or in other schools in the community. The manner in which a child responds to a special program may clarify the basis of his difficulty.

Public schools must provide education for all children. In 1975, Congress passed The Education for All Handicapped Children Act, known as Public Act 94-142, which mandates that State Departments of Education arrange specialized teaching for all children who need it. Some states, like my own state of Connecticut, have provisions for educational programs for handicapped children as young as three years and eight months, and a year earlier for children with hearing deficits.

Federal funds under provision of Public Act 94-142 will provide support for remedial programs. Every school must, by 1980, provide special service for children with a specific learning disability who need supplemental education. Parents, suspecting that their child has a learning disability, who are unsuccessful in obtaining assistance locally should write to the United States Office of Education Information Center, Box 1492, Washington, D. C. 20003. The staff of this office will refer parents to special programs in their areas which offer appropriate evaluation services.

# SCHOOL BEFORE SCHOOL CAN BE THE ANSWER

**What a preventive program can do . . . how to tell if your child needs help . . . what your community can provide**

by Carolyn Luetje

■ This place is fantastic," said Kathy Conner about the Delayed Development Center, part of the Redondo Beach, California, school system, and one of the first public early intervention programs for two-through-six-year-olds diagnosed as having learning problems. Mrs. Conner, well knows how fantastic the Center is. Her own son, Michael, is one of the children there who are receiving individualized help at no cost to their parents.

Four-year-old Michael Conner "improved 100 percent" in less than a year at the Center, according to his mother. "When Michael was three," Kathy Conner relates, "he was speaking at a one to two-year-old level. He usually said only one or two words and when he did speak in a sentence, we were unable to understand him. In addition, his comprehension, attention span and coordination were poor. Now, his speech is almost up to age level, he comprehends what is said to him, he is able to carry on a conversation, and his attention span has improved greatly. The Center is still working with him on his coordination problems but he has made progress in that area, also. It's so important that these problems be caught and helped early so that children don't have trouble in elementary school."

Help at the Delayed Development Center is divided into four areas: speech and language development; conceptual development; motor development; and social and emotional development. Although some children are delayed in only one area, most need several types of assistance.

Each child is originally referred to the Center by a physician, teacher or parent who has noticed that the child's development is delayed in one or more areas. Next he is tested and evaluated by Dr. Antonia Bercovici, a psychologist under contract to the Redondo Beach School District. If Dr. Bercovici believes that the child can benefit from the Center's program, she writes a family profile and specific recommendations for him. Still more testing and screening is done before the youngster enters the program. His motor skills are assessed and a language sample is taken in which everything he says is written down exactly as he says it. Information from the child's parents about his behavior at home, and what he can and cannot do, is also gathered. Then the Center's teachers form quarterly, weekly and daily objectives for him, and draw up lesson plans focused on his specific needs.

On casual observation, a visitor to the Delayed Development Center

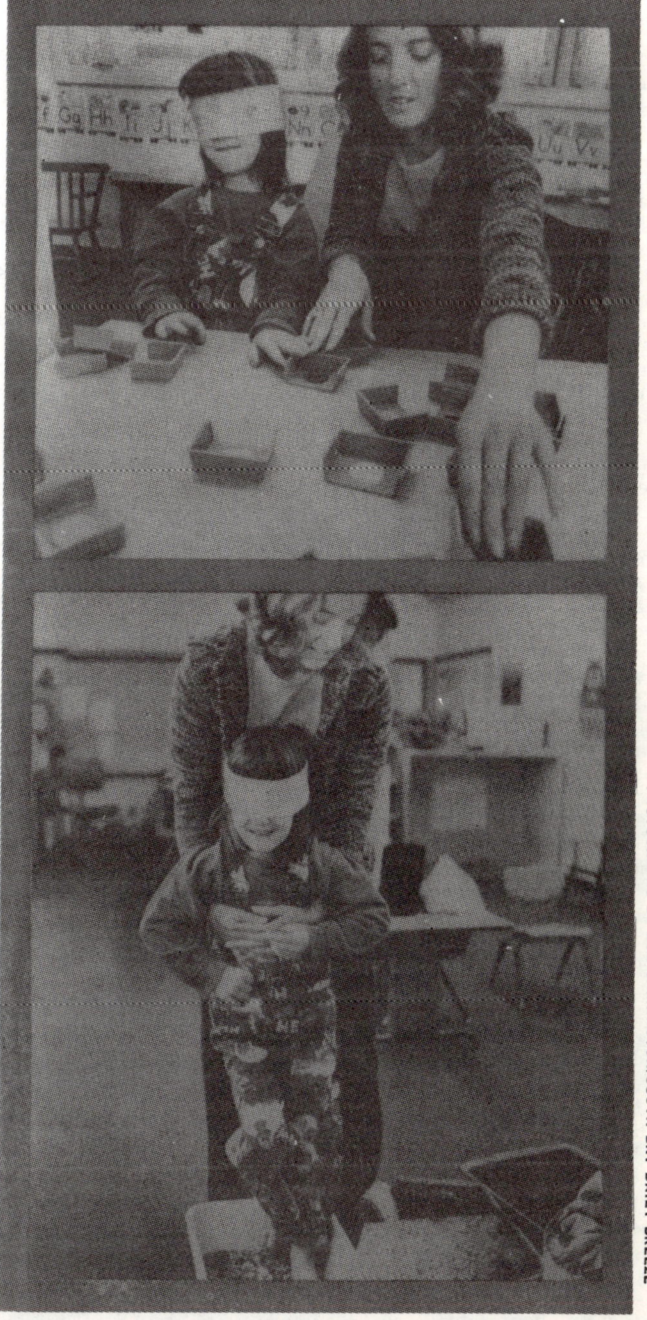

PHOTOGRAPHS BY BOB CARRINGTON/SOUTH BAY DAILY BREEZE

might mistake it for any other well-run, fairly structured preschool. Several activities are in progress at any one time. The children are happy and busy. However, a closer look reveals that these children do, indeed, have problems.

Billy speaks in long paragraphs but the words are so garbled no one can understand him. According to his teacher, his understanding of language is normal, but his articulation is very poor. In contrast, Sam speaks clearly, but his language is bizarre in meaning. Some children leave out various parts of speech, others have trouble with past and future tenses. The teachers constantly provide models of correct speech for the children to imitate and absorb as their own.

As Brian leaves the block area for a quick trip to the bathroom, his teacher tells him, "Please say to Eric, 'I am coming back.'" Brian hesitates and she repeats the sentence. "I—I," Brian struggles. "I—I am— com-ing back," he finishes.

"Good talking, Brian!" his teacher exclaims as she gives him a quick hug. A vital part of the program is the building of self-esteem, and the establishment of a positive self-image. A feeling of self-worth, essential to all, is doubly important for these children. As the activities take place in the Center's classrooms, a steady thread of approval and acceptance runs through the teachers' comments and conversations with the children. Each child is appreciated for what he is and can do. Disruptions and altercations are handled calmly and patiently, with emphasis on what to do rather than on what not to do. Each child's smallest accomplishments are noticed and praised.

"Our goal," says Liz Helm, head teacher at the Delayed Development Center, "is to give early help to these children so they will be able to function in regular classrooms in the future. Children like these have traditionally fallen between the gaps of existing programs. They're not retarded, they're not severely handicapped and most don't belong in classes for the educationally handicapped. But they do have problems and they do need help.

"We are trying to create as many successful experiences as possible, and to capitalize on the successes." Thus the comments are positive and specific—"Good waiting, Fred. You're remembering to wait for your turn." "Good passing, Janet." "Jack, you did a fine job of setting the table for snacks."

Speech and language problems occur most often but other types of delays are often present as well. While one of the Center's classrooms is devoted to activities which increase speech and language skills and concept development, the other classroom contains activities which aid fine motor development. No matter what the child chooses to do in this room,

he will be increasing his fine motor skills as he does it. The children spend 45 minutes in each room every day. During the 45 minute daily outdoor period, the teachers work with the children on gross motor development.

Help with social and emotional development is continuous throughout the three-and-a-half-hour school day. The children are led, in a calm and loving manner, to function as part of a group, to follow directions, to solve their differences with other children in a constructive way, and to relate positively to adults.

A typical day at the Delayed Development Center begins with the children divided into groups of ten. Each group sits in a circle with a teacher and an aide for approximately half an hour. All of the children participate as they update their class calendar, share objects brought from home and work on language development. The teacher and aide guide the session by asking questions which stretch the children's vocabulary and communication skills.

When the group session ends, the children split up—three to the block corner, two to the library, two to the puzzle area and three remaining with Jane Fairchild for a sentence structure game. Choosing from a supply of magazine pictures, which Miss Fairchild has cut out and glued on individual cards, the children make their own sentences by selecting pictures representing a subject, a verb and an object. One by one, they "read" their sentences aloud and their success is applauded. After fifteen minutes, the children switch places in the room, giving each child a fifteen minute daily lesson geared to his needs and a fifteen minute reinforcement period in which he works with the aide on skills he has recently mastered.

Next comes the outdoor period followed by a midmorning snack. Then the children in the language and concept development room go to the fine motor development room (and vice versa) and the process is repeated.

In the fine motor development room, the art table is set up for "face painting." Watching themselves in an eye level mirror, the children use watercolors and a variety of makeup brushes to paint designs on their faces. As the young artists decorate themselves, their teachers again encourage and reinforce language and concept development and motor skills. "I see you made straight lines on your cheeks, Alan." "Can you watch in the mirror and put a red circle right on the end of your nose, Susan?" Tommy dons an Indian headdress and contorts his face, giggling at his image in the mirror. The art table activity differs each day, but the week always includes painting, drawing, cutting and glueing and two construction activities. The school day ends with story time and a songfest.

Each child's progress is evaluated daily and recorded in the detailed

notebooks which the Center's teachers keep for each area of development. Anecdotal records are also kept.

"It's really exciting," Miss Fairchild comments, "to look back through the records and see how the children have progressed. Many who were one to two years below age level when they entered the program are now functioning up to age level."

Approximately 75 percent of the Center's students go on to regular classrooms when they leave the Center. Some need no additional help, some need tutoring to supplement their kindergarten experience and some attend kindergarten classes concurrently with sessions at the Delayed Development Center. The rest continue to need help from the school district's special services department. All, however, have shown impressive growth gains over the period of time they have participated in the Center's program.

Fortunately the help offered to children of Redondo Beach is no longer unique. In Portage, Wisconsin, the Portage Project has helped more than a hundred preschoolers with problems ranging from speech and language delays through physical handicaps and mental retardation. In the Portage Project, parents work with their children under the guidance of trained home teachers. The parents use games, household objects and behavioral techniques to help their children progress. Teaching is based on a sequential checklist of developmental stages supplemented by a set of cards that guide the parents in teaching skills related to particular stages of development. The fact that 80 percent of the children who left the project at the end of a recent school year were placed in regular classrooms testifies to the success of the project.

The school district in Ferguson-Florissant, Missouri, relies heavily on parent participation in their once-a-week Saturday School for both normal preschoolers and those with delays or handicaps. In addition to the Saturday sessions, there is a one-hour weekly teaching visit to small groups of three or four neighboring children, and children with special problems also see a teaching specialist once or twice a week.

In Peotone, Illinois, south of Chicago, all children are screened for possible learning problems before entering kindergarten. Part of the Early Prevention of School Failure program, the screening determines each child's readiness for kindergarten and identifies those children who have one or more learning problems in the areas of speech, language comprehension, hearing, motor coordination and emotional-social development. For those who do have problems, the program provides special classrooms for those who are not ready for regular kindergarten, monitoring of children who enter regular classrooms and help for regular classroom teachers in teaching and evaluating students with learning problems.

As a federally-funded pilot program, the Delayed Development Center in Redondo Beach has served as a model for visitors from surrounding school districts. They have observed the program in action and have taken back ideas and information useful in setting up similar programs modified to meet their communities' needs. With increased public awareness of the vital importance of early intervention for children with learning disabilities, programs such as the Delayed Development Center in Redondo Beach will become more common. Then more children like Michael Conner and his classmates will embark upon their school years with the maximum chance for success.

# A WORKING MODEL FOR DEVELOPING INSTRUCTIONAL MATERIALS FOR THE LEARNING DISABLED

*Carlene VanEtten and Glen VanEtten*

**Meeting the unique educational needs of the learning disabled requires the availability of appropriate instructional materials. The variance in the learning style and behavior of the learning disabled may necessitate the use of completely different materials from one student to the next. Those working with these youngsters often adapt existing materials or develop new materials in order to meet individual differences. It is important that such efforts at developing materials for the learning disabled consider the factors that influence the degree to which an instructional material will be effective. Van Etten and VanEtten have developed a working model to provide guidelines for the development of instructional materials. Four clusters of variables are seen as influencing the effectiveness of such materials: Learner/material interaction variables; content variables; teacher/material interaction variables; and affective variables. — D.D.D.**

In the field of learning disabilities, the selection of instructional materials is a critical variable in the diagnostic/prescriptive process. Without a working model to guide in the development and selection of instructional materials, the classroom teacher has only an intuitive basis as a guide in the selection of appropriate instructional materials. Material developers will continue to produce nonspecific materials of limited value, if a comprehensive working model is not available. Efforts to develop such a model to guide in the selection and development of instructional materials is another step in assuring improved quality of instructional programming for learning disabled students.

One purpose of a model is to provide a framework for communication, but most importantly, a model provides a testing ground for personal principles, hypotheses, and feelings. Finally, a model may identify specific areas toward which research efforts can or perhaps should be directed.

A model which will provide guidelines for the development of instructional materials should identify critical variables which can be considered during the various stages of the product development process. Many currently available materials have been developed by



A Working Model for Developing Instructional Materials for the Learning Disabled, Carlene Van Etten and Glen Van Etten, *Learning Disability Quarterly,* Vol. 1, No. 2, Spring, 1978.

using beliefs, principles, and experience as guidelines, rather than research data from either the classroom or the human learning laboratory. Though common sense and beliefs, based on years of experience, should not be devalued, the chances for poor quality instructional material will remain high if product development is not based upon some predetermined course. Use of any model assures that steps toward the final goal are based on a scientific foundation, rather than following a path of least resistance.

Particular attention should be paid to the word "working" which appears in the title of this article. The choice of this word was not made lightly but was intended to indicate that variables may be altered or deleted, or that new ones may be added as research indicates.

Four clusters of variables are contained in the model: (1) Learner/Material Interaction Cluster; (2) Content Cluster; (3) Teacher/Material Interaction Cluster; and, (4) Affective Cluster. The first three clusters were much easier to identify than the affective cluster, since, for the most part, they have observable and measurable attributes which better satisfy the behaviorist's desire for precise description and tidy endings. Though the temptation was great to ignore affective variables, reason prevailed and they were consequently recognized and included.

## LEARNER/MATERIALS INTERACTION CLUSTER

The variables in the learner cluster are concerned with the learner's interaction with the material or the way in which the material impinges upon the learner.

### Stimulus and Response Characteristics

This variable concerns the modality used in the material to provide input to the learner and the mode of responding. Six modalities are available to humans for the reception of information: auditory, visual, gustatory, olfactory, tactile, and kinesthetic. The auditory and visual modalities are expected to carry most of the load for academic learning, and while the others are sometimes used for support, they are of little value for the learning of symbols or even representational material.

For expression, only two modalities are available: vocal and motor. These two modalities must be adapted to express data received by all six reception modalities and, consequently, options for expression are more restricted than those for reception. Two modalities combined form a channel for communication.

In the present model a channel of communication is composed of a reception modality and an expression modality. Though six reception modalities are available, only two will be considered in this discussion: auditory and visual. These two reception modalities and the two expression modalities are most commonly used in early learning experiences. When the visual and motor modalities are combined and the auditory and vocal modalities are combined, two primary channels are formed.

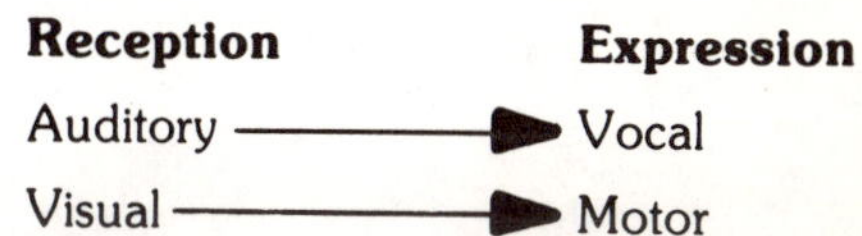


Primary channels allow the learner directly to reproduce the stimulus which is presented. This is the most primitive level of channels of communication.

The secondary channels of communication require much more complex and sophisticated manipulations of the stimuli. These secondary channels are:

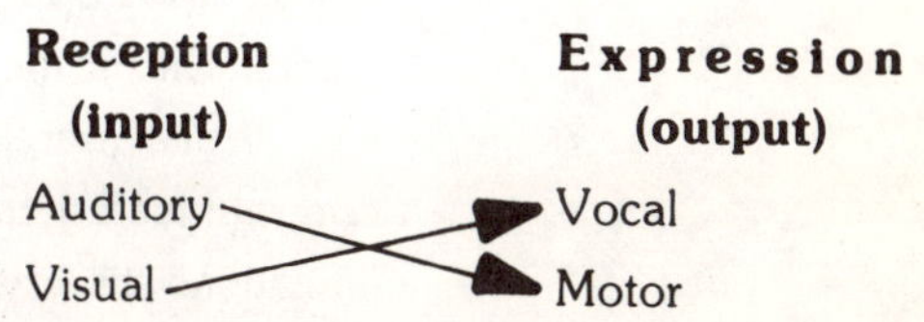

In these channels the direct reproduction of the stimuli is not possible, i.e., it is impossible to reproduce motorically an auditory stimulus. Certain transformations of reception stimuli must be made before a response is possible. Because of a lack of basic research, it is very unclear how these transformations occur. In the past we have relied on such concepts as intraneurosensory and interneurosensory functioning as an explanation. However, these terms do not actually describe what the learner does.

Another important aspect of stimulus-response characteristics must be considered. The developer of a material must consider the complexity of the stimulus presented. The following three levels of stimuli appear to be applicable to instructional materials.

**Concrete information.** Concrete information is essentially the "real thing." A real car is concrete information as is a chair, a banana, or a bed. This is the most primitive type of information. Though it provides a foundation for future learning, concrete information has severe limitations. For example, complex concepts such as love and freedom cannot be fully communicated at the concrete level.

**Representational information.** This type of information includes stimuli designed to represent not only the real thing, but the class to which the real thing belongs. Line drawings of a chair represent not only a single chair, but all chairs. Auditory representation of animal noises would be the sound of a dog barking or a donkey braying. Motor representation occurs as a child imitates a running horse or pretends to be driving a car. In other words, the topography or structure of the stimulus has some resemblance to the real object. While more complex concepts can be communicated than at the concrete level, limitations still exist.

**Symbolic information.** Symbolic information refers to the meaning arbitrarily assigned to sounds or designs. Through the use of these symbols, complex concepts as well as mathematical notations can be communicated. Topographically these sounds or designs may have little relationship to the real object. Most human communication is conducted through use of symbols such as speech, letters (words) or even body language.

The three levels of information may be used either with the reception or with the response modalities. Figure 1 shows how the levels of information interact with the reception modalities. It is apparent that some reception modalities such as olfactory and gustatory cannot be functionally combined with the more sophisticated information levels. Figure 2 shows that both expression modalities (vocal and motor) can utilize all levels of information.

## Feedback/System

This variable concerns the procedure used to provide the learner with information on his/her progress. In order for any learning activity to be effective, the learner must receive feedback about the quality of responses made. Research has consistently demonstrated that feedback which is given immediately after the response results in better learning than when the feedback is delayed. The developer of an instructional material has several options for including provisions for feedback.

**Teacher feedback.** One choice, of course, is to have the feedback provided by the instructor. This frees the product developer from any further responsibility in this area. At the same time, the teacher selecting such a material must be willing to plan the time required for the feedback.

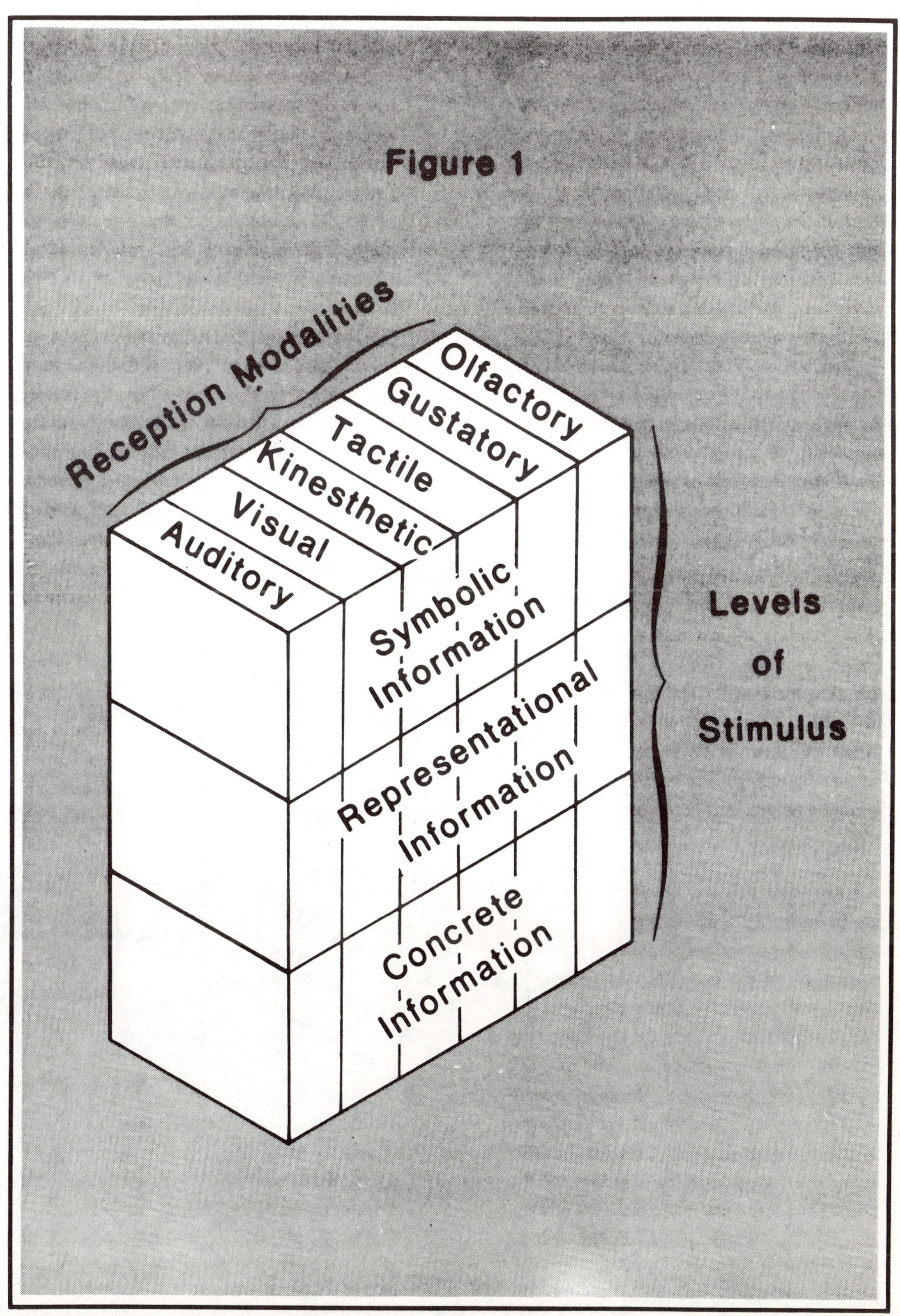

Figure 1
Reception Modalities
Olfactory
Gustatory
Tactile
Kinesthetic
Visual
Auditory
Symbolic Information
Representational Information
Concrete Information
Levels
of
Stimulus

**Self-correcting feedback.** If the product developer opts for this choice, the responsibility for a good feedback system must be accepted and planned as product development progresses. In this instance, feedback may be provided by answer keys, answer booklets, templates, and other such devices. Use of self-correcting feedback assumes a certain level of responsibility and sophistication of the learner.

**Automatic feedback.** Our current level of technological capability allows for rather sophisticated feedback systems. Computers and teaching machines can be programmed to give feedback on an item-by-item basis while chemically treated paper used with special marking pens turns different colors to indicate correct or incorrect answers. Even the simple cassette tape can provide an excellent feedback system.

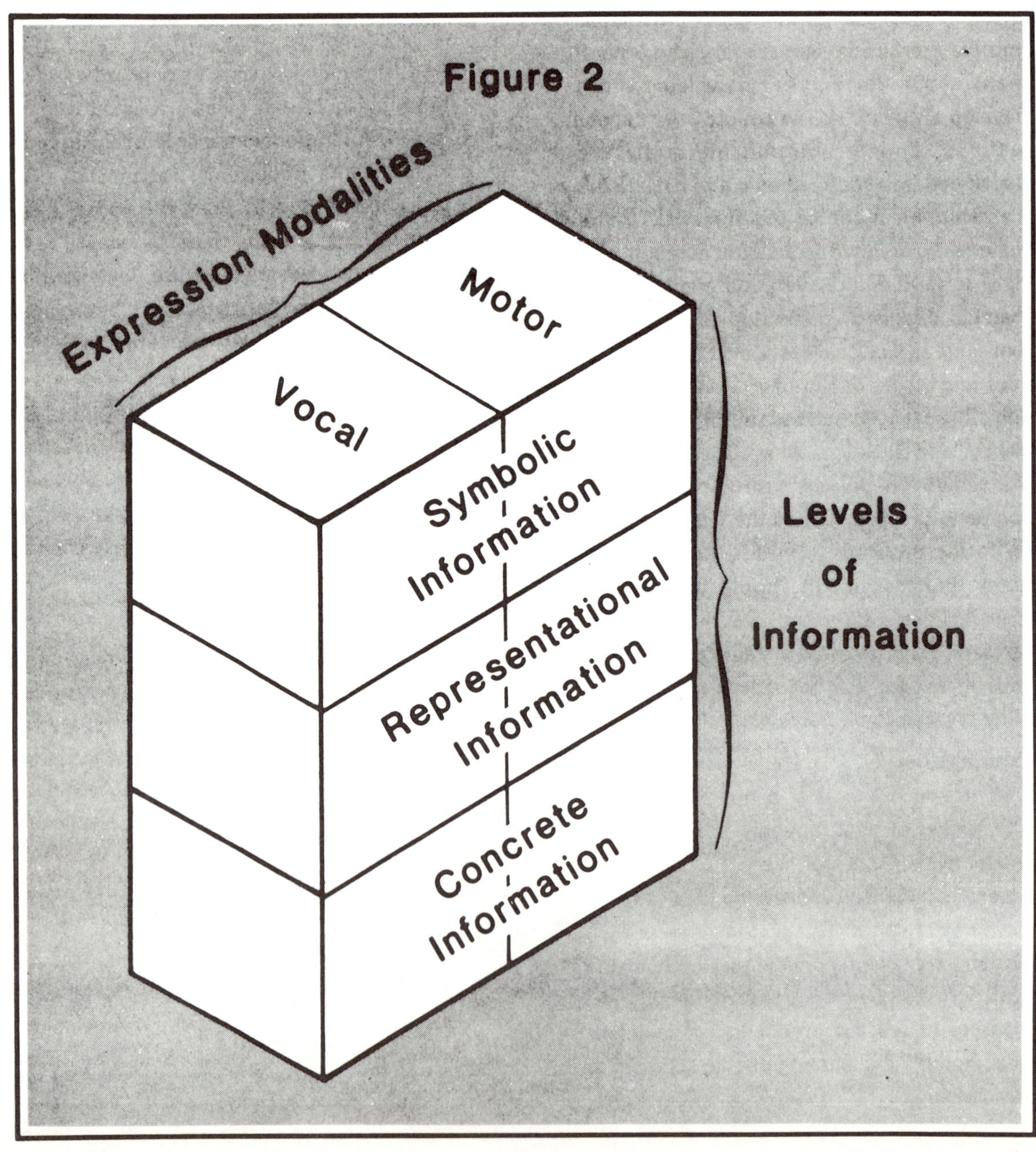

## CONTENT CLUSTER

The content cluster is made up of those variables which most directly affect the complexity and difficulty of the material. Depending upon the manner in which these variables are manipulated, the final product may be a very simple material or a complex one involving many skills and concepts and requiring high levels of cognitive manipulation.

### Instructional Intent

A statement of instructional intent commits the product developer to making a statement about the degree to which he will develop a specific skill or concept. As the objectives for instructional materials are developed, the author should also declare the instructional intent of the material. If the material is designed to build acquisition of a skill, it should look very different from a material designed to develop proficiency in that same skill or concept. Lovitt (1977) identifies four stages of learning: 1) initial acquisition, 2) advanced acquisition, 3) initial proficiency, and 4) advanced proficiency. During the acquisition phases, instruction must accompany practice, but as the learner moves on to the proficiency phases, Lovitt (1977) notes that instruction should be less emphasized and opportunities for practice increased. Early declaration of instructional intent, therefore, will be a deciding factor in other choices to be made along the way.

### Concept Load

The concept load of a material refers to the number of new thoughts or ideas which appear within a lesson or a unit of study. Research evidence supports the idea of single concept learning. Although the value of such teaching has been documented both in the classroom and the clinical research setting, we continue to see the production of materials which require the learning disabled student to respond to several concepts in one exercise, perhaps even on one page. This variable relates closely to instructional intent. If the purpose of the material is to develop advanced proficiency, presentation of pages containing multiple skills and concepts would give a good measure of proficiency and application. However, if the stated instructional intent is the development of skill acquisition, the presentation of single concepts must be the choice.

### Rate of Presentation of Skills and Concepts

This variable deals with the speed of introducing new learnings, as opposed to simply the number of new ideas presented within a lesson. An important factor in attaining proficiency is the opportunity for practice. The faster the introduction rate of new skills and concepts, the less opportunity there will be for practice on previously presented material. Even the presentation of excellent single-concept material (low concept load) to a learner may be of little value if it is followed immediately by another single-concept lesson teaching a totally new concept or skill. Careful consideration must always be given to whether or not opportunity for practice has been sufficient.

### Cognitive Manipulation

This variable concerns the "thinking" processes that the learner must perform to make a response. It is impossible to observe the learner and measure the exact cognitive precedures utilized to solve a problem. However, the selection of the process by which the student will be required to respond can be rather specifically defined. The cognitive manipulation selected by the product developer, along with earlier choices, will be another factor in determining the difficulty level of the finished product. This model identifies four different types of cognitive manipulations which may be required of the learner.

**Type A manipulations.** Manipulations of this type require the learner to reproduce a stimulus (sample). The response required is often referred to as imitation.

Level I Activities: Level I activities require the learner to reproduce a response that matches a stimulus he has just seen or heard. In order to be correct, the response must be identical to the stimulus. Visual stimuli require a motor response, while auditory stimuli require a vocal response. This concept is very similar to Johnson and Myklebust's (1967) concept of intraneurosensory learning. At this level the learner uses only primary channels of communication.

Example: (Visual Model-Motor Response)

| Visual | Motor |
|---|---|
| m | Learner must reproduce letter |

Example: (Auditory Model-Vocal Response)

| Auditory | Vocal |
|---|---|
| sound "mm" | Reproduce sound "mm" |

Level II Activities: Activities at this level are complicated by the need for the learner to use secondary communication channels or to use what has been described as interneurosensory learning (Johnson & Myklebust, 1967). With this type of activity, visual stimuli require a vocal response, while an auditory stimulus requires a motor response.

Example: (Visual Stimuli-Vocal Response)

| Visual | Vocal |
|---|---|
| Letter M is shown | Learner must make the sound of "m" |

Example: (Auditory Stimuli-Motor Response)

| Auditory | Motor |
|---|---|
| Sound of "mm" is given | Learner must write letter "m" |

**Type B manipulations.** These manipulations might be called "match-to-sample." A sample is provided and the learner is required to select from a series of foils an item that is like the sample. The task may require selecting either one or more items that are like the sample or choosing one or more that are different.

Level I Activities: In Level I activities both the sample and the foils utilize the same reception modalities. They are either both visual or both auditory. Here again the learner needs to use only the primary com-

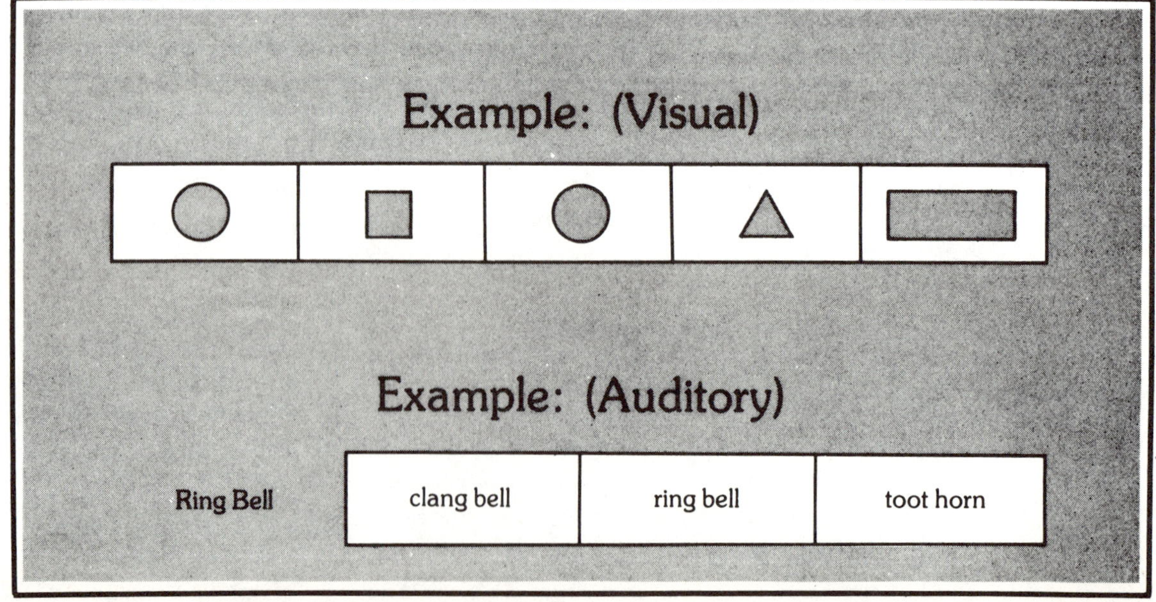

munication channels.

Level II Activities: Level II activities require a similar response, but secondary channels are used requiring the learner to make rather complex translations. At this level the learner might be presented with the auditory sound for "m" and be required to find a picture or drawing (visual) of something beginning with "mm." Another example of a Level II activity is the presentation of a picture of a bell (visual) as the stimulus. The foils might be the auditory presentation of a horn tooting, a ringing bell, and clanging cymbals. The required response in this instance is the auditory match of the ringing bell to the picture of a bell.

**Type C manipulations.** Manipulations of this type require the learner to restructure the stimulus and then construct a response. The stimulus must be restructured because it is presented in such a way that direct matching or copying is not the correct response. These manipulations usually occur in activities which have typically been called concept development. Such a manipulation is required when a learner is asked to name the fifty states or list ten fruits.

We do not know what occurs inside the head of the learner in order to solve such a task. Somehow the stimulus must be reconstructed, which makes it necessary to use only secondary channels of communication. The learner may have to revisualize a list of states or a map of the United States. In the case of naming the fruits, the learner may need to reauditorize the characteristics of the concept of fruit as a class of food different from other classes of food. Or perhaps the learner visualizes foods and selects those that fit the concept of fruit.

Success in Type C manipulations requires the learner to be able to perform what is often called conceptualization. The learner must be able to classify, name objects and events, and to be aware of likenesses and differences.

These concept development skills allow the learner to deal with new stimuli and events.

**Type D manipulations.** These manipulations may be difficult for some learning disabled children since they require the construction of entirely new responses. In effect, the learner must use all past learning to create a new and, for the learner, unique response. Type D manipulations are required in such activities as creative writing, music composition, and in the playing of musical instruments. As in Type C manipulations, the restructuring of the stimulus necessitates the use of secondary channels of communication. Since both Type C and D manipulations require restructuring of the stimulus, only one level (Level II) of activities may occur.

Example:

| **Task** | **Response** |
|---|---|
| What do people from outer space look like? | written description |
| | drawing |
| | vocal description |

Cognitive manipulations of Types A, B, and C should be the focus of remedial instruction. This is not to imply that Type D manipulations are unimportant. Students are, however, placed in learning disability classrooms because of their inability to perform A, B, and C type manipulations.

## TEACHER/MATERIAL INTERACTION CLUSTER

This cluster is concerned with the variables that relate directly to the use of the material by the teacher.

### Management

Due to the current emphasis on individualized educational plans and accountability, teacher expectations of instructional materials are undergoing some changes. With the movement from group to individual instruction, teachers need a selection of materials that will meet both the needs of their personal teaching style and that of overall curriculum management. Basically three options are available.

**Teacher-directed instruction.** Some instructional materials rely on total teacher direction for much of the instruction. An example of such a program is DISTAR. Though such programs may be excellent, the teacher must consider their selection in terms of overall curriculum management.

**Teacher/student shared instruction.** Many materials require an introductory segment to be presented by an instructor, with follow-up instruction as student responsibility. A large majority of presently available materials use this design.

**Student-directed instruction.** The last few years have seen the development of many such materials. A selection of student-directed instructional materials allows the teacher to utilize some totally teacher-directed materials which may meet very special needs of some students. Student-directed instruction also allows for self-paced movement.

### Evaluation Variable

The evaluation variable concerns the procedures for collecting data about pupil progress and for providing the teacher with criteria for knowing when the material has been mastered. VanEtten and VanEtten (1976) described four strategies that can be used for measurement. These include posttest only strategies, pre-post strategies, progress testing, and constant recording.

In posttest only a mastery test is given at the end of an instructional unit to simply measure what the learner knows at the end of instruction. With the pre-test design, a test is given before instruction starts and then again after the completion of instruction. This strategy makes it possible to determine the amount of learning that has occurred. Progress testing, while similar to the pre-post test design, usually requires that the learner meet a predetermined criterion before progressing to the next instructional unit. Constant recording strategies require that learning be measured at least daily. Figure 3 presents various types of instruments and procedures that may be used with the four strategies.

Regardless of the strategy used, it is important that the material developer determine a criterion for mastery so that the user of the material knows what level of mastery is acceptable. This, in turn, allows the learner to progress efficiently through a learning experience and allows the teacher effectively to manage the learning experience.

**Figure 3**

| Posttest Only Strategy | Pre-Post Test Strategy | Progress Test Strategy | Constant Recording Strategy |
|---|---|---|---|
| Standardized Tests | Placement Tests/ | Chapter Tests | Percent Correct |
| Semester Exams | Mastery Tests | Unit Tests | Trials to Criterion |
| Final Exams | (May use the same | Criterion Tests | Duration to Response |
| Achievement Tests | instruments as | | Intensity of Response |
| | posttest-only but | | Response Latency |
| | administered as | | Fluency (rate) |
| | pretest as well) | | |

## AFFECTIVE CLUSTER

There can be little doubt that the most neglected aspect of instructional materials development has been the consideration of affective variables. Traditionally education has focused on how well and how quickly the student mastered the material with little or no interest given to whether or not the student held positive feelings toward the learning experience.

### Ethnic

This variable should consider vocabulary, illustrations, story content, as well as any other element which might effect the appropriateness of a material for a particular ethnic population.

### Sexism

This variable is concerned with the presentation of males and females in a variety of settings and occupational models. Appropriateness of illustrations, vocabulary, and general content in terms of nonsexist presentation should be considered.

### Esthetics

This variable deals with how agreeably or how pleasantly the material is presented to the learner. Logic seems to say that if learning is already a chore, the manner in which information is presented to the learner may deserve some special attention.

### Student Needs or Interests

This variable recognizes that student needs and interests are important. It must be determined not only if students learned the skills or concepts, but whether or not they perceived a need for or had an interest in the material presented.

We would like to say that constraints of space held us to this rather brief discussion of this area. Though space was certainly a limiting factor, we must accept the responsibility for using our alloted pages more fully to discuss other areas. The importance of this cluster, especially for the learning disabled/behavior disordered population, should be carefully investigated. Because learning disabled children usually bring to the special education classroom an impressive record of failure, logic (no data) seems to indicate that such students may respond with intense emotion to any instructional material placed before them. Therefore, if the material is designed to teach specific skills and concepts while also coping with student needs and interests, perhaps more rapid progress may be possible, especially with older LD students.

Over the past few years, educators have made significant progress in the basic knowledge of teaching and human learning. This increased knowledge has resulted in new instructional models and learning theories but unfortunately, progress in the development of instructional materials has not kept pace.

One reason for this may be the lack of a comprehensive model to guide in the development of instructional materials. Without such a model the logical and sequential development of research activities has floundered. It is hoped that the variables described in this model will be subjected to scientific inquiry and eliminated or validated based on research findings. It is inappropriate that the design of instructional materials depend solely upon the inference of basic learning research. Instead, the design of instructional materials must become a separate and valid area of inquiry.

### REFERENCES

Johnson, D.J., & Myklebust, H.R. *Learning disabilities: Educational principles and practice.* New York: Grune & Stratton, 1967.

Lovitt, T.C. *In spite of my resistance I've learned from children.* Columbus, Ohio: Charles E. Merrill, 1967.

VanEtten, C., & VanEtten, G. The measurement of pupil progress and selecting instructional materials. *Journal of Learning Disabilities,* 1976, *9,* 469-480.

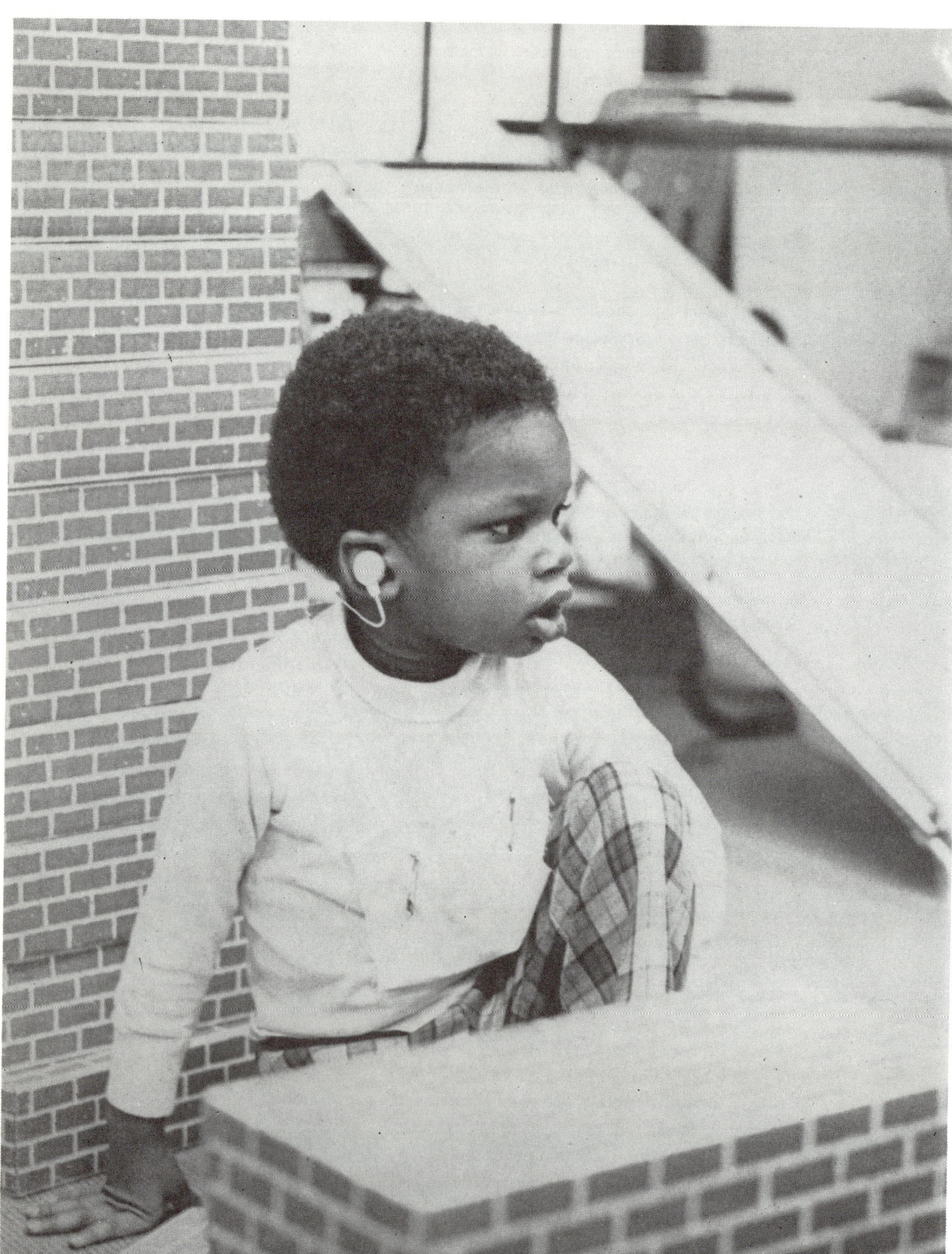

photo:  Office of Human Development Services, DHEW

# PHYSICALLY AND SENSORIALLY HANDICAPPED

The category known as physically and sensorially handicapped is a relatively large category. Included in this group are the deaf or hearing impaired, the blind or visually impaired, the orthopedically impaired, the health impaired, and the speech impaired. This section examines these areas and presents articles which give ideas for successful mainstreaming.

"Sound Minds in a Soundless World" is the first of three articles which deal with the deaf. It is suggested that learning potentials of the deaf are now being met since educational restrictions are no longer as prevelant. "Cued Speech Keeps Deaf Pupils Ahead" presents one method of communicating with the deaf. A parent's view of her child's deafness is then given in the concluding article, "My Child Leads a Full Life."

Blind children have been successfully mainstreamed into regular classrooms for many years. The articles in this section discuss the teacher's role in making this possible. "Mainstreaming: It Can Work for Blind Children" gives insight into the programs used throughout Canada, while the next article discusses precision teaching and its importance in teaching blind children.

Speech impairments comprise the largest group found mainstreamed in public schools. "Help for 10 Million Americans Who Suffer Speech Problems" discusses several impairments and suggest that early detection and treatment can help in remediating speech problems. "St-st-st-st-stuttering" describes one method for remediating the stuttering problem in children and adults.

The remainder of the section deals with the development and mainstreaming of the orthopedically and health impaired. The orthopedically impaired, those with severe skeletal disorders, can be successfully mainstreamed with help from teachers, classmates and the child as shown in "Mainstreaming a Child with Spina Bifida." Health impairments are not usually thought of as a handicap. "What are Health Impairments?" discusses how these problems can be an impairment and what effect they have on development in the child.

# Sound Minds in a Soundless World

Luther D. Robinson, M.D., Sc.D.

### EDUCATIONAL IMPLICATIONS OF DEAFNESS

That far too many deaf children are not deriving maximum benefit from formal schooling is evident in the conclusions of many studies of deaf educational achievement. There is no concensus about the extent of the lag in deaf achievement, but it is clear that the average graduate of a deaf secondary level school is not advanced as his hearing counterpart. In addition, there is the problem of dropout; the studies of Altshuler and Baroff in New York (1969) showed that more than 16 percent of deaf students leave school before 16 years of age, and are thus even further behind in educational achievement. It may be that the tests that have been used to measure the learning progress of deaf students are themselves in need of refinement; recent analyses made by the Office of Demographic Studies at Gallaudet College (March and August 1972, July and September 1973) show this to be so. Analysts there have demonstrated, for example, that the Stanford Achievement Tests commonly used to determine educational achievement and to compare deaf and hearing children contain several sections which are inappropriate for deaf students due to their emphasis on knowledge acquired through auditory means; the staff has modified the test accordingly and is in the process of presenting statistics measuring deaf educational achievement in its proper context. The demographers do not use the new data to compare deaf and hearing students, but they do identify learning problems among deaf students which require immediate attention—for example, weaknesses in reading comprehension, vocabulary and related tests, and a rather slow rate of progress over periods of several years. Language deficiencies were also found in a 1960 study by Roy and Schein of incoming students to Galluadet College; though there was a discrepancy of only 2 to 3 years in achievement between deaf and hearing college candidates, the deaf students scored much higher on nonverbal than on verbal questions. However, the exact nature and extent of the deaf educational lag is not the issue here; what is important for our purposes is that the deaf student is usually not able to take full advantage of his educational opportunities, and that the rea-



Sound Minds in a Soundless World, Luther D. Robinson, M.D., S.D.C., DHEW Publications, 1978.

sons for this problem are once more related to communication handicaps.

It is obvious that if a child goes to school without his native language, and some means of communicating it to others, he or she is going to have a great deal of catching up to do; thus many professionals stress the lack of early education in the home, and the lack of nursery school training, as causative factors in later learning problems. However, the deaf child too often has had to contend with emotional trauma as well, since the pattern in the past has been for parents to place him at an early age in a residential school for the deaf where his contacts with his family and relatives were infrequent and unsatisfying. The child, who often was not adequately prepared for such a displacement, might remain in such a setting until his late teens or early twenties with restricted access to the hearing world; although there were many obvious benefits to be derived from opportunities for friendships with other deaf students, and with concerned teachers and administrators, the residential setting nonetheless served to isolate the deaf child from a broad range of experience. In addition, the child often found that in the residential school, manual communication of any kind was severely restricted, if not forbidden altogether, so that a natural and satisfying mode of self-expression was denied him. Since the ability to learn is intimately tied to psychological security and well-being, and to the capacity to communicate with and absorb from the environment, it is not surprising that large numbers of deaf students failed to fulfill their learning potentials.

Today, however, the situation is changing, and the educational prognosis for the deaf child is constantly improving. The long struggle between purists of the oral and manual schools of thought has been greatly mitigated by the progress of the theory of total communication—that is, that a deaf child should be taught to speak, to speechread, and to communicate with his environment manually as well. There is a decided increase in the number of children who receive preschool training, and a wider range of educational programs from which parents of deaf children may choose. In addition to the public residential schools, there are private residential schools; public and private day classes, which allow a child to live at home; and an ever increasing number of special programs in hearing schools which are designed to keep deaf children close to their families, and integrated with hearing students. On the campus of Gallaudet College are two modern, model institutions which are making great strides in educating the deaf: The Kendall Demonstration Elementary School, opened in 1971; and the Model Secondary School for the Deaf, opened in 1969. Perhaps most importantly, the signing into law of the Education for All Handicapped Children Act (Public Law 94-142) in 1975 ensures Federal commitment to the education of handicapped children (ages 3-21), and to the development of preschool services in local districts and States.

According to Stephen Quigley's 1974 review of the postsecondary scene, the opportunities for deaf students in institutions of higher learning have also shown marked improvement since the early sixties; he estimates that the number of deaf students in postsecondary education quadrupled between 1960 and 1970. Quigley points out that prior to the mid-sixties, the deaf student who was not among the fraction admitted to Gallaudet College did not usually have alternative options for higher education. Now, however, he or she may choose from among an impressive array of possibilities. the National Technical Institute for the Deaf (NTID) at Rochester Institute of Technology in New York offers a program for deaf high school graduates that is connected to the Rochester Institute's regular programs. Deaf students may sign up for special classes for the deaf, or they may participate, with the aid of an interpreter, in classes at the Rochester Institute. Most students combine types of classes and thus benefit from the advantages of integration. Degrees are offered in such areas as electrical or mechanical engineering, photography, printing, business administration, and electronics. Other special programs for deaf students are available at California State University in Northridge (on both undergraduate and graduate levels); Delgado College in New Orleans, Louisiana; Seattle Community College in Seattle, Washington; and the St. Paul Technical and Vocational Institute in St. Paul, Minnesota. The philosophy of all these programs is to provide the deaf student with opportunities for integrated education, and with the necessary knowledge and skills to keep him or her in the mainstream of American life. A recent compilation of postsecondary opportunities for the deaf (Rawlings et al. 1975) describes 43 postsecondary (college) programs distributed throughout the country; in addition, there are hundreds of community colleges which offer regionally oriented vocational programs in which the deaf may and do participate. Gallaudet College, the original institution of higher education for the deaf (it has graduated over 4,000 people since 1864), has greatly expanded its undergraduate and graduate programs during the past decade, thus providing a wider range of choice for the potential student; it has joined the Washington Consortium of Colleges and Universities, which allows a Gallaudet student to take a course in any of the member institutions (with interpreting services provided free of charge); and in 1970 it established a model Center for Continuing Education which provides hundreds of varied course selections for adults. Finally, there are many deaf students who are able to attend regular classes at hearing colleges which have no special programs and/or facilities for them. Thus it can be seen that the severe restrictions in educational opportunities which the deaf individual faced in the past have been greatly diminished, and that professionals in deaf education on all levels are trying to ensure that the deaf student gets an even break. When the learning potentials of deaf children go unrealized through no fault of their own, as has been the pattern in the past, it is necessary for the educational establishment to assume responsibility for reversing the trend. The evidence of the seventies suggests that this is being done, and that educators and administrators at hearing schools, together with their supporters and friends in the general public, are making significant contributions to the effort.

# Cued Speech Keeps Deaf Pupils Ahead

Bart Barnes

Bart Barnes is a staff writer for "The Washington Post." His article is reprinted with permission from "The Washington Post."

*Terry VandenBossche teaches cued speech to, from left, Steven Scher, Tiffany Balderson and Robbie McIntosh.*



Paul Swadley, age 9, is severely deaf, profoundedly deaf, a condition he's had since birth.

Unlike most deaf children he's reading well above the normal level for his age, despite the fact that he's never heard a word of spoken language. It's not unusual for him to read six or seven books a week.

He's enrolled in a regular third grade class with 30 hearing children at Fairfax County's Beech Tree Elementary School in Northern Virginia, where he's getting As and Bs in all his academic subjects.

He participates in all major class discussions and in December he read an original poem at his school's Christmas assembly.

Paul, who enrolled in a regular public school classroom for the first time this fall, is a product of a relatively new and slightly known method of educating deaf children called cued speech—a combination of hand signals and lip reading.

He is one of perhaps a dozen deaf children in the Washington area currently using the cued speech method of learning, some in regular public school systems, some in preschool tutoring and some in an experimental program at the National Child Research Center.[1]

Cued-Speech Keeps Deaf Pupils Ahead, Bart Barnes, *Children Today*, Vol. 7, No. 4, July-August, 1978. Copyright © The Washington Post, 1150 15th Street, NW, Washington, DCc 20071.

## 6. PHYSICALLY

Developed 12 years ago at Gallaudet College in Washington, D.C., by R. Orin Cornett, cued speech is currently in use in about 50 educational programs for the deaf throughout the United States.[2] Its supporters include a small but growing corps of enthusiasts who will argue that because the system is based on phonetics, deaf children who learn that method develop a linguistic agility that many deaf people never acquire.

"The one open window on the world of the hearing which the deaf person should have is reading," says Gallaudet's Cornett. "But the vast majority of prelingually deaf persons do not learn to read well, and thus do not make maximum use of what should be their greatest asset. The basic reason for this is that they do not learn the spoken language before learning to read."

Cued speech, he adds, is simple enough that most parents can learn it in a matter of 12 to 15 hours. "Children then learn the language from their parents, which is the way hearing children learn it."

"With cuing, I can talk to my son like a normal human being. I don't feel held back. I'm talking to a person, not a handicapped child," says Sheila Scher, whose 4½-year-old deaf son Steven is in the cued speech program at the National Child Research Center in Washington, D.C.

Before signing up for the cued method, Steven had been enrolled in a Montgomery County, Maryland program for the deaf that emphasized oral communication and lip reading.

"I felt very stymied and very stifled," says Scher. "I felt very uncomfortable talking to my own son. We just weren't communicating."

"He is just fantastic in the way he receives and the way he expresses himself. We've opened up whole new worlds. We're getting the basic communication that is so important in bringing up children," says Steven's father, Barry Scher.

Developed by Cornett during a six-month leave of absence from Gallaudet, cued speech is, essentially, a manual supplement to lip reading. It consists of eight hand shapes used in four different positions near the lips to make all of the sounds of the English language look different either on the lips or on the hands.

"If all the sounds we use in speech looked clearly different from each other on the lips, a deaf child could learn the spoken language by lip reading," says Cornett.

"But lips identify groups of sounds, not single sounds."

By cuing with hand and finger gestures, enough information is added to the group of sounds identifiable by lip reading to pinpoint visually the single sound being spoken.

"If the parents of a deaf child learn cued speech and use it consistently with the child, the spoken language will be learned in a visual form through normal, everyday communication in the home," says Cornett.

"The child will learn the same verbal elements, the same words, syllables, phrases and syntax that are used

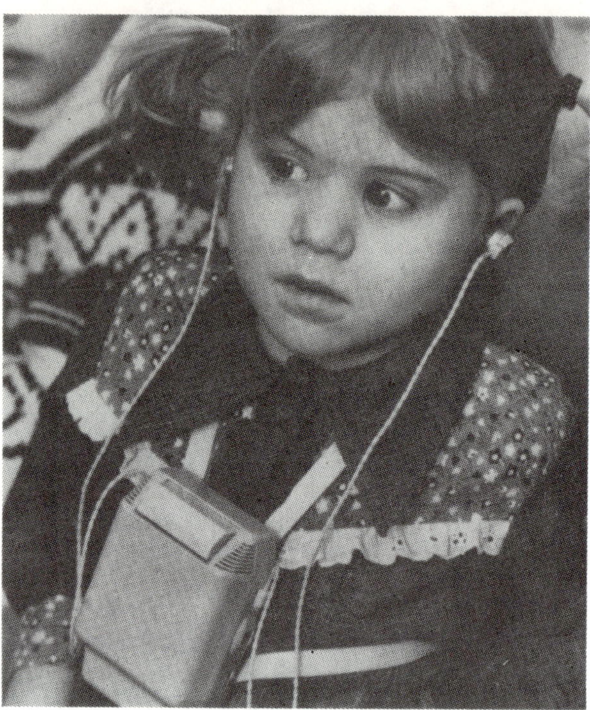

Tiffany Balderson watches cue.

in speech. This can blend together into one language model used for thought and self expression."

A physicist by training, Cornett came to Gallaudet in 1965 as vice president for planning with no previous training in education of the deaf. He soon concluded, he says, that education of deaf persons was failing, at least as far as reading was concerned.

"The average person in a school for the deaf in the United States reads at a fourth grade level at the age of 19. Here at Gallaudet where we get the cream of the crop, 80 percent of the deaf students never read for pleasure and of the 20 percent who do, three-quarters of them were not born deaf."

Sign language, he said, although an effective method of communication among deaf persons, is a language in and of itself, different from English with a different syntax. It is not particularly helpful in the acquisition of reading skills.

Leah Henegar of Glenn Dale in Prince George's County, Maryland, two years old in September, 1966, was the first child to learn cued speech under Cornett's direction.

By the age of seven, she was enrolled in a combined second and third grade class at Glenn Dale Elementary School, reading on grade level.

Throughout grade school, each of Leah's teachers learned cued speech and today, at 13, she is in the eighth grade at Thomas Johnson Junior High School, receiving one hour of special instruction a day, but otherwise functioning in a regular classroom. "She's performing on grade level and she's holding her own," says her mother, Mary Elsie Henegar.

After Leah, the cued speech movement spread, slowly in some places, more rapidly in others.

For more than 100 years, educators of the deaf had been arguing over which method of education was best, manual, using hand signals—or oral, concentrating on lip reading. Cued speech added another element to that dispute.

"I think Cornett's objectives are admirable and desirable," says George Fellendorf, executive director of the Alexander Graham Bell Association for the Deaf, an organization that supports the oral approach.

"The thing that bothers me is that it isn't more widely used. For certain children it does seem to have advantages, but we still think maximum use of residual hearing is the best approach."

Currently, cued speech is used widely in Australia, but sporadically in the United States. In the Washington area, between 30 and 40 deaf children have learned cued speech over the past decade, Cornett estimates, but it was not until the fall of 1973 that the system was put into formal use at the National Child Research Center.

Last fall, three children from that program entered public schools in the Washington area: Paul Swadley to Fairfax County; Tommie Wells, reading two years above grade level in Prince George's County; and Tiri Scott to Montgomery County.

Of the three, Paul's program makes the most extensive use of cued speech. In Montgomery County, Tiri's parents are negotiating for a cued speech program under a new federal law that gives parents of handicapped children increased power to determine what kinds of educational programs will be offered to their children.

Teachers' aides in Tommie's school, Skyline Elementary, have learned cued speech and he's using it in a limited way there.

At Beech Tree Elementary School in Fairfax County, teacher Rosemary Davis decided during the summer that she would like to have Paul in her class and she went to Gallaudet on her own to learn cued speech.

As Davis began the school year, cuing to Paul as she addressed the class, other children soon began imitating her. After a few weeks, she had a cued speech teacher from Gallaudet out to teach cued speech to the class and by Christmas a half dozen of Paul's classmates had learned cued speech well enough to communicate with Paul.

"Cuing to Paul is one of the things that really makes the children feel good about themselves," says Davis. "This is a wonderful opportunity for them to be with a handicapped person and to understand that they can be normal human beings."

"At the beginning of the year, I thought that cued speech would be sort of hard and dumb," said Jennifer Jacoby, one of Paul's classmates. "But it was easy. I like to have conversations with Paul and cue to him."

It was last March, according to Paul's father, the Rev. Charles Swadley, a Methodist clergyman, that Paul's interest in reading soared. "His mother took him to the library one day and they came home with six or seven books. In a few days, he was finished with them and he wanted more. Since then, our problem is to get him to stop reading and go to bed, but that's a good problem to have."

---

[1] The National Child Research Center, 3209 Highland Place, N.W., Washington, D.C. 20008, is a private nursery school. Its total enrollment of 102 includes three deaf children.

[2] Additional information on the cued speech learning method is available from the Office of Cued Speech Programs, Gallaudet College, 7th and Florida Ave., N.E., Washington, D.C. 20002.

# "MY DEAF CHILD LEADS A FULL LIFE!"

**Unlike his four brothers and sisters, 18-year-old Timmy Mackey (*below*) was born deaf. When he was three, his mother had to make the heartbreaking decision to send him away to a special school. Now his accomplishments are outstanding—but his highest achievement is that he can talk! PEARL MACKEY'S story by JOAN RATTNER HEILMAN**

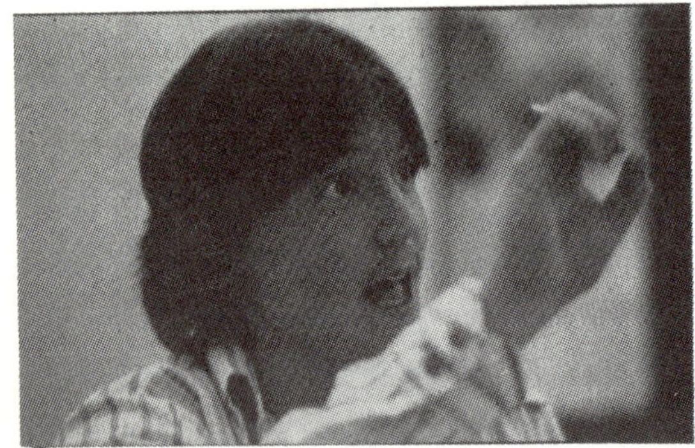



**W**e sat in the Mackeys' cozy, cluttered kitchen, drinking hot coffee, looking past the wood-burning stove, the wooden sink and the laden shelves festooned with drying herbs, through the tilted farmhouse window overlooking the Hudson Valley far below. We could see the foothills of the Berkshires, all the way over the hills dotted with apple trees and close-cropped hayfields, to the Newburgh Bridge crossing the Hudson just below the little farming community of Milton, N.Y. And we talked about Pearl Mackey's son Tim.

Pearl did most of the talking. A large, intelligent, serene woman, Pearl has lived her life on a farm, never further than two miles from where she now sat. Timmy, an alert, handsome 18-year-old, occasionally spoke in painstakingly enunciated syllables, rarely moving his eyes from his mother's face. Timmy Mackey can't hear a word, so he must pay complete attention to lip movements if he's to have any understanding of what is being said. He was born deaf, with no hearing in one ear and only four percent in the other. His accomplishments are astounding: He has one of the highest averages in his school; he has an engaging personality; he is president of the junior class, close to becoming an Eagle Scout, one of the seven deaf members in the entire country in the National Honor Society, a track, basketball and football star; he has awards for swimming, science congeniality, German—virtually anything you can name.

But his highest achievement is that he can talk.

It wasn't easy, and it still isn't. Most people who are deaf at birth are unable to speak intelligibly because, never having heard the language, they can't pick it up effortlessly the way other children do, and perhaps do not realize for years that there are such things as words.

Like most people who can hear, I always assumed that deafness isn't anywhere near as serious a disability as blindness, and I never considered it an almost insuperable problem like stumbling around in total darkness. Perhaps it isn't for those who became deaf after first learning to speak. But for those born deaf or those who lost their hearing before they learned speech, deafness is its own darkness, a more profound one than not being able to see, according to experts (among them Helen Keller), because human beings must be able to communicate with each other. To be shut out of the world of sound can mean total isolation.

The Mackeys, who desperately wanted Tim to be able to live in the world of hearing and not be forever isolated among other deaf people, had to make a vital decision when Timmy was only three. It was a heart-wrenching decision which required months of agonizing thought —they decided to send him away to a residential school for the deaf where he would get the special education he needed if he was ever to learn to communicate with other people. To part with a beloved, dependent child who couldn't understand why he was leaving home was "the hardest thing we've ever had to do," his mother says. "I can understand why other parents don't do it, but for us it was the only answer."

"Educating deaf people," says

*Tim tries out a reconditioned teletype machine, which he uses to call other deaf friends who have this equipment. The TTY is a gift from a group at the phone company where his mother (shown here) works. Younger brother Jonathan, 12, looks on.*



My Deaf Child Leads a Full Life, Joan Rattner Heilman, *Family Circle*, Vol. 91, No. 8, July 10, 1978. Copyright ©1978 Family Circle.

**Timmy, in the cafeteria and in chemistry class at the New York School for the Deaf in White Plains.**

*For 'the past 14 years, Timmy has spent five days a week at this residential school Specially trained teachers use every possible method of speaking, and use them simultaneously. They speak the words distinctly, use sign language and, when necessary, spell the words out 'on their fingers. The trained staff consists of both deaf teachers as well as those who can hear.*

Kendall D. Litchfield, superintendent of the New York School for the Deaf in White Plains, where Tim has been a pupil for 14 years, "is one of the most difficult tasks there is.

"Our language is meant to be learned through imitation, through hearing. Mastering an understanding of each word for a profoundly deaf person is a hard-earned triumph. Then, to be able to approximate normal speech is another almost impossible step."

To a stranger, Tim Mackey's speech is not always totally understandable, but his expressive face and his gestures help get his messages across. However, his family usually knows what he's saying, and his main aim in life, he told me, is to talk so everyone can understand him.

"I made it a point to see that Timmy could talk," his mother says. "How else would he get along in this world? Most people hear. Out there, people don't know sign language; they're not going to wait for him to write everything down. I knew Timmy had a voice—after all, there's nothing wrong with his vocal cords—and he could use it. He's not always going to have his family around to talk for him, and I wanted him to grow up to be a normal person who could work and live and get along."

It's quite clear that Tim is going to make it. And it was his family's determination and total acceptance of him, quite obviously, that has made the difference. Theirs is a strong, closely knit family built on the blocks of hard work, the need to depend on one another for emotional and economic support, an up-front belief in God and the moral standards of the church, and plenty of love. Four of the five children (Tim is the only one who is deaf)—Eddie, 25, Jill, 23, Erin, 21, Tim, 18, and Jonathan, 12—live at home, though Tim's weekdays (and nights) are spent away at school. "Tim is a normal human being who happens to be deaf," Pearl asserts. "He's one of us, he's no different, he is one of God's children. We've always told him his handicap must come second, that he can do everything anyone else can do if he wants to. There's no use feeling sorry for yourself."

The Mackeys are a farm family, the eighth generation on their hilly land.

Visiting them is like going back many years in time because they live in a tiny, 100-year-old farmhouse on the top of a ridge at the end of a dirt lane in apple country. With no hired help, the family works the 135-acre farm themselves. Not only that, but because farming no longer provides a total living, Pearl now works for the telephone company during the day; and Gedney, Tim's colorful, garrulous father, works from 6:00 P.M. till 2:00 in the morning as a custodian at the nearby state university. His brother Eddie, the eldest in the family, who will be the next generation to inherit the land, also labors all day with the cows and crops and has a night job at the college.

"We all work here," says Pearl, who grew up on a farm nearby, "and we always have. We don't buy anything when we don't have

*Weekends at home in Milton, N.Y., Timmy pitches in and does his share of chores, like bringing in the hay, chopping wood and helping to repair farm machinery.*

the cash, and we're not people who want to have debts. The children have worked right along with us, Timmy, too, and we've had a wonderful life. We don't have luxuries and we don't really need them."

It's true that the Mackeys don't have luxuries, except for a color television set in the miniscule living room which Timmy watches and follows with occasional summaries of the action and dialogue from one of his brothers and sisters. And, just the day before my visit, a volunteer group from the telephone company presented Tim with a TTY telephone, a reconditioned teletype machine on which he can call other deaf people who also have the equipment, typing out his message and receiving immediate response. When I arrived, he was enthusiastically talking with a friend from school.

They do have a horse and a goat just for fun, and a number of motor vehicles scattered around the land, most of them not in operable condition. But, as Hannah Manshel, one of Tim's primary school teachers and now supervising teacher of the primary grades, told me, "They're one of the richest families I know. Tim's a happy boy because he's been accepted, treated like the rest of the kids. So many parents of handicapped children aren't like that—they feel they've produced something that's not perfect and are burdened with it."

The Mackeys' chief crop is apples—MacIntosh, Cortlands and Red Delicious—but they also grow plums, peaches and three kinds of pears. They also raise veal calves, with a usual population of about 30 pregnant or nursing cows.

Though Timmy spends very little time with the cows (because he can't hear them coming), he drives the tractor to bring in the hay and the vegetables, chops wood for the stove, helps repair the farm machinery and gathers the crops when he's not in school 80 miles away. The pumpkin patch has always been his and Jonathan's responsibility, and so are the blackberries and raspberries if they want to pick and sell them. Gedney Mackey used to say, "At least we have the farm for Tim. He can always live and work here," but now their hopes for him have gone beyond that. Tim is going to college next year (maybe to Gallaudet, a college for the deaf in Washington, D.C., or, more likely, to Rochester Institute for the Deaf, where the students are taught and live together with hearing students from Rochester Institute of Technology) and plans to become a math teacher. All three older children have gone to college, but everyone agrees Tim has the best academic potential of them all.

Timmy was, as far as anyone could tell, a normal, bright baby. He even said a few words like "mama" and "dada" but just once or twice, and his parents wondered why he never re-

peated them. He was well-behaved and happy, and it wasn't until he was just over two that they began to suspect something was wrong. He didn't talk, and he didn't always respond to their voices.

But one day, walking along the road to the pasture, Timmy let go of his mother's hand and darted into the road. A car was coming and she yelled at him to get out of the way. He never noticed. The car missed him, but Pearl said to Gedney, "He's got to be deaf."

The doctor sent them to a brand new speech-and-hearing clinic at St. Francis Hospital across the river in Poughkeepsie for tests. The tests showed that Timmy was profoundly deaf with very little residual hearing, and that he was undoubtedly born that way. To this day, the Mackeys don't know why—there is no history of deafness in their family. But Timmy obviously had a very high I.Q. He was alert and responsive, and he knew how to lip-read 10 or 15 words. They were told to bring the little boy to the clinic twice a week for special lessons.

### Feelings of Guilt

"It was very hard," Pearl Mackey recalls. "I thought it must have happened because I did something wrong. It had to be my fault. Ged and I were heartbroken. How was he ever going to take his rightful place in the world? If we hadn't learned early in our lives to lean on the Lord, we might not have pulled through the way we did. In a small community like this, everybody knows your problems and that very day the word was all over town—'The Mackey boy is deaf.' That afternoon our minister came over to visit. He was a good friend and a good man. Just like everybody who has a handicapped child or a tragedy in the family, I said, 'Why me?' The minister said, 'Why *not* you? Are you different? Are you special? It's nobody's fault. If you accept it, Timmy will accept it, and you will come out far ahead of anybody else.'

"And sure enough, it was true. 'Thy will be done,' no matter what. That was the turning point in my life, I know it. I had to keep telling myself, you have to accept this, you have to accept this, it's the only way he can flourish."

Two times a week for the next two years, Pearl drove Tim to the clinic, where he was painstakingly taught to sound out words, to know that he could speak, and every morning she worked with him for an hour at the kitchen table after the other children had gone to school, following a correspondence course provided by the John Tracy Clinic in California.

"You had a real object, like a fork, along with a picture of a fork, and a card with the word 'fork' printed on it. It had to be a word you could see on the mouth. 'Spoon,' for example, is too hard to decipher. And 'car' is one of the worst—you can't see it at all. I

would show him the fork, say the word over and over and get him to imitate my mouth; then I'd ask him to give me the fork.' When he learned that, I taught him to recognize the picture of a fork and then the word. You could only work with things, because idea words were too difficult. I used to study up in the book the night before each lesson."

The older children worked with Timmy too, as did his grandparents, who lived a mile down the road at that time. "We tried to make it a game, seeing how many words we could teach him. He was a happy child—that was obvious—but there were times when he got so frustrated. He couldn't express himself the way he wanted, and he threw some terrible tantrums.

"He got his share of spankings when he was bad and hollering when we got tired. It was pretty frustrating for the rest of us, too, when we couldn't make him understand. I'd have to sit everyone down when they started being short with him and explain that he couldn't hear and they'd have to be patient. I'd tell them, 'He's just like you. He's God's child, and he was given to us to raise the same as you.'

Says his sister Jill today, "I don't think we ever found him a problem; he was just our brother. There's something special about Tim—he wants to be number one in everything he does; he has a compulsion to excel. My mother calls him a shining beacon, and he is; everyone loves him. I've never seen anyone try so hard. Maybe it's because he's deaf and he wants to make us all proud of him."

### Easy Acceptance

"Maybe because we live in such an isolated way," Pearl says, "we never had many problems with Timmy being accepted. Mostly we lived just as a family, and everybody knew us. At church on Sundays, some of the children would poke fun at him, but he didn't even know it. I guess our most trying times were when we'd go to town to shop. When Timmy was first learning, his sounds were not like yours and mine, and I guess people thought he was a little crazy, queer anyway. What would really infuriate me, and still does, was people saying, 'He's deaf and dumb.' I wouldn't let them get away with it. I'd walk up to people and say, 'There's nothing wrong with his mind, he's just deaf. Until he learns to speak, this is his language.'"

Timmy learned well, but it was obvious he was going to need some specialized schooling, which wasn't available anywhere near the tiny village. When he was nearing his fourth birthday, the clinic recommended they apply to the New York School for the Deaf, a private school where tuition is subsidized by the state for families who cannot afford the payments. This meant Tim would have to live at the school all week (day students must live within

20 miles), come home every Friday for the weekend and for vacations. "We talked and talked," Pearl reports, "and we decided we had to do what was best for Timmy, and so, when he was accepted, we sent him.

"It was such a hard thing to do," she says with tears rising in her eyes. "It felt like we were abandoning him, giving him away to somebody else. We didn't know what it would do to him. He was only a baby, not even four, a little boy who was so dependent on us. In some ways you get much closer to a child with a handicap because you work with him so much, you want so much for him, you want to protect him."

Pearl and Gedney remember the first time they took him to the school on a Sunday afternoon. "We wondered what he was thinking," his father says. "We wondered what he felt about us, leaving him in a strange place like that. I felt real bad. You couldn't tell him why he was going." Pearl adds, "They told us not to make a big thing out of leaving, just to say good-bye, turn around and go. So that's what we did, and cried all the way home."

They could hardly wait till Friday when it was time to pick him up for the weekend. "I forced myself not to call the school, even that first week. We just went on living."

For the first few weeks, Timmy went back to school happily every Sunday afternoon after church, and Pearl would come home and take long walks in the woods to settle her mind.

But after a few weeks, Timmy began to rebel. He knew that when Sunday school was over, it was time to go home and pack his suitcase, and then, his mother reports, he'd put up a fuss. "A couple of times," Gedney recalls, "we took him to his cottage at school and he grabbed onto my legs and tried to go right out the door with us. The worst thing was, we couldn't explain to him why he had to stay."

However, soon after he made some good friends, there were no more problems. "I think, in a way," his mother told me, "it was a relief for him to get back there. They didn't teach sign language in those days, but the children invented their own and they could talk to each other like they couldn't with us. There were his people. And, tell the truth, it was a relief for us to know he was getting an education we couldn't give him."

For six years, Pearl drove him back and forth each week. Then, after much negotiation, their local school district began providing bus transportation which eased the burden.

In keeping with what she'd been told, Pearl Mackey refused to learn sign language because she knew that it was much easier for the deaf than speaking, and she was determined that Tim would eventually talk. Tim did talk, or try to, and everyone "tuned their ears" to him, but there were times when no one in the family could understand what he was saying. When his sister Erin, three years older than Tim, was about 14, she asked him to teach her finger spelling—the entire alphabet can be spelled out on one hand in a few seconds—and promptly became the interpreter when one was needed. "She's the one he still goes to when he has a problem," Pearl says. "She got us over the worst hurdles."

I asked Erin how it was to have a deaf brother. "It was never difficult for me; it was natural to help him any way I could. In fact, he made me feel kind of privileged. He was special. When we were growing up, it made me feel good knowing I could communicate with him and not many other people could."

With everyone's help, Timmy did flourish, and Pearl is unrestrained in her praise of the school and the residential program. "You can't teach them at home the way they can there. Being there 24 hours a day is a tremendous advantage because even playtime and evening talks are a kind of education when people are trained."

Fourteen years after that traumatic first day of school, Tim is a high achiever, tops in the school, excelling in all his subjects, including chemistry and third year German (the only student to go on to the third year, he uses sign language but he does not speak it).

Even now, he says, learning is a struggle and will remain so. A person born deaf rarely achieves the reading level of an equivalent hearing person. Timmy, his mother estimates, now reads at perhaps 7th grade level although he's in his junior year of high school. Most educated deaf children reach perhaps 5th grade level, and many remain functionally illiterate. "It's a constant fight for language here," states one of Tim's teachers. Today, though Tim is a superb student, his sentence structure and grammar, Pearl says, are more "like Pennsylvania Dutch than English."

### In a Class for Deaf

Many deaf children have remnants of hearing, and in the school Tim attends, every child in the lower grades wears double hearing aids and an amplifier on his chest so he can take advantage of every bit of sound he gets. Tim no longer wears his because, he says, they do him no good, although Erin says they help him with the pitch and loudness of his voice.

I sat in the back of Timmy's history and chemistry classes wondering at the total uninterrupted attention the students paid the teachers, the effort expended in trying to absorb their meaning, the sounds they made in responding. Later I watched a patient therapist in the nursery school painstakingly show three four-year-olds how to form "y" sounds and finally approximate the word "you." Such a simple task for the rest of us.

Timmy Mackey, according to his teachers, always worked very hard. "My children had to do their homework as soon as they came home," Pearl explains, "then they had to attend to their chores. Play was for weekends or after dinner. I wanted Tim treated the same way."

Best of all, Timmy Mackey is radiant, a boy who draws people to him. And he's not afraid. He is looking for a summer job, perhaps as a dishwasher in a nearby resort hotel where no one else is deaf, so he can use his voice. "I can work with hearing people," he says.

"The amazing part of Tim," his mother says, "is his need to succeed. It's like he's been given something extra, something special, to make up for his ears. There isn't anything in the world he can't do. He'll make his mark; I have no qualms about the future for him. I could die tomorrow and he'd be okay."

## TEACHING THE DEAF

Total deafness is a relatively rare problem—about 1,900,000 people in the United States are so disabled that they cannot hear or understand speech, and most of them lost their hearing as adults or after they learned to use language.

Today special education has proliferated, and special schooling is available in every state, although a pupil may have to relocate or enter a residential program to get it. And, of course, the quality of the program varies.

Two years ago, a Federal act that "guarantees free and appropriate education" for all handicapped children went into effect and, starting this September, all children between the ages of 3 and 21 are entitled to it. Most of it will be within the public school systems in what has come to be known as "mainstreaming." It will be almost impossible, however, to give deaf children a good education within the normal school system. Most experts stress the need for special schools and trained teachers.

The deaf, who cannot learn language through hearing, must learn through other means, mainly visual—although only about 30 to 40% of sounds are visible to the eye. A deaf person who "listens" to a speaker must often guess at much of the message. They learn some concepts and words by reading lips, the rest through vibrations and tactile touch.

Until recently, sign language was looked down upon because it was thought it would discourage speech. But during the last decade, there has been a growing movement toward "total communication," which stresses the right of every child to use *every* means of communication available. Schools which have developed this approach teach speech, along with sign language, finger spelling, auditory training, reading and writing, and cued speech.

Sign language is a kind of shorthand using the hands and facial expressions. It is not a translation of English words, but simply conveys simple concepts without tenses or grammar or shades of meaning. Finger spelling literally spells the word, while cued speech is speech along with a set of hand signals that give cues to the existence and pronunciation of invisible sounds. Auditory training, through amplification and other means, makes use of any residual hearing the child may have.

# It Can Work *for* Blind Children

*Much specialized knowledge is necessary for teachers of the visually handicapped*

## Sally Rogow

*Dr. Rogow is an associate professor in the Department of Special Education, the University of British Columbia, Vancouver.*

*"Mainstreaming is concerned with keeping handicapped children of all kinds within the regular school curriculum. Integration focuses on the process of returning the handicapped individual to the mainstream, either part-time or full-time."*[1]

Mainstreaming is based on the idea that children, because they have a handicap, should not be segregated and educated far from their homes and communities. Mainstreaming is intended to provide free and ready access to the world of the non-handicapped and a school experience that is as close as possible to the educational experiences of the non-handicapped peer group.

Blind and visually impaired children, who were traditionally educated in segregated special schools supported by provincial governments or private agencies, are now entering the mainstream. Classroom teachers are concerned about their lack of knowledge of the learning needs of these children and school administrators are at a loss to know how best to provide for children whose numbers may be quite small in a particular district. Classroom teachers and school administrators are questioning the feasibility of integrating children in the absence of sufficient resources and the availability of specialized assistance.

Mainstreaming blind and visually impaired children requires the services of well-qualified specialist teachers, well-developed resource centres (to supply expensive equipment and instructional materials), defined responsibility, and methods of communication among specialist teachers, administrators and classroom teachers. Without the availability of specialist teachers, the blind child is deprived of the means of coping with ordinary classroom activities.

In many instances school districts are unaware of the numbers of blind children in their districts. To their surprise they are finding that they must accommodate a larger number of children than expected. It has only been with the establishment of specialized services that they are learning about the needs of visually impaired children, and the numbers of such children who can benefit from the services of a specialist teacher.

With the development of itinerant teacher services in western Canada, the real numbers of visually impaired children are being revealed. In almost every district where an itinerant teacher has been hired, children with visual handicaps are being newly discovered.

In addition there is a large group of multi-impaired children with greatly restricted vision. These children are to


1. Koopman, P. *"Exceptional Children in Canada    The Disadvantaged Elite",* in *Precepts, Policy and Process: Perspectives on Contemporary Canadian Education,* Stevenson, H.A. and Wilson J.D. (Eds). London: Alexander Blake Associates, 1977.



Mainstreaming: It Can Work for Blind Children, Dr. Sally Rogow, *Education Canada,* Vol. 18, Summer, 1978. Copyright ©1978 Canada Education Association, Suite 5850, 252 Bloor St., W. Toronto, Ontario, Canada M55105.

## 6. PHYSICALLY

be found in child development centres and schools and classes for the mentally and physically handicapped. Many children who combine visual handicaps with mental retardation or cerebral palsy do not turn up in the statistics on blindness. The population of children identified as visually impaired cuts across every other diagnostic category. If these children are to be adequately served, the services of the specialist teacher of the visually impaired must be co-ordinated with other special educational services. The knowledge of the itinerant specialist is a valuable complement to the instructional program designed for multi-handicapped children.

**Whose responsibility?**

The education of children with visual (and other low incidence) handicaps is shared between provincial departments of education and local school districts. Provincial departments of education are responsible for the supply of expensive instructional materials, braille books, braillers, typewriters, tape recorders, large print textbooks and other specialized materials. School boards are also given grants to allow them to employ specialist teachers. The board is responsible for the planning of programs and the accommodation of the children. Three types of public school programs are to be found.

1. The resource room is a part-time classroom located in a public school and is staffed by a specialist teacher. The children come for individual instruction as needed and materials are produced on a day-to-day basis. The resource class teacher is also available at the school to assist with the administration of tests and to adapt classroom materials.

2. The itinerant teacher is employed by a school district or a board to serve children in a number of schools. The itinerant teacher is a specialist whose responsibility is to provide the special instruction, such as braille and arithmetic skills, social and study skills, prepare materials, tests, etc. The main difference between the resource room plan and the itinerant plan is the number of schools served by the itinerant plan and the time available for the individual student.

3. The self-contained special class is designed mainly for younger children who are just learning basic skills and it is intended to be temporary. These special classes are a means of supplying intensive instruction and concentrated attention.

In smaller school districts, where there are small numbers of visually handicapped children of various ages and levels of ability, the most common pattern is the employment of one itinerant teacher to serve all the children.

Specialist itinerant teachers must work closely with all school personnel who are involved with the child. At the secondary level this means teachers of academic subjects, art, music and physical education. The success of the child depends on the co-operation that exists among principals, teachers and itinerant specialists. The success of mainstreaming is dependent on the legislation of services and the integrity of the child's school experience.

This kind of co-operation between specialist and classroom teachers is not possible without the careful co-operation and administration of specialist services. Obstacles to co-ordination derive from the fact that the itinerant teacher is not part of a single school or responsible to one particular administrator. Just how complex the itinerant specialist's role is became evident through a survey (of 23 itinerant teachers in British Columbia, Alberta, Saskatchewan, and Manitoba) that I recently made.

**The survey**

Twenty-two replies were received from the twenty-four questionnaires circulated. These included six replies from British Columbia, seven from Alberta, two from Saskatchewan and seven from Manitoba. There are approximately twenty-four itinerant teachers in the western provinces at present.

1. Most itinerant teachers are serving both braille and print students. Two teachers serve braille students only and three serve only print readers. Seventeen teachers are serving the needs of both.

2. Seventeen teachers are employed by school districts and five teachers are employed by provincial departments of education.

3. Eighteen teachers are working with children in both elementary and secondary schools. Only four teachers work only in elementary schools.

4. Fourteen teachers are working with more than twelve students. Two teachers are working with more than twenty; six serve twelve and only one serves between six and eight students.

5. The teachers of only one province report no difficulty in obtaining needed instructional equipment and teaching materials.

6. Provincial departments of education are responsible for the supply of expensive equipment and the supply and distribution of brailled books and cassette tapes.

7. Most itinerant specialists are serving children who combine visual impairments with other disabilities. Eight teachers are serving children in schools for the mentally retarded; six teachers contribute to special classes for the visually impaired, ten serve children in other types of special classes and one works with a child in his home. One teacher also work with a child who is attending a private school.

8. Fourteen teachers are providing instruction in orientation and mobility (for independent travel within the school and community) and two teachers provide instruction in the use of the Optacon, an electronic reading device. Most teachers also provide personal counselling, life adjustment skills; they also consult with parents, and arrange for other services, where needed.

9. All teachers are finding that they spend a great deal of time with the child's other teachers, principals, and other school personnel. Although itinerant teachers do a great deal of individualized tutoring, they prefer to see their role as supporting the classroom teacher. They should not be thought of as the child's main teacher; this would disrupt the integration process and would remove the child psychologically from the classroom. They also find that they are dependent on the classroom teacher's awareness of their role. Some teachers find it important to spend a great deal of time interpreting the needs of the child to classroom teachers and making sure that expectations are not set too low. The teachers find it frustrating when a child is unable to cope with classroom activities or is inappropriately placed. There are few alternatives in most districts for blind children who cannot cope with the curriculum.

The survey suggests that the success of mainstreaming depends largely on the kind of preparation available to specialist teachers. University special education teacher programs must be developed to meet the requirements of specialist teachers.

An appropriate model for teacher education in the education of visually handicapped children should reflect the multiple roles of these specialist teachers. It should prepare them for the real tasks that must be performed in order to maintain visually impaired children in the classroom. This means that a teacher preparation program must prepare teachers to meet the needs of children from pre-school to secondary school; they must be able to teach braille and use other specialized teaching materials and techniques, and be skilful in the co-ordination and planning of the child's instructional program. How well the specialist teacher is able to function within a school may determine how well the child is able to cope in the classroom. In smaller communities the itinerant specialist may be the only person in the district with a knowledge of blind children. This fact alone places a great responsibility on teacher education programs.

### Specialized knowledge

Teachers of blind and visually handicapped students must have specialized knowledge of the concepts and methods of instruction required by children who do not learn visually. This includes a knowledge of perceptual and cognitive development in children with severe visual restrictions. They must know about the development of the remaining senses, such as tactual and auditory perception. Teaching tactual perception is basic to the acquisition of braille skills and other forms of tactual learning. Listening skills and visual perceptual training are also important. Visual perceptual training is one of the newest developments in the field and is proving productive in promoting visual efficiency even in children with very restricted vision.

These teachers must also be in command of specific methodologies in the teaching of braille. Reading problems and lack of interest in reading occur when braille is not taught systematically and thoroughly.

Teachers must have knowledge of teaching techniques and environmental cues that are meaningful to children who are just learning to move independently within the physical environment. This is called instruction in orientation and mobility. Training in orientation in the classroom and the school building increases the child's comfort and ease in the classroom. How to get about with a cane is the last stage in mobility training and should be taught by a qualified mobility instructor. Some teachers have taken this as additional training.

Teachers must know how to adapt texts and other learning materials. Most materials, especially those designed for younger children, are highly visual and many blind children miss learning basic concepts when they only have a brailled text or cassette tape to rely upon. Specialist teachers must know how to analyze learning materials and present concepts in a meaningful way to blind children.

They should have a knowledge of social development and how to help children initiate social relationships in the classroom.

# The Importance of Precision Teaching in the Education of Visually Impaired Students Being Mainstreamed into Public Schools:

## Sally Mangold

Dr. Mangold is an assistant professor of education in the Department of Special Education, San Francisco State University, California.

*Abstract:* This is the second of two articles (the first appeared in Spring, 1978) on the use of precision teaching techniques with visually impaired children placed in regular public school classes. This focuses upon the educational needs of visually impaired students being mainstreamed and the importance of precision teaching techniques in evaluating the impact of special programs upon the total functioning of each student.

## Mainstreaming

*Trends in Program Development*

Mainstreaming is no longer a new idea. The idea has become a reality.

When a student is mainstreamed he/she spends a portion of the school day in the regular classroom with sighted peers and a portion of the school day in the resource room or with an itinerant teacher. The degree of success experienced by the student in the regular classroom determines the manner in which the student's time is apportioned.

Those responsible for establishing these programs have been occupied primarily with administrative aspects of program development. Little or no effort has been made to evaluate the impact of the programs on the total functioning of the students.

Mainstreaming of visually impaired students was begun in the early twentieth century in the United States. Since then, hundreds of academically oriented students have received education in regular classes alongside their seeing peers.

Visually impaired students have special educational needs which result from their lack of vision. These needs must be recognized and met if the students are to receive a meaningful education anywhere. For many years educators assumed that the special needs of visually impaired students so altered their perceptions, conceptualizations, and acquisition of knowledge that they could best be taught in residential schools and segregated classes.

Today educators recognize that the needs of visually impaired students often can better be met in programs where the students are mainstreamed. Berthold Lowenfeld (1963) attributes the increase in the number of visually impaired students enrolled in public rather than residential schools to three factors: "the increasing integration of the blind into society, the American high regard for public school education, and the recognition of the importance of the family life for the individual child."

One of the reasons that mainstreaming as an approach to educating visually impaired students has grown in popularity is that it has economic advantages over the residential school approach. It costs less to educate students in their home communities than to provide twenty-four hour educational and housing facilities at a residential school.

Even special classes in local schools cost more than mainstreaming. William Smith (1971) pointed out that given the cost of operating classrooms specially set up to handle handicapped children, the shortage of certified special teachers, the evidence that special classes do not offer extra learning advantages, and the fact that many children do not belong there in

 Reprinted by permission of *Education of the Visually Handicapped*, Don L. Walker, Editor.

the first place, state and local officials have joined with those of us concerned with the problem of educating handicapped children, at the federal level, to seek realistic alternatives.

A second reason for the popularity of mainstreaming is that exposure to what is happening in regular classrooms has caused many special teachers to reevaluate their own programs and to experiment with new techniques, many of which prove to be more successful with their visually impaired students and make their programs more accountable. Regular classroom teachers in public schools tend to have higher expectations for their students' performance and tend to give their students a wider variety of experience than traditional programs for visually impaired students have provided in the past.

The personnel in residential schools and special day classes, threatened by the potential loss of students, actively resisted the establishment of mainstreaming programs in their communities for many years. Support came from other areas, however, as increasing numbers of parents resisted sending their children to programs that would stigmatize them as disabled and isolate them from mainstream education (Smith, 1971).

Many special schools and special classes have used outdated curricula and teaching methods, and it was often easier to establish new programs than to bring about the appropriate changes in the behavior of personnel in the existing programs. Opportunities thus were available to experiment with mainstreaming children. Consultants in state departments of education, responding to the requests of parents and local school districts, provided the leadership needed to affect a change. The three blind persons who were most influential in the development of the early programs were John Curtis of Chicago, George Meyer of Minneapolis and New Jersey, and Robert B. Irwin of Ohio and New York. Between the years 1900 and 1910, cooperative and resource programs were established in Chicago, Cincinnati, Milwaukee, Racine, Cleveland, Boston, New York, and Newark. Florence Henderson began California's first resource program in Long Beach, during the 1940s. The success of these programs is attributable primarily to the fact that they had outstanding teachers who really understood what was taking place in the regular classroom.

A few leaders from residential schools shared in the excitement of those early days of mainstreaming. The most enlightened of these leaders pointed out the constantly changing nature of the educational needs of visually impaired children and urged all professionals to keep an open mind to the implications of such changes. Only by such an approach, it was argued, could the educational system continue to function appropriately and effectively.

The philosophy that visually impaired children become an integral part of their community as early as possible received support from state legislatures, which in turn provided economic assistance to local school districts. For example, California in 1947 enacted legislation that required school districts to provide or contract for special educational services for physically handicapped minors and increased the level of state financial support to such districts (Misbach and Sweeney, 1970).

Many educators who believed in the philosophy of mainstreaming did not know how to implement it successfully. Often this was because they had mixed feelings about it. "In the field of the blind there are too many people whose hearts are in the right place but whose minds are muddled with too much emotion. There are far more people who talk about it than believe in it, and there are a lot more who believe in it intellectually, but who have not come to believe in it emotionally as well [Carroll, 1954]."

In selecting an appropriate model for program assessment it must be recognized that visually impaired students are functioning at all levels of intellectual and social strata found in education today. A model must be selected that has been successfully used with students having quite different intellectual and social skills. Precision teaching, because of its emphasis upon individual achievement and individual differences in behavior and social management offers the greatest potential for meaningful curriculum planning.

## Traditional Assessment of Visually Impaired Students

The importance of edumetric precision teaching techniques is even more apparent when contrasted with traditional testing programs. The tests that have been developed for use with sighted students are often inappropriate for use with visually impaired students because they frequently utilize visual, pictorial, or pattern representations.

> development of original tests for use with visually handicapped population is impractical because of the small number of subjects available for test refinement, and standardization. As of 1st January 1973, there were only 24,195 legally blind students enrolled in other than college programs throughout the United States and its provinces [Morris, 1974, p. 33].

Many test developers go to great lengths to obtain "representative" normative groups which their manuals describe in more or less detail. Visually impaired children seldom fit into these groups. Experiences are limited by overprotection, exclusion, lact of appropriate learning materials (Bauman, 1973).

The potential for significant future change would seem to lie in those techniques which can function within the school and home rather than in clinics, offices, and institutions. Current techniques, which can give promise of dealing successfully with those children who have spent time in the schools but who have failed to learn at a rate deemed possible or satisfactory, are still very much needed. Operant techniques offer only the techniques for changing behavior and do not resolve or even assist in the determination of which behaviors, or succession of behavioral goals, a school program should employ (Severson, 1975). Precision teaching can assist the teacher in proper classroom placement by carefully analyzing a student's level of academic performance.

There are serious potential pitfalls in mainstreaming programs. We must be certain that the programs are continuously and stringently evaluated. Keith Sterns and Stewart Swenson point to one potential problem when they say, "The major disadvantage of many resource programs is that they often become no more than part-time segregated classes and duplicate the curriculum of the regular classrooms [Sterns and Swenson, 1973, p. 8]."

Inadequate traditional tests may, in part, be responsible for the confusion as to which students should be mainstreamed and to what degree. Much of the controversy which surrounds traditional achievement tests for the visually impaired student is focused upon the instructions for the tester, and the modifications of the tests designed for normally seeing populations. Questions of validity and reliability are often addressed to the nature or lack of norms applied to the test results. Other problems to be considered are imprecise definitions of populations in terms of degree of visual impairment, ages of onset of visual impairment, and appropriate instructions to students.

According to Ozias (1975), the most popular and well known achievement instrument utilized with visually impaired students is the Stanford Achievement Test (SAT). The SAT was first published in 1923 and, by 1926, the American Printing House for the Blind (APH) had produced the first braille edition. Thus the adaptation and modification of achievement tests for the visually impaired, based upon the tests designed for the sighted, was on its way to being the model for the next quarter of a century. It was thirty-four years later that APH produced a large type edition of the SAT (Morris, 1974). It should be noted that the braille and large type editions, their norms, and their accompanying directions, do not correspond directly to the regular inkprint version.

The revised SAT in braille and large type includes an updated version of all batteries except the Primary Level 1, (because of its highly visual orientation). Some portions still depart drastically from the inkprint because of the limitations inherent in braille transcription.

Gallagher (1974) suggests that maturation in the field of special education appears to be in the generation of techniques and materials designed for the exceptional child, rather than in adaptations from techniques or materials designed for the normal child. This opens the issue of the potential usefulness of criterion-referenced achievement measurements as outlined in precision teaching manuals.

## Summary and Conclusions

Educating visually impaired students with seeing students is not a new idea. Many countries have pointed with pride to individual visually impaired students who have received almost all of their education in public schools with seeing peers. What is significant in educational reform is the large number of students being mainstreamed, our recognition of individual differences, individual rights, and improved strategies for assessing the impact of educational programs upon the total functioning of each student.

Educators of the visually impaired have been so preoccupied with the role of advocate that almost no evaluation of special programs has been attempted.

A problem in moving toward any change is that educators of the visually impaired have seldom been accountable for their efforts. It is very difficult to expect accountability for the individual resource or itinerant teacher who may be the only person in his or her school district with particular responsibilities or competencies which he or she has (Hatlen, 1975).

Traditional assessment measures for the visually impaired are adaptations of tests developed for use with the seeing and in many instances employ raised duplications of visual representations which are meaningless to the visually impaired. The norm-referenced scores which these tests yield do not provide educators with information that will assist in more appropriate curriculum planning. Criterion-referenced measurement specifies the absolute level or quality of performance of a student on some assessment task (Jones, 1973).

Precision teaching should have great appeal for special educators. It is a frequent complaint of special education teachers that, while the traditional assessment instruments communicate the individual's standing in relationship to others, they communicate little about actual skills and level of performance which would assist the teacher in curriculum development. Precision teaching techniques may be applied efficiently to psychological, sociological, and academic areas alike. An astronaut may consider traversing the universe a challenge because of the size of it; however, the precision teacher finds a universe with each pupil (Kunzelmann, 1970).

Precision teaching is a viable structure in which to assess the progress of individual students regardless of prevailing impairment. The major benefits are:

1. Special teachers can use their time with students more efficiently because this structure allows them to pinpoint student needs and monitor the effectiveness of their teaching strategies.
2. Communication between special educators is heightened and they can assist one another in problem-solving.
3. Improved communication between special teachers and regular teachers results in heightened assessment of the student's progress based on empirical data rather than hypothesized improvement based only on subjective evaluation.
4. The reinforcement schedule indicates to the student the correct behaviors for specific situations.

If educators are truly concerned about the large number of unemployed graduates of programs for the visually impaired, and about the fact that they lack well-developed personal management skills, they must initiate assessment procedures which illustrate our weaknesses as well as our strengths. Precision teaching is a viable structure for attaining this goal.

# Help for 10 Million Americans Who Suffer Speech Problems

*Interview With Dr. Christy L. Ludlow, Speech Pathologist*

**People who stutter and lisp in many cases find their social lives and career goals thwarted. But these handicaps may be overcome. Here, an authority tells how early detection and therapy can make life easier.**

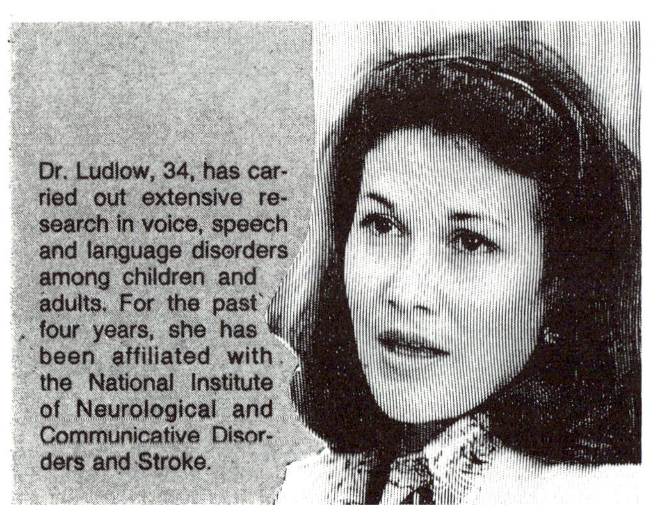

Dr. Ludlow, 34, has carried out extensive research in voice, speech and language disorders among children and adults. For the past four years, she has been affiliated with the National Institute of Neurological and Communicative Disorders and Stroke.

**Q Dr. Ludlow, how many Americans have speech impairments so severe that they require special attention?**

**A** An estimated 10 million children and adults suffer from speech and language problems. About 6 million of these receive treatment.

The problems include such things as stuttering, loss of speech as a result of stroke or disease, and what we call speech-articulation and voice disorders. The latter would include the tendency of some persons to lisp, to mispronounce sounds or to speak too loudly for normal conversation.

**Q Are problems more common among males, or females?**

**A** There are far more males who develop speech disorders than females—by a margin of about 4 to 1. As yet, we do not know why this difference exists.

**Q Do speech impediments result in psychological damage?**

**A** They frequently do. They cause a great deal of ridicule during school years and often foster shyness and lack of self-confidence. There's no easy way to live with a speech problem because it gets in the way of just about everything a person does. I know many people with speech difficulties who changed their professions because they felt they could not enter a career that involved a lot of talking. There is often discrimination in hiring against persons with speech defects, though employers may not do it consciously.

**Q Is stuttering the most common problem?**

**A** No, but it is one of the most noticeable impediments. Approximately 1 million persons in the U.S. are stutterers, and about 1 percent of all children stutter. It's among the most perplexing speech problems because we still do not know why it happens.

**Q Do you have any theories on the cause?**

**A** There seems to be a genetic predisposition to stuttering in about one quarter to one third of those who stutter, where the tendency to stutter may be passed along to successive generations. There are also psychological factors—a jarring or traumatic event, for example—that can sometimes precipitate stuttering, especially in childhood.

In addition, there is a period in the lives of all children in which they become "nonfluent": unable to say what they want to say without stammering. This usually occurs between ages 2 and 4 when children's speech becomes more complex, their grammar and vocabulary more sophisticated. Nearly all children recover from this period spontaneously.

There are also stutterers whose thoughts simply seem to race ahead of their ability to articulate them. We call this cluttering, when people run their words together so rapidly that they become incomprehensible to others.

**Q What happens to the voice mechanism in stuttering?**

**A** There's a temporary, spasmodic contraction of the muscles of the vocal mechanism: a general tightening of the larynx and oral structures, a tension in the neck and facial muscles, and very small tremors in the lips and tongue.

Recent studies show that stutterers do not coordinate the sound produced by the lips and tongue with the initiation of voice from the larynx. For example, a stutterer may be able to make a "p" sound with his lips but be unable to back it up immediately with vocal sound to complete the word.

**Q What therapy is there for stutterers?**

**A** Relaxation techniques are most often employed. We teach people to speak more slowly, to breathe into a word



Reprinted from *U.S. News & World Report*, Vol. LXXV, No. 10, September 11, 1978. Copyright 1978 U.S. News & World Report, Inc.

very gradually instead of pushing right away into a sound. We have also tried biofeedback techniques to reduce tension with some success. In a few instances, very potent relaxation drugs have helped, but we don't usually recommend this avenue because the drugs often have severe side effects.

**Q How high is the success rate after treatment?**

**A** Nearly all stutterers show some improvement after therapy. Roughly half of the children who stutter at the age of 8 can be cured before reaching adulthood. Most of the others may not eliminate their stuttering entirely but can improve to the point where their ability to communicate effectively is not impaired.

Among adults who stutter, the problem is more difficult because many have learned tricks to help them speak which must be eliminated before the therapist can start to work on the stuttering directly. Also, often a person can completely lose his stuttering behavior, then slip back into old habits—and the stuttering reappears.

**Q Are there special clinics to treat stuttering?**

**A** Yes. The American Speech and Hearing Association in Rockville, Md., is a professional society that certifies approved clinics and provides lists of therapists around the U.S. on request.

**Q How long is the normal course of therapy?**

**A** A residential program might require two weeks of intensive group and individual counseling for an individual. Other stutterers may progress over a course of scheduled appointments with a speech therapist. We find that the best method is intense treatment at the beginning and then a long weaning period to reinforce the relaxation techniques.

**Q How should people react to a person who stutters?**

**A** The key is not to get nervous or jittery: Don't look away, tap fingers, suggest a word or finish the sentence. Anything indicating that the listener is uncomfortable will make a stuttering problem worse. The best approach is to remain calm and let the person complete the sentence.

**Q When should parents worry about a child who stutters?**

**A** All children should begin speaking by 2 years of age. Their speech should be easy to understand by the time they are 4. If a child has any speech defect by the time he enters kindergarten, parents should seek out a speech pathologist.

Very often the problem is a minor one, but tension between the parents and child can make it worse. If parents find themselves asking a child to repeat something over and over or if the child seems to avoid saying certain words or sounds, that is a signal to get professional help.

**Q What are other common problems in speech?**

**A** Speech-articulation difficulties are the most widespread. About 3½ percent of schoolchildren receive help for this type of problem, in which speech sounds are substituted or distorted or omitted entirely.

**Q Could you give some examples?**

**A** The lisp is fairly typical. Lisps occur when a sound is produced in a different area of the mouth—so that it's noticeable to others. They are among the most common speech problems, especially among children.

Deaf children have great difficulty with speech development because they can't model their own speech on the voices of others. Then there are birth defects such as a cleft palate or a malocclusion of the teeth that often produce distorted or nasalized sounds. Often this can be corrected by a surgeon or dentist.

**Q What are the most difficult sounds for children to learn?**

**A** In the English language, they are the "r," "l" and "s" sounds. Many children who encounter trouble with these consonants cannot tell the difference between the error that they're making and the normal expected sound.

Speech therapy. "If a child seems to avoid saying certain words or sounds, that is a signal to get professional help."

**Q What kind of therapy helps these children?**

**A** Teaching children to listen to the differences between the speech sounds is most often used. We teach a child to know what sound is desired. Children listen closely to that sound and are taught the correct position of mouth and tongue to reproduce it. Then we teach them how to monitor themselves so that they will avoid the incorrect sound.

**Q Is this treatment available in the schools?**

**A** In most school districts, yes. And speech therapy will become even more available in educational institutions under the new federal law that mandates that public-school systems must provide services for anybody with a handicap.

**Q What happens to speech when someone becomes deaf?**

**A** Deafness causes significant problems. The speech of a person who has gone completely deaf will be affected within a month of the hearing loss, and maintenance of proper speech modulation will be difficult if it is not dealt with early. However, it is possible to retain good speech after deafness occurs. By using instruments and learning to judge the loudness and pitch of the voice, deaf people can monitor their voice levels so that they know just how much force to put behind their speech.

**Q Do stroke victims often have speech difficulties?**

**A** Yes. Language loss, or aphasia, occurs in about one fourth of all stroke victims. The impairment usually follows severe damage to the left side of the brain, where the brain centers controlling speech and language are contained in nearly all individuals. It seems that stroke victims lose the "code" that allows them to use language—put words in the right order and connect meanings.

The severely impaired aphasic patient cannot even decipher speech. It's like being in a foreign country where you don't know the language and can't learn it. It is a very serious problem. There are at least a million and a half persons in the U.S. with aphasia.

**Q What can be done for them?**

**A** We don't teach language to people who have lost it; rather, we facilitate what remains. The most effective way is to stimulate them with language materials, visual symbols, and reading and writing. Everyone has some recovery of language after a stroke, and what the therapist does is to heighten the natural recovery process as much as possible: show people how to use what language is left as best they can.

**Q** **Is there help for those who lose parts of their vocal equipment, such as the tongue or larynx?**

**A** People are quite adaptable to such handicaps.

Many who have had most of their tongue removed can still produce acceptable speech. Great progress is being made in teaching laryngectomy patients to use the back of the throat or the esophagus to make sounds. There are even artificial larynxes that can be hand-held or implanted in the throat to generate sound.

**Q** **Can speech reveal the onset of nonvocal disease?**

**A** Yes. Many degenerative neurological diseases among adults disrupt the neuromotor patterns of speech production and can produce early symptoms in the form of slurred or inarticulate speech. These diseases include Parkinson's disease, multiple sclerosis and Huntington's chorea.

Speech can be a valuable diagnostic tool, and it's an expanding area of research.

**Q** **People, especially children, seem to be shouting more these days rather than talking in a normal tone of voice—**

**A** This problem is of growing concern to speech pathologists. More children seem to shout rather than talk in a normal tone. Of course, all children shout when they get excited or happy or involved in a competitive game, but some children seem to shout nearly all of the time. If this continues over a long period, it strains the larynx and produces small growths called nodules on the vocal cords, causing the child's voice to get husky. The condition can be irreversible if the larynx is sufficiently damaged.

**Q** **Does this occur among adults?**

**A** Singers without professional training often have voice disorders. The late rock singer Janis Joplin was a classic example of someone who overused her voice to the point that she literally became aphonic: She could not speak.

But most singers consult regularly with therapists and learn to adjust the tension in their larynx and control their voice so that nodules do not appear.

**Q** **Can the nodules be removed surgically?**

**A** Yes, but they usually disappear when the patient is simply told not to speak at all for a period of time. We recommend surgery only as a last resort.

# St-st-st-st-st-st-Stuttering

## Help is on the way
## with computers, stopwatches, videotapes.

**By Maya Pines**

"My name is Richard—I could never say, it before, so I had to say Dick . . . ." Though he had stuttered nearly constantly since he was 5, the bearded young man was talking quite normally during a party to celebrate the end of a three-week crash course to eliminate stuttering. "I always liked that name, Richard," he repeated, with obvious pleasure in the sound of it. "For me, the program will really start tomorrow, when I leave," he added. "I know I'll have to keep on practicing what I've learned here. There will always be the possibility of going back to stuttering—but now I know how to control it."

The party was held at the Hollins Communications Research Institute, a small building in Roanoke, Va., across the street from the campus of Hollins, a women's college. The dozen students had just completed an intensive, $750 course, called the Precision Fluency Shaping Program, that made them relearn basic speech patterns with the help of computers, videotape machines, field trips and coaching by speech therapists. Most of the dozen students had tried many other therapies before and were so skeptical of this new one that they had kept their plans secret from relatives and friends. "I didn't tell anyone why I was going to Roanoke," remarked a 40-ish car dealer from Louisiana, the oldest student in the group. "They asked, 'Why Roanoke?' I said I just wanted to see Roanoke, that it was a fascinating place, but they didn't even know where it was!"

The students' handicap, so often treated as a joke, had embarrassed them too often. Some of these people felt unable to order food in a restau-rant. Others could not make telephone calls. One woman had been denied a job because of her stutter. A young man had put off a dreaded interview for admission to graduate school until he had taken the Hollins program. All lived in fear of the sudden, strangling block in their throats that could make them produce ridiculous sounds whenever they tried to say anything.

Some two million American adults—roughly 1 percent of the population—go through such experiences several times a day. Several million children do so as well, since stuttering usually begins in early childhood, when children are just learning to speak. By early adolescence, however, three-quarters of the children are mysteriously cured without any help. For those whose stuttering persists into adulthood, there are real difficulties, because stuttering is notoriously resistant to treatment and exasperatingly quick to recur. And no one really understands what causes it.

It is the subject of violent disagreement among all the therapists who try to help stutterers: speech pathologists, psychologists and psychiatrists. The more traditional ones believe that people stutter for psychological reasons—because of parental pressures about proper speech in childhood, for instance, or because of deep-seated emotional conflicts (of which stuttering just happens to be a symptom). They note that stutterers can usually speak quite clearly to their friends and have no trouble addressing their dogs —but stutter severely when confronted with people in authority.

Other speech therapists seek phy-

*Maya Pines's most recent book is "The Brain Changers: Scientists and the New Mind Control."*

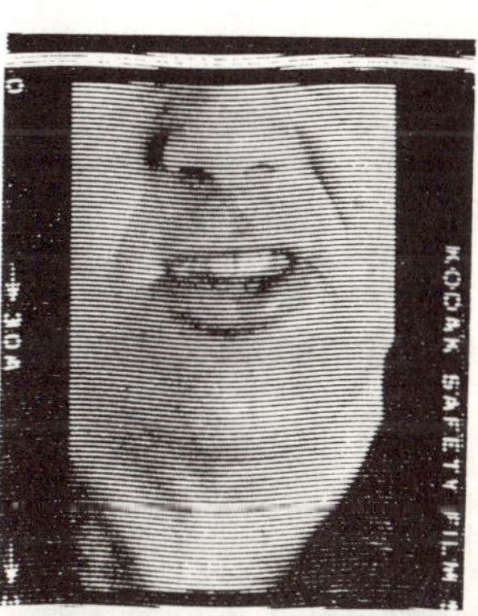
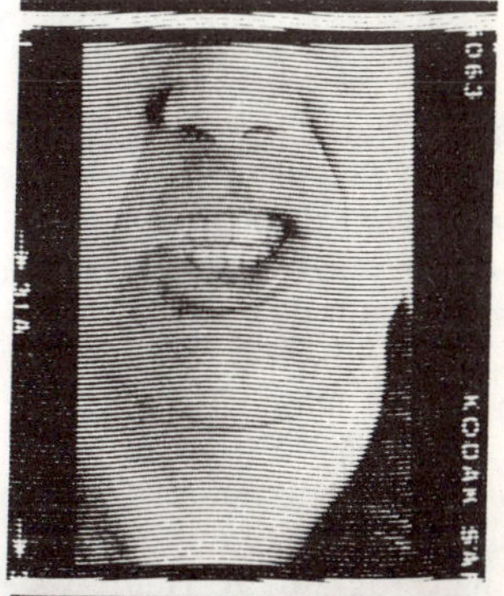
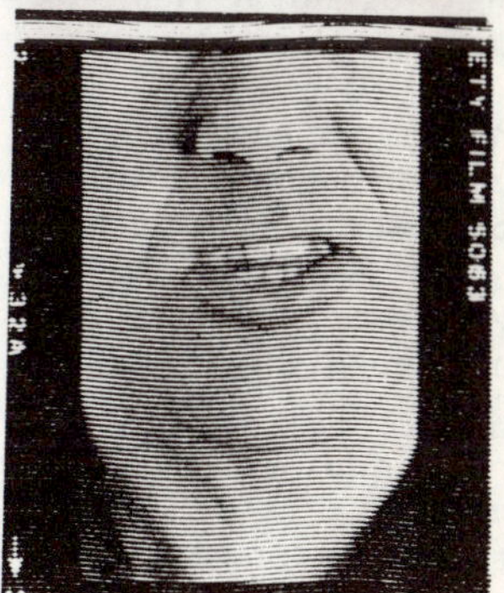

©1977 by *The New York Times* Company. Reprinted by permission.

sical causes for stuttering. They point to the fact that there are at least four times as many men as women who stutter, an indication that the predisposition may be genetic and sex-linked. It cannot be just a psychological problem, they add, since stutterers almost never stutter when they sing, even under the stress of singing in public, and also do miraculously well when speaking to the beat of a metronome, regardless of their emotional state.

Until very recently, most therapists agreed that about one-third of adult stutterers could be greatly improved or cured, one-third somewhat improved, and the rest could not be helped. In the pessimism bred by these figures, they generally focused on eliminating their patients' *fear* of stuttering, rather than the stuttering itself.

Now a small group of therapists has begun to attack stuttering more aggressively, concentrating almost entirely on the physical side of the problem. Whatever its roots, they say, stuttering is a series of learned motor responses which can usually be unlearned through training. And they proceed to teach entirely new ways of speaking, with the help of technological aids. The new programs seem to work in an unusually large number of cases. The Precision Fluency Shaping Program at Hollins, for example, claims success with about 80 percent of its students, despite some relapses. And although it is still controversial, it has been adopted by the Walter Reed Medical Center as well as by speech therapists in several schools around the country.

The program was created by Dr. Ronald Webster, a rather dry and precise professor of psychology at Hollins, after he had spent years making a detailed analysis of stuttering speech. "Speech is awfully complex, so we break it down into many small and easy steps and teach these one at a time,"

he says. Each new skill — whether it involves breathing, voice quality or articulation— must be learned precisely, and each one builds on the one that preceded it, in a tight sequence. Each skill is exaggerated at first and then toned down.

The students' most difficult task is also their first one: slowing down their speech as drastically as Webster requires. This is necessary, Webster explains, in order to hear and work with individual components of speech; they cannot be isolated when people speak at normal rates. The students, equipped with stopwatches, practice in soundproof cubicles in 20-minute stretches, learning to make syllables such as "on" or "my" last for a full two seconds each — "ooooooonnnnnnn" — a nearly unendurable stretch of time. Next, they learn to breathe slowly and deeply, using their abdominal muscles rather than those of the upper chest (Webster has found that stutterers often have problems with their breathing).

Only when they have mastered both these tasks are they ready to work on the skill which Webster considers most critical: making the voice gentler at the beginning of each syllable and then raising it less suddenly than they did before. "There is definitely something wrong with the way stutterers try to start voicing," says Webster. "It's abrupt and excessively forceful, which makes their vocal folds [the valves in their throats] snap shut and prevents their voices from starting again." In every case that he has ever seen, he says, stutterers who succeed in making their voices start up more gently can speak fluently as a result.

A few years ago, Webster designed a small, individual computer, called a voice monitor, that analyzes the gentleness of one's voice and flashes a green light if it is acceptable. By now, he has dozens of these black, radiosized voice monitors. They are

the heart of his program. Beginning on the third day, students may spend as much as six hours practicing lists of individual vowels, consonants, syllables and then words with the voice monitor until they have made approximately 50,000 correct responses. At first, they speak very slowly, with each syllable stretched to two seconds, then they change the monitor setting to one second and, finally, toward the end of the program, for continuous "slow normal" speech with half-second syllables. But at all times they concentrate on their speech onset and subsequent rise in volume. "Aaaahhhhh," went one of the students, demonstrating a voice monitor for me quite loudly. "You see, the light doesn't come on if you have too quick a rise in your voice."

Throughout this process, the students are guided by two therapists and an assistant. (Webster merely supervises.) One of the staff therapists, Ross Barrett, is probably the best walking advertisement for the course. He was a stockbroker until four years ago, when he went to Roanoke to take Webster's program. While correcting his stutter, he found a new vocation. He went back to school, earned a master's degree in speech pathology at the University of Cincinnati, and eventually returned to Hollins.

"I'd been through a lot before that," he says. "I'd tried some traditional speech therapy at a speech and hearing clinic—you know, the psychological kind of therapy, where you discuss what type of problems you have with your speech. That didn't work, so I went to a hypnotist. Then I tried a psychologist. Next, a psychiatrist. I even went to a faith healer. Most stutterers do that: They start with the traditional approach, then go farther and farther out, grasping for whatever seems to hold any hope, because it's all so baffling—you can speak fluently at times, and at other times you can't. Here, at least,

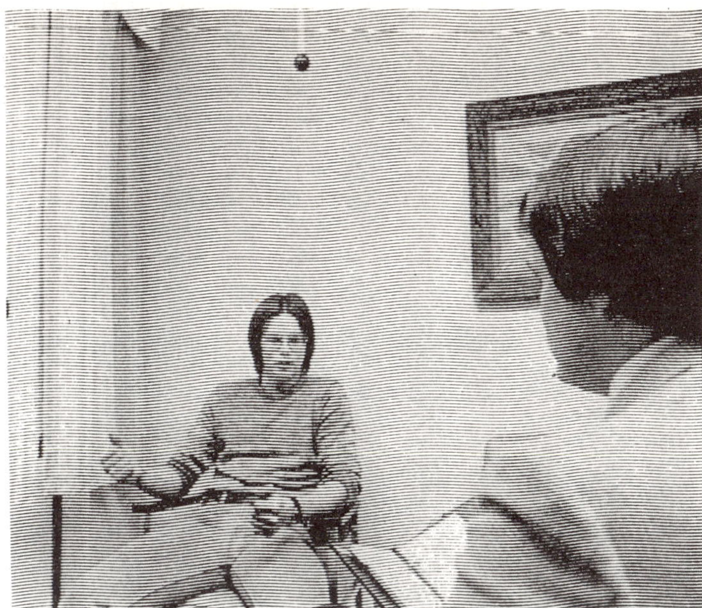

*Concentrating very hard, a stutterer practices vowel sounds with Hollins speech pathologist Ross Barrett, who himself stuttered before taking the Hollins program.*

we teach exactly what to do with your speech to maintain fluency."

Stuttering is so peculiar a disorder that all too often what works in the clinic or lab suddenly becomes inoperative in the real world. A friend who once participated in a research project in stuttering remembers doing speech exercises in a small cubicle several times a week for months. "I g-g-got so that the m-m-m-minute I stepped in that room I did not stutter," he says. "But, hell, I c-c-c-can go home and stay in an empty room and I wo-wo-won't stutter either! The pr-pr-problem was that it wo-wo-wo-worked only while I was in that room."

Webster encountered the same problem when he started to work with stutterers a decade ago. It was relatively easy to make them speak fluently in the laboratory, but he confesses that he was "spectacularly unsuccessful" in teaching them to speak well anywhere else. Therefore, his students are now expected to use their new skills in conversation, in short public speeches before the whole group, and in required encounters with an instrument

that many of them dread — the telephone.

"P-p-p-people hang up if you uh-uh-uh, if you, uh, s-s-stutter too much over the phone," a young man told me, explaining why he never used the telephone. Every stutterer has had unpleasant experiences with it, yet Webster finds it particularly effective as a teaching device. At first, the students make telephone calls only to each other, to practice specific sounds and phrases. But by the end of the course, when their speech begins to sound less bizarre (it just might pass for slow normal speech), they begin to brave the outside world through hundreds of phone calls.

"How . . . late . . . are . . . you . . . open?" each student asks with agonizing slowness as he calls some 50 different stores, restaurants or movie theaters in the area. Alternatively, he may ask, "What . . . time . . . do . . . you . . . close?" I figured that this adds up to about 600 slow-motion calls on the subject in a week. It must drive local merchants crazy, and Webster is embarrassed about it.

Each student also makes about 150 less structured phone calls, mostly in re-

sponse to want ads. The student's side of the conversation is recorded on tape, so the therapists can hear it later. On the last day of the program, I watched an electronics technician from California call about some kittens for sale, and a former pipe fitter on North Sea oil rigs call a tire dealer. Both spoke haltingly, with enormous care, as if treading on eggs. I asked the pipe fitter whether all that concentration on speaking properly didn't interfere with thinking about what he had to say. "*Any* time I've ever spoken, any time I've opened my mouth, I've had to think about stuttering," he replied slowly. "I've had to think about the next word I'm likely to block on and change that word. So I'm used to it. But they say if we practice every day, after we go home, it will eventually become automatic."

The final step, a sort of ordeal by fire, is a series of escorted trips to a shopping center, where students approach strangers to request information while the therapist takes notes. Like the telephone calls, this serves to diagnose their reactions to stress and identify which targets they still need practice on.

Then comes the moment when students see a last-minute videotape of themselves reading and speaking and compare it to the videotape that was made on the day they entered the program. It is not always a happy time. There was not much difference between the two tapes made by one 16-year-old boy, for instance. He had stuttered so badly and struggled so hard on the first tape that his eyes bulged and perspiration showed on his face; he stuttered nearly as much on his last tape. According to the therapists, he had not worked hard enough and would have to repeat the course. Several other students spoke in a robotlike monotone, though they did not stutter. One young woman was clearly disappointed when she heard herself. "It sounded expressionless," she said. "I don't like it." She hoped that the monotone would disappear with time.

For some, the experience was exhilarating. One blond woman in blue jeans, a graduate student, watched and listened to herself in complete silence. "How does it sound?" I asked her. "Not bad," she replied at first, and then with sudden emotion exclaimed, "I've changed so much! God, am I glad!" and hugged her therapist. The Louisiana car dealer said simply, "I'm happier than any time in my life, because of this."

One could only hope it would last. When I asked Webster how he rated their chances, he replied that regressions were possible, as with any motor skills. It all depended on what they did after they went home — whether they practiced on tape recorders and sent in their tapes as required, whether they stabilized their new skills, or whether they got carried away and speeded up too soon. Their monotone did not worry him, he said, for such peculiarities nearly always disappeared within six months after the program. Recently, he completed a follow-up study of 200 out of 329 persons who had been through his program between 1971 and 1974 (a total of about 800 persons have taken the course). They were simply the first 200 he reached by phone after trying three times. His staff checked them first about 10 months after the end of the program, and then rechecked half of them at random two years later. Each discussed what he was doing and read from a magazine or newspaper. The staff then scored the tapes for "disfluencies" (any word on which one could hear forced breathing, repetition of a sound or syllable, a struggle with speech onset, a silent stop, or a repetition of an entire word).

Ten months after treatment, he found, 81.5 percent of the cases scored in the normal range while reading (compared to 94.5 percent on the last day of the course) and 73.5 percent scored in the normal range in conversation (compared to 85 percent on the last day). At the two-year follow-up, these figures had decreased to 80 percent and 73 percent —still far above their scores on entering the program.

According to an article published two years ago, Annie Glenn, the wife of Senator John Glenn of Ohio, the former astronaut, was cured of stuttering by the Hollins program. I decided to call her up, as well as a few other graduates, to do a small follow-up of my own. To my dismay, when I asked to speak to Mrs. Glenn she replied, "Th-th-th-this is Annie." She still stuttered quite severely, though she maintained that the Hollins program had helped her more than any other and blamed only herself for her relapse. "If you had talked to me three years ago [when she finished the program] you would have noticed a tremendous difference," she said, explaining that for the past two years she had been far too busy to practice half an hour a day. Nevertheless, she had retained some real gains: Before going to Roanoke, she was terrified of the telephone, she said, and her husband had to make every call for her. "Now I can make telephone calls for him," she declared. "It's wonderful!"

Other Hollins graduates I called were still doing well, including a 16-year-old boy who was 9 when he went through the program and now has no speech problem whatsoever.

"We don't cure people in the sense that we get at the cause of their stuttering, but we teach them compensatory behavior," emphasizes Webster. "There is an awful lot still to be sorted out. One of our problems in stuttering research is that the level of our measurement is still pretty gross—it's based largely on what you and I hear; we should go beyond that. The voice monitor is a step in the right direction. But we need a computer system that can make a far more detailed judgment of responses, so that it can write individual prescriptions for each stutterer. We're only just getting going." Webster believes, with many others, that stutterers are born with some physical predisposition to it—perhaps a minor defect in the system that provides feedback about their own speech. There is some evidence for this view. In the Hollins lab I tried on some special earphones that prevented me from hearing the sound of my own voice until a fraction of a second later. When asked to read out loud, I managed a few choppy words despite the peculiar delay. But when Webster asked me to say, "Thermodynamics," I suddenly heard myself stuttering, "Thermo-mo-dynamics," and to my surprise, exclaimed, "It's impossible!" Most non-stutterers, who are exposed to a 0.2 second delay in auditory feedback find that they will stutter. Yet stutterers have the opposite reaction: The very same delay turns them into fluent speakers—while it lasts. This implies that there may be something wrong with their feedback loop so anything that prevents a stutterer from hearing his own voice seems to help, including loud "white noise" (like someone saying, "Sh-sh") and deafness. Fluent speakers who go deaf usually become sloppy in their speech, as if they depended on feedback from their own voices, but stutterers who go deaf speak better. Rhythmic beats, as from a metronome, also decrease stuttering, perhaps because they settle the matter of when to speak and reduce the need to rely on auditory feedback.

No one seems to know what the physical predisposition to stuttering—if it exists—might consist of. Webster's own theory—"just a conjecture," he says—is that the muscles of the middle ear are to blame. He has found some indications that among stutterers these muscles contract after the onset of speech, rather than before it, as with normal speakers. Other researchers blame different mechanisms, such as the muscles of the lips and larynx, which they train people to relax through biofeedback.

Dr. Martin F. Schwartz, a research associate professor at N.Y.U. Medical Center, who claims he has "cured" 89 percent of his patients, believes that stuttering begins with a locking of the vocal cords in response to fear, and that the repetitions and blocks of stutterers are actually attempts to unlock these cords. His remedy is to have stutterers inhale and exhale just before beginning to speak, then speak extremely slowly. He, too, emphasizes the need for daily practice to reinforce what he teaches in his one-week training course (which includes practice in shops and restaurants). He is considered even more controversial than Webster, however, largely because he just wrote a book whose title other therapists consider outrageous: "Stuttering Solved."

Another therapy that has become popular recently is the use of a tiny metronome, which is worn like a hearing aid. Stutterers practice speaking in time with the beat, first at a very slow rate and then at more normal speeds, until they learn to do without a metronome altogether.

All such gadgets and speaking tricks are offensive to therapists who emphasize the psychological factor. For one, Dr. Joseph G. Sheehan, a professor of psychology at U.C.L.A., stuttering is "a conflict between expressing yourself and holding back"—as when rats oscillate between their drive for food and their fear of electric shocks. He is skeptical of easy solutions. Eugene Walle, of the Speech and Hearing Clinic at the Catholic University in Washington, D.C., derides Webster and other physically oriented therapists for teaching people "to talk like zombies." He sees them taking stuttering "back to the dark ages of therapy," the early years of the century when commercial stammering schools proliferated, giving gimmicky courses, promising rapid cures and moving on before the inevitable relapses. Walle and Charles Van Riper, a leading spokesman of the more traditional approach who recently retired from Western Michigan University, pin their hopes mainly on early prevention of stuttering in children between the ages of 2 and 6.

Only a century ago, doctors cut the tongues of stutterers, on the theory that people stuttered because their tongues were too long. Fifty years ago, children who stuttered were whipped for it. Today, the chances of early prevention are growing. The quality of research on stuttering is improving. All in all, thanks to the new therapies, this is the best time in history to be an incipient, or even an adult, stutterer — despite the fact that to this day, as a confirmed stutterer put it, "No one r-r-really has th-th-the answer."

# Developing IEP's for Physically Handicapped Students: A Transdisciplinary Viewpoint

**BARBARA SIRVIS**

The individualized education program (IEP) has been identified as a solution—and a problem—for professional special educators. Designed to enhance appropriate educational programing, it also brings to the forefront many of the problems previously encountered in attempts to provide interdisciplinary programing and evaluation for special children. Although much of the information in this article can be applied to other disability areas, it is specifically oriented toward the numerous professionals from many disciplines who may work more with students with orthopedic and other health impairments. The purpose here is to explore the aspects of the IEP that relate to the need for extensive input by these professionals. Initially, it is essential to identify the areas that are crucial to an understanding of the development of the IEP for this population: (1) definition of the population, (2) appropriate skill areas, (3) the transdisciplinary approach as a new approach for intervention, and (4) roles of transdisciplinary team members, parents, and, when feasible, students in the development and implementation of the IEP.



Reprinted from *Teaching Exceptional Children* by Barbara Sirvis by permission of The Council for Exceptional Children.
Copyright ©1978 The Council for Exceptional Children, 1920 Association Drive, Reston, Virginia, 22091.

## DEFINING THE POPULATION

The rules and regulations for Public Law 94-142 define this group of students in two categories:

> "Orthopedically impaired" means a severe orthopedic impairment which adversely affects a child's educational performance. The term includes impairments caused by congenital anomaly (e.g., clubfoot, absence of some member, etc.), impairments caused by disease, (e.g., poliomyelitis, bone tuberculosis, etc.), and impairments from other cause (e.g., cerebral palsy, amputation, and fractures or burns which cause contractures.
>
> "Other health impaired" means limited strength, vitality or alertness due to chronic or acute health problems such as a heart condition, tuberculosis, rheumatic fever, nephritis, asthma, sickle cell anemia, hemophilia, epilepsy, lead poisoning, leukemia, or diabetes, which adversely affects a child's educational performance. (p. 42478)

It is important to note that these students may also have associated disabilities, e.g., mental retardation, learning disabilities, visual and/or hearing impairments, or social-emotional problems. These single and multiple disabilities require adaptation of curricular and instructional strategies which, thus, qualifies these students for special educational services. In addition, many of these students have need for unique, diverse, and often extensive services from several different disciplines.

Reynolds and Birch (1977) noted that this is a somewhat artificial grouping of students because their special instructional needs do not necessarily provide a rationale for bringing them together. They suggest a linkage between physiological, psychological, *and* educational manifestations that may be useful in understanding planning for this population. They cite Stevens (1962) in reference to the definition of impairment, disability, and handicap. *Impairment* refers to the actual physical defect, the condition of the tissue, e.g., absence of limb, cardiac disease, or progressive muscular dystrophy. *Disability* refers to the dysfunction, or lack of ability, manifested by the person with an impairment. *Handicap* is the extent to which the disability becomes a barrier to a "normal way of life," including education.

It is the handicap that is unique to an individual and involves only his or her reactions to the disability. Thus, it is the purpose of this article to examine potential handicaps, i.e., psychological and educational manifestations. It might even be said that one role of the teacher and the entire transdisciplinary team in the development of the IEP is to help the physically disabled student to develop a positive self concept and to encourage motivation, both of which will help to avert the development of an educationally and psychologically handicapping condition.

## APPROPRIATE SKILL AREAS

In order to avoid these potential handicaps, meaningful educational programing for physically disabled students is dependent on accurate assessment data about current levels of performance in skill areas that relate to adaptation:

- Gross motor — general mobility or ambulation.
- Fine motor — including eye-hand coordination.
- Self help — feeding, toileting, dressing.
- Cognitive — preacademic and academic.
- Communication — receptive and expressive (including alternative communication systems for nonvocal students).
- Social — the ability to interact appropriately with others.
- Prevocational/vocational — career potential.
- Recreation — leisure time.

Assessment data will have several applications: (1) clear statement of the child's current ability level, (2) precise identification of the crucial skills to be learned, and (3) specific programing suggestions. For appropriate educational programing and maximum skill development, input and intervention from a variety of disciplines will be crucial. (Sirvis & Edgar, 1978)

## TEAM ROLES AND APPROACHES

In this period of transition as IEP's are first being developed, it is necessary to explore the implementation of a process that will facilitate communication between disciplines. More for the physically disabled student than for those with other handicapping conditions, those disciplines represented are likely to be numerous and to include — but not be limited to — special and regular education teachers, communication disorders specialists, social workers, school psychologists, school principals, school counselors, vocational rehabilitation counselors, physical and occupational therapists, pediatric neurologists, orthopedists, recreation therapists, and community agency representatives.

Public Law 94-142 defines *unrelated services* as "transportation and such developmental, corrective, and other supportive services . . . as may be required to assist a handicapped child to benefit from special education. . . ." The rules and regulations

## 6. PHYSICALLY

identify and define the following specific related services:

> audiology, counseling services, early identification, medical services, occupational therapy, parent counseling and training, physical therapy, psychological services, recreation, school health services, social work services in schools, speech pathology, and transportation (pp. 42479-42480).

These services must be provided as required by the unique needs of the child to enhance the effectiveness of educational instruction. The development process of the IEP requires input by all professional persons who may be involved in the provision of services, as well as by parents. The IEP is not only a written statement for a specific physically disabled student, but it is also an intermediary step in a cyclical educational process that begins with assessment and concludes with implementation and continuous evaluation for sequential reconstruction of an individualized education program:

Assessment ⟶ IEP ⟶ Individual Program Plan ⟶ Evaluation ⟶

The IEP is part of a specific planning process designed to provide systematic organization for educational planning so the end result is individualized, student oriented, and provides a composite statement of a comprehensive plan for the child.

Thomas and Marshall (1977) outlined an "ecological approach" to clinical evaluation and coordination of services. They noted that successful adaptation—physical *and* social—is the primary goal of an intervention model and that the process of adaptation varies from individual to individual and family to family. However, they noted commonalities that exist: information gathering, data pooling, initial programing, and periodic reassessment and program modification. They emphasized the need for communication between the child, his or her family, *and* agency personnel. The concepts of adaptability and flexibility do not end with the child and his or her family but rather extend to all areas of the agency in order to facilitate efforts to meet the unique needs of the child.

Historically, intervention for orthopedically and health impaired children evolved from a medical treatment model. Gradually, the relevance and necessity for educational programing was recognized, but the disciplines often continued to work separately with each child. Varying responsibilities and administrative structures (e.g., school district, public health system, hospital) probably affected—and may still continue to affect—transdisciplinary efforts. Communication often involved only the sharing of written progress reports, each in the respective discipline's own jargon and not readily understood by the other. Although all involved parties agreed that the child's individual needs were the basis for their procedures, communication was not necessarily enhanced by this model.

Weintraub (1977) noted another historical problem related to the relatively small input allowed the teacher in planning/decision making for program delivery. He suggested that such decisions traditionally have been made by psychologists, physicians, social workers, and/or administrators with little regard for the child's performance in the classroom, the skills of the teacher, the learning environment, and the available support services. For example, if a child had a physical disability and thus qualified for placement in a special school for the physically handicapped, it was often assumed that this was the most appropriate placement. Alternatives were not always considered.

## THE TRANSDISCIPLINARY APPROACH

Collaboration at a more sophisticated level, i.e., with disciplines working together in development of programs, should be facilitated by the IEP process. Transdisciplinary means "of, or relating

TABLE I

**Toward a Transdisciplinary Stance**

| | | |
|---|---|---|
| I. | Possessing a sound preparation and competency in one's own discipline. | UNIDISCIPLINARY |
| II. | Believing that (even alone) you and others in your discipline can make an important contribution to the habilitation of individuals at risk or with known neuromotor and neurosensory handicaps and/or mental retardation. | INTRADISCIPLINARY |
| III. | Recognizing that other disciplines, also, have important contributions to make to the habilitation of individuals at risk, or with known neuromotor and neurosensory handicaps and/or mental retardation. | MULTIDISCIPLINARY |
| IV. | Enunciating an activating philosophy that comprehensive services based on the habilitation needs of the individual must be made available to all who are handicapped. | |
| V. | Willing and able to work with other disciplines in the development of jointly planned programs for individuals and groups, and to assume responsibility for providing needed disciplinary services and treatment, as a part of the total habilitation program. | INTERDISCIPLINARY |
| VI. | Committing yourself to teaching/learning/working together with other providers of services across traditional disciplinary boundaries. | TRANSDISCIPLINARY |

to a transfer of information, knowledge, or skills across disciplinary boundaries" (United Cerebral Palsy Associations, 1976, p. 1). The transdisciplinary approach attempts to break the traditional rigidity of discipline boundaries and to encourage a teaching/learning process between team members. It supports the development of a staff that functions with greater unity in meeting the needs of the physically disabled student and his or her family or advocate (see Table 1).

*Note.* From *Staff Development Handbook: A Resource for the Transdisciplinary Process,* United Cerebral Palsy Associations, 1976.

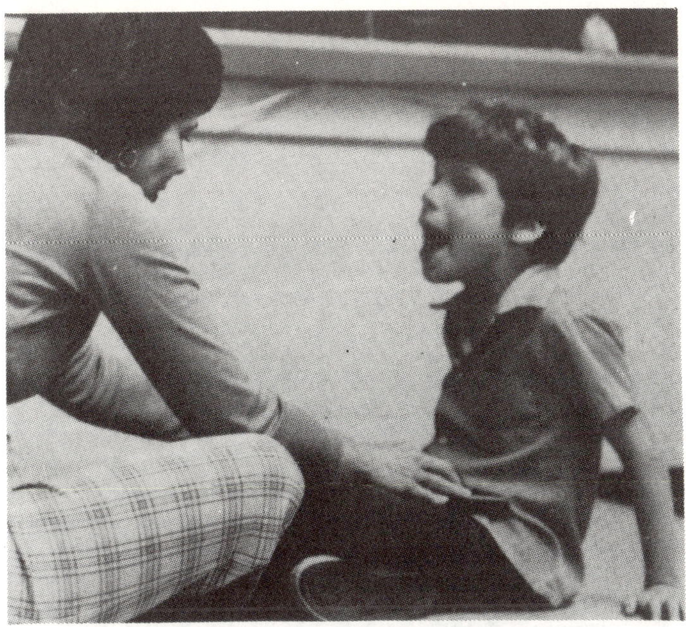

Williamson (1978) identified four factors that influence the movement toward more exchange of knowledge and function between disciplines:

- Decreased "splintering" of the child into segments along disciplinary lines, e.g., the old saying "the hands to the occupational therapist, the legs to the physical therapist, and the brain to the teacher."

- Increased communication among team members.

- Reduced number of professional contacts that the child must endure and facilitation of a trusting relationship with only one or two practitioners.

- Increased services to children regardless of fiscal constraint, e.g., when budgetary restrictions limit the number of full time personnel, some disciplines may still provide input on a consultative basis.

None of these considerations are meant to imply that one individual or discipline assumes total responsibility for a child's program but rather that team members share information and, when appropriate, skills to insure consistency in the child's program.

Jones and Brazelton (1977) provided several examples of the transdisciplinary process in action:

> One teacher indicated that she was able to help the physician in understanding the child because, in seeing him from day to day, performance not demonstrated in a testing situation could be taken into account. For example, in one case a severely physically handicapped child was thought to be mentally retarded because of his behavior in the physician's testing situation. The teacher could report excellent problem solving when the child was not under pressure and was not afraid of failing. (p. 9)

> The therapist contributed to the teacher techniques for handling and positioning children, physical games that lend themselves to simple group activity. Conversely, the teacher contributed to the therapist what concepts the child seemed to be learning so that the therapist could use appropriate materials in her individual work with the child. (p. 9)

Parents and professionals can assist each other in the development of individualized education programs by collecting written data that provide information related to their own discipline/involvement with the physically disabled student: priorities for IEP's, evaluation criteria, suggested strategies for change, strengths and limitations, special aptitudes, performance potential, psychosocial development, specific problems encountered by the student, and specific suggestions for what others can do to facilitate skills development or support other programs.

The individualized education program is to be developed in a formal meeting of parents, teacher, local education agency representative, and, when appropriate, the student. Others may also be invited, but the rules and regulations require that one person be qualified to interpret assessment data. Theoretically, all of the professionals involved with the student could be present at the meeting. However, it is not likely that all of these professionals could gather for an IEP meeting for each student. In addition, this team of professionals might overwhelm many parents if they all descended on the same meeting. Sherr (1977) also noted that "the confidence of parents will not be enhanced if they become involved in a meeting in which there is a wide discrepancy of results on a child or serious disagreements as to diagnosis or levels of functioning. . . " (p. 31).

Thus, it is suggested that the transdisciplinary team might hold a staff meeting to discuss several students prior to the formal IEP meetings with parents. This is *not* meant to suggest that this should be a "closed door session" designed to hide information from the parents. Rather, during this staff meeting, a number of students could be discussed and a general consensus reached about how each child is functioning and some mutual goals for each child. Questions may also be formulated to discuss with the parents or advocate. The purpose of this meeting should not be to plan the educational intervention but rather to share information and to determine if all necessary data are available for the formal meeting. The data discussed at this meeting should be summarized — including disagreements and discrepancies — and discussed in their totality with the parents and, when appropriate, the child.

The formal meeting with the parents is an important part of the transdisciplinary nature of the IEP. It is the time to expand this process of sharing and planning in a collaborative effort to include the parents and, when indicated, the student. It is the time for honest discussion of similarities — and differences — of opinion. It is the place for mutual problem solving and resolution of differences. The formal IEP meeting should result in delineation of priorities for education programing, persons who will provide the necessary interventions, and how the program will be evaluated for possible reconsideration. The IEP also identifies those related services that are to be provided by other members of the transdisciplinary team.

It is time NOW to begin this process of sharing and planning in a collaborative effort. The challenge is clear. As the rules and regulations for Public Law 94-142 are implemented, it is time to begin a concerted effort to provide true transdisciplinary efforts to meet the unique needs of each physically disabled student. The IEP is an annual, cyclical process which necessitates transdisciplinary planning from the onset. It is the time to gather continuous, quality data that affect the student's potential for maximum adaptation and success. Educational programs designed to meet individual differences of physically disabled students have long been an objective of special educators for this population. An effective service delivery system must represent education, medicine, health related professions, psychosocial disciplines, and parent and child consumers. The effectiveness of the system is entirely dependent on the commitment of all involved to the unique and individual needs of the physically disabled student.

# Mainstreaming a child with spina bifida

**Dorothy H. Nelson**

**Dorothy H. Nelson,** a retired teacher,
taught English for 11 years at Wandell
School, Saddle River, New Jersey.

HOW can I be expected to have in my regular classroom, along with the usual assortment of lively, demanding six-year-olds, a little boy with spina bifida, one who cannot walk without crutches, one who has known only the shelter of a special class, one who is incontinent?" First-grade teacher Kay Morris asked herself these questions before school opened last September. Yet, by March Kay looked back upon the past six months with Michael as the most rewarding and enriching time of her entire school career. The rewards were not only to herself, but to Mike, and, most important of all, to each of the students in her class.

The school specialists had placed Michael in Kay's regular class; they felt he should be given this opportunity although they knew it wouldn't be easy. Mike's problem, spina bifida, is a birth defect of the central nervous system, causing a defect in the bony structure of the spinal column. Victims may never control the lower part of their bodies, where they have no feeling. In Michael's case, which is the severest type, it means that he walks with much difficulty, requiring Canadian crutches. It also means that toilet training poses special problems. His assets are a normal upper body with amazingly strong arms, a personable nature, a quick contagious laugh, and normal intelligence. Mike requires glasses, sometimes a side effect of spina bifida, but he has an attractive, lively face and an extremely winning smile.

Once Kay consented and accepted the fact that she would be teaching a handicapped child in her regular public school class, she read everything she could to become acquainted with spina bifida. She visited Mike's home, talked with his mother, and visited the school for the handicapped where Mike had attended kindergarten. She consulted the school nurse and enlisted her cooperation with a bathroom program. And she told herself that together they would make it work.

Mike arrived on the first day of school as planned, so that from the very beginning he'd be considered a regular member of the class. His first school day hadn't gone along too far, however, when the first problem arose. Kay was discussing bulletin board displays, and some of the children were perched on desks as they listened. Suddenly there was a loud crash! Mike, who had tried to sit on his desk, had missed and catapulted to the floor, scattering crutches, books, and crayons. Mike simply picked himself up and made a second swipe at the desk top. That was to be Mike's style; no task was insurmountable.

Usually Kay and Mike together decided when and where to tackle a new mountain. The day he first wanted to go down the slide she lifted, pushed, and finally placed Mike's feet on the ladder, then raced to the bottom to catch him, hoping that the heavy braces wouldn't keep him from sliding. Not only did he learn to control his descent, but he conquered the ladder by himself, with encouragement from his peers.

Mike could go as fast on his crutches as the class could walk, and he never missed an excursion. His first was an autumn nature walk, and he became the envy of his classmates because he could tie his bag of col-

252    Reprinted from *Instructor* Copyright ©March 1979, by the Instructor Publications, Inc., used by permission.

lected treasures to his crutch. In school Mike seldom walked alone, but not because he asked to be accompanied. Some child, unsolicited, would wait for him, carry a book, or act as a shield in the crowded hall. It was astonishing to watch the natural development of kind, thoughtful actions between Mike and his peers.

Within a few weeks, students had become accustomed to Mike's special needs and treated him like everyone else. When he left his crutches in the aisle, someone would say, "Mike, please move those canes; I'm not tripping over them one more time."

Spina bifida is a congenital gap or cleft in the wall of the spinal canal, and this opening is what causes the loss of feeling from the waist down.

The degree of handicap varies with the individual. In Mike's case, he has no control of his bodily functions and has to wear a type of diaper. He has learned to change himself and be responsible for keeping a supply in the office of the school nurse. Because he can't feel the moisture, visits to the nurse were programmed, usually just once a day, immediately following lunch. During the course of the year, Mike has had only three "accidents" serious enough to necessitate a call home for a complete change.

The youngsters are matter-of-fact about this daily routine.

Michael was born with the kind of spina bifida in which the spinal cord does not form properly, and sometimes protrudes from the back. He has undergone a series of spine operations and a brain operation to implant a device called a shunt. This is a thin plastic tube that runs from the brain to the abdomen to drain excess fluid and prevent or limit hydrocephalus. This condition, water on the brain, can enlarge the skull and exert tremendous pressure on the brain, causing mental retardation. Fortunately for Michael, the necessary surgery was performed and the shunt inserted before further damage was done. Often children born with spina bifida also need foot or ankle surgery, and weak ankles are one of Mike's problems.

It is estimated that about 6,000 children are born each year in America with crippling spina bifida. The reason one hears more about spina bifida these days is that more children born with it are surviving now.

Relatively little is known about what causes spina bifida; guesses have ranged all the way from Irish potatoes to poison in the drinking water. There are indications, however, that genetic factors play a causative role. Once parents have had one child with spina bifida, the odds of a second child with the defect rise from two per thousand to about one in twenty. The defect pays little heed to social standing and is found in all socioeconomic levels.

As the year progressed, there were many high points for Mike. One was the school Christmas performance, which provided his first opportunity to try acting. The program was called "Santa in Nurseryland" and Mike played the role of Little Jack Horner. A huge paper-mache pie had been created, and at exactly the appropriate moment he "stuck in his thumb and pulled out a plum" (a purple-painted golf ball drilled with a hole to just fit over his thumb) and raised it high in the air with the widest of grins.

Spina bifida is a serious condition, but the treatments and techniques developed within the past few years make it possible for many of these children not only to grow to adulthood but to live happy, productive lives in spite of their disability. There are many things that doctors and parents can do to minimize the consequences of the condition. With the interest and assistance of dedicated teachers such as Kay Morris, pupils like Michael can make it in a regular classroom.

# Involuntary Deviance: Schooling and Epileptic Children

Werner A. Gliebe, MA

## ABSTRACT

*There exists in schools an unwritten set of pre-suppositions defining "normalcy." Students going beyond these boundaries of normalcy are encouraged (sometimes punitively) to change their behaviors. However, there is a growing awareness that not all children going beyond normalcy do so willingly. The phenomenon here termed "involuntary deviance" represents a way of perceiving and dealing with special students. An example, the case of children with epilepsy, is presented to illustrate the need for health educators and other educators to be familiar with such medical problems and, among their students, to help decrease the social stigma attached to some of these conditions. This need will become more urgent as the practice of mainstreaming students becomes increasingly prevalent.*

## INTRODUCTION

An essential feature of the American experience, unique in world history, is its emphasis on mass involvement and mass opportunity for its citizenry. Institutions have been elaborated to educate the public so that it can participate in government effectively. Over time of course, education has taken on many other responsibilities as well. Schools have become important socializing agents, teaching and encouraging a complete spectrum of knowledge, values, attitudes and appropriate behaviors. As surrogate parents, schools have also provided the legitimate means of upward social mobility by teaching relational and now even vocational skills. Such activities are carried out under an unspoken banner that defines normalcy.

In defining normalcy, we include physical as well as behavioral standards, although physical standards are usually kept implicit. We do not explicitly say that we are differentiating on the basis of sex, race, age, height, weight, physical disability, or physical distortion, perhaps because the affected persons are not the way they are of their own accord. Since they are not in a situation of individual responsibility, it becomes unethical to lay blame in such cases. Of course, despite the immorality of differentiation in such cases, historically we have always done so. However, the practice of isolating such persons from the so-called normals in special schools or other institutions which could handle them (providing custodial care only) without disturbing the experiences and development of others has come under increasing criticism. There is growing awareness that not all children going beyond

**Physiologically, the cause of what are termed convulsions, seizures, or fits is the production of an irregular electrical discharge by cells in the brain.**

normalcy do so willingly, and current thinking favors the integration of all students so that, essentially, the parameters of normalcy can be expanded. The remainder of this paper will focus on one group characterized by involuntary deviance, the child with epilepsy.

### EPILEPSY AND ITS PREVALENCE

Epilepsy has been seen as a physiological disorder (Hippocrates), as being related to supernatural powers, as contagious, as a product of demoniacal possession, and back to brain malfunction.[1,2] Physiologically, the cause of what are termed convulsions, seizures, or fits is the production of an irregular electrical discharge by cells in the brain. Such irregular discharges can be precipitated by high fevers, infections, sudden lack of oxygen or brain tumors, among other causes. If a cause can be identified, it is termed symptomatic epilepsy. When no cause can be found, it is termed idiopathic epilepsy. About 75% of all epilepsy is idiopathic.[1,2] More than 80% of all persons with epilepsy have their first attack before age 20.[1,2] Those persons whose attacks begin later are more likely to have symptomatic epilepsy, while those whose attacks begin during childhood are more likely to have idiopathic epilepsy.[1,2]

Significantly, in over 90% of children who are otherwise normal, incidents can be prevented by using currently available therapy. Estimates of the prevalence of epilepsy among the U.S. population vary from 1 in 200 to as high as 1 in 50. Given its greater incidence among younger age groups, the school will play some part in how such students are handled. This will be considered in more detail later. It is pertinent here to briefly look at the historical experience of the epileptic as a victim of involuntary deviance along with current attitudes of "normal" Americans.

## SOCIAL HISTORY, ATTITUDINAL TRENDS AND INVOLUNTARY DEVIANCE

Preceptions of the epileptic throughout history are as varied as the causal theories of epilepsy alluded to earlier. At various times, epileptics have been socially rejected and deprived of civil rights, scourged and sometimes violently executed. They were sometimes

---

**Trends in public attitudes over the last 25 years show increasing awareness and acceptance of epilepsy in the United States.**

---

rejected by families who kept them hidden away or had them institutionalized. Community avoidance, family shame, and peer taunting were common into this century and have as yet not been eliminated among all persons. In fact, with the development of anti-convulsant drugs, which permit effective management and control of many types of epilepsy, the major problem (or handicap) of epileptics may now be social rather than medical. Treatment of choice for epilepsy today is felt to be multidisciplinary, incorporating medical, social, psychological and vocational problem-solving aimed at improving all facets of the epileptic's life adjustment. [3]

Physicians themselves have been guilty of prejudices against epilepsy, as Bagley has demonstrated in a detailed review. [4] Disturbed behaviors in patients with or without epilepsy have been characterized as epileptic equivalents without any basis for such inferences. What Bagley characterized as a bandwagon effect found its way into research reports as well, with various pathological behaviors being attributed to persons with frontal lobe epilepsy, despite the frequent lack of experimental rigor to warrant such a claim. Many studies postulated a causal connection between epilepsy and disturbed behavior without considering the wide range of possible intervening variables. [4] Szasz, a vocal medical critic of the professional labelling of persons, illustrates the greater importance of social rather than medical interventions:

In the initial decades of this century, much was learned about epilepsy. As a result, physicians gained better control of the epileptic process (which sometimes results in seizures). The desire to control the disease, however, seems to go hand in hand with the desire to control the diseased person. Thus, epileptics were both helped and harmed:

they were benefited insofar as their illness was more accurately diagnosed and better treated; they were injured insofar as they, as persons, were stigmatized and socially segregated.

Was the placement of epileptics in 'colonies' in their best interests? Or their exclusion from jobs, from driving automobiles, and from entering the United States as immigrants? It has taken decades of work, much of it still unfinished, to undo some of the oppressive social effects of 'medical progress' in epilepsy, and to restore the epileptic to the social status he enjoyed before his disease became so well understood. [4]

While the comments are perhaps slightly overstated, they support the need to deal with the social problems associated with epilepsy. To do that, attitudes toward epileptics among the general public should also be examined.

Trends in public attitudes over the last 25 years show increasing awareness and acceptance of epilepsy in the United States. Knowledge of epilepsy was positive for 98% of all professionals but only 85% of those with only an elementary education. Only 5% of all persons objected to their children playing with epileptics. However, more than 2½ million persons still believe epilepsy is a form of insanity. Finally, only 81% of persons thought that epileptics should be employed in jobs like other people, and only 75% of those in the South did so. [5] While still somewhat discouraging, the trends are nevertheless toward more positive orientations. In light of the importance of schools as loci of interaction with peers and other publics, the attitudes of teachers toward epileptics should also be considered.

---

**Significantly, in over 90% of children who are otherwise normal, incidence can be prevented by using currently available therapy.**

---

In one study, 58% of the teachers with no experience with epilepsy often believed that the scholastic record of pupils with epilepsy is always abnormal, while 15% expected the record to depend on the severity of the disease in a particular case. [6] Of teachers experienced with epilepsy, one-third expected the school record always to be normal while 37% of these always expected abnormality. In fact, more than half the school records of the epileptic children were found to be normal. Among those cases whose illnesses are medically controlled, there is no evidence to support grade inferiority due to social stigmatic responses to such involuntary deviance. All the teachers surveyed felt they had no training, and most (60% of those with and 75% of those without experience with epilepsy) were unwilling to teach pupils with epilepsy. [6] The positive responses cited only a general willingness to deal with epileptic pupils. In view of such findings, it is apparent that some educational programs for teachers might be useful, both in changing their attitudes and also the attitudes of other students.

## CHANGE IN THE CLASSROOM:
## HEALTH EDUCATION

Only when teachers are taught how to handle instances of seizures in a classroom and when they understand (at least in general terms) what epilepsy is and what it is not can there be effective efforts in schools to change peer attitudes and provide epileptics the opportunity to succeed as others would in school. The medically controlled cases of epilepsy do not retard students' progress. Rather, socially uncontrolled and uneducated reactions, if anything, can slow some students down to the point of incorporating a negative and inferior self-concept.

If a seizure occurs in a classroom, the teacher must remain calm and act firmly since students will take their reactive cue from the teacher. As the Epilepsy Foundation of America (EFA) points out:

"If the schoolmates recoil in horror and the child is sent home, the experience poses a psychological problem for the child and reinforces the prejudice against those with epilepsy. The child is often encouraged to hide his epilepsy, so he lives in fear of having a seizure in public. That child is denied a full life. If a youngster develops a personality problem, it's usually from the reaction of others to his disorder, not from the epilepsy itself." [7]

## SUMMARY

Thus, we come full circle. Epilepsy has become a social problem. However, it is involuntary deviance for which the epileptic cannot be blamed. It is here, then, that schools can influence students' developing perceptions of normalcy, not only for epileptics but for the entire spectrum of individuals characterized by involuntary deviance. The first level of understanding in this process would be the awareness by students that individuals actually reflect a broader array of physical and behavioral manifestations than simply so-called "normal" children. At the next level, educators should then attempt to foster empathetic and accepting responses, not sympathetic ones. Sympathetic responses would merely constitute an additional obstacle in the achievement of individual acceptance. It is therefore another task that educators, as surrogate parents, will have to assume to meet this responsibility.


### REFERENCES

1. Baird HW: *The Child With Convulsions.* New York, Grune and Stratton, 1972.

2. Scott D: *About Epilepsy.* New York, International Universities Press, 1969.

3. Hudzinski L: Public Rejection of the Epileptic: An impirical investigation. Unpublished Ph.D. dissertation, University of Pittsburgh, 1975.

4. Bagley C: *The Social Psychology of the Child With Epilepsy.* London, Routledge and Kegan Paul, 1971.

5. Caveness WF, Merritt HH, Gallup GH: A survey of public attitudes toward epilepsy in 1974 with an indication of trends over the past twenty-five years. *Epilepsia* 15:523-536, 1974.

6. Pazzaglia P, Pazzaglia LF: Record in grade school of pupils with epilepsy: An epidemiological study. *Epilepsia* 17:361-366, 1976.

7. Staff Report: The educator's role in epilepsy. *Sch Health Rev 4* (2):35-37, 1973.



*Werner A. Gliebe, MA, is Coordinator, Department of Cost Containment & Evaluation, Medical College of Ohio at Toledo, Toledo, OH 43699.*

# What Are Health Impairments?

*Health problems are not necessarily health impairments.*

What are Health Impairments? Alfred Healy, M.D., Paul McAreavey, Ph.D., Caren Saaz von Hippel, Ph.D., Sherry Harris Jones, M.Ed., *Mainstreaming Preschoolers: Children with Health Impairments*, U.S. DHEW, 1978.

# When Is a Health Problem a Handicap?

At birth, Nancy appeared to be a beautiful and healthy baby. Her parents were delighted that she soon smiled, held her head up, and by four months of age was beginning to roll over. They took her regularly to their doctor for immunizations and checkups. At five months Nancy had what appeared to be a brief bout with pneumonia—she had difficulty breathing and had to be hospitalized. Two months after her recovery she suffered another attack, much like the first. By age three, she had been hospitalized five times. Each time she wasn't very sick, but she did have difficulty breathing. Her doctor and parents were not aware that Nancy was having asthma attacks, which occurred when the tubes leading to her lungs narrowed and caused her to wheeze. Nancy was a curious child who enjoyed learning new skills. However, as a preschooler she had attacks almost every day, making her miss many of the preschool's activities. Because she was absent so often, she was always "catching up" with the rest of her playmates, rather than learning along with them.

Nancy didn't wear braces or use crutches. She could see and hear well and was bright. Even so, she was a child with a **handicap.** Her asthma was a health impairment, because it was interfering with her growth and development. She was not able to play as long or as hard as her playmates and she missed almost every other day of preschool. In addition, her special problems called for changes in her activities. Even though she tried very hard, and her parents worked very closely with her teacher, Nancy just couldn't keep up.

Wing, another child in Nancy's group, also had asthma, in a milder form. He took the same medicine as Nancy, but he didn't miss class, and he never had to be in the hospital. Wing had a health problem, but it didn't interfere with his growth or development, and it didn't require special services. So he wasn't considered to be a child with a handicap.

# How Are Health Impairments Defined?

In defining handicapping conditions, Project Head Start distinguishes between **categorical** definitions, which are used for reporting purposes, and **functional** definitions, which describe a child's areas of strength and weakness. The categorical definition uses Project Head Start's legislated diagnostic criteria. An interdisciplinary diagnostic team (or a professional who is qualified to diagnose the specific handicap) must use this definition to make a categorical diagnosis of a child. This diagnosis is used only for reporting purposes. A functional definition or diagnosis, on the other hand, assesses what a child can and cannot do, and identifies areas that call for special education and related services. The functional assessment should be developed by a diagnostic team, with the child's parents and teacher as active participants. Another term for functional assessment or functional diagnosis is **developmental profile.**

According to Project Head Start, the following categorical definition of health impairments is to be used for **reporting purposes** in Head Start programs:

> **These impairments refer to** *illnesses of a chronic nature or*

*with prolonged convalescence,* including, but not limited to, epilepsy, hemophilia, severe asthma, severe cardiac conditions, severe anemia or malnutrition, diabetes, or neurological disorders.

("Transmittal Notice Announcement of Diagnostic Criteria for Reporting Handicapped Children in Head Start," OCD-HS, September 11, 1975.)

The key words in this definition are **chronic** and **prolonged convalescence.** They refer to health problems that severely affect learning.

Many impairments are not considered handicaps by Project Head Start if the conditions do not require special services. For example, a child whose vision can be corrected with eyeglasses is not considered visually handicapped. Children are considered handicapped if they fall within the legislative definition and if, by reason of this handicap, they **require special education and related services.**

# How Do Health Impairments Affect Learning?

The term **handicap** is usually used when a child has a health problem that affects learning: that is, taking in information, thinking about that information, and acting on that information (e.g., moving about or communicating). Almost all handicaps other than health impairments directly interfere with the child's ability to gain information (blindness, deafness) or to use information to communicate (mental retardation). Many also directly interfere with communication itself (speech impairments). Health impairments interfere with the child's opportunity to participate fully in learning activities by affecting the body's supply of energy or the removal of wastes, or by creating severe problems with growth.

# Growth and Development

The terms **growing** and **developing** are often used to mean the same thing, as in "Suzie is growing well," and "Larry is developing nicely." However, growing and developing mean separate things—and each child participates in both while becoming an adult. Growth means an increase in size: becoming taller and heavier. Development means an increase in learning and understanding. Some children grow to the size of adults but never develop an adult's ability to understand. Other children do not gain weight or grow tall, but they develop normal adult intelligence. Ideally, children both grow and develop, given the proper food and varied and stimulating activities.

## Growth

Children's size and rate of growth are characteristics that are determined, in part, by the genes they inherit. Johnny may be growing slowly, like his mother did when she was his age. Mary may be very thin and tall, just as her grandfather was. A small child is not necessarily an unhealthy child.

There are other factors that affect children's size and rate of growth: energy (food and oxygen) and hormones (chemicals produced by the body). We take in energy in order to grow, and we produce hormones to regulate our growth at a regular and "normal" pace. If Mary does not receive enough energy, or if her body is not able to use the energy properly (especially during the first two or three years of life), she may not grow as tall as her genes would have allowed. And if Johnny's hormones are out of balance, he may grow very quickly, instead of slowly.

A doctor can determine whether a child's height and weight appear normal by comparing them to the height and weight of other children of the same age. Doctors do this by using growth charts, which give the average height and weight for each age. This "average" is obtained by weighing and measuring thousands of children of a certain age. For example, if the weights of 100 four-year-old boys were written down in a long column of 100 numbers, you would quickly see that most of the weights were fairly close and it would be easy to arrive at an average weight. However, you would probably also find a few heavy boys and a few light boys on the list. Are the heaviest boy and the lightest boy unhealthy? They may be, but not necessarily.

This could be considered a **screening test** for growth. If the weight of a four-year-old boy is heavier or lighter than the normal range, the child needs to have a medical evaluation to determine if there is anything truly wrong with his growth. Doctors are also interested in the pattern of growth. If a child weighed about 70th in a group of 100 children in October, and in May weighed about 30th in the same group, the uneven growth pattern would alert the doctor that there might be a problem. Just because some children are especially small or

large does *not* mean they are unhealthy—only that they must be reviewed more carefully to see if anything is wrong.

When there is a great difference between a child's weight and height, closer evaluation may be needed to determine if this difference represents a health problem.

# Development

Development can be thought of as a process that enables children to know and do things they didn't know and couldn't do before. For this to happen, children take in information from their environment—or, more exactly, from people, things, and events in their environment. Next, children organize this information in their minds, which makes it usable. Last, they behave in a way that indicates that learning has taken place.

For example, Billy and Mary were playing on a teeter-totter at the playground. They weighed about the same and went up and down easily. When Billy saw his mother coming he quickly jumped off the teeter-totter, while Mary was still up in the air. Of course Mary came down quickly and hit the ground hard. This was the first time either had had this happen. Mary felt the sudden drop and bump, and yelled at Billy, "Don't do that again!" Billy also saw what happened and realized he had caused the problem by suddenly getting off. Mary and Billy now know what happens when you get off a teeter-totter with one person still in the air. That's development— and each day is full of such experiences for every child who is active and healthy.

To grow and develop properly, the muscles and organs of the body are dependent on energy being delivered promptly and on wastes being removed quickly. Any condition that interferes with the body's ability to take in and use energy, or with its ability to remove wastes, can result in a health impairment. This section looks at energy—what it is and how the body uses it.

The body requires two major kinds of energy: calories (units of heat) from the food we eat, and oxygen from the air we breathe. The calories and oxygen are the fuels that combine with other chemicals of the body so that the "work" of the body can be accomplished.

Food passes through the stomach to the intestines, where the calories are removed and carried in the blood through the blood vessels to be stored, or to the different areas of the body that need them. The lungs remove oxygen from the air, and the blood carries it through the blood vessels to areas of the body where it is combined with calories. The heart pumps the blood (and therefore the energy) to the muscles and other organs where energy is needed.

Every part of the body uses energy. Energy is needed when we think, speak, walk, see, hear, breathe, digest food, and even when we sleep. Certain activities take more energy than others. For example, it takes more energy to stand than it does to sit, or to run than it does to walk.

After the energy is used, the by-products (wastes) remaining must be removed from the body. For all of us, there are three main kinds of wastes to be removed:

- **a gas, carbon dioxide, which is removed by the lungs when you exhale**

- **chemicals and acids, which are removed from the blood as it passes through the kidneys, and which leave the body in the urine**

- **remains of the food eaten, which pass through the intestinal tract and leave the body through the rectum. The liver is also indirectly involved, because it is the organ that prepares many of the chemicals so that the lungs and kidneys may remove them from the blood.**

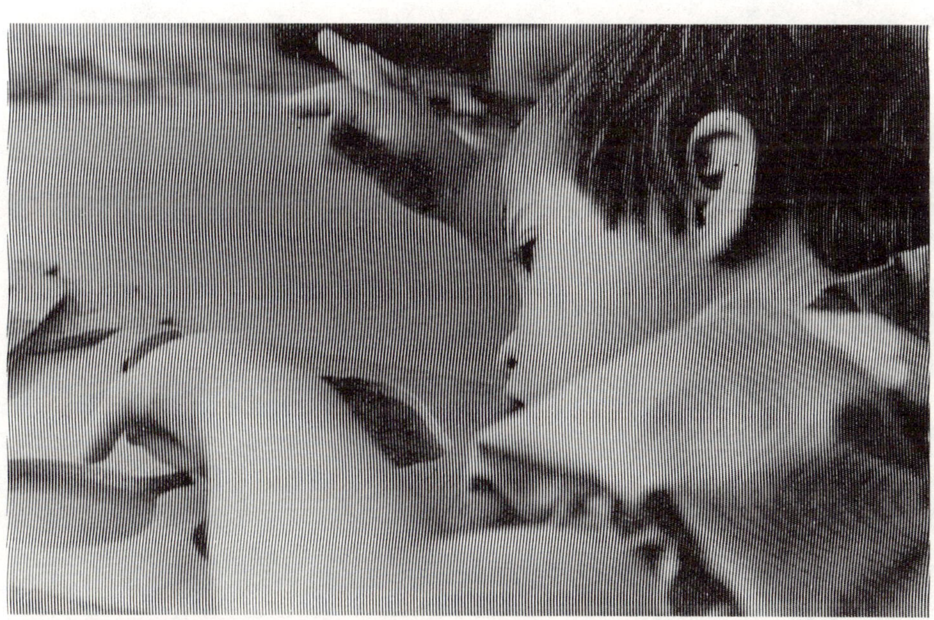

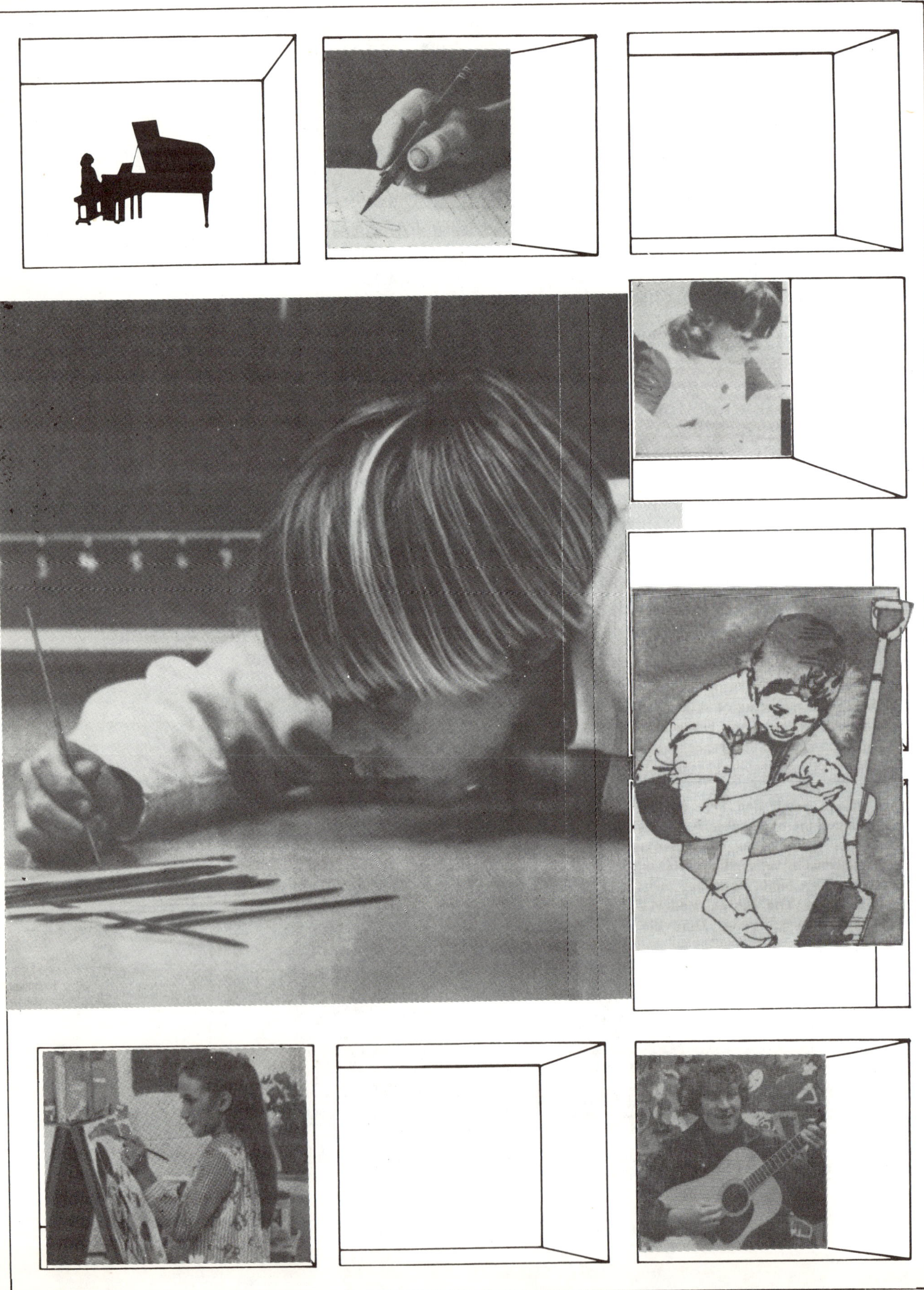

# GIFTED AND TALENTED

Roughly 2.5 million Americans are gifted. Those identified as gifted are ahead of their peers academically, artistically, and/or socially. This group is considered exceptional as is the Mentally Handicapped, Learning Disabled, and Physically Disabled, because they too have special problems. Many gifted children are not identified or if identified, are not given the opportunity to express these talents in curriculums in school. These problems can be handicapping to the child and if not resolved, can cause severe social and emotional problems.

The articles in this section give an overview into the field of gifts and talents. "The Gifted Child" looks at the gifted movement in the United States and discusses the problems of being gifted and ways educators can help to overcome these problems. One view of an instructional method is looked at in the article "The Many paths for Gifts and Talents."

Gifts and Talents are found not only in the white class but also in the black community as well. It is the suggestion of the authors of "Enhancing Self-Concept in Gifted Black Students" that the black self-image is not always presented to gifted black students. A model curriculum is presented to facilitate this idea.

The section closes with a parent's view of her experiences with a gifted child. The problems of growing up gifted are highlighted in this article. The author tells of the family's troubles with contending with a gifted youngster and how they resolve any problems they have.

# The Many Paths for Gifts and Talents

By EDITH BRILL ROTH

Mrs. Roth is on the staff of OE's Office of Public Affairs.

*OE's Office for the Gifted and Talented is helping exceptional students follow the tug of their own talents, whether they lead to laboratory mice or Shakespeare*

When Maritza Holder saw her own first acting performance on videotape, she couldn't believe her eyes. The tape showed her with a group in an improvised playlet about halloween, with Maritza the one chosen to be "scared." There she was, looking truly frightened. She was believable. She was really acting!

Maritza, a 14-year-old inner-city black youngster, hadn't been doing too well in her studies at a New Haven, Connecticut, school. Then the American Shakespeare Theater's Center for Theater Techniques in Education, which seeks to identify and advance creativity in gifted and talented young people through theater games and techniques, tested her and found that, in spite of low achievement in her regular studies, Maritza had creativity and real potential in acting. Given encouragement, she might even show unusual gifts.

Before she joined the center and was steered into acting, Maritza played the violin a bit and thought perhaps she had a future in music. But she was shy and uncommunicative. Learning about the many techniques and skills that combine to make a theatrical performance and working toward acquiring them have changed Maritza into a lively and intense youngster. There has been noticeable improvement in her school work too, especially in social studies, her favorite.

She exhibits a high degree of creativity and much enthusiasm and has turned into a skilled young actress. Yet she has no adolescent fantasies of seeing her name in marquee lights on Broadway.

The uncovering of the true Maritza is no great surprise to Mary Hunter Wolf, director of the Center for Theater Techniques, who says, "There is a process through which we can give a young person experiences that can open up that person to his or her highest potential . . . because the theater embodies all the arts as well as interpersonal relationships. In the exercise of the arts the individual arrives at self-understanding and new experiences that can uncover other gifts."

The Center for Theater Techniques joins with two other programs to make up one of the six national models funded for three years by the Office for the Gifted and Talented in the Office of Education. One of the center's model companions, the Educational Center for the Arts, is a high-school program for talented students in the performing and visual arts. The other, the Independent Study Program, also operates in the high schools of the area, offering highly individualized courses of study to students who have been identified as gifted. All three programs are aimed at disadvantaged young

people who come from culturally diverse backgrounds.

Parts of these three programs form the model program, which offers two years of developmental work and a third in independent study. At the Troup Middle School in New Haven, recruitment for the program starts as early as the sixth grade. By the time they enter seventh grade, the four or five students who scored high in a battery of tests for leadership, creativity, physical ability, general knowledge, emotional maturity—and who rated well in an evaluation by classmates—have been selected. Taking the top four or five thus screened from all the area schools adds up to 45 youngsters. Of that number entering the program, 20 will probably remain for the second developmental year, and most of them will proceed to the third year, which is given to independent study in whatever field a child chooses.

The record shows that the 45 youngsters who work at the center twice weekly for two and a half hours each session will emerge with some sense of direction in their lives and usually with higher grades and goals in their school work. This does not necessarily mean that the center is turning out scenic designers or dancers or musicians, for the work of developing self-awareness and imagination sometimes steers young people to such improvement in other areas that they might eventually choose careers in science or history.

Yet the center's work *does* give the lie to the old persuasion that a bright child is either art- or science-oriented. Mary Wolf feels that most bright young people excel in both the cognitive and the affective areas, one talent feeding the other. "The narrowing into a specialty too early," she says, "makes children develop in an area that is not necessarily their best, because they haven't explored everything. In ages 9 to 13, if a child, on the one hand, has an early interest in science, the tendency is for the parents to see only that. What earns early recognition for the child becomes the emphasis. On the other hand, in the inner city where there is very little exposure to choices, one can't tell what the gifts are. We try to identify ability and then help raise children's self-understanding so that they reach more closely their potential in their studies."

How does the center work to help children focus their abilities? One way, improvisation, is basic to many of the exercises given the youngsters. For instance, a group sits in a circle and one child starts a story that is continued by each member until everyone has twice added episodes to the narrative. The group amends the story until all agree that's the way it should be and then decides how the story is to be interpreted— as comedy, satire, or drama. After selecting a director and cast, the group acts out the story.

There is another game called "Survival," in which one youngster studies the appearance of another who then leaves the room to change five things about the way he or she looks. The first youngster's task is to tell what has been changed. The game calls for observation, concentration, ingenuity, and even more important, the players must survive moments when they might be "stuck" in identifying changes. They learn to overcome these blocks and regain poise and activity through an appropriate question-and-answer technique that, through elimination, isolates the trouble spot and finally pinpoints the answer. The young actor finds that self-consciousness evaporates when involved in a cooperative effort with a partner.

Still another phase of the center's work has to do with "transformations," that is, the translation of an idea from one art medium to another. Given a play, how, for instance, might it be translated into a musical composition? Each character might have a particular identifying musical passage—for example, fortissimo with possible dissonance may suggest the villain. What parts of the action would call for slow music? what parts for fast? and so on. Such transformations steer youngsters toward conceptual thinking and ultimately help them sharpen reading and writing skills.

All sorts of transformations are taking place within the lives of many of the children who come to the center. Reggie Augustine, already a skilled cartoonist, thinks of a future in the visual arts. His art teachers are trying to develop his drawing skills in other directions. At the same time Reggie's work in body-movement exercises and acting has given him a new sense of mastery, which translates into better communication and development of leadership qualities. When his self-image is more fully developed, Reggie may stop drawing superman figures and take off into more serious art.

In funding the six models, OE's Office for the Gifted and Talented also sets aside small sums to train teachers of the gifted. It would seem reasonable that gifted teachers are required to identify, guide, and educate gifted children, and this is an area in which concentration of funds and interest is sorely needed, since there are few universities that offer courses in this special training.

Recently in New York, Dorothy Sisk, director of the Office for Gifted and Talented, addressed a large audience of teachers and administrators on teaching the gifted. She said, "Teachers of the gifted should be real, should develop empathy with the learner, and be expert in *something*." They should, she continued, be flexible to meet the daring minds of the youngsters they teach, and be able to "move with the teaching moment, share their expertise, and communicate well." She added the points that many bright people do not communicate well and that using sarcasm on some little smart aleck is deadly because bright kids can deal back and set up a killing exchange.

Dr. Sisk emphasized the importance of trust and caring. Teachers must help kids clarify what they want to learn and help them to find personal meaning in their studies. She gave the example of the bright little girl who did a beautiful drawing for the school magazine. One of her teachers, amazed at the surfacing of a hitherto unknown talent, asked the child why she didn't do more drawing and why hadn't she come forward before? The child answered simply, "Nobody ever asked me to." Sensitive teachers will see to it that the right questions are asked.

Since ideally all teachers should have these qualifications, Dr. Sisk was asked what makes teaching the gifted *different* from teaching average children. Her answer was "pace and product . . . the gifted child learns faster, and the product he or she delivers is unique and more advanced."

In the Bronx High School of Science there is no problem of identification of gifted youngsters, since all 600 students entering their ninth year are there because they score high in mathematics and science and most come from honors courses in other schools. The 100 exceptions are high-potential youngsters from disadvantaged backgrounds who are given a chance at the kind of stimulation that might open the doors to wider opportunities. The student body of Bronx High is made up of 57 percent boys and 43 percent girls, indicating a rising percentage of women entering science careers.

Money given the school by the Office for the Gifted and Talented helps provide a model project for the creatively gifted in science. The project involves 50 or 60 tenth-year students working intensively in biology, 40 or 45 of whom will be capable of doing independent research on projects of their own during their 11th year. The youngsters picked for the program work under the direction of Milton Kopelman, the assistant principal, and Vincent Gallasso, project coordinator. In the first year at Bronx, model-project students meet six times a week to learn techniques relating to microbiology and instrumentation and to work on introductory laboratory experiments. In the tenth grade the youngsters meet ten times a week instead of six, with increased laboratory work and problem solving directed toward the selection of an individual research problem.

Cori Dauber, a thin little girl of 15 with the usual adolescent stigmata of braces and acne, is working on an experiment with mice. Sitting in the large buzzing and chaotic lab, she is training a mouse to run a maze she has constructed. As she caresses and redirects the mouse, she patiently explains her hypothesis in layman's language. Before her experiment is completed, Cori will have five mice running different and more complex mazes, all checked against the first mouse. She will then be able to determine mathematically the effect of added learning experiences in the case of each mouse. It will take from a few weeks up to six months for Cori to train one mouse to run the maze, made increasingly complicated. That, along with the necessity for Cori to do the experiment twice in order to have a check, gives evidence of the dogged patience required of a young potential scientist.

Then there is Elias Reichel, plump and very serious. He explains that he is working with hydra, tiny animals related to the sponge family. There are 3,000 cells in each hydra, almost unbelievable when one views the pinhead-size specks in a small plastic container that Elias says are hydra. These minute animals, explains Elias, are composed of a type of cell that can divide or differentiate, a type also found in bone marrow and in blood. Elias's quest with the hydra relates to the cells' release of morphogen, a substance that tells the cells whether to divide or differentiate. If morphogen is in great quantity, the cells will differentiate; if it is in low density, the cells will divide, a fact that may have application

**It would seem reasonable that gifted teachers are required to identify, guide, and educate gifted children, and this is an area in which concentration of funds and interest is sorely needed, since there are few universities that offer courses in this special training.**

to human cancers, since morphogen under certain conditions might inhibit the development of wild cells.

Because of Bronx High's reputation, ties with outside research groups are easily made, and are a great aid and inspiration to the young scientists. Students are doing work at the Montefiore Hospital and at various New York museums and universities as part of their research. Messrs. Kopelman and Gallasso are full of wondrous stories about Bronx High geniuses. The National Aeronautics and Space Administration involved Bronx High School youngsters in the Skylab program, and the work of one student, Todd Meister, was flown on Skylab. Todd's experiment was to find out whether the immunizing mechanism of the human body worked in space in test tubes as well as it does here inside earthbound mortals. Todd is now in a six-year medical program at Rensselaer Polytechnic in an accelerated course. At the same time he is teaching courses in neuro-anatomy at Albany Medical College "to cool him off and slow him down a bit," as Mr. Kopelman puts it.

Another grant from the Office for the Gifted and Talented went to the National Commission on Resources for Youth (NCRY), essentially a clearinghouse for model programs that offer young people opportunities to participate in the community and learn ways in which they can make a difference. The commission is inspired and fueled by Mary Conway Kohler, an ex-juvenile court judge, who believes that youth participation in the affairs of the community and the problems of its citizens can bring about creative change in the schools as well.

One of the outstanding characteristics of most gifted people is a passionate altruism and belief that things can—and must—be better, and thus the commission's efforts toward increasing voluntary community in-

volvement is a natural to any program for the gifted. Added to youth participation is the basic idea that the growth of talents and gifts is frequently the result of early interest and encouragement by a significant adult, especially one whose life role and work falls within the interests and goals of the gifted young person.

From the 900 programs in the NCRY files—all of them variations on the youth participation idea—five or six are chosen as dedicated to mentorship programs. Typical of mentorship programing is the Open Living School in Evergreen, Colorado, an alternative school within the public-school system of Jefferson County. Placement with a mentor within the community is made after students put together a personal-interests list, focusing on aspects of community life.

Kevin, a 13-year-old, expressed his keen love of animals. It was therefore arranged for him to meet regularly at the veterinary hospital with an orthopedic specialist, a man who has written the leading textbook on canine orthopedic surgery. The doctor has given Kevin reading assignments to help him understand what is going on. Already Kevin has learned about surgery, x-rays, blood counts, cremation, animal diets, and suturing. "He practiced doing sutures on everything," says Kevin's counselor. "On rats in the school lab and even on grapes at the dinner table." Now Kevin himself teaches pet nutrition and dissection of small animals to a core group of six students at the Open Living School.

Another program typical of NCRY is called Switching Yard, in which the Youth Division of the Marin County (California) Volunteer Bureau matches young volunteers with mentors and community groups and agencies. Working through Switching Yard, 17-year-old Paul chose to volunteer as a planning aide with a bus company. His

mentor, Bruce, a senior planner, needed assistance in developing and testing a rider survey of the district. When Paul got on with the job, he found the kind of bureaucratic halts and hangups that everyone meets in large industry, but for an impatient and bright youngster, the experience served to turn him off "office work" and brought him to the decision that he would one day have to be his own boss.

As Paul puts it, "I don't like the things you have to go through to get things done. First your boss, then his boss, then the general manager, the board of directors...I mean, you could have done it yourself. When I came to the company, one of the first things I needed was a pass to ride the buses free. Bruce called the personnel department to ask for a pass for a volunteer. The man in personnel asked, 'What's a volunteer?' and Bruce explained. Later the man called to say that the policy is that no one may have a pass without being on the payroll, and I wasn't on the payroll. Afterward the personnel man told me to write a letter with signatures of Bruce and his boss, and then it would have to go through the board.

"When I was a little kid I once figured out how to make a round trip on the bus system for only 25 cents just by juggling transfers. Sometimes I think all they need is a little kid around here to figure out some of the things that it takes them months to accomplish."

When Mary Conway Kohler was a family court judge in California, dealing with delinquents, she had to pass judgment on a child who had put together a whole automobile out of stolen parts. "And believe me, that's gifted," she said with a sparkling laugh, making the point that giftedness will be expressed illegally if it doesn't find a normal outlet.

In a more serious vein, Judge Kohler says, "The biggest thing in working with the gifted and talented is providing them an opportunity to assert leadership qualities. And in true leadership, the biggest thing is *caring*. I have found that one gets a different value system by becoming involved with someone else."

Becoming involved and caring have not always been counted as aspects of giftedness. The stereotype has seemed to be more the picture of the lone genius at his piano or in the lab. But the seeds of altruism and the imagination to put one's self into other roles and to "cultivate a concern for the common good" are all present in high degree in most gifted persons if they are given free rein. It is the job of educators to cultivate these scarce commodities and make sure that our potential leaders have basic training in compassion as participants in community life and growth.

# The Gifted Child

No ordinary handbook on child care could possibly have prepared Richard and Sally Hunter for their first baby. When he was just six months old, Kam Hunter began speaking in complete sentences. By the time he was 3, he had taught himself to read. As a first grader, he was allowed to enroll in Spanish courses at a high school near his elementary classroom in Ionia, Mich.; within a year, at the age of 7, he was a full-time high school student. Today, Kam is a sophomore in the Honors College of Michigan State University. He is only 12 years old. "I just want to be treated like any other college student," says the handsome blond youngster. "But I know that's probably not possible."

Kam Hunter is one of the gifted children--roughly 2.5 million young Americans who are endowed with academic, artistic or social talents far beyond those of their peers. They are not just the diagnosed geniuses, but comprise a widely varied group whose gifts range from prodigious prowess in chess or music to extraordinary facility in language, mathematics or the visual arts: a toddler in Seattle who amassed (and read) a library of more than 100 books before she was 2 years old; an 8-year old chess champion from New York City who is well on his way to becoming a grand master; an inner-city 12 year old from Baltimore whose paintings already hang in public galleries.

"They come from all levels of society, all races and both sexes," says Dr. Harold Lyon, former director of the Federal Office for the Gifted and Talented. "These are the future Beethovens, the Newtons, the Jeffersons, the Picassos, Baldwins and Martin Luther Kings. And like other minorities, they need help.

## BEST AND BRIGHTEST

Until recently, gifted children got very little help unless they had parents wealthy enough to send them to good private schools. Most U.S. educators balked at the idea of lavishing public time and money on students whose special talents gave them a head

Andrew Sacks

*Hunter: At 12, a college sophomore—and team manager*

start. The poor and the handicapped desperately needed the extra attention; besides, to single out the best and brightest in public schools struck many as uncomfortably elitist. "Americans have always had trouble on the question of how to handle people who are different-better, rather than different-poorer," explains Sheila Vaughan, an educational psychologist at UCLA. With the exception of the post-sputnik period, when American educators mobilized a frenzied effort to develop superior scientific talent, the public schools have generally ignored gifted students. The assumption was that they would make it on their own.

But no one knows how many gifted children don't make it. Some, it turns out, are so discouraged by everyday schooling that they simply tune out education, and never have a chance to fulfill their promise. Others develop crippling emotional disturbances after years of pressure from parents and teachers and resentment from their peers. And many attend schools where their talents are never recognized--or, even worse, where precocity is viewed as a troublesome trait to be quashed in the name of order and "normality."

During the past six years, however, the fortunes of gifted children have been on the rise. In 1972, Congress established the Federal Office for the Gifted and Talented with the mandate to identify and help develop the nation's most promising youngsters. Since 1976, the office has received $2.5

The Gifted Child, Merrill Sheils, Lucy Howard, Sylvester Monroe, Jon Lowell, and Frederick V. Boyd, *Newsweek,* Vol. XCII, No. 17, October 23, 1978. Copyright ©1978 Newsweek Inc., 444 Madison Avenue, New York, NY 10022.

million a year; about $6 million more is channeled toward exceptional students through other Federal education programs. Thirty states now have full-time consultants on education for the gifted, and all 50 offer special programs--ranging from one hour a week to full-time curriculums--in their public schools. And there may be more help on the way. Provisions in the Education Amendments of 1978, which have been accepted by a House-Senate conference, would increase the authorization for Federal spending on the gifted to $50 million a year by 1983.

Despite the recent resurgence of interest, the problems of dealing with gifted youngsters are far from solved. For one thing, modern research has shown that the old measure of exceptional talent--a score of more than 130 on a IQ test--fails to pick up the extraordinary faculties of many students. Educational psychologists are broadening the yardsticks of giftedness to include creativity, advanced social skills and even exceptional physical aptitude--the kind of finesse that marks the finest surgeons, for example--but the process of developing adequate tests is painfully slow.

## A WHITE ELITE?

Clever students from poor school districts face obvious handicaps. Last year, the U.S. Office for Civil Rights challenged New York City's three public high schools for high achievers on the ground that their student bodies were disproportionately white. OCR eventually withdrew its complaint; city school officials explained that many black and Hispanic junior high schools simply fail to inform students about the entrance exams for the elite high schools, while parochial and private institutions make sure that their own--mostly white--pupils apply on time.

According to Dorothy Sisk, current director of the Federal Office for the Gifted and Talented, many inner-city schools are so fearful of low scores on IQ tests that they hesitate to test children in the first place. "Or if they do," she adds, "they may be reluctant to give up their star students to a special program."

Many experts trace the new interest in the subject to parental pressure. "Parents have seen money spent on the disadvantaged, the handicapped, the children who don't speak English," says Isabelle Rucker, director of Virginia's Office for Exceptional Students. "They haven't seen it spent on the gifted, and they're beginning to ask why."

As a group, gifted and talented children tend to learn faster and retain more than their peers. Almost all, say the experts, show a high tolerance for complexity, and ambiguity at a remarkably young age. Some are individualistic and nonconforming, while others are inquisitive, flexible and open-minded. "A gifted child is a divergent thinker," remarks George Roeper, co-founder of the Roeper School for the gifted in suburban Detroit. "He sees many answers to one question." Gifted kids are also likely to be much more highly motivated than others, competive, even contentious.

## UNTAPPED POTENTIAL

All of these characteristics can be unsettling in an ordinary class. "If a child is always talking out of turn, if he always thinks things are funny, if he's always trying to teach the class, it is not necessarily a sign that he's a troublemaker," explains Robert Rinaldi, Baltimore's assistant superintendent for exceptional students. "It can also mean he has potential that isn't being tapped."

Inexperienced teachers often misinterpret the gifted child's eccentricities as indications that he is mentally handicapped. One Baltimore fourth grader stuttered so severely and did so badly in all his courses that school officials considered him close to retarded. It turned out that the youngster was actually an outstanding artist. Encouraged to develop his talents in a public-school project called G.A.T.E. (Gifted and Talented Education), he began to do well at academic work, too. Last year, he won a statewide contest with a videotape on blacks in Maryland punctuated with a Scott Juplin score and a flawless narration by the erstwhile stammerer.

Insensitive classmates can also make gifted children miserable, by labeling them "freaks," "creeps" and "eggheads." Jack Cahill, a 10-year-old from Brockton, Mass., was overweight, precocious and the butt of classroom jokes. "They'd demand that he spell difficult words for them, and he innocently obliged," recalls his mother. "They were taunting him, and he'd make himself ill rather than go to school." Frequently, gifted children's troubles are compounded at home. Their parents, more likely than not gifted themselves, have often forgotten the loneliness that can plague a youngster who is "different," and they are inclined to expect their talented kids to have social maturity equal to their intellectual development.

Recent research indicates that many gifted children become so alienated by these experiences—and so bored with ordinary schoolwork—that they simply turn off at an early age. Psychiatrists working with ghetto youngsters speculate that many a youthful gang leader may be a talented child who, uninspired by school, has simply turned his skills in an antisocial direction. In Boston, child psychiatrist Shepard Ginandes tells the story of a gifted teen-ager who became a "genius drug-dealer." He was enormously successful at his work, and used his huge profits to restore a colonial house. "If society doesn't give kids like these a channel for their energies," says Ginandes, who works closely with troubled adolescents, "they'll find one—often turning into dragons within the system."

Most experts agree that exceptionally talented students should spend at least part of their time with similarly gifted peers. "They need to know that there are other kids like them," explains Jack Mosier, California's state consultant on gifted children. "Can you imagine what it's like to be playing in a sandbox and thinking about a spacecraft, and the kid next to you has no idea what a spacecraft is? These kids need to be around others who are interested in the same things."

### LEARNING FOR FUN

Educators are trying to answer that need in a variety of ways. Virginia and Maryland both maintain summer programs for gifted children. Pupils for Virginia's "Governor's School," four-week sessions at three Virginia colleges, are selected from schools across the state for extraordinary academic or artistic talent. They take courses ranging from Asian studies and dance to physics and drama. Maryland youngsters work in a similar program at nine sites around the state. At

Wally McNamee—Newsweek

*Sisk: $2.5 million for the stars*

Frostburg State College, for example, last summer's crop learned about forestry and fishery sciences, while at St. Joseph's College, their peers concentrated on madrigal singing, painting, drawing and drama. The idea is to give the children a chance to do things that are simply not available in their hometown schools. "It's an experience in learning for the fun of it," says Virginia's Isabelle Rucker. "The kids applaud it, they're eager to get in there and dig, and they pick your brain until it's sore."

Some districts prefer to enrich schoolwork for gifted children by providing special education during the school year. In Decatur, Ga., for example, 60 talented students spend two hours a week in such classes. Next spring, they will undertake a remarkable project: a simulated archeological dig. Four teams, made up of fifth and sixth graders from rival schools, will create civilizations, complete with their own languages, technologies and religions. Each team will construct appropriate artifacts, including a Rosetta stone that provides the key to the language. They'll then bury the artifacts, and each group will set out to dig up and analyze another's culture. "We are trying to develop a curiosity about the social system, language and art of their own world," explains teacher Jeannette Mc-Clure. "The more concepts they understand, the better they are at making decisions. And these are the kids who are going to be making the decisions that affect history."

### 'WHAT A NICE ORANGE'

Parents who can afford to do so often enroll their talented youngsters in private schools especially designed for them. The 37-year-old Roeper School outside Detroit is a model example. The 500 students on Roeper's 12-acre campus range in age from nursery-school tykes to seniors in high school. For an annual tuition of about $2,500, they are offered informal—but demanding—courses in

*Long (right): They call him 'Brain'*

everything from dance to computer technology. One group of Roeper students has become so proficient at using the school's private computer that they have formed their own company, providing programing services for outside clients.

The teachers at Roeper are acutely aware that gifted children aren't necessarily wizards in all subjects, and they strive to nurture each student's special talents. Ten-year-old Sarah Nishiura, for instance, cares little about math or science, but loves to play with language. She writes short stories, plays, poems and puns with a precocious mix of cleverness, warmth and imagery. And she does it purely for fun, scribbling the lines on scrap paper, then hurling them away; it is up to her teacher to retrieve Sarah's efforts and save them. One tale Sarah wrote last year involves two birds who fly off to

forage for food, and return to find that an orange has fallen into their nest. The papa bird's punch line: "What a nice orange mama laid."

The Avery Coonley School in suburban Chicago offers a much stricter atmosphere. "We are very traditionally minded," says headmaster William L. Kindler. "Ultimately, our concern isn't so much academic orientation as it is to help them build support and self-control. They will get the first in spite of us, but the second is harder—the mind wants to do things that the little body cannot."

All of Avery Coonley's 250 students have IQ's of at least 120, and all perform well above national norms on tests of reading and math achievement. And although all are encouraged to pursue their special interests, they remain in orderly, disciplined grades; the school does not believe in accelerated promotion. "They are children first and gifted second," explains Kindler. Adds teacher Edward Hartig, who has enrolled two of his own children at the school: "What's different here is the attitude. The atmosphere is not down on being able—all the kids know they can do it, and ultimately, no one has anything special to brag about."

Although many experts on gifted children do not approve of accelerating their education, there are a number who encourage it, rather than have talented youngsters languish in classrooms far below their potential. One champion of letting kids progress at whatever rates they can manage is Julian Stanley, a psychology professor at Johns Hopkins University, who seven years ago launched a "Study of Mathematically Precocious Youth." Essentially, SMPY is a talent search for seventh-grade youngsters who rank in the 97th percentile and up on standardized achievement tests given by their schools.

### THE BIGGEST DILEMMA

"The idea is to find the extremely talented youths and make them visible to their schools so that the schools feel obligated to do something special to help them develop," says Stanley. "One of the biggest dilemmas has been that the schools oftentimes have either not known kids had talent or have been very reluctant to admit it when confronted by a parent who says he has a brilliant child." Stanley's program certifies the youngsters' genius. In five contests held since 1972, his team has tested about 9,500 children, of whom 6,500 have shown above-average talent. About 100 of his finds are now studying at Johns Hopkins, many more at other colleges and universities.

Many gifted students seem to thrive on acceleration, and show no sign of serious maladjustment. Michigan State's 12-year-old Kam Hunter, for example, loves mystery stories, plays rock guitar and piano and is an avid sports fan who is one of the managers of the Spartan football team. Bill Sebring, 18, one of Julian Stanley's protégés who graduated from

Johns Hopkins last spring, is a modest, easygoing youth who says that he is "really glad" he skipped through school. "I think it would have been a lot worse if I had stayed behind," he says. "You sort of lose interest, and you don't get stimulated enough." Sebring made most of his college friends through extracurricular activities like backpacking and spelunking. "They may not all have skipped grades," he notes, "but they're as bright or brighter than I am."

### EMOTIONAL TERROR

Most experts, however, think that the ability to handle rapid acceleration depends entirely on the individual student, and that many—perhaps most—cannot take it. "I've known children who had the intellectual ability to skip a lot of grades, but emotionally it would have terrified them," says Jack Nolan, a former elementary-school teacher in Baltimore. "I'd hate to be the teacher who moved a kid up who could handle everything

*Nishiura: A tale of two birds*

academically, but who had no friends."

And it is clear that many gifted kids—given the right school atmosphere—flourish without acceleration. Andrew Lee, a 15-year-old junior at St. Ann's School in Brooklyn, N.Y., is an excellent example. Andy is an "omnibus" prodigy—a child whose every effort yields superlative results. He likes to shoot pool. He plays the flute (and composes his own music), does magic tricks and drafts anagrammatic crossword puzzles. He polished off advanced calculus at the age of 12, and last year, as a sophomore, scored a perfect 800 on the college-board biology exam. Andy is exceedingly popular. Indeed, he seems to be his only critic. "When I say something stupid, it's *really* stupid," he frowns. "Other people can just shrug it off, but not me."

Many gifted children who are now

grownups believe that as long as kids are allowed to do extra work on their own, they can be perfectly happy in ordinary schools. Saul Kripke, now a 37-year-old philosophy professor at Princeton, remembers that his schools in Nebraska did not approve of acceleration. So while his classmates were learning to add and subtract, Kripke, with the help of his parents, taught himself to multiply. When he had mastered that, he bought himself an algebra book, then moved on to calculus. At the age of 5, he taught himself Hebrew. And by seventh grade, he was reading Descartes and Hume—for fun. "I was always being told that things would be over my head," he recalls, "and the principal would try to trip me up. I found it annoying, but I kept saying to myself 'this is not at all incomprehensible'."

Talented youngsters seem to appreciate almost any change from ordinary schooling that gives them more to do. Marvin Long is an eighth grader in Chicago's black ghetto who has shown an extraordinary talent for writing. In elementary school, with his mother's approval, Marvin skipped two grades. Now, at 11, he's one of the smallest boys in his class, and sometimes he finds the public-school atmosphere uncomfortable. "The other kids call me 'Brain' and 'Professor'," he complains. But one half-day a week, Marvin is freed from class for work at one of Chicago's twelve centers for the gifted. There, he concentrates on writing—mostly short stories. "I love it," says Marvin. "I feel more free to express myself there."

## NATIONAL RECOGNITION

But Marvin is lucky. This year, the experts estimate, only about 12 per cent of the ablest American schoolchildren will get the extra attention and academic encouragement that they need. Although those concerned with the education of the gifted are pleased by the current surge of interest in their cause, many of them warn that it is not enough. And they worry that it is just a cyclical phenomenon, one that will soon be eclipsed by another period of egalitarian neglect.

"The issue before us is that we don't honor or nurture intelligence in this country," argues Stanley Bosworth, founder and headmaster of St. Ann's. "For years, we've neglected brains and excellence, while spending billions of dollars on the handicapped and the mediocre." Bosworth and his colleagues do not advocate less attention to disadvantaged youngsters. Instead, they urge national recognition of gifted children as another minority group that needs special help. Unless such help is forthcoming, they warn, the U.S. is in danger of squandering its finest minds, talents and leaders—the most precious natural resources of all.

—MERRILL SHEILS with LUCY HOWARD in Washington, SYLVESTER MONROE in Chicago, JON LOWELL in Detroit and FREDERICK V. BOYD in New York

# The Brightest Kids

## By Cheryl Bentsen

"...There are an estimated 2.5-million gifted children in the nation, 165,000 in New York..."

David speaks a half-dozen languages, says his main interest is comparative philology, calculates mathematical equations, does chemistry experiments, studies the violin, reads the New York *Times* and college textbooks. Recently he asked his parents to find him a physics tutor, because he doesn't understand the different parts of the electromagnetic-radiation spectrum. So his parents are looking for a physicist to explain these mysteries to their four-year-old son.

David is one of an estimated 2.5 million gifted children in this country whose I.Q. scores typically range from 130 upward. They include music, math, and chess prodigies; budding poets, ballerinas, and basketball stars.

The most extraordinary are the prodigies whose abilities, like David's, are far advanced for their age. The most famous have included Mozart, who began composing before age five; violinists Yehudi Menuhin and Isaac Stern, both of whom played with major orchestras before they were teenagers; Puritan writer Cotton Mather, who entered Harvard at twelve; Massachusetts jurist Paul Dudley, a Harvard graduate at fourteen; and John Stuart Mill, who could write Greek with his left hand while writing Latin with his right. Less well known are America's greatest mathematician and the father of cybernetics, Norbert Wiener, who graduated from Tufts University at age fourteen, and French pianist Charles Camille Saint-Saëns, who made his debut at age ten and entered the Paris Conservatory at age thirteen.

Some prodigies, like Arthur Rubinstein or Andrés Segovia, perform at a high level well into their late years, enjoying successful, happy lives. Others end up as mediocrities or failures, such as William James Sidis, a promising mathematician who entered Harvard in 1911 at age 11, but later drifted through mundane jobs and died penniless and unemployed at the age of 46.

The gifted have had an erratic history in public esteem. During times of strong egalitarian concerns—the sixties, for example—their excellence has been viewed with suspicion. It's been commonly thought that the gifted are the least needy of all schoolchildren. But a 1976 New York State Regents report says that without special help these children easily become bored and frustrated and often drop out of school. Now there's a new wave of interest in the gifted. Legislators, educators, and psychologists are once again taking up their cause and studying their needs.

About 3 to 5 percent of all children fall into the category of gifted, depending on how broad a definition is used. These children may excel in one area only or be talented at everything. Bobby Fischer's teachers were surprised to find he was a chess whiz, since he'd been only a fair student at school. Often, gifted children are puzzled at the labels parents and teachers put on them.

Andrew Chen, eight, is a student at St. Ann's School for gifted children in Brooklyn Heights. Andrew sits cross-legged on the floor, books piled beside him, listening intently to older students talk about being gifted. He is studying eighth-grade math. Shyly, in a soft, babyish voice, he interrupts: "I'm not sure I'm gifted," he says. "I'm good at some things, like math. But I'm not so good at other things, like gym." The others giggle and Andrew looks mortified. He continues: "Everybody in fourth grade calls me 'mathemagician.' It makes me feel embarrassed."

At Johns Hopkins University, Dr. Julian C. Stanley, director of the Study of Mathematically Precocious Youth and himself a former gifted child, has tested over 10,000 seventh- and eighth-graders and says his work has shown that math reasoning ability tends to be more hereditary than verbal ability. Math ability seems to show up early in children, regardless of whether they've been exposed to the subject.

Among those Dr. Stanley has helped is Eric Jablow, sixteen, of Brooklyn. Jablow taught himself calculus at age eight and enrolled in Brooklyn College when he was eleven. At fifteen, he became the youngest college graduate in the 130-year history of the city's college system. He was graduated summa cum laude and won a National Science Foundation graduate fellowship to work toward a Ph.D. degree in math at Princeton two years ago, the youngest doctoral candidate the school has ever had.

Last year a writer in the *Smithsonian* magazine described Jablow as somewhat friendless and lacking in spontaneity. "If I offend people just by existing, that is not my fault," Jablow told the writer. Since then he's declined interviews.

Like many highly gifted children, Jablow has been hurt by the way others see him. "There was one teacher," he has said, "he just didn't like me.... He did W. C. Fields imitations when I came into the room.... He must have been afraid of me."

Most of our schools are not prepared for the problems that face the exceptional child. Denise Hurd, sixteen, now a junior at St. Ann's, recalls the humiliations of her early school days.

"In kindergarten in public school I wouldn't say a

Copyright ©1979 by the *New York Magazine* Company, Inc. Reprinted with permission of *NEW YORK* Magazine.

# "…Only 4 percent of the country's gifted children are getting an appropriate education…"

word," she says. "I sat in a corner and read a dictionary. The teacher asked my parents if I were deaf or autistic. It was strange to be four years old and know that everybody else thought I was weird. Everybody made fun of me. One girl constantly hit me and called me 'smartie.' I was always thrown off the monkey bars for being a 'brain.' I was terrified because I was different."

Dr. Dorothy A. Sisk, director of the Federal Office of the Gifted and Talented (located within the Bureau of Education for the Handicapped), says that only 4 percent of the country's gifted children are getting an appropriate education. Her annual budget is $3.78 million. Another $6 million is funneled to gifted children through other federal programs.

But there are signs that the gifted will soon be getting more support. A bill written by Senator Jacob Javits that authorizes $50 million for gifted children's education is now part of federal education law, but the funds have yet to be appropriated. In Albany, State Senator Howard Babbush (D., Brooklyn) has introduced a bill that would authorize $15 million. Current state spending is about $750,000 for an estimated 165,000 gifted students. (The state spends $800 million a year for 210,000 handicapped students.)

But money is just one ingredient to help gifted children fulfill their potential. "Unfortunately, few city teachers are trained in gifted education, and most of the programs designed last year left much to be desired," says Grace Lacy, former regional director of the state office of gifted and talented programs.

"To be incarcerated in an eighth-grade algebra class, forced to sit through 180 50-minute periods, when a student is capable of learning the subject in less than fifteen hours, is deadly for a gifted child," says Dr. Stanley. "When held back, a gifted child can daydream, throw spitballs, grandstand the class, be the class clown, argue, complain, but have nothing good to do. Many children are outrageously victimized by the system, by teachers who put them in a holding operation so they don't get too far ahead."

In listening to parents of gifted children, one hears a litany of public-school abuses. Gifted classes often simply herd together the brightest and provide "enrichment," or just plain busywork. The competition to get into the city's four specialized academic high schools—Bronx Science, Brooklyn Tech, Stuyvesant, Music and Art—is so stiff that approximately six students are turned away for every one admitted.

In recent years the most promising elementary program for the gifted was the Astor classes for gifted children. With a $1.4-million Vincent Astor Foundation grant, Dr. Virginia Z. Ehrlich, former city coordinator for gifted-child studies, designed the program in 1973. Six school districts now have 40 classes for children aged five to ten, but since private funding ran out, the quality of some of the programs has dropped.

Though city educators say they try to have an equal balance in terms of sex and race, often practice doesn't bear out theory. The gifted child most likely to be picked for special classes is still the white, middle-class boy.

But even when a district makes gifted education a priority—if for no other reason than to offer a lure to the white middle class—resentment may run high among parents of children of average intelligence.

"I get a lot of pressure about gifted programs," says Dr. Harvey Garner, superintendent of Brooklyn District 18. "This year we have about $140,000 for all our gifted classes, which is more than most districts, but peanuts when you consider teachers' salaries. Some parents say I am taking money away from their children and diverting it to the gifted. Others say they would leave the city if it weren't for our classes. Another problem is hiring teachers. Many don't want to teach gifted classes because it means more work, with parents looking over their shoulders. Sometimes I try to hire a specialized teacher but the union contract forces me to take the first available."

At age four, with a doctored birth certificate (her father's work) that said she was five, Donnica Moore marched off to kindergarten able and eager to read, write, and compose music. Fortunately, she'd had the foresight to bring along a book, which she read while her classmates explored the alphabet blocks, one letter at a time.

For most of her public-school career Donnica, whose I.Q. is 170, was made to sit patiently while her classmates struggled. Tutored from infancy by a doting father, she was unprepared for attitudes she met at school. Other kids called her a "brain." Teachers stopped calling on her because they knew she knew the answer.

The final humiliation for Donnica took place at her high school senior-awards ceremony. She'd won fourteen scholarship awards. The principal told her that winners were no better than anyone else, just luckier. That fall, at age sixteen, she went to Princeton, the youngest in her freshman class.

"I got through because my father kept telling me I was great," she says at seventeen. "That was all the strength I needed to face setbacks, like teachers who hated me."

Donnica is one of six gifted children in her family— four of whom have I.Q.'s in the 164-to-185 range. Her oldest brother goes to Stuyvesant, and the others are in Special Progress classes.

Last year while Donnica was at Princeton, her eleven-year-old brother, Douglas, was being bullied by classmates at his Brooklyn junior high. Bored, fidgety, and sometimes disruptive, he was criticized by his teachers for being arrogant. "Douglas is doing a lot better," teachers would tell his mother, Toby, a schoolteacher herself. "We're showing him that he's no better than anyone else." In fact, Douglas scores at the twelfth-grade level in reading and math.

Dennis Moore, Douglas and Donnica's father, was the first director of a group of parents called the Concerned Citizens for the Education of the Gifted and Talented. For fourteen years he's argued at PTA meetings and with school administrators for better programs for his children.

"I've been called an elitist, an egotist, reactionary, and even a racist," he says. "Other parents get their backs up when you talk about special programs for the gifted. They think it is elitist because I want my children to have the same attention as the disadvantaged and handicapped get."

Gifted children in the performing arts often get a better break. Each Saturday at Juilliard 280 musical prodigies, including Charles Kim, nine, a violinist, gather for

# "...A five-year-old who has memorized all of Shakespeare cries if she gets 99 on a test..."

a day's intensive training. When Charles's mother brought him to Juilliard three years ago, Olegna Fuschi, director of Juilliard's pre-college division, had doubts whether he was old enough to be in the class. "But once he started I knew he belonged here," she says. "Right now his only limitation is his size, his tiny hands. He is a very, very special child." At his final exam last year his teacher wrote: "Handle with care—a possible national treasure."

Erika Nickrenz gave her first big performance at Town Hall at age eleven. "I was the only kid on the program and I remember sitting backstage waiting, quietly playing through my piece on my lap," she says. "When I went onstage the piano bench was too low. The audience cracked up while the concertmaster raised it."

Erika, now fifteen, wrinkles her nose at the word "prodigy." "I never think of myself as a prodigy," she says. "At fifteen that's kind of old. Prodigy reminds me of Mozart and how he was discontent and grew up sickly and didn't do anything but write music. He had a miserable life and died a pauper in his early thirties.

"My mother doesn't want to rush me. She says if you want to be a concert pianist you have to work your head off. But if you're not really dedicated you shouldn't have to. I guess the idea now is that you work hard when you're a kid and then you shock the world when you're twenty." Next year Erika will audition to play with the St. Louis Symphony.

In Westchester, the parents of David, the four-year-old with a 200 I.Q., have decided to go outside the public-school system to educate their son. In September 1977 they opened a school in Westchester for David and 40 other gifted children. But, because of lack of support, the school was forced to close a month later.

"We did not do this out of arrogance," says his father. "It was the only solution, and we view our responsibility toward David as a genetic mandate."

David's parents knew he was special almost from the day he was born. At age one he picked up a cup in a restaurant and said, "Cooks!" "No dear, cup," his mother said. "Cooks! Cooks!" he insisted. Turning over the cup, his mother saw the manufacturer's name: Cooks.

Helping David's parents start the school was Nora Cohen, coordinator of the mentally gifted program of the Philadelphia school system.

"It's important to reach children like this very early," she says. "The problem is that children this special are outcasts even among other gifted children. David is socially well adjusted, but he can't really share with kids his age. Often these children are in conflict because of their own perfectionism. I know a five-year-old girl who can recite all of Shakespeare from memory. But if she gets a 99 on a test instead of 100 she cries for hours. Unfortunately there is very little validated research on children this special because they are so rare."

Dr. Julian Stanley knows two children with I.Q.'s in the 200 range.

"The girl is doing quite well, excels at math, and is a violin prodigy," he says. "The boy is having a harder time. His mother is not as perceptive about his needs. She is a voluble talker and writes a lot of letters on his behalf looking for suggestions. But she doesn't seem to connect with any of them. I wouldn't wish a child like this on any family not willing to devote an enormous amount of energy. It takes as much time and energy to raise a child like this as it would if he were in the idiot category."

What becomes of these exceptional children as they reach adulthood?

"We hope and expect that these children will have more of a chance to make great contributions to society than anybody else," says Abraham J. Tannenbaum, professor of gifted-child studies at Teachers College of Columbia University.

"But precocity is no guarantee that they will fulfill their potential. Some grow up to be superannuated children, precocious well into their adult years, always promising but never reaching their potential. Some turn out to be highly verbal bores you meet at cocktail parties. They're glib and filled with trivial information, but lack depth and understanding."

Those who attain early success often find it a hard adjustment from whiz kid to adult. Colin Camerer, nineteen, enrolled at Johns Hopkins at fourteen after spending a year each in junior and senior high school and skipping his college freshman year. He completed his B.A. in quantitative studies three years later and is now working on an MBA and Ph.D. in finance at the University of Chicago.

"I don't like to talk about the negative," he says. "But there comes a time when all gifted kids have to face turning 20 or 21. Getting to that age when you're no longer a whiz kid is kind of a comedown. As you enter more competitive environments, people no longer care how old you are, just how well you perform."

In the corporate world, Jud, 21, the youngest manager in his company, feels he must hide his age:

"If the men at my company knew my age, I'm sure I'd be taken less seriously," he says. "My job is mainly interpreting company position to government. Most of the executives feel that our industry is overly regulated, and they criticize the young Carter-administration staffers for being too young to know anything important. Because I am young I've gotten strong signals to slow down. I've learned that sometimes it is more important to slow down and get across an idea than to come across as brilliant."

For some it is a lifelong effort to shed the prodigy image. Merrill Kenneth Wolf, 47, is a professor of anatomy and neuro-anatomy at the University of Massachusetts Medical Center. A former child prodigy in piano—he taught himself to play at two—he earned his B.A. in music from Yale at fourteen, the youngest in the history of the college.

Wolf is reluctant to talk about childhood: "It has no relevance to my adult performance," he says. "As an adult either I am useful to myself and to others or I am not. My childhood was just an anticipation of my adult achievements. It's really quite burdensome to have a freakish kind of childhood that follows one around. When I went to college, a solid midwestern newspaper wrote an editorial denouncing giftedness, saying this was an atypical business, unhealthy, and that I would no doubt come to a bad end. There's less of that attitude today, but then it was quite painful. You can't transform a deviant—whether that deviancy is superior intelligence or an odd set of social or sexual preferences or subnormal intelligence—into something else. You can only help that person be the best he can within the framework he's got."

# THE GIFTED CHILD IN THE UNITED STATES AND ABROAD


Joe Khatena

Marshall University


The gifted movement began in the United States, we might say, with the interest, curiosity and industry of one of our very talented psychologists, Lewis M. Terman, in the early years of this century. His studies of mental tests and precocious children led eventually to two major contributions, namely, the construction and use of the *Stanford Binet* and the *Gentic Studies of Genius,* a monumental longitudinal study of more than 1,500 gifted Californian urban children from kindergarten through high school, followed through mid-life and reported in five volumes by Terman and his associates (e.g. Terman, 1925; Terman & Oden, 1959).

There is much we have learned from his sustained research about the intellectually gifted who as a group:

came from superior intellectual, physical and environmental
  backgrounds, and generally maintain this superiority;

tended to be many-sided intellectually, emotionally stable,
  and well adjusted, maintaining these with little incidence
  of serious problems;

had normal marriages and sexual adjustment;

showed in general a low mortality rate;

were normal to superior in social intelligence, interests and
  play activities, averaging better than most people on
  nearly every personality trait;

were well in advance of their age mates in educational achievement
  and benefitted by acceleration with almost no occurrence of
  failure in school subjects generally obtaining A grades; and

went to college such that 70 percent became college graduates
  (a third with academic distinction), 63 percent went to
  graduate school, and 17 percent obtained doctoral degrees.

However, among the several variables that tend to reduce the generalizability of his findings are three relating to instrumentation. *First,* is the fact that IQ was used as the sole criterion for the identification of gifted children about which Catherine Cox Miles (1960) cites Terman as challenging educators, sociologists and psychologists to produce if they could:




The Gifted Child in the United States and Abroad, Joe Khatena, *The Gifted Child Quarterly,* Vol. XX, No. 3, Fall, 1977.
Copyright ©1977 The National Association for Gifted Children, 217 Gregory Drive, Hot Springs, Ark. 71901.

"..... another concept as effective as the IQ for delimiting of
a group of talent to include the most successful students,
the best achievers in the world, and...in the world of human
relationships and human endeavor generally" (P. 51).

*Second,* is the fact that the *Stanford Binet* used to determine IQ is
biased in favor of the verbally gifted, and so responsible for leaving
out potentially non verbally low socio-economically gifted students
from selection.

And *third,* the *Stanford Binet* was not constructed to include the
screening of divergent thinking so that creatively gifted students
were eliminated from selection.

Of course at the time the Terman studies began (1921) there were
no effective intellectual measures that could yield a better index of
superior abilities than IQ. But that IQ as an index of intelligence
persists in being deified in some quarters, it is necessary to un-
derscore Taylor's critical observation (1959) that "intelligence" is a
concept created by western culture that stresses its important
values, and that intelligence tests in our culture "essentially concerned themselves with how fast relatively unimportant problems
can be solved without making errors," whereas in another culture,
"intelligence might be a measure more in terms of how adequately
important problems can be solved making all the errors necessary
and without regard for time (P. 54).

## MANY KINDS OF GIFTEDNESS

A recognition of the presence of many kinds of giftedness by the
United States Office of Education in its recent report (Educating the
Gifted, 1972) rather than the one kind identified by IQ is a reflection of the change in thought that occurred about giftedness over the
past two decades or so. These have been identified as general intellectual ability, creative or productive thinking, specific academic
aptitude, leadership ability, visual and performing arts abilities and
psychomotor abilities.

*General Intellectual Ability*
Regarding general intellectual ability, thought on the subject has
moved from general intelligence first defined in terms of Mental Age
or MA by Alfred Binet and T. Simon (1905) in France, through Intelligence Quotient or IQ defined as a single index of general intelligence by Lewis Terman (1916) to an IQ differentiated as verbal,
performance and global by David Wechsler (1966) in the United
States.

Perception of intelligence as a univariate phenomenon moved
towards perception of intelligence as a multivariate phenomenon,
with major contributions coming from England and America.
Through simple factorial analyses Charles Spearman (1927) in
England derived his two factor theory of intelligence which saw
general intellectual functioning as governed by some general mental
energy or "g" that entered into the functioning of a number of
specific abilities called "s". Sir Cyril Burt (1949) and P. E. Vernon
(1951) expanded this conception of intelligence into hierarchical

models of human abilities. Both subscribe to the concept of Spearman's "g" as entering into all human mental functioning. *Burt's model* consists of a series of successive dichotomies: the first dichotomy emerges from the head of the hierarchy, the human mind, as the *relations* level or "g" and *practical* level (which includes psychomotor, mechanical and spatial abilities); these dichotomize to the next lower level or *associations* level, which again subdivide into the levels of perception and sensation. *Vernon's model* is headed by "g" which subdivides into two sets of major group factors, namely, verbal-educational or v:ed and kinesthetic motor or K:m factors with the latter being equivalent to Burt's "practical factor." The major factors subdivide into minor factors such that v:ed subdivides into verbal, numerical and educational factors while K:m subdivides into practical, spatial, mechanical and physical factors. These then divide still further into specific factors.

In America, L. L. Thurstone (1938) by using factor analyses discovered that certain grouping of test responses occurred with no presence of "g", and a limited number of elementary factors. This led him to conceive intelligence as consisting of about a dozen or so group factors which he named Primary Mental Abilities most important of which labeled as Verbal, Number, Spatial, Relations, Word Fluency, Memory, and Reasoning. He did find that the primary factors related to each other as a result of further work with his tests and explains this relationship as a function of a "second-order factor".

The expanding concept of intellectual functioning found fullest expression in Guilford's comprehensive theoretical three dimensional model which he called the Structure of Intellect (Guildford, 1967). Ths model consists of five kinds of mental *operations* (cognition, memory, divergent production, convergent production, and evaluation), four kinds of *contents* (figural, symbolic, semantic, and behavioral), and six kinds of informational forms or *products* (units, classes, relations, systems, transformations, and implications), making a total of 120 possible intellectual abilities each different from the rest by its unique combination of mental operation, content and product used. Not only did Guilford's model articulate the multi-faceted nature of ability but also included the dimension of "divergent thinking" (more loosely called creativity) as one of five major thinking operations hitherto omitted by others from their models and measures of intelligence.

*Creative or Productive Thinking*

In the main creative thinking abilities and their measurement have derived from the works of Guilford (1967) and Torrance (1962, 1974) and their associates. Relative to the Structure of Intellect, Guilford defines creative thinking in terms of divergent thinking, redefinition and transformation abilities. Torrance defines creativity as a process of becoming sensitive to problems, deficiencies, gaps in knowledge, missing elements, disharmony, and so on; identifying the difficulty; searching for solutions, making guesses, or formulating hypotheses about the deficiencies; testing and retesting these hypotheses and possibly modifying and retesting them; finally communicating the results (Torrance, 1974).

Their tests of creative thinking in general give major roles to four creative thinking abilities: *fluency* (the ability to produce many ideas to a given task), *flexibility* (the ability to produce different kinds of ideas that show shifts in thinking), *originality* (the ability to produce ideas that are unusual, remote and clever), and *elaboration* (the ability to add details to a basic idea produced). To these four creative thinking abilities Torrance and his associates (1975) have added *synthesis* (the ability to combine two or more figures into a related whole picture) and *closure* (the ability to dely completing a task long enough to make the mental leaps that make possible the production of original ideas). It should be noted that while Guilford tries to measure fluency, flexibility, originality and elaboration in a way that requires a person to do many test tasks, each setting out to give information about one of the 24 divergent thinking abilities, Torrance tries to measure the same four abilities in a way that requires a person to do several complex tasks each designed to make a person show all these abilities at one and the same time.

### Specific Academic Aptitude

This appears to relate to the ability to do one or more academic subjects like language, mathematics, science and social studies. In terms of the Vernon model for instance, much "g" functioning is required to enter into the verbal-educational component of intellect and may call into play one or more of the specific abilities. If the Guilford model is preferred, one or more of the five mental operations may be called to action relative to the kind of content (symbolic and semantic), and product required.

If by specific academic aptitude is meant the potential to do better in certain subject areas than others, then measures of intellectual abilities generally and the sub-tests of these measures specifically may be used to predict aptitude. However, if b specific academic aptitude is meant performance in one or more academic subjects, then a direct approach of evaluating scores obtained in the subject should be the approach. It may be that a combination of these two would fetch the best indices of relevant ability, in which an IQ test and a measure of achievement may be concurrently administered.

### Leadership Ability

To possess leadership ability a person needs to be bright, to have understanding of people, to have a feel for the way people behave in groups, to be sensitive to change, and to be able to creatively and skilfully handle them. In short, such ability requires what Thorndike called "social intelligence". The behavioral component of the Structure of Intellect offers a good explanation of leadership potential as it relates to the single individual assessed where *behavioral content* relates essentially to non-verbal information involving attitudes, needs, desires, moods, intentions, perceptions, thoughts and the like. Acting together with the five mental operations and six product categories, the behavioral component of intellect offers a good assessment model of leadership ability. However, since leadership involves not only the leader but the led, some appraisal of the dynamics of social relations seems to offer a fruitful direction to take. Sociometry as developed by Moreno could be used as a valuable tool to evaluate the social status of the individual in the contest of his group relative to the choice of a leader for a specific assignment. Together these two approaches might provide reasonably good evidence of leadership potential.

*Visual and Performing Arts Ability*

Ability in these dimensions are more appropriately considered as abilities in one or more of the areas in the Fine Arts, and not some single ability that necessarily enters into all activities defined as visual and performing arts. By visual arts we probably mean, drawing, painting, sculptor, designing, musical composition in written form, and all other related forms of art whose products can be observed; by performing arts we probably mean music, dance, oratory, drama, and all other related forms of art that require performance.

Abilities that are required for superior production or performance are not easily measurable; few if any psychological measures are available at present for the purpose; and much reliance has to be placed on observable behavior and products to determine if a person is gifted in the visual and performing arts.

Common to all these art forms is *creativity,* a processing and an energizing agent that differs in degree for its operation depending upon the form of art used. Specific to each art form are highly specialized knowledge and skills that must be acquired by a person before he can express himself in that medium; and often because it takes time to acquire these, it is not unusual to find screening of young children for talent in the arts in terms of potential, difficult. Of course we do find children of exceptional talent that manifests itself early as in the performance of child prodigies in music--but this is quite rare.

For the most part the best way to identify the gifted in these special areas would be through observation by those expert in the field of their products and performances with relevant and important criteria set up for such purpose. Such experts should be alerted to look out for not only superior ability to reproduce but also ability to be innovative and the tendency to break away from the more conventional nature of the art forms. It would be of great value to screen for creative potential as well since the information so obtained would give useful clues about the way in which a person's talent in the visual and performing arts would probably develop.

*Psychomotor Ability*

Psychomotor ability or abilities involve the combined function of body and mind, the "practical intelligence" of Thorndike or Burt; or the kinesthetic-motor (k:m) abilities of Vernon' hierarchical model of intelligence that involve such factors as practical, mechanical, spatial and physical factors; or the Figural dimension of Guilford's Structure of Intellect. Abilities such as these are found in people who are good handymen, mechanics, engineers, draftsmen, clerks, truck drivers, airplane pilots, footballers, athletes, and the like.

If one uses Vernon's model of intelligence then "g" enters into all of psychomotor activity to a greater or lesser extent with highly specialized skills that are involved in a particular psychomotor performance. If one uses the Guilford model, then the Figural dimension as it is processed by the five mental operations and six product categories are involved.

To find out who are gifted in the psychomotor areas, there are a number of good tests available. Where educated observation of psychomotor abilities can be made it should be made. This becomes a necessity when no measures are available; besides, it is also a valuable complement to the assessment procedures for the identification of psychomotor ability.

*Identification of the Gifted in the United States and Abroad*

In the United States while aware of the presence of many kinds of talent in our midst that could be called gifted we have had a special bias for the "intellectually gifted" as the sole category of giftedness, possibly traceable to the mental test movement that began in the first decade of this century and possibly from the term "genius" as derived from high IQ levels as measured by the *Stanford Binet* and the Terman *Genetic Studies of Genius*. Change of thought about the "intellectually gifted" was to a large extent initiated by the changing conceptual models of intellectual abilities precipitated by various advocates into the United States Office of Education recognition in 1972 of six categories of giftedness, namely, general intellectual ability, creative or productive thinking, specific academic aptitude, leadership ability, visual and performing arts abilities and psychomotor abilities.

Generally, and where applicable, in other countries, the official emphasis in the main is still on the "intellectually gifted" with some minor recognition given to talent as manifested in the fine arts. The Binet conception of intelligence and the IQ index of intellectual ability have great prestige abroad, and much reliance is placed upon it and achievement exams for the identification of the gifted, though at times less formal observational screening procedures are used. There has been some growing interest and recognition given to the identification of creative potential abroad, but this is unofficial and negligible. When we stop to think how recent the official recognition in the United States of the six categories of giftedness is, we can better understand the position regarding this abroad.

## Government Provision For The Education of The Gifted

Although our knowledge of the gifted and talented and what we can do for them has increased over the years it has not been without considerable frustration over the obstructionism of a public education system that is essentially geared to a philosophy of egalitarianism. The first really significant step to counteract this problem took the form of an Act of Congress of the United States to include in the Elementary Education Amendments of 1969, signed into law on 13th April, 1970, provisions for gifted and talented (Education of Gifted and Talented Report, 1972). This required the Commissioner of Education to determine the extent to which special educational assistance programs were necessary or useful to meet the needs of gifted and talented children, to evaluate how existing Federal educational assistance programs can be more effectively used to meet these needs, and to recommend new programs, if any, needed to meet these needs; further, the Commissioner was to report his findings together with the recommendations not later than one year after the enactment of this act (Section 806c of Public Law 91-230).

## 7. GIFTED

In 1972, Commissioner Marland launched the Federal Program
for the gifted and talented details of which can be found in the
report itself and in my earlier presentation on this subject (Khatena,
1976). Much of his directions have been translated into action. Some
features of immediate interest are:

(a) establishment of the CEC/TAG Educational Resource
Information Center in Reston, Virginia that collects and
disseminates information on the gifted with the aid of its
computer services;

(b) funding in 1976 of a graduate training program in the
area of the gifted conducted by a consortium of universities
headed by Columbia University such that graduate fellows
may work with some of the best known scholars in the field
whose universities have programs towards degrees in the
area of the gifted.

(c) increased state government involvement in providing
special educational opportunities for the gifted, either
directly via their school systems or Federal and local
special projects, with some states enacting laws for the
educational advancement of their gifted, and in the appointment of personnel to actualize the law

(d) greater university involvement in providing training of
facilitators of the gifted, from single course programs to
certification and degree programs; and

(e) continued conduct of leadership training institutes in
various locations in the United States for the preparation
of professional personnel to assume leadership positions in
the advancement of provisions for the gifted in their state
and colleges.

Conditions abroad do not quite match the efforts in the United
States to provide superior educational opportunity to the gifted. In
fact the latest release by the USOE of Application for Grants Under
Gifted and Talented Program (CFDA no. 13.562) with April 27,
1977 as the closing date for applications defines the gifted and
talent and their need for differentiated education or services beyond
those provided by the regular school system to the average student
in order to realize these potentialities. It also requires comprehensive screening for the identification of these different kinds of
giftedness and in such a way that subjects in each category of giftedness stand an equal chance of selection. Further, that identification of a single category of giftedness is appropriate for a
special program related to it.

However, among the most progressive countries abroad relative to
the provision of special educational opportunities for the gifted are

England, Israel, India, Brazil, Czechoslovakia, Mexico, Syria, and Turkey (Gibson & Chennels, 1976).

(a) *England.* Foremost among these countries is England (and closest to the kind of efforts that exist in the United States) and in addition to various experimental projects, government support comes by way of scholarships, special classes or schools, with opportunities for the gifted to attend the best Universities in the land.

(b) *Israel.* A department for the gifted was established in 1971. Up to 50 percent financial support is given to all programs for the gifted so as to keep fees paid to attend these programs at a relatively low level. There is funding of large and small experimental projects as well. Regional activities for the gifted are encouraged. There is also the development of post secondary boarding schools for the disadvantaged able. Anticipated expansion in 1976 of educational opportunities for the gifted was preceeded by various pilot experiments. Further, government funds and scholarships are available for the advancement of the gifted in the country.

(c) *India.* Government support and commitment in India comes mainly through scholarship especially since 1963. Gifted students are awarded scholarships to attend various projects conducted in the country as for instance, through the National Science Talent Search (1963), the National Rural Talent Search (1971/1972), and the Government of India Merit Scholar in Residential Schools.

(d) *Brazil.* In 1973, a government decree created the National Center for Special Education with the purpose of expanding and improving facilities for teaching exceptional children including the gifted through eleven years of schooling within the regular school. Funds are provided for this by the government through one of its agencies like the Association for the Protection of Gifted Children.

(e) *Czechoslovakia.* The government there supports most of the special educational opportunities given though at times a small fee had to be paid by pupils who for instance attend the People's School of Art.

(f) *Mexico.* Government support is by way of scholarships given to the needy gifted. The aim is to provide special opportunities to all the gifted in Mexico.

(g) *Turkey.* In Turkey the Code of February 16, 1975 clearly defines support of the gifted, and efforts towards this end have been going on since 1948 and includes experimentation, research, grants from TUBITAK or the Government Research Center, special classes (1950/60) and scholarships.

*Another group of countries* have no committed national or Federal support. However, variation in support exists at the regional, state and local levels ranging from none to some special programs and schools for the gifted. Among these countries are Australia, Canada, Ghana, Kenya, Malaysia, New Zealand, Nigeria, South Africa, Tobago and Trinidad.

*Three countries* whose governments recognize the need to provide special opportunities for the education of the gifted are Kuwait,

Syria, and Sri Lanka. However, their programs, in the main, are in the planning stage.

A *fourth group of countries* have governments that do not support or are apathetic towards the needs of the gifted. Among these countries are Denmark, France, Italy and the Netherlands.

A number of factors have influenced the directions that these countries have taken among which are the nature of the political organizations of the country, the degree of their commitment to egalitarianism, the hostility towards an elitism, the relative status of these countries as developing nations, and their economy and wealth.

### Educational Opportunities Provided In
### The United States And Abroad

The educational opportunities provided in the United States and other countries concerned for the gifted vary from special provisions within the regular school to special schools; from grade acceleration to enrichment of the learning environment in the form of enriched curriculum materials and physical surroundings; from development of intellectual and academic abilities relative to language arts, science and mathematics to development of talent in the fine arts and sports to which may be added the provisions for correspondence courses and tutoring, placement in advanced grades and classes, and independent study.

More peculiar to the United States, the provision of educational opportunities have also concentrated on discovering and using superior methodological approaches, on creating psychological climates conducive to optimum learning, on allowing high school students to attend college courses while still in school, on sensitivity training, on individualized instruction through such means as team teaching and non graded plans, on arranging for separate classes with specially trained teachers, supervisors and consultants, special attention to the emotional and social adjustment, and curriculum through programs which emphasize higher level thought (Education of the Gifted & Talented Report, 1972; ERIC--CEC/TAG Selective Bibliography, 1973).

A growing awareness and acceptance of the importance of developing creative and productive thinking of gifted individuals are becoming more noticeable in the United States, and to a lesser extent for instance in England, Australia and Israel.

### Contributions Of National Associations
### To The Gifted Movement

Another very viable influence takes the form of the contributions and activities of national associations. The Association for the Gifted in *Canada* formed in 1975 for instance has set itself the prime function of spurring legislation for the gifted. The National Association for Gifted Children of *France* formed in 1971 levels itself at stirring the French Government, which shuns support for the gifted for fear of being accused of elitism, to do something for the gifted. It organized creativity workshops in 1972 and formed chess clubs in 1974 for gifted children. The National Association for Gifted Children of the *United Kingdom* is more than 20 years old and has championed the cause of the gifted in significant ways, and has recently made some very valuable contributions by organizing the First World Conference in 1975.

The Association for the Gifted and the National Association for Gifted Children of the *United States* are among the chief and loudest voices of support for the gifted, drawing their strength from parents and professionals all over the country. They influence thought to a far greater extent and in many more ways in the United States than do similar bodies elsewhere in the world through national or regional workshops, conferences, and annual conventions; and through participation at USOE organized conferences they have urged special provisions for the Gifted that culminated in the significant legislation of 1970. Both organizations reach their membership in the United States and other subscribing countries, TAG through its newsletter *Talents and Gifts,* and NAGC through its journal the GIFTED CHILD QUARTERLY. Together the message that gifted children are neglected and should be specially provided with unique educational opportunities ring loud and clear. The GIFTED CHILD QUARTERLY in addition is also the leading journal in its field and provides direction for thought and research on matters pertaining to the gifted.

Other developments of interest is the First World Conference held in London, 1975. It was organized by the NAGC of the United Kingdom with the aim of trying to bring together those concerned about the welfare of the gifted from all over the world. In this they were very successful and must be credited with initiative, foresight and industry that has resulted in the establishment of the World Council for the Gifted, the production of a fine book of the proceedings of the Conference entitled *Gifted Children: Looking To Their Future* (Gibson & Chennells, 1976), numerous benefits of contact, and dissemination of knowledge on the gifted whose significance cannot be easily measured.

One direct consequence of the establishment of the World Council has been the emergence of a Second World conference that will be held in August, 1977, in San Francisco, that in its planning has involved the participation of nearly all organizations as well as personnel of the Office of the Gifted in Washington, D.C.

The efforts of all these bodies both national and international towards the cause of the gifted are bound to make significant impact all over the world in time, and we cannot help but anticipate with excitement and pleasure the spread of interest and action universally.

### Summary Conclusions And Implications

This presentation has attempted to link up Terman's studies of the gifted to the development of thought that led to conceptions of many kinds of giftedness, namely, general intellectual ability, creative and productive thinking ability, specific academic aptitude, leadership ability, visual and performing arts ability and psychomotor ability. Further the extent to which education of the gifted is provided by the governments of the United States and by other countries of the world was outlined. In addition, educational opportunities found in the United States and abroad were summarized. The contributions of national associations to the gifted movement and the significance of some of their productions were discussed.

Some very significant steps have been taken in the United States and some smaller but no less important ones have been taken in a few countries elsewhere that recognize the gifted and talented as people who deserve our very special attention and nurture that can only lead to the fuller realization of their potential and unique productions which must enhance their immediate social-cultural group at first, and the rest of the world next.

What, we may ask, are some of the goals we need to set for ourselves in the United States? Here are a few that I think are pertinent:

1. Concerning identification, we still need to formulate procedures that we can use to identify all six USOE categories of giftedness. As it stands now we have but areas of abilities that do not lend themselves to psychological measurement, in which case we will need to consider at least setting up appropriate criteria which can be used with as little bias as possible by observers for selection purposes.

2. We need to move away from the prejudice of considering only the intellectually gifted and academically able as those with exceptional talent and to regard other forms of superior ability as defined by the USOE categories of giftedness.

3. Programs, educational materials and techniques need to have injected into them principles of innovation, flexibility and invention that will allow participants the greatest use of their creative abilities and imagination towards productive learning and self-involvement.

4. Enrichment should be thought of more in terms of specific needs and arrangements for specific development and accelerated learning rather than in more general terms as is customary in the educational system.

5. Acquisition of information from the United States by countries elsewhere about the gifted would be of great value and I see the ERIC--CEC/TAG Clearinghouse as the best facilitator of this. Dissemination of information regarding the availability of its computerized services and some of its low cost publications among the countries of the world would be an extremely valuable service to the cause of the gifted.

6. A closer communication network among the various associations for the gifted can only lead to major thrusts in the advancement of the cause of the gifted, and we should strive for this.

7. The value of having local associations for the gifted affiliated as well with the national organizations while maintaining their own autonomy will no doubt lead all kinds of benefits to the gifted at the local level. This too should be our concern.

8. Research on the gifted dormant for more than a decade has received fresh impetus by the passage of the 1970 Act, certain

financial support from the Office of the Gifted, by the effervescence of activity relating to the gifted all over the country, and by the scholarship of professionals in the gifted movement today. We can expect a fresh blossoming of thought on the gifted in the near future and should both encourage and support it.

9. Already efforts to study the gifted relative to creative energies at work, and to environmental impediment, and the disadvantaged gifted are well under way. These should also find increasing interest.

10. Further, some research directions that are receiving attention are variables affecting the full development of gifted women, the retarding effects of emotional disturbance on the creative energies of the gifted, and the problems affecting the gifted handicapped. These deserve our concern and should be given much encouragement.

In conclusion, the United States is in a position of leadership on matters pertaining to the gifted: in legislation, in measurement, in innovative educational facilities, projects and programs, in storage and retrieval of information through its computerized services, in books and journals, and so on, the United States has much to share with other countries of the world.

# HOW TO TELL IF YOUR CHILD IS GIFTED

By JILL NEWMAN

*Thousands of budding whiz kids go unrecognized each year because their parents and teachers are unable to spot their talents. Here are some easy ways to tell if your own youngster is among them.*

Phoebe Dunn

 Reprinted by permission of *Woman's Day Magazine.* Copyright ©1979 by CBS Publications, Inc.

Boddy is two and a half years old. He reads and speaks English, French, Hebrew, Yiddish and Spanish fluently and is just beginning to learn Danish. He loves science and music and playing the guitar, and his biggest problem, since he's less than three feet tall, is how to hold it under his arms.

Katherine, barely five, has a photographic memory. Because she is only in kindergarten, her teacher does not try to hide the training manual as she tests Karen on a long series of digits. "I think I ought to warn you," says the little girl, "that I can read upside down."

Tim, ten, is building his own computer out of a telephone, using the dial plaque as the data feed-in; while Marsha, eleven, has designed an energy-saving traffic light system that so impressed her classmates they are planning to submit it to President Carter.

Eric is fifteen. After entering college straight out of sixth grade, where he was an A+ student, he is now doing graduate studies at Princeton University, where he hopes to earn his Ph.D. in math.

These youngsters, obviously, are all gifted children. What you may not know, however, is that they are not unique. According to the Office of the Gifted and Talented, a recent offshoot of the U.S. Office of Education, anywhere from 2 to 5 out of 100 school-age children—or approximately 2.5 million youngsters in the country—are gifted, and they cut across all ethnic, racial, sexual and economic lines.

Nor is it only the budding Einsteins or Madame Curies who have been singled out for special mention. Today the term "gifted" applies not just to the person with high intellectual ability (the kid with the genius IQ) or a special academic aptitude (say, the math or science whiz) but to anyone with an unusual flair for leadership, athletics, creativity or the visual or performing arts.

Identifying the gifted child, of course, is not always easy. Some children shine in one subject, but are poor students in others so they wind up with a low total grade average. Others are branded as wild, silly, crazy or weird by their teachers and dismissed as troublemakers or kooks. Still others are bored, frustrated or dissatisfied by classes that are not challenging enough for their talents, and they fail to apply themselves properly or drop out of school altogether. The cases of brilliant men and women who are early underachievers, in fact, are classic: Winston Churchill flunked sixth grade. Einstein was expelled, Picasso played hookey from art school, Louisa May Alcott was told she couldn't write, and Caruso was advised to take up engineering because he had no voice.

Fortunately, these people overcame their early beginnings and went on to achieve later greatness. But educators maintain that other talents and potential are lost because they are not developed or recognized early enough—ideally, before age four—to allow for proper nurturing.

To help you determine whether your own children show exceptional promise, and if so, to suggest how you can insure that they get the special care and attention they deserve, here are some clues from Dorothy A. Sisk, director of the Office of the Gifted and Talented:

**1. Early use of advanced vocabulary:** Most children at two years of age can say things like, "Oh, there's a doggie." A gifted two-year-old, however, uses longer and more complex sentences like "There's a brown doggie in the backyard and he's sniffing our flowers." Older children are increasingly articulate, using highly imaginative or colorful figures of speech, such as "I feel like a caterpillar waiting to become a butterfly."

**2. Keen observation and curiosity:** Gifted children are especially perceptive and have an excellent eye for detail. At an early age, for instance, such a youngster might remember where all his toys belong on the shelf and be able to replace them correctly when he is through playing. Gifted children, too, are highly inquisitive by nature. Most youngsters ask questions continually, but the gifted child poses real stumpers like "How does the moon stay up in the sky?" "When the snow melts, where does the white go?" or "Why doesn't the sticky side of the Scotch tape stay stuck to the other side when you unroll the tape?"

**3. Quick and easy retention of information:** Gifted children have an amazing recall of experiences that the average child easily forgets or hardly notices. For example, one gifted six-year-old returned from a trip to a space museum and reproduced accurately a rocket he had seen being displayed there.

**4. Periods of intense concentration:** Most children are easily distracted and have a short attention span. A gifted one-year-old, on the other hand, can sit for five minutes or more listening to a bedtime story being read to an older brother or sister. Similarly, the gifted school-age child can become so totally absorbed in a project or book—usually designed for someone at least two grades ahead of him—that he literally doesn't "hear" you when you're calling.

**5. Wide and eclectic range of interests:** Gifted children are driven by a need to explore in depth and can become totally immersed in one subject one month—such as dinosaurs or volcanoes—then turn with equal fervor and intensity to something like French literature, stamp collecting or steamboat engines the next.

**6. Ability to understand complex concepts and relationships:** Gifted children are able to free-associate easily and can spot relationships, and their implications, to which their peers are oblivious. For instance, the average child might see a piece of string as something with which to tie a package, and a pencil as a writing tool, but the gifted child would put them both together and come up with a compass. Similarly, the gifted child has a precocious understanding of the abstract. Asked to describe poverty, for example, the average fifth grader might say, "I would be hungry," or "I wouldn't have enough money." The gifted ten-year-old, however, might extemporize that "being poor would only be a problem if others were rich. If everybody had only a little money, then we would all have less to spend and things would be cheaper."

**7. Acute analytical skills and a tendency to self-criticism:** While most young children are highly impressionable and easily influenced, gifted youngsters can more objectively evaluate themselves and others. They notice discrepancies between what people say and what they do, and don't hesitate to challenge the ideas of authorities: "Because you're bigger, does that necessarily mean you're smarter?" one might ask, or "Why do I have to go to school when I can learn so much better on my own?" In their striving for perfection, however, gifted children are usually toughest on themselves: "Why didn't I study harder?" "Why didn't I do better on the test?" "Why wasn't I faster at my homework?" "Why wasn't I first to answer the teacher?" are common concerns.

**8. Nonconformity, a sense of playfulness, independence and acute sensitivity:** Most of the foregoing characteristics are shared by both the intellectually and the creatively gifted. In addition, those with special talents in the arts and athletics usually show their promise early. While their classmates are still struggling, say, to draw the eyes, nose and mouth of a man's face accurately, the visually gifted child might not only draw this man easily, but show him riding on a motorcycle. And children with special creative abilities often have certain characteristics that are quite different from those of the intellectually gifted—notably a reputation for having offbeat or unusual ideas, a highly developed sense of humor and playfulness, an easy ability to relax, a strong tendency toward independent action, a preference for individualized work and a marked sensitivity and empathy for the feelings and situations of others.

If your child fits into one or several of the above categories, what should be your next step? Educators suggest that you present your findings to the youngster's school —and the more evidence you can offer to

### ARE YOU A GIFTED PARENT?

Parents can play an important role in fostering children's growth and creativity. Here are some of the ways you can help—whether the youngsters are gifted, average or actually underachievers. To how many can you truthfully answer yes?

☐ Do you take your children to concerts, libraries, museums, galleries, the theater and other points of interest?

☐ Do you provide a variety of materials—books, toys, puzzles, games—that will challenge the children's abilities and stimulate imagination?

☐ Do you engage in sports and other playful activities with your children?

☐ Do you give the children lessons in music, ballet, art, swimming, judo or whatever else you can afford?

☐ Do you allow your children to use the kitchen, workshop, garage for experiments and activities?

☐ Do you let your children learn about and share in some of your own hobbies and interests?

☐ Do you assign household responsibilities and other tasks that are appropriate to your children's age and coincide with new interests?

☐ Do you help your children make their own plans and decisions, permitting greater independence as their ability to assume responsibility increases?

☐ Do you answer your children's questions with patience and good humor?

☐ Do you avoid comparing one child to a brother, sister, friends or companions?

☐ Do you encourage your children to record thoughts, ideas, in a notebook, diary, scrapbook?

☐ Do you provide materials for your children's hobbies?

☐ Do you find something specific to praise when your children show you their work (a generalized compliment means especially little to the gifted child)?

☐ Do you permit your children ample time for thinking and daydreaming? Remember, just because they don't look as though they're doing anything doesn't mean that their minds aren't going a mile a minute.

*An important reminder:* There is a major difference between promoting and supporting children's talents—and pressuring them into exceeding their limits. You must guard as much against overestimating as underestimating their unique aptitudes. It is here that your real "giftedness" as a parent will come into play.

substantiate your case, the better. You might even want to keep a notebook in which you jot down some of your observations of your child's activities, so as to document your report to teachers—say, your son has read the complete works of Tolkien and he's only seven; your daughter beat the local grand master at chess, and she's eight; your six-year-old made an exact replica of the *Mayflower* out of soap, etc.

In some cases, the child's aptitudes—as in the performing arts or athletics—can be easily demonstrated. The baseball coach can watch your child work out on the field and pretty much tell if he is a budding Babe Ruth. A ballet teacher can observe a child at the barre and usually determine whether another Pavlova or Nureyev is waiting in the wings. Intellectual ability and creativity also can often be gauged through a battery of tests—the Stanford-Binet Intelligence Test, the Wechsler Intelligence Scale for Children (WISC), the Leiter Intellectual Scale, the Torrance Test for Creative Thinking—with a score of 125–135 and above generally considered in the "gifted" range. These tests can usually be administered by a clinical psychologist in the community, with the scores sent to the child's school.

In some cases the teacher may be the first to spot your children's talents. She observes them first hand in the classroom, corrects their tests, reads their papers, fields their questions, and is in an ideal position to judge whether they are superior to their peers and recommend appropriate courses of study.

If the teacher, on the other hand, is not specially trained to identify the gifted, you might want to meet with a school counselor, psychologist, administrator, curriculum specialist, artist, musician or other professional who is better qualified to judge a child's special competencies. Once again, take along your notebook of observations to help them in their evaluation.

Even your child's classmates can serve as mini talent scouts. Do they rave about your son's ability in science? Do they ask your daughter's help with their math homework? Is your youngest child always picked to star in the class play? Your oldest continually elected to the student council? Heed these signs. Your children's peers may be telling you something you yourself are not in a position to know.

If your child is ultimately found to be gifted, you will have to do some rethinking regarding his or her education. While myriad options are open to exceptional youngsters, experts report that actually only 4 percent of them are receiving the kind of learning services that their special aptitudes require. They also warn that despite the persistent belief that the prodigy is perfectly capable of "making it on his own," without proper stimulus and direction his very special talents can either be dissipated or actually wither away.

First, you as a parent will have to accept the fact that yours is an unusual youngster with unique skills and aptitudes and establish an environment at home that will allow these gifts to grow and flower. And second, you will have to scout your community to find out what services are available for the gifted child, and settle with specialists in the field on those that are best suited to your own youngsters needs and skills. Some of the programs and facilities that you might want to consider:

**Resource rooms**--a growing feature of many schools--which are equipped with special materials and teaching aids, where the students can pursue or study in depth subjects that are not usually covered in the classroom.

**Mentorships,** which pair a gifted child with an adult in the community who is highly skilled in the area of the child's interests--such as an illustrious artist, businessman, doctor, scientist--thus enabling the child to develop under the tutelage of an expert.

**Accelerated programs,** which permit a fourth-grader, say, to use sixth-grade books or even accelerate to the sixth grade; or **advanced-placement** programs, which allow a qualified high school student to take university courses prior to graduation, or even enter college before junior of senior year.

**Enrichment courses,** which keep the student at his own grade level, but enable him to pursue specialized interests--through independent study in conjunction with a teacher, or Saturday morning or after-school classes--at a more intensified and advanced level.

**Schools or special classes** for the gifted, where the child can find academic or intellectual peers, and enjoy the benefits of teachers who have been specially trained to instruct gifted youngsters. The names of these schools and programs are available from your State Department of Education, but if there are none in your immediate community, you might want to meet with school officials or your local board of ed to see what can be done to remedy the situation. Here the parents of other gifted children can prove useful allies, and by working together and forming advocacy groups, you may find that much can be achieved.

The important thing is to take some form of affirmative action and to take it fast. To neglect the gifted child, says Dorothy Sisk, to sweep the problem under the rug, to expect him to cope and to excel on his own, is as the director puts it, "to deny that very segment of the population that may one day solve society's problems.

# Enhancing Self-Concept with Gifted Black Students


*Herbert A. Exum and*
*Nick Colangelo*


Gifted Black students have received little attention in terms of their self-concept development. Essentially, self-concept relates to a student's perceptions about his or her adequacy in academic and non-academic situations. This perception is based primarily on evaluations by self, peers, families and teachers.

There have been several studies that show that a positive self-concept is important in the learning process (Bloom, 1977; Jones and Stowig, 1968; Kifer, 1973). Thus enhancing the self-concept of students will likely enhance their ability to learn and achieve.

Gifted Black students, because of their unique abilities and backgrounds, will have some self-concept needs different not only from other Black students, but from non-black gifted students as well. A gifted program that services Black students must provide for building self-concept if these students are to develop effective use of their abilities. This article describes some of the self-concept needs of gifted Black students and presents a model for helping Black students develop positive self-concepts. The model presented is most appropriate for high school students.

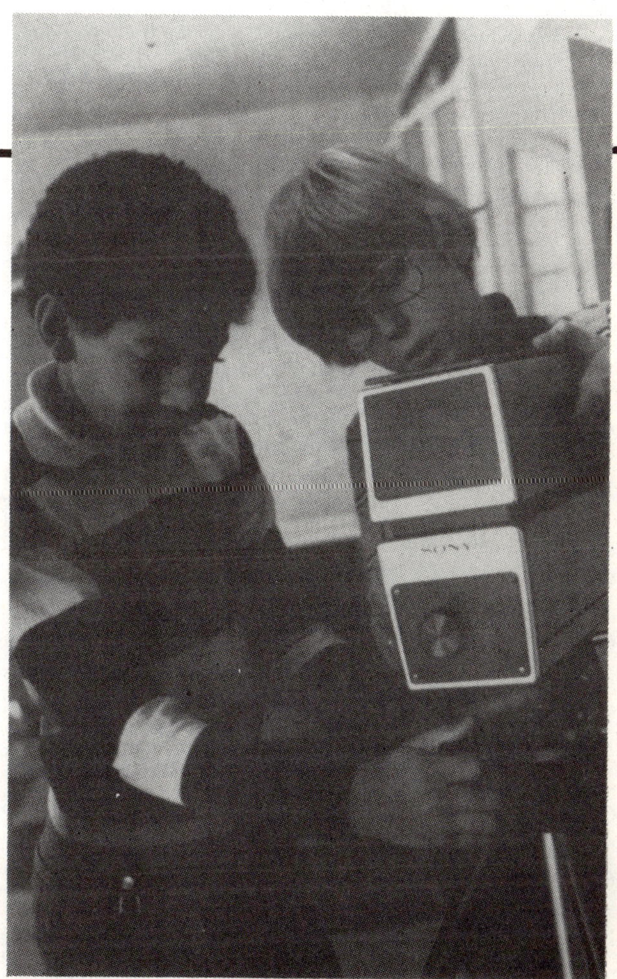

> " Most programs for the gifted are incomplete relative to the needs of Black gifted because they do not focus deliberately on the meaning of the Black experience under conditions of oppression nor do they discuss the concommitant levels or stages of Black awareness existing because of differential responses to oppression. "

### Self-Concept Needs of Gifted Black Students

The sociocultural background of gifted Black students is usually different from that of their gifted white counterparts. These differences must be taken into account by educators in order to understand and provide for these students' needs.

Gifted Black students are:

1. less likely than their white counterparts to be identified as gifted.
2. less likely to have a stimulating intellectual environment either at home or school.

Copyright 1979, *Roeper Review* (Michigan). Reprinted with permission.

# INTRODUCTION TO BLACK PERSONALITY AND IDENTITY

*Introduction: A Statement of Purpose*

This seminar discusses definitions of Black psychology and the role of Black psychologists in defining normalcy. The Cross hypothesis and Carter G. Woodson's concept of mis-education are introduced. Groundwork and expectations are set.

*The African Ontology: A Question of Metaphysics (Part I)*

This seminar addresses itself to the African worldview. During this seminar concepts of good, bad, life and death, are discussed from a non-European perspective. Concept of vital force is introduced. Wade Nobles is introduced.

"Omowale: The Child Returns Home" (Film)

*African Art: A Question of Self-Expression*

The idea of art as communication is explored. The role of sculpture in the transmission of values and ideas is the major focus of this discussion. Students are shown how the influence of African Art has been seen in contemporary Western cultures. The idea of abstraction is discussed.

Filmstrip on African Art and Sculpture.

*Slavery: That Peculiar Institution (Part I)*

The idea of slavery as a human condition is contrasted with that particular brand of slavery which existed in the Western Hemisphere. Attention is focused on the existence of persons of African descent in South America, the West Indies, and Central America.

"Brazil: The Vanishing Negro." (Film)

*Slavery: That Peculiar Institution (Part II)*

Racism as a factor in the maintenance of this system is introduced. Also the ideas of projection and scapegoating are discussed in terms of the "plantation mentality." Stereotyped of the "good" master and the Happy Slave is discussed. Slave revolts are discussed.

"Out of Slavery." (Film)

*Black Reconstruction: A Question of Transition and Direction*

The period of reconstruction facilitated the growth of reactionary posturing on the part of the Ex-Confederates. Advances of Black people are discussed. Discussion focuses on the differences in philosophy between B. T. Washington and W. E. B. Dubois, however.

"Civil War and Reconstruction" (Film)

*Groups, Pressure Groups, and Organizations:*
*A Question of Black Power*

The discussion focuses on the emergence of various organizations and their impact on Black America. Garvism, the Urban League, NAACP, The Black Panthers, and the Nation of Islam in the West is discussed.

*Groups, Pressure Groups, and Organizations: (Part II)*

The Nation of Islam in the West as an organization in transition is discussed.

"Black Power" (Film)

*Groups, Pressure Groups, and Organizations: (Part III)*

"The Negro and the American Promise (Parts I and II) serve as the basis of discussion for this period.

*A Question of Intelligence*

This discussion focuses on defining intelligence as a hypothetical construct. Brief history of I.Q. tests and their influence on the perceptions of Black people about themselves. Jensen and Shockley are discussed. Francis Weising and Robert Williams are introduced.

*A Question of Sanity*

Pathological behavior among Black people is discussed in terms of social learning theory. The concept of Radical Black Behaviorism is introduced. Colonization and neo-colonization are explored. Franz Fannon is discussed.

*A Question of Modern Mythology*

Stereotypes of Black people are discussed along with their maintenance systems.

*A Question of Perception: The Mass Media*

Television and the cinema are discussed in terms of the images they project. Music and advertising are discussed in terms of their negative conditioning ability. Syed M. Khatib (a.k.a. Cedric X. Clark) and Chester M. Pierce are introduced.

*Racism as Mental Illness*

Definitions of racism are explored. Coping systems are discussed. The mental illness conceptualization is the focus of the discussion.

*Integration, Mesgenation, or Separation:*
*A Question of Preference*

Those three modes for existence are discussed in terms of the mind-sets that accompany them. Other alternatives are developed through discussion.

*Third World Membership*

The concept of the Third World is defined. Panafricanism is discussed. Black Americans as world citizens is the focus of this discussion.

*New Directions: Black and Beyond*

This discussion ties it all together and proposes new alternatives.

---

3. more likely to induce negative reactions from their teachers (Shade, 1978).

4. more likely to be cautious, controlled, less trusting, and constricting in their approach to their environment (Shade, 1978).

5. more likely to be shrewd and manipulative of the situations in which they find themselves (Shade, 1978).

6. more likely to be subject to pressure from non-gifted Black peers to not perform well in school.

7. more likely to be sensitive and preoccupied with racial matters and establishing a Black identity.

One of the most important aspects of building a positive self concept among these students is interrelated with building a positive Black identity. Often it seems gifted programs for Black students do not emphasize the importance of building a positive Black identity. Below is a curriculum outline that can be used as one of a gifted program to foster self-concept and identity among gifted Black students. This program has been successfully used with high school age and college-age students.

*Black Identity Facilitation (BIF) Model*

Most programs for the gifted are incomplete relative to the needs of Black gifted because they do not focus deliberately on the meaning of the Black experience under conditions of oppression nor do they discuss the concommitant levels or stages of Black awareness existing because of differential responses to oppression. In order for this to happen: (1) the cognitive portion of the curriculum must represent a psychohistorical examination of the Black experience, (2) the subject or topic of developmental readings must also include references to Black gifted students in particular and (3) lab content must also examine cross-cultural interactions. The Black Identity Formation (BIF) model includes those necessary components.

In order to illustrate an example of a BIF model suitable for gifted adolescents, a sample cognitive curriculum is presented on the following page.

**Summary**

This discussion has presented a model counselors and teachers may use to facilitate self-concept and identity development in gifted Black students. It is imperative that the psychological development of gifted Black students include

commitment — to developing personal standards of Blackness — ending racist and oppressive institutions — and commitment to social responsibility.

The proposed model can be helpful in accomplishing these goals.

*Even though tests show that intellectually she is well advanced for her age, the author's daughter Maria enters any activity with the energy characteristic of a six-year-old.*

# GROWING UP GIFTED AND GETTING ALONG

by Kathleen Kilgore
photography by Neal Menschel



Growing Up Gifted and Getting Along, Kathleen Kilgore, *Yankee,* December, 1978, Vol. 42, No. 12. Copyright ©1978 Yankee Inc., Dublin, NH 03444.

The gifted child has a mind that often runs ahead while the rest of us walk. This can create serious problems that require creative solutions at home and in school. Here the mother of a gifted child reports on both fronts. . . .

□ "DOES THIS SURPRISE YOU?" THE SCHOOL psychologist looked across the desk at me. "Some parents don't know when their child is gifted." "No, it's more like relief. I was afraid no one in the school system would believe me."

The summary of six different types of intelligence tests was neatly typed and corroborated by the teacher's report. "Maria is functioning within the very superior range of intelligence at this time with an extremely rapid rate of mental growth." Then relief changed back to worry.

"Achievement in all areas measured is above present grade level, but below her mental ability level." What was a school system that produces eleventh-graders who can't write their own names going to do with a kid like that?

"I can imagine the past few years haven't been easy for you," the psychologist added sympathetically. "Having a child like Maria for your first would be hard."

* * * *

*She had a formidable ability to reason, but not enough experience to understand that the adult world was not always reasonable.*

The psychologist was right. Since the 1920s, a considerable body of research has been done on the problems of educating the gifted child. Only stray references appear on the problem of parenting the gifted. And even if there were a wealth of professional advice available, the catch is that one finds out about all the problems long before anybody suspects that intelligence might be the cause.

A British teacher of the gifted, Phyllis Pichard, wrote about the advice offered parents at one school for the gifted: "We told all the parents not to worry if their children needed less sleep than other children, but to put in suitable toys for the night so that they could leave their parents in peace." At the time the parents were being told this, they had already experienced at least five years of "less sleep" as well as questions ranging from "Why does the moon follow us wherever we go?" to "If God made the universe, who made God?"

"If only someone had told me from the start!" I used to think wistfully. But no one could have. I couldn't have known when I came home from the Boston Lying-In Hospital with a seven-pound, blue-eyed blonde little girl that I was going to have to bring up the neighborhood's bad baby.

If I had lived in a commune, or maybe even an affluent suburb full of permissive Ph.D.s, my public might not

**"There is still tremendous damage being done to the gifted in schools.**

have been so critical. But in the middle-class, Catholic, Boston community where we lived, they still raised children the old way. Discipline is strict, and begins in infancy. Babies and small children (and consequently, their mothers) are judged on three criteria: number of hours slept per night, amount of food consumed, and ability to keep quiet and

out of the way — and mind Mother without question. On all three counts, my daughter was a dismal failure.

From the first weeks, Maria slept no more than an adult, while other babies logged in 12 hours a night plus naps. If she ate more than half a jar of baby food at a time, it was a triumph, yet she was constantly active, and almost never sick. From the crawling stage, she was always on the go, and an early talker. She rarely broke things — her hands were gentle — but all objects had to be examined, smelled, handled. There were no quiet moments over coffee at my house.

There were desperate times when I needed sleep, and decided I would try the old school methods, but my husband always intervened. After six years on destroyers and a year dodging bullets on patrol boats in the South China sea, he considered a crying baby hardly worth getting excited about. "She wouldn't call if she didn't need me," he reasoned. "How can a little baby be bad?" Night after night, he would sit in an old rocking chair, patting her back with one hand and singing the Navy Fight Song until she dozed off, then try to grab a few hours of sleep before getting up to go to work.

One night when she was about two, I woke up just before dawn and heard their voices. I staggered into the bedroom, and found them making shadow pictures on the wall. "She was afraid of the shadows," he explained. "Because she didn't know what they were. Once she understands something, she isn't afraid of it."

"My hand is too thick for the light to come," Maria added, holding her hand up to the window where the streetlight shone. "It makes the shadow. It doesn't make me afraid."

Working helped, too. A few hours away from a toddler every day can make it all bearable. And I was lucky enough to have a sympathetic sitter, the mother of a severely retarded boy who could not speak. After 12 years of dealing with the effects of brain damage, a few extra questions from a child didn't bother her. "Do you know what she asked me today?" she'd report. "She was sitting on the potty, and she says, 'I was wondering, how do fishes go to the bathroom?'" She laughed. "You know, I never thought of that myself."

But as Maria progressed from baby to toddler to child, I began getting other feedback. Strangers usually noticed her because she was pretty and alert. Our librarian took me aside one day. "I hope you aren't planning on sending her to public school," she cautioned. "She'll be a problem there."

"We don't really have any other choice," I explained. "We supported busing in Boston. We're active in the community. How would it look if she went to private school?"

"I don't think you understand about the public schools," she answered.

I suppose at that time I didn't really understand about Maria either. I carried in my head, as I think most people do, the image of the extra bright child as a skinny recluse with glasses who talked like the *Encyclopaedia Britannica*.

Maria was different. As soon as she was old enough to walk and talk, my house drew kids like a magnet. If no children were available she would visit the retired schoolteacher across the street. She would strike up conversations with grandmotherly ladies on the MBTA, the clerk at the check-out counter, the shoe repair man, or the meter reader.

Aside from an occasional "Get lost, kid," and questions about whether she was a dwarf or worked in the circus, people accepted her with some amusement. Yet there were times when adult resentments would surface. By the age of three or four, she talked pretty much like an adult, larding her conversation with teenage terminology like "neat-o" and "spacey." She had a formidable ability to reason, but not enough experience to understand that the adult world was not always reasonable. Sometimes it was like living with a two-and-a-half-foot tall Mr. Spock.

One summer afternoon we were taking the MBTA to Park Street, and Maria began smiling at the woman sitting next to her.

"How old are you, sweetheart?" the woman asked.

"Four. How old are you?"

The woman's smile faded. "You

Above: *Maria on the swing. "From the crawling stage she was always on the go."* Below: *Mother and daughter share a quiet moment. "Only stray references appear on the problem of parenting the gifted."*

aren't supposed to ask a lady how old she is, sweetie."

"Why not?"

"It isn't polite, dear."

"But," she puzzled, "you asked me first."

"Okay, dear," the woman's smile returned. "If you're four, then I'm five." She held up five fingers helpfully, laughing.

"That's ridiculous." Maria shook her head. "You have wrinkles. Five-year-old kids don't have *wrinkles*. You must be kidding me."

The smile vanished completely. "If that was my kid, she'd get a good spanking," she snapped. "She's got a fresh mouth."

* * * *

For most gifted children, I learned later, the first serious conflict between themselves and the outside world comes in school. Maria was no exception. At first, things went well in pre-kindergarten. She adored her teacher, and liked playing with the other children. But the teacher found it impossible to teach 20 children the names of the primary colors, and one child spelling and arithmetic, at the same time. Maria became the unofficial teacher's aide and messenger while a request to test her percolated through the system.

The psychologist's recommendation read: "Intellectually, socially, emotionally, and academically, the child is advanced for present program, and would profit from Advanced Placement and/or enrichment activities." But the Boston public school system apparently had neither of these alternatives. Maria received permission from the principal to advance from pre-kindergarten to kindergarten so that she could enter first grade early. For a month, she would be "on probation" in the new group.

But after three days in the new class, I was dressing her for school when she began to cry. "I just can't hack it," she sobbed. "The teacher hates me."

"What do you mean? Can't you do what she tells you?"

"Well," she sniffled, "the first thing was I couldn't get the last button of my snowsuit buttoned, and the teacher says, don't help her, she's on probation. And I can't have my own crayons because I'm on probation. And she's keeping a list of all the things I do wrong because I'm on probation. And when she slaps the other kids, it makes me afraid."

I had my first parent-teacher conference the next day. As I walked in the classroom door, something hit me before I realized what it was. The silence. Each child sat on the floor with his hands folded on top of his head, like a prisoner

of war, as they waited to be dismissed. None of them spoke or fidgeted.

As the bell rang, they filed out in perfect order to the hall. If I weren't seeing this, I thought, I wouldn't believe it. But it was real. The teacher was a thin, middle-aged woman with a wintry smile, her hair cropped short. Beyond her desk, the little tables and empty chairs were arranged in perfect order. I pulled up a tiny chair and perched on it, while she sat behind her desk.

"I'm glad you came so soon," she began. "I think you should know that transferring your child was a mistake on your part. She is normal, but not advanced for her age, and I advise you to put her back before any damage is done."

"But, but they did it because of those tests," I groped.

"Those tests rely heavily on vocabulary. Her other teacher mentioned to me that you are a writer. That explains it. It's natural that she would parrot what she hears in the home, but that doesn't mean she has any understanding. I personally think you should disregard tests. Now, I have seen truly gifted children. We had a child here once who could read *Time* magazine. One teacher wanted to put her in the first grade early."

"What happened to her?" I asked.

"We put the child back into kindergarten with her peer group. She is perfectly happy and normal now."

"Well," I ventured, "What if the principal doesn't put her back?"

"I have been keeping notes on her behavior in class." (So the list really existed!) "Look at this one: 'Tore piece of paper and cried.' Very immature. When the time comes, I have the evidence to prove my case. And another thing," she added. "The child seems to have an irrational fear of me. That, too, is simply a question of maturity. Next year, when she has matured, she will be in my class all year, and I'm sure she'll adjust."

Maria had listened silently throughout. As we left the building, she finally spoke. "I'm not going to school anymore. I'm going to stay home, and you can teach me. You can't *make* me go anymore."

All day I wondered. Was she right? Was the psychologist, were the other teachers wrong? Had I been deluding myself for five years? The old classic pushy mother, trying to compensate for my own failures through an innocent child?

As I was leafing through Maria's school files, a folder the librarian had given me fell out. It was about Mensa, an international organization for people with an I.Q. over 130. I called, and got the number of the gifted children's coordinator, who lives in Massachusetts. She is a teacher named Carolyn Mellor.

I poured out my story to her on the phone. "With that many tests, it's practically impossible that you'd get a false positive," she reassured me. "You might get an unusually low score if the child were sick, but you just can't fake that kind of test. Trust your own judgment. Come out here, and we'll talk."

Carolyn Mellor's small ranch house in Framingham was crammed with books. Polished geodes and mineral specimens filled several homemade shelves, and straggling plants covered the windowsills. She welcomed me with homemade cheesecake, and began to enlighten me on the subject of giftedness.

"I wish I could say your experience was unique, but it isn't. Gifted children have not only been kept back in many schools, but even put in classes for the retarded. Just yesterday, I had a letter from a mother in West Virginia — the teacher had proudly told her that her daughter had been gifted, but she had finally slowed her down to normal!

"There is still tremendous damage being done to the gifted in schools. Some teachers feel threatened and use sarcasm and ridicule. And the gifted are very sensitive to this. Gradually they build up walls between themselves and the hurt until no one can reach them. The real tragedy is that gifted people have more to give society than ordinary people, but teachers can kill that off before the child ever has a chance.

"If you go through the literature, you'll find there are all sorts of ways to educate the gifted. I think it depends on the child's personality. Some of them can skip grades. I have one gifted boy now who is younger than the others, but he's tall and mature for his age, and he's the class leader. I've had some children who were gifted and were at the bottom of the pecking order; I had one gifted boy who was so hated that I had to protect him physically — other children would spit on his head as he came down the stairs.

"In Massachusetts today, great emphasis is being placed on the needs of three groups of children: the retarded, the emotionally disturbed, and the handicapped. I don't begrudge them one cent. They need it, and they have it because their parents have organized and pressured their legislators to do something. But parents of the gifted just give up and pay for private schools, and those who can't afford private school just drift along. It's time parents like you got out of the closet and said something."

The national picture, with a few exceptions, seems as grim as that of the state. According to Dorothy Sisk, director of the federal Office of the Gifted and Talented, slightly less than four percent of the nation's gifted are receiving any kind of help in education. Her office, ironically administered under the Bureau of Education for the Handicapped, has a $2.5 million annual budget. The Department of Health, Education and Welfare annually allocates $600 million for the education of the handicapped, and $2 billion for the education of the economically handicapped. In 1972, then U.S. Commissioner of Education Sidney P. Marland, Jr., issued a report to Congress calling the gifted "our most neglected students. Gifted and talented students are, in fact, deprived," he wrote, "and can suffer psychological damage and permanent impairment of their ability to function well which is equal to or greater than the similar deprivations suffered by any other population with special needs served by the Office of Education."

Two bills to raise the federal Office of the Gifted and Talented budget are now under consideration in Congress. Senate bill 1753, sponsored by New York Senator Jacob Javits, a long-time supporter of gifted education, carries a substantial $50 million authorization for fiscal year 1979. The House bill (H.R. 15) was approved by the House Education and Labor Committee in April, and authorizes $10 million for fiscal year 1979. "Both these bills involve direct formula grants to state and local boards of education," Gail Beaumont, education program specialist at the U.S. Office of Gifted and Talented, explained. "Both have provisions for the economically disadvantaged gifted child. But one important provision of the Javits bill is that no state would receive less than $50,000 for this purpose. Up to now, the whole program has been discretionary — a state didn't have to participate. But under the Javits plan, all states would at least start to participate — no board of education is going to turn away money."

Some states, notably Florida and California, have statewide plans for gifted children. Massachusetts does not. The Massachusetts Department of Education has received a $40,000 grant from the federal government to start a program. The grant is currently being administered under the Bureau of Student Services because the only state program that remotely resembled gifted education was a student leadership program for high school students.

Rosalyn Frank at Student Services is working on three objectives: setting up forums for teachers and administrators, identifying existing programs, and eventually setting up a "mentor" network of universities, museums, and even businesses to work with gifted children.

"Ten years ago, there was a state law for three years that funded local programs," Frank explained. "Chapter 766 supplanted this. Originally, the intent of the framers of 766 was to include the gifted in special needs, but because of financial problems, the Commissioner of Education decided to leave out the gifted. Until we are informed otherwise, that's the way it will be.

"We also have a conflict with the federal office," she went on. "The federal office wants us to establish objective, statewide criteria for giftedness. For example, in California, a child has to have a 132 I.Q. on a standard test, period. That may be fine in a state with a homogeneous population, but here we have a lot of communities for whom those standard tests would be meaningless."

According to the federal criteria of giftedness, two percent of any school population can be classified as gifted. In Boston, if that percentage is applied, there are at least 1,400 gifted children in the public schools. But apparently somewhere the decision has been made that gifted children need no special help. Boston still maintains high-level college-preparatory schools on the high-school level, for students who can pass a written exam, but there are many years between pre-kindergarten and the Boston Latin School.

Maria was tested under the 766 program for the retarded, since that was the only testing procedure available, though the examiner was able to waive the requirements for brain-function tests done in a hospital. The 766 coordinator had an honest but discouraging piece of advice for me. "Send her to Milton Academy," she confided. "I've been here awhile. You won't be able to fight the system."

Through the 766 program, I finally worked my way up to Ted Riggen, Associate Superintendent and Director of Special Services. "This is really interesting," he enthused. "This is the first time I've had a request for help for a gifted child. It is strange, come to think of it. There must be others. Well, don't hesitate to call me." But his enthusiasm waned after a consultation with the School Department's lawyers. "I'm sorry about this," he called back. "Gifted doesn't come under my department. They say it isn't viewed as a handicapping condition."

My only hope at this point seemed to be one of Boston's 16 magnet schools. The one I chose had been set up as the first magnet school, and racially balanced 50-50; it has an open classroom system that allows children to progress at their own speed, and offers "enrichment" in art, music, and gym. But, like any good school, it is not easy to get into. It serves as a safety valve for the middle class and professional families in Boston who don't want their children in parochial schools, and there are always more applicants than places.

Soon I ran into a classic Catch 22. I called a friend whose child goes to the magnet school. "The way you get a child in is to have him in kindergarten there. Then he's guaranteed a place in the first grade. And I think it helps if the child is bright."

"But that's the trouble," I wailed. "They thought she was bright, so they transferred her from pre-kindergarten to kindergarten already. She has to go to first grade next year. That is, if she doesn't flunk kindergarten."

"Flunk kindergarten in a Boston public school?" he asked. "Are you kidding or something?"

On a sunny June morning, I was waiting for kindergarten to be dismissed. It was the same kindergarten where the children had sat with their hands on their heads in the winter. After my parent-teacher conference, I had made a deal with Maria. If she stuck it out in kindergarten, I would send her to another school in the fall, no matter what the School Department said, or keep her at home. She had kept her end of the bargain. Every morning she complained, but every morning she went. We marked the days off on a calendar, and now they were almost over.

The kids came up silently, two by two, Maria holding on to a little girl in blue jeans with corn-rowed hair. Thin green slips of paper fluttered in their free hands. I suddenly knew what those papers were. So did the other women waiting.

"Thank God I've got all mine registered for the parochial schools," the woman next to me said.

"The tragedy of busing," her neighbor murmured.

Maria ran up and hugged me around the knees. "I think this is my assignment for next year, Mommy." She handed me the paper. "The teacher wouldn't let us open them. Bye, Kimba!" She called to her partner. "See you on Monday!"

I slit open the envelope. The name of our chosen school leaped out, then "Grade 1."

"You did it," I yelled. "You got in!"

"Please Mommy, you're *embarrassing* me," Maria answered.

"Aren't you thrilled? You got in!"

She shrugged. "Mommy, I really wish you wouldn't *worry* about me all the time." She skipped off down the sidewalk. "I have what it takes."

# Appendix: Agencies and Services for Exceptional Children

Alexander Graham Bell Association for the Deaf
3417 Volta Place, N.W.
Washington, D.C. 20007

Allergy Foundation of America
801 Second Avenue
New York, New York 10017

American Academy for Cerebral Palsy
1255 New Hampshire Avenue, N.W.
Washington, D.C. 20036

American Academy of Child Psychiatry
1800 R Street, N.W.
Washington, D.C. 20009

American Academy of Pediatrics
1801 Hinman Avenue
Evanston, Illinois 60204

American Alliance for Health, Physical Education
and Recreation
1201 16th Street, N.W.
Washington, D.C. 20036

American Association for the Education of the
Severely and Profoundly Handicapped
P.O. Box 15287
Seattle, Washington 98115

American Association for Gifted Children
15 Gramercy Park
New York, New York 10003

American Association of Psychiatric Services
for Children
250 West 57th Street
New York, New York 10019

American Association of Special Educators
107-20 125th Street
Richmond Hill, New York 11419

American Association of Workers for the Blind, Inc.
Suite 637
1151 K Street, N.W.
Washington, D.C. 20005

American Association of University Affiliated
Programs for the Developmentally Disabled
1100 17th Street. N.W.
Washington, D.C. 20036

American Association on Mental Deficiency
5201 Connecticut Avenue, N.W.
Washington, D.C. 20015

American Bar Association
Commission on the Mentally Disabled
1800 M Street, N.W.
Washington, D.C. 20036

American Civil Liberties Union
85 Fifth Avenue
New York, New York 10011

American Coalition for Citizens with Disabilities
1346 Connecticut Avenue, N.W.
Washington, D.C. 20036

American Diabetes Association
18 E. 48th Street
New York, New York 10017

American Foundation for the Blind
15 West 16th Street
New York, New York 10011

American Genetic Association
1028 Connecticut Avenue, N.W.
Washington, D.C. 20036

American Medical Association
535 North Dearborn Street
Chicago, Illinois 60610

American Occupational Therapy Foundation
6000 Executive Boulevard
Rockville, Maryland 20852

American Physical Therapy Association
1156 15th Street, N.W.
Washington, D.C. 20005

American Psychological Association
1200 17th Street, N.W.
Washington, D.C. 20036

American Psychiatric Association
1700 18th Street, N.W.
Washington, D.C. 20009

American Schizophrenia Association
Huxley Institute
1114 First Avenue
New York, New York 10021

American Speech and Hearing Association
9030 Old Georgetown Road
Bethesda, Maryland 20014

Arthritis Foundation
1212 Avenue of the Americas
New York, New York 10036

Association for the Aid of Crippled Children
345 E. 46th Street
New York, New York 10017

Association for Children with Learning Disabilities
5225 Grace Street
Pittsburgh, Pennsylvania 15236

Association for Education of the Visually
Handicapped
1604 Spruce Street
Philadelphia, Pennsylvania 19103

Bureau of the Education of the Handicapped
400 Maryland Avenue, S.W.
Washington, D.C. 20202

Center for Law and Social Policy
1751 N Street, N.W.
Washington, D.C. 2009

Child Study Center
Yale University
333 Cedar Street
New Haven, Connecticut 06520

Child Welfare League of America
67 Irving Place
New York, New York 10003

Children's Bureau
Administration for Children, Youth and Families
P.O. Box 1182
Washington, D.C. 20013

Children's Defense Fund
1763 R Street, N.W.
Washington, D.C. 20009

Children's Foundation
1028 Connecticut Avenue, N.W.
Suite 1112
Washington, D.C. 20036

Closer Look: National Information Center for
the Handicapped
Box 1492
Washington, D.C. 20013

Council for Exceptional Children
1920 Association Drive
Retson, Virginia 22091

Council of National Organizations for Children
and Youth
1910 K Street, N.W.
Washington, D.C. 20005

Day Care and Child Development Council of
America
1401 K Street, N.W.
Washington, D.C. 20085

Down's Syndrome Congress
1709 Frederick Street
Cumberland, Maryland 21502

Education Commission of the States
Handicapped Children's Education Project
300 Lincoln Tower
1860 Lincoln Street
Denver, Colorado 80203

Epilepsy Foundation of America
1828 L Street, N.W.
Washington, D.C. 20036

Goodwill Industries of America
9200 Wisconsin Avenue
Washington, D.C. 20014

International Association of Parents of the Deaf
814 Thayer Avenue
Silver Spring, Maryland 20910

International League of Societies for the Mentally
Handicapped
rue Forestiere 12
B-1050
Brussels, Belgium

International Society for Rehabilitation of
the Disabled
219 East 44th Street
New York, New York 10017

Joseph P. Kennedy, Jr. Foundation
1701 K Street, N.W.
Suite 205
Washington, D.C. 20006

Library of Congress, Division for the Blind and
Physically Handicapped
Washington, D.C. 20542

Mental Health Law Project
1751 N Street, N.W.
Washington, D.C. 20036

Muscular Dystophy Associations of America
810 7th Avenue
New York, New York 10019

National Society for Prevention of
Blindness,Inc.
79 Madison Avenue
New York, New York 10016

The National Association for Gifted Children
8080 Springvalley Drive
Cincinnati, Ohio 45236

National Association for Mental Health
1800 North Kent Street
Arlington, Virginia 22209

National Association for Music Therapy
P.O. Box 610
Lawrence, Kansas 66044

National Association for Retarded Citizens
2709 Avenue E East
Arlington, Texas 76011

National Association of Coordinators of
State Programs for the Mentally Retarded
2001 Jefferson Davis Highway
Arlington, Virginia 22202

National Association of State Directors of
Special Education
1201 16th Street, N.W.
Washington, D.C. 20036

National Association of Private Residential
Facilities for the Mentally Retarded
6269 Leesburg Pike
Falls Church, Virginia 22044

National Association of Private Schools
for Exceptional Children
P.O. Box 928
Lake Wales, Florida 33853

National Association of Social Workers
2 Park Avenue
New York, New York 10016

National Ataxia Foundation
4225 Bolden Valley Road
Minneapolis, Minnesota 55422

National Center for Child Advocacy
U.S. Department of Health, Education and Welfare
Office of Child Development
P.O. Box 1182
Washington, D.C. 20013

National Center for Law and the Handicapped
1236 North Eddy Street
South Bend, Indiana 46617

National Center for Voluntary Action
1735 I Street, N.W.
Washington, D.C. 20006

National Center on Educational Media and
Materials for the Handicapped
Ohio State Unviersity
220 West 12th Avenue
Columbus, Ohio 43210

National Committee
Arts for the Handicapped
1701 K Street, N.W.
Suite 801
Washington, D.C. 20037

National Committee for Citizens in Education
410 Wilde Lake Village Green
Columbia, Maryland 21044

National Council of Community Mental Health
Centers
2233 Wisconsin Avenue, N.W.
Washington, D.C. 20007

National Council for the Gifted
700 Prospect Avenue
West Orange, New Jersey 07052

National Easter Seal Society for Crippled Children
and Adults
2023 West Ogden Avenue
Chicago, Illinois 60612

National Epilepsy League
116 South Michigan Avenue
Chicago, Illinois 60603

National Genetics Foundation
250 West 57th Street
New York, New York 10019

National Information and Referral Service for
Autistic and Autistic-like Persons
302 31st Street
Huntington, West Virginia 25702

National Institute on Mental Retardation
Kinsman NIMR Building
York University Campus
4700 Keele Street
Donsview (Toronoto)
Ontario, Canada M3J 1P3

National Paraplegia Foundation
333 North Michigan Avenue
Chicago, Illinois 60601

National Rehabilitation Association
1522 K Street, N.W.
Washington, D.C. 20005

National Society for Autistic Children
169 Tampa Avenue
Albany, New York 12208

National State Leadership Training Institute on
the Gifted and Talented
316 West Second Street (Suite PH-C)
Los Angeles, California 90012

National Tay-Sachs and Allied Diseases
Association, Room 1617
200 Park Avenue South
New York, New York 10003

Office of the Gifted
400 Maryland Avenue, S.W.
Washington, D.C. 20202

Orton Society
8415 Bellona Lane
Towson, Maryland 21204

Physical Education and Recreation
for the Handicapped: Information and
Research Utilization Center
1201 16th Street, N.W.
Washington, D.C. 20036

President's Committee on Employment
of the Handicapped
1111 20th Street, N.W.
Washington, D.C. 20010

President's Committee on Mental Retardation
Washington, D.C. 20201

Spina Bifida Association of America
P.O. Box G-1974
Elmhurst, Illinois 60126

Therapeutic Recreation Information Center
University of Oregon
1597 Agate Street
Eugene, Oregon 97403

United Cerebral Palsy Association
66 East 34th Street
New York, New York 10016

"Mainstream on Call"*
1-800-424-8089

*A toll free number for individuals to obtain
answers to questions about Federal legislation
concerning the handicapped.

# INDEX

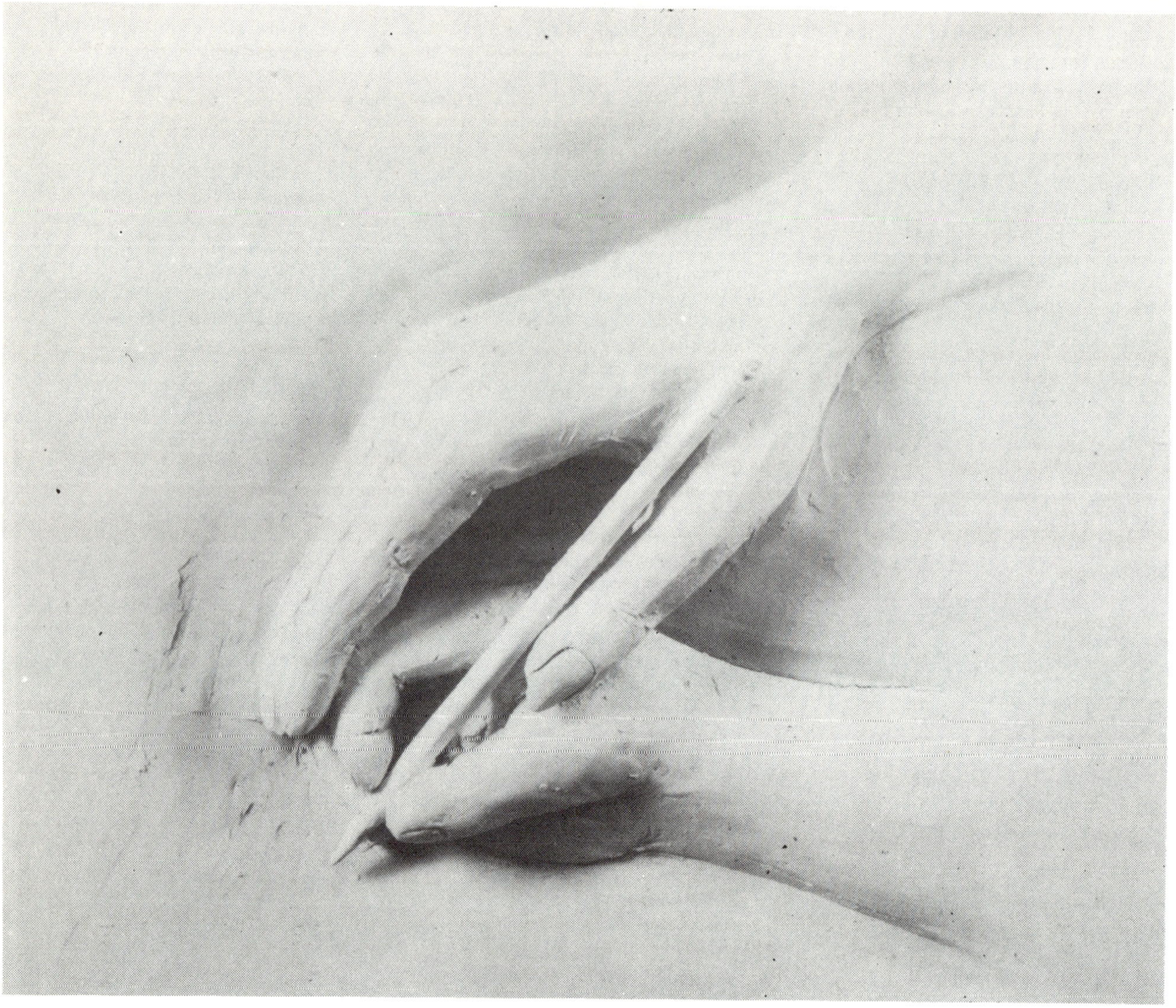

# STAFF

| | |
|---|---|
| **Publisher** | John Quirk |
| **Managing Director** | John Sullivan |
| **Editor** | Roberta Garland |
| **Special Project Editor** | Kathleen Leslie |
| **Permissions Editor** | Vanessa Gessner |
| **Director of Production** | Richard Pawlikowski |
| **Director of Design** | Donald Burns |
| **Typesetting** | Carol Carr |
| **Cover Design** | Donald Burns |

# ORDER FORM

_____ Administration of Special Education (8.75)

_____ Autism (8.75)

_____ Behavior Modification (8.75)

_____ Career & Vocational Education for the
      Handicapped (8.75)

_____ Child Abuse (8.75)

_____ Child Psychology (8.75)

_____ Classroom Teacher & Special Education (8.75)

_____ Counseling Parents of Exceptional Children (8.75)

_____ Curriculum Development for the Gifted (8.75)

_____ Deaf Education (8.75)

_____ Diagnosis & Placement (8.75)

_____ Down's Syndrome (8.75)

_____ Dyslexia (8.75)

_____ Early Childhood Education (8.75)

_____ Educable Mentally Handicapped (8.75)

_____ Emotional & Behavior Disorders (8.75)

_____ Foundations of Gifted Education (8.75)

_____ Gifted & Talented Education (8.75)

_____ Hyperactivity (8.75)

_____ Individualized Education Program (8.75)

_____ Instructional Media & Special Education (8.75)

_____ Law & Special Education: Due Process (8.75)

_____ Learning Disabilities (8.75)

_____ Mainstreaming (8.75)

_____ Mental Retardation (8.75)

_____ Physically Handicapped (8.75)

_____ Pre-school Education for the Handicapped (8.75)

_____ Psychology of Exceptional Children (small) (8.75)

_____ Psychology of Exceptional Children (large) (19.95)

_____ Severely & Profoundly Handicapped (8.75)

_____ Special Education (8.75)

_____ Special Olympics (8.75)

_____ Speech & Hearing (8.75)

_____ Trainable Mentally Handicapped (8.75)

_____ Visually Handicapped Education (8.75)

_____ Vocational Training for the Mentally Retarded (8.75)

_____ Abnormal Psychology: Problems of Disordered Emotional & Behavioral
      Development (8.75)

_____ Development Psychology: The Problems of Disordered Mental
      Development (8.75)

_____ Human Growth & Development of Exceptional Individual (8.75)

1.    Orders will not be processed without *complete* mailing address, including *zip code.*
2.    Orders not accompanied by a purchase order number must be prepaid.
3.    Orders under $15. must be accompanied by check. Add 10% shipping & handling.
4.    Orders less than $100., add 10% shipping & handling.
5.    Orders over $100., add 2% handling, shipping will be charged via specific rate.
6.    Orders of 5 or more of one title receive 20% discount, less than five will be billed at catalog price.

**Checks payable to: SPECIAL LEARNING CORPORATION**
**Allow 3-6 weeks for 4th Class (book rate) delivery**

## BUSINESS REPLY MAIL

First Class Permit No. 142- Guilford

NO POSTAGE
NECESSARY
IF MAILED
IN THE U.S.

Postage will be paid by addressee

**SPECIAL LEARNING CORP.**
**P.O. Box 306**
**Guilford, CT. 06437**

*STAPLE OR TAPE HERE*

# SPECIAL LEARNING CORPORATION

# COMMENTS PLEASE ! ! !

1. Where did you use this book?

2. In what course or workshop did you use this reader?

3. What articles did you find most interesting and useful?

4. Have you read any articles that we should consider including in this reader?

5. What other features would you like to see added?

6. Should the format be changed, what would you like to see changed?

7. In what other area would you like us to publish using this format?

8. Did you use this as a
( )  basic text?                      ( )  in-service?
( )  supplement?                   ( )  general information?

———————————— Fold Here ————————————

Are you a ( ) student  ( ) instructor  ( ) teacher  ( ) parent

Your Name ______________________________________________

School ______________________________________________

School address ______________________________________________

______________________________________________

Home Address ______________________________________________

City ____________________ St. ____________________ Zip ________

Telephone Number ______________________________________________

□   **ORDER PLACED ON REVERSE SIDE**                    *S/E II*

CUT HERE ● SEAL AND MAIL